Following the author's successful biographical dictionaries on Schubert and Mozart, *Beethoven and his World* offers an extremely comprehensive and up-to-date survey of the composer's relations with a multitude of persons with whom he associated on a personal or professional basis: relatives, friends, acquaintances, librettists, poets, publishers, artists, patrons, and musicians. With more than 450 entries, the dictionary is the result of a wide-ranging examination of primary and secondary sources, and it critically assesses the use which scholars have made of the considerable documentation now available. In particular, there are numerous references to Beethoven's correspondence and conversation books, which have recently been published in excellent new editions. The book places the composer and his music in a fuller context and a wider perspective than might be possible in a traditional biography; it will appeal to all music lovers, both the scholar and the non-specialist.

Peter Clive was Professor of French at Carleton University, Ottawa, Canada, for 22 years. His previous publications include a biography of the poet and novelist Pierre Louÿs, *Mozart and His Circle: A Biographical Dictionary*, and *Schubert and His World: A Biographical Dictionary*.

BEETHOVEN AND HIS WORLD
A BIOGRAPHICAL DICTIONARY

BEETHOVEN AND HIS WORLD

A BIOGRAPHICAL DICTIONARY

PETER CLIVE

OXFORD
UNIVERSITY PRESS

OXFORD
UNIVERSITY PRESS

Great Clarendon Street, Oxford OX2 6DP

Oxford University Press is a department of the University of Oxford.
It furthers the University's objective of excellence in research, scholarship,
and education by publishing worldwide in

Oxford New York

Athens Auckland Bangkok Bogotá Buenos Aires Cape Town
Chennai Dar es Salaam Delhi Florence Hong Kong Istanbul Karachi
Kolkata Kuala Lumpur Madrid Melbourne Mexico City Mumbai Nairobi
Paris São Paulo Shanghai Singapore Taipei Tokyo Toronto Warsaw

with associated companies in Berlin Ibadan

Oxford is a registered trade mark of Oxford University Press
in the UK and certain other countries

Published in the United States
by Oxford University Press Inc., New York

© Peter Clive 2001

British Library Cataloguing in Publication Data

Data available

Library of Congress Cataloging in Publication Data

Clive, H. P.

Beethoven and His world: a biographical dictionary / Peter Clive.

p. cm.

Includes bibliographical references and indexes.
1. Beethoven, Ludwig van, 1770–1827—Friends and associates.   2. Beethoven, Ludwig
van, 1770–1827—Dictionaries.   3. Composers—Austria—Biography.   I. Title.
ML410.B4 C62 2001   780'.92—dc21   [B]   00–068836

ISBN 0-19-816672-9

1 3 5 7 9 10 8 6 4 2

Typeset by Graphicraft Limited, Hong Kong
Printed and bound in Great Britain by Biddles Ltd
www.biddles.co.uk

For Megan

Preface

꒭꒰꒱

It is now seventy-five years since Theodor Frimmel published his *Beethoven-Handbuch* which contained an excellent survey of what was then known about the composer and his circle; and it is forty-five years since Paul Nettl brought out his *Beethoven Encyclopedia* in English, a useful dictionary heavily indebted to Frimmel's, though less reliable. Since these two books appeared much further research has been done, yielding a multitude of new facts and conclusions. Moreover, the highly successful execution of two outstandingly important projects has provided scholars with invaluable and reliable new research tools in the form of a definitive edition of Beethoven's conversation books and an authoritative edition of the correspondence (which presents not merely Beethoven's own letters, but also a large number of communications addressed to him, and even some exchanged by other correspondents). Mention should also be made of two very useful collections published in English, *New Beethoven Letters* by D. W. MacArdle and Ludwig Misch, and *Letters to Beethoven and Other Correspondence* by T. Albrecht. Full particulars of all these editions are given in the bibliography.

The time thus appears particularly propitious for the compilation of a new biographical dictionary which takes account of, and assesses, the very considerable documentation now available. This is the purpose of the present book. Wherever possible, primary sources (including some church records) have been consulted, and the use scholars have made of this material has been critically reviewed. As a result, it has been possible in some cases to correct faulty readings on which certain arguments and conclusions were subsequently founded, and, in a few others, to advance fresh interpretations of the material.

The dictionary presents information on more than 450 persons associated with Beethoven: relatives, friends and acquaintances, librettists, poets, writers, publishers, artists, patrons, and musicians. Also included are three persons not known to Beethoven himself, but who are of exceptional interest in this context: Ernst Julius Hähnel, the creator of the celebrated Beethoven statue at Bonn; Caspar von Zumbusch, the sculptor of the no less famous Beethoven monument in Vienna; and the American scholar Alexander Wheelock Thayer, whose biography of the composer remains to this day an essential text for all Beethoven scholars.

SOURCES

Thayer's book has been regularly consulted during the preparation of this dictionary, as has the English edition published by Elliot Forbes. Frimmel's *Beethoven-Handbuch* has also proved very useful, as has Friedrich Kerst's *Die Erinnerungen an Beethoven*, a compilation of recollections set down or otherwise communicated by a host of his contemporaries. Frequent use has, of course, been made of Georg Kinsky's thematic catalogue *Das Werk Beethovens . . .* (completed and edited by H. Halm), as well as of the *Beiträge zur Beethoven-Bibliographie* edited by Kurt Dorfmüller. In addition, a vast number of other studies has been consulted, of which a select list is given in the bibliography. There full particulars will be found of the sources briefly indicated at the end of most entries. (All references to *The New Grove Dictionary of Music and Musicians* are to the 1980 edition.)

BEETHOVEN'S CORRESPONDENCE

With a view to serving the interests of both German-speaking readers and those unfamiliar with that language, precise references to the new German edition by Sieghard Brandenburg as well as to Emily Anderson's English translation of Beethoven's letters are provided in respect of quotations from the correspondence, wherever this has been thought helpful; thus the indication 'A307/B498' signifies that the letter in question is numbered '307' in Anderson's edition and '498' in Brandenburg's. (There may, of course, be differences between the English text appearing in Anderson's version and that given in the dictionary, which is my own.) At the same time, so as not to encumber the dictionary with superfluous information, this method has normally been used only for letters by Beethoven which are either undated or to which different dates have been assigned in the two editions. In the case of his dated letters it has usually seemed unnecessary, where the dates are cited in the text, to give the numbers as well, since the letters in question can be easily identified, both the English and German editions being arranged in chronological order. On the other hand, the number is always indicated in the case of letters received by Beethoven or exchanged by other persons, even if they are dated, so as to alert readers to the fact—of which they might otherwise remain unaware—that these communications are included in Brandenburg's edition. (None of these letters appears in Anderson's English edition.)

CONVERSATION BOOKS

The so-called 'conversation books' are notebooks in which, as his hearing grew worse, Beethoven asked some of the persons with whom he came into contact to write down their remarks. The earliest extant conversation book dates from the year 1818, the last one from the period immediately preceding his death; but there are chronological gaps, notably between September 1820 and June 1822. These are documents of enormous interest, even though Beethoven's own observations are, for obvious reasons, only rarely recorded. The conversation books were among the material of which Anton Schindler took possession after Beethoven's death and which he eventually sold to the Königlich-Preussische Bibliothek in Berlin in 1846. The library thus acquired 137 such books and a number of loose leaves, but Schindler has, rightly or wrongly, been suspected of having destroyed many more.

In the present dictionary all quotations from the conversation books are followed by a precise indication of their location in the new edition prepared by Karl-Heinz Köhler, Grita Herre, Dagmar Beck, et al.; thus '*BKh4/69*' denotes '*Beethovens Konversationshefte*, iv. 69'.

HEILIGENSTADT TESTAMENT

Reference is occasionally made in this dictionary to a letter addressed by Beethoven in October 1802 to his brothers Kaspar Karl and Nikolaus Johann which is generally know as his 'Heiligenstadt Testament', after the village near Vienna (now part of the nineteenth district) where it was written. In it he expressed in moving terms his despair at his increasing deafness and appealed to his fellow men for understanding and sympathy, explaining that what they might regard as churlish and misanthropic behaviour on his part was merely a reflection of the social isolation to which his affliction condemned him. The Testament has been very frequently analysed and repeatedly reproduced in print. Thus, to name but three recent publications, the German text appears in the first volume of the new Bonn edition of Beethoven's correspondence, while English translations will be found in the *Beethoven Compendium* edited by Barry Cooper and in Maynard Solomon's biography of the composer.

WORK NUMBERS

In this dictionary, less well known compositions are regularly followed by their work numbers, as are those which would otherwise not be clearly identified (e.g. particular piano sonatas). In the case of generally familiar works such as the symphonies or the concertos, the work number has been omitted.

VIENNESE ADDRESSES

Because the modern system of numbering houses in Vienna differs from that used in Beethoven's day, no useful purpose would be served by citing the numbers which were assigned to them at that time. However, because readers may be interested to know just where in the city many of the buildings mentioned in the text stood (or still stand), their modern addresses are frequently given within square brackets. It should be borne in mind, however, that the houses which occupy the sites today are not necessarily those which did so in the late eighteenth or early nineteenth century. For the modern addresses, I am mainly indebted to Rudolf Klein's *Beethoven Stätten in Österreich* (Vienna, 1970) and Kurt Smolle's *Wohnstätten Ludwig van Beethovens von 1792 bis zu seinem Tod* (Munich, 1970). I have also consulted Felix Czeike's *Historisches Lexikon Wien* (5 vols., Vienna, 1992–7).

TITLES

Ranks of nobility have been rendered by the most closely corresponding titles in English, e.g. 'Graf' by 'Count'. Honorific titles such as 'Hofrat' have been left in German.

ASTERISK

An asterisk following a person's name at its first appearance in an article indicates that he or she is the subject of a separate dictionary entry. In addition, the asterisk is used in cross-references between articles (e.g. '*see* Mozart*').

TRANSLATIONS

All translations from the German and French are my own.

ACKNOWLEDGEMENTS

Above all, I should like to express my sincere appreciation for the invaluable assistance provided by Callista Kelly and her colleagues Al MacLennan, Lynda Pepin-Massey, Robert Smith, Denize Tan, and Pamela Williamson of the Interlibrary Loans Section at Carleton University. In addition, I wish to thank the following persons who have kindly supplied information or helped in other ways: Silke Bettermann (Beethoven-Archiv, Bonn), Otto Biba (Gesellschaft der

Musikfreunde, Vienna), Mrs C. Davies (Office of National Statistics, Southport), Grita Herre (Staatsbibliothek, Berlin), Hildegard Hnatek (Rollettmuseum, Baden), Liselotte Homering (Reiss Museum, Mannheim), Alastair Laurence (Broadwood Pianos Ltd., London), Dr Leistner (Ostdeutsche Galerie, Regensburg), Brigitte Leucht (Vienna), Norbert Molkenbur (Edition Peters, Leipzig), Patricia O'Kelly (John F. Kennedy Center for the Performing Arts, Washington), Hubert Reitterer (*Österreichisches biographisches Lexikon*, Vienna), Colin Ricketts (City of Westminster Archives Centre, London), Stephen Roe (Sotheby's, London), Armand Roth (Strasbourg), Hans Schneider (Tutzing), Sophie Standford (Royal Philharmonic Society, London), Barbel Stephan (Albertinum, Dresden), Rosemarie Stratmann-Döhler (Badisches Landesmuseum, Karlsruhe), R. L. Vaughn (Broadwood Pianos Ltd., London).

PETER CLIVE

Ottawa
Autumn 2000

Contents

❧

List of Illustrations

❧

A Chronicle of Beethoven's Life[1]

❦

1770   (17 December) Ludwig van Beethoven, second child of Johann van Beethoven, a tenor in the Bonn court Kapelle, and of his wife Maria Magdalene, née Keverich, is baptized at Bonn. He was probably born on the preceding day. His godparents are his grandfather, Ludwig van Beethoven, since 1761 court Kapellmeister, and Gertrud Baum, the wife of the next-door neighbour, Johann Baum, a clerk at the electoral cellar. (The parents were married on 12 November 1767; their first child, also called Ludwig, was born and died in April 1769.)

1773   (24 December) Beethoven's grandfather dies.

1774   (8 April) Beethoven's brother Kaspar Karl is baptized.

1776   (2 October) Beethoven's brother Nikolaus Johann is baptized. (Three further children born to the Beethovens will die in infancy—*see* Johann van Beethoven.*)

1778   (26 March) Beethoven's earliest known public performance, at Cologne. In the announcement of the concert he is described as a pupil of his father's and, erroneously, as being only 6 years old; he is to play 'various piano concertos and trios'.

1782   Christian Gottlob Neefe, who arrived at Bonn in October 1779 to join the Grossmann-Hellmuth theatrical company as its Kapellmeister, is appointed court organist. He may already have been giving Beethoven tuition in thoroughbass and counterpoint by this time. His predecessor, Gilles van den Eeden, is reported to have been Beethoven's first music teacher after his father.

     Either this year, or in any case not later than 1784, Beethoven forms close relations with the Breuning family and with Franz Gerhard Wegeler.

     Publication (late 1782/early 1783): *Variations on a March by Dressler* (WoO 63).

1783   (October/November) Beethoven travels to Holland with his mother. On 23 November he plays at a concert at the court of Prince Willem of Orange-Nassau at The Hague.

[1] The biographical details are followed, where appropriate, by a selected list of publications (in order of work numbers).

(1783–4) During a long leave granted court Kapellmeister Andrea Lucchesi in April 1783, Beethoven assumes some of his duties as organist; he also replaces Neefe as cembalist at theatrical rehearsals.

Publications: Piano Sonatas (WoO 47), Rondo in C major (WoO 48), 'Schilderung eines Mädchens' (WoO 107).

1784   (15 April) Elector Maximilian Friedrich dies; he is succeeded by Archduke Maximilian Franz, a brother of Emperor Joseph II.

(June) Beethoven is appointed a court organist, at a salary of 150 florins. The appointment had been recommended by court chamberlain Count Salm prior to Maximilian Friedrich's death.

Publications: Rondo in A major (WoO 49), 'An einen Säugling' (WoO 108).

1785   Antoine Reicha moves to Bonn with his uncle Josef, who has been appointed cellist and leader of the court orchestra. Later Reicha will state that he and Beethoven had been constant companions at Bonn and afterwards in Vienna, 'like Orestes and Pylades'.

1787   (March–May) Beethoven travels to Vienna via Munich, where he stays on 1 April on the outward and on 25 April on the return journey. (Although the purpose of his journey was to study with Mozart, it is not certain how much, if any, tuition he actually received during the approximately two weeks he spent in Vienna.)

(17 July) Beethoven's mother dies.

1788   (*c.*1 February) Count Waldstein arrives in Bonn, where, on 17 June, he will be made a knight of the Teutonic Order.

1789   (14 May) Beethoven enrols for lectures at Bonn University, at the same time as Antoine Reicha.

(20 November) Beethoven's father retires. It is decreed that one half of his 200-thaler salary should henceforth be paid to Beethoven for the support of his two younger brothers. (However, to keep up appearances, Johann van Beethoven will continue to draw his full salary, of which he then hands one-half to his son.)

1790   (20 February) Emperor Joseph II dies. When the news reaches Bonn Beethoven is invited to set a text by Severin Anton Averdonk, for performance at a commemorative ceremony on 19 March. However, his cantata (WoO 87) is not ready in time. He will later set another text by Averdonk to celebrate the elevation of Joseph's brother Leopold to the rank of emperor (WoO 88).

(25 December) Haydn and Johann Peter Salomon arrive at Bonn on their way to London. The following day they dine with several of the

city's leading musicians. It is not known whether Beethoven was introduced to Haydn during this visit or in 1792 (see below).

1791   (6 March) Performance of a *Ritterballet* devised by Count Waldstein and for which Beethoven has composed at least some of the music (WoO 1).

(September–October) The court musicians, Beethoven among them, visit Mergentheim, where the elector presides over a meeting of the Teutonic Order. On the way there, Beethoven plays for Johann Franz Xaver Sterkel at Aschaffenburg.

Publication: 24 Variations on the Arietta 'Venni Amore' by V. Righini (WoO 65).

1792   (July) Haydn passes through Bonn on his return journey from England. The possibility of his teaching Beethoven is probably discussed on this occasion.

(Early November) Beethoven leaves for Vienna to study with Haydn.

1793   Beethoven studies composition with Haydn and perhaps also with Johann Baptist Schenk.

(19 June) Beethoven travels to Eisenstadt, perhaps to see Haydn, who has been there since May. He will probably be back in Vienna by late July or early August.

(July) Beethoven's variations on 'Se vuol ballare' from Mozart's *Le nozze di Figaro* are published by Artaria & Co. The firm will issue first editions of a considerable number of Beethoven's early works, until a quarrel over the publication rights for the String Quintet Op. 29 will lead to a temporary break in their association in 1802.

Publications: Variations on 'Se vuol ballare' (WoO 40) and on 'Es war einmal ein alter Mann' from Dittersdorf's *Das rote Käppchen* (WoO 66).

1794   (19 January) Haydn leaves for his second visit to England. Beethoven studies with Johann Georg Albrechtsberger until the spring of 1795.

(Spring) Beethoven's brother Kaspar Karl moves to Vienna. Later (1802–6) he will help Beethoven in his dealings with publishers.

(Autumn) Franz Gerhard Wegeler and Lorenz von Breuning arrive in Vienna (Wegeler will stay until 1796, Breuning until 1797).

Publication: 8 Variations on a Theme by Count Waldstein (WoO 67).

1795   (29–30 March) Beethoven makes his first public appearances in Vienna as pianist and composer at concerts of the Tonkünstler-Societät at the Burgtheater, playing the First or Second Piano Concerto at the first concert and improvising at the second.

(July–August) Beethoven's Op. 1, a set of three piano trios, is published, dedicated to Prince Karl Lichnowsky, who, almost from the outset of Beethoven's career in Vienna, has been one of his greatest admirers and most generous patrons. Their friendly relations will come to an abrupt halt in 1806.

(31 March) On the occasion of a performance of *La clemenza di Tito* arranged by Constanze Mozart at the Burgtheater, Beethoven plays a concerto by Mozart (probably K466) between the two parts of the opera.

(20 August) Haydn returns from England. There is no evidence that Beethoven resumes his lessons with him.

(18 December) Beethoven plays one of his first two concertos at Haydn's concert at the Kleiner Redoutensaal.

(26 December) Beethoven's brother Nikolaus Johann arrives in Vienna.

(Late December) Stephan von Breuning arrives in Vienna, where, except for several years from late 1796, he will live for the rest of his life. He will be in intimate contact with Beethoven until about 1815, and again from 1825.

(*c*.1795) Beethoven reportedly proposes marriage to Magdalena Willmann, but is rejected.

Publications: Piano Trios (Op. 1).

1796   (February–July) Extended concert tour, during which Beethoven spends several weeks in Prague (February–April), and visits Dresden (23–*c*.30 April), Leipzig, and Berlin (May–July). While in Prague, he composes the scena *Ah! perfido* (Op. 65); in Berlin he writes the Cello Sonatas Op. 5 for Jean-Louis Duport.

(2 November) Josefa Dušek gives the first performance of *Ah! perfido* at Leipzig.

(23 November) Beethoven gives a concert at Pressburg [Bratislava], from where he reportedly travels to Pest [Budapest].

Publications: Piano Sonatas (Op. 2), String Trio (Op. 3), String Quintet (Op. 4).

1797   (January) Beethoven takes part in a concert given in Vienna by Andreas and Bernhard Romberg, whom he knew at Bonn.

(6 April) First performance of the Piano Quintet (Op. 16), at a concert given by Schuppanzigh at Jahn's, with Beethoven playing the piano part.

Publications: Cello Sonatas (Op. 5), Piano Sonata in E flat major (Op. 7), 'Adelaide' (Op. 46), Variations on a Russian dance from Paul Wranitzky's ballet *Das Waldmädchen* (WoO 71).

1798   (Early 1798) Beethoven is received by General Bernadotte during the latter's residence in Vienna as French ambassador from February to April. According to Schindler, Bernadotte's suggestion that Beethoven should celebrate 'the greatest hero of the epoch' [i.e. Napoleon] in music will lead to the composition of the 'Eroica' Symphony.

(29 March) Beethoven takes part in a benefit concert at Jahn's for Josefa Dušek; he probably plays one of the Op. 12 Violin Sonatas with Schuppanzigh.

(Spring) Karl Amenda arrives in Vienna; he will become an intimate friend of Beethoven.

(Autumn) Beethoven plays his first two piano concertos at concerts in Prague.

Publications: String Trios (Op. 9), Piano Sonatas (Op. 10), Piano Trio (Op. 11), Violin Sonatas (Op. 12, December 1798/January 1799).

1799   Beethoven probably begins his studies with Salieri at this time (but may have done so earlier); they will continue until at least 1801. This year he makes the acquaintance of two well-known foreign musicians, the double-bass player Domenico Dragonetti and the pianist Johann [John] Baptist Cramer (who will spend the whole winter of 1799–1800 in Vienna). Beethoven's hearing deteriorates significantly.

(May) Beethoven makes the acquaintance of the Countesses Therese and Josephine Brunsvik, and gives them piano lessons during their brief stay in Vienna. Following her marriage to Count Joseph Deym on 29 June, Josephine will return to Vienna, where she will remain in close contact with Beethoven.

(Autumn) Amenda leaves Vienna.

Publications: Piano Sonatas Op. 13 (*Sonate pathétique*) and Op. 14; Variations on the duet 'La stessa, la stessissima' from Salieri's *Falstaff* (WoO 73).

1800   Prince Lichnowsky grants Beethoven an annual allowance of 600 florins until he finds a suitable appointment. The payments probably continued until at least 1806.

(2 April) Beethoven gives a concert at the Burgtheater which includes the first performances of the Septet (Op. 20) and the First Symphony.

(18 April) At the Burgtheater, Beethoven plays his newly composed Horn Sonata (Op. 17) with Johann Wenzel Stich [known as Punto], for whom he has written it.

(7 May) Beethoven and Punto perform at a concert in Budapest, probably playing once more the Horn Sonata Op. 17.

(Spring) At Count Fries's house, Beethoven outshines Daniel Steibelt in an informal improvisation contest.

1801   (30 January) At a charity concert arranged by the singer Christine Gerhardi, Beethoven and Punto again perform the Horn Sonata Op. 17.

(28 March) Première of Viganò's ballet *Die Geschöpfe des Prometheus*, for which Beethoven has written the music (Op. 43).

(Spring) In letters to Wegeler (29 June) and Amenda (1 July) Beethoven describes his hearing problems and the distress they cause him.

(Autumn) Beethoven falls in love—probably with Countess Julia [Giulietta] Guicciardi, to whom he will dedicate the Piano Sonata Op. 27, No. 2, next year. Any hopes he may have had of marrying her are frustrated by the difference in their social status.

(Late 1801/early 1802) Ferdinand Ries moves to Vienna, where he becomes Beethoven's pupil.

Publications: First Piano Concerto (Op. 15), Piano Quintet (Op. 16), Horn Sonata (Op. 17), String Quartets (Op. 18), Second Piano Concerto (Op. 19), First Symphony (Op. 21), Violin Sonatas (Opp. 23–4).

1802   (Summer–autumn) Beethoven stays at Heiligenstadt, near Vienna. There, on 6 October (with an addendum on 10 October), he writes the Heiligenstadt Testament.

(Autumn) Antoine Reicha arrives in Vienna, where he resumes his friendship with Beethoven. He will remain in Vienna until 1808.

(November) Beethoven breaks with Artaria & Co., the publishers of many of his early works, over their pirated edition of the String Quintet Op. 29 which he has sold to Breitkopf & Härtel. The legal proceedings will drag on until September 1805, when a settlement is finally reached.

Publications: Septet (Op. 20), Piano Sonatas (Opp. 22, 26–8), String Quintet (Op. 29).

1803   (*c*. January) Beethoven is engaged as composer at the Theater an der Wien and assigned a service flat in the theatre complex. Later in the year he will grapple with the initial project, a setting of Schikaneder's libretto *Vestas Feuer*, but he will soon abandon it.

(5 April) Beethoven's benefit concert at the Theater an der Wien features the first performances of the Second Symphony, Third Piano Concerto, and *Christus am Ölberg*.

(24 May) Beethoven and the violinist George Polgreen Bridgetower give the first performance of the Violin Sonata Op. 47 (later known as the 'Kreutzer' Sonata).

(20 July) George Thomson enquires about Beethoven's fees for composing six sonatas based on Scottish airs. Beethoven replies on 5 October. Thomson considers Beethoven's price excessive, but in later years he will publish Beethoven's arrangements of 125 British folk songs for one or more voices, with newly composed accompaniments for piano trio.

(4 August) Another performance of *Christus am Ölberg*.

(13 September) Ries informs Nikolaus Simrock that Beethoven has ceded the rights to nine of his compositions to his brother Nikolaus Johann, in return for certain favours. (These were presumably of a monetary nature.)

Publications: Violin Sonatas (Op. 30), Piano Sonatas (Op. 31, Nos. 1–2), *Variations* for piano (Opp. 34–5), Romance for violin and orchestra (Op. 40), songs to texts by Gellert (Op. 48), Herrosee (WoO 123), and Metastasio (WoO 124).

1804   Following the death on 27 January of Josephine von Brunsvik's husband, Count Deym (*see* under 1799), Beethoven falls deeply in love with her, his feelings apparently reaching their greatest intensity during the winter of 1804–5. However, Josephine's letters, while affectionate, indicate a desire for a spiritual rather than a physical relationship. (In the view of some modern scholars, she would later be Beethoven's 'Immortal Beloved'—*see* July 1812.)

(May/December) According to Ferdinand Ries, Beethoven is so outraged by Napoleon's decision to become emperor that he tears up the title page of the ('Eroica') symphony he intended to dedicate to him. The incident must have occurred either shortly after Napoleon's proclamation as emperor on 18 May or soon after his coronation on 2 December.

(July) Beethoven quarrels with Stephan von Breuning; they are reconciled a few months later.

(July–September) Beethoven stays at Baden and later at Oberdöbling.

(August) Probably the first private performance of the 'Eroica' Symphony, at Prince Lobkowitz's residence at Eisenberg [Jezeří] in Bohemia.

Publications: Piano Sonata (Op. 31, No. 3), Second Symphony (Op. 36), Third Piano Concerto (Op. 37), *Variations on 'God Save the King'* (WoO 78) and *Variations on 'Rule Britannia'* (WoO 79).

1805   (7 April) First public performance of the 'Eroica' Symphony, at the Theater an der Wien. (In Vienna, it has previously received at least two private performances, at the house of the bankers Baron Andreas Fellner and Joseph Würth on 20 January and at Lobkowitz's palace on 23 January.)

(Summer) Beethoven stays at Hetzendorf.

(Autumn) Ries returns to Bonn, probably in early November.

(13 November) Vienna is occupied by Napoleon's army, which will remain there until 13 January 1806.

(20 November) Première of *Fidelio* at the Theater an der Wien. (The performance of the opera, initially scheduled for 15 October, was forbidden by the censor on 30 September, but the ban was lifted on 5 October as a result of a petition submitted by Joseph Sonnleithner, the secretary of the court theatres and author of the libretto.) Further performances on 21 and 22 November.

(December) At a meeting at Prince Lichnowsky's, Beethoven agrees to make certain changes in the opera.

Publications: 'An die Hoffnung' (Op. 32), Violin Sonata ('Kreutzer') (Op. 47), Romance for violin and orchestra (Op. 50), Piano Sonata ('Waldstein') (Op. 53), *Ah! perfido* (Op. 65).

1806   (29 March) First performance, at the Theater an der Wien, of a new version of *Fidelio* prepared by Beethoven with the help of Stephan von Breuning. The opera is repeated on 10 April.

(25 May) Beethoven's brother Kaspar Karl marries Johanna Reiss.

(4 September) Kaspar Karl's son Karl is born.

(August/September–late October) While staying at Prince Lichnowsky's estate at Grätz in Silesia [now Hradec, Czech Republic], Beethoven composes all or most of his Fourth Symphony. One day they visit Count Oppersdorff, on which occasion Beethoven's Second Symphony is performed. Following a furious quarrel with Lichnowsky, Beethoven leaves precipitately and returns to Vienna. On his arrival there he is reported to have smashed a bust of Lichnowsky in his possession; but this last incident may well not have happened until 1808, after the prince had terminated his annuity.

(23 December) First performance of Beethoven's Violin Concerto, by Franz Clement at the Theater an der Wien.

Publications: Piano Sonata (Op. 54), Third Symphony (Op. 55).

1807   (March) According to press reports, two all-Beethoven concerts are given at the house of 'Prince L.' (presumably Lobkowitz). The works played are the first four symphonies, the Fourth Piano Concerto, the *Coriolan* Overture (its first performance), and arias from *Fidelio*.

(20 April) Clementi, who has established cordial relations with Beethoven during a lengthy stay in Vienna, acquires the English

publication rights for the Fourth Symphony, Fourth Piano Concerto, 'Razumovsky' Quartets, Violin Concerto (as well as a piano arrangement to be made of it by Beethoven), and the *Coriolan* Overture. (But his London firm will eventually publish only the quartets and the two versions of the Violin Concerto.) The contract is witnessed by Baron Ignaz Gleichenstein, who has become one of Beethoven's closest friends.

(24 April) The *Coriolan* Overture is played for the first time in the theatre, preceding a performance of Heinrich von Collin's play.

(13 September) A Mass (Op. 86) commissioned by Prince Nikolaus Esterházy for performance at Eisenstadt during festivities in honour of his wife's name day fails to please the prince, who does not hide his disappointment from Beethoven.

(12 November) Beethoven's Second Symphony is performed at the first of the Liebhaber-Concerte, a series of twenty subscription concerts directed at first by Johann Baptist von Häring, a gifted amateur violinist and a friend of Beethoven, and later by Franz Clement, director of music at the Theater an der Wien; the final concert will be given on 27 March 1808. Beethoven's name appears regularly on the programme. There are performances of the *Prometheus* and *Coriolan* Overtures, as well as of the first four symphonies and the First Piano Concerto. The performance of the 'Eroica' on 6 December was reportedly conducted by Beethoven himself.

Publications: Triple Concerto (Op. 56), Piano Sonata ('Appassionata') (Op. 57), *32 Variations in C minor* (WoO 80).

1808   Beethoven discusses possible opera subjects with Heinrich von Collin; but Collin fails to finish his *Macbeth* and Beethoven hesitates so long over his *Bradamante* libretto that Collin offers it to Reichardt, who sets it.

(March) Beethoven is operated on for a *panaritium* which has almost cost him a finger. That same month his brother Nikolaus Johann settles at Linz, where he has bought a pharmacy. A shrewd businessman, he will accumulate a sizeable fortune.

(13 April) At a charity concert at the Burgtheater, Beethoven conducts his Fourth Symphony, Third Piano Concerto (played by Friedrich Stein), and *Coriolan* Overture.

(May) First public performance of the Triple Concerto at a concert in the Augarten.

(Summer–autumn) Beethoven stays at Heiligenstadt and at Baden.

(27 August) Ferdinand Ries returns to Vienna.

(Late summer/early autumn) The Razumovsky Quartet is founded, consisting of Schuppanzigh, Sina, Weiss, and Linke. It will frequently perform Beethoven's chamber music.

(14 September) Gottfried Härtel, on a visit to Vienna, signs a contract for Opp. 67–70. Altogether, Breitkopf & Härtel will publish first editions of more than twenty of Beethoven's works between 1809 and 1812.

(*c.* October) Beethoven is offered the post of Kapellmeister at the court of Jérôme Bonaparte, king of Westphalia, at Kassel, at a salary of 600 gold ducats.

(15 November) At a charity concert at the Theater an der Wien, Beethoven conducts one of his symphonies, the *Coriolan* Overture, and a piano concerto (in which he may have played the solo part).

(24 November) Johann Friedrich Reichardt arrives in Vienna, on a visit which will last until the following spring. His *Vertraute Briefe* (1809) contain many references to the cultural life of the city and, in particular, to Beethoven and his music.

(22 December) Beethoven gives a benefit concert at the Theater an der Wien. The programme includes the Fifth and Sixth Symphonies, the Choral Fantasia, and one of his piano concertos, in which he appears as soloist.

Publications: Fourth Piano Concerto (Op. 58), 'Razumovsky' String Quartets (Op. 59), Fourth Symphony (Op. 60), Violin Concerto, and its arrangement as a piano concerto (Op. 61), *Coriolan* Overture (Op. 62), 'In questa tomba oscura' (WoO 133), 'Sehnsucht' (WoO 134, No. 1).

1809   (7 January) Beethoven informs Breitkopf & Härtel that he has this day accepted the king of Westphalia's invitation. Soon afterwards, however, he will be involved in negotiations for a contract which would guarantee him an adequate income if he remained in Vienna.

(26 February) Beethoven receives from Archduke Rudolph a contract granting him an annuity totalling 4,000 florins, to be paid jointly by the archduke (1,500 florins), Prince Lobkowitz (700 florins), and Prince Kinsky (1,800 florins). In return, he must undertake to reside in Vienna or in another city in the emperor's hereditary lands. This contract is ratified by the parties on 1 March. It is possible that the instruction in theory and composition which Beethoven will give Rudolph until 1824 results from a commitment made by him at this time.

(5 March) First public performance of the Cello Sonata Op. 69, by Nikolaus Kraft and Baroness Ertmann.

(13 May) Austria having declared war on France on 9 April, Vienna is occupied by Napoleon's army after a heavy bombardment. A week

earlier the imperial family, including Archduke Rudolph, sought refuge in Hungary.

(July) Ries leaves Vienna.

(14 October) Conclusion of the Peace of Schönbrunn.

(20 November) The French troops leave Vienna. Emperor Franz I will return on 27 November, Archduke Rudolph not until later (*see* under 1810).

(24 December) A performance of *Christus am Ölberg* takes place at the Theater an der Wien.

Publications: Fifth Symphony (Op. 67), Sixth Symphony (Op. 68), Cello Sonata (Op. 69), Piano Trios (Op. 70).

1810   Franz Oliva, whom Beethoven has probably already met before this year, begins to help him with his correspondence. In October Beethoven dedicates the *Variations* Op. 76 to him.

(30 January) Archduke Rudolph arrives back in Vienna. His departure, absence, and return are commemorated in Beethoven's Piano Sonata Op. 81a.

(13 February) Josephine Brunsvik-Deym marries Baron Christoph Stackelberg.

(February/March) Beethoven is introduced by Gleichenstein to Jakob Friedrich Malfatti and his family. (He already knows, and has perhaps already consulted, their cousin Dr Johann Malfatti.) During the following weeks he frequently calls on the Malfattis; he is said to have been particularly attracted to the elder daughter Therese.

(27 April 1810) Presumed date (Beethoven's indicates the day and month, but not the year) of the dedication of the Bagatelle WoO 59, probably to Therese Malfatti—*see* Malfatti (family).*

(May) Beethoven makes the acquaintance of Bettina Brentano, and also of her half-brother Franz Brentano, a Frankfurt merchant, and his wife Antonie, who was born in Vienna as the daughter of the diplomat and senior civil servant Johann Melchior von Birkenstock. (According to Schindler, Beethoven had met her already in the 1790s, but she herself denied this.) Birkenstock, whom Beethoven may have known, will die on 30/1 October.

(2 May) Beethoven asks Wegeler (who is living at Koblenz) to obtain and send him a copy of his baptismal certificate. This request has been interpreted by certain scholars as an indication of his intention to marry Therese Malfatti.

(*c.* June) The Malfattis are displeased by Beethoven's conduct—perhaps he proposed to Therese, but this is not certain—and cease personal contact with him.

(15 June) First performance of Beethoven's music to Goethe's *Egmont*. The part of Klärchen is taken by Antonie Adamberger, whom Beethoven has coached in her two songs.

(Summer) Beethoven stays at Baden.

(24 August) Two marches composed by Beethoven for Archduke Anton Viktor (WoO 18, 19) are played at an equestrian spectacle presented at Laxenburg Castle in honour of Empress Maria Ludovica.

Publications: Leonore Overture No. 3 (Op. 72), String Quartet (Op. 74), *Variations* (Op. 76), Piano Sonata (Op. 78), *Egmont* Overture (Op. 84), and songs to texts by Goethe (Op. 75, Nos. 1–3, WoO 134), Halem (Op. 75, No. 4), Reissig (Op. 75, Nos. 5, 6, WoO 137–9), and Matthisson (WoO 136).

1811   Beethoven's annuity declines substantially in real value because of inflation, and also in nominal value as a result of the *Finanzpatent* [financial decree] which comes into effect on 15 March (and is subsequently modified by the court decree of 13 September). Archduke Rudolph readily agrees to maintain the annuity at its original figure, but Beethoven will have to wait longer for a satisfactory arrangement in the case of Prince Kinsky and Prince Lobkowitz.

In the course of this year Beethoven's friendship with Franz and Antonie Brentano becomes closer. On several occasions he seeks to comfort Antonie, when she is ill, by playing for her.

(April) Beethoven empowers Oliva, who leaves on a business trip to Saxony and northern Bohemia, to negotiate with Breitkopf & Härtel, and he entrusts him with a letter to Goethe which Oliva will deliver at Weimar in May.

(Early August) Beethoven arrives at the Bohemian spa Teplitz [Teplice], where he has decided to take the cure on Dr Malfatti's advice. There he meets Oliva and makes the acquaintance of Karl August Varnhagen von Ense and his future wife Rahel Levin, of the poet Christoph August Tiedge and his companion Elisabeth von der Recke, and of Amalie Sebald. While in Teplitz, he quarrels with Oliva; they will not be reconciled until the following spring.

(September) Prince Lobkowitz's annuity payments are suspended until 1815.

(18 September) Beethoven leaves Teplitz to return to Vienna via Prague. There appears to be no firm evidence to support Thayer's statement,

repeated by other scholars, that he visits Prince Lichnowsky at Grätz before travelling back to Vienna.

(22 December) Joseph von Varena, a Graz lawyer, whose acquaintance Beethoven made at Teplitz, arranges a concert at Graz, at which Marie Leopoldine Koschak [later Pachler] is the pianist in the Choral Fantasia.

Publications: Fifth Piano Concerto (Op. 73), Choral Fantasia (Op. 80), Piano Sonata (Op. 81a), three songs to texts by Goethe (Op. 83), *Christus am Ölberg* (Op. 85).

1812   (9 February) The new theatre at Pest [Budapest] opens with performances of Kotzebue's *König Stephan* and *Die Ruinen von Athen*, with music by Beethoven. The plays are repeated on 10 and 11 February.

(11 February) First Viennese performance, by Carl Czerny, of Beethoven's Fifth Piano Concerto. (It has previously been performed by Friedrich Schneider in Leipzig on 28 November 1811.)

(29 March) At another concert put on by Varena in Graz, the *König Stephan* Overture and a march with chorus from *Die Ruinen von Athen*, both still unpublished, are performed from manuscripts provided by Beethoven.

(26 June) Beethoven inscribes the autograph of the Piano Trio WoO 39 for the 9-year-old Maximiliane, a daughter of Franz and Antonie Brentano. (The Trio will not be published until 1830.)

(1–4 July) Beethoven stops in Prague on his way to Teplitz. Prince Kinsky confirms to him the undertaking he gave to Varnhagen van Ense on 8 June that he will adjust both future and still outstanding annuity payments to the level requested by Beethoven. In the meanwhile, he pays Beethoven 60 ducats on account. While in Prague, Beethoven may also have met the Brentanos, who pass through the city en route to Karlsbad.

(5 July) Beethoven arrives at Teplitz.

(6–7 July) Beethoven writes a passionate love letter to an unnamed woman whom he at one point addresses as 'My Immortal Beloved' [more correctly 'My Eternally Beloved']. Her identity has not been established to universal satisfaction. Three candidates are currently receiving serious consideration: Antonie Brentano, Countess Josephine Brunsvik de Korompa [Deym], and Countess Almerie Esterházy de Galántha. Opinions are divided as to whether the letter, which was found in Beethoven's flat after his death, was ever sent.

(July) Beethoven consults Dr Jakob von Staudenheim, who is also staying at Teplitz.

(19 July) Beethoven makes Goethe's acquaintance. They will meet several more times during the following days.

(*c.*25 July) Beethoven moves to Karlsbad [Karlovy Vary], where he is reunited with the Brentanos.

(6 August) Beethoven and the Italian violinist Giovanni Battista Polledro give a concert at Karlsbad in aid of the victims of the fire which largely destroyed Baden, near Vienna, on 26 July.

(August 8) Beethoven arrives at Franzensbad [Františkovy Lázně] together with the Brentanos.

(September 8) Beethoven is again at Karlsbad (where he may have met Goethe once more).

(Latter half of September) Beethoven has returned to Teplitz, where he meets Amalie Sebald again.

(October) Beethoven breaks his return journey to Vienna at Linz to visit his brother Nikolaus Johann.

(3 November) Prince Kinsky dies in Bohemia as a result of a riding accident. It later transpires that he has failed to issue the necessary instructions for the payment of Beethoven's annuity.

(8 November) In Linz, Beethoven's brother Nikolaus Johann marries his mistress Therese Obermayer, thereby putting an end to Beethoven's efforts to break up their relationship.

(November) Beethoven returns to Vienna. It is not known whether he sees the Brentanos again before their final departure for Frankfurt.

(29 December) First performance, by the visiting French violinist Pierre Rode and Archduke Rudolph, of the newly completed Violin Sonata Op. 96 at Prince Lobkowitz's.

(30 December) Beethoven petitions Prince Kinsky's widow to honour her husband's wishes regarding the payment of the annuity. (He will write to her again on 12 February 1813.) The matter will, however, not be settled until January 1815.

Publications: Music to *Egmont* (Op. 84), Mass (Op. 86).

1813   Oliva, who has been assisting Beethoven in various ways since 1810, leaves for Hungary, where he will remain until about the spring of 1819.

(7 January) Another performance of the Violin Sonata Op. 96 by Rode and Archduke Rudolph, again at Lobkowitz's.

(26 March) Première, at the Burgtheater, of Christoph Kuffner's tragedy *Tarpeja*, for which Beethoven has written a march (WoO 2a). The play will receive only one more performance, on 27 March.

(April) Ferdinand Ries settles in London, where, for the next eleven years, he will be an important contact for Beethoven.

(11 April) The oratorio *Christus am Ölberg* is performed at Graz.

(12 April) Beethoven's brother Kaspar Karl, who is gravely ill, makes a written declaration appointing Beethoven guardian of his son Karl in the event of his death. The same day Beethoven grants him a loan of 1,500 florins, for which Kaspar Karl's wife Johanna stands surety.

(1 May) The Fifth Symphony and the March from *Tarpeja* are performed at Schuppanzigh's concert in the Augarten.

(Summer–autumn) At Johann Nepomuk Mälzel's suggestion, Beethoven writes for Mälzel's Panharmonicon a composition celebrating Wellington's victory over the French at Vitoria, in northern Spain, on 21 June. Later he orchestrates the music, and also adds a section depicting the battle. The complete work, *Wellingtons Sieg, oder Die Schlacht bei Vittoria*, will be first performed on 8 December.

(8 December) Beethoven and Mälzel give a charity concert in the great hall of the university for the benefit of Austrian and Bavarian soldiers wounded at the Battle of Hanau (30–1 October). On the programme: the première of *Wellingtons Sieg* and the first public performance of the Seventh Symphony, as well as two marches by other composers played on Mälzel's Mechanical Trumpeter. The concert is a great success (Schindler calls it 'one of the most important moments in the life of the Master').

(10 December) Beethoven cedes to Sigmund Anton Steiner his claim to the 1,500 florins he has lent Kaspar Karl.

(12 December) The concert of 8 December is repeated in the same hall.

Publications: March from *Tarpeja*, in a piano transcription (WoO 2a); 'Der Bardengeist' (WoO 142).

1814   (2 January) Beethoven presents a further concert, this time at the Grosser Redoutensaal, but without Mälzel with whom he has quarrelled about the proprietorship of *Wellingtons Sieg*. Same programme as in December, except that the contributions from the Mechanical Trumpeter are replaced by music from Beethoven's *Ruinen von Athen*.

(Before 13 February) Beethoven sends a suitably inscribed manuscript copy of *Wellingtons Sieg* to the prince regent in London, with a request that he accept it and authorize a similar dedication of the printed score. (The prince regent does not acknowledge receipt of the manuscript.)

(27 February) Beethoven gives another concert at the Grosser Redoutensaal, consisting of the Seventh Symphony, *Wellingtons Sieg*, and the premières of the Eighth Symphony and the trio 'Tremati, empi, tremate' (Op. 116).

(March) Schindler meets Beethoven for the first time (according to Schindler's own later statement).

(25 March) Beethoven conducts the *Egmont* Overture and *Wellingtons Sieg* at the Kärntnertor-Theater,

(11 April) Beethoven, Schuppanzigh, and Joseph Linke give the first performance of the ('Archduke') Piano Trio Op. 97 in the concert hall of the hotel Zum römischen Kaiser.

That same day, Georg Friedrich Treitschke's Singspiel *Die gute Nachricht*, celebrating the entry of the Allies into Paris on 31 March, is first performed at the Kärntnertor-Theater. It features music by several composers, including Beethoven (WoO 94).

(15 April) Prince Karl Lichnowsky dies. There is no evidence that the estrangement which occurred between him and Beethoven in 1806 was ever healed.

(23 May) First performance of a further revised version of *Fidelio*, which Beethoven has prepared with Treitschke's assistance.

(Spring–summer) Having learned that Mälzel has given performances of *Wellingtons Sieg* in Munich on 16 and 17 March, Beethoven institutes legal proceedings against him. These will drag on until the two men are reconciled in 1817.

(*c.* April) Dr Staudenheim becomes Beethoven's regular doctor.

(24 June) The cantata *Un lieto brindisi* (WoO 103), Beethoven's setting of a text by Clemente Bondi, is performed on Dr Malfatti's name day.

(Summer) Beethoven stays at Baden.

(18 July) The new production of *Fidelio* reaches its seventh performance, at which the opera is presented in its final form.

(September) The Congress of Vienna begins.

(Late September/early October) Beethoven asks Ferdinand Ries, who is living in London, to warn English musicians that any performance of *Wellingtons Sieg* which Mälzel might arrange there would be illegal and incomplete. (As far as is known, Mälzel made no attempt to arrange a performance of the work in London.)

(27 November) In Prague, Weber conducts the first performance of *Fidelio* to be given outside Vienna.

(29 November) Beethoven gives a concert at the Grosser Redoutensaal. On the programme: the Seventh Symphony, *Wellingtons Sieg*, and the first performance of the cantata *Der glorreiche Augenblick* (Op. 136). The concert will be repeated on 2 December, and again on 25 December.

(December) Beethoven composes the Polonaise Op. 89 for the empress of Russia. (It will be published in March 1815 with a dedication to her.) He is granted an audience (at an unknown date), at which he receives a gift of 50 ducats, and a further 100 ducats for the violin sonatas he dedicated to the tsar in 1803. Beethoven will also dedicate the piano arrangements of the Seventh Symphony to the tsarina.

(31 December) Count Razumovsky's Viennese palace is largely destroyed by fire.

Publications: *Fidelio* (Op. 72), in a piano arrangement by Ignaz Moscheles (prepared under Beethoven's supervision); 'Germania' (WoO 94), 'An die Geliebte' (WoO 140, 2nd version), and arrangements for piano trio of Irish airs (WoO 152 and WoO 153, Nos. 1–4).

1815

(18 January) A settlement is finally reached with Prince Kinsky's heirs, who agree to pay Beethoven an annuity of 1,200 florins, as well as all arrears.

(25 January) At a concert given at the Hofburg in celebration of the tsarina's birthday, the quartet 'Mir ist so wunderbar' from *Fidelio* is performed, and Franz Wild, accompanied by Beethoven, sings 'Adelaide'.

(10 February) Sir George Smart conducts *Wellingtons Sieg* at the Drury Lane Theatre in London. He will direct another performance on 13 February.

(16–19 March) Häring writes to Smart at Beethoven's request to seek his help in finding London publishers for Beethoven's compositions. Beethoven adds a brief note to Häring's letter.

(19 April) Beethoven's claims against Lobkowitz are settled to his satisfaction, the prince agreeing to resume his part of the annuity at the original rate of 700 florins and to pay all arrears. Thus Beethoven will henceforth receive altogether 3,400 florins (in notes of redemption) annually—less than the original amount of 4,000 florins, but more than he can legally expect.

(20 May) The publisher Sigmund Anton Steiner buys a number of Beethoven's compositions, the most important of which—including the Seventh and Eighth Symphonies, *Wellingtons Sieg*, the String Quartet Op. 95, 'Archduke' Piano Trio, and Violin Sonata Op. 96— will be issued by S. A. Steiner & Co. in 1816–17.

(May) The English musician Charles Neate arrives in Vienna. During the summer he regularly sees Beethoven who has agreed to examine his compositions.

(1 June) Beethoven writes to Johann Peter Salomon in London to ask for his assistance in finding English publishers. Thanks to Salomon, Beethoven will sell certain compositions to Robert Birchall.

(9 June) The Congress of Vienna ends.

(Summer) Beethoven stays at Baden and then at Döbling.

(July) On behalf of the Philharmonic Society of London, Neate buys the Overtures *Die Ruinen von Athen, König Stephan*, and *Zur Namensfeier* for 75 guineas.

(15 July) First performance of Treitschke's Singspiel *Die Ehrenpforten* (inspired by the allied victory at Waterloo and the allied armies' second entry into Paris on 7 July). The final number, 'Es ist vollbracht' (WoO 97), has been set by Beethoven.

(11 October) First performance of *Fidelio* in Berlin, with Josephine Schulz-Killitschky, Schuppanzigh's sister-in-law, as Leonore. At the second performance (14 October) the role is taken over by Anna Milder-Hauptmann, who will sing it with great success ten more times during her present engagement.

(9 November) The Executive Committee of the Gesellschaft der Musikfreunde decides to invite Beethoven to write an oratorio for the society. He will accept the commission, but, despite several reminders over the next ten years, will never write the oratorio.

(14 November) Knowing himself to be near death, Beethoven's brother Kaspar Karl makes his will, in which he first appoints his wife and Beethoven co-guardians of his son Karl, should he die, but then deletes her name at Beethoven's insistence and makes Beethoven sole guardian. Later, however, he adds a codicil in Beethoven's absence, in which he restores the original provision and furthermore stipulates that the boy is to reside with his mother.

(15 November) Kaspar Karl dies.

(22 November) The Lower Austrian Landrecht appoints Johanna guardian and Beethoven associate guardian of Karl.

(28 November) Beethoven appeals to the Lower Austrian Landrecht to entrust the guardianship to him alone. In December, Beethoven will argue his case both in writing and, during an appearance before the tribunal, in person.

(25 December) Beethoven takes part in a charity concert at the Grosser Redoutensaal, at which the Overture *Zur Namensfeier*, the settings for mixed chorus and orchestra of Goethe's poems 'Meeresstille' and 'Glückliche Fahrt' (Op. 112), and the oratorio *Christus am Ölberg* are performed.

(*c.*1 December) The citizenship of Vienna is conferred on Beethoven.

Publications: Polonaise (Op. 89), Piano Sonata (Op. 90), 'Es ist vollbracht' (WoO 97), 'Merkenstein' (WoO 144).

1816
(6 January) Beethoven asks Milder-Hauptmann, who is still in Berlin, to invite Baron de La Motte Fouqué to write an opera libretto for him. (It is not known whether she contacted Fouqué.)

(9 January) The Landrecht rules in Beethoven's favour.

(19 January) Beethoven is formally appointed Karl's sole guardian.

(2 February) Karl is admitted as a boarder to the school run by Cajetan Giannatrasio del Rio.

(24 January) Beethoven writes the two canons WoO 168 in the private album of Charles Neate, who is about to leave for London. Neate takes with him several compositions by Beethoven, for which he is to find English publishers. He will, however, fail to do so.

(11 February) The Schuppanzigh Quartet having been disbanded by Razumovsky, Schuppanzigh gives a farewell concert before leaving for Russia. The programme consists of Beethoven's Quartet Op. 59, No. 3, Quintet Op. 16, and Septet Op. 20. Beethoven is among those present.

(18 February) Joseph Linke, the cellist of the late Schuppanzigh Quartet, gives his own farewell concert, which includes Beethoven's Cello Sonata Op. 69, as well as a piano sonata recently composed by him.

(4 April) Beethoven writes the canon WoO 170 in Hummel's album.

(25 May) Beethoven accompanies Franz Wild in a performance, at a private house, of 'An die Hoffnung' (Op. 94, 2nd version, which, Wild later claims, Beethoven wrote for him).

(Summer) Beethoven stays at Baden.

(July) Beethoven deposits 4,000 florins with Steiner at 8 per cent interest (*see* July 1819).

(18 September) Karl is operated on for hernia by Dr Carl von Smetana.

(15 December) Prince Lobkowitz dies in Bohemia. The cycle *An die ferne Geliebte*, which Beethoven has dedicated to him, appears too late

and Beethoven is obliged to send it to the prince's son Ferdinand. The annuity will be paid regularly until Beethoven's death.

Publications: *Wellingtons Sieg* (Op. 91), Seventh Symphony (Op. 92), String Quartet (Op. 95), Violin Sonata (Op. 96), 'Archduke' Piano Trio (Op. 97), the song cycle *An die ferne Geliebte* (Op. 98), several songs (Opp. 94, 99, 100, WoO 146); arrangements for piano trio of Irish airs (WoO 153, Nos. 5–20, WoO 154, Nos. 1, 3–6, 8–12, WoO 157, Nos. 2, 6, 8, 11).

1817 During much of the year Beethoven is troubled by ill health. In addition, his hearing deteriorates further (on 7 July he asks Johann Andreas Streicher to adjust one of the firm's pianos for him so that it is as loud as possible).

(January) On the advice of Wilhelm Hebenstreit, Beethoven chooses the term *Hammerklavier* in preference to the Italian *Pianoforte* for the German title of the sonata (Op. 101) which S. A. Steiner & Co. are about to publish.

(April) Beethoven quarrels with Dr Malfatti.

(3 May) Greatly moved by the sudden death of his friend Wenzel Krumpholtz the previous day, Beethoven sets a solemn passage from Schiller's *Wilhelm Tell* for three male voices (WoO 104).

(10 May) Johanna van Beethoven signs a contract binding her to contribute at least half her widow's pension to Karl's upkeep.

(9 June) Ferdinand Ries transmits to Beethoven an invitation from the Philharmonic Society to visit London next winter and compose two symphonies for the society, for a total fee of 300 guineas.

(Summer) Beethoven stays at Heiligenstadt and later at Nussdorf.

(9 July) Beethoven accepts the Philharmonic Society's offer in principle, but demands better financial terms.

(15 July) As a result of a revaluation of the currency, Beethoven's annuity of 3,400 florins (in notes of redemption) is fixed at 1,360 florins (in silver).

(August) During a visit to Vienna, the piano manufacturer Thomas Broadwood meets Beethoven.

(19 August) The directors of the Philharmonic Society reject Beethoven's demand, but repeat their previous offer.

(?Autumn) Beethoven makes the acquaintance of Marie Pachler-Koschak. Also around this time, Mälzel returns to Vienna and is reconciled with Beethoven.

(17 December) The Leipzig *Allgemeine musikalische Zeitung* publishes Beethoven's table of tempos, using Mälzel's metronome, for his eight symphonies.

(19 December) Cipriani Potter arrives in Vienna, where he will remain until the following summer. He repeatedly meets Beethoven.

(25 December) At a charity concert, Beethoven conducts his Eighth Symphony.

(27 December) Broadwood sends Beethoven a six-octave grand piano as a gift. It will be delivered to Beethoven at Mödling the following summer and, repaired more than once, will remain a cherished possession until his death.

Publications: Eighth Symphony (Op. 93), Piano Sonata (Op. 101), Cello Sonatas (Op. 102); arrangements for piano trio of Welsh airs (WoO 155).

1818   (24 January) Karl leaves Giannattasio del Rio's school to live with his uncle. He is taught by a private tutor.

(February–March) Beethoven's earliest surviving conversation book dates from this period.

(5 March) Beethoven informs the Philharmonic Society, through Ries, that ill health has prevented him from going to London during the past winter, but that he hopes to take up the society's invitation later that year.

(May–September) Beethoven and Karl stay at Mödling, where, for a time, Karl is taught by the village priest.

(21 September) Johanna van Beethoven petitions the Landrecht for permission to place Karl in the Vienna Stadtkonvikt, since Beethoven, she alleges, is manifestly incapable of providing him with an adequate education. The petition is rejected.

(September–December) Karl attends the Akademisches Gymnasium.

(3 December) Karl, who is still living with Beethoven, runs away to his mother.

(5 December) Karl is removed from his mother's flat with the help of the police and temporarily placed in Giannattasio del Rio's care.

(7 and 10 December) Johanna van Beethoven submits further petitions to the Landrecht.

(11 December) Beethoven, Johanna, and Karl appear before the Landrecht. When asked, during his interview, whether he is of noble birth, Beethoven replies that the Dutch predicate 'van' was not applied exclusively to the nobility, and that he has neither a diploma nor any other proof of his nobility.

(14 December) Karl returns to Beethoven's flat.

(18 December) The Landrecht, whose jurisdiction extends solely to the aristocracy, transfers the case to the Vienna Magistracy.

(Late December/early January) Karl is enrolled as a day pupil at Johann Baptist Kudlich's institute. In March he will become a boarder there.

Publications: Arrangements for piano trio of Scottish airs (Op. 108).

1819   (11 January) Beethoven, Johanna, and Karl appear before the Magistracy.

(17 January) At a charity concert Beethoven conducts the *Prometheus* Overture and the Seventh Symphony.

(1 February) Beethoven addresses a long memorandum to the Magistracy, in which he seeks to demonstrate the excellence of his educational plans for Karl, argues for the permanent exclusion of Johanna from the guardianship, and declares his intention to propose another person to act as co-guardian with himself.

(6 February) A wedding hymn composed by Beethoven (WoO 105) is performed on the occasion of the marriage of Anna [Nanni] Giannatasio del Rio to Leopold von Schmerling.

(15 March) The Philharmonic Society of Laibach [Ljubljana] confers honorary membership on Beethoven.

(Spring?) Oliva returns from Hungary by the spring at the latest. He resumes his secretarial duties and advises Beethoven in different matters.

(26 March) The Magistracy names Beethoven's friend Magistratsrat Mathias von Tuscher Karl's co-guardian, the appointment to take effect the next day.

(23 April) Beethoven applies for a passport for Karl, so that he can be educated by Professor Johann Michael Sailer at Landshut in Bavaria. Tuscher supports the plan. However, in the light of objections raised by Karl's mother, the authorities will reject the application on 7 May.

(May–October) Beethoven stays at Mödling.

(4 June) Beethoven's patron and pupil Archduke Rudolph is elected archbishop of Olmütz [Olomuc]. The *Missa solemnis* which Beethoven is to compose for the installation ceremony on 9 March 1820 will not be completed in time.

(22 June) Karl becomes a pupil at Joseph Urban Blöchlinger's school.

(5 July) Tuscher expresses the desire to give up Karl's co-guardianship.

(13 July) With the money he deposited with Steiner in 1816, Beethoven, on the advice of Baron Eskeles, buys eight shares in the Nationalbank.

(12 September) Beethoven and Karl Friedrich Zelter, who first met in Berlin in 1796, renew their acquaintance during Zelter's current visit to Vienna.

(17 September) Tuscher is relieved of his co-guardianship by the Magistracy, which then appoints Johanna van Beethoven and Leopold Nussböck Karl's co-guardians.

(1 October) Beethoven petitions the Magistracy for his reinstatement as guardian.

On the same day, the first of the Concerts spirituels founded by Franz Xaver Gebauer takes place at the Mehlgrube. During the 1819–20 season Beethoven's first four symphonies, the Sixth Symphony, the Mass in C, and the settings for mixed chorus and orchestra of Goethe's poems 'Meeresstille' and 'Glückliche Fahrt' are performed; during the 1820–1 season there are performances of the Fifth, Seventh, and Eighth Symphonies, as well as of *Christus am Ölberg*.

(4 November) Beethoven's request to be reinstated as guardian is refused. A further application dated 20 November will be rejected on 20 December.

Publications: String Quintet (Op. 104), an arrangement of the Piano Trio Op. 1, No. 3; Piano Sonata (Op. 106).

1820   (7 January) Beethoven submits his case to the Lower Austrian Court of Appeal.

(March) Beethoven dedicates the song 'Abendlied unter gestirntem Himmel' (WoO 150) to Dr Anton Braunhofer.

(8 April) The Court of Appeal rules in Beethoven's favour, and, as he has requested, he and Karl Peters are appointed co-guardians. Johanna van Beethoven's subsequent appeal to the emperor proves unsuccessful. However, Peters, who is travelling abroad, will not be able to assume his duties until October. He will thereafter exercise them until he moves to Prague in April 1825.

(May–October) Beethoven stays at Mödling.

(29 December) Steiner asks Beethoven to repay the 3,000 florins he owes him.

(December) Oliva leaves for Russia, where he will remain until his death in 1848.

1821   Beethoven is ill during a large part of the year.

(31 March) Death of Josephine Brunsvik-Deym-Stackelberg (*see* under 1799, 1804, and 1810).

(Summer–autumn) Beethoven stays at Unterdöbling (June–September) and at Baden (September–October).

(*c.* December) The Steiermärkischer Musikverein [Styrian Music Society] elects Beethoven an honorary member.

Publication: Piano Sonata (Op. 109).

1822   (Late March) Rossini arrives in Vienna, where a three-month season of his operas opens in April. During his stay, he is introduced to Beethoven by the Italian poet Giuseppe Carpani.

(April) There are conflicting accounts as to whether Schubert personally delivers to Beethoven a copy of his newly published *Variations on a French Song* which are dedicated to Beethoven.

(18 May) The Leipzig music publisher C. F. Peters contacts Beethoven. Over the next three years negotiations between them will focus primarily on the publication of a Mass; but they will lead nowhere, and in 1825 Beethoven will return to Peters the advance of 360 florins he received from him in August 1822.

(May–June) Beethoven stays at Oberdöbling.

(Late May–early August) Friedrich Rochlitz, the editor of the Leipzig *Allgemeine musikalische Zeitung*, who is visiting Vienna, probably meets Beethoven several times.

(6 July) Beethoven asks Ries how much the Philharmonic Society would pay for a new symphony (*see* 10 November below).

(31 July) Beethoven asks his brother Nikolaus Johann, to whom he already owes 200 florins (which he will repay in February 1823), for a further loan. He also mentions that he still owes Steiner some 3,000 florins (*see* under 1820; this debt will not be completely repaid until 1824). Johann will lend him some money (the amount is not known), in return for which Beethoven will assign to him the rights to certain compositions.

(September) Beethoven stays at Baden.

(3 October) The newly rebuilt Theater in der Josefstadt is inaugurated with two works by Karl Meisl, *Die Weihe des Hauses* (an adaptation of Kotzebue's *Die Ruinen von Athen—see* under 1812) and *Das Bild des Fürsten*. For *Die Weihe des Hauses* Beethoven has composed a new overture (Op. 124) and a chorus (WoO 98). He conducts all the music himself, assisted by Franz Gläser.

(3 November) A *Gratulations-Menuett* (WoO 3) composed by Beethoven is performed at a ceremony in honour of Karl Hensler, the manager of the Theater in der Josefstadt. On the same day *Fidelio* is revived at the Kärntnertor-Theater, with Wilhelmine Schröder as Leonore. Beethoven attends the performance, which is conducted by Michael Umlauf.

(4 November) Hensler gives a dinner at the Theater in der Josefstadt, at which Beethoven is present. Schindler's first genuine entries in the conversation books date from this occasion. (All earlier ones, going back as far as 1819, have been identified as forgeries.) His closer contact with Beethoven seems to date from this period, and he will soon undertake a multitude of tasks and errands for Beethoven.

(9 November) Prince Golitsïn, writing from St Petersburg, commissions 'one, two, or three new quartets'. Beethoven accepts, and will in due course compose the String Quartets Opp. 127, 132, and 130 (in that order) for the prince.

(10 November) In reply to his enquiry (*see* 6 July above), the directors of the Philharmonic Society of London decide to offer Beethoven £50 for a new symphony in manuscript. Ries transmits the offer to Beethoven on 15 November. Beethoven will accept it on 20 December.

(28 December) The Royal Swedish Academy of Music issues a diploma appointing Beethoven a foreign member.

Publications: Piano Sonata (Op. 110), the settings of Goethe's poems 'Meeresstille' and 'Glückliche Fahrt' (Op. 112).

1823
(23 January) Having decided to sell the *Missa solemnis* by subscription at 50 gold ducats a copy, Beethoven begins to send out invitations to European courts and certain music societies. He will in due course receive ten positive replies.

(30 January) Beethoven learns that the post of court composer, for which he has applied, is to be abolished. (The previous occupant, Anton Tayber, died on 18 November 1822.)

(5 February) In a letter to Ries, Beethoven writes that, if his health improves, he hopes to travel to London in 1824.

(February) Beethoven, heavily in debt, is obliged to sell one of his eight bank shares.

(1 March) Louis Schlösser calls on Beethoven. They subsequently meet several more times before Schlösser's departure in May.

(6 March) In a letter to his lawyer Johann Baptist Bach, Beethoven appoints his nephew Karl his sole heir.

(19 March) Beethoven offers a presentation copy of the *Missa solemnis* to Archduke Rudolph.

(Spring) Buoyed by the successful revival of *Fidelio*, Beethoven contemplates writing another opera. In this connection, he discusses two possible subjects, *Drahomira* and *Melusina*, with Grillparzer.

(May–August) Beethoven stays at Hetzendorf.

(12 April) Beethoven composes a short cantata (WoO 106) for the birthday next day of Prince Ferdinand Lobkowitz.

(13 April) The 11-year-old Liszt, who has previously called on Beethoven, gives a recital at the Kleiner Redoutensaal, at which Beethoven may have been present.

(*c.*24 April) Beethoven signs a contract with Diabelli for the publication of the *Missa solemnis*, but later withdraws from the arrangement.

(26 April) Beethoven composes a canon (WoO 184) as a greeting for Schuppanzigh who has recently returned from Russia.

(29 April) At her Dresden debut, Wilhelmine Schröder is highly acclaimed in a performance of *Fidelio* conducted by Weber.

(14 June) Schuppanzigh resumes his quartet recitals (with Karl Holz, Franz Weiss, and Joseph Linke).

(July) Friedrich Wieck is introduced to Beethoven by Matthäus Andreas Stein.

(Summer) Beethoven's suffers from ill health, including eye trouble.

(August–October) Beethoven stays at Baden.

(29 August) Karl leaves Blöchlinger's school.

(17 September) Beethoven informs Spohr that he has already begun setting Grillparzer's libretto (*Melusina*). However, no sketches have survived.

(27 September) Beethoven composes a canon (WoO 202) for Marie Pachler-Koschak, whom he has met at Vöslau, and perhaps also at nearby Baden.

(28 September) Johann Reinhold Schultz visits Beethoven at Baden, together with Tobias Haslinger and Joseph Blahetka.

(5 October) Weber calls on Beethoven at Baden, with Haslinger, Ferdinand Piringer, and Julius Benedict.

(October) Karl enrols at the university, where he studies principally philosophy and languages. He will be obliged to repeat the first year of his studies and will eventually withdraw from the university (*see* April 1825).

Publications: Piano Sonata (Op. 111), *Diabelli Variations* (Op. 120).

1824   (*c.* February) Schott's Söhne write inviting Beethoven to send them new works for publication and to contribute to their journal *Cäcilia*.

(February) Beethoven is presented with a petition signed by thirty-one Viennese music lovers urging him to perform the *Missa solemnis* and his new (Ninth) symphony in Vienna, and to compose a new opera. The petition is printed in the *Allgemeine Theaterzeitung* and the *Wiener allgemeine musikalische Zeitung*.

(10 March) Beethoven writes to Schott's Söhne, politely refusing the request to contribute to *Cäcilia* but offering his new Mass and symphony, as well as a string quartet. (The firm will publish, among other compositions, both the Mass and the Ninth Symphony, as well as the String Quartets Opp. 127 and 131.)

(April) Dr Anton Braunhofer replaces Dr Staudenheim as Beethoven's regular doctor.

(7 April) First complete performance of the *Missa solemnis*, arranged by Prince Golitsïn in St Petersburg.

(27 April) A manuscript copy of the Ninth Symphony is handed to Franz Christian Kirchhoffer, who will send it to the Philharmonic Society in London.

(7 May) Following lengthy discussions concerning date and venue, Beethoven gives a concert at the Kärntnertor-Theater which includes the Overture *Die Weihe des Hauses*, the Kyrie, Credo, and Agnus Dei from the *Missa solemnis*, as well as the first performance of the Ninth Symphony (with Sontag, Unger, Haizinger, and Seipelt as soloists). Beethoven assists Michael Umlauf, who is in overall charge of the concert.

(23 May) The concert is repeated at the Grosser Redoutensaal, without the Credo and Agnus Dei of the Mass, but including the trio 'Tremate, empi, tremate' (Op. 116) and the aria *Di tanti palpiti* from Rossini's *Tancredi*, both performed by singers of the Italian opera company currently appearing in Vienna.

The receipts from the concerts, and especially those of the second, disappoint Beethoven who blames Louis Antoine Duport, the manager of the theatre and the Redoutensaal, and also Schindler. As a result, his close relations with the latter are suspended.

(May–November) After a short time at Penzing, Beethoven rents accommodation at Baden.

(July) Ferdinand Ries leaves London for Godesberg, near Bonn.

(Late September) Johann Andreas Stumpff, on a month's visit to Vienna, calls on Beethoven at Baden with Haslinger. He meets Beethoven several more times, and arranges and supervises the overhaul of his Broadwood piano by Matthäus Andreas Stein. (*See also* December 1826.)

(19 December) The directors of the Philharmonic Society decide to offer Beethoven 300 guineas to visit London during the forthcoming season (February–June) and compose a symphony and a concerto to be performed during his stay.

(20 December) Neate informs Beethoven of the society's offer.

Publication: Variations for piano trio on 'Ich bin der Schneider Kakadu' (Op. 121a).

1825

(15 and 27 January) Beethoven indicates his willingness to accept the Philharmonic Society's offer (*see* 19 December 1824), provided he also receives travelling expenses of 100 guineas.

(1 February) Neate notifies Beethoven that the Philharmonic Society cannot increase the financial terms it has offered.

(6 March) Schuppanzigh directs the first performance of the Quartet Op. 127. The performance is generally considered inadequate.

(18 March) After intensive rehearsals supervised by Beethoven himself, Joseph Michael Böhm directs a satisfactory performance of the Quartet Op. 127. He will direct further performances on 23 March (when the quartet is played twice) and 7 April.

(19 March) Beethoven informs Neate that he is unable to travel to London this spring, but holds out the vague possibility of a visit in the autumn.

(21 March) Sir George Smart conducts the first English performance of the Ninth Symphony.

(30 March–4 May) Ludwig Rellstab visits Vienna, where he calls on Beethoven more than once. On 3 May Beethoven sends him a farewell note which includes the canon WoO 203.

(April) Karl, having withdrawn from the university, enrols at the Polytechnisches Institut for studies in commerce. The institute's vice-principal, Franz Michael Reisser, replaces Peters as his co-guardian. Karl will lodge with Mathias Schlemmer, near the institute.

(2 April) Karl Holz calls on Beethoven, apparently to consult him about the tempos of the Fourth Symphony which Holz is due to conduct two days later. By the summer they will enjoy close relations, and Holz will take Schindler's place as Beethoven's assistant in various matters.

(Mid-April to mid-May) Beethoven suffers from an abdominal complaint.

(May–October) Beethoven stays at Baden.

(13 May) Beethoven sends Dr Anton Braunhofer a report on his condition from Baden, together with the humorous canon WoO 189.

(23 May) At the Niederrheinisches Musikfest at Aix-la-Chapelle, Ries conducts Beethoven's Ninth Symphony and *Christus am Ölberg*. On 9 June he will send Beethoven a fee of 40 louis d'or.

(2 September) Friedrich Kuhlau visits Beethoven at Baden. They dine at an inn, together with Conrad Graf, Haslinger, Holz, and the oboist Joseph Sellner. Beethoven writes a canon on Kuhlau's name (WoO 191), which he will send to Kuhlau the next day.

(4 September) Maurice Schlesinger visits Beethoven at Baden.

(7 September) A rehearsal of the Quartet Op. 132 takes place in Schlesinger's rooms at the hotel Zum wilden Mann in the Kärtnerstrasse.

(9 September) First (private) performance of the Quartet Op. 132 by Schuppanzigh, Holz, Weiss, and Linke at the hotel Zum wilden Mann, before some fourteen persons, including Beethoven. The quartet is played twice. On this occasion Beethoven is introduced to Sir George Smart, who has come to Vienna mainly in order to ascertain from him the tempos of his symphonies.

(10 September) Schlesinger pays Beethoven 80 ducats for the Quartet Op. 132.

(11 September) At another private concert at Schlesinger's hotel, attended by a larger company, Schuppanzigh, Linke, and Carl Czerny perform one of the Trios Op. 70 and the 'Archduke' Trio, after which the Quartet Op. 132 is once again played. After the concert Beethoven dines with the performers and a few other persons, among them Sir George Smart. Finally, Beethoven improvises.

(16 September) Smart travels to Baden to visit Beethoven, who presents him with the canon WoO 192.

(15 October) Beethoven returns to Vienna and moves into what will be his final lodgings there, at the Schwarzspanierhaus [15 Schwarzspanierstrasse]. He will henceforth be in close contact with Stephan von Breuning and his family, who live nearby.

(6 November) First public performance of the Quartet Op. 132 by the Schuppanzigh Quartet, at Linke's benefit concert at the Musikverein. Also on the programme: the 'Archduke' Trio, played by Karl Maria von Bocklet, Schuppanzigh, and Linke.

Publications: Overture *Zur Namensfeier* (Op. 115), 'Opferlied' (Op. 121b), Overture *Die Weihe des Hauses* (Op. 124).

1826   (Late January) Beethoven again suffers from abdominal and eye complaints. He once more consults Dr Braunhofer.

(31 January) At a meeting of the *Repräsentanten* [representatives] of the Gesellschaft der Musikfreunde, the executive committee's proposal that honorary membership be conferred on Beethoven is accepted.

(21 March) The Schuppanzigh Quartet gives the first performance of the Quartet Op. 130 with the fugue (later Op. 133).

(25 April) Anton Halm delivers to Beethoven his arrangement for piano duet of the fugue from Op. 130, but Beethoven considers it unsatisfactory and will make his own (Op. 134).

(6 August) Karl attempts suicide in the ruins of Rauhenstein Castle, near Baden. (The date is not absolutely certain.) He is injured and taken to his mother's lodgings in Vienna.

(7 August) Karl is admitted to the Allgemeines Krankenhaus [General Hospital].

(23 September) Samuel Heinrich Spiker calls on Beethoven with Haslinger. When he leaves Vienna on 9 October, Spiker will take with him a specially bound manuscript copy of the Ninth Symphony, corrected by Beethoven, for King Friedrich Wilhelm III of Prussia to whom the work is dedicated.

(September) Stephan von Breuning becomes Karl's co-guardian.

(25 September) Karl is discharged from the hospital.

(28 September) Beethoven and Karl leave Vienna to stay at Nikolaus Johann van Beethoven's country estate at Gneixendorf, near Krems, where they will arrive the next day.

(27 November) Probable date of Beethoven's and Karl's departure from Gneixendorf.

(28 November) Probable date of their arrival in Vienna.

(*c.*3 December) Beethoven falls ill and keeps to his bed. On this or the following day he writes to Holz asking him to call. (The canon WoO 198, which Beethoven includes in his note, may be prompted by a recent dispute between them for which Beethoven seems to accept some responsibility.)

(5 December) After Dr Braunhofer and Dr Staudenheim have failed to respond to Beethoven's summons, Holz contacts Dr Wawruch, who comes promptly.

(*c.*13 December) After showing some improvement, Beethoven's health deteriorates dramatically. He suffers from dropsy and jaundice.

(14 December) Beethoven receives Stumpff's gift of Samuel Arnold's forty-volume edition of Handel's works, which gives him great pleasure.

(20 December) Beethoven undergoes an operation to withdraw fluid from his abdomen.

(December) Karl is interviewed by Baron Stutterheim, who, at Stephan von Breuning's request, accepts him into his regiment. The grateful Beethoven will dedicate the Quartet Op. 131 to Stutterheim.

Since his return to Vienna, Beethoven has resumed his contact with Schindler who will remain in close attendance until the end.

Publications: March with chorus from *Die Ruinen von Athen* (Op. 114), trio 'Tremate, empi, tremate' (Op. 116), Overture *König Stephan* (Op. 117), *Elegischer Gesang* (Op. 118), Ninth Symphony (Op. 125), String Quartet (Op. 127).

1827   (2 January) Karl departs for Iglau (Jihlava), where his regiment is stationed.

(3 January) In a letter to his lawyer, Johann Baptist Bach, Beethoven appoints Karl his sole heir. (*See also* 23 March.)

(8 January) Second abdominal operation.

(11 January) Dr Malfatti takes part in a doctors' conference, at which he recommends consumption of frozen fruit punch and rubbing the patient's abdomen with ice-cold water. These remedies are applied for a time.

(19 January) Beethoven and Dr Malfatti are reconciled.

(2 February) Third abdominal operation.

(27 February) Fourth abdominal operation.

(28 February) The directors of the Philharmonic Society decide to make Beethoven a gift of £100. The money is sent to Sebastian Rau, who delivers the equivalent sum (1,000 florins) to Beethoven on 17 March. The banknotes will be found intact after Beethoven's death.

(7 March) Raphael Georg Kiesewetter, vice-president of the Gesellschaft der Musikfreunde, sends Beethoven the diploma (dated 26 October 1826) appointing him an honorary member of the society.

(8 March) Hummel, accompanied by Ferdinand Hiller, calls on Beethoven. He will visit him again on 13, 20, and 23 March.

(*c.*20 March) According to one report, Schubert is among Beethoven's visitors.

(23 March) On the advice of Stephan von Breuning (who considers Karl still very irresponsible), Beethoven writes out a will in which he stipulates that, while Karl shall be his sole heir, the capital of the estate shall fall to Karl's natural or testamentary heirs.

(*c.*23 March) Beethoven receives the last rites.

(24 March) In the evening Beethoven falls into a coma.

(26 March) Beethoven dies, reportedly between 5 and 6 o'clock in the afternoon. Anselm Hüttenbrenner, who is one of probably only two persons present, later claims to have been responsible for closing his eyes. The identity of the other person is uncertain.

Some Further Notable Nineteenth-Century Dates

1827   (27 March) Dr Johann Wagner carries out the autopsy on Beethoven's body.

(28 March) Joseph Franz Danhauser takes Beethoven's death mask.

(29 March) Beethoven's funeral. Following a service at the Trinitarier-kirche [17 Alserstrasse], the coffin is transported to Währing Cemetery [now Schubert Park]. At the entrance to the cemetery, an oration written by Grillparzer is delivered by the well-known actor Heinrich Anschütz.

(March/April) Publication of the *Missa solemnis*.

(3 April) At a service for Beethoven at the Augustinerkirche Mozart's Requiem is performed.

(5 April) At a service for Beethoven at the Karlskirche Cherubini's (first) Requiem is sung.

(22 April) The Schuppanzigh Quartet gives the first performance of the Quartet Op. 130 with the new finale.

(4 June) Stephan von Breuning dies. He is succeeded as Karl's guardian by Jakob Hotschevar.

(September) Publication of the String Quartets Opp. 132 and 135.

1828   (20 November) Death of Therese van Beethoven.

1832   (May) Karl van Beethoven resigns from the army.

(16 July) Karl marries Karolina Barbara Naske. They will have five children.

1840   Schindler's *Biographie von Ludwig van Beethoven* is published at Münster.

1845   Publication, at Münster, of the second edition of Schindler's Beethoven biography (identical with the first, except for the addition of two annexes).

(12 August) Ernst Julius Hähnel's statue of Beethoven is unveiled at Bonn.

1848   (12 January) Death of Nikolaus Johann van Beethoven.

1858   (13 April) Death of Karl van Beethoven.

1860   The third, completely revised and expanded, edition of Schindler's Beethoven biography is published at Münster.

1863   (13 October) Beethoven's body is exhumed and reburied at Währing Cemetery.

1866   Vol. i of Thayer's Beethoven biography is published in Berlin, in a German version (*Ludwig van Beethovens Leben*) prepared by Hermann Deiters.

1868   (2 February) Death of Beethoven's sister-in-law Johanna van Beethoven.

1872   Vol. ii of *Ludwig van Beethovens Leben* appears in Berlin.

1879   Publication of vol. iii of *Ludwig van Beethovens Leben* in Berlin. (This is the last part of the biography to appear in Thayer's lifetime; vols. iv and v will appear at Leipzig in 1907 and 1908 in editions prepared by Hugo Riemann, who will subsequently bring out revised editions of vols. i–iii.)

1880   (1 May) Caspar von Zumbusch's statue of Beethoven is unveiled in Vienna.

1888   (22 June) Beethoven's remains are transported from Währing Cemetery to the new Central Cemetery (Group 32A, Grave 29).

Five generations of the Beethoven Family

Ludwig van Beethoven (1712–73), the composer's grandfather
m. (1733)
Maria Josepha Poll (c.1714–75)

Maria Bernhardine Ludovika
(1734–5)

Markus Joseph
(b. & ?d. 1736)

Johann
(c.1740–92)
m. (1767)
Maria Magdalene Laym, née Keverich
(1746–87)

Ludwig Maria
(b. & d. 1769)

Ludwig
(1770–1827)

Kaspar Karl
(1774–1815)
m. (1806)
Johanna Reiss
(c.1786–1868)

Karl
(1806–58)
m. (1832)
Caroline Naske
(1808–91)

Nikolaus Johann
(1776–1848)
m. (1812)
Therese Obermayer
(1787–1828)

Anna Maria
(b. & d. 1779)

Franz Georg
(1781–3)

Maria Margarete
(1786–7)

Karoline Johanna
(1831–1919)
m. (1854)
Franz Weidinger
(1823–82)

Maria Anna
(1835–91)
m. (1857)
Paul Weidinger
(1828–1904)

Ludwig Johann
(b. 1839, d. between 1890 and 1916)
m. (1865)
Maria Nitsche
(1846–1917)

Gabriele
(1844–1914)
m. (1864)
Robert Heimler
(1833–1910)

Hermine
(1852–87)
m. (1876)
Emil Axmann
(1850–1935)

DICTIONARY

Adamberger, Antonie (b. Vienna, 31 December 1790; d. Vienna, 25 December 1867). Actress and singer; daughter of the tenor Johann Valentin Adamberger (1740/3–1804), the original Belmonte in Mozart's *Die Entführung aus dem Serail*, and of the actress and singer Maria Anna Adamberger, née Ja(c)quet (1752–1804). Antonie made her debut at the Burgtheater as Antonia in Heinrich von Collin's* *Der gestörte Abschied* on 22 February 1804, and was a full-time member of the company from 1807 to 1817.

She was cast as Klärchen in the first Viennese production of Goethe's* *Egmont* (24 May 1810). It was, however, not until the fourth performance, on 15 June, that the play was given with Beethoven's music. This included, in addition to the now well-known overture and several other numbers, two songs for Klärchen: 'Die Trommel gerühret' (Act I) and 'Freudvoll und leidvoll' (Act III). In a letter to Thayer* on 5 January 1867, Adamberger recalled how patiently Beethoven had coached her in those songs.

In 1812 she became engaged to Theodor Körner,* in whose plays *Toni* (17 April 1812) and *Hedwig* (11 January 1813) she took the leading roles. After his death in the Wars of Liberation she continued her acting career until her marriage in June 1817 to the historian and numismatist Joseph Cales von Arneth (1791–1863). She knew Schubert well and became a much admired interpreter of his Lieder.

(Arneth, Berger[2], Clive[2], Zimmer)

Adlersburg, Karl Schwabel von [from 1843, Baron] (b. 1774; d. Vienna, 20 March 1855). Lawyer. He advised Beethoven in his quarrel with Mälzel,* in his negotiations with Prince Lobkowitz* and with Prince Kinsky's* heirs about his annuities, and, until about the summer of 1818, in his litigation with Johanna van Beethoven.* From 1820 he was a member of the law faculty at Vienna University; in 1834 he served as the university's rector. He was granted the title 'Hofrat' in 1850.

(Ullrich[5])

Albrechtsberger, Johann Georg (b. Klosterneuburg, near Vienna, 3 February 1736; d. Vienna, 7 March 1809). Organist and composer. He was greatly admired as a master of counterpoint and much sought after as a teacher (his many pupils include Hummel* and Mozart's* son Franz Xaver Wolfgang).

Following Haydn's* departure for London in mid-January 1794, Beethoven studied counterpoint with Albrechtsberger until the spring of 1795. Albrechtsberger was a very thorough, if somewhat dry, teacher. (The exercises which

Beethoven wrote under his guidance were later closely examined by Gustav Nottebohm.) Beethoven remained in friendly contact with Albrechtsberger after he ceased to be his pupil, as is shown by three letters he received from his former teacher between December 1796 and June 1797 (*Corr.* B24, 29, 31). Two of these mention an orchestral arrangement which Albrechtsberger made of a 'trio' by Beethoven and which was to be performed at a private concert (perhaps at the house of Count Browne,* to whom the three String Trios Op. 9 were dedicated in July 1798).

Beethoven seems to have retained a high regard for Albrechtsberger. Cipriani Potter* relates that when he asked Beethoven, during his stay in Vienna in 1817–18, to recommend a teacher, Beethoven answered: 'I have lost my Albrechtsberger and have no confidence in anyone else.' And in 1825, when requested by the young German organist and composer Carl August Reichardt to recommend a treatise of counterpoint, he apparently suggested Albrechtsberger's *Gründliche Anweisung zur Composition* (*see BKh7/296*). It was probably also out of respect for Albrechtsberger that he offered to give lessons in musical theory to the latter's grandson Carl Friedrich Hirsch* in 1816–17. As for Albrechtsberger's opinion of Beethoven's compositions, Jan Emanuel Doležálek* later told Otto Jahn that he had once asserted that Beethoven 'has learned nothing and will never produce anything of real value'. It should be pointed out, though, that Doležálek's conversation with Jahn took place some fifty years after the remark was said to have been made and may not have been accurate. Moreover, Doležálek does not specify the precise date of the alleged observation, so it is not possible to know which of Beethoven's works were known to the public by then. It would not be surprising, however, if Beethoven's style of composition had indeed displeased the much older Albrechtsberger, whose musical tastes were quite different.

(Freeman, Nottebohm[1], Staehelin[6])

Alexander I, emperor of Russia (b. St Petersburg, 28 December 1777 (NS); d. Taganrog, 1 December 1825 (NS)). Son of Emperor Paul I (1754–1801). He married Princess Luise of Baden [Elisabeth Alexievna*] in 1793, and became emperor in 1801. In 1803 Beethoven dedicated to him the three Violin Sonatas Op. 30, but he did not receive his reward until years later (*see* the article on Elisabeth Alexievna). During the Congress of Vienna, in which Alexander was a prominent participant, Beethoven was presented to him and the empress.

Alexander's sister Maria Pavlovna (1786–1853), who was married to the future Grand Duke Karl Friedrich of Saxe-Weimar-Eisenach, was likewise present in Vienna. It was at her request that Beethoven's concert, originally announced for 20 November, then for 22 November and subsequently for 27 November 1814, was postponed yet again, this time until 29 November. (Its programme included the Seventh Symphony, *Wellingtons Sieg*, and the first performance of the oratorio *Der glorreiche Augenblick*.)

In 1823 Alexander was among the subscribers to the *Missa solemnis*. Beethoven planned to dedicate the Ninth Symphony to him; following Alexander's death, he dedicated it to King Friedrich Wilhelm III* of Prussia instead.

Amenda, Karl (b. Lippaiken, Courland [Lipaikciems, Latvia], 4 October 1771; d. Kandau, Courland [Kandava, Latvia], 8 March 1836). Clergyman; violinist. He attended school at Mitau [Jelgava], where he received violin lessons from Franz Adam Veichtner, Konzertmeister to the Courland court. After studying theology and music at Jena (1792–5), he spent two years as a music teacher at Lausanne. In the spring of 1798 he arrived in Vienna together with his friend and compatriot Gottfried Heinrich Mylich, a competent musician who played the violin, viola, and guitar. In Vienna Amenda found employment in the household of Prince Lobkowitz;* later he was engaged by Mozart's* widow Constanze as tutor for her sons.

During his stay in Vienna he became extremely friendly with Beethoven. According to one source, he made Beethoven's acquaintance through Constanze Mozart; according to another, they met at the house of 'friends' of Amenda's (perhaps the Palais Lobkowitz) on the occasion of a chamber music session in which Amenda took part. He and Beethoven frequently made music together, sometimes with Mylich. When Amenda decided to return to Courland in the summer of 1799, Beethoven presented him with a copy of his String Quartet Op. 18, No. 1, on which he inscribed a fond dedication. (Later Beethoven would ask Amenda not to show the quartet to anyone, as he had considerably revised it.)

It is clear from their correspondence that for both men their friendship formed one of the most profound experiences of their lives. 'You are no ordinary man,' Amenda wrote some time after his return to Courland. 'I consider anyone who knows you as I do and feels only ordinary love for you to be unworthy of the divine emotion of love . . . Oh my Beethoven! Never forget a friend who, though he may be separated from you for ever, will do all he can to be worthy of your love. You still fill his heart completely . . . My beloved friend, I long for you' (*Corr.* B51). (Lest any modern critic be misled by the highly charged language, so dear to young men in the Romantic age, and perceive in it homosexual overtones, it should be added that in the same letter Amenda informed Beethoven that he had fallen in love with 'a pretty, young, and talented girl from Geneva' (Jeanette Benoit); he was to marry her in 1802.) Beethoven's affection, though expressed in more sober terms, was manifestly no less sincere: 'A thousand times the thought of the best human being I have ever met comes to my mind,' he assured Amenda, in a letter probably written around June 1801 (*Corr.* A52/B66). 'Of the three persons who have possessed my whole love, of whom one is still alive, you are the third. The memory of you will never die in me.' (The other two friends were probably Franz Gerhard Wegeler,* and Lorenz von Breuning* who had died in 1798.) In a letter written shortly afterwards, Beethoven told Amenda, in strict secrecy, of his progressive loss of hearing and described the anguish it caused him (*Corr.* A53/B67).

Not all of Amenda's letters to Beethoven have survived. One, which dates from 1815 (*Corr.* B791), appears to have been written after a lengthy break in correspondence, yet it displays all the old affection. In it Amenda suggests that Beethoven ought to undertake a grand musical tour, perhaps as far as Russia: 'If you were to pass through Mitau and Riga on your way to St Petersburg, how warmly you would be received there! And I would hasten to embrace you, I would bring you to my house for a few days—oh, how happy I should be to have you, my most dearly beloved Beethoven, as a guest in my house!' Amenda had become a pastor in 1802, and in 1815 was living with his wife and his five children at Talsen [Talsi]. With his letter, he sent Beethoven an operatic libretto by his friend Rudolf vom Berge.* No doubt Beethoven received further news of Amenda's activities the following year, when he was visited by Karl von Bursy.*

Anschütz, Heinrich (b. Luckau, Nieder-Lausitz, 8 February 1785; d. Vienna, 29 December 1865). Actor. After a successful stage debut at Nuremberg in 1807 as the younger Klingsberg in Kotzebue's* comedy *Die beiden Klingsberg*, he spent the next thirteen years attached to different German theatres. In 1821 he was engaged at the Burgtheater in Vienna, and he remained with the company for more than forty years, becoming one of its most distinguished and revered members. He last appeared on 4 June 1864 as the musician Miller in Schiller's* *Kabale und Liebe*, one his most famous roles; others were the title roles in Lessing's* *Nathan der Weise*, Schiller's *Wilhelm Tell* and *Wallenstein*, and Shakespeare's* *King Lear* and *Macbeth*. By 1835 his repertoire comprised no fewer than 114 roles, and he is reported to have played altogether 257 parts in 243 plays at the Burgtheater.

He made Beethoven's acquaintance at Döbling in the summer of 1822. In his posthumously published memoirs (*Heinrich Anschütz: Erinnerungen aus dessen Leben und Wirken*, Vienna, 1866), he recalls how, while walking in the countryside, he came across Beethoven, absorbed in the act of composition, with his head cupped in his left hand and 'his gaze fixed upon a sheet of music paper, on which, with his right hand, he was inscribing mystical runes, drumming with his fingers when not writing'. They spoke briefly and subsequently met on several occasions.

After Beethoven's death Anschütz, who was an outstanding speaker of both verse and prose and much in demand at official ceremonies, was asked to deliver the funeral oration composed by Grillparzer.* This he did, on 29 March 1827; for religious reasons, the oration was delivered not at the grave itself, but at the entrance to Währing district cemetery. (Anschütz was also the orator at the unveiling of Ludwig von Schwanthaler's statue of Mozart* at Salzburg on 4 September 1842.)

Anton Viktor, Austrian archduke (b. Florence, 31 August 1779; d. Vienna, 2 April 1835). Eighth son of Leopold (1747–92), grand duke of Tuscany [later Emperor

Leopold II], and of Maria Ludovica [Luisa] of Bourbon (1745–92). He was chosen to follow Maximilian Franz* as prince bishop of Münster and elector of Cologne in 1801, but was unable to assume those positions for political reasons. In 1803 he became a knight of the Deutscher Orden [Teutonic Order], and the following year its grand master. He remained, until his death, head of the Order (the functions of which were in 1809 restricted to Austrian territory under the terms of the Peace of Schönbrunn). In his capacity of grand master, he was also owner of the 'Hoch- und Deutschmeister Regiment', an infantry regiment stationed in Vienna.

Beethoven composed two military marches (WoO 18, 19) for him at the request of his brother, Archduke Rudolph.* 'I note that Your Imperial Highness wishes to try out the effect of my music also on horses,' Beethoven wrote to Archduke Rudolph, probably in August 1810. 'Very well, I will see if it will enable the riders to turn some skilful somersaults . . . The desired music for horses will be conveyed to Your Imperial Highness . . . at a very quick gallop' (*Corr.* A274/B462). Both marches were played at an equestrian spectacle presented at Laxenburg Castle on 24 August 1810 in honour of Empress Maria Ludovica. In one of the extant autographs of WoO 18, the dedication to Anton Viktor was replaced by Beethoven by the inscription 'Für die Böhmische Landwehr' [For the Bohemian territorial army], while in the first edition (Berlin, Schlesinger,* 1818/19) the march was dedicated, perhaps by the publisher, to the 'Yorck'sche Korps', i.e. the corps bearing the name of General [later Field Marshal] Count Hans David Ludwig Yorck von Wartenburg.

Anton Viktor was a noted botanist, a patron of the Institute for the Blind, and, from 1831 (following the death of Archduke Rudolph) until 1835, 'patron' of the Gesellschaft der Musikfreunde.*

(Hamann[1])

Arnim, Elisabeth [Bettina] **von** (b. Frankfurt am Main, 4 April 1785; d. Berlin, 20 January 1859). Writer; sister of Clemens Brentano, half-sister of Franz Brentano, and sister-in-law of Antonie Brentano (on all these, *see* Brentano*). In December 1810 she became engaged to the poet and novelist Achim von Arnim (1781–1831), whom she married on 11 March 1811.

In the spring of 1810 she travelled to Vienna in the company of her sister Kunigunde [Gunda] and the latter's husband Friedrich Karl von Savigny, in order to visit Franz and Antonie Brentano. In Vienna she made Beethoven's acquaintance and was quickly subjugated by the force of his personality. Henceforth she was to revere the man as well as his music, as she already did Goethe* and his literary works. In *Goethes Briefwechsel mit einem Kinde* (Berlin, 1835), allegedly a record of her correspondence with Goethe, she printed a letter, dated 28 May 1810, in which she gives a detailed account of her first meeting with Beethoven. Unfortunately, the letter is a fabrication, like so many others included in that collection. This does not mean, however, that it is entirely devoid of value, for the incidents and conversations described in it may well be substantially true; above all, it reflects faithfully the hero worship which he inspired in her. Moreover, she really did later express her feelings for Beethoven to Goethe in writing (on 28 July 1810) and probably also in person, for Goethe informed Beethoven on 25 June 1811 (*Corr.* B509) that 'dear Bettina Brentano . . . speaks of you with delight and the greatest affection, and counts the hours she spent with you among the happiest in her life'.

In 1839 the Nuremberg periodical *Athenaeum für Wissenschaft, Kunst und Leben* published what were said to be three letters addressed by Beethoven to Bettina. These letters, which were dated 11 August 1810, 10 February 1811, and 15 August 1812, were subsequently reprinted, with some stylistic and other differences, in Bettina's *Ilius Pamphilius und die Ambrosia* (Leipzig, 1847–8). However, only the second of these letters (*Corr.* A296/B485), the autograph of which has survived, is now regarded as incontrovertibly authentic. In it, Beethoven refers to two letters he has received from Bettina ('I carried the first letter around with me during the entire summer, and it often made me blissfully happy') and assures her of his affection—which is, indeed, evident from the very tone of his letter, as well as being explicitly affirmed in a remark concerning her brother Clemens ('the sister already has so large a share of [my affection] that not much will be left for the brother'). The letter concludes: 'Now farewell, dear, dear B., I kiss you on your forehead, and I thereby imprint on it, as with a seal, all my thoughts for you. [In this sentence, unlike anywhere else in the letter, Beethoven uses the familiar 'Du'.] Write soon, soon, to your friend Beethoven.' There can thus be no doubt of Beethoven's warm feelings towards Bettina (who was about to be married, as Beethoven well knew, since earlier in the letter he had sent his best wishes to her and her future husband). He may well have flirted with her a little in Vienna in 1810; but the suggestion once advanced by some writers that she was perhaps his 'Immortal Beloved' was discarded long ago. It was based in part on the fact that Beethoven met her again during the summer of 1812 at Teplitz [Teplice], where she was staying with Achim.

(Arnim[1], Gottschalk)

Artaria, Mathias (b. Mannheim, 1793; d. Vienna, 22 April 1835). Art dealer and music publisher; son of Domenico (II) Artaria (1765–1823). He was trained in the business by his father who directed the Mannheim branch of the firm, and he gathered further experience while employed for some two years in a London bookshop. By 1818 he had settled in Vienna, where he formed an association with the art dealer Daniel Julius Sprenger. In 1821, two years after Sprenger's death, he married his widow Karolina [Charlotte], and in 1822 he obtained a licence to carry on the business in his own name. In 1833 his firm was taken over by Anton Diabelli & Co.*

On 9 January 1826 Beethoven sold his new String Quartet in B flat major (Op. 130) for 80 ducats to Mathias Artaria, who had been recommended to him by Karl Holz.* Subsequently, at Artaria's instigation, Holz persuaded Beethoven to replace the original fugue (which was to be published separately as Op. 133) by a new finale, for which Artaria paid him a further 15 ducats. In addition, Artaria commissioned Anton Halm* to make an arrangement of the fugue for piano duet. However, Halm's arrangement did not satisfy Beethoven, who thereupon made his own (Op. 134) which he sold to Artaria for 12 ducats. The quartet with the new final movement, as well as the fugue and its arrangement for piano duet, were all published by Mathias Artaria in May 1827, a few weeks after Beethoven's death.

(Slezak[4])

Artaria & Co. Music publishers. The Viennese branch of the firm was founded by the cousins Carlo Artaria (1747–1808) and Francesco Artaria (1744–1808), who started to deal in engravings in 1770, and in 1778 set up their own music publishing business. They ran the firm, at times together with Giovanni Cappi* and Tranquillo Mollo,* until the early years of the nineteenth century. They were succeeded by Francesco's son Domenico (III) [Dominik] Artaria (1775–1842), who formed partnerships with Pietro Cappi (*see* Giovanni Cappi*) and Carlo Boldrini* before assuming sole proprietorship from 1824 until 1830, when his son August (1807–93) joined the business.

Beethoven's association with Artaria & Co. began soon after he settled in Vienna in 1792: in July 1793 the firm published his variations for violin and piano on Figaro's aria 'Se vuol ballare' from Mozart's* *Le nozze di Figaro* (WoO 40). Subsequently, Artaria issued the first editions of a considerable number of Beethoven's early works, including notably the following: in 1795, the three Piano Trios Op. 1; in 1796, the three Piano Sonatas Op. 2, the String Trio Op. 3, and the variations for piano on 'Menuett à la Viganò' from Jakob Haibel's ballet *Le nozze disturbate*; in 1797, the two Cello Sonatas Op. 5, the Piano Sonata Op. 7, the song 'Adelaide', and two sets of variations (WoO 45 and WoO 71); in 1799, the variations on 'La stessa, la stessissima' from Salieri's* *Falstaff* (WoO 73); and in 1801, the piano arrangement of the ballet music *Die Geschöpfe des Prometheus* (Op. 43).

But shortly after the publication in September 1802 of the Rondo for piano Op. 51, No. 2, and of the six dances WoO 15, Beethoven broke with Artaria over its pirated edition of the String Quintet Op. 29 (*see* Breitkopf & Härtel*). The legal proceedings, in which Beethoven was advised by Johann Nepomuk Zizius,* dragged on for almost three years before a settlement was finally reached on 9 September 1805. The publication by Artaria of the Trio Op. 87 in April 1806 may presumably be regarded as a sign of reconciliation between the two parties. It did not, however, herald a significant resumption of Beethoven's association with the firm. Apart from Ignaz Moscheles's* piano reduction of the final version of *Fidelio* (1814), the only other first editions issued by Artaria & Co. between 1806 and 1819 were of the songs 'An den fernen Geliebten' (Op. 75, No. 5), 'Der Jüngling in der Fremde' (WoO 138), 'Der Liebende' (WoO 139), and 'Der Zufriedene' (Op. 75, No. 6), all four in 1810, and 'Sehnsucht: Die stille Nacht umdunkelt' (WoO 146) in 1816. Even then, the publication of these songs, as a part of larger collections, was not arranged by Beethoven, but by the author of the texts, Christian Ludwig Reissig.* In 1819, on the other hand, there was an important, if temporary, re-establishment of the association. That year, Artaria & Co. published the first editions of the 'Hammerklavier' Sonata (Op. 106) and of the String Quintet Op. 104 (arranged by Beethoven from his Piano Trio Op. 1, No. 3), as well as the first continental edition of his variations on six foreign songs (Op. 105). No further first editions were issued by Artaria during Beethoven's lifetime, but it is worth noting that the firm was among those negotiating for the publication rights of the *Missa solemnis*. In 1830 Artaria & Co. issued the first edition of the Octet Op. 103.

(Hilmar, Slezak[3,4], Ullrich[5])

Atterbom, Per Daniel Amadeus (b. Åsbo, 19 January 1790; d. Stockholm, 21 July 1855). Poet, best known for the fairy play *Lycksalighetens ö* [The Isle of Bliss]. He merits a place in Beethoven literature as a man who 'almost met' the composer. He first saw Beethoven when, in the course of a journey which took him through Germany and into Italy, he was present on 17 January 1819 at a concert in Vienna, at which Beethoven conducted the *Prometheus* Overture and the Seventh Symphony. Atterbom gave a description of the occasion, accompanied by a few remarks about Beethoven's mode of life, in *Minnen från Tyskland och Italien* [Recollections of Germany and Italy], of which a German translation by F. Maurer appeared in Berlin in 1867.

Some years later—probably in the summer of 1826—Atterbom once more visited Vienna. Ignaz Jeitteles,* knowing how much he longed to meet Beethoven, escorted him to the Schwarzspanierhaus. Finding the door to the flat unlocked, they entered and found Beethoven in the act of composing. Standing with his back to them and unaware of their presence owing to his deafness, he continued to write down and conduct his music, and even struck a few notes on the piano, while his bemused visitors watched in awe. After a time they withdrew discreetly. The story, based on Jeitteles's account of the incident, was told in the article 'Beethoven *in flagrante*' which appeared in the Viennese journal *Blätter für Musik, Theater und Kunst* in 1855. (The statement in P. Nettl's *Beethoven Encyclopedia* that Jeitteles introduced Atterbom to Beethoven on this occasion is clearly incorrect.)

Averdonk, Severin Anton (bapt. 21 September 1768). He provided the text for two cantatas composed by Beethoven at Bonn in 1790, the first (WoO 87) on the death of Emperor Joseph II,* the second (WoO 88) on his brother Leopold's elevation to the rank of emperor. (Joseph II died on 20 February; Leopold was elected Roman emperor on 30 September and crowned at Frankfurt on 9 October.) It was one of these two cantatas which Beethoven showed to Haydn* in 1790 or 1792 (*see also* Schneider*).

Averdonk, who was then studying theology, was the brother of the contralto Johanna Helene Averdonk (b. Bonn, 11 December 1760; d. 18 August 1789). She was a pupil of Johann van Beethoven,* who presented her to the public at the same concert at Cologne on 26 March 1778 at which the young Ludwig made his own debut as a performer. She subsequently studied with Pietro Pompeo Sales at Koblenz, was engaged as a singer at Bonn on 8 November 1780, and was a member of the court Kapelle from 1782 until 1789. She must have been on very friendly terms with Beethoven's parents, for she was a godmother of their fifth son Franz Georg.

Bach, Johann Baptist (b. Graffenberg, near Eggenburg, Lower Austria, 16 June 1779; d. Vienna, 25 September 1847). Lawyer. Son of a landowner; uncle of the prominent politician Baron Alexander Bach (1813–93). Following his father's death, he moved to Vienna in *c.*1789, and there he was brought up by his uncle Alois Maria Bach, a well-known lawyer. He obtained a doctorate in law in 1803 and later probably worked in his uncle's office. After teaching law for several years, he set up his own practice in 1817. He enjoyed an excellent reputation, both professionally and for his considerable personal qualities. From 1837 to 1839 he was dean of the law faculty at the university.

Bach became Beethoven's legal adviser in the autumn of 1819, and from then on his name is frequently mentioned in the conversation books, in which he himself also made numerous entries. In particular, he counselled and represented Beethoven in his legal battle to exclude Johanna van Beethoven* from the guardianship of her son Karl.* Bach was largely responsible for securing the favourable decision by the Court of Appeal in April 1820, under which Beethoven and Karl Peters* were appointed joint guardians. Beethoven also consulted Bach about other matters relating to Karl. His warm feelings towards Bach found expression in his letter of 24 January 1823, which conveyed an invitation to lunch: 'It appears hardly necessary to tell you with what pleasure and affection we [i.e. Beethoven and Karl] are looking forward to seeing you, for you have long had proof of our feelings.' Beethoven discussed his last will with Bach on more than one occasion. In his letter of 3 January 1827, in which he named Karl his sole heir, he wrote: 'I appoint you *his trustee* and ask you to act as a father to him, together with his guardian Hofrat [Stephan von] Breuning.* May God preserve you. A thousand thanks for the love and friendship you have shown me.'

According to Schindler,* who worked for a time in his chambers, Bach was a competent cellist and enjoyed playing quartets. His admiration for Beethoven's music is clearly reflected in some of his entries in the conversation books.

(Ullrich[5], Wurzbach[1])

Bähr [Beer] **(Franz) Joseph** (b. 19 February 1770; d. Vienna, 7 August 1819). Clarinettist. From 1787 to 1794 he was in the service of Prince Kraft Ernst of Öttingen-Wallerstein, who sent him to Würzburg to study with the famous clarinet teacher Philipp Meissner. In 1794 he went on a concert tour to Potsdam with the cellist Friedrich Witt, and in 1796 both were in Vienna, where Bähr made a great impression ('Bähr blows like a God,' Witt wrote to a friend). By 1797 he had been engaged by Prince Johann Joseph of Liechtenstein.

In Vienna he soon established contact with Beethoven, and it is significant that almost all of Beethoven's chamber music compositions with important parts for the clarinet were written during the period 1796 to 1802. Beethoven and Bähr took part in performances of the Quintet Op. 16 at Schuppanzigh's* concert of 6 April 1797 and at a concert of the Tonkünstler-Societät on 2 April 1798. It was in the latter year that Beethoven composed his Trio for clarinet, cello, and piano (Op. 11), and it was reportedly at Bähr's suggestion that he used a theme from Joseph Weigl's* opera *L'amor marinaro* in the variations of the final movement of the trio; the theme had attained great popularity since the opera's première on 15 October 1797. Bähr also played in the first public performances of the Septet Op. 20 (2 April 1800) and the Sextet Op. 71 (April 1805). His performance of the first clarinet part in the sextet was described in the Leipzig *Allgemeine musikalische Zeitung* as 'absolutely perfect'.

(Weston[1,2,3])

Bauernfeld, Eduard von (b. Vienna, 13 January 1802; d. Vienna, 9 August 1890). Dramatist. After studying philosophy and law at Vienna University, he was employed in the civil service (1826–48). The great interest which he showed in literature and the theatre from an early age brought him a commission to contribute translations to the Shakespeare* edition in German which Joseph Trentsensky published in Vienna in 1824–6. The first of his own plays to be produced at the Burgtheater, *Der Brautwerber* (5 September 1828), was only modestly successful, but the next one, *Leichtsinn aus Liebe, oder Täuschungen* (12 January 1831), established him as a promising young playwright. His vast literary output was to consist predominantly of comedies of manner, but it also included poetry (*Gedichte*, 1852), a novel (*Die Freigelassenen*, 1875), and memoirs (*Aus Alt- und Neuwien*) which provide a fascinating record of Viennese intellectual life in his time. He was fond of music and a competent pianist, having studied with Johann Baptist Schenk.*

According to his memoirs, he met Beethoven several times at the house of Cajetan Giannattasio del Rio,* at a time when Karl van Beethoven* was a pupil at Giannattasio's school. These meetings must therefore have taken place in 1816–17, when Bauernfeld was only 15 or 16 years old. He relates that when he was introduced to Beethoven as a young poet, the composer said to him: 'Write an

opera for me. About Brutus, or a similar subject. Others are of no use to me.'
(Bauernfeld assumes that this was a sly reference to the operatic libretto *Melusina*
which Grillparzer* had prepared for Beethoven; but he is mistaken, for Grillparzer's
text was not written until several years later.) Also of interest to Beethoven
scholars is Bauernfeld's account of the tuition which, he claims, Beethoven
received from Schenk.*

(Bauernfeld)

Beethoven, Johann van (b. ?Bonn, *c.*1740; d. Bonn, 18 December 1792).
Beethoven's father; son of Ludwig van Beethoven.* After elementary school he
attended a high school run by Jesuits for a year or two; there, in September 1750,
he sang and acted in a school play. By 1752 he sang as a boy soprano in the court
Kapelle, and in 1756, by which time his voice had settled into the tenor range, he
was appointed an (unpaid) court musician; the appointment was confirmed on
24 April 1764, with a salary of 100 reichsthaler. He remained a member of the
Kapelle for twenty-five years. In addition to carrying out his official duties, he
was able to supplement his income by giving private music lessons. According
to Gottfried Fischer,* his pupils included the children of certain ambassadors,
as well as members of prominent local families. On 12 November 1767, at Bonn,
he married Maria Magdalene Leym (née Keverich: *see* Maria Magdalene van
Beethoven*). They had seven children: Ludwig Maria (bapt. 2 April 1769; d. 8
April 1769); Ludwig, the future composer; Kaspar (Anton) Karl;* Nikolaus
Johann;* Anna Maria Franziska (bapt. 23 February 1779; d. 27 February 1779);
Franz Georg (bapt. 17 January 1781; d. 16 August 1783); and Maria Margarete
Josepha (bapt. 5 May 1786; d. 26 November 1787).

Johann never attained the comfortable financial situation which his father had
enjoyed. Biographers have tended to attribute his money problems to weakness of
character and, especially, to an overindulgence in wine, but recent writers have
tried to correct what they regard as an undeservedly negative appraisal of his
character. The final period of his life was marked by a series of misfortunes. His
voice declined to such an extent in quality that in a report on the court Kapelle
prepared for the new elector Maximilian Franz* in 1784 it was characterized as
'ganz abständig' [quite worn-out]. Moreover, his last three children all died in
infancy, and in July 1787 he lost his wife. A few days after her death he requested
an advance of salary, explaining that the heavy expenses he had incurred during
her long illness had already obliged him to sell or pawn some of his personal
effects. In 1789 his services were dispensed with and his salary was reduced by half,
the other half being henceforth allotted to his son Ludwig; but, so as not to hurt
his pride, the full amount was still paid to Johann, who then handed one half
of it to Ludwig. Little is known about the latter's feelings for his father, but he is
generally believed to have been less fond of him than of his mother. However, the

Beethoven-Haus in Bonn has in its collection a copy made by Johann of part of Carl Philipp Emanuel Bach's *Morgengesang am Schöpfungsfeste*, which Ludwig had carefully preserved and on which he had inscribed the words 'written by my beloved father'.

(Schiedermair[1,2], Schmidt-Görg[4])

Beethoven, Johanna van, née Reiss (b. Vienna, *c.*1786; d. Baden, near Vienna, 2 February 1868). Daughter of Anton Reiss, an upholsterer, and his wife Theresia, née Lamatsch. On 25 May 1806 she married Beethoven's brother Kaspar Karl;* their son Karl* was born on 4 September of the same year.

Little is known about her life, and what there is reflects small credit on her. In 1804 she was accused of stealing from her parents, but was not prosecuted. Far more seriously, she was convicted of embezzlement on 30 December 1811, having falsely reported as stolen a pearl necklace valued at 20,000 florins, which she had taken on consignment. She was sentenced to one year's severe imprisonment, but this was reduced, first to two months' severe imprisonment, and then, in response to her husband's appeals, to one month's ordinary detention and finally to one month's detention in police cells. In the end, she did not fully serve even this milder sentence. It was mainly on her conviction for this felony that Beethoven consistently founded his allegation that she was morally incompetent to serve as guardian to her son. In a submission to the Lower Austrian Landrecht in December 1818, Johanna claimed that her husband had been more at fault than she herself, and her lawyer Jakob Hotschevar,* who was related to her, made a similar statement in his memorandum of 11 December 1818. But this allegation was clearly contrary to the conclusions reached by the various courts in 1811–12.

The marriage appears to have been troubled by personal differences as well as financial problems; the latter grew more serious after Kaspar Karl was stricken with tuberculosis in 1812. Beethoven tried to alleviate the situation, but by the time Kaspar Karl died in 1815 the couple was heavily in debt (for further information, *see* under Kaspar Karl van Beethoven*). Relations between Johanna and Beethoven were less than cordial even then, and in the codicil to his will Kaspar Karl urged them to strive for greater harmony for the sake of his son Karl whom he was entrusting to their joint guardianship (*see* under Karl van Beethoven*). His appeal fell on deaf ears, and over the next several years Beethoven and Johanna engaged in acrimonious legal proceedings over the custody of the child, for he was determined to deprive her of all influence over Karl, on the grounds that she was deficient in the requisite moral and intellectual qualities. He succeeded in severely limiting her access to the boy, but at considerable cost to his own nervous energy and peace of mind, as well as to Karl's happiness. The matter was finally settled on 8 April 1820 when the Court of Appeal overturned a ruling made by the Vienna Magistracy in Johanna's favour on

17 September 1819. (The Magistracy had taken the view that the offence for which Johanna had rightly been punished in 1811 should no longer be considered an impediment to her appointment as guardian in 1819, and that the other allegations of immoral behaviour made by Beethoven constituted no more than unproven gossip.) The Court of Appeal now granted Beethoven's request to be appointed the boy's guardian jointly with Karl Peters.* As a last resort, Johanna submitted the case to the emperor, but on 24 July 1820 she was informed that her appeal had been rejected.

She was no doubt deeply disappointed by the result of the litigation, but Maynard Solomon is probably unduly chivalrous in regarding that disappointment as the reason for the pregnancy which led to the birth of her daughter Ludovika Johanna that year: 'Grief-stricken and weary from her long struggle, eager to build a new life, and perhaps to replace her stolen child, Johanna became pregnant in the spring of 1820.' In reality, she became pregnant some time before then, for the records of the Schottenkirche show that Ludovika Johanna was born and baptized on 12 June 1820. Conception is therefore likely to have taken place in the late summer or early September of 1819, around the time when the Vienna Magistracy ruled in her favour and several months before she finally lost the custody battle. The space in the church register reserved for the father's name has been left blank, whilst the mother is identified as 'Johanna Hofbauer, single'. The man who acknowledged paternity (privately, though not in the register) was, in fact, the wealthy bell founder ['Hofglockengiesser'] Johann Kaspar Hofbauer (*c.*1771–1839), who duly made her an allowance and helped her pay off at least some of her debts (*see BKh* 2/325 and 9/189, 287, 399); their relationship dated from at least 1818 (see below). But according to Nikolaus Johann van Beethoven* (*see BKh* 2/327), Ludovika Johanna's true father was the Hungarian-born physician Samuel Raics de Nagy-Megyer, a fact of which Hofbauer was said to be unaware. (Ludovika died in 1891.)

Johanna was chronically short of funds, even after she had sold on 2 July 1818, for 16,000 florins, the house in the Alservorstadt [Alser suburb] which she had bought jointly with her husband in 1813 (*see* Kaspar Karl van Beethoven*). (Following his death, her share in the house had risen from one-half to three-quarters, with Karl owning the remaining quarter; later, under the terms of the settlement of Karl's inheritance on 10 May 1817, she had acquired full ownership.) However, the proceeds from the sale of the house were insufficient to clear all her debts. It appears nevertheless from her letter to Sigmund Anton Steiner* of 28 March 1818 that she had managed to repay loans of 700 florins and 1,500 florins to him (the latter amount probably representing the claim which Beethoven had ceded to Steiner in 1813—in this connection, *see* the article on Steiner). Beethoven subsequently assumed responsibility for the interest still due on those earlier debts. It appears from an entry in the conversation books (*BKh* 9/287) that it was Hofbauer who had arranged the sale of the house in 1818. Perhaps, among the debts he helped her to pay off was the money she owed Steiner (or, at any rate, the principal of the loans).

In January 1824 Johanna asked Beethoven for financial help, but he replied that he was unable to offer her any just then. Instead, he told her to keep henceforth for her own use the half-portion of her widow's pension which she had in 1817 undertaken to contribute to Karl's educational and living expenses. Yet despite such occasional conciliatory gestures, Beethoven's feelings towards Johanna did not soften with the passage of time. As late as September 1826, in a letter to Magistratsrat Ignaz Czapka (*Corr.* A1502/B2206), he described her as an 'extremely depraved person' and her character as 'evil, malevolent, and treacherous'. Some scholars have taken the view that Beethoven's furious denunciations were not wholly justified and, at least in part, due to extreme prejudice. But there does appear to be strong evidence of her dishonesty and dissolute character. In this connection, weighty support for Beethoven's standpoint was later provided by none other than Jakob Hotschevar—who, as already mentioned, had assisted her in her legal actions against Beethoven and was also her relative. In a statement made some time after 25 September 1830 he informed the Magistracy that he had declined her request to assume Ludovika's guardianship because 'her far from praiseworthy moral conduct is of such a nature as to make it unacceptable to me to enter into closer contact with her as guardian of her illegitimate child'.

In view of the hostility which existed between Beethoven and Johanna, most scholars have assumed that Anselm Hüttenbrenner* must have been mistaken when he told Thayer* in June 1860 that Johanna had been at Beethoven's bedside when he died. Soon afterwards, in a letter to Thayer on 20 August of the same year, Hüttenbrenner mentioned the presence of 'the wife of Johann van Beethoven, property owner and pharmacist' instead. Quite possibly, both statements are incorrect, for Beethoven's relations with Nikolaus Johann's wife were scarcely better than those he maintained with Karl's mother. Gerhard von Breuning* states in *Aus dem Schwarzspanierhause* (Vienna, 1874) that shortly before Beethoven's death—which he did not witness himself—he had seen Johann and the housekeeper Sali [Rosalie] in his room. Hüttenbrenner could have mistaken the servant for one or the other of Beethoven's sisters-in-law, or his memory may have failed him more than thirty years after the event described.

Beethoven would surely not have been pleased had he known that one of the most intimate of his personal documents, the Heiligenstadt Testament, would come into Johanna's hands. It was handed to her by Jakob Hotschevar, who, as Karl's guardian, had received it from Domenico Artaria* on 21 November 1827. (Artaria had either bought it at the auction of Beethoven's effects or had, in his capacity of a member of the appraisal committee, kept it back with the intention of passing it on to the family.) In 1840 Johanna, as ever in need of money, asked Liszt* to find a buyer for the Testament in England. It was bought in 1842 by the celebrated violinist Heinrich Wilhelm Ernst, but its sale did not realize the price of 50 guineas which Johanna had demanded. Liszt, with his usual generosity, offered to augment the payment out of his own pocket. Ernst later gave the autograph to the pianist and composer Otto Goldschmidt and his wife Jenny Lind. In September 1888 Goldschmidt presented it, in his own and his late wife's name—she had died the previous year—to the Hamburg Stadtbibliothek. It is today preserved at the Staats- und Universitätsbibliothek in that city.

(Asow, Brandenburg[7], Reinitz[1,2], Solomon[2], Tellenbach[3], Weise)

Beethoven, Karl van (b. Vienna, 4 September 1806; d. Vienna, 13 April 1858). Beethoven's nephew; son of Kaspar Karl* and Johanna van Beethoven.* Nothing is known about his early years, but he probably received some musical instruction from his father. Later he took lessons with Friedrich Starke,* Carl Czerny,* and Joseph Czerny,* and became a competent pianist.

For more than four years following his father's death on 15 November 1815 he was the subject and innocent victim of a fierce legal battle between his mother and Beethoven for control over his life. It would be impracticable to attempt to give full particulars of the complicated legal proceedings here and accordingly only the most important decisions are mentioned below. (For more detailed surveys, *see* the publications by Dagmar Weise and Stefan Wolf listed in the Bibliography; Wolf's book is also recommended for its informative summary of Karl's education.) At the heart of the dispute was Beethoven's determination to deprive Johanna of any opportunity to influence Karl by himself assuming the sole guardianship of the boy and by severely restricting her access to him. Beethoven's justification for thus separating mother and son was his stated conviction that she was not qualified, either morally or intellectually, to bring him up herself (*see also* the article devoted to Johanna).

The struggle for control over Karl began even before Kaspar Karl's death, as is evident from the text of his will executed on the preceding day. For while he initially appointed Johanna and Beethoven joint guardians, he later crossed out her name, evidently at his brother's urging; but in the latter's temporary absence he then added a codicil, no doubt under pressure from Johanna, in which he reinstated her as co-guardian and specified that the boy was to reside with her. Beethoven subsequently stated that Kaspar Karl had immediately regretted having written the codicil and had sent an urgent message to his lawyer instructing him to delete it, but the lawyer had not been at home. Beethoven alleged furthermore that Kaspar Karl had later sent him on a similar, but equally fruitless, errand; and that Kaspar Karl had thus died before his wish could be carried out. (It is worth noting that Kaspar Karl had already made a written declaration appointing Beethoven guardian in April 1813, when he thought he was dying.)

On 22 November 1815, the Lower Austrian Landrecht, on the strength of the codicil, named Johanna principal guardian and Beethoven associate guardian. However, following representations by Beethoven, it reversed itself on 9 January

1816, and on 19 January he formally assumed the function of sole guardian. Thereupon the 9-year-old Karl was removed from his mother's care, and on 2 February he was placed by Beethoven in Giannattasio del Rio's* boarding school, of which he was to remain a pupil until 24 January 1818. In the meantime, a settlement had been reached on 10 May 1817 regarding the disposal of Karl Kaspar's estate; in it Johanna agreed to pay to Beethoven one-half of her pension as a contribution towards the costs of Karl's education (her initial failure to do so was to lead to further disputes). This does not mean, however, that she had resigned herself to the loss of the guardianship; on the contrary, she was to claim it once more in 1818 and again the following year (see below).

After leaving Giannattasio del Rio's school in January 1818, Karl lived with Beethoven who engaged a private tutor for him. That autumn he attended the Akademisches Gymnasium. On 3 December 1818 he ran away to stay with his mother, but he was promptly recaptured with the help of the police and spent some time under strict supervision at Giannattasio's house before returning to Beethoven's flat. Subsequently, in addition to lessons from his tutor, he also received instruction at Johann Baptist Kudlich's* institute; in March 1819 he became a boarder there. (For several months in 1819, Mathias von Tuscher* acted as Karl's co-guardian.) After Beethoven's plan to have Karl educated by Johann Michael Sailer* at Landhut had met with official disapproval, and since Giannattasio del Rio refused to take him back as a pupil, Karl became a boarder on 22 June 1819 at a school run by Joseph Blöchlinger von Bannholz.* He pursued his studies there until 29 August 1823. During that time, the dispute concerning the guardianship was at last settled: on 8 April 1820 the Court of Appeal overturned a ruling made in Johanna's favour by the Magistracy of the City of Vienna on 17 September 1819, and granted Beethoven's request to be appointed co-guardian, together with Karl Peters.* (After Beethoven had acknowledged that 'van' in his name was not a nobiliary particle, the case had been referred in December 1818 by the Lower Austrian Landrecht, which dealt with aristocratic litigants only, to the Vienna Magistracy.)

In October 1823 Karl, who was by then once more living with Beethoven, enrolled at the university, where he studied principally philosophy and languages. His academic performance was unsatisfactory and he was obliged to repeat the first year of his studies. Eventually he withdrew from the university, and in April 1825 he began to study commerce at the Polytechnisches Institut, whose vice-principal Franz Michael Reisser* henceforth replaced Peters as Beethoven's co-guardian. Karl now found lodgings near the institute, at Mathias Schlemmer's.* He hoped, at the completion of his courses, to obtain employment at the well-known bank Arnstein & Eskeles (*see also* Eskeles*); but he once again encountered difficulties in coping with his studies.

It is possible that fear of failing his examinations and having to face his uncle's reprimands was one of the reasons which drove him to attempt suicide, probably on 6 August 1826, in the ruins of Rauhenstein Castle near Baden. It was assuredly not the only one, for the past eleven years must have been extremely stressful for him. Removed from the family home soon after losing his father; denied virtually all contact with his mother (about whom, moreover, he probably heard many unflattering tales—whether true or not, their effect was likely to be traumatic); placed in the care of a much older uncle who, however well intentioned and loving, was singularly ill fitted by temperament and also, increasingly, by reason of his deafness and declining physical condition, to deal sympathetically with a teenage boy; subjected to frequent reproaches of lack of affection and gratitude, and struggling (though perhaps not always whole-heartedly) to meet his uncle's expectations of academic excellence—Karl was undoubtedly exposed over the years to a multitude of pressures which could well account for a certain instability in his behaviour and may, in the end, have proved too burdensome for him. It is likely that he did not pursue his studies as conscientiously and diligently as he should have done, and he may at times have acted in an undisciplined and reckless manner, as Stephan von Breuning* alleged in a letter in January 1827, in which he counselled Beethoven to restrict Karl's inheritance to the interest on the money he bequeathed to him, until such time as Karl had become a sufficiently 'mature and responsible man' to handle the capital (*Corr.* B2247). But it must be remembered that Karl was, after all, barely 20 years old when Breuning wrote that letter. In any case, his character and comportment are unlikely to have been as disgraceful and despicable as Beethoven described them on occasion, and as Schindler* was to portray them for posterity in his Beethoven biography. In fact, the conversation books—especially those covering the years 1826–7—show him in a decidedly favourable light, genuinely concerned about his uncle's well-being and eager to relieve him of many responsibilities.

The suicide attempt failed, one bullet missing altogether and a second merely injuring Karl. He was transported to his mother's rooms in Adlergasse in the inner city, where the wound was treated, and the next day he was admitted to the Allgemeines Krankenhaus [General Hospital], from which he was discharged on 25 September. Three days later he left Vienna together with Beethoven to stay at Nikolaus Johann van Beethoven's* estate at Gneixendorf. By then Karl had abandoned all ideas of a business career and decided to join the army instead. Reluctantly, Beethoven gave his consent. With the help of Stephan von Breuning, who held a senior post in the war department, he was accepted into Baron Joseph Stutterheim's* regiment. Soon after he returned to Vienna with Beethoven (probably on 28 November) he was interviewed by Stutterheim and, on 2 January 1827, he left Vienna to join the regiment at Iglau [Jihlava]; he never saw his uncle again. On 3 January, in a letter to his lawyer Johann Baptist Bach,* Beethoven named Karl his sole heir; but in a document he drew up a few days before his death on the advice of Breuning (who, as already mentioned, regarded Karl as still very irresponsible) he excluded him from the enjoyment of the capital itself, which was to go to Karl's own heirs. Breuning, who had, with some hesitation, agreed to become Karl's co-guardian the previous September, assumed sole responsibility for him after Beethoven's death. But he was to die himself on 4 June, and was then succeeded as guardian by Jakob Hotschevar.*

Karl resigned from the army in May 1832, not long after being commissioned a second lieutenant; for most of the rest of his life he lived in Vienna. On 16 July 1832 he married Karolina Barbara Naske (b. Iglau, 1 February 1808; d. Vienna, 15 November 1891). They had five children: Karoline Johanna (1831–1919), Maria Anna (1835–91), Ludwig Johann (b. 1839; d. between 1890 and 1916), Gabriele (1844–1914), and Hermine (1852–87).

(Köhler[2], MacArdle[1], Schmidt-Görg[4], Weise, Wolf)

Beethoven, Kaspar (Anton) Karl van (bapt. Bonn, 8 April 1774; d. Vienna, 15 November 1815). The elder of Beethoven's two surviving brothers. In the spring of 1794 he moved to Vienna where he gave music lessons and even did a little composing ('I derive pleasure from music,' he informed the editor of the Leipzig *Allgemeine musikalische Zeitung* in 1802, 'and also play several instruments' (*Corr.* B94)). From 1800 he worked as a clerk in the Department of Finance, but his duties left him sufficient free time to assist Beethoven, especially in his dealings with publishers. 'You may fully trust my brother who, in general, conducts all my business affairs,' Beethoven wrote to Breitkopf & Härtel* on 22 April 1802.

To judge from the numerous letters which Kaspar Karl addressed to publishers on Beethoven's behalf, he promoted his brother's interests with a good deal of determination, if not with a maximum of tact. 'Charl [*sic*] Beethoven is the greatest miser in the world,' Ferdinand Ries,* who disliked him intensely, wrote to Nikolaus Simrock* on 6 May 1803. 'For the sake of a ducat he takes back fifty undertakings he has given, and as a result he makes some bitter enemies for his brother' (*Corr.* B136). In another letter Ries assured Simrock that 'all the publishers here [in Vienna] fear him more than fire, for he is a terribly coarse man' (*Corr.* B155). Kaspar Karl certainly did not mince words when it came to defending his brother's reputation. When Breitkopf & Härtel, concerned that their rights to the Quintet Op. 29 were about to be compromised by Artaria & Co.,* angered Beethoven by initially holding him responsible for the situation, Kaspar Karl replied haughtily (5 December 1802, *Corr.* B119): 'You have written my brother a letter which might possibly be appropriate for a schoolboy, but not for an artist such as Beethoven.' (At the same time, however, realizing that the restoration of good relations with such a well-known firm was important for Beethoven's career, Kaspar Karl asked Georg August von Griesinger* to intercede.) When, the following year, an unnamed correspondent stated in the *Allgemeine musikalische Zeitung*, which was published by Breitkopf & Härtel, that the oratorio *Christus am Ölberg* had met with a poor reception in Vienna, Kaspar Karl wrote to Gottfried Christoph Härtel: 'It really is of no significance whether my brother is disparaged or not in your journal, for the greatest proof that the truth is otherwise lies in the numerous orders which we receive from everywhere. But it is remarkable that you should print such garbage in your journal' (*Corr.* B163). It is not altogether surprising that it was only after Beethoven had himself begun to negotiate with Breitkopf & Härtel that he was able to form a fruitful association with the firm. Another publisher did not hide his irritation at Kaspar Karl's often presumptuous style and, in particular, at his habit of associating himself with his brother's compositions through the use of the plural pronoun. 'I still understand German quite well,' Simrock wrote to Kaspar Karl on 30 July 1805, 'but I fail to comprehend what you wish to convey by the word "our" publishers and by "we". I bought the sonata Op. 47 from Louis van Beethoven, and in his letter about it there is no mention of a company' (*Corr.* B229). Writing to Ferdinand Ries, Simrock called Kaspar Karl's letter (*Corr.* B228) 'impertinent' and Kaspar Karl himself 'apparently incorrigible' (*Corr.* B230).

Beethoven, however, was glad to leave his affairs in Kaspar Karl's hands—it is evident that he did not see all the correspondence himself—and appears generally to have been on good terms with him during this period. When Beethoven moved into a service flat in the building complex housing the Theater an der Wien in 1803, Kaspar Karl moved in with him; and in 1804 Beethoven recommended him warmly to Countess Josephine Deym (*see* Brunsvik de Korompa*), whose assistance Kaspar Karl was hoping to obtain in a certain matter: 'Although *evil persons* have spread rumours that he does not act honourably towards me, I can assure you that this is untrue and that, on the contrary, he has at all times taken care of my affairs with complete integrity. There used to be something *rough* in his manner, and this is what turned *people* against him. However, this roughness has completely disappeared since he undertook some trips in connection with his work' (*Corr.* A103/B203).

On 25 May 1806 Kaspar Karl married Johanna Reiss (*see* Johanna van Beethoven*), the daughter of Anton Reiss, a well-to-do upholsterer. On 4 September their only child, Karl,* was born. Following his marriage, Kaspar Karl seems to have largely ceased his activities as Beethoven's part-time secretary-cum-business manager. Relations between them then became less cordial. In a letter to Gleichenstein in June/July 1807, Beethoven describes Kaspar Karl as being 'animated by a spirit of revenge' against him (*Corr.* A148/B287); and in 1809 he complained to Nikolaus Johann van Beethoven* about Kaspar Karl's callousness: 'If only God would grant my other brother, just for once, instead of his unfeelingness, some feeling. I suffer infinitely because of him. After all, with my bad hearing I always need somebody, and whom shall I trust?' (*Corr.* A205/B369).

In 1812 Kaspar Karl contracted tuberculosis. There is no doubt that Beethoven assisted him financially, though it is impossible to know whether he was altogether truthful when he informed Princess Kinsky* in December that he 'was obliged to completely support an unfortunate sick brother and all his family'

(*Corr.* A403/B607). On 12 April 1813 Kaspar Karl, believing his days to be numbered, made a written declaration appointing Beethoven his son's guardian after his death. That same day, Beethoven granted him a loan of 1,500 florins, for which Johanna stood surety. It is tempting to speculate that Beethoven may have insisted on the declaration as a condition for the loan. Kaspar Karl's forebodings of imminent death proved, however, unwarranted; his health improved, at any rate temporarily. When he failed to repay the loan within six months as arranged, Beethoven sued Johanna as the guarantor of the debt. An agreement was reached on 22 October for its repayment by instalments. However, Beethoven's recourse to legal proceedings infuriated Kaspar Karl, which in turn prompted Beethoven to complain to a correspondent (Joseph Reger) on 18 December that 'My brother, whom I have helped with countless acts of generosity and for whose sake I have myself got into some financial difficulty, is—my greatest enemy!' A week before he wrote this letter, Beethoven had ceded his claim against Kaspar Karl and Johanna to Sigmund Anton Steiner.* In the autumn of 1814 Steiner secured a lien on Johanna's half of the house which she had acquired jointly with her husband on 26 September 1813. It may seem strange that at the very time when Kaspar Karl was just about due—but seemingly unable—to repay the loan granted to him by Beethoven in April, he and Johanna should have purchased a large house in the Alservorstadt [Alser suburb] for some 11,600 florins (its site corresponds to the present 2 Kinderspitalgasse). In fact, though, they probably paid little or no cash for it, since it carried encumbrances of 10,000 florins, which they took over. (On its eventual sale, *see* Johanna van Beethoven;* on the further history of the loan, *see* Steiner.*)

Eventually, Kaspar Karl's health declined again, and on 8 March 1815 he submitted a formal request to be relieved of his duties at the department of finance. Although the official decision, which was negative, was not issued until 23 October, it is likely that he had absented himself from his work for some time during the intervening period. He died three weeks after his request was refused.

The assistance which Beethoven furnished Kaspar Karl and his family during the final years of Kaspar Karl's life undoubtedly entailed a serious drain on his resources, especially since his brother's illness coincided with a period in which his own income was greatly reduced (*see* Ferdinand Kinsky* and Lobkowitz*). In a letter to Ferdinand Ries* on 22 November 1815, he claimed to have spent altogether some 10,000 florins 'to make [Kaspar Karl's] life easier'. But even if this high figure is correct, the burden was far less onerous, in its effect on Beethoven's life, than the responsibility he so eagerly sought and assumed after his brother's death, namely the care of his son Karl.

(Brandenburg[7], Reinitz[1,2])

Beethoven, Ludwig van (bapt. Mechelen [Malines], 5 January 1712; d. Bonn, 24 December 1773). Beethoven's grandfather. Son of Michael van Beethoven

(1684–1749), a baker and dealer in lace, and his wife Maria Louise, née Stuyckers (1685–1749). In 1717 he became a chorister at St Rombaut's Cathedral at Mechelen; from 1725 he received instruction from the cathedral organist Anton Colfs, so that he might be able to play at Mass at St Rombaut's and other churches. In November 1731 he was engaged as a tenor in the choir at St Peter's Church at Louvain, where he also substituted for the Kapellmeister. In September 1732, by which time his voice was presumably fully developed, he was taken on as a bass at St Lambert's Church at Liège; but he stayed only a short time, for in March 1733 he joined the court Kapelle at Bonn. It is possible that the elector of Cologne, Clemens August, who was also suffragan bishop of Liège, had heard Ludwig sing during one of his visits to that city and had offered him the position. On 7 September 1733, at Bonn, Ludwig married Maria Josepha Poll (c.1714–75). They had three children, of whom two died in infancy; the third, Johann,* became the composer's father. On 16 July 1761 Ludwig was appointed court Kapellmeister by the Elector Maximilian Friedrich.* He appears to have been a very competent musician and was, moreover, highly respected both for the conscientiousness with which he carried out his duties and for his sterling character. His brother Kornelius (1708–64), a merchant by trade, had also settled at Bonn by 1733; and their parents were to spend their final years there.

Beethoven hardly knew his grandfather, who died when he was barely 3 years old. Yet Franz Gerhard Wegeler* recalled that he cherished his memory and in his youth frequently spoke about him to his friends. Later he asked, moreover, to have (?Leopold) Radoux's portrait of his grandfather sent to him in Vienna, and he treasured it for the rest of his life. It was subsequently owned by Karl van Beethoven* and then by his descendants; eventually it came into the possession of the Historisches Museum der Stadt Wien in Vienna. A copy can be seen at the Beethoven-Haus in Bonn.

(Schmidt-Görg[4])

Beethoven, Maria Magdalene van, née Keverich (b. Ehrenbreitstein, near Koblenz, 19 December 1746; d. Bonn, 17 July 1787). Beethoven's mother; daughter of Johann Heinrich Keverich (1702–59), head cook at Ehrenbreitstein Castle, and his wife Anna Klara, née Wistorff [Westorff] (1704–68). On 30 January 1763 she married Johann Leym (1733–65), valet to the elector of Trier; he died on 28 November 1765. Two years later, on 12 November 1767 at Bonn, she married Johann van Beethoven, to whom she bore seven children (*see* Johann van Beethoven*).

It was presumably news of his mother's illness which led Beethoven to cut short his stay in Vienna in the spring of 1787 (*see* Mozart*). He was greatly attached to her. 'She was such a kind, loving mother to me, my best friend,' he wrote to Joseph Wilhelm von Schaden* after her death (*Corr.* A1/B3).

Beethoven, Nikolaus Johann van (bapt. Bonn, 2 October 1776; d. Vienna, 12 January 1848). The younger of Beethoven's two surviving brothers; known originally as Nikolaus, he later chose to be called 'Johann'. He was apprenticed to the court pharmacist at Bonn, and in Vienna, where he arrived in December 1795, he was employed as an assistant in different pharmacies and also passed the necessary professional examinations. Almost nothing is known about his relations with Beethoven during the early years of his life in Austria. Some biographers have interpreted as an indication of hostility the fact that in his Heiligenstadt Testament of October 1802 Beethoven on three occasions left blank the space where Nikolaus Johann's name should have appeared, but others have speculated that the omission may have been due simply to Beethoven's uncertainty as to which of his brother's names he ought to use. On 13 September 1803 Ferdinand Ries* informed Nikolaus Simrock* (*Corr.* B155) that Beethoven, in return for certain favours Johann had shown him, had ceded to him the rights to nine of his compositions (Op. 52, Nos. 2–4, 6–8, WoO 55, and WoO 117, together with a further song which is lost). It is tempting to conclude that the favours were of a monetary nature.

Eager to set up in business on his own, Johann tried to acquire a pharmacy in Vienna, Graz, and elsewhere, but without success. His luck changed in 1808 when he managed to scrape together sufficient money to buy the pharmacy 'Zur goldenen Krone' in Linz, together with the house in which it was located. The following year he landed some lucrative contracts for medical supplies with the occupying French army. Thrifty by nature and perhaps not entirely scrupulous in his business practices, he was to accumulate a sizeable fortune.

Johann rented a part of his house at Linz to a physician, Dr Georg Johann Saxinger, and his wife Agnes; the latter's sister Therese (*see* Therese van Beethoven*) came to live with them, and before long she became Johann's house-keeper and mistress. At the time Johann met her, she already had an illegitimate child, Amalie Waldmann, born on 30 January 1807. When Beethoven visited Linz in October 1812 (perhaps on his way back from Teplitz [Teplice]), he was dismayed by the situation and did all he could to break up the liaison; but the result of his interference was the very opposite from the one he desired, for on 8 November Johann married Therese and adopted her daughter. For the next nine years there are only a few indications—and those not absolutely certain—of contacts between the two brothers; but from 1822 there is ample evidence that they were enjoying close relations. Johann's fortunes had prospered during the intervening years. He had sold his pharmacy in Linz in December 1816 and soon afterwards opened a new one across the Danube at Urfahr [then an independent community, since 1919 part of the city of Linz]; in August 1819 he had bought a country estate at Gneixendorf, near Krems, and in 1821 another house in Linz. During the winter he usually occupied a flat in the house belonging to Therese's brother Leopold Obermayer* in the Windmühle suburb of Vienna [now part of the sixth district, Mariahilf].

It is clear from Beethoven's correspondence and conversation books in 1822 and subsequent years that he was glad to have his brother's assistance and advice in business matters. 'C'est moi qui a [*sic*] le soin des affaires de mon frère,' Johann informed the Paris publisher Antonio Pacini* somewhat grandiloquently in December 1822 (*Corr*. B1518). Beethoven even proposed that he and Johann should share a flat, and when nothing came of that idea, he took rooms in July 1822 in a house adjoining the one in which Johann spent his winters (*see* Obermayer*). That same year, moreover, Johann lent Beethoven a sum of money (the amount is not known), in return for which Beethoven assigned to him the rights to some more of his compositions (Opp. 121b, 122, 124, 126, 128).

Several of Beethoven's letters to Johann are affectionate in tone, or, at any rate, contain passages which are; but, as in his relations with so many other persons, the nature of his feelings tended to vary. Typical of this ambivalence are two letters to his lawyer Johann Baptist Bach* relating to testamentary dispositions. In the first (6 March 1823) he appointed Bach as the curator of his estate and left him free to choose as his nephew Karl's* guardian anyone he wished, with the exception of Johann. In the second (1 August 1824) he wrote, after confirming that Karl was to remain his sole heir: 'but since one must also bequeath something to one's relatives, even if one feels no kinship with them, my worthy brother shall have my piano from Paris' (i.e. the piano he had received in 1803 from Sébastien Érard; in 1824/5 Beethoven would give it to Johann, who presented it to the Oberösterreichisches Landesmuseum at Linz in 1845). Apart from periodically doubting his brother's trustworthiness—he more than once referred to him as his 'pseudo-brother', on at least one occasion in a letter addressed to Johann himself—Beethoven seems to have had a low opinion of his intelligence ('asinaccio' being one of the terms he applied to him). It is true that Johann appears to have been widely regarded as pretentious and eager to derive prestige from being Beethoven's brother; Count Moritz Lichnowsky* told Beethoven in 1823 that everyone made fun of Johann and that his sole merit was that 'he bears your name' (*BKh3*/28). Among Johann's severest critics are Schindler* and Gerhard von Breuning,* but the reliability of their statements has been questioned by some biographers.

Beethoven's declining respect for his brother was in no small measure due to the exasperation, not to say contempt, which the spectacle of Johann's toleration of Therese's dissolute behaviour inspired in him. Beethoven's feelings for her, which are unlikely to have ever been more than lukewarm, turned violently hostile when Schindler informed him in July 1823 that she and her daughter had completely neglected Johann during a serious recent illness, and that she had even brought a lover to the flat (*Corr*. B1688). Beethoven, who was at Hetzendorf at the time, was so incensed that he contemplated reporting her to the police.

Thereafter he repeatedly urged Johann, though in vain, to break with Therese and Amalie, to whom he referred respectively as 'Fettlümmel' [Fat lout] and 'Bastard'. According to Schindler, a further cause of friction between the two brothers was Beethoven's demand that Johann should appoint Karl his heir rather than Therese; but the couple had, in fact, concluded a contract on 23 December 1820, in which each named the other as sole heir. Beethoven long refused to visit Gneixendorf so as not to meet Therese; but in September 1826, after Karl's attempted suicide, he thought it advantageous that his nephew should leave Vienna, and they both then spent some two months on Johann's estate. During Beethoven's final illness Johann visited him repeatedly; he was at his bedside on the day Beethoven died, but not present at the death itself.

The later history of Johann and Therese is not devoid of a certain drama, for after Therese's death in 1828 it was discovered that in a will executed on 21 May 1827 she had cancelled her part of the aforementioned contract of 1820, and had named her daughter Amalie her sole heir in place of Johann. Amalie accordingly inherited one-half of her parents' joint estate, and after her death on 10 March 1831 her husband Karl Stölzle, whom she had married the previous year, came into possession of the inheritance. According to Johann's biographer Otto Zekert, Johann 'was never able to recover from the consequences of [Therese's] will'. This statement is, however, contradicted by certain documents cited by Zekert himself. According to these, the couple's assets, at the time of Therese's death, amounted to some 41,000 florins, of which one-half was paid out to Amalie, leaving Johann about 20,000 florins. Yet when he died in 1848, his estate was valued at over 42,000 florins, i.e. more than twice that sum. In *c.*1835 he had sold the estate at Gneixendorf; but the previous year he had bought a house at Urfahr which he kept until 1843. Finally, in 1845, he had acquired a house at Weikersdorf, near Baden. The sole heir to his estate was none other than his nephew Karl, so Beethoven's wish was ultimately fulfilled, after all.

(Wacha[1,2], Zekert)

Beethoven, Therese van, née Obermayer (b. Vienna, 18 August 1787; d. Gneixendorf, near Krems, Lower Austria, 20 November 1828). Daughter of Wolfgang Obermayer, a baker, and his wife Theresia, née Waldmann; sister of Leopold Obermayer.* She married Beethoven's brother Nikolaus Johann* on 8 November 1812. At that time she already had an illegitimate daughter, Amalie (1807–31), who was given her grandmother's maiden name 'Waldmann'. The marriage of Nikolaus Johann and Therese was childless. (For some details of their married life and Beethoven's opinion of Therese, as well as some other pertinent information, *see* the article on Nikolaus Johann; *see also* Johanna van Beethoven.*)

Berg, Conrad Matthias (b. Colmar, 27 April 1785; d. Strasbourg, 14 December 1852). Composer, teacher, and writer on music. He studied the violin with Ignaz

Fränzl at Mannheim (1804–5) and the piano at the Paris Conservatoire (1806–7). In 1808 he settled at Strasbourg, where he became a highly respected piano teacher. In the course of a visit to Vienna in 1816 he met several prominent local musicians, including Beethoven, to whom he was introduced by Peter Joseph Simrock.* Many years later Simrock told Thayer* that he had asked Beethoven if Berg might dedicate some piano trios to him and that Beethoven had said, with a laugh, 'Nun, wenn er keinen Bessern hat, so kann er die mir dedizieren.' [Very well, if he can't find anyone more worthy, he may dedicate them to me.] P. Nettl, in *The Beethoven Encyclopedia* (article 'Simrock, Peter Joseph'), translates, almost certainly incorrectly, 'Well, all right, if you don't have anything better.' (Nettl even adds, by way of explanation, that Beethoven 'did not think too much of these compositions'.) The trios were published the following year by S. A. Steiner & Co.,* with a dedication to Beethoven.

Among Berg's other compositions were string quartets, violin sonatas, piano sonatas, and three piano concertos; his published writings include a pedagogical work, *Ideen zu einer rationellen Lehre der Methode der Musik mit Anwendung auf das Clavierspiel*, and a survey of music at Strasbourg during the period 1790–1840.

(Fétis)

Berge, Rudolf vom (b. Herrendorf, Silesia, 3 January 1775; d. Breslau [Wrocław, Poland], 13 August 1821). Dramatist. He studied law at Breslau, Frankfurt an der Oder, and Erlangen, and later worked as a civil servant in Breslau and Berlin. In 1803 he moved to Courland [now part of Latvia] where he earned his living at first as an actor and writer at Libau [Liepaja] and Mitau [Jelgava], and later as a private tutor at Puhnen [Puhne] and then at Talsen [Talsi]. There he became a close friend of Karl Amenda.* He published a volume of poetry and a comedy, *Frauentriumph*, at Mitau in 1810. He also wrote a number of tragedies, one of which, *Das Haus Barcelona*, was produced at the Burgtheater in Vienna on 3 June 1824, with music by Ignaz von Seyfried.* It received altogether fifteen performances there, the last one on 16 August 1830.

On 20 March 1815, Amenda sent Beethoven a copy of Berge's libretto for a grand lyric opera, *Bacchus*. Beethoven told another friend of Amenda's, Karl von Bursy,* the following year that it was quite good and would, with a few changes, be suitable for setting to music; but he never used it himself.

(Alth/Obzyna, Goedeke)

Bernadotte, Jean Baptiste Jules (b. Pau, 26 January 1763; d. Stockholm, 8 March 1844). Army commander, diplomat. He was elected crown prince of Sweden on 21 August 1810, and on 5 February 1818 succeeded Karl XIII as king of Sweden and Norway, under the name Karl XIV Johan.

On 11 January 1798 Bernadotte was appointed French ambassador in Vienna. He arrived there on 8 February, but was forced to relinquish his post some two months later, after the display of the tricolour from the embassy's balcony had provoked a riot. Schindler* states that Beethoven was among the distinguished persons of different ranks whom Bernadotte received in his salon, that Bernadotte suggested to Beethoven that he should compose a work celebrating 'the greatest hero of the epoch' (i.e. Napoleon)—a suggestion which, Schindler claims, led to the composition of the 'Eroica' Symphony—and that Beethoven was about to hand Bernadotte a fair copy of the score for forwarding to Paris when he learned that Napoleon had had himself proclaimed emperor, whereupon he tore off the title sheet and threw it on the floor (*see* Napoleon I*).

The overall credibility of Schindler's statements is seriously impaired by his placing the whole sequence of events in the year 1804, whereas Bernadotte's appointment in Vienna was, as already mentioned, limited to a few weeks in 1798; he had thus left the city several years before 18 May 1804, the day on which Napoleon was proclaimed emperor. It does not follow, however, that Schindler's account of Bernadotte's role in the history of the composition of the symphony must necessarily be incorrect. He even sought to substantiate his assertion by the following footnote: 'The present writer heard from Beethoven's own lips, on the occasion when he addressed a letter to the king of Sweden in 1823, that the idea for this work originally came from General Bernadotte.'

Many scholars have nevertheless been reluctant to take Schindler's word in this matter, in view of the faulty chronology of his account and his well-established untrustworthiness as a source. There is also the fact that five years were to elapse between Bernadotte's presence in Vienna and Beethoven's first sketches for the symphony. Certain arguments hostile to Schindler's assertion rest, however, on less valid ground. Thus D. W. MacArdle, in his English version of Schindler's biography (Chapel Hill, NC, 1966), wrongly translates the above-cited footnote as signifying that Beethoven had made the alleged statement in his letter to Bernadotte, instead of verbally to Schindler, and this error leads him to comment: 'Schindler's statement is not borne out by the facts. The only known letter from Beethoven to King Karl XIV Johann of Sweden . . . makes no reference to Napoleon or to the "Eroica" symphony.' (In fact, Beethoven addressed two letters to the king—see below.)

Schindler may or may not have been justified in tracing back the composition of the 'Eroica' Symphony to a suggestion made by Bernadotte. On the other hand, he was undoubtedly correct in stating that Beethoven had been received by him. In 1823 Bernadotte, by then king of Sweden and Norway, was among the eminent personages whom Beethoven invited to subscribe to the *Missa solemnis*. The formal request, dated 26 February 1823, was followed on 1 March by a more personal letter, in which Beethoven recalled their meetings twenty-five years earlier ('La présence de Votre Majesté à Vienne, et l'intérêt qu'elle prit avec quelques Seigneurs de sa suite à mes médiocres talents'). After once again soliciting a subscription to the Mass, Beethoven expressed his desire to write a composition for the crown prince [the future King Oscar I], who, he had been informed, possessed great musical talent. The king does not appear to have responded to either letter. It is perhaps worth mentioning that Bernadotte had again visited Vienna in June and October 1809, but no one has so far suggested that he saw Beethoven on those occasions.

(Palmer[1], Schindler[1])

Bernard, Karl Joseph (b. Horatitz, near Saaz [Hořetice, near Žatek, Czech Republic], 1780/6; d. Vienna, 31 March 1850). Librettist, journalist, and editor. He settled in Vienna in 1800. From 1810 to 1813 he edited *Thalia*, a periodical founded by Ignaz Franz Castelli.* He also worked on Johann Valentin Schickh's* *Wiener Zeitschrift für Kunst, Literatur, Theater und Mode* (especially in 1818–20) and was editor-in-chief of the *Wiener Zeitung* (1819–47). From 1849 he was in charge of the conservative daily *Austria*. He wrote the librettos for Spohr's* opera *Faust* (produced in Prague on 1 September 1816, and at the Theater an der Wien in Vienna on 7 July 1818) and for Conradin Kreutzer's* *Libussa* (Kärntnertor-Theater, 4 December 1822).

Beethoven's correspondence and the conversation books testify to his intimate friendship with Bernard, especially during the years 1816–23. He frequently discussed personal matters with Bernard, particularly his relations with his nephew Karl* and Johanna van Beethoven,* as well as Karl's education. At Beethoven's request, Bernard accompanied him to Karl's schools and also to court sessions, and helped him draw up various legal documents and petitions. Sometimes Beethoven called Bernard jokingly 'Bernardus non sanctus'—evidently to distinguish him from the well-known saint (*see also* the canon WoO 175 and certain entries in the conversation books).

Beethoven's professional association with Bernard was less rewarding than their personal relationship. Early in 1814 he set, or at any rate began to set, *Europens Befreyungsstunde*, a text believed to have been written by Bernard. He intended to present the cantata at his forthcoming concert on 27 February, but its performance was forbidden by the censor. Later that same year he used a text by Bernard in *Chor auf die verbündeten Fürsten* (WoO 95), which paid homage to the illustrious personages who were due to attend the Congress; however, as far as is known, the chorus was not performed at the time. Another work, in the preparation of which Bernard reportedly had a hand, did, however, achieve public performance that same year: the cantata *Der glorreiche Augenblick* (Op. 136)—of which the original text (by Aloys Weissenbach*) had, according to Schindler,* been revised by Bernard at Beethoven's request—was sung at three concerts (29 November, 2 and 25 December 1814). Several years later Bernard was involved in another unsuccessful venture. Having been chosen to furnish the libretto for the oratorio which Beethoven had undertaken to compose for the Gesellschaft der Musikfreunde,* he produced a text entitled *Der Sieg des Kreuzes* in late 1823, after a long delay punctuated by patient reminders from the society. Beethoven promptly pronounced the text inadequate, a judgement supported by several friends he consulted. There was talk of an abridgement and revision, but nothing ever came of the project.

Beethoven remained in contact with Bernard, but their relationship appears to have become less close after Bernard married Magdalena Grassl in 1823. But as late as June 1825 Beethoven was still asking Bernard to keep an eye on his nephew while he was himself staying at Baden, and he invited Bernard to visit him there together with his wife and Karl (*Corr.* A1387/B1991). At Beethoven's funeral Bernard acted as a torchbearer.

(Czeike)

Bernhard, Elisabeth von, née Kissow (1784–1868). When 12 years old, she was sent by her father from her native Augsburg to Vienna to study the piano with Johann Andreas Streicher,* who had moved there in 1794. In Vienna, she lived at the house of a Russian diplomat named von Klüpfell* (or Klüpfeld). Through Klüpfell and his superior, Count Razumovsky,* she gained access to the musical circles of Viennese high society. As she told Ludwig Nohl at Augsburg in 1864, she had numerous occasions to observe Beethoven and to hear him play, both at Klüpfell's and elsewhere. She herself was frequently asked to perform, notably at Prince Lichnowsky's.* A letter written by Beethoven to Streicher, perhaps in August or September 1896 (*Corr.* A18/B22), attests to the fact that he regarded Elisabeth as a gifted pianist. In fact, he states that her performance of an 'Adagio' composed by himself had moved him to tears. (The context suggests that he may have been referring to the Adagio section of one of the Piano Trios Op. 1, which he had published the previous year and dedicated to Lichnowsky.) He assured Streicher that he would follow Elisabeth's progress with interest and do what he could to encourage her. And she herself told Nohl that from then until she left Vienna in 1800 Beethoven would regularly send her a copy of his newly published compositions.

(Nohl[4])

Bertolini, Joseph von (b. Cles, Tyrol [now in Italy], 26 September 1784; d. Vienna, 3 March 1861). Physician; assistant of Dr Johann Malfatti.* He attended Beethoven from 1806, and also became a personal friend. According to a declaration made by Artaria & Co.* during their quarrel with Tobias Haslinger* in 1831–4 concerning their respective rights to the publication of *Fidelio*, it was Bertolini who had arranged the purchase by Artaria of the score of the opera in 1814. That same year, Beethoven had composed the cantata *Un lieto brindisi* (WoO 103) for a party which Bertolini arranged in celebration of Malfatti's name day on 24 June. (*See also* Elisabeth Alexievna.*)

On 28 September 1816 Bertolini called on Beethoven with an Englishman, Major-General Alexander Kyd, who was anxious to commission a symphony but was unwise enough to specify that it should be shorter and simpler than Beethoven's recent symphonies and more in the style of his earlier ones. Furious at being dictated to on artistic matters, Beethoven refused peremptorily, and he furthermore felt resentful towards Bertolini who had conveyed Kyd's offer to him. The incident seems to have put an end to their friendship, and their contacts are said to have ceased altogether after Beethoven quarrelled with Malfatti in 1817.

When Bertolini was gravely, and as he thought fatally, ill with cholera in 1831 he had all the letters and notes he had received from Beethoven destroyed. He recovered, however, and was able to share his recollections of Beethoven with Otto Jahn in 1852 (Jahn's notes on their conversation are published in F. Kerst's *Die Erinnerungen an Beethoven*) and with Thayer* in the early 1860s.

(Hilmar, Kerst, Slezak[4])

Bigot (de Morogues), Marie, née Kiené (b. Colmar, 3 March 1786; d. Paris, 16 September 1820). Pianist. In 1791 she moved with her parents to Neuchâtel in Switzerland. There, on 9 July 1804, she married Paul Bigot de Morogues (b. Berlin, 1765; d. ?1852). Soon afterwards the couple moved to Vienna, where Bigot was employed as a librarian by Count Razumovsky.*

Marie was introduced to Salieri and to Haydn* (who is reported to have effusively complimented her on her playing), and in May 1805 she performed at a concert in the Augarten. She may have received some instruction from Beethoven, or at least some coaching in the performance of his compositions, for which she felt the greatest admiration. The closer contacts between Beethoven and the Bigots probably date from the winter of 1806–7, when he was a frequent visitor to Razumovsky's palace. It was no doubt at that time that Marie astonished Beethoven by brilliantly sight-reading the 'Appassionata' Sonata from his rain-damaged autograph. (The source of this frequently told story is a note which Paul Bigot wrote many years later on a printed copy of the sonata owned by the French pianist Mortier de Fontaine.) At Marie's request, Beethoven presented the autograph to her following the publication of the sonata in February 1807; it is now at the Bibliothèque Nationale, Paris.

Beethoven's extant letters to the Bigots show that he was, for a time at any rate, on very friendly terms with them, and also that he found Marie highly attractive. Unfortunately, certain jocular remarks, such as 'Kiss your wife very often—I could not blame you for it' (*Corr.* A161/B269) appear to have displeased the husband, who was, after all, five years older than Beethoven and more than twenty years older than Marie. Beethoven provoked an even more hostile reaction when, evidently aware that Bigot did not wish Marie to go out with him alone, he proposed, in a letter to her on 4 March 1807, that she and 'Caroline' should go for a drive with him that day. Marie refused Beethoven's invitation, and it is clear from letters written by Beethoven during the following two days—one to Paul Bigot, the other jointly to Paul and Marie—that they had expressed their displeasure in no uncertain terms. Beethoven protested at great length the innocence of his intentions, and he assured them that it was one of his foremost moral principles 'never to have relations other than those of friendship with another man's wife' (*Corr.* A139/B273).

Emily Anderson assumed that 'Caroline' was 'the Bigots' infant daughter' (*Corr.* A138 n. 3), presumably because Beethoven had told Marie Bigot to 'wrap Caroline in swaddling clothes from head to foot [in Windeln von Kopf bis zu füssen], so that no harm can come to her'. But this identification is incorrect, for the records of the Protestant community in Vienna show that the Bigots' daughter—who was, in fact, named 'Gustavie Adele'—was not born until 28 October of that year. (A son, Andreas Paul, had been born on 3 November 1805.) The Caroline in question was, no doubt, Marie's sister of that name (to whom Marie dedicated her *Andante varié* published by Artaria & Co.*). Perhaps Caroline had been ill, or maybe Beethoven's reference to swaddling clothes was simply a joke, for she was certainly no longer an infant in 1807. In another note to Paul Bigot which probably dates from the same period, Beethoven wrote that he was looking forward to hearing Caroline play (presumably the piano) the next day (*Corr.* A161/B269). And Johann Friedrich Reichardt,* who met Caroline at a musical evening given by the Bigots in January 1809, on which occasion she served tea to the guests, described her as 'very pretty and highly cultivated'. It is thus highly unlikely that she had really still been in swaddling clothes two years earlier.

Nothing is known about any later contacts between Beethoven and the Bigots, although they doubtless continued to meet socially (*see also* Esterházy von Galántha, Almerie*). Reichardt, for one, provides evidence of Marie's continuing enthusiasm for Beethoven's music. Thus a concert given by her at the Kleiner Redoutensaal in December 1808 consisted almost entirely of works by Beethoven 'who appears to be her musical God'. The programme included a symphony and the Overture to *Coriolan*, and Marie herself performed one of the piano concertos, as well as the *Thirty-Two Variations* in C minor. Reichardt praised her great virtuosity (especially the strength of her left hand) and the perfect clarity with which she played even the most difficult passages. At the previously mentioned *soirée* in January 1809 'she played five great sonatas by Beethoven in quite masterly fashion', including some violin sonatas with Schuppanzigh.*

In 1809, the year of the resumption of the war against Napoleon and the occupation of Vienna by the French, Paul and Marie Bigot left for Paris. There her playing continued to attract high praise. In his *Biographie universelle des musiciens*, F.-J. Fétis pays tribute to her 'exquisite sensitivity [which] gave her a rare understanding of every masterpiece'. She also gave piano lessons, among others to the young Mendelssohn.

(Fétis, Perreau, Reichardt)

Bihler, Johann. A qualified physician of Swiss origin. He was employed as tutor to the children of Baron Johann Baptist Puthon,* and in 1823/4 became tutor to the sons of Archduke Karl. The earliest mention of Bihler in a dated letter by Beethoven occurs on 30 July 1817, but he almost certainly knew Bihler well before then. (An undated note from Beethoven to Bihler (*Corr.* A646/B659) is tentatively ascribed to the year 1813 in the new Bonn edition of his correspondence.) His relations with Bihler must have been fairly close, for when he arranged for Johanna van Beethoven* to come to his flat to see her son Karl* on 31 July 1817, he asked Bihler (as well as Nikolaus Zmeskall von Domanovecz*) to be present. Shortly afterwards he provided Bihler, who was about to leave on a trip to Switzerland, with letters of introduction to Hans Georg Nägeli* and Xaver Schnyder von Wartensee.* In the note to Nägeli, he twice referred to him as his 'friend'.

Bihler was acquainted with several persons who belonged to Beethoven's circle. In fact, Joseph Blahetka—Leopoldine Blahetka's* father—told Schindler* that it was Bihler who had introduced him to Beethoven. Bihler also knew Joseph Czerny* (who told Beethoven in December 1819 that Bihler 'frequently thinks of you' (*BKh*1/134)) and Cajetan Giannattasio del Rio* (who wrote about him in 1823: 'Great *embonpoint*! A true Swiss' (*BKh*3/98)). Presumably Johannes Büel* had Bihler in mind when, in a letter to a friend, he mentioned 'Bühler, a Swiss, my confidant, one of the gentlest and most upright of men'. Whether the 'I. N. Bihler' who signed the letter presented by Viennese music lovers to Beethoven in February 1824 is identical with the subject of this article is not certain, but quite possible.

Birchall, Robert (b. ?London, *c.*1760; d. London, 19 December 1819). Music seller, instrument dealer, and publisher. He was in business by 1783, first in partnership with T. Beardmore and subsequently, from 1783 to 1789, with Hugh Andrews; thereafter he ran the firm on his own until 1819.

Birchall's association with Beethoven's music began with his publication of the Violin Sonata in A major, Op. 47, in May 1805. The circumstances leading up to it are unclear, for Birchall is not known to have been in contact with Beethoven at that time. According to Alan Tyson, the direct source of Birchall's edition is not known; in any case, his edition is not a reprint of the one which had been issued the previous month by Nikolaus Simrock* at Bonn.

In 1815, through Johann Peter Salomon,* Beethoven sold Birchall his own piano arrangement of *Wellingtons Sieg*, Anton Diabelli's* piano reduction of the Seventh Symphony, the Violin Sonata in G major, Op. 96, and the Piano Trio in B flat major, Op. 97. The English editions of these works appeared in 1816–17, soon after those published by S. A. Steiner & Co.* in Vienna, except for the arrangement of *Wellingtons Sieg* which first came out in London. Beethoven had some correspondence with Birchall's firm in connection with these and possible further publications (since Birchall himself was in poor health, his employee

Christopher Lonsdale wrote on his behalf). On 14 August 1816, Birchall suggested that Beethoven might compose some 'Variations to the most favourite English, Scotch or Irish Airs for the Pianoforte with an Accompaniment either for the Violin or Violoncello' (*Corr.* B958). In his reply on 1 October 1816 Beethoven indicated that he was willing to do so, for a fee of £30. At the same time, he offered Birchall the Piano Sonata in A major (Op. 101) and a piano trio (on which he was presumably working at that time, but which he never completed). However, these different offers and projects came to nothing, in the main because Birchall considered the fees demanded by Beethoven too high, and also because Birchall's failing health made him less eager to add new pieces to his catalogue.

(Tyson[3])

Birkenstock, Johann Melchior von (b. Heiligenstadt, Thuringia, 11 May 1738; d. Vienna, 30/1 October 1809). Austrian diplomat and senior civil servant. Son of the imperial treasurer-general Johann Konrad von Birkenstock (1703–80, ennobled 1745) and his wife Maria Ursula, née Güntzer. After studies at Erfurt and Göttingen he joined the Austrian government service and was subsequently employed in several Austrian embassies before assuming a number of senior posts in Vienna. In these he distinguished himself by his enlightened ideas; he is, in particular, credited with an important reform of the educational system. He retired in 1803, with the title 'Hofrat'. Through his marriage to Carolina Josepha von Hay (1755/6–88) on 1 March 1778 he became Joseph von Sonnenfels's* brother-in-law. The couple had four children, of whom only two, Hugo Konrad (1778–1825) and Antonia [Antonie] (1780–1869), reached adulthood. Antonie married the Frankfurt merchant Franz Brentano (on both, *see* Brentano*).

Birkenstock was a man of very great erudition. Several of his writings appeared in print, including a posthumously published Latin poem on Antonio Canova's splendid funerary monument for the Archduchess Marie Christine in the Augustinerkirche. He owned a large house in the Landstrasse suburb (on the site now numbered 19 Erdbergstrasse). The house was filled with books, works of art, and scientific objects, reflecting their owner's wide-ranging interests. After his death, these treasures, together with the house itself, passed into the possession of his daughter Antonie, who sold a large number of them at auctions in Vienna in 1812. The house itself was bought in 1832 by the pharmacist Joseph Gerold, a brother of the bookseller and printer Carl Gerold.* The building was demolished in 1911. (The sale catalogue of Birkenstock's collection lists no fewer than 551 paintings, many of them by celebrated artists. Even so, by no means all the pictures from the collection were included in the sale. The others, including some of the best, were transported, together with most of the engravings, to Antonie's Frankfurt home where they were to form the nucleus of the Brentanos' own collection. The latter was eventually sold at auction at Frankfurt in 1870, together with the rest of Antonie's property.)

There is ample evidence that Beethoven was a frequent visitor to the house when Antonie and her husband Franz Brentano lived there after her father's death (1809–12); but Beethoven's biographers have reached differing conclusions as to whether or not he had been personally acquainted with Birkenstock himself. The matter is complicated by being linked to the debate concerning the date of his first meeting with Antonie. Schindler* states that Beethoven made Antonie's acquaintance at her father's house soon after arriving in Vienna in 1792, from which it would evidently follow that he met her father also at that time. For Thayer,* the question was settled beyond all doubt in 1872 by a written declaration from the then 'head of the [Brentano] family', which reached him through the American consul general at Frankfurt, W. P. Webster. This declaration contains the statement that Beethoven's close association with Antonie and her husband had their origin in the friendly relations he enjoyed with Birkenstock when she arrived in Vienna to visit her sick father in 1809. In a covering note, Webster informed Thayer that he had learned (presumably from Brentano) that Birkenstock had been a friend of Beethoven's, that he had frequently received Beethoven at his house, and that Beethoven had met Antonie prior to her marriage. Yet Ludwig Nohl reports in his 1867 edition of Beethoven's letters that Antonie herself had 'categorically' asserted to him that the first time she met Beethoven was when she accompanied Bettina Brentano (*see* Arnim*) to his lodgings in 1810.

While Antonie's declaration makes it unlikely that Birkenstock met Beethoven before she moved to Frankfurt in 1798, it does not entirely rule out the possibility of a later association between the two men. Maynard Solomon has firmly dismissed such a possibility, but his conclusion is partly founded on a mistranslation of Brentano's statement, which leads him to reject as 'improbable' Brentano's report that 'Beethoven first met Birkenstock on his deathbed'. In fact, though, Solomon had mistakenly understood the key phrase that Beethoven was on friendly terms with Birkenstock *already at the time* when Antonie visited her father in Vienna ['schon zur Zeit, in welcher Frau Brentano ihren Vater in Wien besuchte'] as signifying '*since the time*'. Clearly, Brentano's declaration in no way implied a first meeting between Beethoven and Birkenstock at the latter's deathbed. Solomon, furthermore, accuses Webster of 'misreading' Brentano's communication in his covering note. But Webster's information almost certainly derives from a personal conversation he had with Brentano and not from his reading of Brentano's written declaration. To sum up: while it cannot be established with certainty that Beethoven knew and visited Birkenstock, Solomon's arguments against the possibility of such personal contact are at least partly flawed. (For further information on Antonie, *see* Brentano.*)

Finally, it may be of some interest to music lovers that the house next to Birkenstock's mansion became in 1809 the property of Anna Watteroth, the wife of Professor Heinrich Joseph Watteroth, and that Schubert's friends Johann

Mayrhofer and Joseph von Spaun lived there for a time, as did perhaps, briefly in 1816, Schubert himself. His cantata *Prometheus* was first performed in its garden on 24 July 1816.

(Czeike, Nohl[1], Schindler[1], Solomon[2,5])

Blahetka, (Anna Maria) Leopoldine (b. Guntramsdorf, Lower Austria, 16 November 1809; d. Boulogne-sur-Mer, 17 January 1885). Pianist, composer, and teacher; daughter of Joseph L. Blahetka (1783–after 1847), a teacher and journalist, and his second wife Barbara Sophia Traeg, a niece of the music publisher Johann Traeg.* She attracted Beethoven's attention when she was only 5 years old, and at the age of 8 she was hailed an infant prodigy after performing Hummel's* variations on a theme from Georg Joseph Vogler's* opera *Castor e Polluce* in public. She gave her own first concert on 28 March 1819. Her piano teachers were Joseph Czerny,* Frédéric Kalkbrenner, and Ignaz Moscheles,* and she studied composition with Simon Sechter.* In 1829 Chopin called her 'the finest woman pianist in Vienna'. She enjoyed an international career before settling at Boulogne-sur-Mer, probably some time before 1840. There she became a greatly admired teacher.

In a letter to Schindler* on 8 September 1839 (which is quoted by Schindler's biographer Eduard Hüffer), Joseph Blahetka stated that he had been introduced to Beethoven by Johann Bihler.* He furthermore declared that without Beethoven's encouragement and without the close interest he took in her progress, Leopoldine would never have become the outstanding pianist she was. Beethoven, he wrote, had set her written exercises, advised her mother (who was evidently her first teacher) how best to instruct her, and forbade her to play any compositions other than Mozart's* for an entire year; later he chose Joseph Czerny as her teacher.

(Clive[2], Hüffer, Jancik[1])

Blöchlinger von Bannholz, Joseph Urban (b. Goldingen, Canton St Gallen, Switzerland, 9 September 1788; d. 1855). In 1804 he went to Vienna, where he studied medicine, one of his teachers being Johann Adam Schmidt.* However, he did not pursue these studies for long, but turned to teaching instead. For a time he was employed at Friedrich Krause's school, but in 1814 he opened his own school in the Landstrasse suburb; that same year he married Henriette von Fischer, a daughter of court secretary Karl Emanuel von Fischer.

He was an admirer of Johann Heinrich Pestalozzi; whether, as is sometimes stated, he was a pupil or even a friend of Pestalozzi is less certain. It is true that Beethoven, in a letter to Archduke Rudolph on 15 July 1819, calls him 'ein schüler [pupil] pestalozzis', but this could mean a follower rather than a pupil. It is, after all, worth remembering that Pestalozzi did not found his famous boarding school at Yverdon until 1805, by which time Blöchlinger was in Vienna. It is possible, though not absolutely certain, that Blöchlinger's remark 'I know him personally' in a conversation book in March 1820 (*BKh*1/345) refers to the Swiss educationist. If he did indeed know Pestalozzi personally, the acquaintance is unlikely to have been a close one, for the thirteen-volume edition of Pestalozzi's letters (Zurich, 1946–71) does not contain a single one addressed to Blöchlinger, nor does his name figure in the index to any of the volumes.

On 22 June 1819, a few days after Giannattasio del Rio* had declined to take Beethoven's nephew Karl* back into his school, he became a pupil at Blöchlinger's institute which was then located in the Palais Chotek [39 Josefstädter Strasse]. Beethoven's early relations with Blöchlinger were somewhat tense, owing to his insistence that Karl's mother Johanna* be denied free access to her son, but they soon became quite amicable when Blöchlinger carried out his instructions to his satisfaction. Blöchlinger's son Karl later recalled that Beethoven, who had at first taken rooms near the school, used to call on his father several times a week and would often play chess with him. Beethoven's nephew remained at the school until August 1823. Some time afterwards, and at any rate not later than 1825, Blöchlinger moved to a house in Favoritenstrasse, opposite the Theresianische Akademie.

(Geiser)

Boer, Samson Moses de: *see* De Boer.*

Böhm, Joseph Daniel (b. Wallendorf, near Zips [Spišske Vlachy, Spiš, Slovak Republic], 15 March 1794; d. Vienna, 15 August 1865). Sculptor and medallist. He arrived in Vienna in 1813 and during the next six years studied at the Akademie der bildenden Künste, where his teachers were the painter Johann Ender and the sculptors Johann Martin Fischer, Joseph Straub, and Franz Anton Zauner.

He is known to have been in contact with Beethoven in 1819–20, for the conversation books for those years contain a number of references to him, as well as some entries in his own hand. He made two drawings of Beethoven out walking, one showing him from the side, the other from the back; he subsequently engraved these drawings on silver. The original engraving and the original sketches appear to have been lost. To-day, the sketches are known from facsimiles printed in the *Leipziger illustrierte Zeitung* in 1892 of tracings taken from the engraving. In addition, Böhm planned to make a medal bearing Beethoven's portrait. There are several references in the conversation books to the project, and Beethoven sat for Böhm at least once; in December 1819, Karl Joseph Bernard* told Beethoven that Böhm would like a further sitting (*BKh*1/164). Some two months later, Karl Peters* assured Beethoven that Böhm had created an excellent likeness (*BKh*1/297). Only a plaster cast made from the wax model prepared by Böhm has survived.

Böhm spent the years 1821–2 and 1825–9 in Italy. In 1831 he received the title of 'Kammermedailleur', and in 1836 he was appointed director of the

Graveur-Akademie at the Hauptmünzamt [Mint] in Vienna. His son Joseph Edgar (1834–90) enjoyed a highly successful career as a sculptor in England where he settled in 1862.

(*ALBK*)

Böhm, Joseph Michael (b. Pest [Budapest], 4 April 1795; d. Vienna, 28 March 1876). Violinist and composer. He was taught the violin and piano by his father and reportedly also received instruction from Pierre Rode.* In 1816 he made a very promising debut in Vienna, playing works by Rodolphe Kreutzer* and Franz Weiss;* later he toured with great success in Italy, Germany, and France. He was greatly admired, not only for his technical skill, but also for his artistic taste. In addition, he was very highly esteemed as a teacher; in 1819 he was appointed the very first professor of violin at the Conservatoire, and he remained on its faculty until 1848. Among his pupils were Heinrich Wilhelm Ernst, Georg Hellmesberger, and Joseph Joachim.

Böhm frequently played at concerts in Vienna until 1827, when he gave up performing in public; he was, in particular, an enthusiastic champion of chamber music. In 1816 he arranged six concerts at the hotel Zum römischen Kaiser, which were mainly devoted to quartets by Beethoven and Haydn.* In 1821 he launched a series of chamber music recitals together with Karl Holz,* Franz Weiss, and Joseph Linke.* The excellence of their performances prompted one critic to write: 'This is how Beethoven's and Mozart's quartets should be played.' Böhm also frequently appeared at the 'evening entertainments' of the Gesellschaft der Musikfreunde,* mostly performing in chamber music. In addition, he was a member of the court Kapelle from 1821 to 1868. His own compositions were written mainly for the violin.

Böhm was among the musicians whom Beethoven invited to take part in the concert he gave on 7 May 1824. In 1825, following the disappointing first performance of the Quartet in E flat major (Op. 127) by the Schuppanzigh* Quartet on 6 March, Beethoven asked Böhm to direct some further performances of the work. After intensive rehearsals supervised by Beethoven himself, Böhm was able to achieve the hoped-for success in a series of performances (on 18 March, on 23 March, when the quartet was played twice, and on 7 April).

Böhm was a torchbearer at Beethoven's funeral.

(Moser[1], Wurzbach[1])

Boldrini, Carlo (b. Blevio, 9 January 1779; d. Vienna, 16 January 1850). Music publisher; son of Giuseppe Boldrini and Cecilia Boldrini, née Cappi; nephew of Carlo Artaria. After moving to Vienna in 1801 he was employed at Artaria & Co.* In 1810 he was made a partner by Domenico (III) Artaria, and soon afterwards married Elisabeth Martini, whose father owned the house in which the firm's premises were located in Kohlmarkt. He remained with the firm until 1824, when he sold his share to Domenico and retired. During the following years he and his wife frequently stayed at Baden, the well-known spa near Vienna; later a street there was named after them, in recognition of their benefactions to the town and the region. A portrait of Boldrini by Johann Baptist Lampi (1807–57) can be seen at the Rollett Museum at Baden.   .

Beethoven knew Boldrini quite well and sometimes addressed him as 'Falstaff', for the publisher—like the violinist Schuppanzigh,* on whom Beethoven bestowed the same sobriquet—had a corpulent figure.

(Slezak[4])

Bonaparte, Jérôme (b. Ajaccio, 15 November 1784; d. Villegenis, near Paris, 24 June 1860). Brother of Napoleon I.* After serving in the French navy in the West Indies, he lived in the United States (1803–5) and, while there, married Elisabeth Patterson (1785–1879). However, after his return to France the marriage was annulled on Napoleon's orders, and in 1807 he married Princess Katharina of Württemberg (1783–1835). On 18 August 1807 he became king of Westphalia, a kingdom created under the terms of the Treaty of Tilsit (7 and 9 July 1807) with Kassel as its capital. He arrived in that city in December 1807, and over the next six years he led a life devoted mainly to pomp and pleasure, not to say dissipation; as a result, he became known as 'König Lustig' [King Merry]. He took part in Napoleon's Russian campaign and later fought at Waterloo. By then, in the aftermath of the Battle of Leipzig (16–19 October 1813), he had lost his kingdom; he left Kassel for good on 26 October 1813. After the final collapse of the Napoleonic regime he lived in exile in Württemberg and Italy, and it was not until 1847 that he was allowed to return to France. In 1852, following the *coup d'état* of his nephew Louis-Napoleon [Napoleon III], he became president of the senate.

In the autumn of 1808 Beethoven received through Count Friedrich Ludwig Waldburg-Capustigall, the high chamberlain at the Westphalian court, an invitation to take up the post of Kapellmeister at Kassel. The precise date when Beethoven received this offer is not known, nor are the circumstances which led to it. The earliest datable reference to the offer in Beethoven's extant correspondence occurs on 1 November 1808, in a letter to Count Franz Oppersdorff.* Contrary to some reports, Johann Friedrich Reichardt,* who had been Kapellmeister at Kassel since the beginning of that year, had nothing to do with the matter. Indeed, when he arrived in Vienna towards the end of November he was surprised to learn of the offer and even tried to dissuade Beethoven from accepting it. (*See also* Willmann, Ignaz.*)

Beethoven was immediately attracted by the invitation, not because he disliked living in Vienna, but because he felt frustrated by his inability to a achieve a secure financial situation there. He was accordingly greatly tempted by the proposed annual salary of 600 gold ducats, plus 150 ducats for travelling expenses, in exchange for which payments he was to have no other obligation than to play occasionally for the king and to conduct his infrequent concerts. On 7 January 1809 Beethoven informed Breitkopf & Härtel* that he had that day written to confirm his acceptance of the post; he would make his travel arrangements as soon as he received the certificate of appointment. Yet, in the end, he did not depart for Kassel. Instead, he accepted a proposal made by three highly placed Viennese music lovers (Archduke Rudolph,* Prince Kinsky,* and Prince Lobkowitz*) who, dismayed at the prospect of his imminent departure, guaranteed him an annual income of 4,000 florins, in return for his promise to reside in Vienna or in another city within the Austrian crown lands for the remainder of his life. The contract was dated 1 March 1809. In many ways, therefore, Jérôme's invitation was the best thing that ever happened to Beethoven.

In his memoirs, Baron Trémont,* who arrived in Vienna soon after the Battle of Aspern-Essling (21–2 May 1809), wrote: 'When Napoleon took possession of Vienna for the second time, his brother Jérôme, the king of Westphalia, proposed to Beethoven that he should become his *maître de chapelle*, at a salary of 7000 francs. As I was then in Vienna, he asked my advice, in confidence. I think I did well to advise him not to accept the offer, but to adhere to the arrangement for the agreed annuity.' If accurate, Trémont's remarks must signify that Beethoven was still wondering in the spring of 1809 whether he had made the right decision. It is not known exactly when he formally declined Jérôme's invitation.

(Fischer-Dieskau, Kircheisen)

Bonaparte, Napoleon: *see* Napoleon I.*

Bondi, [Abbate] **Clemente (Donnino Luigi)** (b. Mezzano Superiore, near Parma, 27 June 1742; d. Vienna, 20 June 1821). Poet and translator. He joined the Society of Jesus in 1760; after its suppression by Pope Clement XIV in 1773 he lived for a time at Padua, Parma, and Venice, before finding employment as a librarian at Mantua. In *c*.1790 he moved to Milan, where he came into contact with the governor general of Lombardy, Archduke Ferdinand, and his wife Maria Beatrix d'Este. When they were obliged to leave Milan in 1796, he followed them, first to Brünn [Brno], where he was appointed the archduchess's librarian, and later to Wiener Neustadt, where some members of Ferdinand's family temporarily resided. Bondi finally settled in Vienna in 1810.

His poems were highly regarded, but he made an even greater name for himself with his translations of Virgil's *Aeneid* and Ovid's *Metamorphoses*. He wrote the text for the cantata *Un lieto brindisi* (WoO 103) which Beethoven composed for a party given by Dr Joseph von Bertolini* in honour of Dr Johann Malfatti* on 24 June 1814.

(Barbarisi, Wurzbach[1])

Bossler, Heinrich Philipp Carl (b. Darmstadt, 22 June 1744; d. Gohlis, near Leipzig, 9 December 1812). Music printer and publisher. Information about his early life is sketchy, but there is some evidence that he was working as a copper engraver in 1769. In 1779, while residing at Heilbronn, he invented a machine for engraving music, which both speeded up the process and improved its quality. In 1780, together with Caspar von Beecke, a brother of the composer Ignaz von Beecke, he founded a publishing house at Speyer, for which he assumed sole responsibility the following year. Later, especially from 1791, his son Friedrich assumed an increasingly important role in the firm, which moved to Darmstadt in 1792 and to Leipzig in 1799. It remained in business until 1828.

In 1782 Bossler launched a weekly publication, *Blumenlese für Klavierliebhaber beyderley Geschlechts*, in which he printed songs and piano music written mainly by south German composers; it appeared until 1787. He furthermore published the periodical *Musikalische Realzeitung* (1788–90), subsequently renamed *Musikalische Korrespondenz* (1790–2). In 1783 Beethoven's Rondo in C major (WoO 48) and the song 'Schilderung eines Mädchens' (WoO 107) were printed in *Blumenlese*, and in 1784 his song 'An einen Säugling' (WoO 108; *see* Döring*) was published there. Bossler also issued the first edition of Beethoven's three Piano Sonatas WoO 47 in 1783.

(Matthäus[1], Plesske)

Boucher, Alexandre-Jean (b. Paris, 11 April 1778; d. Paris, 29 December 1861). Violinist. An infant prodigy, he played at court at the age of 6 and at the Concerts spirituels at 8. From 1795/6 to 1805 he was attached as violinist to the court of King Charles IV of Spain. A violinist of exceptional technical accomplishment, he increasingly indulged in empty feats of showmanship, to the detriment of the music he was performing.

During a stay in Vienna from 4 March to 23 June 1822, he gave three concerts (26 March, 21 April, 2 May) together with his wife Céleste, an excellent pianist and harpist who was no less eccentric a performer than her husband. The concerts were not well received by the Viennese critics. On the other hand, Boucher was warmly welcomed by Beethoven, mainly because he carried a letter of introduction from Goethe.* On the occasion of his visit (29 April 1822), Beethoven composed for him a seven-bar piece for two violins (WoO 34), the autograph of which is now at the Bibliothèque Nationale, Paris.

(Vallat, Warrack[1])

Bouilly, Jean-Nicolas (b. La Coudraye, near Tours, 23/4 January 1763; d. Paris, 25 April 1842). Librettist and playwright. Trained as a lawyer, he practised first in Paris and, from 1789, at Tours. It was there that he began writing for the stage. His libretto *Pierre le Grand* was set by Grétry and the opera was performed at the Comédie-Italienne in Paris on 13 January 1790. Bouilly himself returned to Paris in 1795, and three years later he quit the legal career in order to devote himself entirely to literary activities. Certain incidents which, according to his memoirs

(*Mes récapitulations*, 1836–7), he had witnessed while serving as head of a military commission at Tours led him to write the libretto *Léonore, ou L'Amour conjugal* for Pierre Gaveaux; the historical persons involved are believed to have been a Count René Semblançay and his wife Blanche. Gaveaux's opera was produced at the Théâtre Feydeau on 19 February 1798, with the well-known soprano Julie-Angélique Scio in the title role and with Gaveaux himself as Florestan. Bouilly's later works include the libretto for Cherubini's* enormously successful *Les Deux Journées* (Théâtre Feydeau, 16 January 1800), and the vaudeville *Fanchon la vielleuse*, written in collaboration with Joseph Pain, for which Joseph-Denis Doche composed the music (Théâtre du Vaudeville, 19 March 1803). Bouilly also wrote two popular collections of moral tales for children, as well as the above-mentioned memoirs.

Subsequent to Gaveaux's opera, Bouilly's *Léonore* was set in Italian versions by Ferdinando Paer* (*Leonora, ossia L'amore coniugale*, Dresden, 3 October 1804) and Simon Mayr (*L'amor coniugale*, Padua, 26 July 1805). Neither Gaveaux's nor Mayr's opera was ever given in Vienna, but Paer's received a private performance (most probably in the original Italian version) at Prince Lobkowitz's* palace in February or March 1806, and was produced at the Kärntnertor-Theater on 8 February 1809 with a German text by J. F. Rochlitz.*

Joseph Sonnleithner's* libretto for Beethoven's *Fidelio* was likewise based on Bouilly's text. (On the possible influence of Paer's *Leonora* on *Fidelio*, *see* the article on Paer.)

(Pendle)

Brauchle, Joseph Xaver (1783–1838). Tutor of Countess Erdödy's* son August and perhaps also music teacher of her two daughters. In addition, he seems to have fulfilled certain other functions in her household. In a letter to Breitkopf & Härtel* on 4 January 1812, she wrote that she very greatly esteemed him 'not only for his services to my family, but also for his considerable musical talent'. He accompanied her on her various journeys, and eventually to Munich. At her death in 1837 she bequeathed to him her personal property, including the letters she had received from Beethoven. He was survived by his wife Elise (1803–86).

Brauchle was on friendly terms with Beethoven. However, there appears to be little truth in Schindler's* story that Beethoven, heartbroken at losing Julia [Giulietta] Guicciardi,* disappeared while staying with Countess Erdödy at her Jedlesee house, leading her to think that he had returned to Vienna; but that he was found on the third day by Brauchle in a distant part of the garden, supposedly intent on committing suicide by starvation, and that from that time on he treated Brauchle with special courtesy.

Brauchle wrote a number of pieces for the solo piano, as well as some chamber music and songs. Most of these works were published by Tobias Haslinger,* and a string quartet was issued by Breitkopf & Härtel. According to G. Haupt,

Brauchle's compositions 'are no better than those of an amateur, albeit a talented one'.

(Haupt[1], Schindler[1])

Braun, Josephine, Baroness, née von Högelmüller (b. Vienna, *c*.1765; d. Vienna, 13 February 1838). Wife of Baron Peter Braun.* Beethoven dedicated to her the two Piano Sonatas Op. 14 in 1799, the Sonata in F major for piano and horn (Op. 17) in 1801, and the arrangement of the Piano Sonata Op. 14, No. 1 for string quartet in 1802. Like her husband, she appears to have been an excellent pianist.

Braun, Peter Anton, Baron (b. Vienna, 18 October 1764; d. Vienna, 15 November 1819). Civil servant, industrialist, and theatre manager; son of Hofrat Johann Gottlieb Braun. He served as a court secretary, but subsequently left government service and in 1789 opened a factory for the manufacture of silk articles, which employed workers from Lyons, then the centre of the European silk trade, and proved highly successful. (However, P. Nettl's statement, in his *Beethoven Encyclopedia*, that Braun 'introduced silk industry in Austria' appears to be wide of the mark: according to the *Österreich Lexikon* (1995), that industry had flourished in Austria since the seventeenth century, and by 1784 provided work for some 10,000 persons in Vienna.) Later Braun engaged in other commercial ventures. He was granted a barony in 1795.

Braun also played a prominent role in Vienna's cultural life. According to J. F. von Schönfeld's *Jahrbuch der Tonkunst von Wien und Prag* (1796), he was himself an excellent pianist and a competent composer. From August 1794 until December 1806 he leased and personally managed the two court theatres. In his *Biographisches Lexikon des Kaiserthums Oesterreich* Constantin von Wurzbach—who, having been born in 1818, had not been a personal witness to the events of this period—greatly praises Braun's character as well as his administration of the theatres, which he describes as representing their 'golden age'. But some of Braun's contemporaries were evidently less enthusiastic, for J. F. Reichardt* heard 'incredible stories' about him in Vienna in 1809, in which it was alleged that he had shown himself utterly indifferent to the arts and intent only on his personal gain; he was moreover held responsible for the decline in the standard of orchestral playing. 'Only the personal protection of the court can explain that in a city such as Vienna, known for its passionate interest in the arts of music and the theatre, a man so totally lacking in any feeling and taste for music should have been able to tyrannise the court, the public, and the artists in a manner that would not be tolerated in many smaller towns' (*Vertraute Briefe*, letter of 5 April 1809). Regrettably, Reichardt does not name his informants; but, irrespective of whether or not the accusations were justified, it is not surprising that Braun made enemies, for his hold over theatrical and operatic performances in Vienna, already very strong as a result of his position at the

Kärntnertor-Theater and Burgtheater, became even more powerful when, in February 1804, he bought the Theater an der Wien from Bartholomäus Zitterbarth. (Four years earlier he had unsuccessfully attempted to prevent its construction by Emanuel Schikaneder.*) Braun ran the three theatres until the end of 1806, at which time the lease of the court theatres was acquired by a group of noblemen, who at the same time purchased the Theater an der Wien from him. (*See also* Hoftheater-Musik-Verlag.*)

The precise nature of Beethoven's relations with Braun is far from clear, but they are unlikely to have transcended professional contacts. In 1799 and again in 1801 he dedicated compositions to Baroness Braun.* In 1802, however, he had cause for vexation, as his brother Kaspar Karl* informed Breitkopf & Härtel* on 22 April: 'My brother would have written to you himself, but he is in no humour to do anything at present because the director of the theatre, Baron Braun, who, as is well known, is a stupid and boorish man, has refused him the use of the theatre for his concert, and has given it to other, very mediocre, artists' (*Corr.* B85). Nevertheless Beethoven dedicated yet another newly published work to the baroness a few months later. The memory of Braun's refusal continued, however, to rankle and was probably the main reason for his allegation in a letter to Joseph Sonnleithner* in February or March 1804 (*Corr.* A88/B177) that Braun had always disliked him. He was therefore convinced, he wrote, that if he were to ask for a larger service apartment at the Theater an der Wien in place of the inconveniently small one he had occupied for the past year, his request would be turned down by Braun, who was the theatre's new owner. (In May he moved to lodgings in the Alsergrund suburb.)

Despite his misgivings about Braun's attitude towards him, the Theater an der Wien was to play a not insignificant part in his career during the following three years. It was there that he conducted the first public performance of the 'Eroica' Symphony on 7 April 1805, at a concert which also featured the Third Piano Concerto, the oratorio *Christus am Ölberg*, and some of the music for *Die Ruinen von Athen*; and it was also there that Franz Clement* gave the first performance of the Violin Concerto on 23 December 1806. And it was, of course, at the Theater an der Wien that the première of *Fidelio* took place on 20 November 1805 and the revised version of the opera was presented on 29 March and 10 April 1806. If neither production proved particularly successful, the fault can hardly be laid at Braun's door, even though the second one reportedly produced some tensions between the baron and the composer. Joseph Röckel,* the Florestan in the new version, told Thayer* in 1861 that Beethoven, who was entitled to a percentage of the receipts, believed himself to have been cheated by Braun's officials and told the baron of his suspicions. Braun affirmed his trust in his employees and attributed the unsatisfactory receipts to the fact that Beethoven's music had not yet attracted the gallery public—which even Mozart* had not disdained when writing his operas. Beethoven thereupon shouted 'I do not compose for the gallery' and marched out of the theatre, taking his score with him. (A more detailed account of the supposed quarrel was given by R. Bunge.)

It is interesting to set Röckel's recollections, related several decades after the event they purport to describe, beside a contemporary, quite different explanation for the withdrawal of the revised *Fidelio* after only two performances. In a letter to his sister Eleonore and her husband, Franz Gerhard Wegeler,* on 2 June 1806, Stephan von Breuning* puts the blame on a 'cabal' organized by Beethoven's enemies, 'several of whom he [had] insulted, especially at the second performance'.

(Bunge, Czeike, Hess[8], Schönfeld)

Braunhofer, Anton (b. Prague, 18 December 1780; d. Vienna, 1845). Physician. He studied medicine at the University of Vienna, qualifying in 1816. Following the death in 1817 of Professor Vinzenz Blaha, who had been professor of general natural history and technology since 1801, Braunhofer took over his duties; in 1819 he was himself appointed to the chair.

There is no documentary proof that Braunhofer treated Beethoven as early as 1820, as is sometimes stated (e.g. in Kinsky/Halm), There is, however, evidence that they knew each other by that time, for Beethoven dedicated to Braunhofer his song 'Abendlied unterm gestirnten Himmel' (WoO 150), composed on 4 March 1820 and published as a music supplement to the *Wiener Zeitschrift für Kunst, Literatur, Theater und Mode* on 28 March of that year. It is therefore quite possible that Beethoven had already consulted Braunhofer professionally before then. What is certain is that Braunhofer replaced Dr Staudenheim* as Beethoven's regular doctor from April 1825. Afflicted with severe stomach pains but unable to consult Staudenheim, Beethoven had sent for Braunhofer, who visited him promptly (*see also* the article on Staudenheim). According to Schindler,* Braunhofer was no less strict than his predecessor in the way he handled his headstrong patient, but his 'Viennese gruffness' made a favourable impression on Beethoven, who, at least for a time, conscientiously respected the doctor's instructions to abstain from wine and coffee and follow the prescribed diet.

In response to Braunhofer's request for an autograph, Beethoven sent him, on 13 May 1825, a short canon (WoO 189) from Baden, where he had moved on the doctor's advice (*see also* WoO 190). But Beethoven would not have been Beethoven if he had not very soon suspected his new physician of shortcomings. Thus he complained to his nephew Karl* on 18 May: 'B[raunhofer]'s prescriptions have already proved unsuccessful on several occasions and he strikes me altogether as very mediocre and rather a fool.' Braunhofer nonetheless succeeded in alleviating the painful bowel inflammation from which Beethoven was suffering and he earned Beethoven's gratitude by generally building up his strength sufficiently to enable him to resume composing. When Beethoven's health deteriorated once more early in the following year, he again called in Braunhofer, who came quickly, prescribed some powders, banished coffee and wine, and fairly quickly brought about an improvement in Beethoven's condition (which the composer described as an attack of rheumatism or gout, but which was probably, at least in part, a recurrence of the earlier abdominal complaint). But when Beethoven, once more in need of medical attention, summoned Braunhofer on his return to Vienna in December 1826, the doctor did not respond to the call. It is assumed that Beethoven must have offended him by an outburst of ill temper earlier that year.

(Bankl/Jesserer, Czeike, Neumayr)

Breitkopf & Härtel. Music publishers in Leipzig; the head of the firm during its association with Beethoven was Gottfried Christoph Härtel (1763–1827). Relations, initiated by the publishers in late 1801 or early 1802, soon soured when Artaria & Co.* issued a pirated edition of the Quintet Op. 29 which Beethoven had sold to the Leipzig firm. But Beethoven's anger at the reproaches addressed to him by Härtel quickly abated, thanks to the diplomatic efforts of Georg August von Griesinger.* However, apart from two sets of variations (Opp. 34–5) of which the firm brought out the first editions in 1803, the connection yielded no further results during the next few years, mainly because Härtel balked at the prices demanded. It was probably no coincidence that the association did not flourish until after the abrasive Kaspar Karl van Beethoven* had more or less ceased to handle his brother's business affairs, following his marriage in May 1806. (In 1805 Härtel had even suggested to Beethoven (*Corr.* B226) that any future negotiations should be conducted 'without the intervention of a third party'.)

In June 1808, after a break of some eighteen months in their correspondence, Beethoven was persuaded by Griesinger to try his luck once more with Breitkopf & Härtel. This time matters proceeded much more smoothly, and on 14 September of that year, during a visit by Härtel to Vienna, a contract was signed for Opp. 67–70. Between 1809 and 1812, the firm brought out first editions of more than twenty works by Beethoven. Among these were the Fifth and Sixth Symphonies, the Cello Sonata Op. 69, and the Piano Trios Op. 70, in 1809; the Fifth Piano Concerto, the Sextet Op. 71, the String Quartet Op. 74, the Piano Sonata Op. 78, and a piano reduction of the revised score of *Fidelio,* as well as songs by Goethe,* Halem,* Matthisson,* and Reissig* (Op. 75 and WoO 136–7), all in 1810; the oratorio *Christus am Ölberg*, the music to *Egmont*, the Choral Fantasia, the Piano Sonata Op. 81a, and the Goethe songs Op. 83, in 1811; and the Mass in C major (Op. 86) in October 1812. Thereafter Sigmund Anton Steiner* replaced Härtel as Beethoven's principal publisher. In July 1816, in response to new requests for compositions from the Leipzig firm, Beethoven proposed a number of works, but the offer was not accepted, probably because his prices were considered too high. Finally, in 1822, Breitkopf & Härtel published the Overture in E flat to *Fidelio*, which Beethoven had composed in 1814.

In 1851 the firm published a thematic catalogue of Beethoven's compositions (*Thematisches Verzeichnis sämmtlicher im Druck erschienenen Werke von Ludwig van Beethoven*). It was edited by a certain 'Geissler' (probably Karl Geissler). A second, revised edition prepared by G. Nottebohm appeared in 1868. Furthermore, Breitkopf & Härtel published between 1862 and 1865 an edition of Beethoven's collected works in twenty-four series; a supplementary series followed in 1888. A list of compositions omitted from this edition later appeared in Willy Hess's *Verzeichnis der nicht in der Gesamtausgabe veröffentlichen Werke Ludwig van Beethovens*, which the firm published in 1957. Subsequently Hess was responsible for editing the fourteen volumes of *Supplemente zur Gesamtausgabe* published between 1959 and 1971. The Breitkopf & Härtel edition is now being superseded by the edition which the Beethoven Archiv, Bonn, has been publishing since 1961. (Regarding the *Allgemeine musikalische Zeitung*, which was published by Breitkopf & Härtel, *see* especially Rochlitz.*)

(Hase[1], Hitzig[2,3])

Brentano (family). A multi-branched family of Italian origin, some of whose members established themselves in business at Frankfurt in the seventeenth century. It owes its association with Beethoven to some of the children of Peter Anton [originally Pietro Antonio] Brentano, who was born at Tremezzo on Lake Como in 1735, became a citizen of Frankfurt in 1762, and there ran the import and trading firm of 'Domenico Martino Brentano' with his brothers until 1771, when he founded his own business in a house named 'Zum goldenen Kopf' [The Golden Head] in Grosse Sandgasse. He married three times: in 1763, Josepha Maria Walpurga Paula Brentano-Gnosso (1744–70); in 1774, Maximiliane von La Roche (1756–93); and in 1795, Baroness Friederike Anna Ernestine Rottenhoff (1771–1817). These marriages produced, respectively, six, twelve, and two children. Peter Anton died in 1797.

Of interest to Beethoven biographers are the following members of the Brentano family: Franz, an offspring of Peter Anton's first marriage; his wife Antonia; their daughter Maximiliane; and Clemens and his sister Elisabeth [Bettina] (see Arnim*), both children of Peter Anton's second marriage.

Franz (Dominik Maria Joseph) (b. Frankfurt am Main, 17 November 1765; d. Frankfurt am Main, 28 June 1844) at first joined his father's business, but in 1792 he set up a separate firm in his own name, specializing in the sale of spices and dyes and in the negotiation of bills of exchange. Upon his father's death in 1797 he became head of the large family, since his elder brother Anton was mentally retarded. He promptly merged the two firms into one, which he then managed with his half-brother Georg, Maximiliane's eldest son. Subsequently the Brentanos added banking to their business interests. Their fortunes prospered and Franz became one of the wealthiest citizens of Frankfurt. In 1806 he acquired a splendid summer house at Winkel on the Rhine, some 25 kilometres west of

Mainz (Goethe* was a guest there in 1814), and in 1820 he moved his family into a new town house in Neue Mainzerstrasse, situated in the most fashionable quarter of Frankfurt; it was built to plans by the famous architect Karl Friedrich Schinkel. Franz Brentano was highly respected in his community; in 1816 he was elected a city senator, and in 1827 he became a magistrate. The firm was wound up on 31 December 1840.

On 23 July 1798, in Vienna, Franz married (**Johanna**) **Antonia [Antonie]** (**Josepha**) **von Birkenstock** (b. Vienna, 28 May 1780; d. Frankfurt am Main, 12 May 1869). They were to have six children: Mathilde Josepha Maximiliane (1799–1800); Georg Franz Melchior (1801–52), Maximiliane Euphrosine Kunigunde (1802–61—see below), Josepha Ludovica (1804–75), Franziska Elisabeth Magdalena (1806–37), and Karl Joseph (1813–50).

Antonie was the daughter of Johann Melchior von Birkenstock,* a senior Austrian civil servant and noted art collector, who, though born in Germany, resided in Vienna for most of his life. Following her mother's death in 1788, she was educated for the next seven years at an Ursuline convent at Pressburg [Bratislava]. At 18, in obedience to her father's wishes, she married the 32-year-old Franz Brentano. The early years of her marriage were marked by much loneliness and unhappiness, somewhat relieved by the pleasure she took in her growing family (although the first child, a daughter, died nine months after birth) and by her biennial visits to her beloved Vienna to see her father to whom she remained deeply attached. At Frankfurt she had to preside over a large household which included twelve of her husband's younger siblings. For her husband, who was still a stranger to her when she married him (it was several months before she grew accustomed to addressing him with the familiar 'Du'), she felt both respect and affection, for he was an extremely kind man who was greatly loved by all his brothers and sisters. In 1809, when her father had fallen ill, she moved to Vienna with her children in order to spend the last weeks of his life with him; he died at the end of October. She spent the next three years in Vienna, mainly for the purpose of winding up his very considerable estate, but in part also because she was often unwell and, in any case, eager to delay returning to the still alien Frankfurt. Franz had joined her in Vienna and carried on his business from there.

According to Schindler,* Beethoven had originally met Antonie at her father's house during the 1790s, and a member of the Brentano family made a similar statement in 1872 (*see* Birkenstock*). On the other hand, Ludwig Nohl quotes Antonie as declaring categorically that she had first met Beethoven in 1810, when she called on him together with Bettina Brentano (*see* Arnim*). She was already in her eighties at the time of her conversation with Nohl, but one must assume that her recollections of what was one of the most important events in her life were accurate. (In this connection, *see also* Birkenstock.*) It is, in any case, well established that she and her husband developed close relations with Beethoven during their stay in Vienna. He is said to have visited them frequently, to have attended chamber music concerts at their house, and to have played for their pleasure. Moreover, Antonie later told Otto Jahn that many times when she was indisposed and unable to leave her room, Beethoven, with whom she had formed a 'tender friendship', would call, seat himself at the piano in her anteroom and improvise, and after he had 'told her everything and offered her comfort' in his language, he would depart without speaking to anyone. He was also on good terms with the children who, according to Brentano family lore, brought him fruit and flowers, whilst he gave them chocolates. For the eldest girl, Maximiliane, he wrote a piano trio (see below).

In the summer of 1812 Beethoven, as well the Brentanos, spent several weeks at spas in Bohemia. Beethoven travelled via Prague, where he probably briefly met the Brentanos, to Teplitz [Teplice]. There, on 6–7 July, he wrote the famous letter to his 'Immortal Beloved'. Maynard Solomon, who has written extensively about Antonie, believes firmly that she was the person to whom Beethoven addressed the letter (which he may never have sent) and that it reflected the dramatic climax of a love affair which had been 'under way by late 1811'. Solomon's conclusion has been widely, though not universally, accepted (regarding other candidates, *see* Brunsvik de Korompa and Almerie Esterházy de Galántha*). Subsequently Beethoven and the Brentanos stayed for several weeks at Karlsbad [Karlovy Vary] and Franzensbad [Františkovy Lázně], after which Beethoven travelled back to Karlsbad and thence to Teplitz. Solomon surmises that during their reunion at Karlsbad and Franzensbad 'in some way the trio managed to pass through the crisis into a new stage of their relationship' and that 'passion was apparently undergoing sublimation into exalted friendship'. To anyone who accepts the identification of Antonie as the 'Immortal Beloved', as well as the further premiss that Franz was aware of the alleged affair, this will no doubt seem an attractive and satisfying scenario. A further intriguing aspect of the situation, as far as subscribers to Solomon's theory are concerned, is the birth on 8 March 1813 of Antonie's son Karl Joseph, a few months after her return to Frankfurt and almost seven years after the birth of her then youngest child, Franziska. Antonie was therefore in the early stages of pregnancy during the previous summer, presumably already at the time when Beethoven wrote his letter to the 'Immortal Beloved' and certainly during the period when he and Antonie supposedly sublimated their passion into exalted friendship, thereby enabling the three of them to reach a new—and evidently, in view of their future contacts, highly amicable—stage in their relationship.

Finally, the mystery surrounding the famous letter and its background has been given a further twist by one firm supporter of Solomon's identification of the beloved with Antonie. In *Raptus: A Novel about Beethoven Based on the Source Material* (the novel is preceded by several closely argued introductory articles), Susan Lund asserts that Karl Joseph was actually Beethoven's child; and, moreover, that Franz—who, she maintains, had no intimate relations with his wife during the crucial period—could have been in no doubt about the true circumstances when he learned that his wife was pregnant. (Solomon himself has prudently characterized any speculation regarding Karl Joseph's paternity as 'fruitless', since 'it is in the nature of such matters that they will always remain open questions'.) Karl Joseph was to have an unhappy life, for an illness which afflicted him when he was 4 years old left him mentally retarded for the rest of his life. He died in 1850.

Beethoven broke his return journey from Teplitz to Vienna at Linz to visit his brother Nikolaus Johann,* and did not reach Vienna until November. It is not known whether he arrived before the Brentanos moved back to Frankfurt or whether their final meeting had taken place at Franzensbad. Although he never saw Antonie and Franz again, he remained in correspondence with them. In 1813/14, when he found himself in financial difficulties owing to the suspension of Prince Kinsky's* and Prince Lobkowitz's* annuities, Franz granted him a loan. It was also he who commissioned Joseph Stieler* to paint Beethoven's portrait in 1820. Later he acted more or less as Beethoven's agent in the latter's discussions with Nikolaus Simrock* concerning the possible publication of the *Missa solemnis*; he even advanced to Beethoven the fee of 900 florins which Simrock would have paid for the work. (After the negotiations had broken down, Beethoven repaid the fee in two instalments in 1823–4.)

Beethoven frequently expressed his affection for the Brentanos and the gratitude he felt towards them, for instance in the following passages: 'I recall to my mind with pleasure the hours I spent in the company of both of you, which are the most unforgettable of my life' (letter to Antonie, 6 February 1816); 'I greatly miss your company and that of your wife and your dear children, for where could I ever find anything like it here in Vienna' (letter to Franz, 15 February 1817); 'B. [is] such an obliging, kind, and unselfish man' (letter to Adolph Martin Schlesinger,* 12 December 1821); 'I shall always be grateful to you' (letter to Franz, 13 September 1822); 'two of the noblest human beings, who, when I was almost destitute, lent me this sum, free of interest, out of pure affection' (letter to Johann Baptist Bach,* 1 August 1824). In 1823 he dedicated his *Diabelli Variations* to Antonie.

As for Antonie, there is no doubt that she revered Beethoven both as a composer and a man. Writing to Clemens Brentano in January 1811, she declared that he walked 'like a God among mortals' and that she felt great veneration for him; and in 1819, in a letter to Johann Michael Sailer,* she described him as 'this great and excellent man' who was 'even greater as a man than as an artist', spoke of his 'soft heart' and 'ardent nature', and summed up his character as 'guileless, straightforward, wise, and wholly benevolent' (*Corr.* B1289).

Franz and Antonie were very interested in the arts and themselves possessed a very fine collection (*see* Birkenstock*); their house was, moreover, frequented by many well-known writers and artists. As already mentioned, these included Goethe, with whom Antonie corresponded over several years (their letters, edited by R. Jung, were published at Weimar in 1896). Both Antonie and Franz are buried in Frankfurt Cathedral, to which Antonie bequeathed in her will, in her own and her late husband's name, Anthony van Dyck's magnificent *Descent from the Cross*.

Maximiliane [Maxe] (**Euphrosine Kunigunde**) (b. Frankfurt am Main, 8 November 1802; d. Brunnen, Switzerland, 1 September 1861) was the daughter of Franz and Antonie Brentano. On 30 December 1842 she married Baron Friedrich Landolin Karl Blittersdorf (1792–1861).

Beethoven wrote for her the Piano Trio in B flat major (WoO 39) in 1812, 'in order to encourage her in her piano playing'; she is reported to have taken lessons with Wilhelm Karl Rust. In 1821 Beethoven dedicated the Piano Sonata Op. 109 to her. Her association with Beethoven even extended beyond his death, for in 1852 Moritz von Schwind* portrayed her in his painting *Die Symphonie* as the pianist taking part in a rehearsal of the Choral Fantasia.

Clemens (**Wenzel Maria**) (b. Ehrenbreitstein, near Koblenz, 9 September 1778; d. Aschaffenburg, 28 July 1842), a poet and novelist, was the son of Peter Anton and Maximiliane Brentano, and half-brother of Franz Brentano. In January 1811, through his sister-in-law Antonie Brentano who was then in Vienna (see above), he sent Beethoven a text inspired by the death of Queen Luise of Prussia on 19 July 1810. He hoped that Beethoven would set it as a cantata (*see Corr.* B483), but Beethoven informed Clemens's sister Bettina (*see* Arnim*) on 10 February that the event was not regarded as a sufficiently important one in Vienna to justify such a musical composition. Clemens's text was found among Beethoven's effects after his death.

Clemens himself arrived in Vienna for an extended stay in early July 1813 and, while there, made Beethoven's acquaintance, apparently at a coffee house. The meeting inspired an effusive letter (*Corr.* B683), in which he expressed his profound admiration for Beethoven's music. He also stated his intention of calling on Beethoven in the near future, in order to 'offer you my Muse for whatever use you wish to make of it'. Nothing is known about the projected visit, or indeed about any further meetings between the two men, but some time later (perhaps on 2 January 1814, *see Corr.* B689) he sent Beethoven the following four poems, under the general title of *Vier Lieder von Beethoven an sich selbst*: 'Einsamkeit, du stummer Bronnen', 'Gott! Dein Himmel fasst mich in den Haaren', 'Du hast die Schlacht geschlagen', and 'Meine Lyra ist umkränzet'. These poems were clearly not intended to be set to music, but were conceived as a declaration of homage to Beethoven.

Elisabeth [Bettina]: *see* Arnim.*

(Brentano, Gelderblom, Günzel, Lund, Nohl[1], Schiel[1,2], Solomon[2,5])

Breuning (family). Prominent Bonn family with which Beethoven had close connections. The father, Hofrat **Emanuel Joseph von Breuning** (b. 11 October 1740; d. 15/16 January 1777), was a senior court official who lost his life as a result of injuries suffered during a fire at the palace. His wife **Helene**, née Kerich (b. 3 January 1750; d. 9 December 1838), whose father had been a court physician, brought up the four children (Eleonore, Christoph, Stephan, Lorenz) with the assistance of her brother-in-law, Canon Lorenz von Breuning. Beethoven became closely acquainted with the family when, on the recommendation of Franz Gerhard Wegeler,* he was engaged—probably in 1782 and, in any case, not later than 1784—to give piano lessons to Eleonore and Lorenz. In a letter to Beethoven on 28 December 1825, Wegeler recalled that the Breunings' house 'became your home more than your own house, especially after you had lost your excellent mother' (*Corr.* B2100). And in *Biographische Notizen* Wegeler wrote: 'Beethoven was treated as a member of the family; he used to spend not only the major part of the day, but even many nights there.' Wegeler added that Frau von Breuning had considerable influence over the often difficult young man. Beethoven would later refer to the Breunings as the 'guardian angels' of his youth and he always remained grateful to Helene for frequently reprimanding him, and particularly for protecting him from certain acquaintances who might have had a bad effect on his artistic development: 'She knew how to keep the insects away from the blossoms,' he told Schindler.*

Ludwig Schiedermair describes **Eleonore** (bapt. 23 April 1771; d. 13 June 1841) as Beethoven's 'first serious love'. Certainly, the two extant letters from Beethoven to her—the first (*Corr.* A9/B4) probably written in the summer of 1792 while he was still in Bonn, the second (*Corr.* A7/B11) sent from Vienna a year after his arrival there—indicate a profound attachment on his part. Their close relationship was, however, at least temporarily damaged, some time before he left Bonn, by a quarrel which he soon greatly regretted and for which he assumed full blame. The two above-mentioned letters are full of contrition and of regret at the harm done to what had been a close friendship; it is difficult to find in them the inimical sentiments perceived by Maynard Solomon who describes them in his Beethoven biography as revealing 'a strong mixture of affection and hostility'. At the same time, it must be stressed that Emily Anderson's translation of the opening of the second letter—'Verehrungswürdige Eleonore!'—as 'Adorable Eleonore!' is greatly misleading inasmuch as it suggests an intimacy that is in no way conveyed by the German adjective, which expresses respect and admiration rather than adoration. Beethoven dedicated the variations for violin and piano on 'Se vuol ballare' (WoO 40) to Eleonore in 1793; he also wrote for her the Piano Sonata WoO 51. He never saw her again after leaving Bonn in 1792. His references to her in letters to Wegeler, whom she married on 19 March 1802, are warm and friendly. For her part, Eleonore evidently retained affectionate feelings for him, to judge by her postscript to her husband's letter of 1 February 1827 (*Corr.* B2255), in which she urged Beethoven to visit them at Koblenz, thereby fulfilling 'one of my dearest wishes'.

Like Eleonore, the eldest son, **Christoph** (bapt. 13 May 1773; d. 24 October 1841), contributed to the autograph album with which some of Beethoven's friends presented him on his departure from Bonn in 1792. Apart from this, nothing is known about his relations with Beethoven. Following legal studies at Bonn, Jena, and Göttingen, he worked, according to Max Braubach, as a lawyer in Vienna during the first months of 1796; if so, he could have seen little of Beethoven since the latter was travelling elsewhere during most of that period. In a letter to Wegeler, probably written in June 1801 (*Corr.* A51/B65), Beethoven mentions his intention of writing to Christoph, but no such letter has survived. In the course of a manifestly successful career as a lawyer, judge, and teacher, Christoph lived in Bonn, Koblenz, Cologne, and finally Berlin. He retired in 1838.

The second son, **Stephan**, known as 'Steffen' (bapt. 17 August 1774; d. 4 June 1827), maintained for many years an affectionate relationship with Beethoven, which was, however, marred by at least one bitter quarrel in 1804, and later interrupted by an estrangement probably lasting some ten years. After studying law at Bonn and Göttingen, Stephan lived in Vienna from late December 1795 until October 1796. He subsequently worked for the Teutonic Order at Mergentheim and later in Vienna. From 1803 he was employed at the war ministry in Vienna; he was granted the title 'Hofrat' in 1818. During most of this period, until about 1815, he was in intimate contact with Beethoven. On 29 June 1801 Beethoven wrote to Wegeler: 'Steffen Breuning is now here and we meet almost every day. It is a great pleasure for me to revive the old feelings of friendship. He has really become an excellent and splendid fellow who is well informed and who has his heart, like most of us, more or less in the right place.' In the spring of 1804 Beethoven moved to the Rotes Haus, a very large apartment complex where Stephan was then living. He appears almost immediately to have left his new rooms in order to stay in Stephan's apartment, but he forgot to cancel his lease. This omission, which obliged him to continue to pay rent for his own rooms, led in July to a fierce altercation between them, which seems, however, to have been as much the culmination of various accumulated irritations as the result of a single dispute. They were reconciled a few months later when Beethoven presented Stephan with his portrait by Christian Hornemann.* Thereafter they enjoyed a close association, and in 1806 Stephan revised for Beethoven the original libretto of *Fidelio*. The new version was produced at the Theater an der Wien on 29 March (and repeated on 10 April). Stephan also composed poems for the premières of both the original and the revised versions, which he had printed and handed out at the theatre. In 1806 Beethoven set to music (WoO 132) Stephan's translation of the text of a romance from *Le Secret*, an *opéra comique* by Jean-Pierre Solié first performed in Paris in 1796 (it was produced in Vienna in 1808 under the title *Das Geheimnis*).

In April 1808 Stephan married **Julie** (1791–1809), a daughter of Dr Gerhard von Vering.* Beethoven visited them frequently, and on many occasions used to play duets with Julie who had studied with Johann Baptist Schenk* and was a good pianist. In August 1808 he dedicated his Violin Concerto to Stephan, and his own arrangement of it as a piano concerto to Julie. She died less than a year after the wedding. During the following years Beethoven still saw a great deal of Stephan, as is evidenced by Stephan's statement in a letter to his mother in 1811 that Beethoven regularly dined with him at his apartment at the Rotes Haus. In 1812 Stephan married Constanze Ruschowitz (1784–1856); with her, also, Beethoven is said to have been on friendly terms. But a few years later relations cooled between Beethoven and Stephan, perhaps, as Schindler states, because Stephan offended Beethoven by advising him against assuming the guardianship of his nephew Karl.* If that was indeed its cause, the estrangement could date from late 1815.

While Beethoven and Stephan may have met occasionally during the following years, there is no firm evidence of any further contact until the year 1825, except for the later statement by the notoriously unreliable Louis Schlösser* that at a performance of *Fidelio* in November 1822 he had caught sight of Beethoven in the company of two men whom Schubert had identified for him as Schindler and Stephan von Breuning. In late March or early April 1825, however, the conversation books reveal that Nikolaus Johann van Beethoven* had had a long talk with Stephan, who, so Karl informed his uncle, 'sends you his regards, will look into the matter, and will then visit you' (*BKh*7/203). Perhaps the subject of the long conversation was Karl's recently announced intention to break off his studies at the university and be trained in commerce at the Polytechnisches Institut (*see Corr.* A1360/B1956). Stephan called on Beethoven shortly before the latter left for Baden on 7 May. Some of his entries in the conversation book, notably certain information about his family ('I have three children'; 'A boy of 11 and girls of 4 and 6 years' (*BKh*7/262–3)), point to a lengthy break in their personal contact. But after Beethoven took an apartment later that year at the Schwarzspanierhaus, close to the Rotes Haus where Stephan was still living, they soon resumed their earlier intimate and affectionate relations. During Beethoven's final illness, Stephan visited him daily, together with his son (*see* the separate article on Gerhard von Breuning). Stephan also became increasingly involved in the planning of Karl's future; and it was he who arranged for his admission into Baron Stutterheim's* regiment. Stephan even agreed to become Karl's guardian (Beethoven signed the relevant document on his deathbed); but he outlived Beethoven by little more than two months, and the guardianship was then taken over by Jakob Hotschevar.*

The youngest of the Breuning brothers, **Lorenz** (bapt. 25 September 1776 (according to the records of the local church); d. 10 April 1798), was known as 'Lenz'. (In *Aus dem Schwarzspanierhause*, Gerhard von Breuning states mistakenly that Lorenz was born 'half a year after his father's death, posthumously, in the summer of 1777', and Thayer* repeats the incorrect date.) Lorenz studied medicine, and in this connection he went to Vienna in 1794, together with Wegeler; one of his teachers there was Johann Nepomuk Hunczovsky.* In Vienna, Lorenz continued to receive instruction in piano playing from Beethoven, and he also saw him frequently outside the lessons. 'He thinks very highly of me,' Lorenz informed Wegeler at one point. Later Stephan told his son Gerhard that Lorenz 'was perhaps Beethoven's most intimate friend'. Beethoven wrote in Lorenz's album before he left Vienna in the autumn of 1797: 'Never shall I forget the time I spent with you in Bonn and here.' Lorenz died from meningitis a few months after returning to Bonn. Both E. Anderson and S. Brandenburg suggest, in their editions of Beethoven's correspondence, that he had Lorenz and Karl Amenda* in mind when he wrote to Ferdinand Ries* in 1804: 'I have found only two friends in the world with whom I have never had a misunderstanding. But what men they were! One is dead, the other is still alive' (*Corr.* A94/B186; *see also* A52/B66).

(Braubach[7], Breuning, Ley[1], Schiedermair, Wegeler/Ries)

Breuning, Gerhard von (b. Vienna, 28 August 1813; d. Vienna, 6 May 1892). Son of Stephan and Constanze Breuning.* Beethoven grew extremely fond of Gerhard during the final period of his life, when he had moved to the Schwarzspanierhaus and resumed his intimate association with Gerhard's parents. Noticing how attached the boy was to his father and how close he always kept to him, Beethoven nicknamed him 'Hosenknopf' ['trouser button'], because he 'stuck to him like a button to trousers'. (It is touching to find that in 1816 Beethoven had signed a letter to his nephew Karl* with the same sobriquet: 'Dein Hosenknopf' (*Corr.* A657/B975).) He also called Gerhard, who was an extremely lively boy, 'Ariel' after the character in Shakespeare's *The Tempest*. In his book *Aus dem Schwarzspanierhause*, published in Vienna in 1874, Gerhard offers a host of fascinating recollections of Beethoven, many of which testify to the renewal of the composer's intimate relations with Stephan. Gerhard last saw Beethoven half an hour before he died.

Gerhard qualified as a physician in 1837 and, after serving as a doctor in the army, he had a flourishing private practice in Vienna.

(Breuning)

Bridgetower [Bridgtower], **George (Augustus) Polgreen** (b. Biala [now merged with Bielsko as Bielsko-Biala], Poland, ?1779; d. Peckham, London, 29 February 1860). Mulatto violinist. His family background and many aspects of his life still remain to be established. His father Friedrich Augustus, of West Indian or African origin, was for a period during the 1780s in the service of Prince Nikolaus I Esterházy at Esterháza, a fact which lends some credibility to his son's later claims that he had been taught by Haydn.* His mother Maria Anna was probably a German or Austrian.

He made his professional debut at a Concert spirituel in Paris on 11 April 1789, playing a concerto by Giovanni Mane Giornovichi 'avec une netteté, une facilité, une exécution & même une sensibilité, qu'il est bien rare de rencontrer dans un âge si tendre' (*Le Mercure de France*). He played the same composition again at a further concert on 13 April (which no doubt accounts for the erroneous statement in *New Grove* that he made his debut on the latter day). Later that year he moved with his father to England, where he achieved increasing fame during the next ten years. He played before the king and queen at Windsor, gave his first public recital at Bath on 5 December 1789, and first played in public in London at the Drury Lane Theatre on 19 February 1790 (on which occasion he again played a concerto by Giornovichi). He gained, moreover, the attention and admiration of the music-loving prince of Wales (the future George IV*), who had him play at his London residence, Carlton House, and took him under his protection when serious friction developed between the boy and his father (whom the prince obliged to leave England). The prince arranged for Bridgetower to study composition, theory, and keyboard with Thomas Atwood and the violin with François-Hippolyte Barthélemon. Altogether, between 1789 and 1799, Bridgetower performed in some fifty public concerts either as soloist or as principal violinist in leading orchestras. (*See also* Clement.*)

In 1802 he received permission to visit his mother at Dresden, where she was living with another son who was a cellist. While at Dresden, he gave at least two concerts, on 24 July 1802 and 18 March 1803, which were highly successful. From Dresden he travelled to Vienna, where, bearing letters of introduction to several of the leading music patrons in that city, he arrived sometime before 16 April 1803. On that day he took part in a chamber music session in Schuppanzigh's* rooms, at which Beethoven was present. He may well have made Beethoven's acquaintance already earlier. In an short, undated letter printed by Thayer,* Count Dietrichstein,* who did his best to open the doors of the Viennese aristocracy to Bridgetower, informed him that he was to dine the following day at Prince Lichnowsky's* and that the prince would afterwards call with him on Beethoven 'in order to obtain his consent to your wishes'. This letter has been taken as an indication that it was Lichnowsky who introduced Bridgetower to Beethoven. Bridgetower most probably wished to ask Beethoven to take part in a concert he was planning to give in Vienna; he may even have asked him to provide a new composition for the occasion. In the event, Beethoven did both. On 24 May 1803 he and Bridgetower gave the first performance of the Violin Sonata in A major, Op. 47. In actual fact, though, not the whole of the sonata was newly written for the concert, for Beethoven had previously made sketches for the first and perhaps the second movements, and he used in the last movement music originally intended for the Sonata Op. 30, No. 1. But the final version of the Andante con variazioni was indeed so freshly completed that the violinist was obliged to play it from Beethoven's manuscript.

In addition to participating in Bridgetower's concert, Beethoven helped him in other ways. Thus he furnished him with a letter of introduction (*Corr.* A73/B137) to Baron Alexander Wetzlar von Plankenstern, in which he described 'Hr. Brischdower' as 'a highly skilled virtuoso, in full command of his instrument', and he arranged for him to be received in other aristocratic households (*see Corr.* A74–5/B150–1). His friendly feelings towards Bridgetower are evident not only from the very cordial tone of one of his notes, but also from the droll dedication of an autograph (now at the Beethoven-Haus, Bonn) of an early partial version of the first movement of the Violin Sonata Op. 47: 'Sonata mulattica Composta per il Mulatto Brischdauer gran pazzo e compositore mulattico.' But when Beethoven published the sonata in 1805 (Simrock,* Bonn), he dedicated it to Rodolphe Kreutzer* (hence its nickname to this day). Bridgetower later alleged that they had quarrelled over a girl towards the end of his stay in Vienna.

Bridgetower spent the third week of July 1803 at Eisenstadt, where he probably again met Haydn, in one of whose London concerts he had performed in 1791. He left Vienna around the end of that month, returning to England via Dresden. In 1811 he took the degree of Bachelor of Music at Cambridge. He became an associate member of the Philharmonic Society* upon its foundation in 1813 and performed at some of its concerts. Later he was to spend many years on the Continent, especially in Paris and Rome, before eventually returning to England.

(Edwards, Matthews, Schmidt[3], Wright)

Broadwood, Thomas (bapt. London, 7 January 1787; d. Lower Beeding, near Crawley, Sussex, 6 November 1861). Piano manufacturer; son of John Broadwood (1732–1812) and his second wife Mary, née Kitson (1752–1839). In 1761 John Broadwood had begun working for Burkat Shudi [Tschudi] (1702–73), a leading London harpsichord maker of Swiss origin. In 1769, upon his marriage to Shudi's daughter Barbara (1749–76), he was made a partner in the firm, henceforth known as 'Shudi & Broadwood'; in 1771 he effectively became its head. In 1781 he married Mary Kidson. James Shudi Broadwood (1772–1851), a son from his first marriage, was made a partner in 1795, and the firm's name changed to 'John Broadwood & Son'. Finally, Thomas, who had been managing the firm's accounts since 1803, was taken into partnership in 1808, and the company thereupon became 'John Broadwood & Sons', a name it was to retain even after the father's retirement (1811) and death (1812).

By that time the firm's instruments enjoyed a reputation for excellence not only in Britain, but throughout Europe and even beyond. As early as 1765, Frederick the Great had ordered four harpsichords for his new palace at Potsdam (one of them was used by Mozart* at a London concert before being sent to Prussia); Empress Maria Theresa had purchased one in 1773, and Haydn* in 1775. However, in keeping with developing musical tastes and technical advances, the manufacture of harpsichords was being increasingly replaced by that of pianos during the 1780s, and the company had entirely ceased production of the former by the mid-1790s. During his first visit to London in 1791, Haydn used Broadwood grands at all his benefit concerts. John Broadwood's extraordinary success can be judged from the fact that at his death his personal estate was valued at more than £100,000. His two sons carried the fortunes of the company to still greater heights. Altogether, it made 124,048 pianos between 1780 and 1861, 75,700 of them during the last thirty-five years of that period. In 1842 the firm was among the twelve largest employers in London, with a staff of some 500 men. James Shudi Broadwood was to leave a personal estate of close to £320,000 in 1851, and Thomas one of £350,000 in 1861.

After the end of the Napoleonic wars, Thomas Broadwood travelled widely in Europe, and in August 1817 he visited Vienna, where he was introduced to Beethoven by the banker Giuseppe Antonio Bridi who had been a close friend and great admirer of Mozart. Broadwood called on Beethoven several times. As he later told Vincent Novello, the composer 'was kind enough to play to me, but he was so deaf and unwell'. Beethoven was spending most of that summer at Nussdorf, but he occasionally returned to his rooms in the Landstrasse suburb, so it was probably there that Broadwood visited him.

After his return to London, Broadwood decided to present Beethoven with a six-octave grand. It was dispatched via Trieste on 27 December 1817. 'The case was Spanish mahogany, inlaid with marquetry and ormolu, the brass carrying-handles formed as laurel wreaths. The piano was triple-stringed throughout, with two pedals, the left a soft pedal and the right divided into two, the right side damping the treble, the left side the bass' (D. Wainwright). In addition to the inscription of Beethoven's name and a Latin legend recording the gift and the donor's name, the piano bore the signatures of five prominent musicians then active in London who apparently wished to share in the gesture: the pianist and composer Frédéric Kalkbrenner, Ferdinand Ries,* the composer Giacomo Gotifredo Ferrari, Johann Baptist Cramer,* and the singer Charles Knyvett. Broadwood informed Beethoven of the gift on 3 January 1818 (*Corr.* B1217), and Beethoven expressed his delight at the generous gesture in his reply of 3 February. The piano was delivered to Beethoven several months later in Mödling, where he had moved for the summer. He appears to have thought highly of it (in December 1823 he lent it to Moscheles* for his Viennese concerts); but his deafness prevented him from properly appreciating its tonal quality and led him, moreover, to thump on it so ferociously that he almost wrecked the instrument. It had to be repaired in 1824 (*see* Stumpff*) and again in 1826 (*see* Stein (family)* and Graf*).

The piano remained in Beethoven's possession until his death, and at the auction after his death it was bought for 180 florins by Anton Spina, a partner in Anton Diabelli & Co.* Liszt* intended to play on it at the Beethoven Festival in Bonn in 1845, but the idea was abandoned when it was realized that the instrument could not compete with more recent types of pianos. The following year—

probably in March, when Liszt gave a series of concerts in Vienna—Spina, whose firm was among Liszt's publishers, presented the piano to him. Thereafter the Broadwood grand stood for many years in Liszt's rooms at the Altenburg in Weimar; later it was stored, still at Weimar, together with certain items belonging to Princess Sayn-Wittgenstein. In 1873 Liszt decided to present it, with other memorabilia, to the Hungarian National Museum in Budapest; but it was not until 1887 that the Museum received it, after the princess's death, from her daughter Princess Marie Hohenlohe-Schillingsfürst (Liszt himself had died the previous year).

Finally, two other links between the firm and Beethoven merit a mention. When, at the Beethoven Centenary Festival held at Bonn in August 1871, Charles Hallé appeared as soloist in the Choral Fantasia and the 'Emperor' Concerto, he used a concert grand which had been specially sent over by Broadwoods from London. And at a concert given at the Queen Elizabeth Hall, London, on 4 May 1978 in celebration of the 250th anniversary of the founding of Burkat Shudi's company in 1728, Malcolm Binns played music by Beethoven on a Broadwood grand dating from 1819 which was similar to the one presented to him by Thomas Broadwood. At this concert Binns played altogether on five Broadwood pianos built between 1787 and 1978.

(Gábry, Geiser, Sakka, Wainwright, Wegerer)

Broderip & Wilkinson. London music publishing firm directed by Francis Broderip and C. Wilkinson from 1798 to 1807. (F. Kidson mistakenly identified 'Broderip' as 'without doubt Robert Broderip, the musician, organist at Bristol', who was probably Francis's brother.) From 1776 to 1798 Broderip had been a partner in the firm Longman & Broderip, which had been very prominent in the areas of music publishing and instrument making, but had in the end gone bankrupt.

In addition to publishing new compositions, Broderip & Wilkinson reissued some of the music previously published by Longman & Broderip. Above all, the new firm concentrated on selling sheet music. In 1799 it published 'La tiranna' (WoO 125; for further details, *see* Wennington*). After Broderip's death in 1807, the firm continued under the name 'Wilkinson & Co.' until 1810.

(Humphries/Smith, Kidson, Tyson[10])

Browne [Browne-Camus], **Anna Margaretha**, Imperial Countess (b. Riga, 12 January 1769; d. Vienna, 13 May 1803). Daughter of Geheimrat Otto Hermann von Vietinghoff [Scheel] (1722–92) and his wife Anna Ulrika, née Countess Münnich. She married Imperial Count Johann Georg Browne [Browne-Camus]* on 22 August 1790.

In April 1797 Beethoven dedicated to her the *Twelve Variations* for piano on a Russian dance performed by Maria Casentini* in Paul Wranitzky's* ballet *Das*

Waldmädchen (WoO 71); her husband thereupon presented a horse to him. Beethoven furthermore dedicated to the countess the Piano Sonatas in C minor, F major, and D major (Op. 10) in 1798; and the *Six [Eight] Variations* for piano on the trio 'Tändeln und scherzen' from Franz Xaver Süssmayr's Singspiel *Soliman der Zweite, oder Die drei Sultaninnen* (WoO 76) in December 1799. (Wranitzky's ballet was first performed on 23 September 1796; Süssmayr's Singspiel had its première at the Kärntnertor-Theater on 1 October 1799.)

(*DBL*, Dorfmüller, Slezak[2])

Browne [Browne-Camus], **Johann Georg**, Imperial Count (b. Riga, 20 September 1767; d. January 1827). Son of Imperial Count George Browne (b. County Limerick, Ireland, 15 June 1698; d. Riga, 18 September 1792) and his second wife Eleonora von Vietinghoff, née Baroness Mengden (d. 1787); husband of Countess Anna Margaretha Browne.* The father was an officer in the Imperial Russian army from 1730, took part in several campaigns, attained the rank of general, and became governor general of Livonia and Estonia.

Johann Georg Browne, who had also served as a senior officer in the Russian army, moved with his wife to Vienna in 1794 or early 1795. There his wealth, mainly derived from his estates in Livonia, enabled the couple to live in considerable style. They were among Beethoven's earliest patrons in Vienna, and he was a frequent visitor to their house (*see also* Albrechtsberger*). In the dedication of the three String Trios Op. 9 in 1798, he called Browne '[le] premier Mécène de sa Muse'. His contacts with Browne continued for some time after the countess's death in May 1803. It was through Browne that he met Hofrat Johannes Büel,* who, in June of that year, became the count's major-domo and tutor to his son Moritz (1797/8–1820). Büel later described Browne as 'one of the strangest of men, on the one hand full of excellent talents and splendid qualities of heart and mind, and on the other full of weaknesses and depravity'; on another occasion he referred to him as 'the most intelligent fool I have ever known'.

Beethoven dedicated the following compositions to Browne: in 1798, the three String Trios Op. 9; in 1802, the variations for piano and cello on the duet 'Bei Männern, welche Liebe fühlen' from Mozart's *Die Zauberflöte* (WoO 46), and the Piano Sonata in B flat major (Op. 22); and in 1803, *Sechs Lieder* based on poems by Gellert* (Op. 48). The fact that these pious songs were published in August 1803, only three months after the countess's death, led certain scholars to speculate that their composition might have been prompted by that event. But the Gesellschaft der Musikfreunde* in Vienna possesses a manuscript copy of the songs specially made for the Princess of Liechtenstein,* on which Browne had inscribed the date 'Montags den 8t März 1802'. The *terminus ad quem* of the composition of the songs must accordingly be early March 1802.

Browne is also associated with the composition of four other works by Beethoven. Ferdinand Ries* states in *Biographische Notizen* that he asked

Beethoven to write the three Marches Op. 45; and according to the title inscribed on an autograph of 'Der Wachtelschlag' (WoO 129), the song was composed for him in 1803. However, Beethoven dedicated none of these works to Browne when they were published in Vienna in 1804: the marches were dedicated to Princess Maria Esterházy,* while the edition of 'Der Wachtelschlag' appeared without any dedication.

(*DBL*, Noll, Schmidt-Görg[7], Wegeler/Ries)

Brunsvik de Korompa (family). Hungarian aristocrats. The following children of Count Anatol Brunsvik (1745–93) and his wife Anna Barbara, née Baroness Seeberg (1752–1830), were to be closely associated with Beethoven: Therese (b. Pressburg [Bratislava], 27 July 1775; d. Pest [Budapest], 23 September 1861); Franz de Paula (b. Pressburg, 25 September 1777; d. Pest, 24 October 1849/50); and Josephine (b. Pressburg, 28 March 1779; d. Vienna, 31 March 1821). Another daughter, Karoline [Charlotte] (1782–1840/3), also knew Beethoven, but less intimately. The Brunsviks usually lived either in Budapest or at their country house at Maratonvásár, some 30 kilometres outside the city, but they also sometimes stayed at Korompa [Krupá], near Pressburg, on an estate owned by Anatol's brother Joseph.

In May 1799 the widowed Countess Anna took **Therese** and **Josephine** to Vienna where several of her sisters-in-law were then living. They called on Beethoven, and he agreed to give the two girls piano lessons, which he did every day at their hotel during the fourteen days they spent in Vienna. On 23 May he wrote in their album a setting of 'Ich denke dein', the first strophe of Goethe's* poem 'Nähe des Geliebten', together with four variations on it for piano duet (in 1803 he composed and wrote out for them two further variations, and the whole set (WoO 74) was published in 1805 with a dedication to them).

During their brief stay in Vienna, Countess Anna and her daughters also met Herr Müller, the owner of an art gallery, whose real name and title was Count Joseph Deym von Stritetz (1752–1804); he had adopted his new name after temporarily fleeing the country following a duel. The gallery, famous for its wax portraits and copies of classical works of art, was housed in an enormous building near the Donaukanal, which also contained, in addition to Deym's personal living quarters, some eighty rooms for rent. (The building stood on a site [left vacant after the Second World War] which extended almost the whole distance from the present Rotenturmstrasse to the Schwedenplatz; it was demolished in 1889.) Deym fell in love with Josephine, and her mother, mistakenly believing him to be wealthy and well regarded in society, obliged her to accept his proposal, even though he was close to thirty years older. They were married at Martonvásár on 29 June 1799 and immediately afterwards left for Vienna, where Josephine soon discovered that her husband was heavily in debt. The four and a half years of her marriage were marked by grave financial problems which were aggravated by her mother's refusal to pay the substantial dowry she had promised. It never-theless appears from correspondence exchanged by the sisters at the time that Josephine's life was by no means as uniformly unhappy as Therese's later memoirs might suggest. One major source of pleasure was her frequent contact with Beethoven who gave her more piano lessons and performed at her musical soirées. After one of these parties, on 9 December 1800, she reported happily to her sisters that 'Beethoven played his cello sonata [perhaps Op. 17] and I played the first of the three violin sonatas [Op. 12, No. 1], together with Suppanzi [Schuppanzigh*] . . . and Beethoven, like a true angel, let us hear his new, still unprinted, quartets [Op. 18] which are the *non plus ultra* of musical compositions.' Beethoven furthermore composed five pieces (WoO 33) for Deym's mechanical instruments, for which Mozart* had likewise written music.

Josephine had four children from this marriage, the last of whom was born after her husband had died on 27 January 1804. She continued to see Beethoven, and from a series of letters he wrote to her it is clear that he fell deeply and pas-sionately in love with her. The fourteen extant letters—all but one undated—were first published by J. Schmidt-Görg in *Beethoven: Dreizehn unbekannte Briefe an Josephine Gräfin Deym, geb. v. Brunsvik* (Bonn, 1957), and 'Neue Schriftstücke zu Beethoven und Josephine Gräfin Deym' *(Beethoven-Jahrbuch,* 2nd ser., 1965/8 (1969)). Beethoven's feelings appear to have reached their greatest intensity during the winter of 1804–5. Josephine responded with assurances of affection and friendship, but her remarks reflect a desire for a spiritual, platonic relation-ship rather than a physical one. Her family may also have advised her not to marry Beethoven. There were several long periods during which they did not see each other. Thus Josephine and her children spent the autumn and winter of 1805–6 in Budapest with her mother, and during a part of the spring and summer of 1806 she and Therese were in Transylvania, on a visit to Charlotte who had married Count Emerich Teleki the previous year. There is evidence that Beethoven still saw her frequently in 1807, but it is generally believed—though this is largely speculation—that his love for her had cooled by then. From August 1808, for close to a year, she was again away from Vienna, this time travelling with Therese and two of her children in Germany, Italy, and Switzerland. There is no record of any further contact with Beethoven after this lengthy journey (but see below). In Switzerland she had met Baron Christoph Stackelberg (1777–1841), an Estonian nobleman, and in February 1810 he became her second husband. The marriage, during which she bore him three daughters, turned out even more unhappily for her than her first. When she refused in 1815 to follow him back to Estonia, where he had come into an inheritance, he left Vienna with the children, whom he then entrusted to the dean of Trautenau [Trutnov, Czech Republic]. He returned briefly two years later, before taking the children away for good to live with him at Reval [Tallinn]; there he had a successful career as an educationist.

Josephine stood for a long time high on the list of candidates for the distinction of having been the 'Immortal Beloved' to whom Beethoven addressed his celebrated letter in 1812; it was even speculated that her last child, Minona, born on 9 April 1813, might have been fathered by Beethoven. Many scholars now accept Maynard Solomon's identification of Antonie Brentano* as the 'Immortal Beloved', but Josephine still has some supporters (*see*, notably, Harry Goldschmidt, *Um die unsterbliche Geliebte: Eine Bestandsaufnahme*, Leipzig, 1977, and especially Marie-Elisabeth Tellenbach, *Beethoven und seine 'Unsterbliche Geliebte' Josephine Brunswick: Ihr Schicksal und der Einfluss auf Beethovens Werk*, Zurich, 1983); *see also* Esterházy de Galántha, Almerie*. Apart from the above-mentioned *Variations* WoO 74, Beethoven never dedicated any composition to Josephine; the song 'An die Hoffnung' (Op. 32), which he wrote for her in March 1805, was published later that year without a dedication.

Therese was also briefly considered as a possible candidate for the 'Immortal Beloved', but any claims on her behalf have long been dismissed. There is no doubt that she met Beethoven repeatedly during the years following those early piano lessons, both in Hungary (he reportedly visited the Brunsvik homes at Buda and Martonvásár in 1800, and may have been at Martonvásár again at a later date) and in Vienna, where she stayed with Josephine after Deym's death. In 1810 she sent him a painting (probably a copy of her portrait by the older Johann Baptist Lampi), and that same year he dedicated to her the Piano Sonata Op. 78. Therese never married. The extended visit which, together with Josephine, she paid to Johann Heinrich Pestalozzi's school at Yverdon, on Lake Neuchâtel, in 1808 had a profound effect on her, and she was to devote many years of her life to the care of children. On 1 June 1818 she opened the first Hungarian day nursery in her mother's house in Budapest. She subsequently founded several other nurseries, in Budapest and elsewhere.

Beethoven enjoyed a particular warm friendship with Josephine's and Therese's brother **Franz**, whose acquaintance, according to Therese, he made not long after Josephine's marriage to Deym. In one letter he called the count his 'dear friend and brother' (*Corr.* A427/B665) and they addressed each other with the familiar 'Du'. (P. Nettl is, however, incorrect in stating in his *Beethoven Encyclopedia* that Therese and Josephine used the same intimate pronoun in addressing Beethoven.) Like his sisters, Franz was musical, his preferred instrument being the cello. He was a great admirer of Beethoven. Schindler,* who saw him frequently while living in Budapest in 1827–9, described him as 'one of the most perceptive connoisseurs' of Beethoven's music, and his wife Sidonie as an outstanding interpreter of Beethoven's compositions for the piano. Beethoven dedicated the 'Appassionata' Piano Sonata to Franz in 1807, and the Fantasia for piano (Op. 77) in 1810.

After 1815 Franz lived mostly in Budapest; from 1819 to 1822 he was director of the theatre at Pest. There is no reliable evidence of any direct or indirect contact between him and Beethoven during the final years of the latter's life, but three entries in Schindler's hand in the conversation books relate to him. In March 1824, Schindler reported that Count Brunsvik intended to attend Beethoven's forthcoming concerts, perhaps together with his wife, and that he wanted to take Beethoven back to Hungary with him afterwards (*BKh*5/214). In May of the same year, Schindler announced his intention of writing to the count (*BKh*6/188). And on 31 March or 1 April 1826 he referred to a remark which he alleged Beethoven had made to the count the previous year (*BKh*9/134). But since all three entries have been identified as later additions by Schindler, it is difficult to attach any credence to them.

(Czeke, Czeke/Révész, Goldschmidt[2,3], La Mara[1,2], Massin, Schmidt-Görg[3,8,11], Tellenbach[1,2,3])

Büel, Johannes (b. Stein am Rhein, Switzerland, 12/13 August 1761; d. Stein am Rhein, 7 October 1830). Schoolmaster and educationist. In addition to teaching at Hemishofen from 1784 until 1802, he was employed as an inspector of schools and involved in the planning of reforms of the Swiss educational system. In 1802 he travelled to Saxony, where his wife Louise von Auleben had been born. He was offered the post of assistant librarian at Altenburg by Duke Ernst of Saxe-Gotha, to be occupied at his convenience. In fact, he never did take up the position, but that did not prevent Duke Ernst's successor August from conferring the title 'Hofrat' upon him in May 1804. The news reached him in Vienna, where he had arrived in April 1803; except for one major interruption, that city was to remain his place of residence for the next fourteen years.

Büel was blessed with a character and manner which opened all doors to him and won him friends wherever he went. In Vienna he enjoyed particularly close relations with Karoline Pichler, and had access to the houses of Count Fries* and Prince Karl Philipp Schwarzenberg, among others. He also became acquainted with Count Johann Georg Browne,* and after the death of Countess Anna Margaretha* in May 1803 he accepted the count's invitation to become his major-domo and tutor to his 5-year-old son Moritz. In addition to educating Moritz, Büel spent the next thirteen years effectively running the household, for his employer became increasingly manic in his behaviour, especially in the way he squandered his money, and had to be hospitalized more than once.

Through Browne Büel met Beethoven, with whom he was soon on a friendly footing. 'Van Beethoven, full of enthusiasm, inspired, slightly hypochondriac, who yesterday, when Browne read him a letter of mine, gave free rein to his tears', he reported to his friend Johann Georg Müller on 1 March 1805. And to another correspondent (J. J. Freuler) he wrote on 27 April of the same year: 'What you write about Beethoven and his compositions is excellent, I shall not fail to mention it to Beethoven himself at the first opportunity, for it is certain to give him pleasure.' He had recently (7 April) been present at the first (public) perform-ance of the 'Eroica' Symphony. The very cordial nature of their relationship is attested by Beethoven's entry in Büel's album on 29 June 1805, in which he addresses Büel with the intimate 'Du' and calls himself 'your devoted friend'. At that point Büel was about to leave Browne's service and depart from Vienna, but he returned in late 1806 to resume his duties. There is no record of any later contacts between Büel and Beethoven. Moritz joined the army in November 1816 (he died in 1820); Büel went back to Switzerland in June 1817.

(Geiser, Noll)

Bürger, Gottfried August (b. Molmerswende, near Halberstadt, 31 December 1747; d. Göttingen, 8 June 1794). Magistrate and university teacher; poet. After studying theology at Halle and law at Göttingen, he was employed as a magistrate at Altengleichen (1772–84). He subsequently taught at Göttingen University, first as an unpaid lecturer and, from 1789, as a professor. As a poet, Bürger was associated with the young romanticists who founded the Göttinger Hainbund and published their works in the *Göttinger Musenalmanach*. It was in that periodical that Bürger's most famous poem, 'Lenore', was printed in 1774. In 1778 he published a collection of poems under the title *Gedichte*; a further, two-volume, edition appeared the following year. Bürger is credited with having created the Romantic ballad; he is also admired as a lyric poet of considerable accomplishment.

Beethoven set texts by Bürger in the following songs: 'Das Blümchen Wunderhold' and 'Mollys Abschied', both early compositions composed in Bonn and included in his *Acht Lieder* (Op. 52) published by the Kunst- und Industrie-Comptoir* in Vienna in 1805; 'Seufzer eines Ungeliebten—Gegenliebe' (WoO 118), a double song based on two separate but related poems, which was probably composed in 1794 or early 1795 and was published by Anton Diabelli & Co.* in 1837; and 'Minnesold' (Hess 139), the music of which has been lost. The melody of 'Gegenliebe' was later used by Beethoven in the Choral Fantasia.

(Häntzschel)

Bursy, Karl von (b. Blieden, Courland [Blidene, Latvia], 26 November 1791; d. Mitau [Jelgava, Latvia], 25 September 1870). Physician residing in Courland. A friend of Karl Amenda,* who had provided him with a letter of introduction, he was cordially received by Beethoven when he called on him in July 1816. He visited Beethoven more than once that month, and later published (censored) extracts from his travel diary describing their conversations in the *St. Petersburger Zeitung* (1854) and *Belletristische Blätter aus Russland* (1856). The full text, including the deletions made by the Russian censor, was printed by F. Kerst in *Die Erinnerungen an Beethoven*. Shortly before Bursy left Vienna in late July or early August 1816, Beethoven wrote some words from Leonore's 'Abscheulicher' aria in his copy of *Fidelio*.

(*DBL*, Kerst)

Cappi, Giovanni [Johann] (b. Blevio, Lombardy, 30 November 1765; d. Vienna, 23 January 1815). Music publisher. He arrived in Vienna in 1773 and became first an employee and, in 1793, a partner in the firm of Artaria & Co.* In 1801 he set up his own publishing business under the name 'Johann Cappi', with the assistance of his nephew Pietro [Peter] who had likewise been working for Artaria. Pietro returned to Artaria in 1803. (In 1816 Pietro would found his own firm, 'Peter Cappi', which was renamed 'Cappi & Diabelli'* when Anton Diabelli* joined it in 1818; and in 1824 he formed together with Giovanni Cappi's son Carlo [Karl] the firm 'Cappi & Co.', which, after his share had been bought by Joseph Czerny* in 1826, became 'Cappi & Czerny'.*)

In 1802 Giovanni Cappi published the following four works by Beethoven: the Serenade for flute, violin, and viola (Op. 25), and the three Piano Sonatas Op. 26 and Op. 27, Nos. 1–2. (*See also* Neidl.*)

(Slezak[4])

Cappi & Czerny. Firm of music publishers directed by Carlo [Karl] Cappi and Joseph Czerny* from spring 1826 until November 1827 (*see* Giovanni Cappi*). In April 1827 it published piano arrangements for two and four hands of Beethoven's military march WoO 24. (The original orchestral score was issued by Breitkopf & Härtel* in 1864.)

(Slezak[4])

Cappi & Diabelli. Firm of music publishers directed by Pietro Cappi and Anton Diabelli* from late 1818 until December 1823 (*see* Giovanni Cappi*). In 1823 it published Beethoven's *Thirty-three Variations on a Waltz by Diabelli*.*

(Slezak[4])

Carpani, Giuseppe (b. Villalbese, near Como [Albavilla, Brianza], 28 December 1751 (according to H. C. Jacobs, who rejects the usually cited year 1752); d. Vienna, 21/2 January 1825). Librettist, critic, and poet. After training in law at Pavia and Milan, he lived until 1795 in the latter city where he soon made his mark as a poet and playwright. Giacomo Rust's opera *Gli antiquari in Palmira*, to Carpani's libretto, was successfully performed at La Scala in the autumn of 1780. Carpani also translated a number of French librettos for the theatre at Monza. From 1796 he lived mainly in Vienna, where he wrote, notably, the librettos for Ferdinando Paer's* *Camilla, ossia Il sotterraneo* (Kärntnertor-Theater, 23 February 1799) and Joseph Weigl's* *L'uniforme* (Schönbrunn, 1805). He furthermore translated Gottfried van Swieten's* text for Haydn's* *Die Schöpfung* into Italian, and the oratorio was first performed in Vienna in this version on 27 March 1808, in honour of Haydn's seventy-sixth birthday four days later. For some years, at the turn of the century, he served as manager of the theatres in Venice.

His great interest in contemporary music led him, in particular, to write a book on Haydn (*Le Haydine, ovvero Lettere su la vita e le opere del celebre maestro Giuseppe Haydn*, Milan, 1812). Today he is remembered by musicologists primarily as the author of the poem 'In questa tomba oscura', which Beethoven, among others, set in 1807 (WoO 133) at the request of Countess Rzewuska. (For details, *see* Rzewuski.*)

Carpani was personally acquainted with Beethoven. Rossini* told Ferdinand Hiller* (in 1856) and Eduard Hanslick (in 1867) that it was Carpani who had introduced him to Beethoven, just as he had previously taken him to meet Salieri.* Carpani greatly admired Beethoven's instrumental music, but detested *Fidelio*, which he regarded as the antithesis of the operas of his adored Rossini. In an article published in the Milanese periodical *Biblioteca italiana* in April 1818, he dismissed the work as 'highly erudite, frenzied music', contrary to nature and good sense ('Ma la voglia di battere un sentier nuovo lo [i.e. Beethoven] fé dare in musicali frenesie dottissime che la natura condanna, ed il buon senso non può approvare'). However, by the time he prepared the second edition of *Le Haydine* (1823), he had sufficiently moderated his distaste for *Fidelio* to acknowledge Beethoven as the only composer among his idol's contemporaries who was great and original enough not to feel obliged to 'rossineggiare', i.e. to imitate Rossini ('Beethoven . . . resterà sempre grande ed originale').

(Jacobs², Marchi, Zanetti)

Cartellieri, Anton Kasimir (b. Danzig [Gdańsk, Poland], 27 September 1772; d. Liebshausen [Libčeves, Czech Republic], 2 September 1807). Composer; son of the singers Antonio Cartellieri (1746–1817) and his wife Elisabeth (b. 1756; d. between 1809 and 1819). He arrived in Vienna in the early 1790s and studied with Albrechtsberger* and Salieri.* His oratorio *Gioas, re di Giuda* was performed at the concerts given by the Tonkünstler-Societät at the Burgtheater on 29 and 30 March 1795 (the first part on 29, the second on 30 March). In addition, a symphony composed by him was played on both evenings, and a bassoon concerto on the second night. The concert on 29 March is of particular interest to Beethoven scholars since it marked Beethoven's first public appearance in Vienna as composer and virtuoso pianist. The work which he played on that occasion, between Cartellieri's symphony and the first part of the oratorio, was either the C major or the B flat major Concerto. At the second concert he improvised on the piano.

In 1796 Cartellieri was engaged by Prince Joseph Franz Maximilian Lobkowitz* as assistant Kapellmeister of his private orchestra; he also gave the prince instruction in singing. By then Cartellieri was no doubt personally acquainted with Beethoven, and he must have had further opportunities to meet him at the prince's palace. He is reportedly the source of certain well-known anecdotes about Beethoven. His wife Franziska was a daughter of Anton Kraft.*

(Antonicek¹, Macek², Wurzbach¹)

Casentini [Cassentini], **Maria**. Solo dancer at the Vienna court opera (1796–1801, 1803–4). She made her debut at the Kärntnertor-Theater on 30 March 1796 in *Alonzo e Cora*, a ballet by Giuseppe Traf(f)ieri to music by Joseph Weigl.* After attending a performance of that ballet the following year, Wilhelm von Humboldt wrote to his friend Christian Gottfried Körner, Theodor Körner's* father: 'Casantini [*sic*] was excellent . . . [She] is not nearly as graceful as Vigano [i.e. Salvatore Viganò's* wife Maria Viganò], but she is an incomparably better dancer and combines incredible strength with admirable lightness.'

On 23 September 1796 Casentini danced at the première of *Das Waldmädchen*, another ballet by Trafieri, to music by Paul Wranitzky.* Beethoven composed a set of twelve variations (WoO 71) on a Russian dance which she executed in that ballet; they were published by Artaria & Co.* in April 1797. In 1801 Casentini took the leading female role in Salvatore Viganò's ballet *Die Geschöpfe des Prometheus*, for which Beethoven had written the music (Op. 43). The première on 28 March 1801 was a benefit performance for her. The spectacle was less than rapturously received, a fact for which the choreographer was blamed more than the composer; but the prima ballerina herself did not escape criticism. A reviewer in the *Zeitung für die elegante Welt* (19 May), who referred to her as 'the famous dancer, Demoiselle Casentini' and 'our popular Casentini', complained: 'Although Casentini could never dance badly, there is no doubt that, merely with a little more effort, she would have made the ballet far more attractive.' The ballet's success was nonetheless sufficiently great to justify thirteen more performances that year, as well as nine the following year (according to Robert Haas, who supports these figures with a list of dates; Thayer* gives the number of performances as sixteen for 1801 and thirteen for 1802).

(Haas[1], Humboldt, Raab)

Castelli, Ignaz Franz (b. Vienna, 6 March 1781; d. Vienna, 5 February 1862). Dramatist, librettist, poet, and editor; civil servant. He was also a great wag and a gifted raconteur, and in his memoirs (*Memoiren meines Lebens: Gefundenes und Empfundenes, Erlebtes und Erstrebtes*, 1861) he recalled that Beethoven greatly enjoyed listening to his jokes and anecdotes. While still at school, he conceived a passionate love for the theatre, spent all his free time at performances and in the company of actors, and soon began writing for the stage; he also had some success as an amateur actor. Furthermore, having studied the violin, he sometimes played in the orchestra at the Freihaus-Theater auf der Wieden. In 1810 he founded the journal *Thalia*, which was devoted to the theatre. For his librettos, of which he was to produce some two hundred, he frequently turned to French models; one of his earliest successes was the text for Joseph Weigl's* opera *Die Schweizerfamilie* (première: Kärntnertor-Theater, 14 March 1809). In September 1811 he was appointed house dramatist at the Burgtheater, a position he held until July 1814.

It is not known when Beethoven first met Castelli. The earliest mention of Castelli in his correspondence occurs on 3 July 1811, in a letter to Georg Friedrich Treitschke* who had promised to write an opera libretto based on Guilbert de Pixérécourt's drama *Les Ruines de Babylone, ou Le Massacre des Barmécides* (first produced at the Théâtre de la Gaîté, Paris, on 30 October 1810). Together with his letter, Beethoven sent Treitschke Castelli's translation of the play, which he had received from Count Ferdinand Pálffy.* Beethoven added that Treitschke was unlikely to find Castelli's version very useful, but this may have been a reflection on the unsuitability of literal translations for operatic purposes rather than a criticism of the quality of Castelli's German text. Treitschke does not appear to have got very far with the libretto, and in September, while staying at Teplitz [Teplice], Beethoven tried, with some success, to interest Karl August Varnhagen von Ense* in the project; however, nothing came of the idea. Later Beethoven seems to have considered collaborating directly with Castelli, for in a letter probably written in late May 1813 (*Corr.* A423/B651) he asked to see some of Castelli's librettos. It is not known whether he was ever shown any. The nearest they got to an artistic association occurred in the case of Beethoven's setting of Rupprecht's* poem 'Merkenstein' (WoO 144). It was printed as a supplement to the 1816 issue of the almanac *Selam* which was published by Castelli.

In his memoirs, which contain several anecdotes about Beethoven, Castelli speaks of him with the greatest admiration, calling him a 'giant' and 'one of the greatest practitioners of his art, the Shakespeare of music'. He also wrote an 'anecdote' in verse, 'Ein Mittagmahl Beethoven's', which tells how Beethoven, totally absorbed in composition ('with an eye from which shines forth Prometheus's fire'), not only forgot to order his meal at a restaurant, but later believed that he had actually eaten it. (*See also* Sechter.*)

(Castelli)

Chappell & Co. London firm of music publishers, concert agents, and piano manufacturers, founded in December 1810 by Johann Baptist Cramer,* Francis Tatton Latour, and Samuel Chappell (*c*.1782–1834); the last named had previously worked for Robert Birchall.* Cramer withdrew from the partnership in 1819, and Latour in 1826.

More or less simultaneously with the edition issued by S. A. Steiner & Co.* in Vienna in May 1824, Chappell & Co. and Goulding & Co.* published Beethoven's variations for piano trio (Op. 121a) on 'Ich bin der Schneider Kakadu', a song from Wenzel Müller's popular Singspiel *Die Schwestern von Prag* (first produced in Vienna on 11 March 1794). According to the title page, the London edition was published 'for the proprietor', who has been identified by Alan Tyson as Johann Reinhold Schultz.* He had presumably acquired the rights to the English edition of the trio during his visit to Beethoven in September 1823 and had then brought back a copy of the music.

Beethoven had known of the firm's existence for several years. In a letter to Ferdinand Ries* on or shortly before 19 May 1818 (*Corr.* A898/B1258), in which he begged his friend to find English publishers for certain of his works (*see* Regent's Harmonic Institution*), he mentioned that Cipriani Potter* had described '*Chapphell* [*sic*] in der *Bond Street* Gasse' as being among the leading London publishers.

(Husk/Jones, Redlich/Harman, Tyson³)

Cherubini, Luigi (Carlo Zanobi Salvadore Maria) (b. Florence, 8/14 September 1760; d. Paris, 15 March 1842). Composer, theorist, and teacher. He arrived in Vienna in July 1805, having been invited to compose an opera for the court theatre. He was no stranger to Viennese music lovers. Schikaneder* had put on *Lodoïska* at the Theater an der Wien on 23 March 1802, and later that same year two different productions of *Les Deux Journées, ou Le Porteur d'eau* were presented on successive days at the Theater an der Wien (under the title *Graf Armand, oder Die zwei unvergesslichen Tage*, on 13 August) and at the Kärntnertor-Theater (as *Die Tage der Gefahr*, on 14 August). Next came *Medea* [*Médée*] at the Kärntnertor-Theater (6 November 1802), followed by *Der Bernhardsberg* [*Eliza*] at the Theater an der Wien (18 December 1802), and *Der portugiesische Gasthof* [*L'Hôtellerie portugaise*] at the Kärntnertor-Theater (22 September 1803). According to Grillparzer,* Cherubini met Beethoven at the house of Joseph Sonnleithner* not long after his arrival in Vienna. Sonnleithner, who wrote the libretto for *Fidelio* which was produced on 20 November of that year, also provided the text for Cherubini's new opera *Faniska*, first performed on 25 February 1806.

Beethoven expressed high regard for Cherubini's operas on more than one occasion. In a letter to Cherubini in March 1823 (*Corr.* A1154/B1611) he declared that he valued them more highly than any other compositions written for the stage, and he expressed regret that, at any rate in Germany, no new theatrical work of his had been produced for a long time. He moreover assured Cherubini that his praise was sincere and in no way occasioned by the fact that he was about to request a favour. The purpose of the letter was, in fact, to ask Cherubini to persuade the king of France to subscribe to the *Missa solemnis*. (In the event, Cherubini never received the letter, but Louis XVIII, to whom Beethoven had already written separately on 1 March, subscribed anyway.) There is no doubt that Beethoven genuinely admired Cherubini's music. In a letter to Peter Gläser* in 1824 (*Corr.* A1275/B1814), he wrote that, like 'those great composers Haydn,* Mozart,* and Cherubini', he never hesitated to make cuts or additions in his scores. And when Cipriani Potter asked him, in 1817 or 1818, to name the greatest living composer, apart from himself, he replied, after a moment's thought: 'Cherubini'.

His admiration was not reciprocated. Cherubini was not at all impressed with *Fidelio*, which, in his view, showed Beethoven to be inadequately trained in the art of vocal writing. He therefore sent for a copy of a manual which was used at the Paris Conservatoire and presented it to Beethoven (in whose library it remained until his death). Nor did Cherubini think highly of Beethoven as a pianist. As he told Schindler* in Paris in 1841, he had found his playing 'rough' and therefore had drawn his attention to Clementi's* manner of playing the instrument. Beethoven, he added, had been grateful for the advice. Lastly, Cherubini evidently did not take to Beethoven as a person, for in his conversations with Schindler he criticized Beethoven's behaviour and repeatedly complained that 'il était toujours brusque'. (His wife, on the other hand, tended to defend Beethoven.) Indeed, he was so offended by Beethoven's manner that in 1809 he refused Baron Trémont's* request for a letter of introduction with the following explanation: 'I will give you one to Haydn, and that excellent man will make you welcome, but I will not write to Beethoven; I should be mortified if he refused to receive someone I had recommended. He is an churlish fellow ['un ours mal léché'].'

Following Beethoven's death, Mozart's Requiem was sung at the Augustinerkirche on 3 April 1827, and Cherubini's first Requiem was performed at the Karlskirche on 5 April and at the Augustinerkirche on 26 April. Interestingly enough, Beethoven, according to Karl Holz,* had considered Cherubini's Requiem a more suitable Mass for the Dead than Mozart's, for such a work should, in his opinion, be a quiet, melancholic recollection of the dead; there was no call for noisy music, for the sounding of the last trumpet, or for dramatic references to the Last Judgment.

(Prod'homme[1], Schindler[1])

Clam-Gallas, Josephine: *see* Clary.*

Clary [later Clam-Gallas], **Josephine**, Countess (b. Prague, 9 July 1777; d. Prague, 12 December 1828). Daughter of Count Philipp Clary-Aldringen (1742–95) and his wife Barbara, née Countess Schaffgotsch (1750–after 1812). She married Count Christian Clam-Gallas (1771–1839) in November 1797. According to J. F. von Schönfeld's *Jahrbuch der Tonkunst von Wien und Prag* (1796), she 'sang charmingly'; she also played the mandolin.

Beethoven made her acquaintance during his visit to Prague in February–April 1796. While there, he composed the scena *Ah! perfido* (Op. 65). On the title page of a corrected manuscript copy of the work he wrote 'Aria composta e dedicata alla Signora di Clari di L. v. Beethoven'. However, an announcement in the *Leipziger Zeitung* on 19 November 1796 of a concert due to be given by Josefa Dušek* in Leipzig two days later stated that *Ah! perfido* (of which she was about to give the first public performance) had been composed for her. As for the printed edition published by Hoffmeister* & Kühnel in Leipzig in 1805, it bore no dedication at all.

Four other compositions by Beethoven are tentatively associated with the countess and were probably composed for her during his stay in Prague in 1796: the Sonatinas in C minor (WoO 43a) and C major (WoO 44a), the Adagio in E flat major (WoO 43b), and the *Theme and Variations* in D major (WoO 44b), all written for mandolin and piano. An autograph of the Adagio (a slightly variant version from that published in the Supplement to Breitkopf & Härtel's* collected edition) is inscribed 'pour la belle J.'

Beethoven is believed to have renewed his contact with Josephine, by then Countess Clam-Gallas, when he again visited Prague in 1798. Václav Tomášek* later recalled having heard him play at that time at the house of 'Count C . . .', which initial probably stood for Count Clam-Gallas. Schönfeld states that the Clam-Gallas family was well known in Prague for its love of music.

(Chitz, Schönfeld)

Claudius, Matthias (b. Reinfeld, Holstein, 15 August 1740; d. Hamburg, 21 January 1815). German poet, journalist, and translator. His poems, which are characterized by piety, simplicity, and a delight in the pleasures of life and nature, have inspired many composers, among them Hiller,* Reichardt,* Schubert* ('Abendlied', 'Der Tod und das Mädchen', etc.), Zelter,* and, in the twentieth century, Othmar Schoeck. Beethoven turned to Claudius for only one song, 'Urians Reise um die Welt' (Op. 52, No. 1). According to Wegeler,* this was one of his earliest compositions. It appeared in print in 1805, as one of the *Acht Lieder* by Beethoven published by the Kunst- und Industrie-Comptoir.*

(Wegeler/Ries)

Clement, Franz (Joseph) (b. Vienna, 17 November 1780; d. Vienna, 3 November 1842). Violinist, conductor, and composer. He made his public debut in 1788, appeared at some concerts in Vienna the following year, and was then taken by his father on a three-year tour to Germany, Belgium, and England. At one of his highly acclaimed London concerts, at the Hanover Square Rooms on 2 June 1790, he appeared together with another child prodigy, George Polgreen Bridgetower.* The two boys performed together a concerto for two violins by Jean-Baptiste Davaux, and Clement also played a concerto of his own composition, which was so well received that he repeated it at a concert in 1791, and also at one of the concerts given at Oxford University in July of that same year on the occasion of Haydn's* installation as doctor of music. After his return to Vienna in late 1792 he made several further successful appearances as a concert artist.

When he was 19 he was engaged at the court theatre as soloist and as assistant to the Kapellmeister of German opera, Franz Xaver Süssmayr. In 1804 he was appointed leader of the orchestra at the Theater an der Wien, and in 1805 he became 'Musikdirektor', a position he held until 1811. In addition, he directed concerts there and elsewhere in the city, including those which took place at the house of the bankers Würth and Fellner in 1803–5. The 'Eroica' Symphony received its first public performance, under its composer, on 7 April 1805 at one of Clement's benefit concerts at the Theater an der Wien. In 1807–8 Clement directed the last fifteen of the twenty Liebhaber-Concerte (*see* Häring*). Among the music performed at these concerts were Beethoven's First, Second, and Fourth Symphonies, as well as his First Piano Concerto, which was played by Johann Baptist Stainer von Felsburg (*see* Dietrichstein*). The most famous instance of Beethoven's association with Clement is the Violin Concerto, which was written for Clement and first performed by him at another of his benefit concerts at the Theater an der Wien, on 23 December 1806. But although Beethoven wrote on the autograph 'Concerto par Clemenza pour Clement primo Violino e direttore al theatro a vienna', he dedicated the printed edition to Stephan von Breuning* in 1808.

Beethoven had met Clement at the latest in 1794, in which year he made an entry in the boy's album (now at the Nationalbibliothek in Vienna). Clement was admired for his technical mastery, as well as for the elegance, delicacy, and expressiveness of his playing. Schönfeld, who devotes almost two pages of his *Jahrbuch der Tonkunst von Wien und Prag* (1796) to 'this darling of the Muses', writes: 'One has at times the impression that his own soul inhabits the violin and dissolves into sounds.' Clement was, moreover, able to place a phenomenal memory at the service of his great musical gifts. Its exceptional quality, which astounded his contemporaries, is well illustrated in an anecdote related by Joseph August Röckel* (who sang Florestan in the 1806 *Fidelio*). At the meeting held at Prince Karl Lichnowsky's* apartment in December 1805 for the purpose of persuading Beethoven to shorten the original score of the opera, Princess Lichnowsky* played the music on the piano while Clement, sitting in a corner of the room, 'accompanied with his violin the whole opera by heart, playing all the solos of the different instruments'.

In 1811 Clement toured in Russia, and in 1813 he was recruited by Carl Maria von Weber,* the newly appointed conductor of the Estates Theatre in Prague, as leader of his orchestra. On 6 April 1816 he directed a performance of *Wellingtons Sieg* there. Weber left Prague in October 1816, and the following year Clement returned to his old position at the Theater an der Wien. In 1821 he gave concerts in south Germany jointly with the famous soprano Angelica Catalani, and in the middle and late 1820s he undertook further tours of Germany, but the final part of his career did not live up to the triumphs he had achieved in his youth. Indeed, if one can believe a highly critical report by Franz Oliva* of a concert which Clement gave in Vienna on 4 April 1819, his musical skills were already on the decline even at that time: 'Poor stuff, empty, quite ineffective. Your theme was in poor hands [Clement had played some variations on a theme by Beethoven] . . . You can imagine what one had to put up with! . . . He has lost a great deal, and seems too old to be entertaining with his capers on the fiddle' (*BKh1/44*). The last remark may refer to Clement's delight in rather frivolous displays of show-manship. Perhaps Beethoven remembered such criticisms when he insisted in 1824 that the orchestra at his forthcoming concert should be directed by Schuppanzigh* and not by Clement. On the other hand, he may simply have been motivated by his great affection and esteem for the former rather than by any serious reservations about the musical competence of the latter. As a result of his preference for Schuppanzigh, the concert, which included the first perform-ance of the Ninth Symphony, took place on 7 May at the Kärntnertor-Theater and not at the Theater an der Wien.

Clement does not appear to have harboured a grudge, for on 12 July 1825 he travelled with Karl Holz,* Joseph Linke,* and the violinist Franz Xaver Pecháček* to Baden, where Beethoven had moved for the summer. The purpose of their journey was to ask him for the score of his new String Quartet in E flat (Op. 127). As it turned out, they did not find Beethoven at Baden, for he had gone to Vienna for the day; but by chance they met him at Neudorf [Wiener Neudorf] station, while they were returning to Vienna and he was heading back to Baden. In tell-ing his nephew Karl* about it, Beethoven remarked: 'The attachment shown by such first-rate musicians is not to be despised and, indeed, gives one pleasure' (*Corr.* A1394/B2006).

(Biba², David/Charlton, Haas², Merk)

Clementi, Muzio [Mutius Philippus Vincentius Franciscus Xaverius] (b. Rome, 23 January 1752; d. Evesham, Worcestershire, 10 March 1832). Composer, key-board player, teacher, music publisher, and piano manufacturer. He had a highly successful career as a pianist and composer, although Mozart,* for one, was little impressed either by his playing (he described him as 'a mere *mechanicus*', totally devoid of taste or feeling) or by his sonatas ('anyone playing or hearing them will realize that they are worthless compositions'). Beethoven, on the other hand, thought highly of the sonatas, and 'his admiration for Clementi . . . was at its most intense during the first part of his so-called second period, when he followed the Italian Master's lead not merely in matters of pianistic style but in thematic inspiration as well' (A. L. Ringer). Examples of that influence cited by Ringer include the Piano Sonatas Op. 28 and 53, and the *contredanse* theme of the *Variations* Op. 35 (derived from Clementi's Piano Sonata in G minor, Op. 7, No. 3), which Beethoven had previously used in the *Prometheus* music and would use again in the 'Eroica' Symphony. Beethoven also retained all his life a high regard for Clementi's *Introduction to the Art of Playing on the Piano Forte* (1801), for in 1826 he went to some trouble to obtain a copy of it for the young Gerhard von Breuning.* In sending it to Gerhard's father, Stephan von Breuning,* he wrote:

'If he uses it in the way I shall show him, it is certain to produce good results' (*Corr.* A1532/B2203).

In 1798 Clementi, who had been living mainly in England since 1766/7, founded a firm of music publishers and instrument manufacturers in London together with Josiah Banger, Frederick William Collard, David Davis, Frederick August Hyde, and John Longman. The firm was originally known as 'Longman, Clementi & Co.', but after Longman left to set up on his own, it became 'Clementi, Banger, Hyde, Collard & Davis', and simply 'Clementi & Co.' Between 1802 and 1810 Clementi travelled widely on the Continent, mainly in order to find customers for his company's pianos and negotiate with publishers and composers concerning English publication rights for recent compositions. In the course of this extensive business trip he stayed in Vienna on several occasions: for a few days in October–November 1802; from early 1804 until May of that year; from November 1806 to late April 1807; and from December 1808 until the summer of 1810. Ferdinand Ries* relates that Beethoven wanted to call on Clementi as soon as he had arrived in Vienna in 1804, but was persuaded by his brother Kaspar Karl* that it was for the Italian to pay the first visit. Even though he was considerably older, Clementi might have done so (for Beethoven stood high in the list of composers whose English publishing rights he wished to acquire), if the matter had not become the subject of public gossip. As a result, a ludicrous situation developed, in which the two composers, who knew each other by sight, frequently dined at the same table at the Zum weissen Schwan restaurant in the Kärntnerstrasse, together with their respective pupils Ferdinand Ries and August Alexander Klengel, without any of them acknowledging the presence of the others.

However, Beethoven's unfriendly attitude in no way dampened Clementi's enthusiasm for his music. Shortly after leaving Vienna, he bought the English rights to the Piano Sonata Op. 31, No. 3 from the Zurich publisher Hans Georg Nägeli,* and his firm published the sonata in September 1804, at about the same time as it issued the *Variations on 'God Save the King'*. (These two works, incidentally, were not the first compositions by Beethoven to be printed by Clementi, for in Lesson 39 of the *Introduction to the Art of Playing on the Piano Forte* (1801) he had presented one of the *Ländlerische Tänze* WoO 11.) Also in 1804, Clementi entered into an arrangement with Breitkopf & Härtel,* under which the latter were to purchase all of Beethoven's future compositions and subsequently cede to Clementi the copyright for the British Dominions; but this agreement yielded no results, since Beethoven did not sell any new works to the Leipzig firm during the next few years.

In 1807 Clementi at last succeeded in establishing a close association with Beethoven. On 22 April he reported to his partner Frederick William Collard: 'I have at last made a compleat conquest of that *haughty beauty*, Beethoven: who first began in public places to grin and coquet with me which of course I took care not to discourage: then slid into familiar chat, till meeting him by chance one day in the street—"Where do you lodge?" says he; "I have not seen you this long while!"—upon which I gave him my address. Two days after I find on my table his card, brought by himself, from the maid's description of his lovely form. This will do, thought I. Three days after that, he calls again and finds me at home. Conceive the mutual ecstasy of such a meeting!'

Two days earlier, on 20 April 1807, Clementi had acquired, for £200, the English rights for the Fourth Piano Concerto, the three 'Razumovsky' Quartets, the Violin Concerto (as well as an arrangement to be made of it by Beethoven as a piano concerto), and the *Coriolan* Overture. There appear, however, to have been delays in the delivery of the scores, perhaps due in part to the Napoleonic wars, and in the end the firm published only the quartets (probably in 1809) and the two versions of the Violin Concerto (in the late summer of 1810); Beethoven did not receive any payment until 1810. But Clementi's contacts with Beethoven, which he renewed during his stay in Vienna in 1808–10, were to produce splendid results after his return to London. Between autumn 1810 and spring 1811 his firm issued what were in fact the earliest editions of no fewer than ten works, among them the 'Emperor' Concerto, the String Quartet Op. 74, and the Piano Sonatas Opp. 78, 79, and 81a. Finally, it brought out in 1823 editions of the Piano Sonatas Opp. 110 and 111, and also, under the title *Trifles for the Piano Forte*, what Alan Tyson has identified as 'the first and only authentic edition' of the full set of the eleven Bagatelles Op. 119, the first six of the pieces being here published for the first time.

(Platinga, Ringer, Tyson[3], Unger[2], Wegeler/Ries)

Collin, Heinrich Joseph von (b. Vienna, 26 December 1771; d. Vienna, 28 July 1811). Dramatist and poet; civil servant; son of a well-known Viennese physician of the same name (1731–81). Several of Collin's verse dramas glorify man's freedom and strength of will. His most successful play was *Regulus* (Burgtheater, 3 October 1801); the others include *Coriolan* (24 November 1802) and *Polyxena* (15 October 1803). As a poet, he became best known for his patriotic *Lieder österreichischer Wehrmänner* (1809), inspired by the war against Napoleon. A six-volume edition of his works was published in 1812–14 by his brother Matthäus (1779–1824), who was himself a poet and playwright, as well as an influential critic.

It is not known when Collin's first met Beethoven, but Joseph August Röckel* names him as one of the persons who met at Prince Karl Lichnowsky's* apartment in December 1805 with the intention of persuading him to shorten the original score of *Fidelio*. No information is available to explain why Beethoven should have decided early in 1807 to write an overture to *Coriolan*. At its première on 24 November 1802 the tragedy had been rather coolly received, although the actors, especially Joseph Lange in the title role, were enthusiastically applauded. It was performed four more times that year, six times during 1803, four times in

1804, and just once, on 20 February, in 1806. The play was next given on 24 April 1807, with Beethoven's overture; but scholars believe that this performance is more likely to have been prompted by the existence of the overture than to have been the reason for its composition. The overture had previously been played at concerts at Prince Lobkowitz's* and Prince Lichnowsky's. The edition of the overture, published by the Kunst- und Industrie-Comptoir* in 1808, was dedicated to Collin. No further performances of *Coriolan* took place in 1807, or during the years 1808–10; subsequently the play received eight more performances at the Burgtheater, the last one on 3 December 1825. Apart from Beethoven's overture, *Coriolan* inspired a well-known painting by Friedrich Heinrich Füger. (Incidentally, Shakespeare's *Coriolanus* was produced at the Burgtheater on 13 and 15 April 1789, in a German version by Johann Friedrich Schink, and then not again until 10 June 1851.)

Beethoven, eager to find a suitable libretto for another opera, looked to Collin as a possible collaborator. Two subjects, in particular, were discussed by them: the stories of Macbeth and of Bradamante, the heroine of Ariosto's *Orlando furioso*. Beethoven was sufficiently interested in the former topic to ask Röckel to read the first act of Collin's *Macbeth* and he even made some musical sketches; however, the play was never finished. Regarding the second topic, Beethoven had some reservations, mainly because of similarities between Collin's plot and the Traf(f)ieri–Weigl* ballet *Alcina* which had first been performed at the Kärntnertor-Theater on 25 January 1798 (*see Corr.* A165/B332); and even after Collin had finished his libretto for *Bradamante*, Beethoven hesitated to set it. Collin finally lost patience and in November 1808 offered the text to Johann Friedrich Reichardt,* who was then on a visit to Vienna and who immediately accepted it. Beethoven thereupon suddenly felt much more enthusiastic about the project: 'Great and enraged poet!!!!!! Forget Reichardt—use my music for your poetry,' he implored Collin (*Corr.* A185/B344); but it was too late. Reichardt completed his score by February 1809, and following some rehearsals at Prince Lobkowitz's palace, a concert performance of the opera was presented there on 3 March, with Anna Milder-Hauptmann* in the title role. In the audience were many prominent musicians, among them Clementi,* Gyrowetz,* Kozeluch,* Ferdinand Ries,* Salieri,* Michael Umlauf,* Weigl,* and Beethoven himself. Because of the unsettled conditions—the following month Austria was to declare war against Napoleon and in May Vienna would be occupied by the French—the time was thought inopportune for a stage production, and although there was talk of one later, none ever took place.

(Collin, Hess[6], Laban, Reichardt)

Cramer, Johann [John] **Baptist** (b. Mannheim, 24 February 1771; d. London, 16 April 1858). Composer, pianist, and publisher. According to Schindler,* Cramer spent the whole winter 1799–1800 in Vienna and during that time saw a good deal of Beethoven. Their relations, at first very friendly, later reportedly became somewhat strained as a sense of rivalry developed between them. Even if that is true, it did not lessen their mutual admiration. Beethoven told Cipriani Potter,* in 1817 or 1818, that Cramer had given him greater pleasure than any other pianist, and Ferdinand Ries* states in *Biographische Notizen* that Cramer was the only pianist whom Beethoven had praised as being truly excellent. Cramer, for his part, considered Beethoven to be the supreme improviser. As for his opinion regarding Beethoven's works, nothing is known apart from a remark by Beethoven (in a letter to Johann Peter Salomon on 1 June 1815) that Ries had informed him in a recent communication that Cramer had publicly criticized his compositions. Since this particular letter from Ries to Beethoven is lost, it is difficult to decide what significance to attach to Beethoven's statement; in any case, he appears not to have borne any grudge and would have been quite ready to sell his music to Cramer, had the latter wished to buy it. (Cramer had founded Chappell & Co.* with Samuel Chappell and Francis Tatton Latour in 1810. He left the firm in 1819, and in 1824 set up another one together with Robert Addison and T. F. Beale. This new company, which later became known as 'J. B. Cramer & Co.', published editions of many of Beethoven's works.) When Schindler met Cramer in Paris in 1841, he was favourably impressed by the warm manner in which Cramer spoke about Beethoven.

Although Cramer composed nine piano concertos and no fewer than 124 sonatas, he is known today almost solely for the eighty-four studies for the piano which he published in two sets of forty-two in 1804 and 1810 under the title *Studio per il pianoforte*. According to Schindler, Beethoven considered the studies an excellent preparation for the performance of his own sonatas, so much so that he selected and annotated twenty of them for the benefit of his nephew Karl.* Schindler later transcribed Beethoven's alleged annotations into a copy of Cramer's studies. (Actually, the number of annotations he thus attributed to Beethoven concerned twenty-one, not twenty, studies.) At the same time, he added his own annotations—in which he claimed to have followed the spirit of Beethoven's remarks—to almost all the remaining studies. In 1880, Schindler's copy of Cramer's studies containing all these various annotations was acquired by the Königlich-Preussische Bibliothek in Berlin, and it is today in the possession of that library's successor, the Deutsche Staatsbibliothek.

Since the discovery of Schindler's numerous forged entries in Beethoven's conversation books, scholars have increasingly questioned the authenticity of the annotations he attributed to his 'teacher'. The case against Schindler has been most forcefully put by D. Back and G. Herre in their article 'Anton Schindlers "Nutzanwendung" der Cramer-Etüden: Zu den sogenannten Beethovenschen Spielanweisungen'. Their conclusion, based on a closely argued examination of the matter, is that Schindler concocted these annotations himself between 1849 and 1854.

(Beck/Herre[2], Graue, Newman[1], Wegeler/Ries)

Cramolini, Ludwig (b. Vienna, 1805; d. Darmstadt, 29 October 1884). Tenor. Having made his debut in Nicolas Isouard's *Joconde* on 25 February 1824, he sang to great acclaim at the Kärntnertor-Theater until 1830, in which year he accepted an engagement at the court theatre at Brunswick. From 1847 until his retirement from the stage in 1874 he was one of the stars of the Darmstadt court theatre, where his popularity was such that the cafés offered 'Cramolini cakes' and his admirers wore 'Cramolini collars'.

He came to know Beethoven in August 1818 when he stayed with his mother in a house at Mödling, in which Beethoven had also taken rooms. (In Cramolini's recollections of Beethoven which Hermann Knispel published in the *Frankfurter Zeitung* on 29 September 1907, he states that his mother spent the month of August there in each of the years 1816–18. The only year during that period in which Beethoven is known to have been at Mödling is 1818.) Cramolini tells of following Beethoven on his walks in the country near Mödling, and picking up the sheets of music paper which he absent-mindedly dropped, and handing them back to him later at the house; on one occasion, Beethoven rewarded him with a coin.

Cramolini's next, and final, personal contact with Beethoven did not occur until the composer was dying. Together with his fiancée Nanette Schechner* he visited Beethoven at the Schwarzspanierhaus—but not 'on 15 or 16 December 1826', as he mistakenly recalled, but in February 1827. He was also incorrect in stating that Schechner had recently appeared in *Fidelio*—in fact, according to his account, it was that performance which led to the visit, for his mother, who had not heard the opera before, was so moved by it that she suggested that he should call on Beethoven, who would probably still remember them. But there is no record of a performance of *Fidelio* in Vienna in 1826 or 1827 (nor indeed at any time between March 1823 and March 1831). However, Cramolini's memories of the visit itself could well be largely correct. He describes Beethoven as receiving his guests very graciously. Cramolini sang 'Adelaide' for him, and Schechner sang 'Leonore's great aria from *Fidelio*'. Beethoven, who was unable to hear them, watched them intently and afterwards congratulated them on having sung his music with such great feeling.

(Kerst, Kutsch/Riemens)

Cressener, George (b. 1700; d. Bonn, 17 January 1781). British ambassador at Bonn from 1775 until his death. According to the cellist Bernhard Mäurer, who was a member of the electoral orchestra from 1777 to 1780, Cressener (whose name Mäurer deformed into 'Krescher') supported the Beethoven family financially. When he died, Beethoven composed a cantata in his memory, which he submitted to Kapellmeister Andrea Lucchesi* for his comments. Although Lucchesi declared that he could not understand it, he agreed to its being rehearsed and even performed by the orchestra. With each rehearsal appreciation of the originality of the work increased, and it was well received at its performance. Mäurer called it Beethoven's first attempt at composition.

Scholars have hesitated to accept this story, in the first place because Mäurer could not have been speaking from personal memory, having left Bonn several months before the events he claimed to be describing. In addition, there is no mention of this cantata in any other contemporary account of Beethoven's youth, nor has any trace of it been found to this day.

(Kerst)

Crevelt, Johann Heinrich (bapt. Bonn, 28 June 1751; d. Bonn, 25 August 1818). Physician. Following medical studies in Vienna and Paris, he practised at Bonn from 1782. A man of wide cultural interests, he was a founding member of the Bonn *Lesegesellschaft* [Reading Society] which was established in 1787. (It was for the society's planned memorial celebration of the death of the Emperor Joseph II* that Beethoven composed his cantata WoO 87 in 1790 (*see* Averdonk* and Schneider*), but it was not ready in time.) Crevelt was himself something of a poet; several odes and other pieces written by him appeared in *Beiträge zur Ausbreitung nützlicher Kentnisse*, published at Bonn in 1784/5. He was a close friend of the Koch* family.

He made an entry, which he signed 'Your admirer and friend', in the album presented to Beethoven upon his departure for Vienna in 1792, but nothing is known about their relations. When, as president of the society, he made a speech in July 1813 on the occasion of the twenty-fifth anniversary celebrations of its founding, he arranged for a composition by Beethoven to be played beforehand. Max Braubach, who reports this (but without identifying the work), states further that when Beethoven sent an engraving of his portrait to the society in 1815, he asked that it should be handed to Crevelt 'as a memento of an old friendship', once the society had received the painting which he was planning to present to it. As far as is known, he never sent the painting.

(Braubach[7,8])

Czerny, Carl (b. Vienna, 21 February 1791; d. Vienna, 15 July 1857). Composer, pianist, piano teacher, and writer on music. Son of Wenzel Czerny (1750–1832), a piano teacher and violinist of Bohemian origin, who first went to Vienna in 1786 and settled there permanently after spending the years 1791–c.1795 in Poland; he was Carl's first and principal teacher. By the time he was about 10, Carl could play almost all the piano works of Mozart,* Clementi,* and other well-known composers competently and from memory. He made his public debut in 1800, playing Mozart's C minor Concerto (K491) at a concert in the Augarten.

It was at about that time (in 1800 or 1801) that the violinist Wenzel Krumpholtz,* a friend of his father's as well as of Beethoven, who had awakened and nurtured Carl's interest in Beethoven's sonatas, took the boy to play for him. After listening to Carl play Mozart's Piano Concerto in C (K503) and the *Sonate pathétique*, and accompany his father in the song 'Adelaide', Beethoven offered to teach him. At first Carl was made to practise scales in all the different keys and was taught the correct hand and finger positions and how to use his thumb, after which he progressed to exercises taken from Carl Philipp Emanuel Bach's *Versuch über die wahre Art das Clavier zu spielen*. The lessons were not given regularly and, in any case, did not extend beyond the year 1802. In a later account of a conversation he had with Beethoven in 1804, Czerny stated that he had then not seen him for two years and, furthermore, that Beethoven was annoyed with his father for having broken off the lessons. The tuition must nonetheless have been of great value to Czerny, inasmuch as, other likely benefits apart, it conferred an exceptional authority on his performances of Beethoven's music. In 1804–5 Prince Lichnowsky,* to whom he had been presented by Krumpholtz, asked him to come to his palace several times a week and play Beethoven's sonatas to him. As Czerny was able to perform all of them from memory, the prince contented himself with calling out the opus number of the particular composition he wished to hear.

Czerny remained on friendly terms with Beethoven and continued to meet him on various occasions. When, having become a highly sought after teacher, he started in 1816 to have regular Sunday concerts for his pupils at his house, Beethoven attended some of them and even improvised on occasion. Moreover, at Beethoven's request, Czerny gave piano lessons in 1816–18 to his nephew Karl.* He furthermore made himself useful to Beethoven by preparing piano arrangements of several of his works, a task he accomplished with competence and speed. Thus he prepared a piano reduction of the second version of *Fidelio*, assisted with the arrangements of some of the orchestral works purchased by S. A. Steiner* in 1815, adapted the score of the Eighth Symphony for two pianos, revised the arrangement made of it for two hands by Tobias Haslinger,* and transcribed the Overture *Die Weihe des Hauses* for solo piano and piano duet. Thus, for one reason or another, Beethoven had good reason to feel 'affection, gratitude, and esteem' for Czerny (*see* his letter of 8 October 1824). After Beethoven's death, Heinrich Albert Probst* published, between 1827 and 1829, Czerny's arrangements for piano duet of all the nine symphonies. (*See also* Diabelli & Co.*)

In 1842 Czerny wrote an autobiographical sketch ('Erinnerungen aus meinem Leben') which is preserved in the archives of the Gesellschaft des Musikfreunde* and from which some of the above information is derived. Ten years later he wrote down some recollections about Beethoven for Otto Jahn ('Anekdoten und Notizen über Beethoven') which are now at the Staatsbibliothek, Berlin. In addition to these documents, which contain many fascinating remarks about Beethoven the man and the musician, the *Complete Theoretical and Practical Piano School* which Czerny published in 1839 (and dedicated to Queen Victoria) is of considerable interest to the Beethoven scholar, since it offers extremely valuable observations on the performance of his piano sonatas. (*See also* Sonnleithner.*)

(Kahl², Mitchell, Schünemann)

Czerny, Joseph (b. Wrbnol [Vrbno, near Melnik, Czech Republic], 14 June 1785; d. Vienna, 22 September 1831). Composer, piano teacher, and music publisher; no relation of Carl Czerny.* He was highly regarded as a teacher and counted among his pupils the well-known pianists Fanny Sallamon and Leopoldine Blahetka.* He had been very strongly recommended to the latter's father by Beethoven. 'He forced Joseph Czerny on me as a teacher against my inclination,' Joseph L. Blahetka wrote to Schindler* in 1839, 'for I would have preferred Carl Czerny . . . But Beethoven was right: Joseph Czerny was an excellent teacher.' In 1820 Czerny began teaching Karl van Beethoven* who was then attending Joseph Blöchlinger's* school. An entry by Czerny in a conversation book in March of that year reads: 'He played for me today a sonata by Mozart and the *Sonate pathétique*, so I now know his ability. In the next lesson I shall start him on something suited to his capacity' (*BKh*1/313). The conversation books indicate that Beethoven was in close contact with Czerny in the early 1820s; many of their meetings took place at restaurants or coffee houses. Czerny made arrangements of Beethoven's *Egmont* Overture for piano duet, and of the *Coriolan* Overture and the Quintet Op. 16 for two pianos.

In the spring of 1826 he bought Pietro [Peter] Cappi's half-share in the firm 'Cappi & Co.', thereby becoming the partner of Giovanni Cappi's* son Carlo [Karl]; the new firm traded under the name of 'Cappi & Czerny'.* In November 1827 Carlo Cappi withdrew from the business and sold his part to Czerny, who registered his own firm 'Joseph Czerny' in March of the following year. In February 1831 it was acquired by the lithographer Joseph Trentsensky. Czerny was particularly important as the publisher of a number of first editions of Schubert's works.

(Hüffer, Slezak⁴)

Dale, Joseph (1750–1821). Organist, composer, and music publisher, in business in London from 1783. Among his early publications were William Shield's operas *The Flitch of Bacon* (which had been produced at the Little Theatre in London in 1778) and *Rosina* (Covent Garden, 1782). In 1805 his son William became a partner in the firm, which was then called 'Joseph Dale & Son' (or 'Joseph & William Dale'). After William left to establish his own business in 1809, Joseph continued alone. Among other composers whose works he published were Clementi,* Jan Ladislav Dussek, Krumpholtz,* Daniel Steibelt,* and Stephen Storace; he himself composed a number of concertos and sonatas. He was also organist at the Church of St Anthony and John the Baptist in Watling Street.

In 1803 he brought out an edition of Beethoven's seven Bagatelles for piano (Op. 33), which had originally been issued in May of that year by the Kunst- und Industrie-Comptoir* in Vienna. Kinsky/Halm characterize Dale's edition as a '*Nachdruck*'; but according to Alan Tyson, the edition, which was entered at Stationers Hall in London on 12 October 1803, was 'not a *Nachdruck* of the Viennese edition', but 'seems to be based on an *Abschrift* or proof copy sent by the Bureau [i.e. the Comptoir] to London'. Tyson states furthermore that he has found 'some evidence of a business link between the Bureau and Dale'.

(Smith/Jones, Tyson[3])

Danhauser, Joseph Franz (Vienna, 19 August 1805; d. Vienna, 4 May 1845). Painter; son of the furniture designer and manufacturer Joseph Ulrich Danhauser (1780–1829), and grandson of the woodcarver Joseph David Danhauser (1753–96). He was musically gifted and studied the violin with Mayseder,* but by 1820 he had decided to make art his career and accordingly enrolled at the Akademie der bildenden Künste, where his principal teacher was Johann Peter Krafft. In 1826 he spent several months studying Italian art in Venice, at the invitation of Ladislaus Pyrker who was then patriarch (i.e. archbishop) of that city. Later that year Pyrker was appointed archbishop of Erlau [Eger], where, thanks to his patronage, Danhauser was to receive several important commissions during the following decade. However, after his father's death in 1829 he devoted most of his time, for several years, to managing the furniture factory in Vienna. In 1838 he was engaged as 'Korrektor' at the Academy, and in 1841–2 he held the position of a professor. As a painter, Danhauser specialized in depicting social scenes drawn from contemporary life; his genre pictures achieved great popularity. (*See also* Graf.*)

Danhauser, who first exhibited at the Academy in 1826, showing three paintings illustrating scenes from Pyrker's epic poem *Rudolphias*, was still virtually unknown when he was authorized to make Beethoven's death mask. The explanation for what may seem a surprising choice is furnished by a note from Stephan von Breuning* to Schindler,* dated 27 March (printed and also reproduced in facsimile in Schindler's biography of Beethoven). Breuning writes: 'A certain Danhauser wishes to make a plaster cast of the body tomorrow morning.

He says it will take five or at the most eight minutes. Write and tell me whether I should agree or not. The taking of such casts is often permitted in the case of famous men, and if one does not permit it one might later be accused of having failed to consider the interests of the public.' Evidently Schindler took the same view, and Danhauser was granted access to Beethoven's room the next morning, 28 March. His visit is likely to have lasted a good deal longer than five, or even eight, minutes, for before he could make the cast it was necessary to shave off the beard which Beethoven had grown during his final illness. According to his brother Carl's later account (see below), this task was performed by Johann Matthias Ranftl, a friend of Danhauser's who had accompanied him to the Schwarzspanierhaus (and who would eventually also become a well-known painter). Then, in addition to the mask, Danhauser made a drawing of Beethoven on his deathbed, and also two sketches in oils (now at the Beethoven-Haus, Bonn), one of his face, the other of his hands.

Some uncertainty has been expressed as to whether the mask was made before or after Dr Johann Wagner's* autopsy on Beethoven's body. Yet the report of the autopsy is clearly dated 'die 27. Martii MCCMXXVII'. It is therefore evident from the date and content of Breuning's letter, on the one hand, and from the date of Dr Wagner's report, on the other, that the autopsy (27 March) preceded the making of the death mask (28 March). If still further proof were needed, it would be supplied by the lithograph which Danhauser made from his drawing of Beethoven: it bears the printed legend 'Beethoven drawn on his deathbed 28 March 1827'. In any case, the mask reveals the effect of the dissection, in the course of which the temporal bones had been removed. There can thus be no doubt as to the true sequence of the two events.

Many years later Carl Danhauser gave a detailed and credible account of the manner in which the plaster cast had been made by his brother Joseph, with the help of an assistant named Hof[f]mann. At the same time, Carl's recollections are manifestly unreliable in certain other respects—not surprisingly, since he was describing events which had occurred almost sixty-five years earlier. Thus he places Beethoven's death in the night of 25–6 March, writes that they gained access to his rooms the following morning [i.e. 26 March], and omits any mention of Stephan von Breuning having granted the necessary permission. The document is nevertheless of considerable interest. It has been reproduced several times, for instance by F. Glück in his contribution to the *Festschrift* for Otto Erich Deutsch (Kassel, 1963).

Both the Beethoven-Haus, Bonn, and the Historisches Museum der Stadt Wien possess positive copies of the death mark. The Viennese copy was at one time owned by Liszt;* at his death in 1886 it passed into the possession of Princess Carolyne Sayn-Wittgenstein, and after her death in 1887 into that of her daughter Princess Marie Hohenlohe-Schillingsfürst, who presented it that same year to the newly founded Historisches Museum. The museum also has a copy of a bust of Beethoven which Danhauser made some time after the composer's death. (*See also* Klein.*)

(Badura-Skoda⁵, *Danhauser*, Glück³, Steblin²)

De Boer, Samson Moses (1771–1839). A Dutchman who visited Beethoven at Baden on 3 August 1825, on which occasion he made a number of entries in the conversation books (*see BKh*8/35–8). He introduced himself as a member of the Academy of Fine Arts in Amsterdam, and, among other remarks, assured Beethoven that his quartets and his opera had been very well received in that city. (*Fidelio* had been first performed at Amsterdam on 13 November of the preceding year.) De Boer was himself an amateur cellist. Beethoven presented a short canon (WoO 35) to him, which he erroneously inscribed to 'Monsieur S. M. de Boger'. (The autograph is now at the Houghton Library of Harvard University.) In a letter addressed to one of the Academy's committees on 15 March 1827, De Boer gave a detailed account of his visit.

The *Wiener Zeitung*, which reported his stay in Vienna (from 4 July to 14 August 1825), described him as a man of private means. Ludwig Nohl wrongly believed that the visitor might have been the Parisian surgeon Alexis Boyer (1760–1833), while Theodor Frimmel was equally mistaken in his conclusion— which is restated in Kinsky/Halm—that he was the Dutch painter and amateur musician Otto de Boer (1797–1856).

(Frimmel⁵, Nohl¹, Van der Zanden)

Decker, Johann Stephan (b. Colmar, 26 December 1783; d. Grinzing, near Vienna, 25 June 1844). Painter and lithographer. After studying with Jacques-Louis David and Jean Jacques [Casimir] Karpff in Paris, he returned to Colmar in 1811/12. In 1818 he moved to Pest [Budapest], and in 1821 to Vienna. There he painted portraits of several prominent persons, including the duke of Reichstadt, and also gave drawing lessons to members of Archduke Karl's family, notably to his daughter Maria Theresia, later queen of the Two Sicilies.

In May 1824, at a time when Beethoven's two big concerts focused considerable public interest on his latest compositions, Decker was commissioned by the Lithographisches Institut to paint his portrait (*see BKh*6/211, 240, 250). Decker's lithograph, based on a chalk drawing, was issued by the Institut on 3 June and printed as a supplement to the Vienna *Allgemeine musikalische Zeitung* on 5 June. In 1827 Artaria & Co.* published an engraved copy of the portrait, prepared by Joseph Steinmüller. Carl Czerny* reportedly considered Decker's portrait a very good likeness, but Schindler* dismissed it as a 'bit of fantasy'. It has been suggested that it may have served as the model for Kriehuber's* 1832 lithograph (*see* Hochenecker*).

(*ALBK*, Frimmel³, Schindler¹)

De Gamerra, Giovanni (b. Leghorn [Livorno], 1743; d. Vicenza, 29 August 1803). Poet, librettist, and dramatist. He took minor orders, then studied law at Pisa, and eventually opted for a military career in the Austrian army, in which he served from 1765 until 1770. He was then appointed poet at the Teatro Regio Ducal, Milan (1770–4), and during his tenure of that post he wrote the libretto for Mozart's* *Lucio Silla*, which was produced at that theatre on 26 December 1772. From 1774 to 1776, and again from 1793 to 1802, he held the position of court poet in Vienna. There he wrote librettos for several well-known composers, notably Salieri* (who set seven) and Joseph Weigl* (who set two).

De Gammera's libretto for Felice Alessandri's opera *Medonte, re d'Epiro* (first produced at Milan on 26 December 1774) was later set by several other composers, including Giuseppe Sarti, whose opera was first performed at Florence on 8 September 1777 and in Vienna on 9 February 1794. In 1801–2 Beethoven made sketches for a new setting of one of the numbers in the libretto, the trio 'Tremate, empi, tremate'. It is not known exactly when he completed the composition (Op. 116), in which the voices are accompanied by the orchestra. It was given its first performance by Anna Milder-Hauptmann,* Giuseppe Siboni, and Karl Weinmüller* at Beethoven's concert at the Grosser Redoutensaal on 27 February 1814. The trio was also on the programme of Beethoven's concert of 23 May 1824. It was published by S. A. Steiner & Co.* in February 1826.

(Dorfmüller, Rice)

Degenhart, Johann Martin (bapt. Bonn, 26 May 1768; d. Bonn, 11 November 1800). Son of the town adjutant Lieutenant Peter Degenhart. He studied philosophy (1783–5) and law (1785–91); in 1799 he became a notary.

He evidently had close relations with the young Beethoven. On 23 August 1792 the latter wrote a duo for two flutes (WoO 26) 'for my friend Degenharth [*sic*]'. Together with Matthias Koch,* Degenhart was responsible for putting together the album in which some of Beethoven's friends recorded their farewells on the occasion of his departure for Vienna later that year. Degenhart himself contributed a very affectionate entry.

Dembscher, Ignaz (*c.*1776–1838). Government official. Originally of modest means, he had reportedly inherited a fortune from a wealthy benefactor, tentatively identified in the new edition of Beethoven's conversation books (*BKh*8/404–5) as Vinzenz Hamschka or Vinzenz Hamson. A bachelor, he lived with his three sisters; in late 1824 or early 1825 he moved to a new house on the Löwelbastei. There were frequently string quartet sessions at his home, which were usually directed by Joseph Mayseder* and at which he himself often played the cello. In 1825, following the unsatisfactory first public performance of Beethoven's String Quartet in E flat (Op. 127) under Schuppanzigh* on 6 March, the work was played more competently at Dembscher's under Mayseder's direction on 15 April and again later that month (*see also* Joseph Michael Böhm*). But in February 1826 Karl Holz* took back the parts of the Quartet in A minor (Op. 132) which Beethoven had lent to Mayseder for a performance at Dembscher's, because he had come to the conclusion during rehearsals that the musicians were finding it too difficult (*BKh* 9/38). Soon afterwards Beethoven was annoyed to learn that Dembscher had not subscribed to Schuppanzigh's concert of 21 March, at which the B flat Quartet (Op. 130) was to receive its first performance, but had boasted that he would arrange a performance by better artists at his house. When told that he must send Schuppanzigh the 50-florin subscription price before he could borrow the music, he apparently exclaimed 'Muss es sein?' [Must it be?] or 'Wenn es sein muss' [If it must be]. Thereupon Beethoven wrote the canon 'Es muss sein, es muss sein' [It must be] (WoO 196), and he used its theme in the last movement, 'Der schwergefasste Entschluss' [The difficult decision], of the Quartet in F (Op. 135) which he composed that summer.

Demmer. The original Florestan. Scholars have had difficulty identifying the Demmer who created the role, for, as was then customary, only the singer's surname appeared on the programme of the première on 20 November 1805. Thayer* states that Demmer had been trained at Cologne, and he quotes a report dating from the year 1799, when Demmer was appearing at Frankfurt, according to which he possessed 'a strong, steady voice with a high range' and excelled in comic tenor roles. Thayer believed furthermore that he might have been identical with the Joseph Demmer who had sung as a bass in the Bonn court Kapelle before being engaged (as a tenor) at Weimar in 1791 and whom Beethoven must have known in his years at Bonn. Theodor Frimmel similarly speculates in his *Beethoven-Handbuch* that the Joseph Demmer of the Bonn Kapelle 'is probably identical with the tenor Demmer who sang Florestan in *Fidelio* in Vienna in 1805'. This supposition has never been substantiated, and more recent scholars have settled on a different candidate. Kurt Dorfmüller, citing Friedrich Slezak as his source, affirms that 'the Florestan of the first performance was Friedrich Christian (not Joseph) Demmer', and Willy Hess, in his detailed study of Beethoven's opera, reproduces a lithograph which he labels 'Fritz Demmer, the first Florestan'.

According to Slezak/Dorfmüller, Friedrich [Fritz] Demmer was probably born in Berlin in either 1785 or 1788. (J. Bindtner, in his edition of Ignaz Castelli's* *Memoiren meines Lebens*, gives his dates as 1786–1838.) One may wonder whether such a demanding principal male role could really have been entrusted to a singer who was, at the most, 20 years old. The answer must be that this is by no means impossible. After all, the Leonore, Anna Milder (*see* Milder-Hauptmann*), was herself no older—she would not be 20 until 13 December 1805—and

Joseph August Röckel,* who replaced Demmer shortly afterwards, apparently to Beethoven's full satisfaction, was then no more than 22. On the other hand, Thayer quotes Röckel as telling him in 1861 that he had been engaged at Salzburg by an agent of Baron Braun* who had gone there 'in search of a young and fresh tenor to succeed Demmer, whose powers had rapidly declined lately'—which, if true, would seem to point to a man considerably older than 20. Perhaps Thayer misunderstood Röckel, or the latter's memory—he was almost 80 when he spoke to Thayer—may have been somewhat vague regarding events which had occurred more than half a century earlier. (Emily Anderson, in asserting that Röckel 'replaced the rather elderly Demmer in the part of Florestan' (*Corr.* A186 n. 3), may simply be following Thayer's story.)

However, if Röckel was indeed correct in describing the first Florestan as an older singer, it might be fruitful to look for a candidate among Friedrich Demmer's own relatives, for he belonged to a theatrical family. Thus his father, Karl Demmer, who reportedly came from Cologne, and his uncle Christian were both professional singers and actors in Vienna. In his memoirs, Castelli states that one of the brothers performed at the court theatre and the other at the Theater an der Wien, and that, at one time, they 'acted and sang the role of the Seneschal in *Johann von Paris* concurrently, each at his theatre'. (Boieldieu's *Jean de Paris* was produced at the Kärntnertor-Theater, with a German text by Castelli, on 28 August 1812, and at the Theater an der Wien, with a German text by Joseph von Seyfried,* on the following day.) Since the role of the Sénéchal was written for a baritone, either Karl or Christian, if not both, presumably possessed a voice which fell essentially within that range. If, nonetheless, one of them was chosen to assume the higher-lying role of Florestan, might that account for the reproach expressed by the critic of the Leipzig *Allgemeine musikalische Zeitung* that 'Demmer sang almost constantly below pitch' [Demmer intoniert fast immer zu tief]? All this is, of course, speculation.

What is certain, on the other hand, is that the singer's performance failed to please. Thayer even states that it was judged inadequate by all contemporary critics. Röckel told R. Bunge many years later that Beethoven attributed the failure of his opera entirely to Demmer; and, whether or not his memory was faulty in other respects, he was undoubtedly right in speaking of Beethoven's profound dissatisfaction with his first Florestan. The proof is that Demmer was the only member of the original cast to be dropped in the 1806 production.

During his career, Friedrich Demmer appeared at the Theater an der Wien, at the court theatre, at the theatres in Graz and Pest [Budapest], and at the Theater in der Josefstadt in Vienna. Incidentally, the male members of the family were not the only ones to pursue theatrical careers. Friedrich's mother, Karolina Friederike Wilhelmine Demmer, was an actress at the Burgtheater from 1804 until her death in 1813; and his sisters Johanna [Jeanette], Josephine, and Thekla

(1802–32) all went on the stage (Thekla sang Marcellina in the 1822 revival of *Fidelio*).

(Bunge, Castelli, Dorfmüller, Eisenberg, Hess[8], Thayer[1])

Deym, Josephine: *see* Brunsvik de Korompa.*

Diabelli, Anton (b. Mattsee, near Salzburg, 6 September 1781; d. Vienna, 7 April 1858). Publisher, teacher, and composer. After he moved to Vienna in 1802 he earned his living primarily as a piano and guitar teacher, and as a composer. In 1815 he became a proof-reader at the music publishing firm of S. A. Steiner & Co,* and through this work he met Beethoven, who appears to have taken a liking to him and facetiously called him 'provost marshal' and 'Diabolus diabelli'. In late 1818 Diabelli founded the firm 'Cappi & Diabelli'* together with Pietro Cappi (*see* Giovanni Cappi*); their association lasted until December 1823. Subsequently Diabelli obtained a new licence as an art and music publisher, and in June 1824 he formed a partnership with the lawyer Anton Spina, who assumed responsibility for the management of the firm while Diabelli attended mainly to musical matters. Under the name 'Anton Diabelli & Co.'* they traded very successfully for more than twenty-five years. After Diabelli retired in January 1851 and Spina at the end of that year, the firm, now run by Spina's son Carl, took the name 'C. A. Spina'.

Diabelli wrote numerous compositions, both sacred and secular; he also made many arrangements of the works of other composers, including Beethoven (notably piano reductions for two and four hands of the Seventh Symphony, which were published by S. A. Steiner & Co. at the same time as the full score in 1816). But Diabelli's enduring fame rests above all on his having written the waltz which formed the basis of the so-called *Diabelli Variations*. Starting in 1819, he invited contributions from various musicians, each of whom furnished one variation, with the exception of Beethoven, who provided thirty-three, which Cappi & Diabelli brought out separately in 1823; the complete set was published the following year by the new firm Anton Diabelli & Co. (*see* the following article).

(Kantner, Slezak[4])

Diabelli & Co. [complete name: Anton Diabelli & Co.]. Music publishing firm directed by Anton Diabelli* and Anton Spina from 1824 until 1851. Its highly successful career was launched with the publication of the *Diabelli Variations* in 1824. These were issued in two parts, of which the first offered a new edition of the Beethoven set already published by Cappi & Diabelli* the previous year, while the second consisted of the contributions, amounting to forty-nine variations and a coda, which had been received from other musicians.

The firm did not bring out any first editions of Beethoven's works while he was still alive, but it was later to be the first to publish the following compositions: Rondo *a capriccio* (Op. 129) in 1828; Rondo for two oboes, two clarinets, two bassoons, and two horns (WoO 25) in 1830; and the songs 'Seufzer eines Ungeliebten' and 'Gegenliebe' (WoO 118) and 'Die laute Klage' (WoO 135) in 1837. In addition, Anton Diabelli & Co. published, in 1829, the Rondo in B flat for piano and orchestra (WoO 6) which may originally have been intended as the final movement of the Second Piano Concerto (for this edition the piano part, which Beethoven had at times merely sketched out, was completed by Carl Czerny*). Finally, the firm issued in 1838 a piano arrangement (WoO 62) made by Diabelli of a fragment of a string quintet. Beethoven had promised, as early as 1824, to write a flute quintet for Diabelli, but never did so; in autumn 1826 he began work on this string quintet, which, however, he did not complete. As far as is known, Beethoven never even began work on the sonata for piano duet which Diabelli had commissioned in 1822 and which Beethoven had undertaken to compose that year; he had renewed his promise to write the sonata in 1824.

One other matter merits a mention. In late March 1823, some two months after Beethoven had decided to offer the *Missa solemnis* in manuscript to the sovereigns of Europe for a fee of 50 gold ducats, Diabelli offered to publish it by public subscription within two months. Beethoven, anxious not to jeopardize the hoped-for success of his own plan, asked Diabelli to hold back his publication for a year, a suggestion which Diabelli rejected. Eventually, an agreement was reached and Beethoven signed a contract with Diabelli on or about 24 April 1823, but soon afterwards he asked for the document to be returned to him, whether for the purpose of making changes or for other reasons is not known; the contract has not survived. He later withdrew from the arrangement, despite Diabelli's protests and even, according to Schindler,* some threats to take him to court. Beethoven's personal relations with Diabelli do not appear to have suffered as a result and remained cordial until the end. During his final illness, Diabelli presented him, to his great delight, with a lithograph which the firm had published of the house in which Haydn* was born.

(Slezak[4])

Dietrich, Anton (b. Vienna, *c.*1796; d. Vienna, 26 April 1872). Sculptor. He enrolled at the Akademie der bildenden Künste in 1808, and from 1811 studied sculpture with Hubert Maurer and Johann Martin Fischer; another of his teachers was Joseph Klieber. In 1820 he was awarded a prize for modelling from life.

Today Dietrich is known above all for his association with Beethoven. In an article published in the Leipzig periodical *Signale für die musikalische Welt* in 1871, C. F. Pohl, the archivist and librarian of the Gesellschaft der Musikfreunde,* stated that in 1821 Dietrich had made a half-length drawing and also a bust of Beethoven, both from life, and that he had made some ten copies of the bust.

Pohl adds that, having destroyed the original mould because it misrepresented the style in which Beethoven wore his hair, Dietrich subsequently made a new model from one of the busts, which he modified so as to portray Beethoven with the longer hair he actually favoured. (The bust at the Historisches Museum der Stadt Wien is presumably a copy of the second model.)

Although Pohl stressed that the information he was presenting in the above-mentioned article had been seen and confirmed by Dietrich himself, he is incorrect in placing Dietrich's first professional contact with Beethoven in the year 1821, for Dietrich had already shown a bust of Beethoven at the Academy's exhibition of April 1820. The bust mentioned by Pohl is therefore likely to date from 1820, as is the drawing (a reproduction of the latter in the new Bonn edition of Beethoven's correspondence (iv. 384) is, in fact, ascribed there to that year). Moreover, if Franz Glück and the most recent editors of the conversation books are correct in concluding that a certain entry made in July 1820 (*BKh*2/180–1) is in Dietrich's hand, then he was at that time planning to make a full-length portrait of Beethoven to show at the following year's exhibition. However, nothing seems to have come of this idea, but the catalogue of the 1822 exhibition once again listed a bust of Beethoven by Dietrich. This was perhaps the 'corrected' version of the 1820 bust, showing Beethoven with a fuller head of hair. In later life Dietrich prided himself on having been the only sculptor whom Beethoven ever permitted to model him from life.

Dietrich's remark, in the above-mentioned entry in the conversation books, that Beethoven's head stands between those of Haydn* and Mozart* suggests that the 1820 bust had been commissioned by Johann Andreas Streicher* for his music room (*see also* Klein*). Dietrich is believed to be also the sculptor of a bust of Streicher himself, of which a copy was at one time exhibited at the Rollett Museum at Baden near Vienna. He is furthermore known to have made a bust of Schubert, to whose circle he belonged (he appears in Moritz von Schwind's* celebrated drawing *A Schubert Evening at Joseph von Spaun's*). It is not certain whether the bust, which is lost, was made before or after Schubert's death.

In 1825, having been recommended by the painter Moritz Michael Daffinger to Count Ladislaus Festetics, Dietrich left Vienna to work for several years on the latter's estates in Hungary. He probably did not return to Vienna until 1830 at the earliest; during the 1840s he had his own studio in the Wieden suburb. In 1865 he was commissioned, at his own request, to make the Beethoven and Schubert busts for the loggia of the new opera house. He died destitute.

(Badura-Skoda[5], Glück[3], Krasa-Florian, Pohl[1], Steblin[2])

Dietrichstein von Proskau-Leslie, Moritz (Joseph Johann), Count (b. Vienna, 19 February 1775; d. Vienna, 27 August 1864). Son of Prince Johann Karl Dietrichstein (1728–1808) and his wife Maria Christina, née Countess Thun (1738–88), a sister-in-law of Mozart's* great patroness Countess Wilhelmine

Thun-Hohenstein,* to whom Beethoven dedicated his Piano Trio Op. 11. In 1800 Dietrichstein married Countess Therese Gilleis (1779–1860).

After serving in the Austrian and Neapolitan armies (1791–9) and spending a year in captivity in France, Dietrichstein returned to Vienna, where he devoted the remainder of his life to cultural activities, among which music played an important part. He studied with the Abbé Stadler* and composed a certain amount of vocal music, both sacred and secular; he also wrote a number of dances and was invited to contribute to the *Diabelli* Variations*. He was, furthermore, one of the founder members of the Gesellschaft der Musikfreunde.* In 1815 he was given responsibility for the education of Napoleon's son, the duke of Reichstadt. Four years later he was appointed Hofmusikgraf [count responsible for court music] and during his tenure of that post he established a music collection within the court library [now the Österreichische Nationalbibliothek] and strengthened the court Kapelle by engaging a number of younger musicians. In 1821 he became, in addition, director of the court theatres, but he relinquished both posts in 1826 on his appointment as director of the court library; he remained in charge of it until 1845.

Beethoven's association with Dietrichstein was of a professional rather than personal nature. Thus they were in contact during the winter of 1807–8 in connection with the Liebhaber-Concerte, for the organization of which the count was largely responsible, while Beethoven was involved in the series both as composer and conductor (*see also* Clement* and Häring*). When, exasperated by an inadequate performance of his First Piano Concerto by Johann Baptist Stainer von Felsburg on 31 January 1808, Beethoven threatened to withdraw from the series, he wrote to Dietrichstein: 'Everything I did was done to please you . . . To please you, I have put up with many things which I would otherwise never have tolerated' (*Corr.* A929/B320). For his part, Dietrichstein revered Beethoven. When the position of court composer, for which Beethoven had applied after the death of Anton Tayber, was abolished in 1823, Dietrichstein— who was then Hofmusikgraf—was reluctant to give the bad news to Beethoven and turned instead for help to their mutual friend Count Moritz Lichnowsky:* 'I do not want to write to Beethoven about it and give hurt to a man whom I admire so sincerely. I therefore ask you to tell him when a suitable occasion presents itself' (*Corr.* B1578). In the same letter he referred to the composer as 'our great Beethoven'.

In his *Beethoven Encyclopedia* P. Nettl states that 'Beethoven dedicated his song 'Merkenstein' (version in the Almanach Selam of 1816) to the Count'. This statement is erroneous in several respects. Of the two settings which Beethoven's made of J. B. Rupprecht's* poem, the one for single voice (WoO 144) published in the almanac *Selam* for the year 1816 bore no dedication. It was the version for vocal duet (Op. 100), issued by S. A. Steiner & Co.* in September 1816, which was dedicated to Dietrichstein—though not to Count Moritz but to his relative

Count Joseph Karl Dietrichstein-Hollenburg (1763–1825). Lastly, the wording of the title suggests that it was not Beethoven, but the poet alone who was responsible for the dedication ('*Merkenstein near Baden*. A poem most respectfully dedicated to His Excellency the Governor of Lower Austria Count Joseph Karl Dietrichstein by Johann Baptist Rupprecht, and set to music for voices with piano accompaniment by Ludwig van Beethoven.'). It was to Count Joseph Karl Dietrichstein that Beethoven applied early in 1825 for permission to use the Landstädtischer Saal in Vienna for a concert on 1 April. Although permission was granted, the concert did not take place.

(Antonicek[2], Biba[2], Weidmann)

Dittersdorf, Carl Ditters von (b. Vienna, 2 November 1739; d. Neuhof, Pilgram [Nový Dvůr, Pelhřimov, Czech Republic], 24 October 1799). Composer and violinist. When his Singspiel *Das rote Käppchen, oder Hilft's nicht so schadt's nicht* was produced at Bonn early in 1792, its great success prompted Beethoven to compose some variations for the piano on the arietta 'Es war einmal ein alter Mann' (WoO 66). These were published in 1793 by Nikolaus Simrock,* who, that same year, also issued Christian Gottlob Neefe's* variations on 'Das Frühstück schmeckt viel besser hier', another number from the same work. It is suggested in Kinsky/Halm that Beethoven may have used Neefe's variations as his model.

Doležálek, Jan Emanuel (b. Chotěboř, near Iglau [Jihlava, Czech Republic], 22 May 1780; d. Vienna, 6 July 1858). Composer, instrumentalist, and teacher. He went to Vienna to study law, but then switched to music; among his teachers was Johann Georg Albrechtsberger.* He became an excellent pianist, organist, and cellist.

Doležálek was a great admirer of Beethoven, to whom he had been introduced by his compatriot Wenzel Krumpholtz* in 1800. He was among Beethoven's visitors during his final illness. In 1852 he spoke to Otto Jahn about his contacts with Beethoven, and also about the unsympathetic and even hostile attitude of certain Viennese composers towards him. Jahn's notes on their conversation were published by F. Kerst in *Die Erinnerungen an Beethoven*.

(Kerst, Simpson[1], Štědroň[1])

Döring, Johann von (b. Lüneburg, 5 August 1741; d. 1818). Poet. He served as a royal Danish chamberlain at Altona from 1781 and held a senior civil service appointment at Sonderburg and Norburg from 1790. Some of his poems appeared under the pseudonym 'Wirths' or simply 'Ws.' In 1778, at Wolfsbüttel, the composer Johann Friedrich Hobein published some piano pieces based on poems by Döring.

Döring's poem 'An einen Säugling' was printed in the *Göttinger Musenal-manach* in 1779. Four years later it was set to music by Beethoven (WoO 108). The song (with only the first of its four stanzas) was originally published in H. P. C. Bossler's* *Blumenlese für Klavierliebhaber beyderley Geschlechts* at Speyer in 1784.

(Dorfmüller, Schürmann)

Dragonetti, Domenico (Carlo Maria) (b. Venice, 7 April 1763 (according to F. M. Palmer); d. London, 16 April 1846). Virtuoso double-bass player. He gained recognition at an early age as an outstanding performer on his favourite instrument (he had also studied the guitar and violin) and played in orchestras at St Mark's as well as in the city's opera houses. In September 1794 he set out for England, where he was to fulfil countless engagements over the next fifty years, at chamber music recitals, orchestral concerts, and theatrical and operatic performances. His association with the Philharmonic Society* extended from 1816 to 1842. Very frequently he shared a desk with the fine English cellist Robert Lindley (H. F. Chorley praised 'the intimacy of their mutual musical sympathy'). On 27 June 1844, at the age of 81, he took part in the farewell concert in London of the violinist François Cramer. The following year he headed the double basses at the Beethoven Festival at Bonn. He continued to play in public until shortly before his death.

Dragonetti met Beethoven during a visit to Vienna in 1799. Many years later he told Samuel Appleby (his solicitor, and a great music lover) that, at Beethoven's request, he had played with him the Cello Sonata Op. 5, No. 2, and that afterwards Beethoven had impulsively embraced both Dragonetti and his double bass. Dragonetti's mastery of the double bass is likely to have given Beethoven a deeper understanding of the possibilities of that instrument and may well have influenced his orchestral writing. Indeed, some musicians believed that certain passages for double basses, for instance in the Recitative in the last movement of the Ninth Symphony, were written for Dragonetti. (In fact, in the early performances of that work by the London Philharmonic Society in which he took part —on 17 April 1837, 23 April 1838, and 3 May 1841—this passage was played by him as a solo.) Dragonetti undoubtedly met Beethoven again during his further, extended, stay in Vienna from 1810 until the spring of 1814, but no information is available about their contacts other than that Dragonetti was among the well-known musicians who played at Beethoven's concert of 8 December 1813. When Cipriani Potter* called on Beethoven in 1817 with a letter of introduction from Dragonetti, he was at once warmly received.

While Dragonetti played in some London performances of the Ninth Symphony (see above), he had not taken part in the very first performance on 21 March 1825, because the Society had been unwilling to pay the fees he demanded for his participation in that season's concerts. 'Have the goodness to inform the Directors of the Philharmonic', he had written on 21 January, 'that I will accept the engagement for the ensuing Season at 10 guineas per night, and play all the Solo's in Beethoven's new symphony, but if I am called upon to play any other solo's, I shall expect to receive 5 Guineas for each night that I am so called upon. I beg leave to add that I saw the score of Beethoven last Sunday, and had I seen it before I sent in my terms I would have asked double. I must be paid likewise 5 Guineas for each trial of Beethoven's symphony.' Dragonetti's terms were rejected by the directors, and the double basses were led by J. P. Anfossi at the first performance of the symphony. (*See also BKh*8/122.)

In a letter to the editor of the *Musical World* dated 31 March 1846 (and published in that journal on 11 April), J. A. Stumpff* gave the following account of his recent visit to the dying Dragonetti: 'I found him in his bed; on beholding me, he stretched his hand towards me, which I pressed warmly, saying—"That was the hand Beethoven desired me to press, and which I came here to perform now in my own name, as well as that of his great friend Beethoven, who is now composing sublime symphonies in purer regions." At this moment his withered countenance visibly cleared up and grew animated, uttering—"I am glad to see you very much."' This incident was evoked, in a slightly embroidered form, by C. F. Pohl in his article on Dragonetti in *Grove's Dictionary of Music and Musicians*. It resurfaced, though in a garbled version, in John M. Levien's 1927 monograph on Beethoven's association with the Philharmonic Society, where the remark is attributed to Dragonetti himself ('Dragonetti . . . said with emotion . . . "This is the hand which Beethoven, our great friend, whose spirit now dwells in purer regions, pressed."')

(Chorley[2], Levien, Palmer[2], Redlich, Slatford[1,2])

Dressler, Ernst Christoph (b. Greussen, near Schwarzburg-Sondershausen, Thuringia, 1734; d. Kassel, 6 April 1779). Poet; composer, singer (tenor), and writer on music. He led a highly peripatetic existence, both as a student and later. Thus he studied theology at Halle, philosophy at Jena, and law, poetry, singing, and the violin at Leipzig; and he held various appointments, as a musician as well as in other capacities, at Bayreuth, Gotha, and Wetzlar, and travelled as far as Vienna, where he sang for the Emperor Joseph II.* Finally, in 1774, he was engaged as a tenor at Kassel, where he sang in opera and with the Kapelle. He published some collections of settings of his own songs (*Melodische Lieder für das schöne Geschlecht* (1771), *Freundschaft und Liebe in melodischen Liedern* (1774–7)), but, according to Max Friedländer, he was 'a thoroughly mediocre poet and musician, not deserving serious consideration'. Of greater interest are his writings on the state of German opera, with suggestions for improving it: *Fragmente einiger Gedanken des musikalischen Zuschauers, die bessere Aufnahme der Musik* *in Deutschland betreffend* (1764), *Gedanken die Vorstellung der 'Alceste' betreffend* (1774), and *Theater-Schule für die Deutschen, das ernsthafte Singe-Schauspiel betreffend* (1777).

One of Beethoven's earliest compositions was a set of *Variations on a March by Dressler* (WoO 63), which, 'in order to encourage him', Christian Gottlob Neefe* arranged to have published at Mannheim in 1782 (or early 1783).

(Allroggen[1], *Dressler*, Friedländer, Wolff)

Duncker, Johann Friedrich Leopold (b. ?1768; d. Berlin, 21 August 1842). Prussian civil servant. He accompanied King Friedrich Wilhelm III* to the Congress of Vienna in 1814 as first secretary; while in Vienna, he stayed with Giannattasio del Rio.* He was in contact with Beethoven, who composed some music (WoO 96) and orchestrated the funeral march from the Piano Sonata in A flat (Op. 26) for Duncker's tragedy *Leonore Prohaska*, which told the story of a heroic Prussian girl who enlisted in male disguise in the Wars of Liberation and died from wounds received in battle. Duncker's hopes for a performance of the play in Vienna were, however, not fulfilled, mainly because the subject had already been treated in Piwald's *Das Mädchen von Potsdam* which had been produced at the Theater in der Leopoldstadt on 1 March 1814.

Nothing is known about Duncker's meetings with Beethoven during his stay in Vienna in 1814–15, but the relationship must have been a mutually agreeable and cordial one, for Beethoven recalled it with exceptional warmth in a letter to Duncker in February 1823, which began: 'My esteemed friend, How often I am with you in spirit!' and concluded: 'Now I shall close, my beloved friend. I only wish that we could meet once again and that our souls could once more communicate with each other. But even if this cannot be, I shall always preserve the memory of your love and friendship, and your splendid intellectual qualities are also very frequently present in my mind. Ever with love and admiration, your most devoted Beethoven' (*Corr.* A1139/B1571). Without doubting the genuineness of Beethoven's feelings, it is possible that some of the hyperbolic language of this letter is due to the fact that its prime purpose was to enlist Duncker's help in persuading the king of Prussia to subscribe to the *Missa solemnis*. (In this connection, Beethoven also wrote to Carl Friedrich Zelter,* as well as to the king himself; and Friedrich Wilhelm III was indeed the first subscriber to the Mass.)

Duport, Jean-Louis (b. Paris, 4 October 1749; d. Paris, 7 September 1819) and **Jean-Pierre** (b. Paris, 27 November 1741; d. Berlin, 31 December 1818). Brothers; cellists and composers. In 1773 Jean-Pierre accepted an invitation to become first cellist of the Prussian court Kapelle in Berlin; from 1787 to 1806 he held the post of court Intendant [director of entertainments]. His younger brother, who had once been his pupil, became principal cellist in Berlin, in his turn, in 1789 and lived there until 1806, when he returned to France; Jean-Pierre remained in Berlin.

According to Ferdinand Ries* (*Biographische Notizen*), Beethoven composed the two Cello Sonatas Op. 5 'for Duport (first cellist of the king)' and performed them with him during his visit to Berlin in the spring of 1796. There has been some uncertainty as to which brother Ries had in mind, but most modern scholars are of the opinion that he was referring to Jean-Louis.

(Johnson[2], Lockwood[1,2], Wegeler/Ries)

Duport, Louis Antoine (b. Paris, ?1 January 1785; d. Paris, 18 October 1853). Dancer, ballet-master, and theatre director. He married the dancer Therese Mathilde Franziska Neumann (1797/8–1876) in 1812; they were divorced in 1840. (Therese was a sister of the actress Emilie Neumann, for whom Helmina von Chezy wrote her play *Rosamunde, Fürstin von Zypern*, to which Schubert composed his famous incidental music.) Duport made some guest appearances in Vienna in 1808, the first of them on 19 May in Pierre Gabriel Gardel's ballet *Die Tanzsucht* [*La Dansomanie*] to music by Étienne-Nicolas Méhul. For the next three years he performed at St Petersburg, but in 1812 he was engaged as dancer and ballet-master in Vienna. From 1814 to 1817 he performed at Naples, and in 1819 he appeared in London.

During the whole, or at any rate the major part, of the period when Domenico Barbaia was lessee of the Kärntnertor-Theater (January 1822–March 1825, April 1826–April 1828), Duport was responsible for the management of that theatre. It was for that reason that Beethoven negotiated with him in 1824 (mainly through Schindler*) for the use of the theatre for the important concert he was planning. The concert eventually took place on 7 May; it included the first performance of the Ninth Symphony. The concert was repeated on 23 May with substantially the same programme at the Grosser Redoutensaal, for which Duport was likewise responsible. The low receipts from the first concert and the disappointing results of the second led the ever suspicious Beethoven to conclude that he had been cheated by the management. He was furthermore annoyed at having to apologize to Tobias Haslinger* for the erroneous announcement, for which he blamed Duport, that the vocal trio 'Tremate, empi, tremate' (Op. 116) performed at the second concert was a 'new' work. It had, in fact, been largely composed as long ago as 1802, had been performed by Anna Milder-Hauptmann,* Giuseppe Siboni, and Karl Weinmüller* at Beethoven's concert of 27 February 1814, and its publication rights had been acquired in 1815 by Haslinger and Sigmund Anton Steiner* (who did not, however, publish it until 1826). Beethoven gave way to his anger in a letter to Prince Golitsïn on 26 May, in which he alleged that he had been the 'victim' of Duport, adding: 'Allow me to omit the vulgar details which would outrage and disgust you as much as their repetition and description would incense and revolt me.'

It is worth mentioning, however, that Duport, acting on behalf of Barbaia, encouraged Beethoven on at least two occasions to write a new German opera for the Kärntnertor-Theater. In 1823–4 the subject under consideration was Grillparzer's* *Melusina*; in 1826 Duport sent Beethoven the libretto *Die Mainacht, oder Der Blocksberg*, which he had commissioned from Friedrich August Kanne.* Nothing came of either project.

Later, from 1 September 1830 until 31 March 1836, Duport was himself the lessee of the Kärntnertor-Theater.

(Raab)

Dušek, Josefa [Duschek, Josepha], née Hambacher (bapt. Prague, 6 March 1754; d. Prague, 8 January 1824). Soprano; daughter of the Prague pharmacist Adalbert Hambacher and his wife Maria Domenica Columbia, who was a daughter of the prominent Salzburg merchant Ignaz Anton von Weiser. Josefa studied with the Czech composer, pianist, and teacher František Xaver Dušek (1731–99); she married him in 1776. Mozart was on friendly terms with the Dušeks, and while he was preparing the première of *Don Giovanni* in 1787 he and Constanze stayed at the Villa Bertramka (now a Mozart museum), the Dušeks' summer residence in the Smichov suburb of Prague. He wrote for Josefa the scene *Ah, lo previdi . . . Ah, t'invola agl'occhi miei* (K272) in 1777 and *Bella mia fiamma . . . Resta, o cara* (K528) in 1787. She was greatly admired for the beauty of her voice, and for the expressiveness and the dramatic quality of her singing. Her concert career, which lasted from the 1770s into the nineteenth century, took her to Salzburg and Vienna and several German cities, as well as to Warsaw; but her base remained Prague. According to J. F. von Schönfeld's *Jahrbuch der Tonkunst von Wien und Prag* (1796), she was also an excellent pianist.

Beethoven's contacts with her were considerably less frequent and intimate than Mozart's. Unless he had made her acquaintance earlier, of which there is no evidence, he may be presumed to have done so during his stay in Prague in early 1796, even though there is no documented proof of a meeting even then. On 21 November of that year, at Leipzig, she gave the first public performance of *Ah! perfido* (Op. 65) which Beethoven had composed while he was in Prague (*see also* Clary*). In 1798 Josefa Dušek performed in Vienna. At her benefit concert at Jahn's* on 29 March, Beethoven played one of his violin sonatas (probably one of the Op. 12 set) with Schuppanzigh.*

(Poštolka[1], Schönfeld)

Eder, Joseph Jakob Martin (bapt. Vienna, 26 July 1760; d. Vienna, 17 February 1835). Music publisher. He set up as an art and music dealer in 1792, and in 1796 established a partnership with Ignaz Sauer (*see* Sauer & Leidesdorf*) which was dissolved two years later. He then ran the business by himself until 1812, when his son-in-law Jeremia Bergmann became a partner and the firm's name was restyled 'Joseph Eder & Co.' After Eder retired in 1817, Bergmann ran the firm under his own name. His son Joseph became a silent partner in 1828, and an active partner in 1836. The firm was renamed 'J. Bergmann & Sohn'.

In September 1798 Eder published the first edition of Beethoven's three Piano Sonatas Op. 10, dedicated to Countess Browne.* According to Kinsky/Halm, he also issued the first editions of the *Sonate pathétique* and of the variations for piano on the trio 'Tändeln und scherzen' from F. X. Süssmayr's opera *Soliman II* (WoO 76), but it has since been established that the editions which Eder published of these two compositions in 1799 did not constitute their first appearance in print; the credit for that belongs to Franz Anton Hoffmeister.*

(Dorfmüller, Slezak[4])

Eeden [Eede, Ede, Eethe, Eden, Vandeneet], **Gilles** [Aegidius] **van den** (b. ?Liège, *c*.1708; d. Bonn, 17 June 1782). Organist and composer; son of Henri van den Eeden, a singer (bass), whose name was included in 1695 in a list of members of the court Kapelle at Liège and who subsequently moved to Bonn, where he appears in lists of the court Kapelle for 1716, 1719, 1722, and 1724. (The bishopric of Liège had been acquired by the elector of Cologne, Joseph Clemens, in 1694.) Gilles was appointed second organist at Bonn by Joseph Clemens in March 1723, lost the position sometime after the latter's death in November of that same year, but was re-engaged by Joseph Clemens's successor, Archbishop Clemens August, in February 1727, though initially without salary . He served as principal organist to the court until his death, when the post was assumed by Christian Gottlob Neefe,* who had been designated his successor the previous year.

To van den Eeden belongs the distinction of having been Beethoven's first music teacher after his father, if credence can be given to the statement later made by Bernhard Mäurer, a cellist in the Bonn Kapelle from 1777 until 1780, that the boy became van den Eeden's pupil in his eighth year. If correct, this would mean in 1778, but there was some uncertainty in Bonn circles as to the true year of Beethoven's birth. (It will be remembered that at his first concert on 26 March 1778 he was presented by his father as a 6-year-old boy.) No reliable information is available concerning the subjects which van den Eeden taught his young pupil, but Beethoven probably studied the piano and organ with him, and perhaps also thoroughbass. There is, on the other hand, some evidence of van den Eeden's long-standing friendly relations with the Beethoven family, going all the way back to the marriage of the composer's grandfather (Ludwig van Beethoven*) to Maria Josepha Poll on 7 September 1733, at which he was a witness.

(Braubach[5], Schiedermair[1], Schmidt[6])

Elisabeth Alexievna, empress of Russia, née (Marie) Luise (Auguste) of Baden (b. Karlsruhe, 24 January 1779; d. Belev, 16 May 1826 (NS)). Daughter of Prince

Karl Ludwig of Baden (1755–1801) and his wife Amalie Friederike, née princess of Hesse-Darmstadt (1754–1832); Karl Ludwig was the oldest son and heir of Margrave Karl Friedrich of Baden (1728–1811), but died before his father. On 9 October 1793 Luise married Grand Duke Alexander (from 1801 Emperor Alexander I*); she took the names 'Elisabeth Alexievna'.

She was in Vienna at the time of the Congress, at which her husband played a major role. Beethoven, reportedly at the suggestion of Dr Bertolini,* took advantage of her presence to compose and dedicate to her the Polonaise Op. 89. He had an audience with her, at which she gave him 50 ducats, and he received a further gift of 100 ducats when she learned that he had never been rewarded for the Violin Sonatas (Op. 30) which he had dedicated to the tsar in 1803. In addition to the Polonaise, he dedicated to her the piano arrangements of his Seventh Symphony. (The Polonaise was published in March 1815, the piano reductions of the symphony at the same time as the full score, in November 1816.)

Also in Vienna at the time of the Congress were Elisabeth's brother Karl Ludwig Friedrich (1786–1818), then the reigning grand duke of Baden, and her sister Karoline Friederike (1776–1841), consort of King Maximilian I Joseph of Bavaria.*

Eppinger. Beethoven was in contact with at least three persons of that name. **Heinrich Eppinger** (*c*.1776–1823) was a violinist and composer. In his *Jahrbuch der Tonkunst von Wien und Prag* (1796), J. F. von Schönfeld singles him out as 'one of our most excellent violinists', adding that he was 'one of the best pupils of the splendid Zissler [i.e. the violinist Joseph Zistler or Zissler]'. In 1789, while still a young boy, he performed to general admiration and acclaim at a concert in aid of Christian widows and orphans. He regularly played at private concerts, arranged musical soirées himself, and also composed. He often took part in chamber music sessions, for instance in a performance of Beethoven's Septet Op. 20 at Prince Odescalchi's* (in about 1801—*see Corr.* A56/B52). In 1803 he was engaged by Count Ferdinand Pálffy von Erdöd* as his director of music. In that same year he supported Beethoven in his dispute with Artaria & Co.* over their publication of the String Quintet Op. 29, affirming in a written statement that their edition was of little practical use to a performer.

It is not known whether Heinrich was related to the brothers **Emanuel Eppinger** (1768–1846) and **(Leopold) Joseph Eppinger** (1775/6–1860). The former was lessee of the hotel Zum römischen Kaiser [1 Renngasse], where Beethoven may have stayed in the winter of 1816–17 (*see* Hirsch*). The hotel had a large hall that was frequently used for concerts. It was there, for instance, that the 'Archduke' Trio was first performed, on 11 April 1814. Around that same period a small group of music lovers formed an association under the name 'Reunion', which organized regular Tuesday evening concerts at the hotel during the winter. According to Leopold von Sonnleithner,* the musical fare usually consisted of music for piano or string instruments; but sometimes larger works for full orchestra were also attempted. Sonnleithner adds that on 1 March 1814 he sang in the chorus at a performance of the oratorio *Christus am Ölberg*, conducted by Beethoven himself. (The journal *Friedensblätter*, in its issue of 9 March 1815, carried a report of another performance of the oratorio, again conducted by the composer, which Emanuel Eppinger had arranged at the hotel on 5 March in aid of a soldiers' charity fund.) During Carnival, the 'Reunion' society held a few balls at the hotel. The person mainly responsible for organizing the musical programme of these various entertainments was Emanuel's brother Joseph, a lawyer by training, who also used to sing at private concerts (for instance, those given by the blind pianist Maria Theresia von Paradis) and was the composer of a number of songs. Sonnleithner states that he was well known in Vienna for his offensively assertive character and the inflated opinion he had of his musical capabilities. Sonnleithner concedes nevertheless that, despite these defects, his activities produced good results at times. It was Joseph Eppinger, incidentally, who escorted Anselm Hüttenbrenner* to Beethoven's flat in 1816 and introduced him to the composer.

(Sonnleithner, Wurzbach[1])

Erdödy, Anna Maria [Marie], Countess, née Countess Niczky (b. Arad, Rumania, 21 August 1778 (according to F. Czeike, *Historisches Lexikon Wien*; according to Kinsky/Halm: 8 September 1779); d. Munich, 17 March 1837). Both she and her husband, Count Peter Erdödy (b. 1771), whom she married on 6 June 1796, came from old Hungarian aristocratic families. They had two daughters, Maria [Mimi] (b. 1799) and Friederike [Fritzi] (1801–19), and a son, August [Gusti] (1802–16). The couple lived apart from 1805; there is not a single reference to the husband in the extant Erdödy–Beethoven correspondence.

Beethoven's earliest documented contact with the countess dates from the year 1808, but he had almost certainly become acquainted with her much earlier; she had been living in Vienna since about 1803. During the winter of 1808–9 Beethoven occupied rooms in her apartment in Krugerstrasse [10 Krugerstrasse/9 Walfischgasse]. The countess, who was herself a competent pianist, frequently held musical soirées. Johann Friedrich Reichardt,* who was staying in Vienna at that time, mentions in his *Vertraute Briefe* attending several of these private concerts, at which Beethoven played some of his compositions and also improvised; on one occasion Schuppanzigh* performed with his Razumovsky* Quartet. Reichardt described the countess as a very pretty young woman, who, despite a chronic ailment, was of a very cheerful disposition. Watching her and a friend listening to Beethoven's music with rapt attention and evident admiration, he reflected: 'Fortunate the artist who can count on such listeners!'

Beethoven was clearly fond of the countess, but it is thought unlikely that he was in love with her; according to Schindler,* he called her his 'Beichtvater' [father confessor]. From a letter he wrote to Baron Gleichenstein,* probably in January 1809 (*Corr.* A198/B352), it appears that she took part in the negotiations which resulted his being granted annuities by Archduke Rudolph,* Prince Kinsky,* and Prince Lobkowitz.* But their friendship became seriously strained in the spring of 1809, when a dispute over a servant led Beethoven to seek new lodgings. The quarrel seems to have been quickly patched up, for in June and August of that year his two Piano Trios Op. 70 appeared with a dedication to her. A further, much longer break in their relations occurred between 1810 and 1815. However, in the latter year they resumed their close contact and Beethoven visited the countess on several occasions at her villa at Jedlesee, near Vienna [now part of the twenty-first district, Floridsdorf]. It was very probably for her and the cellist Joseph Linke,* who was staying at the villa at the time, that he wrote the two Cello Sonatas Op. 102 that summer. (They were first published, without a dedication, by Nikolaus Simrock* in Bonn in 1817; but the Viennese edition issued by Artaria & Co.* in 1819 bore a dedication to the countess.) Beethoven was also on friendly terms with Joseph Xaver Brauchle,* a member of her household.

At the end of September 1815 the countess went to her family estate at Pancovecz [Popovača], near Agram [Zagreb] in Croatia, and from there she moved to Padua, where she is believed to have spent about a year. Her son died there on 18 April 1816. Beethoven wrote to commiserate with her as soon as he heard the news (*Corr.* A634/B935). She spent the years 1817–19 in Croatia, except, perhaps, for brief visits to Vienna; for New Year 1820 Beethoven sent her his best wishes in the form of a canon (WoO 176). She was to stay in Vienna more frequently in the years 1820–3, which were reportedly difficult ones for her, although the nature of her problems is not fully known; G. Haupt concluded, after examining various police records, that she was the victim of an intrigue conducted by a sister-in-law who falsely denounced her, as well as Brauchle. In the end she left Vienna, either of her own free will or by order of the authorities, and from 1824 until her death she lived in Munich. She does not seem to have had any further contact with Beethoven. The villa at Jedlesee, which she sold before her departure, burnt down in 1863 and was subsequently rebuilt in a different form. A small Beethoven museum opened in the new building [17 Jeneweingasse] in June 1974.

(Czeike, Haupt[1], Reichardt, Schöne)

Ertmann, (Catharina) Dorothea, Baroness, née Graumann (b. Frankfurt am Main (according to H. Federhofer), 3 May 1781; d. Vienna, 16 March 1849). The daughter of a Frankfurt businessman, Georg Carl Graumann (1747–1810), she married the Austrian army officer Baron Stephan Ertmann (d. 1835) at Frankfurt on 5 August 1798; a captain at the time, he would eventually rise to the rank of lieutenant-field marshal. She was an outstanding pianist. Nothing is known about her early life, nor about her music teachers, but it is evident from the catalogue of the musical scores which were in her possession in 1797 that she was then already a highly competent performer, with a wide-ranging acquaintance with contemporary works. Among the items listed are sixteen early works by Beethoven—variations for the piano for two or four hands, compositions for piano and violin, the Piano Trios Op. 1, the Piano Sonatas Op. 2, and the Cello Sonatas Op. 5.

The Ertmanns were living in Vienna by early 1803 at the latest, for a report (probably written by August von Kotzebue*) on musical activities in the Austrian capital, which appeared in the Berlin periodical *Der Freimüthige* in April of that year, praises the 'amazing precision, clarity, and delicacy' of her playing. Dorothea later told her niece, the famous singing teacher Mathilde Marchesi, that she had made Beethoven's acquaintance at Tobias Haslinger's* music shop, where she was sight-reading some of his recently published sonatas. She reportedly became his pupil, which probably signifies that he helped her gain a better understanding of his piano works, for which she felt a special affinity. At the beginning of 1804 she received a card conveying New Year's greetings 'from her friend and admirer Beethoven'.

Dorothea Ertmann greatly impressed everyone with her superb technical and interpretative skills. After hearing her play a Beethoven sonata, Johann Friedrich Reichardt* wrote in one of his *Vertraute Briefe* in 1809: 'Never have I encountered such power allied to such exquisite delicacy, not even in the greatest virtuosi.' On another occasion he heard her performing 'a great fantasia by Beethoven [presumably the Sonata Op. 27, No. 2, which was one of her favourite pieces] with a power, wealth of feeling, and perfection which delighted us all'. And in yet another letter he reports that when Muzio Clementi* first heard her, he was so delighted with her playing that he repeatedly called out 'Elle joue en grand maître'. It has been stated that she received instruction in Vienna from the excellent young German pianist Wilhelm Karl Rust, but this seems unlikely since he did not arrive in Vienna until 1807 (when he was 20), by which time her fame was already well established. Reichardt no doubt puts their association into a more correct perspective when he attributes Rust's increasing understanding of the music of Bach and Handel to her influence: 'For the past year he has had the good fortune to practise the sublime works of both with this great artist (for she plays them also in a masterly fashion) and has much profited from the experience.' Among Dorothea's foremost admirers was Schindler,* who devotes a lengthy passage in his Beethoven biography to a description of her 'unequalled' playing of his compositions. He pays, moreover, warm tribute to the considerable and beneficial influence she exercised on the musical taste of Viennese society. In his words, 'she was a conservatory all by herself'.

In February 1817, at about the time when she moved from Vienna to nearby St Pölten, where her husband's regiment was stationed, Beethoven dedicated to her his Piano Sonata in A flat (Op. 101). Three years later Baron Ertmann was posted to Milan. It is possible, as A. C. Kalischer states, that during the following years Dorothea 'not infrequently visited Vienna and did not fail to contact her revered teacher and composer', but there is no trustworthy evidence to support this assertion. Kalischer would appear to have based it entirely on an entry in the conversation books in April 1824, in which Schindler mentions having recently played the Piano Trio Op. 97 with the baroness and goes on to assure Beethoven that he would derive much pleasure from hearing how she now performs it (*BKh*6/83). However, this entry has since been identified as one of Schindler's forgeries, and the information is therefore suspect. On the other hand, there is firm evidence that the Ertmanns met Beethoven when they stayed in Vienna from 30 May to 16 September 1826. One of the meetings may have taken place at the house of Dorothea's sister Anna Maria (*c*.1786–1838) at Dornbach. (Anna Maria was married to the prominent merchant and banker Johann Jacob von Franck who handled some of Beethoven's financial transactions.) It was while the Ertmanns were in Vienna that Karl van Beethoven* attempted suicide. He and Beethoven hoped afterwards that Baron Ertmann would take him into his regiment, but Ertmann was either unable or unwilling to do so. Stephan von Breuning* was subsequently able to arrange for Karl to join Baron Stutterheim's* regiment.

(Federhofer[4], Kalischer, Reichardt, Schindler[1])

Eskeles (family). Wealthy Viennese family whose head, **Bernhard** (b. Vienna, 12 February 1753; d. Hietzing, near Vienna, 7 August 1839), became in 1785 a partner of the bankers and wholesale merchants Nathan Adam Arnsteiner and Salomon Herz. After Herz retired in 1805, the firm, which long played a prominent role in national financial affairs, was renamed 'Arnstein & Eskeles'. Some ten years later Eskeles took over the management of the business. He was one of the founders of the Nationalbank in 1816; he was ennobled in 1797 and made a baron in 1822.

In 1800 he married **Cäcilia** Wulff (1760–1826), a daughter of the Berlin banker Daniel Itzig, who was divorced from her first husband; her sister Franziska [Fanny], who had married Nathan Adam Arnsteiner in 1776, became one of Vienna's most celebrated hostesses. Eskeles and his wife likewise held many brilliant receptions at their mansions at Hietzing and in central Vienna. Their town house [11 Dorotheergasse] now contains the Jewish Museum of the City of Vienna.

Beethoven had some dealings with Eskeles's bank. It was moreover on Eskeles's advice that Beethoven bought eight shares in the Nationalbank in July 1819. This was the most important investment he made in his whole life. (He later sold one of the shares; the others, which he bequeathed to his nephew Karl,* were found after his death in a secret drawer in his rooms.) Another of Beethoven's known associations with the Eskeles family is of a musical nature: on 20 January 1823 he made a setting (WoO 151) of the lines 'Der edle Mensch sei hülfreich und gut' from Goethe's* poem 'Das Göttliche' for the private album of either Baroness

Cäcilia or her daughter **Marie** (1801–62). It is even possible that he later made a similar entry in the album belonging to the other of the two ladies (*see BKh6/221*, and *BKh8/126*). Marie, and perhaps also her mother, were apparently present at the private performance of the String Quartet in A minor (Op. 132) on 9 September 1825 (*see* Smart*) and at the meal which followed it. On that occasion Maurice Schlesinger* assured Beethoven that Marie was an excellent pianist and that she adored his compositions; and she herself told his nephew Karl that she enjoyed playing his uncle's music more than that of any other composer. She furthermore offered to help Karl obtain a position in her father's firm, but, for different reasons, his hopes for a commercial career were not fulfilled (*see also* the article on Karl). Marie, who married Count Franz Wimpffen (1797–1870) in October 1825, assembled a large collection of musicians' autographs, which her son eventually bequeathed to the Gesellschaft der Musikfreunde.* Among the items was Beethoven's autograph of WoO 151.

Esterházy de Galántha, Almerie Franziska Ursula [Almérie-Françoise-Ursule], Countess (b. Valenciennes (?Paris), 24 December (?September) 1789; d. Öden-burg [Sopron], 25 January 1848); elder daughter of Count Valentin Ladislaus Ferdinand Esterházy de Galántha (1740–1805/13) and his wife Maria Franziska Ursula, née Countess Hallweil [Hallewyl] (1766–1814). The late Czech music historian and writer Jaroslav Celeda believed that Almerie was Beethoven's 'Immortal Beloved' (for other current candidates, *see* Brentano* and Brunsvik de Korompa*).

The typescript, completed in the 1960s, in which Celeda set out the results of his research and the conclusions he drew from them has remained unpublished until now, but it is due to appear in print in Prague in late 2000 in an edition, pre-pared by Oldrich Pulkert and further revised by Hans-Werther Küthen, which is to form part of the compendium *Ludwig van Beethoven im Herzen Europas: Leben und Nachleben in den böhmischen Ländern* (edited by the same two scholars). The present article is based on an English translation of this edition by William Meredith which appeared in the Summer 2000 issue of the American Beethoven Society's *Beethoven Journal*. (See *also* Meredith's 'Mortal Musings: Testing the Candidacy of Almerie Esterházy against the Antonie Brentano Theory' in the same issue.)

Altogether the biographical data given by Celeda, some of which are cited above, need to be treated with great caution (in this connection see the final para-graphs below). He relates that the family was split up by the French Revolution, because the count, a general in the Hussar regiment and a long-time confidant of Louis XVI and Marie Antoinette, left France in *c.* 1791 to seek refuge abroad, notably in St Petersburg, whilst his wife remained in Paris with their children until 1805 (but during his exile the count is said to have still paid an occasional visit to Paris, which would explain Celeda's statement that the countess gave birth there to a son, Ladislaus, in July 1797). Eventually, Celeda writes, the family was reunited and settled in Eisenstadt and Vienna in 1805.

Celeda does not pretend to know for certain where Beethoven and Almeria could have first met, but he suggests that it might have been at Eisenstadt in September 1807 (on the composer's brief stay there at that time *see* Esterházy von Galántha, Nikolaus (II)*). It is, in any case, Celeda's contention that they were deeply in love by 1811. He speculates further that Beethoven may have decided to visit Bohemia in 1812 only after learning of Countess Esterházy's intention of going there with her two daughters; that the letter he wrote to his 'Immortal Beloved' after arriving at Teplitz [Teplice] in early July was meant for Almerie, who is known to have stayed at Karlsbad from 29 June until 15 September with her mother and younger sister Everilde (the count is also said to have been there during part of that period); that Beethoven sent the letter to Almerie; and that their relationship was discovered by her parents, who were adamantly opposed to the idea of one of their daughters marrying a person other than an aristocrat, 'particularly if the potential bridegroom was an artist with an uncertain existence . . . and furthermore was said to be an only too well known enemy of the nobility and the ruling Austrian house' (a rather sweeping statement, in view of Beethoven's often close relations with some of his aristocratic patrons and with Archduke Rudolph). Given the parents' attitude, Celeda concludes, their decision 'could hardly have been other' than to send the discovered letter back to Beethoven and to prevent any further contact between him and Almeria. Beethoven, having learnt of the parents' hostility or suspecting that 'something bad had happened', hastened to Karlsbad at the end of July, but was not able to see Almerie during the approximately ten days he spent there. Celeda believes, however, that during his further stay at Karlsbad in September Beethoven succeeded in meeting her one afternoon, when he came across her 'alone in the countryside'. Having unsuccessfully tried to persuade her to leave her family there and then and come away with him, he 'spun around without a word and disappeared quickly without saying good-bye'. They never spoke to each other again. (Celeda took some details, including the lovers' alleged final, dramatic encounter at Karlsbad, from Carl Pidoll's *Verklungenes Spiel*, a book which relates certain episodes in Beethoven's life as they were supposedly described in the—in fact, entirely fictitious—memoirs of his friend Nikolaus Zmeskall von Domanovecz.*)

On 6 September 1815 Almerie married Count Albert Joseph Murray de Melgum (1774–1848), a high military officer, to whom she was to bear four daughters. According to Celeda, Beethoven was, however, to encounter her on one further occasion; for he surmises that she was the woman with whom Beethoven exchanged glances as she drove by him one July day at Baden and whom, in an emotional note about the incident, he identified merely by the initial 'M'. Celeda ascribes this incident to the year 1818. (Joseph Schmidt-Görg, on the strength of the watermarks in the paper, dated the note to the year 1807, and identified 'M' as Marie Bigot;* but it is presumably not impossible that Beethoven could have used some of the paper he acquired in 1807 at a later date.)

Celeda's exposition of his theory is interesting and, in part, quite persuasive— indeed, it could in certain respects be regarded as more plausible than some of the arguments which have been put forward in support of the candidacies of Antonie Brentano and Countess Josephine Brunsvik. But the fact remains that no firm evidence has so far been found that Beethoven and Almerie ever actually met, let alone fell passionately in love. All this speculation therefore needs more solid backing if the theory is to gain general acceptance.

His identification of Countess Almerie Esterházy as the 'Immortal Beloved' leads Celeda to a further deduction which may not convince everyone: if Beethoven started, in February 1815, to make 'bitter and satirical' use of high military titles in his communications to the publisher S. A. Steiner* and the latter's associates, the reason must be that he had learnt of Almerie's plans to wed Count Murray de Melgum from the reports of the forthcoming marriage which 'at the beginning of 1815 . . . began to circulate in Viennese society'. (No evidence is cited to prove the existence of these alleged reports.) Beethoven, Celeda asserts, was attempting to compensate for his powerlessness, of which he was all too painfully conscious, by mocking the social class whose members were depriving him of his every chance of happiness.

Whether Beethoven's intention, in resorting to these terms, was really 'to debase the high military' may be a matter for debate. It should, in any case, be pointed out that Beethoven's letter to Steiner of 1 February 1815, in which this terminology first occurs in his correspondence, is merely his earliest *known* communication to that publisher, but almost certainly not his very first, seeing that their contacts went back at least to 1813 (*see* the article on Steiner). It is therefore by no means certain that he had not already employed these titles on earlier occasions, before any rumours of Almerie's forthcoming marriage could have circulated. Besides, war had been 'in the air' for many years and Beethoven had already signalled his own interest in military matters by composing *Wellingtons Sieg* in 1813. Moreover, Steiner was to buy the latter composition in May 1815 (and his firm would publish it the following year), so its purchase may well already have been under discussion between himself and Beethoven at the beginning of 1815 or even earlier; perhaps it was during these negotiations that Beethoven came to adopt military terminology in his dealings with his prospective publishers. (Incidentally, Wellington himself arrived in Vienna on 1 February 1815—the very day on which Beethoven wrote the aforesaid letter to Steiner—in order to take part in the Congress.) It is also worth remembering that at the time of the Congress Vienna was filled with high-ranking and distinguished military officers of various nations who must have offered its citizens a highly impressive spectacle of colourful uniforms and glittering decorations. One of the most splendid military parades of that period took place in the Prater on 18 October 1814 before the monarchs of Austria, Russia, and Prussia, in commemoration of the Battle of Leipzig the previous year. Might not the presence in Vienna of all these soldiers have been at least one reason for Beethoven's jocular (or satirical?) use of these military terms?

Finally, it is curious that no mention is made in this edition of Celeda's manuscript (at any rate, there is no such mention in the English version) of the fact that certain of his biographical data concerning Count Esterházy and his family differ from those given in the count's own memoirs, published by Ernest Daudet in Paris in 1905. (This is especially strange as there is a reference to these memoirs, and even a quotation from them.) The differences are far from minor. Thus Celeda writes that the count's 'date and place of birth are unknown' and adds that 'it is however very probable that he was born in 1740 or 1741', whereas the count himself declares firmly: 'I was born on 22 October in the year 1740.' Furthermore, whilst Celeda gives Almerie's date of birth as 24 September 1789 and the place as Paris, the count states that she was born on 24 December 1789 at Valenciennes. Also, according to the count's memoirs, the birth in 1797 of his son Ladislaus [Ladislas] did not take place in Paris, as Celeda says, but in Russia, where the countess had joined her husband in January 1793. Her arrival there is, moreover, amply confirmed by the count's letters, two series of which were published by E. Daudet in 1907 and 1909.

In short, most of Celeda's (or his editors') remarks about the couple's activities during the Revolution need to be re-examined, and in several instances corrected, in the light of the account presented in the memoirs and the correspondence. In particular, the statements that after her husband's emigration 'his twenty-four-year-old wife remained with her children in Vincennes', throughout the horrors of the Revolution and until 1805, and that 'for fifteen years [i.e. from *c.* 1791] Valentin Esterházy only communicated with his family through letters' are entirely contradicted by the evidence presented by the memoirs and the correspondence, which show that the Esterházys left France in the summer of 1790 and that none of them were in Paris during the Reign of Terror. The family spent the autumn of 1790 and the succeeding winter in England, and they were living at Tournai when the count was sent to St Petersburg at the end of August 1791 as representative of the two brothers of Louis XVI. In the spring of 1792 the countess and her children moved to Aix-la-Chapelle, and in January 1793 they joined the count in Russia. During the following years they lived there and in the part of Poland which was then under Russian domination. In fact, Daudet, in his introduction to the count's memoirs, records that Esterházy died, 'surrounded by his family', at the village of Grodek in Volhynia [now part of Ukraine] on 23 July 1805 (in his memoirs, the count mentions that tsar Paul I has granted him possession of Grodek). According to Celeda, on the other hand, the count died, aged seventy-two, 'at the end' of 1813 (it is not stated where—whether in Hungary,

Eisenstadt, or Vienna); and Celeda adds that his forty-eight-year-old widow gave birth to his posthumous son Karl, apparently in Vienna, on 18 September 1814(!).

Clearly, it will be necessary to check Daudet's and Celeda's conflicting statements about Count Esterházy's death, and also to revise Celeda's remarks about Almerie's youth. Especially misleading is the suggestion, in reference to her initial contacts with Beethoven, that he might 'have been interested in her on account of . . . the events which she had actually experienced jointly with her mother [in Paris] and which occupied Beethoven's strong interest at this time in connection to his *Sinfonia eroica*'. Almerie was less than one year old when she left France with her mother in August 1790.

(Celeda, Esterházy[1,2,3], Pidoll, Schmidt-Görg[6])

Esterházy de Galántha, Maria (Josepha Hermenegild), Princess (b. 13 April 1768; d. 8 August 1845). Daughter of Prince Franz Joseph of Liechtenstein (1726–81); sister of Field Marshal Prince Johann (Joseph) of Liechtenstein (1760–1836), a soldier of great renown. On 15 September 1783 she married Prince Nikolaus (II) Esterházy de Galántha.* Beethoven dedicated to her the three Marches Op. 45 in 1804.

Esterházy de Galántha, Nikolaus (II), Prince (b. 12 December 1765; d. Como, 25 November 1833). Son of Prince Paul Anton Esterházy (1738–94), and grandson of Nikolaus the 'Magnificent' (1714–90) who was Haydn's* employer for almost three decades; husband of Maria (Josepha Hermenegild) Esterházy.* An ardent music lover and generous patron (he was among the subscribers to Beethoven's Trios Op. 1), he revived the orchestra at Eisenstadt which his father had disbanded. Among the highlights of the year were the festivities in honour of the princess's name day, 8 September, which included notably the celebration of a special Mass in the palace chapel on the following Sunday. Haydn composed several of his Masses for these events.

Early in 1807 the prince commissioned Beethoven to supply the Mass for that year's celebrations. (Beethoven may have received the commission already in late 1806.) After some delays, he was able to complete the work (Op. 86) in time, but in a letter on 26 July, in which he promised to deliver the score by 20 August, he added that he would do so 'with considerable apprehension, since you, most noble Prince, are accustomed to having the inimitable masterpieces of the great Haydn performed for you'. His anxiety was justified, for when the Mass, which was indeed different in style from Haydn's, was performed on 13 September, it failed to please the prince. The latter appears, moreover, to have made his disappointment known to the composer who had gone to Eisenstadt to direct the performance, though the prince may not have done so in the rather bizarre manner described by Schindler.* Schindler did not, of course, know Beethoven at the time and must have heard the story several years later. Thus the question he attributes to Esterházy—'But, my dear Beethoven, whatever have you composed this time?'—may be as inaccurate as the date (1810) and the prince's name (Paul) which appeared in his version of the incident in the first edition of his Beethoven biography. Nevertheless, of Esterházy's dissatisfaction there can be no doubt, for in a letter to Countess Henriette Zielinska he wrote: 'Beethoven's Mass is unbearably ridiculous and detestable . . . I feel angry and humiliated.' Beethoven, who was to have remained some time at Eisenstadt and was even due to give a concert there, cut short his stay. But Schindler is incorrect in stating that he left on the day of the performance; he departed on 16 September.

In view of the unfavourable reception of the Mass by Esterházy, it is a little surprising to read in Beethoven's letter to Breitkopf & Härtel* of 8 June 1808 that 'it has been produced in several places, including Prince Esterházy's residence, where it was performed to great applause in honour of the princess's name day'; but then Beethoven was trying, in 1808, to sell the Mass to the Leipzig publishers. More significant is the fact that, although the manuscript copy preserved in the Esterházy archives bears in the title (which is not in Beethoven's hand) a dedication to the prince, when the Mass was published in 1812 it was dedicated to Prince Ferdinand Kinsky* instead. Furthermore, Beethoven clearly still remembered Esterházy's criticism when he sent him an invitation to subscribe to the *Missa solemnis* in 1823. 'I doubt that it will be successful,' he told Schindler, 'for I believe that he is not well disposed towards me, at any rate judging by his attitude years ago' (*Corr.* A1188/B1662). As he had predicted, the prince declined to subscribe.

(Harich, Schindler[1])

Fischenich, Bartholomäus Ludwig (b. Bonn, 2 August 1768; d. Berlin, 4 June 1831). Jurist; teacher. After studying at the universities of Cologne and Bonn, he was appointed professor of natural law at the University of Bonn on 27 April 1791, with the understanding that he would not take up the position until the following year, but would pursue advanced studies in natural and international law under Gottlieb Hufeland at Jena in the intervening period. While he was at Jena, he formed a close friendship with Friedrich Schiller* and his wife Charlotte. After his return to Bonn he soon won the respect and admiration of his students, and in 1793 he was granted the title 'Hofrat'; from 1800 he taught jurisprudence at the Zentralschule. Before long, however, he left academia. In 1811 he became president of the court of justice at Aix-la-Chapelle, and in 1819 he joined the Prussian ministry of justice in Berlin with the rank of Geheimer Oberjustizrat.

Fischenich knew the young Beethoven well; what is more, he early on appreciated his genius. On 26 January 1793 he sent Beethoven's setting of Sophie Mereau's* poem 'Feuerfarb' (Op. 52, No. 2) to Charlotte Schiller, introducing it as the work of 'a young local man whose musical talent is highly praised by everyone'. He further mentioned that Beethoven was planning to set Schiller's 'An die

Freude', strophe by strophe; and he added: 'I expect something splendid, for, from what I know of him, he is interested only in what is great and noble.'

(Braubach[1])

Fischer, Gottfried (Bonn, 21 July 1780; d. Bonn, 23 February 1864). The house in the Rheingasse in Bonn in which he grew up had been owned by his family for several generations. Among its tenants were Beethoven's grandfather Ludwig, who had a flat there for some thirty years, and Beethoven's parents. Beethoven himself lived in the house [24 Rheingasse] for some ten years as a young boy, from *c*.1775.

In about 1838 Fischer, a baker by profession, began writing down his recollections about the Beethoven family, together with those of his sister Cäcilia (1762–1845). It was no accident that he decided to do so then, for the composer was the subject of much local interest at that time: Franz Gerhard Wegeler's* and Ferdinand Ries's* *Biographische Notizen über Ludwig van Beethoven* appeared that year (at Koblenz), there was a renewed debate about the location of the house in which Beethoven was born, and plans were going ahead for the erection of a local monument to him (*see* Hähnel*).

Cäcilia's contributions to the text were of considerable value, for, being eighteen years older than her brother, she was able to provide information about the Beethoven family of which Fischer had no direct knowledge. The final manuscript was completed at the earliest in the 1850s. Fischer tried to find a publisher for it, but failed. After his death, it was placed in the archives of the city of Bonn; later the city presented it to the Verein Beethoven-Haus. The integral text was first published by J. Schmidt-Görg (*Des Bonner Bäckermeisters Gottfried Fischer Aufzeichnungen über Beethovens Jugend*, Bonn, 1971). It is of undoubted interest to Beethoven scholars, inasmuch as it offers certain information not available elsewhere. The house in Rheingasse, which Fischer sold before 1850, was destroyed in an air raid in October 1944.

(Fischer[4])

Fischhof, Joseph (b. Butschowitz [Bučovice, Czech Republic], 4 April 1804; d. Baden, near Vienna, 28 June 1857). Pianist, teacher, and music historian. He studied medicine at the University of Vienna, and music with Anton Halm* and Ignaz von Seyfried.* In 1827 he decided to make music his career. He gave private lessons and, from 1833 to 1848, also taught at the conservatoire of the Gesellschaft der Musikfreunde.* His library, which, in addition to a vast number of printed and manuscript scores, contained many books and documents, was bought after his death by the Berlin music dealer Julius Friedlaender, who sold the bulk of it to the Königlich-Preussische Bibliothek [now Staatsbibliothek] in Berlin.

Among the items thus acquired by the Berlin library was a manuscript copy of various texts by or about Beethoven; the copy had been made for Fischhof in 1842 or earlier. Most of the contents were taken from an earlier copy of the material, made soon after Beethoven's death in preparation for a biography which Anton Gräffer, an employee of Artaria & Co.,* was planning to write, perhaps together with Jakob Hotschevar* and Karl Holz.*

The so-called Fischhof Manuscript comprises forty-four sheets and presents documents, correspondence, and a diary by Beethoven dating from the years 1812–18, as well as anecdotes and reminiscences about the composer. For a modern transcription (excluding the diary), *see* Brenneis[2] in the Bibliography and for modern editions of the diary, *see* Solomon[1].

(Brenneis[1,2], Johnson[1])

Ford, Richard (1796–1858). Writer and traveller, best known for his *Handbook for Travellers in Spain* (1845) and *Gatherings from Spain* (1846); he was also a contributor to the *Edinburgh Review*, *Quarterly Review*, and *Westminster Review*. On 28 November 1817 Beethoven composed for him a twenty-three-bar string quartet movement. The autograph was discovered in England in 1999 and sold at auction by Sotheby's in London on 8 December of that year, when it was acquired by the Bodmer Foundation of Zurich. The movement had been played by the Eroica String Quartet at Sotheby's on 8 October.

(Cooper[5])

Förster, Emanuel Aloys (b. Niederstein, Silesia, 26 January 1748; d. Vienna, 12 November 1823). Composer, pianist, theorist, and teacher. During the 1780s he settled in Vienna, where he came to be highly respected as a musician; among his acquaintances were Haydn* and Mozart.* After the latter's death he applied for the now vacant position of court chamber composer (unsuccessfully, for the position was eliminated). In a testimonial in his support, a certain Augustinus Erasmus Donath claimed that he had frequently heard Mozart tell Förster that he was 'without a doubt the most excellent and skilful keyboard player after himself'. In his *Jahrbuch der Tonkunst von Wien und Prag* (1796), J. F. von Schönfeld describes Förster more soberly as 'one of our good pianists'. As a composer, Förster is known principally for his string quartets; he also wrote variations and sonatas for the piano, as well as some other works.

Beethoven met Förster at the chamber music sessions which were regularly held at Prince Karl Lichnowsky's.* Franz Gerhard Wegeler* describes in some detail (in *Biographische Notizen*) one particular occasion on which Beethoven took part there in the performance of a new quartet by Förster. According to information later supplied to Thayer* by one of Förster's sons (to whom Beethoven had given piano lessons in 1802 and again in 1804), Beethoven also played in quartets at Förster's and frequently visited him at other times. It is even possible that Beethoven may have briefly studied quartet composition with him. He certainly had a high opinion of Förster as a teacher, for he recommended him to Count Razumovsky,* Charles Neate,* and Cipriani Potter.* Förster's son stated further that Beethoven had encouraged his father to publish his manual *Anleitung zum Generalbass* (Leipzig, 1805); it contains references to some of Beethoven's works.

(Longyear, Orel[3], Wegeler/Ries)

Forti, Anton (b. Vienna, 8 June 1790; d. Vienna, 16 July 1859). Singer (baritone). He began his musical career as a violist in the Theater an der Wien orchestra, but in 1807/8 he was engaged as a singer at Prince Esterházy's* theatre at Eisenstadt, where he remained for three years. From 1813 until 1834 he performed at the Kärntnertor-Theater, except for a brief engagement in 1830 at the Königstädtisches Theater, Berlin (following a successful guest appearance there the previous year). He was particularly admired for his interpretation of Mozart* roles: Count Almaviva, Sarastro, and, above all, Don Giovanni.

He did not, as stated in *New Grove*, sing Pizarro at the first performance of the final version of *Fidelio* in 1814; on that occasion (23 May 1814) the role was taken by Johann Michael Vogl.* Forti did, however, substitute for the indisposed Vogl at the seventh performance on 18 July. On 14 July Beethoven wrote to Archduke Rudolph: 'As a result of Vogel's [*sic*] illness, I have been able to realize my desire to give the role of Pizarro to Forti, whose voice is better suited to the part.' The Leipzig *Allgemeine musikalische Zeitung* reported that 'Herr Forti . . . was entirely successful in the role.' When, after an absence of more than three years, *Fidelio* returned to the Kärntnertor-Theater in a new production on 3 November 1822, Forti once again appeared as Pizarro. He was also associated with another Beethoven work, the cantata *Der glorreiche Augenblick*, at the first performance of which, on 29 November 1814, he took one of the solo parts. However, when it came to choosing the singer for the solo bass part in the Ninth Symphony, Beethoven preferred Joseph Preisinger to him (in the end, though, Preisinger withdrew, and at the first performance on 7 May 1824 the part was sung by Joseph Seipelt).

Forti's wife Henriette Theimer (1796–1818) was a soprano who sang at the Theater an der Wien and later at the court opera.

(Czeike, Forbes[1], Kutsch/Riemens, Ledebur)

Fouqué, Friedrich (Heinrich Carl), Baron **de La Motte** (Brandenburg an der Havel, 12 February 1777; d. Berlin, 23 January 1843). Dramatist, novelist, and poet. In 1808–10 he published a mythological trilogy in verse (*Der Held des Nordens: Sigurd der Schlangentöter, Sigurds Rache, Aslauga*), based on the Icelandic *Edda*. He followed it in 1811 with the fairy tale *Undine*, the most successful of his works. A three-volume novel, *Der Zauberring*, with a plot which combined the chivalric with the magic, appeared in 1813, and in 1815 he published the romance *Die Fahrten Thiodulfs des Isländers*. By 1816 Fouqué was thus a very popular and highly regarded writer whose quintessentially Romantic works were closely attuned to contemporary taste.

In a letter on 6 January 1816 Beethoven asked Anna Milder-Hauptmann,* who had been appearing with great success in *Fidelio* in Berlin, to invite Fouqué to 'invent a subject for a grand opera' for him, which would at the same time have a suitable role for her. Beethoven assured her that she would thereby 'render a great service to myself and to the German theatre'. He would compose the opera exclusively for Berlin, 'for I shall never manage to persuade our miserly management here to produce a new opera of mine'. If Milder-Hauptmann sent a reply to Beethoven's letter, it has been lost. As far as is known, Beethoven made no further attempt to approach Fouqué.

A few months after Beethoven wrote to Milder-Hauptmann, E. T. A. Hoffmann's 'magic opera' *Undine*, based on Fouqué's story, was produced in Berlin (3 August 1816). Years later Beethoven considered setting Grillparzer's* libretto *Melusina* which treated a kindred subject.

(Schulz)

Frank [Franck], **(Johann) Peter** (b. Rothalben, Baden, Germany, 19 March 1745; d. Vienna, 24 April 1821). Physician and hygienist. After qualifying at Heidelberg in 1766, he started his medical career at Bitsch in Lorraine [now Bitche, France], and subsequently served as court physician to Margrave August Georg of Baden-Baden at Rastatt (1769–71) and, from 1772, as medical officer at Bruchsal; in addition, he was from 1775 the personal physician of Count August Limburg-Styrum, prince bishop of Speyer. In 1784 he left Bruchsal to teach medicine at the University of Göttingen; in 1785 he took up a post at the University of Pavia, and the following year he became director of the town's hospital. Shortly afterwards he was placed in charge of all medical services in Lombardy. In 1779 he had begun to publish what was to be his *magnum opus*, the six-volume *System einer vollständigen medicinischen Polizey* (1779–1819).

In 1795 Frank was appointed professor of medicine at the University of Vienna and director of the Allgemeines Krankenhaus [General Hospital] which had been founded in 1784 and was then the most important hospital in Europe. His son **Joseph** (1771–1842) temporarily took over his duties in Padua before himself accepting a senior post at the same hospital in Vienna. In 1804 both father and son left for Vilna [Vilnius, Lithuania], where they had been offered professorships. However, whereas Joseph spent the next twenty years at Vilna, his father moved in 1805 to St Petersburg. There, as rector of the Academy of Medicine and Surgery, he planned and carried out significant pedagogical and institutional reforms. He left Russia in 1808 and the following year, in Vienna, Napoleon invited him to become his personal physician and, at the same time, inspector-general of medical services in Paris, but Frank declined the offer. Instead, he settled for a time at Freiburg im Breisgau, and, while there, devoted his time to writing. In 1811 he returned to Vienna where he was to spend the remainder of his life. Frank is regarded as the founder of hygiene as an independent science. Though some of his ideas proved controversial, he was, as his career amply demonstrates, one of the most respected and influential medical practitioners of his time. His son Joseph also had a successful, if less illustrious, career, during which he instituted important reforms in the medical services of Vilna; he also published extensively.

Beethoven knew both Peter and Joseph Frank. In a letter to Franz Gerhard Wegeler* on 29 June 1801 he mentions having been treated by 'Frank' for his chronic diarrhoea and increasing deafness, but with no resulting improvement. (Since he does not give the doctor's first name, it is not possible to determine whether he means the father or the son.) Furthermore, Leopold von Sonnleithner* told Thayer* that both Peter and Joseph Frank, but especially the latter, had been very fond of music and that Beethoven had regularly performed at the musical soirées which Joseph Frank had arranged at his father's house [20 Alserstrasse] near the hospital (*see also* the article on Joseph's wife Christine Gerhardi*). Sonnleithner added that Beethoven used to correct the cantatas which Joseph composed for his father's birthday and name day.

(Biach, Breyer)

Franul von Weissenthurn, Johanna, née Grünberg (b. Koblenz, 16 February 1773; d. Vienna, 17 May 1847). Actress and playwright, under the name 'Johanna Weissenthurn'. She was engaged at the Munich court theatre in 1787; the following year she performed at the municipal theatre at Baden, near Vienna, and from 1789 at the court theatre in Vienna. In 1791 she married A. Franul von Weissenthurn. She remained a member of the Burgtheater company until 1842, and was also the author of numerous comedies and romantic dramas.

An autograph of Beethoven's song 'Man strebt die Flamme zu verhehlen . . .' (WoO 120) in the possession of the Gesellschaft der Musikfreunde* is inscribed 'pour madame Weissenthurn par louis van Beethoven'. The composition is believed to date from *c*.1795. The original title of the poem and the poet's name are not known. The song was not published in Beethoven's lifetime.

(Czeike, Eisenberg)

Frey, Michael (bapt. Ladenburg, near Heidelberg, 19 September 1786; d. Mannheim, 10 August 1832). Composer, violinist, and Kapellmeister. In 1807 he was appointed a court musician in the grand duchy of Baden, and in the winter of 1808–9 he studied with Spohr* at Gotha. From about the middle of November 1815 until the following April he stayed in Vienna where he received instruction from Förster* and Salieri.* The diary which he kept during this time bears testimony to the wealth of musical activities which a visitor to Vienna could then enjoy, and in some of which Frey himself participated. He met many of the leading amateur and professional musicians who were then in Vienna, among them Beethoven, on whom he called several times. On the first occasion, on 24 November 1815, Beethoven told him, 'with tears in his eyes', of his brother Kaspar Karl's* recent death.

Frey had the greatest admiration for Beethoven's music, and the musical experiences he was able to savour in Vienna only served to convince him of Beethoven's greatness and originality. He attended several concerts given by the Schuppanzigh* Quartet at the hotel Zum römischen Kaiser. After hearing them play the String Quartet Op. 74, he wrote in his diary: 'This marvellous quartet inspired in me, like all his compositions, the greatest admiration for his genius. It is, like all his compositions, so original and inventive that it is difficult to follow the composer's ideas while one is listening to it.' After hearing *Fidelio* for the first time (he subsequently attended a further performance), he noted: 'Never has an opera by a contemporary composer made such an impression on me.' He visited Beethoven for the last time a week before he left Vienna.

Frey later became Kapellmeister of the Mannheim court orchestra. In 1824, according to a report in the Leipzig *Allgemeine musikalische Zeitung*, he was director of the Mannheim opera. In a letter to the publishers Schott* in June 1827, the singer and stage director Wilhelm Ehlers refers to 'Herr Musikdirektor Frey' as 'a pupil of Beethoven' (*Corr.* B2178 n. 5). There is nothing in Frey's Viennese diary to support this statement.

(Frey)

Friedelberg [Friedlsberg], **Joseph** (b. ?1780/1; d. 19 September 1800). Poet. A number of his poems appeared in the *Wiener Musenalmanach* between 1794 and 1796. When, in the latter year, in the face of a likely invasion of Austria by Napoleon, volunteer corps were formed at various points in the country, Friedelberg joined the one established in Vienna. A poem he wrote to mark the departure of the corps was set to music by Beethoven in 'Abschiedsgesang an Wiens Bürger' (WoO 121) and the composition was published by Artaria & Co.* in November 1796, with a dedication to the corps commander, Major von Kövesdy. The following April, by which time Napoleon had advanced deep into Austria and was approaching Vienna, Beethoven set a further poem by Friedelberg in 'Kriegslied der Österreicher' (WoO 122); the setting was published, again by Artaria & Co., at the end of that month. Friedelberg later served as a sublieutenant in the war and reportedly died as a result of wounds he had received at the Battle of Möskirch (5 May 1800).

(Schürmann)

Friedlowsky, Joseph (b. St Margareth, near Prague, 11 June 1777; d. Vienna, 14 January 1859). Clarinet virtuoso and teacher. After studying the clarinet and basset-horn with Nejebse, the principal clarinettist of the orchestra at the Prague theatre, he was appointed first clarinettist in the town band. At the beginning of the winter season 1802 he joined the orchestra of the Theater an der Wien, and he was to spend the remainder of his life in Vienna where he was greatly admired. Reporting on his performance at a concert at the hotel Zum römischen Kaiser on 3 November 1817, the critic of the Leipzig *Allgemeine musikalische Zeitung* wrote: 'The virtuosity of this clarinettist has for long been universally acknowledged here; his ravishing, magical sound and the beauty of his expressive playing pierce the heart.' Spohr,* who directed the Theater an der Wien orchestra from 1813 to 1815, wrote the clarinet part of his Octet (Op. 32) for him in 1814. In 1832 Friedlowsky joined the court orchestra. He enjoyed an equally successful career as a teacher, and from 1821 until 1847 taught at the Conservatoire.

According to Schindler,* Friedlowsky was among the small number of contemporary Viennese musicians for whom Beethoven felt profound admiration. Schindler states furthermore that it was Friedlowsky who 'taught our composer the mechanics of the clarinet', but this latter assertion is unconvincing, since almost all of Beethoven's solo clarinet parts were composed between 1796 and 1802, before Friedlowsky arrived in Vienna (*see* Bähr*). However, Beethoven no doubt benefited from his advice in later years. There are some laudatory references to Friedlowsky in the conversation books. Thus Karl van Beethoven* observes in February 1825 that 'Friedlowsky plays the clarinet very beautifully' (*BKh*7/142); and in January 1826 Karl Holz* singles him out as the best wind instrument player in Vienna (*BKh*8/242) Holz's praise may have been prompted by Friedlowsky's playing in a performance in Beethoven's Septet Op. 20, on 24 December 1825.

Two notes written by Beethoven to Friedlowsky have survived (*Corr.* A1108, 1042/B1597–8). They are very brief and unfortunately undated (in the new Bonn edition of Beethoven's correspondence they are tentatively ascribed to the beginning of March 1823); but both are extremely cordial in tone. One is an invitation to lunch ('I am greatly looking forward to seeing you once again at my home'), while in the other one Beethoven requests Friedlowsky to call on him to discuss a small matter, adding: 'I am counting on the kindness you have always shown me.' Pamela Weston believes that it was Archduke Rudolph* who introduced Friedlowsky to Beethoven. In Gustav Schilling's *Beethoven Album* (1846), a collection of tributes from the leading musicians of the day, Friedlowsky wrote: 'Dear unforgettable friend! With sincere emotion I remember the time when I was so fortunate as to perform your beautiful compositions under your direction and learned to appreciate them to the full.'

Friedlowsky's four children were all musically gifted. Anton (1804–75) was a well-known clarinettist and teacher; Franz (b. 1802), who studied the violin with Joseph Michael Böhm* and the piano with Moscheles,* also became a music teacher; and Eleanore (b. 1803) and Marie (b. 1806) had careers as professional singers.

(Schindler[1], Weston[1,2,3])

Friedrich Wilhelm II, king of Prussia (b. Berlin, 25 September 1744; d. Potsdam, 16 November 1797). Son of Prince August Wilhelm (1722–58); nephew of Frederick the Great whom he succeeded on the throne in 1786. His position allowed him to indulge freely in his two great passions, women (he had four wives and numerous mistresses) and music. He was taught to play the cello by Ludwig Christian Hesse and Carlo Graziani, and later by Jean-Pierre Duport.* Friedrich Wilhelm became an excellent cellist, loved chamber music, and, even before his accession to the throne, established a private orchestra in which he would sometimes play himself.

He was in contact with several well-known composers. In January 1786 Luigi Boccherini became his chamber composer; in 1787 Haydn* dedicated to him the six 'Prussian' String Quartets (Op. 50); and in 1789 the king commissioned Mozart* to write several string quartets and some piano sonatas (as a result, Mozart composed the Quartets K575, K589, and K590, and the Sonata K576). During his stay in Berlin in 1796, Beethoven repeatedly played before the king. He also composed the two Cello Sonatas Op. 5, probably for Jean-Louis Duport,* and took part in their performance at court. Upon his departure he was rewarded with a gold snuff-box filled with louis d'or. He may even have received an invitation to join the Prussian court permanently, but this cannot be confirmed. The cello sonatas were published in Vienna by Artaria & Co.* in February 1797, with a dedication to the king.

A curious consequence of his contacts with Friedrich Wilhelm II was the rumour that he was, in fact, the king's illegitimate son. This startling possibility was first mentioned in the *Dictionnaire historique des musiciens, artistes et amateurs, morts ou vivants* published by Alexandre Choron and François Fayolle in Paris in 1810–11. The report resurfaced (with Fayolle being cited as its source) in Friedrich Arnold Brockhaus's *Conversations-Lexikon* (Leipzig, 1814), but was eventually dropped in the eighth edition (1833) of that encyclopedia, reportedly at Schindler's* insistence. Beethoven was aware of the rumour at the latest by 1819, when reference was first made to it in the conversation books, but he made no statement denying it. In a letter on 28 December 1825, his old friend Franz Gerhard Wegeler* reproached him for the 'culpable indolence' which kept him from publicly defending his mother's honour and which Wegeler attributed to Beethoven's 'innate reluctance to allow anything other than music to be published in print' (*Corr.* B2100). Beethoven let almost a year go by before explaining his silence in this delicate matter in a letter to Wegeler on 7 December 1826: 'I have made it a principle neither to write anything about myself nor to reply to anything that has been written about me. I therefore gladly leave it to you to proclaim to the world my parents' rectitude, and in particular that of my mother.' Perhaps Beethoven was not altogether averse to being considered the offspring of a royal father.

(Bissing, Dorfmüller, Solomon[5])

Friedrich Wilhelm III, king of Prussia (b. Potsdam, 3 August 1770; d. Berlin, 7 June 1840). Son of King Friedrich Wilhelm II * and his second wife, Friederike von Hessen-Darmstadt; reigned 1797–1840. It is quite likely that he met Beethoven during the latter's visit to his father's court in 1796 and again at the time of the Congress of Vienna, in which he participated. He attended Beethoven's concert on 29 November 1814 (but, according to an eyewitness, the Weimar bookseller Carl Bertuch, left after the first part of the programme).

In 1823 he was among the ten rulers and noblemen who, in response to Beethoven's invitation, subscribed to a manuscript copy of the *Missa solemnis* for the sum of 50 gold ducats. Three years later Beethoven dedicated the Ninth Symphony to him. He had considered several other possible dedicatees, last among them Alexander I,* but when he learned that the tsar had died on 1 December 1825 he offered the symphony to Friedrich Wilhelm. Through his ambassador to Austria, Prince Franz Ludwig Hatzfeld zu Trachenberg, the king authorized the dedication (*see Corr.* A1472/B2136). Beethoven then decided to present him with a manuscript copy of the score; handsomely bound, it was handed to Samuel Heinrich Spiker* in Vienna at the end of September or beginning of October 1826, together with a letter from Beethoven to the king (*Corr.* A App.D6/B2214). The copyist, or principal copyist, of the manuscript has been tentatively identified by Alan Tyson as Wenzel Rampl* (and not Peter Gläser,* as was earlier thought). It has not been possible so far to establish with certainty whether the copy (now preserved in the Staatsbibliothek, Berlin) was executed specially for the king or whether, as is thought more likely, Beethoven availed himself of a previously completed one which was then in his possession. The manuscript contains numerous marginal corrections by Beethoven, as well as calculations of the copyist's fees in his writing. A special title sheet bears Beethoven's dedication of the work to the king. (The printed score was sent to the king directly by the publishers, B. Schott's Söhne.*)

The king acknowledged the gift in a letter dated 25 November (*Corr.* B2231), together with which he sent Beethoven 'a diamond ring as a token of my sincere admiration'. Both the letter and the ring reached Beethoven through the Prussian embassy in Vienna in December. A mystery surrounds the ring. According to a note written by Schindler* on the back of the king's letter, Beethoven discovered to his amazement, on opening the case containing the ring, that it was set not with a diamond, but with a stone of reddish colour. The Viennese court jeweller, when consulted, valued it at no more than 300 florins. Beethoven then reportedly considered returning it to the embassy, on the assumption that an error had been made, but in the end, needing the money, sold it to the jeweller for the above-mentioned sum. Schindler obliquely raises the possibility that the stone had been substituted for the original diamond by someone at the Prussian embassy. Given Schindler's general untrustworthiness as a person and as a source, it is unlikely that the truth of the matter will ever be ascertained. He made no mention of the story in his Beethoven biography, but, characteristically, forged an entry referring to the sale of the ring in the conversation books (*BKh*10/320).

Beethoven also had some contact with the king's daughter Charlotte Luise [Alexandra Feodorovna] who married the future Tsar Nicholas I in 1817. As he proudly informed Spiker, she had asked him to choose a Viennese piano for her.

(Kalischer, Paulig, Spiel, Tyson[7])

Friedrich Wilhelm IV, king of Prussia (b. Berlin, 15 October 1795; d. Potsdam, 2 January 1861). Son of King Friedrich Wilhelm III* and his first wife, Princess Luise von Mecklenburg-Strelitz; reigned 1840–61 (but, following his two strokes, his brother Wilhelm (afterwards emperor) acted as regent from 1858).

On 7 March 1821 Beethoven wrote to Adolph Martin Schlesinger,* with reference to the forthcoming publication of the *Schottische Lieder* (Op. 108): 'You are at liberty to dedicate the work to the crown prince of Prussia, even though I had planned to offer it to someone else.' In the event, however, Schlesinger subsequently decided to dedicate the edition of the songs, which appeared in 1822, to Prince Antoni Henryk Radziwill.* In 1846 the first edition of the full score of *Die Ruinen von Athen* (Op. 113) was dedicated by Artaria & Co.* to Friedrich Wilhelm, by then king of Prussia.

Fries, Moritz (Christian), Count of the Realm (b. Vienna, 6 May 1777; d. Paris, 26 December 1826). Industrialist and banker; prominent collector and patron of the arts. Son of Count Johann Fries (1719–85) who, with his Swiss compatriot Baron Johann Jakob Gontard, had founded the firm 'Fries & Co.' in Vienna in 1766. Moritz studied law at Leipzig (1794–7), and on his return to Vienna took charge of the family business (his elder brothers, Johann and Joseph, had died in 1770 and 1788 respectively). In addition to the bank, in which he owned a major share, the business included important textile mills and extensive landholdings.

He eventually came to be regarded as the richest man in Austria; his art collection was famous and he also possessed a library of 16,000 books. He and his wife, Princess Maria Theresia Josepha Hohenlohe-Waldenburg-Schillingsfürst, whom he married on 15 October 1800 (she died in 1819), were known for the lavish hospitality they offered at their splendid town residence [5 Josefsplatz], an imposing mansion built for Moritz's father by the celebrated architect Johann Ferdinand Hetzendorf von Hohenberg. They also owned Vöslau Castle, near Vienna, which now serves as Vöslau's town hall. Fries was, moreover, a great music lover and a generous patron; he was a member of the first executive committee of the

Gesellschaft der Musikfreunde,* and served as the society's vice-president from 1815 to 1817. It was at one of his musical parties, in the spring of 1800, that Beethoven triumphed over Daniel Steibelt.*

Fries commissioned the String Quartet Op. 29, and probably also the Violin Sonatas Opp. 23–4; Beethoven dedicated all three works to him, as well as the Seventh Symphony. (The sonatas were published in 1801, the quintet in 1802, and the symphony in 1816.) Among other musicians who dedicated works to the count were Haydn* (String Quartet Op. 103) and Schubert* (the song 'Gretchen am Spinnrade'). It is also possible that Beethoven initially intended to dedicate the *Variations on the Duet 'Bei Männern, welche Liebe fühlen' from Mozart's* 'Die Zauberflöte' (WoO 46) to Countess Fries, before he offered them to Count Browne,* for the autograph bears a note (though not in the composer's writing) to that effect. As well as benefiting from the count's personal patronage, Beethoven found it convenient to use his firm for banking transactions and also for the dispatch of music abroad (e.g. in his dealings with George Thomson* and with Schott's Söhne*).

In the end, Fries's extravagant lifestyle proved disastrous even for his immense fortune. In 1825 he was replaced in the management of the bank by his son Moritz (1804–87); the latter was obliged to declare bankruptcy on 29 April 1826. 'You will doubtless have learned of the misfortune which has befallen Fries and Co.', Beethoven wrote to Schott's Söhne on 20 May. 'I should therefore prefer that you make out your bills of exchange to Arnstein & Eskeles.' At the end of that year, the elder Count Moritz Fries died in Paris where he had been living with his second wife, the dancer Fanny Münzenberg. His Viennese mansion was acquired by the banker Georg Simon Sina, his property at Vöslau by another banker, Johann Heinrich Falkner-Geymüller. (However, Vöslau Castle was later bought back by the younger Moritz Fries and remained in the family until 1901.) The famous art collection was sold between 1823 and 1828. Fries's dramatic fall from extreme wealth is believed to have inspired Ferdinand Raimund's play *Der Verschwender*.

(Fries, Mikoletzky[1,2], *ÖBL*, Pohl[1])

Frühwald, Joseph

Frühwald, Joseph (b. Höbenbach, Lower Austria, 19 January 1783; d. Vienna, 20 April 1856). Singer (tenor). He attended the school attached to Göttweig Monastery and became a choirboy there. In 1798 he settled in Vienna, and from 1807 until 1821 he was a member of the court opera. There, on 23 May 1814, he sang Jacquino at the first performance of the final version of *Fidelio*. He also sang for many years at St Stephen's Cathedral. In addition, he was appointed choirmaster at the Schottenkirche in 1809, and, following the death in 1831 of Philipp Thaddäus Korner, he was entrusted with the musical training of the choirboys of the court Kapelle and at the same time he became a singer in the Kapelle. He and Korner had been engaged in 1817 as the first singing teachers at the newly established Conservatoire of the Gesellschaft der Musikfreunde.* He remained on its faculty until 1848.

(Pohl[3], Wurzbach[1])

Fuchs, Aloys [Alois] (b. Raase, Austrian Silesia [Razová, Czech Republic], 22 June 1799; d. Vienna, 20 March 1853). Civil servant; musicologist and collector. He was educated at the Franciscan monastery at Troppau [Opava], where he received organ and cello lessons and sang in the choir. According to Otto Jahn, who probably had the information from Fuchs himself (see below), the latter sang at Troppau in 1811 in a performance of Beethoven's Mass in C, conducted by the composer, but the accuracy of that statement is doubtful (*see* Karl Lichnowsky*). After studying philosophy and law at the University of Vienna (1816–23), Fuchs took up a post at the war office. He played the cello in amateur orchestras and sang bass in the choir of the court Kapelle. In 1820 he began to form a music library which would ultimately contain a wealth of autographs and editions, as well as portraits; in 1851 he informed Schindler* that he owned more than 1,400 autographs and over 2,500 portraits of composers. In further letters to Schindler in 1852–3, he mentioned that he had been assembling material on Beethoven for some thirty years, and that it filled some ten to fifteen folders. He made this material, as well as his extensive notes on other composers, available to Jahn, when the latter visited Vienna in 1852.

Fuchs's own publications dealt predominantly with the lives and works of Gluck and Mozart* (in 1851 his thematic catalogue of Gluck's works was printed in the *Neue Berliner Musikzeitung*); but in 1845, in the *Allgemeine Wiener Musikzeitung*, he published what was the first comprehensive survey of Beethoven portraits ('Verzeichnis der sämtlichen Portraits des Komponisten Ludwig van Beethoven'). At the auction of Beethoven's effects in 1827 he had bought two of the composer's sketchbooks, as well as the autographs of the Kyrie from the Mass in C (he later acquired also the Gloria) and of the Piano Sonata Op. 27, No. 2 (to his chagrin, the title page and the first fourteen bars were missing).

(Schaal[4], Staehelin[1], Wessely[8])

Galitzin: *see* Golitsïn.*

Gallenberg, Wenzel Robert, Count (b. Vienna, 28 December 1783; d. Rome, 13 March 1839). Composer and theatre administrator. A pupil of Albrechtsberger,* he wrote many compositions for the piano, but was best known for his ballet music. Soon after his marriage to Countess Julia [Giulietta] Guicciardi* on 3 November 1803 he moved to Naples, where he later came into contact with Domenico Barbaia who was appointed manager of the royal opera houses there in 1809. When Barbaia took over the administration of the Kärntnertor-Theater at the beginning of 1822, Gallenberg returned to Vienna and was made a member of the newly established board of management of that theatre. In 1828 he became himself the lessee of the Kärntnertor-Theater, but he lost a good deal of money in the venture. He left Vienna in 1830 and spent the rest of his life in France and Italy.

He knew Beethoven before his departure for Naples. Indeed, he assured Schindler* in 1823 that they had enjoyed very cordial relations (*BKh*3/50), but Beethoven retained less pleasant memories of their contacts: 'Il etoit toujours mon ennemi,' he told Schindler (*BKh*2/366). There is no record of any meetings between them after Gallenberg's return to Vienna, but his name appears frequently in the conversation books for early 1823 when Beethoven was trying to find a manuscript copy of the score of *Fidelio* to send to Carl Maria von Weber,* who was planning to produce the opera at Dresden. At Beethoven's request, Schindler repeatedly called on Gallenberg who was responsible for the library of the Kärntnertor-Theater, which possessed a copy of the music, and he reported on their discussions in the conversation books. At first Gallenberg was less than friendly (according to Schindler, he described Beethoven as 'an insufferable fellow'), but he changed his tone after receiving a letter from Beethoven (which is unfortunately lost). He now proclaimed his profound admiration for Beethoven, described him as the most brilliant star in the musical firmament, expressed a great desire for a new opera from his pen, and invited him to dinner. At one time he even offered to have the score copied, but it is not clear whether the manuscript which was eventually dispatched to Dresden was the work of Gallenberg's own copyist or of a copyist sent to the theatre by Beethoven. It reached Weber on 10 April, and he conducted the first Dresden performance of the opera on 29 April, with Wilhelmine Schröder-Devrient* in the title role.

Beethoven was an occasional visitor to the house of Gallenberg's sister, Countess Maria Eleonora Fuchs (1786–1842).

(Branscombe[1], Landon[1])

Gebauer, Franz Xaver (b. Eckersdorf, near Glatz, Silesia [Kłodzko, Poland], 1784; d. Vienna, 13 December 1822). Organist, conductor, and composer. After moving to Vienna in 1810 he was active there as a cellist and piano teacher, and in 1816 was appointed choirmaster at the Augustinerkirche. In 1819 he founded the Concerts spirituels which were held on alternate Friday afternoons (except during the summer months) at the building known as Zur Mehlgrube [on the site now occupied by the Ambassador Hotel]. A symphony was played at each concert, in addition to the choral work which was to be performed at the church on the following Sunday; the initial concert took place on 1 October 1819. The works performed during the first season included Beethoven's first four symphonies and the 'Pastoral' Symphony, the Mass in C, and the settings of Goethe's songs 'Meeresstille' and 'Glückliche Fahrt'; among those played in the second season (1820/1) were the Fifth, Seventh, and Eighth Symphonies, and *Christus am Ölberg*.

The concerts proved popular, even though the quality of these sight-reading performances was inevitably uneven. In a letter to S. A. Steiner & Co.* in 1820, Beethoven calls them 'Winkelmusik', a pejorative term suggesting incompetence (*Corr*. A1066/B1380). As for Gebauer, Beethoven plays on his name unflatteringly —'Geh' Bauer' [Go, peasant]—in the same letter (*see also BKh*2/52), and Karl Joseph Bernard* alleges, in another entry in the conversation books, that he 'cannot conduct and, what is worse, cannot compose' (*BKh*2/72); but Franz Oliva* declared that the quality of the sacred music performed at the Augustinerkirche had greatly improved under his direction (*BKh*2/52). Gebauer was also associated with the Gesellschaft der Musikfreunde* and conducted some of its early concerts.

There can be little doubt that he must have been personally acquainted with Beethoven; indeed, certain entries in the conversation books have been attributed to him. There is, however, no indication that their relationship was a close one, and there is no record of any correspondence between them, for it has now been established that a letter which was believed to have been addressed to him (*Corr*. A791/B1144) was in fact written by Beethoven to Benjamin Gebauer, an orchestral player at the Theater an der Wien who occasionally did some copying for him. (The letter A127/B233 was probably addressed to the same person.)

(Hanslick, Pohl/Warrack)

Gelinek [Gelineck, Jelínek], **Joseph** [Abbé] (b. Sedletz, near Selčan [Sedlec, near Sedlčany, Czech Republic], 3 December 1758; d. Vienna, 13 April 1825). Composer, pianist, and piano teacher. His aptitude for improvisation reportedly led Mozart*, while he was in Prague in 1787, to recommend him to Count Philipp Kinsky. Sometime between 1789 and 1792, the count took him to Vienna, where he served for fifteen years as domestic chaplain, piano teacher, and tutor to the Kinsky family; later he became domestic chaplain to Prince Nikolaus II Esterházy.* He was greatly admired as a pianist and much sought after as a teacher. As a composer, he concentrated on writing variations, especially on operatic themes and arias.

When, not long after Beethoven's arrival in Vienna, Gelinek had occasion to match his musical skills against the newcomer's, he found himself outclassed, as both a pianist and an improviser: 'That young man is possessed by the devil,' he told Carl Czerny's* father. 'Never have I heard anyone play the piano like that. And he improvised on a theme I had given him in a manner I have not heard even Mozart equal.' Learning that Beethoven required further instruction in counterpoint, Gelinek reportedly persuaded Johann Baptist Schenk* to teach him. In his autobiography, Schenk states that relations between Beethoven and Gelinek soon deteriorated. If this is correct, then the estrangement was evidently not a permanent one, for in 1804 Giovanni Cappi* published an arrangement for the piano of Beethoven's First Symphony 'par son ami l'abbé Gelinek'. It would not be surprising, however, if Gelinek found it increasingly difficult to appreciate

Beethoven's later works—Václav Tomášek* records in his memoirs certain critical observations allegedly made by Gelinek after attending a rehearsal of the Seventh Symphony. He would certainly not have been the only musician of the older school to be disconcerted by Beethoven's compositional style. Nonetheless Gelinek wrote some variations for piano on the Allegretto of the Seventh Symphony which S. A. Steiner & Co.* published in 1816.

(Komma/Vernillat, Poštolka², Schünemann)

Gellert, Christian Fürchtegott (b. Hainichen, Saxony, 4 July 1715; d. Leipzig, 13 December 1769). Poet, playwright, and novelist. He is best known for his *Fabeln und Erzählungen* (1746–8), a collection of fables and tales in verse, and *Geistliche Oden und Lieder* (1757), a volume of religious poems and hymns. From the latter work Beethoven took the texts for the songs 'Bitten', 'Busslied', 'Die Ehre Gottes aus der Natur', 'Die Liebe des Nächsten', 'Gottes Macht und Vorsehung', and 'Vom Tode'. The songs were published together by T. Mollo* in the autumn of 1803 under the title *Sechs Lieder von Gellert am Klavier zu singen* (Op. 48). (Regarding the date of composition of these songs, *see* Johann Georg Browne.*)

George IV [George Augustus Frederick], king of Great Britain and Ireland (b. London, 12 August 1762; d. London, 26 June 1830). Eldest son of George III (1738–1820) and Charlotte Sophia of Mecklenburg-Strelitz (1744–1818); prince regent 1811–20, king 1820–30.

Early in 1814 Beethoven had a manuscript copy made of the as yet unpublished *Wellingtons Sieg* which had recently been performed with great success in Vienna (*see also* Mälzel*). The copy bore a dedication to the prince regent, together with a request that he graciously accept it and furthermore authorize a similar dedication of the printed score. Prince Razumovsky* arranged for the copy to be transmitted to the prince regent. To Beethoven's disappointment, the latter did not even acknowledge the gift, let alone reward it. Beethoven's vexation increased when he learned the following year that the score had been made available for public performance at Drury Lane Theatre, without his deriving any benefit from the performances (*see* Smart*). The presence in Vienna of the hero of his composition no doubt ensured that Beethoven did not forget the slight and the harm he felt he had suffered; for the Duke of Wellington replaced Viscount Castlereagh on 1 February 1815 as the English representative at the Congress of Vienna (a fact not usually mentioned by Beethoven biographers). Beethoven expressed his frustration at the unsatisfactory financial situation in which he found himself as a result of the prince regent's silence in a long letter to Razumovsky on 5 June 1815. In the end, even though he had not received the prince regent's permission, Beethoven dedicated to him both the Viennese edition of the *Wellingtons Sieg* (published by S. A. Steiner & Co.* in February 1816) and the London edition of his own piano reduction of the work (published by Robert Birchall* in January 1816). These dedications also failed to produce the hoped-for result.

In 1823 Beethoven made a further attempt to extract some financial reward from the dedicatee who had by now become King George IV. Enlisting the help of Caspar Bauer, a secretary at the Austrian embassy in London, and of his old friend and pupil Ferdinand Ries,* who was now living in London, he tried to have a printed copy of *Wellingtons Sieg* delivered to the king, together with a letter referring to the earlier manuscript presentation copy (see *Corr.* A1142/B1579 and B 1641). However, neither Bauer nor Ries found an opportunity to approach the king directly; eventually, though, Ries was able to arrange for a royal page who greatly admired Beethoven's music to hand the letter (and presumably the printed score) to the king. But once more Beethoven's expectation of a pecuniary recompense was dashed. He had apparently already earlier abandoned his original intention of inviting the king to subscribe to the *Missa solemnis*.

(Wegeler/Ries)

Gerhardi [later Frank], **Christine** (b. *c*.1777). Amateur singer (soprano). On the certificate of her marriage to Dr Joseph Frank (*see* Frank*) on 20 August 1798 she is stated to be the daughter of Christian Gerhardi, the director of a cotton factory in Moravia, and of his wife Sophie, née Monti. Her delightful and flexible voice, her sensitive musicianship, and her attractive appearance made her a favourite performer at the private concerts sponsored by the association of aristocratic music lovers [Gesellschaft der Associerten] formed by Baron Gottfried van Swieten.* These concerts were held at the Palais Schwarzenberg* and the Palais Lobkowitz.* She won particular praise for her interpretation of the solo soprano parts in Salieri's* *Axur*, Gluck's *Alceste*, Handel's* *Acis and Galatea*, and Haydn's* *Die Schöpfung* (she sang at the first performance, under the composer's direction, on 29 April 1798). Count Johann Karl Zinzendorf, a discerning critic, wrote in his diary after hearing her at Lobkowitz's one evening: 'Madame Frank sang like an angel.'

Beethoven knew her well. His published correspondence includes three letters to her, two before her marriage, the third in 1801. It is evident that between the first one, a formal note written to thank her for a poem in praise of his music (*Corr.* A23/B33), and the second one, addressed to 'Dear Chr.' and concluding with a jocular 'Go to the devil' (*Corr.* A24/B34), their relationship had become a fairly intimate one. They both performed at the musical soirées arranged by Joseph Frank at his father's house. On 30 January 1801 she organized a charity concert at the Grosser Redoutensaal for the benefit of the wounded soldiers of the imperial army. Several well-known artists took part, including Ferdinando Paer* (who directed the orchestra accompanying the singers), Haydn (who conducted two of his own symphonies), and Beethoven (who played the Horn Sonata Op. 17 with Giovanni Punto*). A few days before the event Beethoven had written to

Christine to complain about an announcement of the forthcoming concert in the *Wiener Zeitung* on 21 January, which mentioned only the name of Frau Frank, 'the celebrated amateur in the art of singing', and made no reference to any of the other artists who were offering their services in this good cause. He strongly criticized this action, for which he apparently held her husband responsible, and demanded that the omission be rectified in any further announcement (*Corr.* A45/B56). However, the text appeared unchanged in two more issues of the newspaper. At the concert, Christine sang an aria from Sebastiano Nasolini's opera *Merope*, and took part in a duet from the same opera with the tenor Joseph Simoni and in numbers from Cimarosa's *Gli Orazi ed i Curiazi* with Simoni and the soprano Magdalena Willmann*.

The Franks left Vienna in 1804 for Vilna [Vilnius, Lithuania]. There, Christine is known to have sung in 1809 in a Polish-language performance of *Die Schöpfung* conducted by Daniel Steibelt.*

Gerold, Carl (b. Vienna, 12 June 1783; d. Vienna, 23 September 1854). Bookseller and printer. He was the publisher of *Musenalmanach für das Jahr 1814* (ed. Johann Erichson), in which Beethoven's song 'Der Bardengeist' (WoO 142) appeared as a music supplement.

Gesellschaft der Musikfreunde (Vienna). The society was formally established, with the emperor's approval, in 1814, with Archduke Rudolph as its 'Protektor' [Patron]. The driving force behind its foundation was Joseph Sonnleithner,* who served as its (unpaid) secretary until his death twenty-one years later. Beethoven's music was frequently presented at its concerts. The following of his works were performed during the first five seasons: the Second Symphony (7 January 1816), the second and third movements of the Violin Concerto and the *Egmont* Overture (10 March 1816), the Seventh Symphony (2 February 1817), the *Coriolan* Overture (1 March 1818), the first movement of the 'Eroica' Symphony (3 May 1818), the Second Symphony (18 April 1819), the *Prometheus* Overture (9 May 1819), the 'Eroica' Symphony (20 February 1820), the Fifth Symphony and a chorus from *Christus am Ölberg* (9 April 1820).

At its meeting of 9 November 1815 the executive committee decided to invite Beethoven to compose an oratorio for the society. The invitation was conveyed to Beethoven by Nikolaus Zmeskall.* Beethoven accepted the commission in a letter to Zmeskall on 9 February 1816, and proposed a fee of 400 gold ducats; he added that 'H.[err] von Seyfried' (presumably Joseph von Seyfried*) was already at work on the libretto. The society then made a counter-proposal of 300 gold ducats, to which Beethoven agreed. When no progress had been made two years later, the task of preparing the text was entrusted (apparently by the society) to Karl Joseph Bernard,* who undertook to write a libretto on the subject *Der Sieg des Kreuzes*. However, the matter dragged on for several more years, to the frustration of the society which had, moreover, paid Beethoven an advance of 400 florins in 1819 (*see also* Odescalchi*). Bernard eventually provided Beethoven with the first part of the libretto, but later asked for its return because he wished to change it; not until October 1823 was he able to supply the text to the composer and the society, whereupon Beethoven promptly declared it to be in need of considerable revision (letter to Raphael Georg Kiesewetter* of 23 January 1824). The oratorio was never composed (*see also* Kuffner*).

On 29 November 1825 Kiesewetter chaired a meeting of the executive committee, at which it was decided to draw the attention of the society's members to the desirability of electing further honorary members, in which connection the committee proposed the names of fifteen composers, Beethoven among them. This recommendation was accepted at a meeting of the *Repräsentanten* [representatives] on 31 January 1826; but it was not until 7 March 1827 that the diploma (which was dated 26 October 1826) was actually sent to Beethoven, together with a letter signed by Kiesewetter on the society's behalf (*Corr.* B2272).

(Perger/Hirschfeld, Pohl[3])

Giannattasio [Giannatasio] **del Rio** (family). Family on friendly terms with Beethoven between 1816 and 1820. The father, **Cajetan** (1764–1828), had opened a private school for boys in Vienna in 1798, which he ran with the help of his wife **Katharina**, née Quenzer (1762–1825). They had two daughters: **Franziska** [Fanny] (1790–1873) and (**Maria**) **Anna** [Nanni] (1792–1868). According to his granddaughter, Cajetan's ancestors were Spanish noblemen who had settled in Austria earlier in the eighteenth century. He himself had been a tutor in an aristocratic household, first in Vienna, and later in Hungary where his daughters were born.

After visiting the school with his friend Karl Joseph Bernard* on 24 January 1816, Beethoven arranged for his nephew Karl* to be admitted as a boarder on 2 February. He must have found Giannattasio and his family highly congenial company, for he took almost at once to spending many evenings with them, especially during that first winter. His visits delighted his hosts, and particularly the daughters, whose interest in Beethoven and his music had been greatly stimulated by J. F. L. Duncker,* when he stayed at their house at the time of the Congress of Vienna. They were very well educated, played the piano, and are said to have had pleasant voices; on rare occasions during his association with them Beethoven accompanied them in performances of his songs. In view of his celebrity, the difference in age, and, not least, his often forbidding manner, they naturally stood in some awe of him, but when he was in a merry and relaxed mood the relationship became a very friendly one, with a good deal of teasing on his part and general laughter. He appears to have preferred Nanni (so, at any rate, her sister thought, regretfully), mainly because she was more outgoing and gay. Nanni was then already engaged to Leopold von Schmerling, a merchant whom she was to marry in 1819 (see below) and whose brother Joseph, a lawyer, advised Beethoven in matters pertaining to the guardianship of Karl. In 1817 Beethoven composed the canon 'Glück fehl' dir vor allem . . . niemalen' (WoO 171) as a birthday greeting for Nanni.

Fanny, in contrast to her sister, was rather melancholy by nature, and she had been greatly saddened by the recent death of a man she loved. Within a short time she developed deep feelings for Beethoven, whom she admired both as a musician and a man. These feelings she recorded and analysed in her diary, from which numerous passages were later published by Ludwig Nohl in *Eine stille Liebe zu Beethoven: Nach dem Tagebuch einer jungen Dame*. Soon after making his acquaintance, she wrote: 'I am very much afraid that during a prolonged and closer association with this good and excellent man I shall come to feel for him more than mere friendship, and that I shall experience many troubled hours as a result.' And on 2 March 1816: 'Is it really possible that he has become so important, so dear to me that I should have been irritated and hurt by my sister's facetious advice not to fall in love with him? . . . When I come to know him better, I am certain that he will become dear, very dear, to me.' In September of that year, she overheard Beethoven tell her father 'something which very deeply distressed me and confirmed a long-held suspicion: he is in love, but unhappily'.

At one time, Beethoven, no doubt out of a desire to be closer to Karl, considered occupying a flat in the garden house belonging to the Giannattasios, who had moved from the inner city to the Landstrasse suburb [3 Reisnerstrasse] in the summer of 1816; but he rejected the idea for health reasons. Instead, he found rooms near the school, of which Karl remained a pupil until 24 January 1818. Karl then went to live with his uncle, who at first had him taught by a tutor and later, from September to December of that year, sent him to the Akademisches Gymnasium. But after Karl had run away from Beethoven to his mother's flat in early December 1818, Giannattasio agreed to have him stay temporarily, under strict supervision, at his house. He was, however, to refuse Beethoven's request six months later that he accept Karl once more as a regular pupil. (From late December 1818/early January 1819 until June 1819 Karl had attended Johann Baptist Kudlich's* institute.) Karl was enrolled as a boarder at Blöchlinger's* school in late June.

It is clear from the above that Beethoven did not break off all contact with Giannattasio's family after withdrawing Karl from his school in January 1818. On the occasion of Nanni's wedding to Leopold von Schmerling on 6 February 1819 he even composed a special 'Hochzeitslied' (WoO 105), to words by Anton Joseph Stein.* It was sung upon the couple's return from the church service, the performers and Beethoven hiding in a corner of the room; afterwards he presented the manuscript to the bride. Beethoven made two versions of the 'Hochzeitslied' (*see* W. Hess, 'Zu Beethovens Hochzeitslied vom Jahre 1819'). The autograph of the second version was eventually acquired by an English publisher and the composition was published in London, with an English text by John Oxenford, as a 'Wedding Song' dedicated to Victoria, princess royal of Great Britain, on the occasion of her marriage on 25 January 1858 to Prince Friedrich Wilhelm of Prussia [later King Friedrich III].

On 19 April 1820, 'after we had not seen him for almost a year', Fanny visited Beethoven with an unnamed companion (perhaps Nanni). 'It seemed to me that he was glad to see us again,' she noted in her diary. He presented her with the recently composed song 'Abendlied unterm gestirnten Himmel' (WoO 150).

(Hess[6], Hitzig[1,4], Nohl[3], Oldman)

Gläser, Franz (Joseph) (b. Obergeorgenthal [Horní Jiřetín, Czech Republic], 19 April 1798; d. Copenhagen, 29 August 1861). Composer and conductor; son of Peter Gläser,* and father of the organist and composer Joseph Gläser (1835–91). He received his musical training first as a choirboy at Dresden and then at the Prague Conservatoire. In 1817 he moved to Vienna, where he at first earned his living by copying and arranging music. On 22 August 1817 his first work for the stage, *Bärnburgs Sturz*, was produced at the Theater in der Leopoldstadt. The following year he was appointed assistant Kapellmeister at that theatre; from 1819 until 1827 he was Kapellmeister at the Theater in der Josefstadt, and from 1827 to 1830 he held a similar post at the Theater an der Wien. He then became Kapellmeister at the Königstädtisches Theater, Berlin, and, finally, moved from there in 1842 to Copenhagen, where he was appointed court composer. During his years in Vienna he wrote a very considerable number of farces, parodies, and pantomimes for the theatres to which he was attached; but his best-known works were composed in Berlin, the most successful of them being *Des Adlers Horst*, to a libretto by Karl von Holtei.

While he was at the Theater in der Josefstadt, it fell to him to prepare and supervise the performance of Beethoven's music for Karl Meisl's* *Die Weihe des Hauses* on 3 October 1822 (*see* Hensler*). Beethoven himself conducted, but Gläser, who stood by his side, was obliged to take over the direction of certain passages which the composer, due to his failing hearing, had difficulty in handling. Gläser later described the event in his autobiography. He states furthermore that he subsequently remained in contact with Beethoven.

(Branscombe[2], Gläser)

Gläser, Peter (Paul) (1776–1849). Father of Franz Gläser,* whom he accompanied to Vienna in 1817. By trade a weaver, he had a large family but little money. How he acquired the necessary skills is not known, but he eventually became a music copyist at the Theater in der Josefstadt, where his son was Kapellmeister from 1819 to 1827. In August 1823, shortly after Wenzel Schlemmer's* death, Schindler* told Beethoven that Gläser would like to work for him. Schindler considered him to be a man of great probity and, moreover, 'sufficiently musical' for the task; his weak point was his poor handwriting which 'was often unacceptable even for the theatre' (*BKh*4/36). By April 1824 Gläser was kept busy by Beethoven working on scores of the *Missa solemnis* and the Ninth Symphony, even though his efforts did not always satisfy his employer: 'I asked you to write everything exactly as I had done, yet *the words* [in the last movement of the Ninth Symphony] have been written in the very way I did not want, just as if it was done on purpose,' Beethoven complained in one letter (*Corr.* A1275/B1814). It used to be thought that Gläser was responsible for the copy of the Ninth Symphony presented to King Friedrich Wilhelm III,* but Alan Tyson, in his 1970 article on Beethoven's copyists, stated that most of the credit for that particular manuscript should probably be given to Wenzel Rampl.*

(Gläser, Tyson[7])

Gleichenstein, Ignaz von [from 1808 Baron] (b. Staufen, near Freiburg, Breisgau, 24 May 1778: d. Heiligenstadt, near Vienna, 3 August 1828). Son of Hofrat Baron Carl Benedict Gleichenstein (1725–1813) and his wife Franziska, née von Bayer (1753–1832); the father was in the service of the prince abbot of St Blasien. After attending school at Freiburg and Konstanz, Ignaz studied law at Freiburg University (1794–8). In August 1800 he moved to Vienna, where, in November 1801, he obtained a post in the war department.

Beethoven was in contact with the Gleichenstein family by early 1797, for on 20 February of that year Albrechtsberger* transmitted to him an invitation from 'old Baron Joseph Gleichenstein' to a concert the following evening (*Corr.* B29). The letter also indicates that the baron had asked Beethoven to teach his son Ignaz and was anxious to have Beethoven's reply. Sieghard Brandenburg, in his recent edition of Beethoven's correspondence, states that the 'Ignaz' in question was none other than the subject of this article, who may have been a relative—but evidently not, as Albrechtsberger states, the son—of Baron Joseph, and that Ignaz could very well have spent some time in Vienna already prior to settling there in 1800. While this is a feasible explanation, it is presumably not impossible that Baron Joseph himself really had a son named Ignaz. Beethoven's response to the request is not known. (It has not been possible so far to identify Baron Joseph Gleichenstein. As a matter of fact, the Gleichensteins were not granted the rank of Freiherr [baron] until 1808. Perhaps Albrechtsberger was merely following the well-known Viennese custom of gratuitously bestowing honorific titles.)

It is uncertain, then, whether Beethoven met his future friend as early as 1797, or only a few years later when he may have been introduced to him by Stephan von Breuning,* who became Gleichenstein's colleague at the war ministry in 1803. In his earliest known letter to Gleichenstein (*Corr.* A160/B276), Beethoven still addresses him with the formal 'Sie', but it is evident from its contents that Gleichenstein was then already helping Beethoven with his correspondence and running errands for him. The undated letter is likely to have been written not later than 20 April 1807, the day on which Gleichenstein was a witness to Beethoven's contract with Muzio Clementi.* In a letter on 13 June of the same year Beethoven already uses the more intimate 'Du'; moreover, three days later, he writes 'I embrace you with all my heart', and on 23 June, 'I am very fond of you'. Erich Münch, in his biography of Gleichenstein's great friend Julius Schneller,* describes the baron as one of the kindest men he had ever met and as a person of the greatest probity. He liked music and played the cello; in 1809 Beethoven dedicated his Cello Sonata Op. 69 to him. In a letter introducing Gleichenstein to the composer Peter Winter, Beethoven wrote that while he was not a connoisseur of music, he was attracted to everything that was beautiful and good (*see Corr.* A173/B357).

At the beginning of 1809 Gleichenstein advised Beethoven in his negotiations concerning the annuities which he was to receive from Archduke Rudolph,* Prince Kinsky,* and Prince Lobkowitz.* In February of that year he left Vienna, apparently on an intelligence mission to observe French troop deployments in Germany and France before and during the imminent new war against Napoleon. On his return in February 1810 he was eagerly greeted by Beethoven. Shortly afterwards he introduced Beethoven to the Malfatti* family.

On 28 May 1811 Gleichenstein married Anna Malfatti. That summer the couple left for the Breisgau, where Gleichenstein took over the management of his parents' estate at Oberrotweil, near Freiburg. While Gleichenstein reportedly stayed in Vienna on several occasions during the next fifteen years, there is no record of any further meetings with Beethoven. In 1827, however, he visited his dying friend on more than one occasion. He returned to Vienna early the following year and was treated during his final illness by Dr Johann Malfatti.*

(Brandenburg[2], Münch)

Gleim, Johann Wilhelm Ludwig (b. Ermsleben, 2 April 1719; d. Halberstadt, 18 February 1803). Poet, best known for a collection of anacreontic verse, *Versuch in scherzhaften Liedern* (1744/5), and for a volume of patriotic Prussian poems, *Preussische Kriegslieder in den Feldzügen 1756 und 1757 von einem Grenadier* (1758).

Beethoven set one of his poems in 'Selbstgespräch' (WoO 114). The song, composed at Bonn in 1792, was not published in Beethoven's lifetime. He also made a brief sketch for a setting of Gleim's poem 'Flüchtigkeit der Zeit'.

(Kriegleder)

Glöggl, Franz Xaver (b. Linz, 21 February 1764; d. Linz, 16 July 1839). Musician; art and music dealer. He was for many years a dominant figure in the musical life of Linz, where he was active as conductor, theatre manager, and, from 1797, Kapellmeister at the cathedral; in 1803 he opened an art and music shop. He wrote a number of books, among them pedagogical works such as *Allgemeine Anfangsgründe der Tonkunst für Ton-Schulen* (1810), and *Kirchenmusik-Ordnung:*

Erklärendes Handbuch des musikalischen Gottesdienstes (1828), a guide to music for different church functions; he also edited some (short-lived) periodicals. Among his pupils was Tobias Haslinger* (*see also* Holz*). His important collection of rare instruments, autographs, and portraits was acquired by the Gesellschaft der Musikfreunde* in 1824.

Beethoven met Glöggl during his stay at Linz in the autumn of 1812. His arrival was announced in Glöggl's *Musikalische Zeitung für die österreichischen Staaten* on 5 October: 'We now have the long-desired pleasure of welcoming to our city the Orpheus and greatest composer of our time, Herr L. van Beethoven, who arrived here a few days ago. If Apollo is favourably disposed towards us, we shall also have an opportunity to admire his art.' In the event, Beethoven did not give a public concert at Linz, but he did improvise at a soirée given by Count Ludwig Nikolaus Dönhoff. The occasion was described by Glöggl's son Franz in the recollections of Beethoven which he wrote down shortly before his death and made available to Thayer.* He also recalled that Beethoven had visited his father almost daily during his stay at Linz. During one of these visits Beethoven composed, at his host's request, the Equali (WoO 30) for four trombones. (For Beethoven's funeral, Ignaz von Seyfried* adapted two of these for four male voices.)

Franz Glöggl (1796–1872) owned a music shop and founded a school for singing in Vienna; he also published a journal, *Neue Wiener Musikzeitung* (1852–60), and served as archivist of the Gesellschaft der Musikfreunde. He met Beethoven repeatedly at Sigmund Anton Steiner's* music shop and elsewhere.

(Pohl[3], Wessely[1,6,7])

Goeble, H. Beethoven set one of his poems in 'Abendlied unterm gestirnten Himmel' (WoO 150) in 1820. The extant autograph is dated 4 March, and the song was published in the music supplement to the *Wiener Zeitschrift für Kunst, Literatur, Theater und Mode* on 28 March. It was dedicated to Dr Anton Braunhofer.* Nothing is known about Goeble's life.

Goeckingk, Leopold Friedrich Günther von (b. Gröningen, near Halberstadt, 13 July 1748; d. Deutsch-Wartenberg, Silesia, 18 February 1828). Prussian civil servant, ennobled in 1789; poet. He contributed to various periodicals, and from 1776 to 1778 edited the *Göttinger Musenalmanach*. He was best known for his *Lieder zweier Liebenden* (1777); his collected poems (*Gedichte*) first appeared in three volumes in 1780–2, his prose writings (*Prosaische Schriften*) in 1784. Beethoven left a short sketch for a setting of the poem 'An Amarant', from *Lieder zweier Liebenden*.

(Mix)

Goethe, Johann Wolfgang von (b. Frankfurt am Main, 28 August 1749; d. Weimar, 22 March 1832). Beethoven revered Goethe all his life. 'When I see someone who loves you as sincerely, as fervently as [Beethoven], I forget the whole world,' Bettina Brentano (*see* Arnim*) wrote to Goethe in 1810.

Beethoven made Goethe's acquaintance at Teplitz [Teplice] in July 1812; they may have met again at Karlsbad [Karlovy Vary] in September. (They had exchanged letters the previous year—*see Corr.* A303/B493, B509.) Very dissimilar in temperament, background, education, and social position, they also differed considerably in their views on life and art; in particular, Goethe's musical understanding, which was greatly influenced by the ideas of his friend Carl Friedrich Zelter,* who was initially highly critical of Beethoven's music, did not predispose him to feel very sympathetic towards Beethoven's compositions. Yet he sensed Beethoven's greatness and was impressed by the force of his personality. After his first meeting with Beethoven on 19 July, he wrote to his wife: 'Never have I seen a more intensely focused, dynamic, or fervent artist.' On 20 July he travelled with Beethoven to the nearby town of Bilin [Bílina], and the next day he called on Beethoven. In his diary he noted: 'In the evening at Beethoven's. He played delightfully.' He visited Beethoven again on 23 July; a few days later Beethoven left Karlsbad. Clearly, Goethe was fascinated by Beethoven. On 2 September he wrote to Zelter: 'I made Beethoven's acquaintance at Teplitz. His talent astounded me. Unfortunately, though, he has a wholly uncontrolled temperament, and while doubtless not altogether wrong in regarding the world as detestable, he assuredly does not make it more enjoyable either for himself or others by thinking so. Still, he is to be readily forgiven and much to be pitied, for he is losing his hearing, which has perhaps a less harmful effect on the musical part of his nature than on the social one.' As for Beethoven, his fiercely independent spirit made him somewhat critical of the deference Goethe was wont to show to his social superiors: 'Goethe is more fond of the court atmosphere than is seemly for a poet,' he complained to Breitkopf & Härtel* (9 August 1812). This did not, however, lessen his admiration for Goethe's works, and he had reported with evident gratification in an earlier letter to the publishers (24 July) that Goethe had promised to write something for him.

Beethoven worked on settings of Goethe texts at various times throughout his life, beginning while he was still in Bonn, but there seems to be no particular pattern either to their composition or their publication. In 1805 he published 'Maigesang' ['Mailied'] and 'Marmotte' (in *Acht Lieder*, Op. 52), and 'Ich denke dein' (WoO 74; the song is followed by six variations for piano duet). Next came 'Neue Liebe, neues Leben' (the first version of Op. 75, No. 2) in 1808. The most important year was 1810, which saw the publication of four different settings of 'Sehnsucht: Nur wer die Sehnsucht kennt' (WoO 134; the autograph bears the following note: 'I did not have time to produce a good setting, therefore several attempts'); of the three songs 'Mignon: Kennst du das Land', 'Neue Liebe, neues Leben' (second version), and 'Aus Goethes *Faust*: Es war einmal ein König' (Op. 75, Nos. 1–3); and of the music to *Egmont* (Op. 84). In 1811 Beethoven published three further songs (Op. 83): 'Wonne der Wehmut', 'Sehnsucht: Was zieht mir das Herz so?', and 'Mit einem gemalten Band'; in 1822, 'Meeresstille' and 'Glückliche Fahrt' (Op. 112), which he dedicated to Goethe; and in 1825, 'Bundeslied' (Op. 122). Lastly, he set verses from the poem 'Das Göttliche' in WoO 151 and WoO 185. He also left sketches for some songs, among others, 'Erlkönig' and 'Heidenröslein'.

There are several indications that Beethoven would have liked to compose music for *Faust*, and it is possible that he discussed the possibility with Goethe at Teplitz. How Goethe might have viewed such a project and whether he indicated any willingness to prepare a libretto is not known; he certainly never did so. Beethoven still cherished the idea a few years before his death. In April 1823 he told a visitor: 'I am composing, not what I should most like to compose, but what I need to compose, because of the money. This does not mean that I compose only for the sake of money. But once the present period is over, I hope to compose at last what is noblest for myself and in art—*Faust*' (*BKh* 3/148).

Goethe apparently did not write to Beethoven when Breitkopf & Härtel, at the composer's request, sent him the music to *Egmont* in January 1812, nor when he received in May 1822 the settings of 'Meeresstille' and 'Glückliche Fahrt'. Yet he is known to have been very satisfied with the *Egmont* music, at any rate. In a letter to Marianne von Willemer, on 12 July 1821, he praised Beethoven for having 'worked wonders' ['Beethoven hat darin Wunder getan']. She had written to him, in June: 'I wish that Beethoven would set those marvellous poems [the *West-östlicher Divan*] to music; he, and no one else, would fully understand them. I felt this vividly when I heard the music to *Egmont* last winter: it is heavenly!'

On 8 February 1823 Beethoven wrote once more to Goethe. After expressing the hope that Goethe had safely received the compositions dedicated to him the previous year (i.e. Op. 112), Beethoven solicited his help—this was, of course, the real purpose of the letter—in persuading the grand duke of Weimar to subscribe to the *Missa solemnis*. As far as is known, Goethe did not reply; Grand Duke Karl August did not subscribe.

(Dalton, Goethe[3], Jacobs[1], Mies[1], Sternfeld)

Golitsïn [Galitzin], **Nikolay Borisovich**, Prince (b. 19 December 1794 (NS); d. Bogorodskoye, Kursk govt., 3 November 1866 (NS)). Russian nobleman whose family had associations with Vienna. A relative, Prince Dmitry Michailovich Golitsïn (1720/1–93), was Russian ambassador and minister plenipotentiary to the Austrian court from 1762 to 1792, and to this day a hill overlooking the city on which he built his summer residence is known as the 'Gallitzinberg'. Nikolay Borisovich himself spent part of his childhood (1804–6) in Vienna.

In November 1822 the prince commissioned Beethoven to write 'one, two, or three new quartets' for him (*Corr.* B1508). His choice of the string quartet was no accident, for he was a competent cellist and delighted in playing chamber music.

Beethoven readily agreed to compose three quartets for him; and from then until his death he remained in regular contact with Golitsïn, either directly or through the prince's St Petersburg bankers Stieglitz & Co. The main reasons for this extensive correspondence were, in the first place, Beethoven's delay in delivering the quartets—thus the first (Op. 127), promised for the end of February or the middle of March 1823, was not completed until February 1825—and, later, Golitsïn's delay in paying for them. The financial situation was confused by the fact that, in addition to undertaking to pay 50 ducats for each quartet, Golitsïn in due course also subscribed to the *Missa solemnis*, and since he received the Mass before the first quartet, the sum deposited by him in Vienna for the quartet was paid out to Beethoven for the Mass. (Beethoven eventually received also the fee for the quartet.) Although Golitsïn was to assert in later years that he had not only met, but even exceeded, his commitments towards Beethoven prior to the composer's death, his statement appears to be contradicted by their correspondence. It is true that in a letter (*Corr.* B2230) on 22 November 1826 (NS) Golitsïn promised to send within a few days the 125 ducats which, according to Beethoven, were still due to him: 50 ducats each for the last two quartets (Op. 132 and Op. 130, with the Fugue Op. 133 as its last movement) and 25 ducats for the overture *Die Weihe des Hauses* (Op. 124) which he had dedicated to the prince in 1825. Yet the very last letter Beethoven is known to have written, which is dated 21 March 1827, was another reminder to Stieglitz & Co. that the amount had still not been received.

In fact, the matter was not settled until after Beethoven's death, and then only by instalments: first 20, then 30 ducats (for which, according to Thayer,* Karl van Beethoven* signed a receipt on 9 November 1832), and finally 75 in 1852, but Golitsïn made this last payment conditional on its not being regarded as the repayment of a debt. (Golitsïn had been infuriated by the version of the affair which Schindler* had published in the first two editions of his Beethoven biography. In his account, which is indeed full of errors, Schindler alleges that Beethoven received no money whatsoever for the quartets.) The ultimate event in the Golitsïn–Beethoven relationship occurred in the autumn of 1858, when Nikolay Borisovich's son, the conductor and composer Prince Yury Nikolayevich Golitsïn (1823–72), presented a sum of 125 ducats to Beethoven's heirs (Karl had died earlier that year) as a token of the admiration which Russian musicians felt for his music.

Apart from prompting the composition of three of Beethoven's greatest quartets, Golitsïn has other claims to a place of distinction among the composer's patrons. Not only did he subscribe to the *Missa solemnis*, but he was at least partly responsible for Tsar Alexander I* likewise becoming a subscriber. Having looked through the score of the *Missa solemnis*, he wrote to Beethoven: 'Je lui ai trouvé cette Sublimité qui préside à toutes vos Compositions, et qui rendent vos œuvres inimitables' (*Corr.* B1752, 29 November 1823). He could moreover take the credit for organizing the first complete performance of the Mass, which took place at St Petersburg on 7 April 1824 (NS). In a subsequent letter to Beethoven, he described the work as 'un trésor de beauté' (*Corr.* B1807). Lastly, his admiration for Beethoven's music led him to arrange several of the piano sonatas for string instruments. In March 1826 he offered Schott's Söhne* nine quartets, three trios, and a quintet, arranged from Beethoven's 'plus belles œuvres pour le Piano'. He had already previously published a quartet in St Petersburg, of which the first and final movements were taken from the Piano Sonata Op. 53 and the middle movements from the Cello Sonata Op. 69 and the Piano Sonata Op. 7. Furthermore, in a letter to Karl van Beethoven on 16 April 1852, he stated that sometime after Beethoven's death he had published at Brunswick and St Petersburg, at his own expense, two string quartets and a string quintet likewise based on works by Beethoven. In one way or another, Golitsïn made a significant contribution to the growth of Beethoven's reputation in Russia.

Golitsïn wrote to Beethoven on 21 July 1825: 'J'ambitionne le bonheur de faire personnellement vôtre [*sic*] Connaissance' (*Corr.* B1997); but they never met.

(Fischman[2], Ginsburg[1,2,3])

Götz, Johann Michael (bapt. Mannheim, 7 February 1740; d. Worms, 15 February 1810). Music publisher. Son of the court trumpeter and violist Joseph Götz. He began publishing music in 1773, and in 1776 he was given an exclusive patent for twenty years within the Palatinate; it was extended in 1782 to include Bavaria (the two countries had been united in 1777). Compositions by Mannheim composers figured prominently in his list. At various periods, Munich and Düsseldorf are mentioned as places of publication, at the same time as Mannheim. In 1799 he moved his business to Worms. The original firm at Mannheim was run for a time by his former partner Joseph Abelshauser.

In March 1782 Götz published Beethoven's *Variations on a March by Dressler** (WoO 63). This was the first of Beethoven's works to appear in print (*see also* Neefe*). On the other hand, the statement in Kinsky/Halm that Götz also published Beethoven's variations on Righini's arietta 'Venni Amore' (WoO 65) in 1791 is erroneous; the first version of that composition was issued by Bernhard Schott. (The second version was published by Johann Träg in 1802.)

(Brandenburg/Staehelin, Schneider, Walter[1], Würtz)

Goulding & Co. English firm of music sellers and publishers, founded in *c.*1786 by George Goulding, whose name was associated with it until about 1834. Over the years he took several different partners, notably Thomas D'Almaine, and business was carried on under various names. In 1824, Beethoven's *Variations* for piano trio Op. 121a were published by Chappell & Co. and Goulding & Co. (*see* Chappell & Co.*).

(Kidson/Smith/Jones, Tyson[3])

Graf, Conrad (b. Riedlingen, Württemberg, 11 November 1782; d. Vienna, 17 March 1851 (dates according to D. Wythe; *New Grove* has 17 November 1782 and 18 March 1851)). Piano manufacturer. He originally studied cabinetmaking, and began working in that trade in 1796. In 1798/9 he moved to Vienna where, after a period of military service in the Jäger-Freikorps, he was taken on by the keyboard instrument maker Jakob Schelkle [Schelke]. After the latter's death he married his widow Katharina in 1804 or 1805 and took over the firm; by 1809 he was employing ten workmen. His business continued to prosper, and in 1824 he was appointed court piano maker. In 1826 he bought the 'Mondscheinhaus' [5 Technikerstrasse], a large building which had for many years housed a celebrated ballroom and in which he was able to carry out his plans of further expanding the firm: 'By the late 1820s Graf's business had become a factory, rather than a workshop . . . Pianos were produced by a group of workers organized in eight divisions, each specializing in a particular job' (D. Wythe). The firm was then employing some forty workers. In 1835 Graf won the gold medal in the piano category at the first Austrian industrial exhibition. In 1842 he sold the business to Karl Andreas Stein, a grandson of the famous Augsburg piano manufacturer Johann Andreas Stein (*see* Stein (family)*). Deborah Wythe estimates Graf's total output at some 3,000 pianos.

Two of his instruments are particularly famous. One is the piano he built as a present for Clara Wieck upon her marriage to Robert Schumann on 12 September 1840. The other is the piano he lent Beethoven when the latter's Broadwood* had to be repaired in 1826. Graf had specially adapted his piano to the needs of the almost deaf composer, and Beethoven kept it even after the Broadwood had been restored to working order. Gerhard von Breuning* describes the two pianos standing 'Bauch to Bauch' [curve to curve] in one of Beethoven's rooms at the Schwarzspanierhaus. After Beethoven's death Graf once more took possession of his piano. It was later acquired by the bookseller Franz Wimmer, who gave it to his daughter Charlotte (1814–67) upon her marriage to Joseph Otto Widmann (1816–73) in 1841. When, the following year, the young couple moved to Liestal, near Basle, the piano was transported there after it had been repaired by Franz Rausch, a former employee of Graf's. It remained in the family's possession until Joseph Otto's son, Joseph Viktor Widmann (1842–1911), sold it to the Verein Beethoven-Haus, Bonn, in September 1889. It had previously been shown at an exhibition at Zurich in 1883 and at one at Manchester in 1887, after which it appears to have remained in England (where it may also have been exhibited in London), and it was eventually dispatched directly from there to Bonn. By then it had lost most of its original tone quality. It was completely restored in 1963 by the Nuremberg firm J. C. Neupert.

In 1840 Joseph Danhauser* painted Graf's portrait. That same year he was commissioned by Graf to paint a portrait of Liszt* playing a Graf piano, surrounded by a group of distinguished friends (the Countess Marie d'Agoult,

George Sand, Victor Hugo, Alexandre Dumas, Paganini, and Rossini*). Anton Dietrich's* bust of Beethoven stands on the piano.

(Breuning, Geiser, Hirt, Mies², Sakka, Wythe)

Griesinger, Georg August von (b. Stuttgart, 8 January 1769; d. Vienna, 9 April 1845). Diplomat; son of Georg Christoph Griesinger (1734/5–82), a lawyer and senior civil servant residing at Stuttgart. Georg August studied theology at Tübingen, but did not go into the Church; later he worked for several years as a tutor in an aristocratic household at Morges in Switzerland. In 1797 he moved to Leipzig, and two years later to Vienna, where he was employed for the next six years as tutor to a son of the Saxon ambassador Count Johann Hilmar Adolph Schönfeld. Vienna was to remain Griesinger's principal place of residence for the rest of his life. In 1804 he was appointed secretary at the Saxon embassy, and later he was promoted to counsellor and eventually chargé d'affaires. He was ennobled in 1819.

Griesinger became very friendly with Joseph Haydn* and played an important role in the latter's dealings with Breitkopf & Härtel.* Shortly after Haydn's death, he published his 'Biographische Notizen über Joseph Haydn' in the *Allgemeine musikalische Zeitung* (July–September 1809); the following year Breitkopf & Härtel issued a revised version of the text in book form. Griesinger came to know Beethoven quite well in 1802, after Breitkopf & Härtel had asked him to inform Beethoven of their desire to publish some of his compositions. Beethoven sent them his String Quartet in C major (Op. 29), which they published in December of 1802; but the publication was to involve Beethoven in a dispute with Artaria & Co.* and in a rather acrimonious correspondence with Breitkopf & Härtel. It is no small tribute to Griesinger's character and tactfulness that Kaspar Karl van Beethoven* should have informed Breitkopf & Härtel, at the height of the dispute, that he would probably need to send for Griesinger to calm his brother, for 'he [Beethoven] likes him a great deal' (*Corr.* B119). For his part, Griesinger held Beethoven in high esteem. 'Ludwig van Beethoven', he assured the Leipzig publishers at one point, 'is a man devoid of duplicity and deceit,' and he underlined the statement for greater emphasis. He duly succeeded in smoothing out the tensions between the two parties.

Beethoven's published correspondence provides evidence of later approaches made by Breitkopf & Härtel through Griesinger in 1808 (*see Corr.* A167/B327) and 1822 (*see Corr.* B1470), in the hope of obtaining further compositions from him. The first of these efforts proved extremely fruitful, for Breitkopf & Härtel became Beethoven's principal publishers during the years 1809–12, but the second was unsuccessful. On 7 January 1823 Beethoven turned to Griesinger for advice on how he might induce European sovereigns to subscribe to the *Missa solemnis*, and at same time he expressed the hope that Griesinger would assist him in the matter, presumably with regard to the Saxon court. It was therefore probably at

Griesinger's suggestion that Beethoven sent a formal invitation to King Friedrich August I through the Saxon ambassador in Vienna, Count Friedrich Albert von der Schulenburg auf Closterroda, on 23 January. The invitation was not taken up. However, a further attempt to secure a subscription from the king, in July of the same year, brought the desired result, thanks to the support of Archduke Rudolph.* On 20 November 1823 Beethoven was able to inform Griesinger that his nephew Karl* would that day be delivering to him the manuscript copy of the Mass intended for the king. This is the last known written communication between Beethoven and Griesinger.

(Griesinger, Hitzig², Rheinwald)

Grillparzer, Franz (b. Vienna, 15 January 1791; d. Vienna, 21 January 1872). Dramatist and poet. The first time he saw Beethoven was at a musical soirée given by his uncle Joseph Sonnleithner* in about 1805. He probably came to know Beethoven fairly well in the summer of 1808, when his family shared a house with the composer at Heiligenstadt, near Vienna.

Grillparzer's tragedy *Die Ahnfrau* (Theater an der Wien, 31 January 1817) made him famous overnight. The success of his next play, *Sappho*, produced at the Burgtheater on 21 April 1818, earned him the post of resident poet at that theatre; and the trilogy *Das goldene Vliess* (Burgtheater, 26–7 March 1821) confirmed his position as the leading dramatist of the younger generation. Yet it was not until 1823 that the possibility of an artistic collaboration with Beethoven arose. Buoyed by the successful revival of *Fidelio* in November 1822, Beethoven was contemplating writing a new opera, perhaps as a vehicle for Wilhelmine Schröder* who had been so highly acclaimed in the role of Leonore. It was probably at Count Moritz Lichnowsky's* suggestion that Grillparzer prepared the libretto *Melusina* for Beethoven; he may also have been encouraged to do so by Count Moritz Dietrichstein,* the director of the court theatres. Beethoven appears to have expressed general approval of the text, though not without suggesting some changes which he discussed with Grillparzer in the spring and summer of 1823. On 17 September of that year Beethoven informed Louis Spohr* that he had already begun work on Grillparzer's libretto, and in December Louis Antoine Duport* enquired on what terms he was prepared to sign a contract for the opera. However, nothing ever came of the project, and not a single sketch has come to light which has been identified as belonging to *Melusina*. Yet Beethoven thought highly enough of the libretto to send it in February 1826, through Adolph Martin Schlesinger,* to Count Karl Friedrich Moritz Brühl, the general manager of the Königliches Theater in Berlin (*see Corr.* B2125). Brühl, while enthusiastic about Beethoven's willingness to write a German opera for his theatre, considered the story of *Melusina* too similar to the plot of Fouqué's* story *Undine*, on which E. T. A. Hoffmann* had based his opera of the same title, first produced in Berlin in 1816. (*Melusina* was later set by Conradin Kreutzer and, somewhat ironically, had its première in Berlin, though not at the Königliches Theater but at the Königstädtisches Theater, in 1833.) Another subject proposed to Beethoven by Grillparzer, *Drahomira*, based on a Bohemian legend, did not get past the initial discussions.

Grillparzer was a torchbearer at Beethoven's funeral. He was also entrusted with the far more important task of writing the oration which Heinrich Anschütz* delivered at the entrance to Währing Cemetery. A year later, on 29 March 1828, the second of the three Equale WoO 30, arranged for voices by Ignaz von Seyfried,* was sung at the consecration of the tombstone of Beethoven's grave to words written for the occasion by Grillparzer.

(Orel[2])

Grosheim, Georg Christoph (b. Kassel, 1 July 1764; d. Kassel, 18 November 1841). Composer, teacher, and writer on music. The son of an orchestral player, he was for many years a prominent figure in the musical life of Kassel. He taught at the teachers' training school attached to the Lyceum Fridericianum from 1782 [?1784] to 1835, played the viola in the court Kapelle (1782–5), and held the post of Musikdirektor at the local theatre (1800–2). Between 1798 and 1813 he furthermore arranged numerous concerts of sacred music at his home and organized some public charity concerts. He also lectured on music and published a number of books and articles; and he was among the contributors to Gustav Schillings's *Enzyclopädie der gesamten musikalischen Wissenschaften* (1837). His own compositions included Lieder and several operas (of which the most successful was *Das heilige Kleeblatt*, produced in 1794).

In 1816 he published '*Über Glückseligkeit und Ehre': Ein Gedicht von J. G. Seume, mit einer Vorrede von G. C. Grosheim*. In his introduction, he drew attention to what he considered to be significant correspondences between the opening movement of Beethoven's Piano Sonata Op. 27, No. 2 and Seume's poem 'Die Beterin' (in which a woman prays for the recovery of her gravely ill father); and he expressed the hope that Beethoven, once he had been made aware of the similarities, would arrange the music as a setting for Seume's text. He sent a copy of his publication, doubtless with an accompanying letter, to Beethoven, who does not seem to have rejected the suggestion outright but explained that ill health prevented him from acting upon it straightaway. (Both Grosheim's letter and Beethoven's answer are lost.) On 10 November 1819, Grosheim wrote once more (*Corr.* B1352), this time enclosing ten songs he had composed to texts by Ernst Friedrich von der Malsburg and which had been published the previous year by Schott's Söhne,* with a dedication to Beethoven. There is no evidence that Beethoven ever thanked him and he seems to have simply ignored Grosheim's renewed request that he should set 'Die Beterin'. For in a letter to Spohr* (27 July 1823), in which he mentioned the recent visit of a singer who had presented introductions from Spohr and Grosheim, Beethoven remarked that he owed the latter a reply and promised to write to him shortly. However, there is no record of his having done so, or of his having set Seume's poem.

(Brennecke, Engelbrecht)

Guicciardi, Julia [Julie, Giulietta], Countess (b. Trieste, 23 November 1784; d. Vienna, 22 March 1856). Daughter of Count Franz Joseph Guicciardi (*c.*1752–1830), a senior Austrian civil servant, and his wife Susanna, née Brunsvik (*c.*1756–1813), who was an aunt of Count Franz Brunsvik and his sisters (*see* Brunsvik de Korompa*). In 1800 Count Guicciardi took up a post at the Austro-Bohemian court chancellery in Vienna. Through their Brunsvik relatives, the Guicciardis were introduced to Beethoven, and he was persuaded to give piano lessons to Giulietta who had previously been taught by Franz Xaver Kleinheinz.* Beethoven appears to have been greatly taken with his beautiful young pupil, and she seems to have returned his feelings. On 16 November 1801 he wrote to Franz Gerhard Wegeler:* 'Now I am once more living more pleasantly . . . This change has been wrought by a dear, enchanting girl who loves me and whom I love. During the past two years I have again known some moments of bliss, and for the first time I feel that—marriage might bring me happiness. Unfortunately, she belongs to a different class.' Very likely the 'enchanting girl' was Giulietta.

In March 1802 Beethoven dedicated the Piano Sonata Op. 27, No. 2—the so-called 'Mondschein' [Moonlight] Sonata—to her. She herself told Otto Jahn in 1852 that Beethoven had originally given her the manuscript of the Rondo in G (Op. 51, No. 2), but had asked her to return it when he needed to dedicate a composition to Countess Henriette Lichnowsky,* and that he had subsequently dedicated the piano sonata to her in its place. (In the circumstances, it seems rather curious that the Rondo, duly dedicated to Countess Lichnowsky, should not have been published until September 1802, six months after the sonata.) Perhaps Beethoven wished to offer Giulietta a more important composition than the rondo, and one which, maybe, held a more personal significance for him. Indeed, some writers, starting with Schindler,* have suggested that the sonata was inspired by his love for her; but Giulietta herself appears to have made no reference to her personal relations with Beethoven in her conversation with Jahn.

Another composition which has been associated with Beethoven's affection for Giulietta is the song WoO 123 (*see* Herrosee*) which was published by Johann Traeg* in June 1803, together with 'La partenza' (WoO 124). It is tempting to speculate that the juxtaposition of these two songs—one expressing the joys of reciprocated love, the other the grief felt at parting from one's beloved—was not entirely fortuitous, for by June 1803 Beethoven must have abandoned any expectation of ever marrying Giulietta. In fact, his hopes of doing so had been severely shaken when, in January 1802, he had received from Countess Susanna Guicciardi a gift—perhaps a purse filled with coins (*see Corr.* B77 n. 3)—in recompense for the tuition he had given her daughter. His angry response reflects his hurt pride at being treated like a person intent on financial gain rather than as a friend and equal who had freely given of his time because it pleased him to do so (*Corr*. B77, 23 January 1802). At the same time, the gesture must have made him painfully aware that his chances of ever bridging the social gap which separated him from Giulietta were slight. This realization, which no doubt deepened during the following months, has been cited as one probable cause of the despair that gripped him in the autumn of 1802 and produced the Heiligenstadt Testament.

On 3 November 1803 Giulietta married the 19-year-old Count Wenzel Robert Gallenberg.* The couple soon left for Italy, where they were to reside for the next eighteen years. But before their departure Giulietta apparently visited Beethoven and made advances to him which he rejected. This, at any rate, appears to be the meaning of an entry made in the conversation books by Beethoven himself in 1823 (*BKh*2/365–7)—an entry rendered rather obscure by his poor French (a sample: 'elle cherchait moi pleureant, mais je la meprisois'). Thayer's* contention that the visit took place after the Gallenbergs' return in 1822 is not borne out by the text. In the same entry Beethoven assured Schindler that Giulietta had loved him more than she ever did her husband. But Schindler's assertion, in his Beethoven biography, that she was the 'Immortal Beloved' has long been disproved. Beethoven did, though, treasure all his life a miniature portrait of her, which she had presumably given to him herself. It was found among his effects after his death.

(Grasberger[2,5], Kalischer, Tyson[9])

Gyrowetz, Adalbert [Jirovec, Vojtěch Matyáš] (b. Budweis [České Budějovice, Czech Republic], 20 February 1763; d. Vienna, 19 March 1850). Composer and conductor. He visited Vienna in 1784–5, but did not settle there until 1793; except for a short period towards the end of the century, he lived there for the rest of his life. In 1804 he was appointed conductor and resident composer at the court theatre, and he remained on its staff until 1831. His most successful opera, *Der Augenarzt*, was produced there on 1 October 1811.

Gyrowetz, whose model throughout his career was Haydn,* found Beethoven's music difficult to digest. When Jan Emanuel Doležálek* mentioned that he had bought a copy of the 'Razumovsky' Quartets, Gyrowetz told him that he had wasted his money. For his part, Beethoven seems to have had little admiration for Gyrowetz's operas, to judge by a facetious remark in a letter to Georg Friedrich Treitschke* (*Corr*. A467/B699).

Gyrowetz was a pallbearer at Beethoven's funeral.

(Stenzl)

Hähnel, Ernst Julius (b. Dresden, 9 March 1811; d. Dresden, 22 May 1891). Sculptor. After studying architecture with Joseph Thürmer at Dresden and

Friedrich von Gärtner in Munich, he switched to sculpture under the influence of Ernst Rietschel and Ludwig von Schwanthaler. He continued his studies in Italy (1831–4), first in Florence and later in Rome, before returning to Dresden in August 1834. The following year he moved to Munich, where he created the figure of Homer for the Staatsbibliothek and the figures of Perugino and Poussin for the Alte Pinakothek. In 1838 Gottfried Semper, whom he had met during his stay in Rome, invited him back to Dresden, and there he resided for the remainder of his life. Among his early works at Dresden were the figures of Aristophanes, Molière, Shakespeare, and Sophocles for the façade of the new court theatre, and those of Flora and Pomona for the Orangerie. His name soon became more widely known throughout Germany thanks to the Beethoven statue he created for Bonn.

On 17 December 1835 the executive committee of the association Bonner Verein für Beethovens Monument ['Bonn Association for Beethoven's Monument'], which had been formed earlier that year, launched an appeal for funds. The response was disappointing, and the committee was obliged to issue a further appeal in November 1838, by which time its original chairman, August Wilhelm Schlegel, had been replaced by Heinrich Karl Breidenstein, the director of music at Bonn University. Donations were, however, still slow in coming, and on 3 October 1839 Franz Liszt,* having learned of the association's plight, wrote from Pisa offering to provide whatever amount might ultimately still be needed for the realization of the project. In return, he requested the privilege of designating the artist, his choice falling on the well-known Italian sculptor Lorenzo Bartolini, for whom he had sat in Florence the previous year. Although Breidenstein responded positively to Liszt's proposal, the committee was, in reality, determined that the commission should go to a German artist. It was, moreover, reluctant to let Liszt guarantee to pay a sum which, though still undetermined, was certain to be very considerable; for it feared uncharitably that he might later be credited with having financed the whole project. Accordingly, Liszt was invited to make a specific contribution to the fund there and then— he generously donated 10,000 francs—and he was persuaded to accept the idea of a public competition. In actual fact, this was to be restricted to Germans candidates.

The competition was announced by the committee in October 1840; entries were to be submitted by 1 March 1841. After examining the twenty-five sketches and models received, a specially selected jury of artists and scholars expressed its preference for the designs proposed by Hähnel and by the Berlin sculptor Gustav Hermann Bläser. Finally, on 21 January 1842, the decision was taken to award the commission to Hähnel; the contract was signed on 23 February (not 8 August 1842, as stated by Kahl—*see* Schaal[5]). The statue, cast by the Nuremberg founder Jakob Daniel Burgschmiet, arrived in Bonn on 23 July 1845 and was unveiled on 12 August in the Münsterplatz, in the presence of the king and queen of Prussia, Queen Victoria and Prince Albert, and numerous other distinguished personages and prominent musicians from Germany and elsewhere. The ceremony was the centrepiece of a Beethoven festival (10–13 August), in which Liszt played a prominent role, as organizer, conductor, pianist, and composer (for some details, *see* the article on Liszt).

Notable among Hähnel's later achievements were the statues of the Emperor Karl IV in Křižovnické Námĕsti [Crusaders' Square] in Prague (1848), of Prince Elector Friedrich August II of Saxony (1866) and the poet Theodor Körner* (1871) at Dresden, and of Field Marshal Prince Karl Philipp Schwarzenberg in Vienna (1867). He also made several allegorical figures for the Vienna opera house. In 1891 Hähnel donated his collection of some 350 plaster casts and models of his works to the Albertinum in Dresden.

(*ALBK*, Kahl[6], Schaal[5], Schmoll, Springer)

Haizinger [Haitzinger], **Anton** (b. Wilfersdorf, Lower Austria, 14 March 1796; d. Karlsruhe, 31 December 1869). Tenor. His singing teachers included Joseph Mozatti and Salieri.* In 1821 he was engaged at the Theater an der Wien, where he made his debut as Giannetto in Rossini's* *La gazza ladra*. Among his other early roles at that theatre and at the Kärntnertor-Theater were Don Ottavio in Mozart's* *Don Giovanni* and Lindoro in Rossini's *L'italiana in Algeri*. At the revival of *Fidelio* at the Kärntnertor-Theater on 3 November 1822 he sang Florestan, opposite Wilhelmine Schröder's* Leonore, and on 25 October 1823 he created Adolar at the première of *Euryanthe*. At Beethoven's concert on 7 May 1824 he took part in the first performance of the Ninth Symphony and in sections of the *Missa solemnis*.

In 1826 Haizinger accepted a contract at Karlsruhe, and he remained a member of the court theatre there until 1850. He also sang repeatedly in other German cities and elsewhere, notably in Paris in 1829–30, England in 1833, and St Petersburg in 1835.

(Kutsch/Riemens)

Halem, Gerhard Anton von (b. Oldenburg, 2 March 1752; d. Eutin, 4 January 1819). Poet, dramatist, narrative writer, and historian. A lawyer by profession (he studied at Frankfurt an der Oder and Strasbourg, and eventually qualified in Copenhagen), he is considered an important champion of the ideas of the Enlightenment in north-west Germany. Much of his work, both in verse and prose, is of a didactic nature. His historical studies, notably a three-volume history of the dukedom of Oldenburg (1794–6) and biographies of Count Burkhard Christoph Münnich (1803) and Peter the Great (1803/4), were highly regarded.

He is the author of the poem set by Beethoven in the song 'Gretels Warnung', which, composed before 1800 and later revised, was published by Breitkopf & Härtel* as one of the *Sechs Gesänge* (Op. 75) in 1810.

Halm, Anton (b. Altenmarkt, near Wies, Styria, 4 June 1789; d. Vienna, 6 April 1872). Pianist, composer, and teacher. He received his musical training in Graz, later served in the army in campaigns against Napoleon (1809–11), and was subsequently active as a pianist and teacher in Graz. In 1813 he went to Hungary, where he was employed as a music teacher. During his stay there he became acquainted with Count Franz Brunsvik,* who reportedly provided him with a letter of introduction to Beethoven which he duly presented to the composer after moving to Vienna in 1815. According to Schindler,* he got on well with Beethoven who liked his breezy military manner. In 1816 Beethoven accepted the dedication of one of his piano sonatas.

In Vienna Halm successfully continued his career as pianist and teacher; among his pupils were Joseph Dachs, Julius Epstein, Joseph Fischhof,* Stephen Heller, and Adolf Henselt. Even before arriving in Vienna, Halm is known to have performed at least one Beethoven work in public, the Third Piano Concerto at a concert at Graz on 18 March 1814. In Vienna he took part in various performances of Beethoven works, including a disastrous rendition of the Choral Fantasia at the Kärntnertor-Theater on 15 November 1817, when his failure to observe the correct tempos resulted in the chorus coming to grief and the performance being temporarily halted, to whistles from the audience. The incident prompted one of Beethoven's more ingenious wordplays. When asked about the concert by the pianist and composer Johann Peter Pixis, he wrote on the copy of the Fantasia which Pixis had just purchased at Steiner's* music shop: 'Nicht jeder Halm gibt Ähren!'—literally: 'Not every stalk bears ears of corn!', but with the double pun 'Halm' ['stalk' and the pianist's name] and 'Ähren—Ehren' ['ears of corn' and 'honour(s)']. However, Beethoven does not appear to have nursed a lasting grudge against Halm over the fiasco. In 1826 Halm was, with Beethoven's blessing, commissioned by Mathias Artaria* to make an arrangement for piano duet of the *Grosse Fuge* (Op. 133), which Beethoven had initially composed as the final movement for the String Quartet Op. 130. Halm sent his transcription to Beethoven on 24 April 1826 (*see Corr.* B2149), but it failed to satisfy Beethoven, who thereupon made his own arrangement (Op. 134) which Artaria & Co.* published in May 1827. As a composer, Halm wrote almost entirely pieces in which the piano plays either the sole, or at any rate an important, role. The main exceptions are a Mass, and the opera *Marvorio* (which was never produced or printed).

Halm and his wife Maria (1782–1843) were involved in a bizarre episode which he related to Thayer* many years later. Halm had asked Karl Holz* to transmit to Beethoven Maria's request for a lock of his hair, and in due course she received some hairs which were said to be Beethoven's but had in reality been cut from a goat. When Beethoven heard of the deception he was furious, apologized to Halm, and sent Maria some genuine 'Beethoven hair' which he had snipped off himself. (Schindler's account of the incident implicates Beethoven himself in the hoax, while yet another version attributes the deception to Beethoven's nephew Karl* rather than to Holz.)

(Deutsch[2], Federhofer[1], Suppan)

Hammer-Purgstall, Joseph, Baron (b. Graz, 9 June 1774; d. Vienna, 23 November 1856). Diplomat, orientalist, writer, and translator. Son of Joseph von Hammer (1738–1818), a civil servant. He studied at the Orientalische Akademie in Vienna (1789–99), specializing in Turkish and Persian; his principal teacher was Thomas Chabert. In 1799 he was posted to Istanbul as a linguist, and he was subsequently employed in Egypt, England, and Eastern Europe, before joining the court chancellery in Vienna in 1807; he was awarded the title 'Hofrat' in 1817. He married Karoline von Henikstein (1797–1844), a daughter of Joseph von Henikstein,* in 1816. In 1835, under the will of the widowed and childless Countess Johanna-Anna Purgstall, he became proprietor of her estates in Styria, and upon adopting her name he was granted the hereditary rank of Freiherr [baron].

He was a prolific writer and translator who, through his publications, was instrumental in acquainting scholars, as well as a wider public of cultured readers, with a wealth of information and insights regarding the life and literature of various oriental countries. Indeed, it has been suggested that his services to oriental studies in Germany were no less profound than those rendered by Antoine Isaac Silvestre de Sacy in France and by Sir William Jones in England. His major publications include *Geschichte des osmanischen Reiches* (10 vols., 1827–33), *Geschichte der osmanischen Dichtkunst* (4 vols., 1836–8), and *Gemäldesaal der Lebensbeschreibungen grosser moslemischer Herrscher* . . . (6 vols., 1837–9). He also published some poems and plays. Among his literary translations, the version of Hafiz's *Divan* deserves special mention, not so much for any extraordinary intrinsic quality, but because it prompted Goethe* to write his *West-östlicher Divan*. Hammer-Purgstall was mainly responsible for the foundation of the Akademie der Wissenschaften in Vienna in 1847, and was elected its first president. Years before his death he designed his tombstone at the cemetery at Weidling am Bach; shaped like a Turkish *türbe*, it bears inscriptions in ten languages.

In his posthumously published memoirs (*Erinnerungen aus meinem Leben, 1774–1852*), he states that he first met Beethoven during the 1790s at the house of Dr Thomas Franz Closset (who had been Mozart's* personal physician during the final year of his life). Hammer-Purgstall furthermore recalls having been present on more than one occasion in Beethoven's rooms when the composer's increasing deafness prevented him from noticing that the piano on which he was playing was badly out of tune.

Beethoven's published correspondence includes two communications to Hammer-Purgstall (*Corr.* A227/B391, A206/B1291). The purpose of the first one, which probably dates from the summer of 1809, was to ask Hammer-Purgstall to help Joseph Ludwig Stoll* obtain free, or at least cheap, transport to Paris. The second letter is of greater interest. On 24 February 1819 Hammer-Purgstall, having apparently learnt from Johann Schickh* that Beethoven wished to set to music 'an Indian chorus of a religious character', sent him a manuscript copy of an Indian pastoral play (*Dewajani*) which he had recently written. He also submitted for Beethoven's consideration two further original works, a Persian Singspiel (*Anahid*) and the libretto for an oratorio on the subject of the Flood (*see Corr*. B1290). Beethoven promptly returned *Dewajani* and *Anahid*, explaining that his heavy artistic commitments did not allow him time for examining them properly just then, but he promised to visit Hammer-Purgstall when he was less occupied, in order to discuss the Indian play as well as the proposed oratorio (*Corr*. A206/B1291). There is no firm evidence that he ever reverted to the matter again, but the following passage in Hammer-Purgstall's memoirs relating to the year 1815 could indicate that he did so: 'At about this time he had asked me to write the text for his setting of *Die Sintflut* [*The Flood*]. I can only regret that my libretto did not meet his expectations.' The year 1815 is clearly wrong. As for the statement itself, it is clear from the correspondence that Hammer-Purgstall had not originally written the libretto at Beethoven's suggestion. Accordingly, either he retained only a confused recollection of what had happened (which would not be surprising, since he did not commence writing his memoirs until 1841) or Beethoven may have asked him to produce a revised text, which he then rejected.

(Hammer-Purgstall, *ÖBL*, Solomon[4], Wurzbach[1])

Handel, George Frideric [Georg Friederich or Friedrich] (b. Halle, 23 February 1685; d. London, 14 April 1759). Composer. Beethoven's profound admiration for Handel's music may well owe a good deal to the influence of Baron Gottfried van Swieten,* whose house he frequently visited during his early years in Vienna. At any rate, the various concerts arranged by Swieten will have afforded him exceptional opportunities to become better acquainted with Handel's works. Swieten owned, moreover, the scores of many of Handel's compositions.

Beethoven's enthusiasm for Handel's music is well documented. 'Of all composers, Beethoven valued Mozart* and Handel most highly, then S. Bach,' Ferdinand Ries* reports. 'Whenever I found him with music in his hands or saw some lying on his desk, it was certain to be a composition by one of these idols.' When Cipriani Potter* asked Beethoven in 1817 whom he regarded as the greatest composers of the past, he 'answered that he had always considered Mozart as such, but since he had become acquainted with Handel he had put him at the head'. Johann Reinhold Schultz* tells of hearing him assert, at a dinner in 1823, that Handel was 'the greatest composer that ever lived'. Schultz continues: 'I cannot describe to you with what pathos, and I am inclined to say, with what sublimity of language, he spoke of the *Messiah* of this immortal genius. Everyone of us was moved when he said, "I would uncover my head, and kneel down at his tomb!" ' And Johann Andreas Stumpff* was so impressed by Beethoven's avowed devotion to Handel that he later presented him with Samuel Arnold's splendid forty-volume edition of Handel's works. Johann Baptist Streicher* wrote to Stumpff (in English) on 5 January 1827: 'It will be highly gratifying to you to learn that your present gave poor Beethoven, miserably as he is confined to his sick-bed, the greatest joy, and made him forget his melancholy situation. A book from an acquaintance of his in London [H. A. Reichard's *Taschenbuch für Reisende durch Deutschland und die angrenzenden Länder*, sent by Sir George Smart*] was delivered to him at the same time with your Handel; he took it into his hand, and laid it aside without uttering a syllable. He then pointed with his finger to Handel's works, and said, with feeling and emphasis, "Das ist das Wahre" [There lies the Truth]' (*Corr.* B2247a). Later that same day Beethoven showed the volumes to the young Gerhard von Breuning.* 'I have long wished to own them,' he told him, 'for Handel is the greatest, the most accomplished composer. I can still learn from him.' He then asked Gerhard to bring the scores over to his bed: 'He leafed through one volume after another as I handed them to him, sometimes stopping at particular passages, and at once placed one volume after another to his right on the bed against the wall until they finally formed a high pile. They remained in that position for several hours, for I still found them there in the afternoon.' At the auction of Beethoven's effects on 5 November 1827 the edition was acquired by Tobias Haslinger;* it later came into the possession of Giacomo Meyerbeer.

In 1797 Beethoven published a set of variations for piano and cello on the chorus 'See the conqu'ring hero comes' from Handel's oratorio *Judas Maccabaeus* (WoO 45). When, in 1826, he considered composing an oratorio on the subject of Saul, for which Christoph Kuffner* was to write the text, he is reported by Karl Holz* to have closely studied Handel's *Saul*. However, nothing came of the project.

(Breuning, Potter, Schultz, Wegeler/Ries)

Häring, Johann Baptist von (b. *c.*1761; d. Vienna, 17 May 1818). Son of Regierungsrat Franz Anton von Häring (d. 1792). He was the first love of the future writer and society hostess Karoline von Greiner [later Pichler], but their close association ceased in 1788. She was to draw a rather unflattering portrait of him as Ferdinand Blume in her novel *Leonore* (1804) and gave a more factual, though inevitably one-sided, account of their relations in the autobiographical *Denkwürdigkeiten aus meinem Leben* (1844). He eventually married Nancy [?von] Atkins. His early financial situation was somewhat troubled, but later he seems to have lived a comfortable enough life. He was in business with his brother-in-law Ignaz von Schwab, and also became co-owner, together with Franz Joseph Breuss von Henikstein, of a cotton mill at Ebergassing, in Lower Austria.

J. F. von Schönfeld, in his *Jahrbuch der Tonkunst von Wien und Prag* (1796), places Häring among the outstanding amateur violinists in Vienna. Michael Frey,* no doubt repeating information he had received from local sources during his visit to Vienna in 1807–8, states in the diary he kept during his stay there that Häring 'had frequently had the honour of playing quartets with Mozart'. It is known, in any case, that on one occasion—on 9 April 1790—he took part with Mozart and others in performances of the String Trio K563 and the Clarinet Quintet K581 at Count Johann Karl Hadik's house. Johann Friedrich Reichardt,* who heard Häring on several occasions during his visit to Vienna in 1808–9, particularly admired the 'good taste and clarity' of his playing in some Haydn* quartets.

Häring made a significant contribution to Viennese musical life. Thus he was named director of the orchestra when the Liebhaber-Concerte were established in 1807. He was responsible for the first five concerts (12 November–13 December 1807), after which he relinquished the position, apparently as the result of some disagreement; he was succeeded by Franz Clement.* (The series ran altogether to twenty concerts, the last on 27 March 1808.) During his tenure of the post, the orchestra performed Beethoven's Second and Third Symphonies, as well as the *Prometheus* and *Coriolan* Overtures. The 'Eroica' Symphony was conducted by Beethoven himself, but it is not known whether he conducted any other of his works which were performed during the series. On 16 and 19 March 1815, Häring led the second violins in performances of Handel's* *Messiah*, in which altogether 144 violinists took part. And when, later that year, the Gesellschaft der Musikfreunde* established its own series of regular concerts, he became leader of the second violins of the orchestra. He was furthermore in charge of the first 'evening entertainment' presented by the Gesellschaft on 12 March 1818, at which he also played in a quartet by Franz von Contin, a quintet by Spohr,* and a violin sonata by Beethoven. At his death, he owned five violins, including an Amati, a Guarneri, and a Stradivarius.

Thayer* believes that Häring was on friendly terms with Beethoven by 1794, but there is no formal evidence of their association at that time. Certainly, there must have been frequent consultations between them in connection with the Liebhaber-Concerte (see above). However, the most regularly documented contacts between them occurred during the years 1815–16, when Häring helped Beethoven with his correspondence with Robert Birchall,* Charles Neate* (whom he had introduced to Beethoven in the spring of 1815), Sir George Smart,* and George Thomson.* Having spent more than a year in England as a young man and having visited that country again as recently as 1814, Häring wrote excellent English, and he now placed his knowledge of the language at Beethoven's service. At the same time, a note from Beethoven in November 1816, in which he addresses Häring as 'Your Honour' [Euer Wohlgebohrn] and signs himself 'Your Honour's most devoted servant'—without, as far as one can tell, any hint of persiflage—seems to indicate that their relations were far from intimate (*Corr.* A689/B1001).

(Biba[2], Pichler[2], Perger/Hirschfeld, Pohl[3])

Haslinger, Tobias (Carl) (b. Zell, near Zellhof [Bad Zell], Upper Austria, 1 March 1787; d. Vienna, 18 June 1842). Art and music dealer; composer. He was trained as a boy chorister by Franz Xaver Glöggl,* and then worked in the latter's music shop; from 1807 to 1810 he was employed by the art and music dealer Friedrich Imanuel Eurich. In 1810 he moved to Vienna where he worked for the bookseller Katharina Gräffer. (In 1815 he married her daughter Karoline (1789–1848).)

In 1813 Sigmund Anton Steiner* engaged him as manager of his art and music shop; two years later he became Steiner's partner. According to F. Slezak, the contract was dated 3 March 1815, and the new firm, S. A. Steiner & Co., was registered on 3 July. Over the following ten years, the firm acquired an excellent reputation, and its premises in Paternostergässchen [21 Graben] became a favourite meeting place for local and visiting musicians. After the partnership was dissolved on 11 March 1826, Haslinger obtained a licence to trade under his own name. His business prospered and he eventually employed some fifty persons. His list of composers included Albrechtsberger,* Hummel,* Liszt,* Moscheles,* Spohr,* and Weber,* and he also published almost all the compositions of Johann Strauss the Elder, as well as the later works of Joseph Lanner. He left a fortune of more than 50,000 florins. After his death, the firm (which had moved to the nearby Trattnerhof on the Graben in 1835) was run by his widow and their son Carl (1816–68) under the name 'Tobias Haslinger's Witwe & Sohn', and, following Karoline's death in 1848, by the son alone as 'Carl Haslinger quondam Tobias'.

Beethoven's correspondence contains numerous letters and notes addressed to Haslinger. The earliest known communication probably dates from March 1815, but their acquaintance undoubtedly went back at least to the preceding year; the last extant letter was written on 7 December 1826. There are, moreover, regular references to him in Beethoven's letters to Steiner. In the military hierarchy which Beethoven invented for the members of Steiner's establishment, Steiner himself was designated 'Generalleutnant' and Haslinger 'Adjutant'. Almost all of Beethoven's written communications to Haslinger employ a humorous tone, and quite a few reflect real affection, if only in the frequent use of diminutives and other amusing forms of address ('Adjutanterl', 'Tobiasserl', 'Best of all Tobiases', etc.). According to his brother-in-law Franz Gräffer, Haslinger was 'cordiality and amiability itself', and he appears to have enjoyed an almost unclouded and unusually warm friendship with Beethoven, which survived their rare disagreements unscathed. Apparently he did not even take offence when Beethoven's satirical 'romantic biography' of Haslinger was printed in the Mainz periodical *Cäcilia* in April 1825.

Beethoven later claimed that he had sent the text to Schott's Söhne,* the publishers of the journal, as a private joke, and had not wished it to be printed, at any rate not without Haslinger's consent.

Beethoven wrote for Haslinger the canon 'O Tobias! O Tobias! Dominus Haslinger! o! o!' (WoO 182, inserted in his letter of 10 September 1821), as well as a few musical jokes in other letters (WoO 205 c, g–k). Haslinger visited Beethoven during his last illness, and he acted as a torchbearer at his funeral.

As well as seeing some editions of Beethoven's works through the press, Haslinger undertook certain personal errands for him, and he also called on him socially, sometimes accompanying foreign visitors like Spiker* or Johann Reinhold Schultz* or Weber.* Having had a sound musical training, he was himself a composer—mainly of occasional pieces, such as *Der Brand in Baden*, a 'musical sketch for the pianoforte' about the fire which destroyed much of that famous spa in 1812. He furthermore made arrangements of the works of other composers, including piano reductions for two and four hands of Beethoven's Eighth Symphony. The firm 'Tobias Haslinger' published the first edition of *Elegischer Gesang* (Op. 118) in July 1826; after Beethoven's death, it issued the first editions of the Fugue for string quintet (Op. 137) in the autumn of 1827, of the cantata *Der glorreiche Augenblick* (with the original words as well as with a new text entitled *Preis der Tonkunst*—*see* Rochlitz* and Weissenbach*) in 1837, and of the Overture Leonore No. 1 in 1838. The first edition of the song 'Gedenke mein' (WoO 130) appeared in 1844 under the imprint 'Tobias Haslinger's Witwe und Sohn'. (For first editions published by S. A. Steiner & Co., *see* the article on that firm.)

Haslinger's association with Beethoven produced one further notable project. Over a period of several years (1817–21), he had a de luxe manuscript set of Beethoven's works prepared by Mathias Schwarz and Friedrich Warsow; Schwarz copied the music, while Warsow did the titles. This collection, consisting of sixty-one volumes, was acquired in 1823 by Archduke Rudolph.* There was sufficient blank space available in the original set to accommodate later compositions, but a further volume was subsequently added for the String Quartets Opp. 130 ff. Today the whole set, supplemented with the copy of the *Missa solemnis* which Beethoven presented to the archduke, is in the archives of the Gesellschaft der Musikfreunde.* Haslinger's later plan to issue a printed edition of Beethoven's collected works was frustrated by the refusal of a number of publishers (notably Artaria & Co.* and Breitkopf & Härtel*) to cede their rights in respect of certain works.

(Slezak[4])

Hatzfeld, (Maria Anna) Hortensia, Countess, née Countess Zierotin (b. Vienna, 1750; d. ?Vienna, 31 December 1813). Daughter of Count Johann Carl Zierotin (1719–76) and his wife Maria Josepha Theresia, née Countess Königsegg-Erps; great-niece of Maximilian Friedrich,* elector of Cologne (1761–84). She married the court chamberlain [later Lieutenant-General] Count Clemens August Hatzfeld (1743–94) at Bonn in 1772.

She was a leading patroness of music, both in Vienna and at Bonn. She was, moreover, herself a brilliant pianist and soprano. In his *Jahrbuch der Tonkunst von Wien und Prag* (1796), J. F. von Schönfeld praises her great vocal agility and her 'marvellous trill', and states that her execution 'surpasses in many respects the skills of the ordinary amateur'. She took important roles in several operatic performances at Prince Johann Adam Auersperg's private theatre in Vienna, including that of Elettra in the first Viennese performance of Mozart's* *Idomeneo* on 13 March 1786. She was a subscriber to Mozart's Trattnerhof concerts in 1784, and was known to be a great admirer of his music. In dedicating to her his variations for piano on the march of the priests from Mozart's *Zauberflöte* (Bonn, 1793), Christian Gottlob Neefe,* who owed his position as court organist at Bonn in part to the countess's support, expressed his conviction that 'any, even the smallest, echo of the music of her favourite composer Mozart' would be agreeable to her. (Her husband's half-brother, Count August Clemens, was a close friend of Mozart.)

In 1791 Beethoven dedicated his variations for piano on Vincenzo Righini's arietta 'Venni Amore' (WoO 65) to the countess.

(Clive[1])

Haugwitz, Paul, Count (b. Reichenbach, 22 January 1791; d. Dresden, 8 September 1856). According to K. E. Schürmann, he was a 'Landrat', i.e. district administrator. He is the author of the text set by Beethoven in his song 'Resignation' (WoO 149) which was first published in Johann Schickh's* *Wiener Zeitschrift für Kunst, Literatur, Theater und Mode* on 31 March 1818. Schindler* reports that Beethoven was so pleased with the song that he asked Schickh to convey his gratitude to the poet for providing the stimulus for such a 'happy inspiration'.

(Schindler[1], Schürmann)

Hauschka, Vinzenz (b. ?Mies [Stříbo, Czech Republic], 21 January 1766; d. Vienna, 13 September [?January] 1840). Civil servant; musician. He received his early musical instruction from his father, Thaddäus Hauschka, a teacher and organist, and at St Vitus' Cathedral, Prague, where he was a chorister. He became an excellent cellist and performer on the baryton, and as a result was engaged to play in the private orchestra of Count Johann Joseph Anton Thun-Hohenstein. Following the count's death in 1788, he performed in various towns in Germany. By 1793 he had settled in Vienna, where he was employed as a finance officer in a government department. At the same time, he quickly made a name for himself as an outstanding amateur musician. In his *Jahrbuch der Tonkunst von Wien und Prag* (1796), J. F. von Schönfeld calls him 'one of our most brilliant cellists', adding: 'At the most elegant concerts he is much in demand not simply as an accompanist, but also, and especially, as a soloist.'

He was among the original fifty representatives [*Repräsentanten*] of the Gesellschaft der Musikfreunde* and a member of its first executive committee. In addition, he had overall responsibility for the society's concerts from 1815 to 1827. He himself conducted many of the early concerts, including the very first one on 3 December 1815 which offered music by Mozart,* Righini, Hummel,* Handel,* Cherubini,* and Salieri.* On 10 March 1816, Hauschka conducted the Overture to *Egmont*, and during the following seasons he conducted the Seventh Symphony (2 February 1817) and the first movement of the 'Eroica' Symphony (3 May 1818).

It is not known when Beethoven made Hauschka's acquaintance, nor in what circumstances their friendship developed, but their contacts are likely to pre-date Hauschka's participation in the first performance of *Wellingtons Sieg* on 8 December 1813. Beethoven's published correspondence contains only four short letters to Hauschka, the first of which probably dates from December 1816 or January 1817 (*Corr.* A716/B1026); the last one was written in September 1824 (*Corr.* A1309/B1882). In all of them Beethoven uses the familiar 'Du', and his tone is at times downright affectionate. Two, or perhaps three, of the letters contain references to the oratorio which the Gesellschaft der Musikfreunde had invited Beethoven to compose. In *Corr.* A903/B1259 (written some time after 19 May 1818) Beethoven expressed his acceptance in a brief setting of the words 'Ich bin bereit! Amen' (WoO 201). Another musical token of their friendship is the canon WoO 172.

Hauschka himself wrote a number of compositions for the voice and some chamber music, with parts for the cello or baryton.

(Komma, *ÖBL*)

Haydn, (Franz) Joseph (b. Rohrau, Lower Austria, 31 March 1732; d. Vienna, 31 May 1809). Composer. Franz Gerhard Wegeler* relates in *Biographische Notizen* that when Haydn stayed at Bonn on his return journey from his first visit to London (i.e. in July 1792), Beethoven showed him a cantata he had written (*see* Joseph II*), and that Haydn thought highly of it and encouraged him to pursue his studies. This was, however, not necessarily Beethoven's first meeting with Haydn, which may have occurred when the latter passed through Bonn on his way to England in December 1790. (It is even possible that Beethoven had shown his cantata to Haydn already on that occasion.)

Early in November 1792, the Elector Maximilian Franz* sent Beethoven to Vienna to study with Haydn. The arrangements for this journey had probably been made while Haydn was at Bonn in July. As for the nature of the instruction which Beethoven received, Gustav Nottebohm concluded, on the strength of an analysis of Haydn's corrections of some of his exercises in counterpoint, that

Haydn was 'not a systematic, thorough, or meticulous teacher'. But a modern scholar, Alfred Mann, has argued that Nottebohm failed to 'take into account the complexity of the two artistic personalities involved, or fully reckon with the awkwardness of the didactic situation', and that the corrections in question ought accordingly to be considered in a different light. A further matter for discussion is the degree of reliance which should be placed on certain statements made by Johann Baptist Schenk* in 1830.

There is also some disagreement concerning the credence to be given to allegations—usually based on anecdotes told many years after the events described—of a temperamental conflict and mutual distrust between Beethoven and Haydn, especially during the period of Beethoven's pupillage. This period undoubtedly began soon after Beethoven's arrival in Vienna in late 1792 and presumably continued, though not without interruption, more or less until Haydn left once again for England in January 1794. If their relations did indeed suffer any strain during this period—of which there is no firm evidence—it might conceivably have resulted from Haydn's correspondence with Maximilian Franz in late 1793. On 23 November Haydn sent the elector five compositions by Beethoven, which, he suggested in his accompanying letter, were proof of his diligence. He expressed moreover his conviction that Beethoven would one day become one of Europe's greatest composers. In the same letter he requested the elector to increase the allowance already granted to Beethoven, since his present one had proved inadequate and he had himself been obliged to supplement it (*Corr.* B13). In a tart reply (of which only a draft, dated 23 December 1793, has survived), the elector stated that four of the five compositions in question had been written by Beethoven prior to his departure for Vienna, and had even been performed in Bonn; and that, as far as his income was concerned, he was in fact receiving a considerably higher amount than Haydn had indicated (*Corr.* B14; *see also* Maximilian Franz*). Whether Beethoven deliberately misinformed Haydn about his income and about the date of composition of his works (which he presumably revised in Vienna, even if he did not compose them there) it is impossible to say. A modern scholar, James Webster, has suggested that the elector may never have sent his letter or that it may not have reached Haydn before he left for England on 19 January 1794, but this is, of course, mere speculation. If, however, Haydn did receive the letter, he would have been justified in feeling some annoyance. Perhaps it was for this reason that he decided not to take Beethoven to England with him; but, then again, it is by no means certain that he had ever intended to do so, even though Christian Gottlob Neefe* had stated in the *Berliner Zeitung* on 26 October 1793 that when Beethoven was sent to Vienna, it was in the expectation that he would accompany Haydn on his next journey to London. There is no evidence that the tuition was ever resumed after Haydn's return from England in the summer of 1795.

In 1796 Beethoven dedicated his three Piano Sonatas Op. 2 to Haydn, though without identifying himself in the title as the latter's pupil, as, according to Ferdinand Ries,* Haydn had wished him to do in his early compositions in Vienna. (Beethoven refused to do so, he reportedly told Ries, because he 'had never learnt anything from him'.) There may well have been a certain ambivalence in Beethoven's attitude towards Haydn, then and later, as there was no doubt in Haydn's feelings for him. Thus, while Haydn recognized Beethoven's outstanding qualities and respected his judgement in musical matters, and was therefore gratified to hear from Georg August von Griesinger* that Beethoven had expressed high praise for *Die Schöpfung* and *Die Jahresheiten*, he complained about what he regarded as Beethoven's arrogance towards him (*see* Griesinger's letter to Breitkopf & Härtel* of 4 January 1804); and Ignaz von Seyfried* recalled that Haydn had, in his last years, sometimes referred to Beethoven as 'our Grand Mogul'.

As for Beethoven, his determination to shed whatever influence Haydn's music had exercised on his compositional style and to plough an independent furrow did not blind him to the excellence of many of Haydn's works, and he stated his admiration for them on more than one occasion. Writing to Prince Nikolaus Esterházy* on 26 July 1807, he spoke of his apprehension at offering his Mass (Op. 86) to a prince who was accustomed to hearing 'the inimitable masterpieces of the great Haydn'. Lest this be regarded as flattery, not so much for the composer as for the nobleman who employed him, two other examples are worthy of mention. On 17 July 1812, in replying to a 'fan letter' from a young girl, he wrote: 'Do not rob Handel,* Haydn, and Mozart* of their laurel wreaths: they are entitled to them, I do not yet merit mine.' And in 1824 he wrote to his copyist Peter Gläser:* 'I am of the same opinion as those great men Haydn, Mozart, and Cherubini,* who never hesitated to delete, shorten, or lengthen [a piece of music]' (*Corr.* A1275/B1814). But the most touching evidence of Beethoven's lasting and profound regard for Haydn dates from the period of his final illness. Both Schindler* (in a letter to Ignaz Moscheles on 14 March 1827, *Corr.* B2282) and Gerhard von Breuning* (in *Aus dem Schwarzspanierhause*) describe his great delight when Anton Diabelli* gave him a newly published lithograph of the Haydn family's house at Rohrau, in Lower Austria. 'Just look at this small house —to think that such a great man was born in it,' he said to Gerhard; and Schindler reports him as addressing similar words to Johann Nepomuk Hummel*: 'My dear Hummel, just look at the house in which Haydn was born. I was given it as a present to-day, and I am tremendously pleased with it. That such a great man should have been born in a modest peasant hut!'

(Griesinger, Landon², Mann¹,², Nottebohm¹, Reinöhl, Walter²,³, Webster¹, Wegeler/Ries)

Hebenstreit, Wilhelm (b. Eisleben, Thuringia, 24 May 1774; d. Gmunden, 17 April 1854). Writer. Hebenstreit lived in Vienna from 1811 until about 1836, when he moved to Gmunden. He was joint editor of the *Wiener Zeitschrift für Kunst, Literatur, Theater und Mode* from 1816 to 1818 (*see* Schickh*), and subsequently worked for *Der Sammler* and also, from 1819 to 1821, for the *Wiener Conversationsblatt*.

Hebenstreit's contention that the Italian musical terms ought to be Germanized caught the attention of Beethoven, who was particularly interested in finding a suitable German term for 'pianoforte'. Shortly before 5 January 1817 he wrote to Tobias Haslinger:* 'I would ask you not to show Hebenstreit's letter about the Germanization of *piano forte* to anyone, but to send it back to me.' He added that he was in the habit of seeking Hebenstreit's advice (*Corr.* A666/B1056; Hebenstreit's letter is lost). At that time Beethoven was choosing a title for the Sonata in A (Op. 101) which S. A. Steiner & Co.* were about to publish. Soon afterwards he concluded that a suitable German term might be 'Tasten- und Hammerflügel', but, he told Haslinger, he intended to consult a 'scholar' on the subject (*Corr.* A748/B1069). It is tempting to think that the scholar was Hebenstreit. Finally, he informed Steiner on 23 January that 'after examining the matter ourselves and after consulting our *Council*, we have decided and decide that henceforth for all our compositions where the title is in German, *Hammerklavier* is to be used instead of *Pianoforte*.' This was duly done in the case of the first edition of Op. 101, where, on the bilingual title page, 'Pianoforte' appears in the French text and 'Hammerklavier' in the German. The same principle was applied to the Sonata in B flat (Op. 106) which was issued by Artaria & Co.* in September 1819 in parallel editions bearing a French and a German title respectively; but it was not followed in the case of the Sonata in E (Op. 109), published by A. M. Schlesinger* in Berlin in 1821 with a German title only which reads 'Sonate für das Pianoforte'. As for the last Piano Sonatas (Opp. 110–11), they were originally issued with a French title only. However, a copy of Op. 110 now in the possession of the Gesellschaft der Musikfreunde* bears the title 'Sonate für das Hammerklavier', in Beethoven's writing.

(Wurzbach[1])

Heckel, (Johann) Christoph

Heckel, (Johann) Christoph (b. Mannheim, 12 August 1792; d. Mannheim, 1 December 1858). Painter and lithographer. Son of the composer and Kapellmeister Johann Jakob Heckel (1763/5–1811) who was active as a music teacher at Mannheim from *c*.1790, moved to Vienna in 1796, and died at Gumpoldskirchen, Lower Austria. (For Johann Jakob Heckel's part in the publication of the settings of 'In questa tomba oscura', *see* Rzewuski.*)

Christoph was a brother of the composer, publisher, and piano manufacturer Karl Ferdinand Heckel (1800–70). The latter was born in Vienna and received his early musical education there, then studied with J. N. Hummel* at Weimar, and eventually settled at Mannheim, where he opened a music shop in October 1821; he also founded a publishing house and manufactured pianos. The firm's publications included editions of Mozart's* operas in piano reductions and the earliest miniature scores of the Viennese classics.

Christoph studied painting at the Akademie der bildenden Künste in Vienna. He is best known to-day for his 1815 portrait of Beethoven which is now at the Library of Congress in Washington. According to an unconfirmed story, the composer sat for him in Johann Andreas Streicher's* music room. By 1823 Christoph was living at Mannheim, where he worked in close association with his brother's firm, which, in addition to its other activities, sold lithographs of portraits of many musicians.

(*ALBK, Heckel, ÖBL*)

Held, Johann Theobald (b. Hohenbruck [Třebechovice pod Orebem, Czech Republic], 11 December 1770; d. Prague, 20 June 1851). Physician; composer and musician. After qualifying in 1797, he was for thirty years on the staff of the hospital run by the Order of the Knights of St John of Jerusalem in Prague; in 1822 he was also appointed a senior physician at the General Hospital. He was greatly esteemed for his personal as well as professional qualities. Five times elected dean of the medical faculty at the University of Prague, he served as the university's rector in 1826–7. He was a notable music lover, possessed a good baritone voice, and played the violin and guitar very competently. In addition, he wrote a number of compositions, mainly for the voice.

In his autobiography Held recalls that, while on a visit to Vienna in April 1803, he and a companion, Count Prichowsky, who knew Beethoven, happened to meet the composer in the street. Beethoven took them along to Schuppanzigh's,* in whose rooms there was to be a run-through of certain arrangements for string quartet which 'Kleinhals' (i.e. Kleinheinz*) had made of some of Beethoven's piano works. Among the musicans present (and presumably taking part) were Wenzel Krumpholtz* and George Polgreen Bridgetower.* Held states that he subsequently met Beethoven on numerous occasions at concerts.

(Thayer[1], Wurzbach[1])

Henikstein, Joseph von (b. Leimen, near Heidelberg, 16 December 1768; d. Vienna, 29 April 1838). Wealthy merchant, head of the bank Henikstein & Co.; eldest son of Adam Adalbert Hönig von Henikstein (1740/5–1811) and his wife Karoline, née Seligmann (1748–1823). Adam was a prominent merchant and director of salt works in Galicia; he converted from Judaism to Catholicism in 1781, and was ennobled in 1784.

Like his brothers and business partners Karl and Johann and like his sister Josepha, who had been taught by Mozart,* Joseph was a good amateur musician; he was an excellent cellist and mandolinist, and had a fine bass voice. He told Vincent Novello in 1829 that he used to visit Mozart and try out different musical numbers of *Don Giovanni* as they were being composed, with Mozart accompanying him from his manuscript. His wife Elise, née von Sonnenstein (1770–1823), is described as an 'absolutely delightful singer' in J. F. von Schönfeld's *Jahrbuch der Tonkunst von Wien und Prag* (1796). The Heniksteins regularly gave concerts which attracted many well-known performers. Schönfeld writes: 'The muse of music has, as it were, taken up her residence in this house. Not only does the eldest son [i.e. Joseph] arrange small weekly concerts of instrumental music, when the guests consist solely of those participating in the performance, but on any evening throughout the year there is vocal music. Since a large number of our most competent amateurs and even many professional musicians gather there, one has endless opportunities to hear beautiful music.' Henikstein was among the founding members of the Gesellschaft der Musikfreunde* and was elected one of its fifty *Repräsentanten* [representatives].

Beethoven had both personal and business relations with Henikstein. A note written by him to Baron Gleichenstein* in April 1810 indicates that Henikstein had invited both of them, as well as Clementi,* to lunch on the following day (*Corr.* A252/B432). There must have been other such social contacts. Beethoven also used the bank for financial transactions, as in his dealings with Prince Golitsïn;* the latter, for his part, used the bank established at St Petersburg by Baron Ludwig Stieglitz, who, according to Nikolaus Johann van Beethoven,* was Henikstein's son-in-law (*see BKh*7/111)). In addition to handling money transfers, Henikstein assisted Beethoven in other ways. Thus he arranged the transportation from Trieste to Vienna of the piano presented to Beethoven by Thomas Broadwood* in 1818, and sent to Golitsïn a copy of the *Missa solemnis* in 1823, and the scores of the Overtures *Zur Namensfeier* and *Die Weihe des Hauses* in 1825. Eventually, believing that Henikstein had given him an unfavourable rate of exchange, Beethoven apparently asked Golitsïn to have his payments sent to Count Fries's* bank instead (*see BKh*9/57 and n. 141, and *Corr.* B2106).

Henikstein's daughter Karoline (1797–1844) married the orientalist Baron Joseph Hammer-Purgstall.*

Henning, Carl Wilhelm (b. Öls, 31 January 1784; d. Berlin, March 1867). Conductor and composer. A violinist by training, he joined the orchestra of the Nationaltheater in Berlin in 1807 and the Prussian court Kapelle in 1811; in 1822 he was accorded the title of a royal Konzertmeister. In 1823 he was designated music director of the Königstädtisches Theater which eventually opened on 4 August 1824. He remained in this post until 1826 when he resumed his position of Konzertmeister of the Kapelle; in addition, he conducted the concerts of the Philharmonische Gesellschaft from 1832 to 1836. In the latter year he was appointed royal music director, and in 1840 royal Kapellmeister; he retired in 1848. His compositions include music for plays and ballets, instrumental music, cantatas, and the opera *Die Rosenmädchen* which was produced at the Königstädtisches Theater on 22 March 1825.

As it was proposed that the Königstädtisches Theater should be inaugurated with a performance of *Die Weihe des Hauses*, the festival piece with which the new Theater in der Josefstadt had opened on 3 October 1822 and for which Beethoven had provided the music (*see* Hensler* and Meisl*), Henning called on Beethoven during a visit to Vienna in November 1823, in order to request permission to use his music. He was accompanied by the director designate of the theatre, Heinrich Eduard Bethmann. In due course Beethoven was paid 56 louis d'or by Bethmann for the score. (Bethmann was subsequently obliged to resign for financial reasons in March 1824, before the Königstädtisches Theater opened.)

Later a dispute was to arise concerning the terms of the contract (which has not survived). Henning believed that it covered the music originally written for *Die Ruinen von Athen*, on which *Die Weihe des Hauses* was based, as well as the new overture specially composed by Beethoven in 1822 (Op. 124). Beethoven, on the other hand, considered that, unlike the music for *Die Ruinen von Athen*, the overture had not become the property of the Berlin theatre under the terms of the contract; and while he did not object to its being performed there— the overture was, in fact, the only part of the music used in Vienna at the performance of *Die Weihe des Hauses* which was actually played at the opening of the Königstädtisches Theater on 4 August 1824—he was outraged to learn at the beginning of 1825 that the Berlin bookseller and music dealer Trautgott Trautwein had recently published Henning's arrangement of the overture for piano duet. He was all the more vexed because he had just sold the overture to Schott's Söhne.* (In April and July 1825 Schott published arrangements of the overture made by Carl Czerny* for two and four hands; they published the full score in December 1825.)

In his reply to a furious letter from Beethoven (1 January 1825), Henning offered not to publish any of the other arrangements he had made of the overture, but he declared himself unable and, indeed, unwilling to withdraw the one already on sale, the publication of which, he claimed, was in any case perfectly legal (*Corr.* B1923, 13 January 1825). Dissatisfied with this response, Beethoven had a notice printed in the *Wiener Zeitschrift für Kunst, Literatur, Theater und Mode* (5 March) and elsewhere, denouncing not only the illegality but even more what he considered the extremely poor quality of Henning's arrangement. Trautwein and Henning thereupon denied all the charges in a declaration inserted in the Dresden journal *Wegweiser im Gebiet der Künste und Wissenschaften* on 23 March. Finally, Schott asserted their proprietary interest in the overture in several statements printed in *Intelligenzblätter*, the supplement to the firm's periodical *Cäcilia*. In these statements, the appearance of which coincided with their publication of Czerny's arrangements of the overture, Schott emphasized furthermore that Czerny had worked under the composer's close supervision. This seems to have been the end of the dispute, but Beethoven still felt sufficiently angry about the matter the following year to complain to the singer Wilhelm

Ehlers that 'the Kapellmeister of the Königstädtisches Theater has made a wretched piano arrangement of the Overture in C' (letter of 1 August 1826).

(Becker)

Hensler [Hennsler, Hennseler], **Karl Friedrich** (b. Vaihingen, Württemberg, 1 February 1759; d. Vienna, 24 November 1825). Playwright and theatre manager; son of a physician. He studied theology at the University of Tübingen. In 1784 he moved to Vienna, where he was to devote the remainder of his life to the theatre, first as an author and subsequently, for some twenty-two years, as a manager.

Beginning in 1786, he provided the Theater in der Leopoldstadt, then owned and directed by Karl Marinelli, with a multitude of comedies (including many 'Lokalstücke' featuring a local setting and often inspired by current events), plays using subjects drawn from German or Viennese history and legend, and texts for Singspiels. Among his most popular works were *Das Donauweibchen* (1798, with music by Ferdinand Kauer) and *Die Teufelsmühle am Wienerberg* (1799, adapted by him from a text by Leopold Huber, with music by Wenzel Müller). Following Marinelli's death on 28 January 1803, Hensler became the lessee and director of the theatre, which he ran with considerable success until August 1816. He remained as administrative director under a new lessee until January 1817, and later tried, unsuccessfully, to lease the theatre again himself. For a short time (January–August 1817) he was director of the Theater an der Wien under Count Ferdinand Pálffy,* and in 1818 he assumed responsibility for the theatres at Pressburg [Bratislava] and Baden, near Vienna. Finally, in 1821, he acquired the licence for the Theater in der Josefstadt [26 Josefstädterstrasse]. Before he took charge, the owner, Wolfgang Reischl, had the original building pulled down and a new, larger and more modern theatre constructed in its place. The new theatre was to open on 3 October 1822.

Soon after Beethoven arrived in Baden early in September 1822, he received from Hensler free tickets for himself and his nephew Karl* to enable them to attend a performance of his Overture to *König Stephan* (Op. 117) at the local theatre. While this is the earliest documented evidence of contacts between them, Schindler* states in his Beethoven biography that Beethoven already knew Hensler well by then. At all events, he now readily accepted Hensler's invitation to compose music for the imminent inauguration of the new Theater in der Josefstadt. For this occasion Karl Meisl* adapted Kotzebue's* *Die Ruinen von Athen*, which had been presented, with music (Op. 113) by Beethoven, at the opening of the Pest [Budapest] theatre in 1812. For Meisl's text, entitled *Die Weihe des Hauses*, Beethoven composed an overture (Op. 124) and a chorus (WoO 98); in addition, some of the music he had written for Budapest was again performed, in part to new words. Beethoven conducted, assisted by Franz Gläser,* while Schindler led the orchestra. The entertainment also included another work by Meisl, *Das Bild des Fürsten*, with music by Joseph Drechsler.

Beethoven evidently enjoyed very amicable relations with Hensler at this time, for in the month following the opening ceremony he composed a *Gratulations-Menuett* (WoO 3) which was performed by the entire company of the theatre on the evening preceding Hensler's name day, 4 November. On the latter day, Beethoven was among the guests at a dinner given by Hensler, probably at Reischl's restaurant.

After Hensler's death his daughter Josepha von Scheidlin took over the management of the theatre.

(Czeike, Kindermann, *ÖBL*)

Herder, Johann Gottfried (b. Mohrungen, East Prussia, 25 August 1744; d. Weimar, 18 December 1803). Philosopher, poet, critic, and translator. His ideas played an important role in the formation of the 'Sturm und Drang' movement. Beethoven set poems by Herder in the songs 'Die laute Klage' (WoO 135) and 'Der Gesang der Nachtigall' (WoO 141). The former song, the composition of which has been tentatively assigned by Sieghard Brandenburg to the year 1815, was published by Anton Diabelli & Co.* in 1837; the latter, written in 1813, was first printed in 1888 in Breitkopf & Härtel's* *Gesamtausgabe*.

(Brandenburg[1])

Hermann, Franz Rudolph (b. Vienna, 1787; d. Breslau [Wrocław, Poland], 8 April 1823). Writer whose works included a dramatic trilogy about the Nibelungs, as well as a number of stories, poems, and essays. In November 1813 Beethoven set his poem 'Der Bardengeist' (WoO 142). The song appeared in the *Musenal-manach für das Jahr 1814* which was edited by Johann Erichson and published by the bookseller and printer Carl Gerold.*

(Wurzbach[1])

Herrosee, Karl Friedrich Wilhelm (b. Berlin, 31 July 1754; d. Züllichau, 8 January 1821). Protestant clergyman; son of a cantor. He attended the University of Frankfurt an der Oder (1775–7) and subsequently worked for some years as a private tutor in Berlin. In 1788 he was appointed pastor at Züllichau.

He wrote the text of a church hymn ('Danket dem Herrn, wir danken dem Herrn') which achieved a certain popularity, as well as the libretto used by Johann Heinrich Rolle in the oratorio *Gedor, oder Das Erwachen zum bessern Leben*. But if he is at all remembered today, it is as the author of the poem 'Duett eines sich zärtlich liebenden Ehepaars', published in the Leipzig journal *Für ältere und neuere Lectüre* in 1785. It was set to music by Johann Heinrich Egli, Karl Hanke, Gottfried von Jacquin—and by Beethoven in WoO 123. His composition exists in two versions which, musically, are almost identical, but which differ textually: one (probably the earlier one) is a setting of the third, fourth, and sixth stanzas of Herrosee's ten-stanza poem, while in the other one the whole poem has been compressed into five stanzas. The former version was published by Johann Traeg* in June 1803 with the simple title 'Lied' (together with 'La partenza', WoO 124); it also survives in an autograph in the possession of the Gesellschaft der Musikfreunde.* The latter version is known from a copy included in the manuscript set of Beethoven's compositions prepared under Tobias Haslinger's* direction, where the song is entitled 'Zärtliche Liebe'.

(Friedländer, Grasberger[2,5], Moser[2])

Hiller, Ferdinand (von) (b. Frankfurt am Main, 24 October 1811; d. Cologne, 11 May 1885). Conductor, composer, and teacher. He studied with Hummel* at Weimar from 1825 to 1827, and in the latter year travelled with his teacher to Vienna. While there, they called on the dying Beethoven on four occasions. Hiller provided detailed accounts of these visits in *Aus dem Tonleben unserer Zeit*, as well as in a talk he later gave to a group of Viennese journalists and writers, the text of which was printed in the periodical *Nord und Süd* in February 1880.

(Hiller[1,2])

Himmel, Friedrich Heinrich (b. Treuenbrietzen, Prussia, 20 November 1765; d. Berlin, 8 June 1814). Composer and pianist. After studying with Johann Gottlieb Naumann in Dresden, he was appointed chamber composer by King Friedrich Wilhelm II,* who then sent him on a journey to Italy (1793–5). On his return to Berlin he became royal Kapellmeister in place of Johann Friedrich Reichardt.* When Beethoven visited Berlin in 1796 he at first saw a great deal of Himmel, according to Ferdinand Ries,* but their relations grew cooler following an occasion on which they both improvised. Beethoven played first; when Himmel, in his turn, had been playing for a while, Beethoven asked him: 'Now then, when will you start in earnest?' Himmel, who believed he had already performed splendidly, was furious and a quarrel ensued. 'I thought he was just warming up,' Beethoven told Ries. A reconciliation took place, but, Ries writes, 'Himmel forgave, but he never forgot.' This probably explains the final episode in their association, for which Ries is the sole source. After his return to Vienna, they reportedly corresponded (none of their letters have survived), until one day Himmel, irritated by Beethoven's persistent requests for news from Berlin, informed him of the recent invention of a lamp for the blind. Beethoven passed on this exciting news to his Viennese acquaintances and, having met with much curiosity which he was unable to satisfy, he told Himmel that he should have supplied a more detailed description of the invention. Himmel's reply, Ries states, 'does not bear repeating'. Himmel was at Teplitz in the summer of 1811 at a time when Beethoven was also there, and he probably visited Vienna at a later date; but there are no reports of any further meetings with Beethoven.

As a musician, Beethoven does not appear to have rated Himmel very highly (*see also* Louis Ferdinand*). Yet Himmel met with considerable success in his time, in Germany as well as elsewhere, as both a pianist and a composer. His very considerable output includes sacred music, songs, and instrumental compositions, as well as works for the stage, notably the Singspiel *Fanchon das Leyermädchen* which was produced in Berlin in 1804. As a man, he must have been less than lovable. A writer in 1797 described his way of life as being 'composed of debauchery and drinking', and K. A. Varnhagen von Ense* drew an equally stark portrait in *Denkwürdigkeiten des eignen Lebens*, in which he characterized him as a 'dissolute eccentric, whose life now [in 1811] mainly alternates between periods of blissful drunkenness and wretched sobriety'.

(Allroggen², Varnhagen¹, Wegeler/Ries)

Hippius, Gustav Adolph (b. Nissi, Estonia, 1 March 1792; d. Reval [Tallinn], 24 September 1856). Painter and lithographer. He studied painting with Eduard Höppner and Karl Siegmund Walther. In 1812 he was in Prague, and from 1814 to 1816 in Vienna; later he lived at Munich and in Rome. From 1820 to 1850 he resided in St Petersburg, where he painted the portraits of numerous Russian statesmen, scholars, and artists. While in Vienna, he made a pencil drawing of Beethoven which is now at the Beethoven-Haus at Bonn.

(*DBL*, Neumann²)

Hirsch, Carl Friedrich (1801–81). Pupil of Beethoven. He told Frimmel in 1880 that his father Franz Thomas, who was married to Albrechtsberger's* youngest daughter Anna, had made Beethoven's acquaintance at the hotel Zum römischen Kaiser [1 Renngasse], where both often took their evening meal and where Beethoven had rooms at the time. Beethoven offered to give the son some instruction in musical theory, which he did for several months. The period of these lessons is likely to have extended from about November 1816 to May 1817. Hirsch's statements provide the only known indication that Beethoven may have temporarily stayed at the hotel during the winter of 1816–17. By late April or early May he had given up the apartment he had rented since the autumn of 1815 in Seilerstätte and had moved into new lodgings in Landstrasse.

(Frimmel¹)

Hochenecker [Hochnecker], **Joseph** (1793–1876). In 1987 Rita Steblin discovered in an antique shop in Vienna a pencil-drawn portrait of Beethoven which had been signed by Hochenecker and was dated '1819'. In an article published in the *Journal of the American Musicological Society* in 1992, Steblin claimed that this drawing was used by Kriehuber* in 1832 as the model for his lithographed portrait of the composer. This assertion was strongly disputed by S. Brandenburg who argued that it was Hochenecker's drawing which was derived from Kriehuber's lithograph (itself inspired by Johann Stephan Decker's* portrait) and not the other way around; and he accordingly concluded that the date 1819 could not be the true date of the drawing ('Drawings allow themselves to be predated'). In her response to these statements, Steblin stoutly defended her position. (Both Brandenburg's obervations and Steblin's further communication appeared in the *Journal of the American Musicological Society* in 1994.)

(Steblin[1])

Hoechle, Johann Nepomuk (b. Munich, 6 January 1790; d. Vienna, 12 December 1835). Painter and lithographer. Son of the Austrian court painter Johann Baptist Hoechle (1754–1832) who moved to Vienna from Munich in *c*.1800, following the death of the elector of Bavaria Karl Theodor, whose court painter he had been for some twenty years.

Johann Nepomuk Hoechle studied under Ferdinand Kobell in Munich and later under Friedrich Heinrich Füger and Michael Wutky at the Akademie der bildenden Künste in Vienna (1804–8). Under the influence of Ignace Duvivier he turned to the depiction of battle scenes, a genre for which he was to become famous. He furthermore excelled at drawings, which formed a major part of his output. Among them are three of interest to Beethoven biographers. One of these shows the composer, muffled up in a long overcoat, walking abroad in bad weather. This unsigned and undated drawing (partly highlighted in watercolour) was attributed to Hoechle by Leo Grünstein and Theodor Frimmel, and has been tentatively ascribed to the period 1820–5; its present whereabouts are unknown. After Beethoven's death, Hoechle also made drawings of the composer's room at the Schwarzspanierhaus (now at the Historisches Museum der Stadt Wien) and of the funeral procession.

(*ALBK*, Bettermann, Frimmel[3], *ÖBL*)

Höfel, Blasius (b. Vienna, 27 May 1792; d. Aigen, near Salzburg, 17 September 1863). Copperplate engraver and lithographer. After studying at the Akademie der bildenden Künste under Johann Baptist Hagenauer and Hubert Maurer, he worked as an engraver for Quirin Mark (1807–11). Later he became greatly interested in woodcutting.

In 1814, presumably during the Congress of Vienna, he was commissioned by Artaria & Co.* to make an engraving of Louis Letronne's* drawing of Beethoven. Dissatisfied with Letronne's portrait, he applied himself diligently to creating a better likeness of the composer, whose frequent visits to Artaria offered Höfel many opportunities to study his features. Beethoven granted him moreover two sittings in his rooms. The superiority of Höfel's portrait over his model becomes very apparent when the two are juxtaposed. It was judged to be an excellent likeness by his contemporaries. Aloys Fuchs* told Thayer* in 1851: 'This is just how he looked when I first met him.' Beethoven himself thought highly of the engraving and in 1816 he sent it to both Franz Gerhard Wegeler* and Antonie Brentano.* To the latter he wrote: 'I am sending you a copper engraving on which my face is portrayed. Some persons maintain that it also clearly reveals my soul, but I will express no opinion on that' (*Corr.* A607/B897).

Höfel taught drawing at the Military Academy at Wiener Neustadt from 1820 until 1837; in 1824 he became a member of the Akademie der bildenden Künste. His brother Johann Nepomuk (1788–1864) was well known for his historical and altar pictures.

(*ALBK*)

Hoffmann, E(rnst) T(heodor) A(madeus) [Ernst Theodor Wilhelm] (b. Königsberg [Kaliningrad, Russia], 24 January 1776; d. Berlin, 25 June 1822). Writer, critic, and composer (notably of the opera *Undine*, based on Fouqué's* story). He is credited with having significantly contributed to the growing appreciation for Beethoven's music in Germany, particularly by his (unsigned) articles and reviews in the Leipzig *Allgemeine musikalische Zeitung*, for which he wrote from 1809 until 1815. A searching analysis of the Fifth Symphony (4 and 11 July 1810) was followed by stimulating assessments of the Overture to *Coriolan* (5 August 1812), the Piano Trios Op. 70 (3 March 1813), the Mass in C (16 and 23 June 1813), and the music to *Egmont* (21 July 1813). An essay, 'Beethovens Instrumentalmusik', which made use in part of the earlier discussions of the symphony and the trios, was first published in the Leipzig *Zeitung für die elegante Welt* in December 1813 and subsequently reprinted in the first volume of Hoffmann's *Fantasiestücke in Callots Manier* (1814–15). A modern writer, Scott Burnham, has described Hoffmann as 'the author of the first chapter of Romantic music criticism and the charter member of the musico-literary coalition which created the mythologization of Beethoven'.

In March 1820 Beethoven sent a friendly and flattering note to Hoffmann (*Corr.* A1014/B1373) through Adam Neberich,* who had spoken to him about Hoffmann while on a visit to Vienna. Hoffmann's name prompted Beethoven to write the canon 'Hoffmann, sei ja kein Hofmann' [Hoffmann, don't ever be a courtier]. The canon (WoO 180), a good example of Beethoven's perennial love of punning, was printed in the journal *Cäcilia* in April 1825 under the title 'On a person named Hoffmann', which Beethoven had chosen himself.

(Burnham, Ehinger[2], Schmitz, Schnaus)

Hoffmeister, Franz Anton (b. Rothenburg am Neckar, 12 May 1754; d. Vienna, 9 February 1812). Music publisher and composer. He arrived in Vienna in 1768 to study law, but subsequently made music his career. A prolific and popular composer, he wrote over sixty symphonies, some sixty concertos, an enormous amount of chamber music, and several Singspiels, of which the most successful was *Der*

Königssohn aus Ithaka, to a libretto by Emanuel Schikaneder* (first produced at the Freihaus-Theater on 27 June 1795).

He began to publish in Vienna in 1784 and ran his business, somewhat fitfully and at different addresses, until 1806. He issued first editions of several of Mozart's* works, including the Violin Sonatas K481 and K526 and the Quartets K478 and K499 (the latter being known as the 'Hoffmeister' Quartet). Among other composers on his list were Albrechtsberger,* Dittersdorf,* and Ignace Joseph Pleyel.* In 1800 he established the Bureau de musique at Leipzig, together with the organist Ambrosius Kühnel. Its publishing activities were conducted in rather loose association with the Viennese firm. When Hoffmeister returned to Vienna in 1805, Kühnel remained in sole charge of the Bureau de musique; after his death in 1813, the business was acquired by the Leipzig bookseller Carl Friedrich Peters.* Hoffmeister himself withdrew from publishing in 1806 (*see* Steiner*) and devoted all his time to composition.

Beethoven knew Hoffmeister by 1799 at the latest, for towards the end of that year Hoffmeister published the first editions of the *Sonate pathétique* and the variations on the trio 'Tändeln und scherzen' from Süssmayr's opera *Soliman II* (WoO 76). In 1801–2 the first editions of the following works were published simultaneously by Hoffmeister & Co. in Vienna and Hoffmeister & Kühnel (Bureau de musique) at Leipzig: the Second Piano Concerto, the First Symphony, the Piano Sonata in B flat major (Op. 22), and the Septet (Op. 20). Lastly, the following compositions were first published at Leipzig by Hoffmeister & Kühnel (Bureau de musique): *Zwei Praeludien* for piano or organ (Op. 39), Romance for violin (Op. 40), Serenade for piano and flute (Op. 41), all in December 1803; Notturno for piano and viola (Op. 42), the Overture to the ballet *Die Geschöpfe des Prometheus* (Op. 43), and Variations for piano trio (Op. 44), all in January 1804.

(Slezak[4], Weinmann[2,11])

Hoftheater-Musik-Verlag. When the court theatres were taken over by a group of noblemen [*Kavaliere*] in 1807, the Hoftheater-Musik-Verlag, the publishing house attached to the theatres, which had been founded by Baron Peter Braun* in 1796 and managed by Thaddäus [Thadé] Weigl, a brother of Joseph Weigl,* ceased its activities for several years. In 1811 it was acquired by Prince Joseph Franz Maximilian Lobkowitz,* one of the *Kavaliere,* who ran it until his death in 1816. During that period more than 200 items were published. Among them were the first editions of the piano transcriptions of Beethoven's march for Christoph Kuffner's* tragedy *Tarpeja* (WoO 2a) in 1813, and of his music for the final scene of Georg Friedrich Treitschke's* *Die gute Nachricht* (WoO 94) in 1814.

(Slezak[4])

Hölty, Ludwig Christoph Heinrich (b. Mariensee, near Hanover, 21 December 1748; d. Mariensee, 1 September 1776). Poet. The son of a pastor, he studied theology at Göttingen University. In 1774 he returned to Mariensee, where he earned his living as a translator and private tutor. He died two years later from tuberculosis.

Hölty was a member of the Göttinger Hainbund, a group of young poets united in their fervent admiration for Klopstock,* and he contributed to H. C. Boie's *Göttinger Musenalmanach*. His poems were not published in volume form until after his death—in 1783, by Johann Heinrich Voss and Friedrich Leopold Stolberg, with some 'improvements' of the original text by Voss. Unlike Schubert,* who made over thirty settings of poems by Hölty, Beethoven turned to him only once, for the song 'Klage' (WoO 113). It was composed in Bonn around 1790 and did not appear in print in Beethoven's lifetime.

Holz, Karl (b. Vienna, 3 March 1799; d. Vienna, 9 November 1858). Minor official in the finance office of the Lower Austrian Landstände; violinist and conductor. Son of Wolfgang Holz (b. 1756), of Bavarian origin and described in the church records as a 'Chirurg' [surgeon], and of his wife Anna Maria, née Hörmann (b. 1764), who came from Hainfeld in Lower Austria. Nothing is known about Holz's education, but he is likely to have attended high school (perhaps the Schotten-Gymnasium), though not the university; one of his entries in the conversation books indicates some knowledge of classical literature. As for his musical training, Thayer* believed, on the strength of an observation by Karl van Beethoven* (*BKh* 7/206), that Holz had studied with Franz Xaver Glöggl* in Linz, but it has since been shown that the remark referred not to Holz, but to Tobias Haslinger.* Holz probably received some tuition from Ignaz Schuppanzigh,* who, on one occasion (*BKh* 5/205), punningly referred to him as his 'hölzerner Schüler' [wooden pupil]. He was a competent violinist and perhaps played the viola as well; he also gave violin lessons. He became the second violinist in the quartet directed by Joseph Böhm* in the early 1820s, and from 1823 occupied the same position in the new quartet formed by Schuppanzigh after his return from Russia. He thus took part in many performances of Beethoven's chamber music. In addition, he conducted at the Concerts spirituels and elsewhere.

His intimate association with Beethoven dates from 1825, though he may be assumed to have made his acquaintance earlier. On 2 April 1825 he called on Beethoven, apparently in order to consult him about the tempos of his Fourth Symphony which Holz was to conduct at a concert of the Gesellschaft der Musikfreunde* two days later. By the summer their relations had become close. Beethoven at first employed Holz as a copyist, but he very soon used him for more personal matters, and in a general manner Holz came to occupy the position previously assumed by Schindler,* who had fallen out of favour. 'A thousand thanks for your devotion to me and for your affection,' Beethoven wrote on 24 August 1825, from Baden. 'Do write again, or better still, come to see me.' And he asked Holz not to forget to visit his 'Benjamin', i.e. Karl, which proves that Holz had by then been admitted to his more intimate circle. This situation continued until Beethoven went to Gneixendorf in September 1826. Holz's work as a civil servant was far from demanding and he seems to have devoted much of his free time to Beethoven, as is evident from the latter's correspondence and from Holz's countless entries in the conversation books. His remarks show him to be intelligent and well informed, and are occasionally spiced with an amusing touch of irony. He must have been an agreeable companion, and he reportedly had a great liking for wine. During this period he continued to perform Beethoven's music, sometimes in the composer's presence. One such occasion, when he had, not very successfully, substituted for Schuppanzigh as first violinist in private performances of the Quartets Opp. 127 and 132, resulted in Beethoven composing the musical joke WoO 204. (The canon WoO 197 is also associated with Holz.)

Beethoven wrote to Holz immediately after his return to Vienna at the beginning of December 1826, but he seems to have mislaid the letter before he could send it. A few days later he wrote a further letter (*Corr.* A1541/B2234), in which he mentioned having fallen ill and asked Holz to visit him. (There is a hint in this letter of a recent quarrel, for which Beethoven takes responsibility; this, at any rate, may well be the explanation for the canon WoO 198 included in the letter—*see* Kirnberger.*) Holz came promptly, and it was he who contacted Dr Wawruch* when Dr Braunhofer* and Dr Staudenheim* failed to call after being summoned. Soon afterwards, however, in circumstances which are unclear, Schindler resumed his former position, while Holz largely withdrew from the scene. Although he visited Beethoven several times during the following months and Beethoven still made occasional use of his services, their relationship appears to have lost some of its intimacy. This was no doubt due in part to the presence and influence of Schindler, who disliked Holz intensely, but in part also to the fact that Holz had become engaged; he was to marry Elisabeth von Bogner on 16 May 1827.

At Holz's request, Beethoven gave him written authorization on 30 August 1826 to write his biography. Schindler states that Beethoven later regretted this (*see also* Rochlitz*), but did not ask Holz to return the document. However, Holz never wrote his biography, and on 4 November 1843—by which time Franz Gerhard Wegeler's* and Ferdinand Ries's* *Biographische Notizen,* as well as Schindler's biography, had been published—he formally transferred the authorization to the Viennese-born composer and writer on music Ferdinand Simon Gassner, who was then director of music at Karlsruhe and editor of the *Zeitschrift für Deutschlands Musik-Vereine und Dilettanten.* (In this connection, *see also* Fischhof* and Hotschevar.*) But Gassner, who died in 1851, did not complete the project either.

(Brenneis[1], Ullrich[4])

Holzmann, Barbara (b. 1755). Beethoven's longtime housekeeper, first engaged on 30 May 1822. He quickly took against her, disliking her manner and deploring the quality of her cooking. Accordingly his letters contain numerous derogatory remarks about the performance of 'Die Alte' [The old woman]—the term by which she is most frequently designated. Other, less innocuous, epithets are 'The old beast', 'The old witch', and 'The old devil'; on at least two occasions she is referred to as 'Frau Schnapps'. She also figures prominently in the conversation books, in which, moreover, she herself made a number of largely illiterate entries. Yet, although Beethoven repeatedly expressed his intention of dismissing her and, at various times, searched for a suitable replacement, she remained in his employment—with, possibly, a short break or two—until early 1826. Even then her absence was apparently only temporary, for she reportedly re-entered his service in December of that year (*see BKh*10 n. 104).

Honrath, Jeanette d'. Beethoven's first love, according to Franz Gerhard Wegeler.* She lived at Cologne, but frequently spent several weeks at Bonn as a guest of the Breunings.* Wegeler describes her as 'a beautiful and vivacious blonde' who enjoyed music and had a pleasing voice. She married the Austrian recruiting officer at Cologne, Captain Carl Greth, who later rose to the rank of lieutenant-field marshal and became owner of an infantry regiment and commanding officer at Temesvar [Timisoara, Romania]; he died on 15 October 1827.

(Wegeler/Ries)

Hornemann, Christian (b. Copenhagen, 15 August 1765; d. Copenhagen, 7 March 1844). Miniaturist, pastellist, and lithographer. After studying at the Copenhagen Academy of Fine Arts, he lived between 1786 and 1803 in Italy, Germany (Dresden, Leipzig, Berlin), and Austria. The last five years of that period he spent in Vienna, where he had arrived with a letter of introduction from the German sculptor Johann Gottfried Schadow to the director of the Vienna Akademie der bildenden Künste, Friedrich Heinrich Füger. In Berlin he had, together with the miniaturist H. H. Plötz, painted portraits of King Friedrich Wilhelm III* (1797) and Queen Luise (1798).

In Vienna his subjects included Beethoven, whose portrait he painted on ivory in 1802. This miniature is the best of the early portraits of Beethoven. The composer presented it in November 1804 to Stephan von Breuning,* with whom he had recently become reconciled after a quarrel that had kept them apart since July. In the accompanying letter he wrote: 'May what has passed between us for a time, my dear good St., be forever hidden behind this painting—I know that I tore your heart apart, but the torment within me, which you must have noticed, has sufficiently punished me for that . . . My portrait has long been intended for you' (*Corr.* A98/B197). It is today at the Beethoven-Haus at Bonn.

(*ALBK*)

Hotschevar, Jakob (*c.*1780–1842). Civil servant; married to Judith Förschl, a stepsister of Johanna van Beethoven's* mother. He helped Johanna in her dispute with Beethoven over the guardianship and education of her son Karl* by drawing up her petitions to the Landrecht of 21 September and 11 December 1818 and supporting them with an extensive statement, in which he sought to demonstrate Beethoven's unsuitability to act as sole guardian of his nephew. When, at a hearing before the court on 11 December, she was asked where she would find the means to provide for her son, she replied that Hotschevar was prepared to defray the expenses. His attitude towards her changed after she had an illegitimate daughter in 1820, and he refused her request to assume the guardianship of the child (*see* Johanna van Beethoven*).

After Beethoven's death, Stephan von Breuning* became Karl's guardian; but, following Breuning's death on 4 June 1827, Hotschevar was appointed guardian in his place. He thereby came into possession of certain documents concerning Beethoven, and he reportedly made these available to Anton Gräffer who was planning to write a biography of the composer, perhaps together with the help of Karl Holz* and of Hotschevar himself. (Eventually these documents were given by Gräffer to Ferdinand Simon Gassner—*see also* Fischhof* and Holz.*)

In his capacity as guardian, Hotschevar succeeded in obtaining the London Philharmonic Society's* agreement not to seek to reclaim the gift of £100 (=1,000 florins) which it had made to Beethoven, but to allow the sum to form part of Karl's inheritance (*see* Rau*). Hotschevar remained Karl's guardian until he attained his majority in September 1830.

Huber, Franz Xaver (b. Beneschau [Benešov, Czech Republic], 10 October 1755; d. Mainz, 25 July 1814). Dramatist, librettist, and journalist. He was active as a writer and journalist in Prague in 1780, and in Vienna from 1781 on. On 28 September 1797 he married the pianist (Maximiliana Valentina) Walburga Willmann (1769–1835), a sister of Magdalena Willmann.* A champion of the Enlightenment, Huber helped to found a number of liberal newspapers which provided him with a forum for his anticlericalism and his social and political ideas. His support for the French Revolution forced him to flee to Germany, but he was back in Vienna at the turn of the century. In 1809 he was, however, obliged to leave the country once more after expressing his admiration for Napoleon in his journal *Morgenbote*, and this time he does not appear to have returned.

He had some success as a playwright; his most successful work, *Julchen, oder Liebe Mädchen, spiegelt euch!* was produced at the Burgtheater on 1 September 1793. He also furnished the librettos for Franx Xaver Süssmayr's operas *Die edle Rache* (Kärntnertor-Theater, 27 August 1795) and *Soliman der Zweite* (1 October 1799), and for Peter Winter's *Das unterbrochene Opferfest* (14 June 1796). In 1802–3 he provided Beethoven with the text for the oratorio *Christus am Ölberg*, which was first performed at the Theater an der Wien on 5 April 1803. Beethoven later claimed that the work 'was written by myself and the poet in the space of two weeks; but the poet was musical and had already written several texts to be set to music, and I could discuss the work with him at any moment' (letter to Raphael Georg Kiesewetter* of 23 January 1824). In fact, as Barry Cooper has persuasively argued, Beethoven was probably closely involved in planning the dramatic structure and perhaps even in writing the text of this oratorio, which was a 'direct, conscious and almost immediate response to his personal crisis as embodied and brought to a head in the Heiligenstadt Testament'.

This does not mean, however, that Beethoven felt fully satisfied with either text or music, especially since critical reaction at the first performance was less than enthusiastic. He accordingly made some changes in the music in 1804. The text itself was substantially revised prior to the publication of the oratorio by Breitkopf & Härtel* in 1811, but these changes were made at the instigation of the publishers who made various suggestions, some but not all of which Beethoven accepted. 'I know that the text is extremely bad,' he wrote to the publishers from Teplitz [Teplice] on 23 August 1811. 'But once one has thought out a whole work from even a bad text, it is difficult to avoid damaging that whole by making changes here and there, and as for single words which sometimes carry great significance, they must stand. A good composer is one who seeks and is able to produce as good a work as possible even from a poor text; and if he is incapable of doing so, the composition as a whole will certainly not be improved by a few alterations. I have accepted some, since they really are improvements.' However, not all of Beethoven's decisions were followed by the publishers, nor is it by any means certain that all the textual changes which were made had first been submitted to him for his approval.

The only known written communication from Beethoven to a person named Huber (*Corr.* A518/B749) may not have been addressed to the subject of this article. Together with this note, Beethoven sent his correspondent a lithographed portrait of himself which he signed 'Your friend who sincerely esteems you'. According to Theodor Frimmel, the lithograph in question was the one executed by Blasius Höfel* from Louis Letronne's* portrait; it bore the date 1814. It has been suggested, with some plausibility, that the portrait was made during the Congress of Vienna, and therefore not earlier than the autumn of 1814. Huber had died in July of that year.

(Asshoff, Brandenburg[4], Cooper[4], Tyson[5])

Hummel, Johann Nepomuk (b. Pressburg [Bratislava, Slovak Republic], 14 November 1778; d. Weimar, 17 October 1837). Pianist, composer, and teacher. While still a young boy, Hummel studied with Mozart* and even lodged with his family, probably in 1786–7. It is therefore possible that he made Beethoven's acquaintance during the latter's brief stay in Vienna in 1787. The following year Hummel departed on a concert tour which was to last some four years, and by the time he returned to Vienna early in 1793 he had gained international renown as a pianist of prodigious accomplishments. Although no details are known about his contacts with Beethoven during the following decade, the two men are certain to have met on various occasions. Their relations are moreover likely to have benefited from the absence of any constant and overt rivalry on the concert platform, since Hummel made few public appearances, preferring to devote his time mainly to study, composition, and teaching. For his part, Beethoven was able to gain rapidly a reputation as an outstanding pianist and, more gradually, as a composer of exceptional talent and originality.

From 1804 until 1811 Hummel was Konzertmeister to Prince Nikolaus Esterházy* at Eisenstadt. It was there that Beethoven's Mass in C major, which the prince had commissioned, was first performed on 13 September 1807. According to Schindler,* this performance was the cause of an estrangement between Beethoven and Hummel (who, in any case, 'had never been on intimate terms'), because Hummel appeared to agree with the prince's criticism of the music (*see* the article on Esterházy). Schindler also gives further reasons for Beethoven's alleged hostility towards Hummel. However, as in the case of certain other statements made by Schindler, several modern scholars are doubtful about the truth of these assertions. In 1811 Hummel returned to Vienna and there, on 16 May 1813, he married the singer Elisabeth Röckel (1793–1883), a sister of Joseph August Röckel.* Like so many other prominent musicians, he participated in performances of *Wellingtons Sieg* in the winter of 1813–14. At the first two performances, on 8 and 12 December, he played the big drum; at subsequent performances on 2 January and 27 February he took over the direction of the percussion instruments from Salieri.* In this connection, a note from Beethoven (*Corr.* A466/B700) asking him 'to conduct the drums and cannonades with your excellent Kapellmeister's and artillery commander's baton' at the last of these performances is noteworthy for its very friendly tone and, especially, for its opening: 'Allerliebster Hummel!' [Beloved Hummel], which clearly indicates that if Beethoven had ever felt any coolness towards Hummel, it had by then been replaced by feelings of affection. On 4 April 1816, on the occasion of Hummel's appointment as Kapellmeister at Stuttgart, Beethoven wrote the canon 'Ars longa, vita brevis' (WoO 170) in Hummel's (now lost) album, together with the words 'Bon voyage, my dear Hummel. Think sometimes of your friend Ludwig van Beethoven.' A curious aspect of this inscription—copied by Ludwig Nohl and first published by him, with the canon, in 1867—is Beethoven's use of the formal 'Sie', whereas he had used the familiar 'Du' in the above-cited letter of 1814. While in Stuttgart, Hummel conducted the first performance of *Fidelio* in that city, on 20 July 1817. In January 1819 he became grand ducal Kapellmeister at Weimar.

As far as is known, the two men did not correspond after Hummel had left Vienna. But they were to see each other again in March 1827, when Hummel, who was in Vienna with his wife and his young pupil Ferdinand Hiller,* visited the dying Beethoven. Altogether, Hummel called on Beethoven on four occasions (on 8, 13, 20, and 23 March), each time with Hiller and at least once accompanied by his wife. In a letter to Ignaz Moscheles* on 14 March, Schindler related that Hummel had burst into tears at the sight of his stricken friend (*Corr.* B2282). Hummel was a pallbearer at Beethoven's funeral. A fellow mourner, Paul Friedrich Walther, recalled in 1860 what happened at the cemetery: 'Hummel threw into the grave three wreaths of laurel—one on the head, one on the feet, and one on the centre of the body—and then, with tears in our eyes, we left this most memorable spot.' On 7 April Hummel played, as he had promised Beethoven, at a concert given at the Theater in der Josefstadt for Schindler's benefit. For his improvisation he took as his principal theme the Allegretto from the Seventh Symphony.

Hummel published arrangements for piano quartet of a number of Beethoven's works, including the first seven symphonies.

(Benyovszky, Hiller[1,2], Sachs, Walther)

Hunczovsky, Johann Nepomuk (b. Čech, [Čechy pod Kosiřem], near Prossnitz [Prostějov, Czech Republic], 15 May 1752; d. Vienna, 4 April 1798). Surgeon. After studying in Vienna, Milan, Paris, and London, he taught various aspects of medicine and, especially, surgery, at a military hospital in the Gumpendorf suburb of Vienna, and from 1785 lectured at the new Josefs-Akademie [Josefinum]; later he specialized in gynaecology. In 1791 he accompanied Leopold II on a journey to Italy, and was subsequently appointed personal surgeon to the emperor. He was the author of a number of scientific publications, notably *Anweisungen zu chirurgischen Operationen* (1785). He was, moreover, a highly cultured man who spoke several languages and collected paintings and etchings. Stephan von Breuning,* after a visit to the Austrian capital in 1796, described him as 'the most charming man I came to know in Vienna'.

There is no evidence that Beethoven ever consulted Hunczovsky professionally, but he certainly met him socially on numerous occasions. Lorenz von Breuning mentions in a letter to his sister Eleonore in 1795 that he frequently met Beethoven at Hunczovsky's. And on 8 October 1796 Lorenz wrote to his mother: 'Some 4 days before Stephan left Vienna, Hunczovsky and his family, together with a certain Böcking [Dr Wilhelm Böcking, a colleague of Hunczovsky's], visited us in my room and spent the whole evening with us. We entertained them with music, to which [Andreas Jakob and Bernhard Heinrich] Romberg, who are at present in Vienna, and Beethoven contributed splendidly.'

(Czeike, Ley[1], Neumayr, Puschmann, Wegeler/Ries, Wurzbach[1])

Hüttenbrenner, Anselm (b. Graz, 13 October 1794; d. Ober-Andritz, near Graz, 5 June 1868). Composer and pianist. After studying theology and Semitic languages at Rein Monastery, near Graz (where he was a novice in 1812–13, but which he left without taking his vows), he enrolled as a law student at the University of Graz; he also studied music with the Graz Cathedral organist Matthäus Gell. While on a visit to Vienna, probably early in 1815, he became a pupil of Salieri.* From then on, he attended law courses during the winter in Vienna and in the summer at Graz. After completing his studies in 1818 he at first worked in local government at Graz, but in 1819 he took up a position in the civil service in Vienna. However, following his father's death, he was obliged to leave Vienna in 1821 to take charge of the family's estate in Styria. He took a very active part in the musical life of Graz.

Hüttenbrenner met Schubert* in 1815 while both were studying with Salieri. The next year, according to his own account, he was introduced to Beethoven by Joseph Eppinger.* The essential source for information regarding Hüttenbrenner's contacts with Beethoven is Thayer,* who was able to draw both on a conversation he had with Hüttenbrenner at Graz on 5 June 1860 and on a long letter which Hüttenbrenner addressed to him on 20 August of that year. At their first meeting Beethoven said, after looking at two compositions by Hüttenbrenner: 'I am not worthy that you should visit me'—a remark which still puzzled Hüttenbrenner decades later: 'If this was humility, it was divine; if it was irony, it was excusable.' Hüttenbrenner does not speak of any further meetings with Beethoven during his stay in Vienna in 1816, though he mentions observing Beethoven frequently during the latter's visits to Steiner's* music shop. In March 1827, having heard of Beethoven's grave illness, he travelled to Vienna in the hope of seeing him once more. He told Thayer that he had visited Beethoven about a week before his death, together with Schubert and Schindler,* and that he had again called at Beethoven's lodgings on 26 March and was present at his death: 'I closed the half-open eyelids of the dead man and kissed them, then also his forehead, mouth and hands.' He stated, moreover, that only one other person had been in the room during Beethoven's last moments. In his conversation with Thayer he identified that person as Johanna van Beethoven,* while in his letter he named Beethoven's other sister-in-law, Therese.* Strong doubt has, however, been expressed by scholars about the likelihood of either woman having been there that day, and it has been suggested that the other person was in fact the housekeeper Sali [Rosalie] (*see also* Teltscher*). In June 1827, Tobias Haslinger* published a musical tribute to Beethoven (*Nachruf an Beethoven, in Akkorden am Pianoforte*) by 'his most fervent admirer Anselm Hüttenbrenner'.

Anselm's brother Joseph (1796–1882), a government official and amateur musician, also knew Beethoven. After the first performance of the Ninth Symphony on 7 May 1824, at which he sang in the chorus, Beethoven invited Joseph to ride back with him in his carriage, together with his nephew Karl* and Schindler, to his rooms in Landstrasse. (Joseph's note describing this incident is preserved at the Stadtbibliothek in Vienna.)

(Clive², Suppan)

Jahn, Ignaz (b. Hungary, 1744; d. Vienna, 26 February 1810). Restaurateur and caterer. In 1772 he was appointed caterer at Schönbrunn by Empress Maria Theresa, and in 1775 he opened a restaurant in the Augarten, the imperial property which Joseph II* threw open to the general public that year and which soon became a favourite pleasure park for the Viennese. There, in addition to providing excellent food, Jahn was presently to launch, in a large room specially set aside for the purpose, a series of regular concerts which were to play a significant part in the musical life of the city. These concerts, which took place at an early hour of the day (at 8, or even 7 o'clock), were given by an orchestra composed for the most part of amateurs. At the first one, on 26 May 1782, Mozart* conducted one of his symphonies (perhaps K338) and played his concerto for two pianos (K365) with Josepha Barbara Auernhammer. From *c*.1798 the concerts were directed by Ignaz Schuppanzigh.* Some well-known musicians, such as the violinists Joseph Mayseder* and Franz Xaver Pecháček* and the cellist Joseph Linke,* reportedly made their professional debut in Vienna at an Augarten concert; Marie Bigot,* Carl Czerny,* Ferdinand Ries,* and Ignaz Moscheles* were among the pianists who took part. A number of Beethoven symphonies and piano concertos were performed at the concerts, and on 24 May 1803 the composer himself accompanied George Polgreen Bridgetower* in the first performance of his 'Kreutzer' Sonata.

Even more famous than Jahn's establishment in the Augarten was his restaurant in the inner city, which, after locations in the Kärntnerstrasse (from 1774) and later the Neuer Markt, occupied from 1788 part of a house [6 Himmelpfortgasse] adjoining the winter palace built earlier in the century for Prince Eugène of Savoy. Jahn at first rented the premises, then bought the house on 15 February 1792, and it remained in his possession until 6 April 1808 when he sold it to a merchant, André Joseph Popper. Here also he had at his disposal a large room capable of accommodating some 400 persons, which was regularly used for concerts from *c*.1790, but had already served for that purpose on some earlier occasions, including a performance in 1788 of Handel's* *Acis and Galatea* under Mozart's direction. It was also at Jahn's hall that Mozart made his final appearance as a soloist on 4 March 1791, playing his Piano Concerto in B flat major (K595). His Requiem was performed there on 2 January 1793.

Beethoven performed as pianist on at least two occasions at Jahn's hall. On 6 April 1797, at a concert given by Schuppanzigh, he took part in the first performance of his Piano Quintet (Op. 16). According to the programme, he furthermore accompanied 'Madame Willmann' in an aria composed by himself. The aria has not been identified; the singer was either the former Magdalena Willmann,* who had married Antonio Galvani the previous year, or more probably her stepmother Marianne Tribolet-Willmann. And on 29 March 1798 Beethoven played a violin sonata—perhaps one from Op. 12—with Schuppanzigh; among the other artists appearing at that concert was Josefa Dušek.* It is also worth mentioning that the first public performance of Beethoven's Septet, directed by Schuppanzigh, took place at Jahn's on 20 December 1799.

By his wife Katharina, née Österreicher, Jahn had three sons and one daughter. After his death the restaurant was run by his son Franz (*c*.1780–1833) until the mid-1820s.

(Goldschmidt[2], Gugitz, Klein[6])

Jeitteles, Alois Isidor (b. Brünn [Brno], 20 June 1794; d. Brünn, 16 April 1858). Physician; writer, poet, translator, and editor. He studied medicine at Prague, Brünn, and finally in Vienna, where he qualified in 1819; his later years were spent as a doctor at Brünn. He began his literary activities while still a student; in or before 1816 he composed his cycle of poems *An die ferne Geliebte*. Ignaz Franz Castelli* published several of his poems in his almanac *Selam*, and in 1818 he collaborated with Jeitteles in *Der Schicksalsstrumpf*, a parody of the 'Schicksals-tragödie' [fate tragedy], a dramatic genre then enjoying considerable popularity. Jeitteles also wrote a number of comedies, two of which were produced at the Burgtheater: *Der Liebe Wahn und Wahrheit* on 9 April 1842, and *Die Hausgenossen* on 18 April 1843. His translation of Agustín Moreto y Cabaña's *La fuerza del sangre* [*Die Macht des Blutes*] was presented at the Burgtheater on 10 April 1829. In 1848 he became editor of the *Brünner Zeitung*.

It was in 1816 that Beethoven composed the six-song cycle *An die ferne Geliebte* (Op. 98). It is believed that Jeitteles, who was perhaps introduced to him by Castelli, had sent him a handwritten copy of the poems. According to Schindler,* Beethoven was delighted with them. The cycle was published in October 1816 by S. A. Steiner & Co.;* it was dedicated to Prince Joseph Franz Maximilian Lobkowitz.*

Beethoven's funeral prompted Jeitteles to write the poem 'Beethovens Begräbnis' ('Im Lenz in heitrer Abendstille, da trugen sie Dich hinaus. Wir folgten schweigend Deiner Hülle bis in ihr unerwünschtes Haus . . .'). The words, if taken literally, would indicate that Jeitteles had been in the funeral procession, but this cannot be confirmed. The poem was set for four voices and piano by Ignaz von Seyfried* to music taken from the third movement of Beethoven's Piano Sonata in A flat major (Op. 26). This setting was published later in 1827 by Tobias Haslinger.*

(Kerman, *ÖBL*)

Jeitteles, Ignaz (b. Prague, 13 September 1783; d. Vienna, 19 June 1843). Cousin of the preceding. Lawyer, businessman, and writer. According to the brief biography written by August Lewald to accompany Jeitteles's posthumously published book *Eine Reise nach Rom* (Siegen, 1844), he very frequently dined with Beethoven at the Seitzerhof restaurant [7–7A Tuchlauben] during the winter of 1821–2. Lewald, who was present on several occasions, states that their conversation—on

Beethoven's part, in writing—usually focused on possible operatic subjects, and in particular on one dealing with Bacchus. (No conversation books have survived for the period in question.) In 1826 Jeitteles called on Beethoven at the Schwarzspanierhaus together with the Swedish writer Per Daniel Amadeus Atterbom,* but Beethoven, in his deafness, apparently did not notice the visitors, who watched him while he was composing but left without speaking to him (for further details *see* the article on Atterbom). Jeitteles later published an *Ästhetisches Lexikon* (1835–7) which contains some unimportant references to Beethoven.

Jenger, Johann Baptist (b. Kirchhofen, near Freiburg im Breisgau, 23 March 1793; d. Vienna, 30 March 1856). Civil servant; pianist. He was employed at the regional military headquarters at Graz from 1815 until 1825, when he was posted to the war department in Vienna. In Graz he became friendly with Julius Schneller,* Marie Pachler,* and Anselm Hüttenbrenner,* among others. He was also associated from its earliest days with the Steiermärkischer Musikverein [Styrian Music Society] which was founded in 1815; he was a member of its executive committee in 1819, and served as the society's secretary from 1820 to 1825. In that capacity he was one of the persons who signed the diploma dated 1 January 1822, by which the society conferred honorary membership on Beethoven. After his transfer to Vienna he quickly assumed an important place in the musical life of that city. He was much in demand as a pianist, and especially as an accompanist; in particular, he frequently partnered Baron Karl Schönstein, the most admired Schubert* singer of his time after Johann Michael Vogl.* Jenger was also an intimate friend of Schubert himself. In addition to his activities as a pianist, Jenger was much involved in the activities of the Gesellschaft der Musikfreunde.*

Jenger was eager to make Beethoven's acquaintance and asked Marie Pachler for a letter of introduction. However, the letter she wrote on 15 August 1825 (*Corr.* B2031) failed to reach him until the following year, and it was not until December 1826 that he called on Beethoven, armed with the original letter as well as with a further one she had written on 5 November of that year (*Corr.* B2226). He was cordially received, but, as he reported to Marie Pachler on 29 December, he had been shocked to find Beethoven looking ill and unshaven, and his room in total disorder. In this letter Jenger describes his visit as having taken place 'some ten days ago', which would place it on or around 19 December. However, the conversation book in which he made an entry during his visit (*BKh*10/309), was, according to the latest editors of the books, used from 7 until probably 12 December. The visit may therefore have taken place somewhat earlier than Jenger indicated.

Jenger, who in his letter had mentioned Beethoven's first operation (on 20 December), wrote to Marie Pachler again on 12 January to report on the doctors' conference the previous day, at which Dr Malfatti* had recommended a new treatment. (Jenger seems very well informed, having probably learned the details from Schindler,* to whom he had referred as 'my friend' in his previous letter to Marie Pachler.) Jenger's later letters tell of Beethoven's death and funeral. He cut off several locks of Beethoven's hair and sent one of them to Marie Pachler, for whom he also bought several items at the sale of Beethoven's personal effects on 5 May.

In 1829 Jenger acted as deputy secretary of the Gesellschaft der Musikfreunde, and he did so again after Joseph Sonnleithner's* death in 1835, and also in 1838. In 1840 he was placed in charge of the secretariat. At the same time he continued to be in demand as a pianist. Marie's son Faust wrote of Jenger in 1866: 'The name of this man became inextricably interwoven with the history of music-making in Vienna. Although an amateur pianist of no more than average accomplishments, Jenger was drawn into all circles of society, including, eventually, the very highest, because he knew better than anyone else how to provide sensitive accompaniment for the singer's voice and how to transpose music, while playing, to another key.'

(Clive[2], Deutsch[1], Pachler)

Joseph II, emperor of Austria (b. Vienna, 13 March 1741; d. Vienna, 20 February 1790). Schindler* states that, according to certain of Beethoven's friends (whom he does not identify), only two well-known persons made a profound and lasting impression on Beethoven during his brief visit to Vienna in 1787: Mozart* and the Emperor Joseph. After Joseph's death, news of which reached Bonn on 24 February 1790, Beethoven wrote a funeral cantata for solo voices, chorus, and orchestra (WoO 87) to a text by Severin Anton Averdonk* (*see also* Schneider*). It was to be performed at a memorial celebration held by the Bonn *Lesegesellschaft* on 19 March, but was not ready in time. It may have been this cantata which Beethoven showed to Joseph Haydn,* at Bonn either in 1790 or in 1792, and which prompted Haydn to encourage him to continue to compose. A later admirer of the cantata was Brahms who, in a letter to Eduard Hanslick in May 1884, praised its 'beautiful and noble pathos' and claimed to discern in the two outer sections (for chorus and soloists) 'all the characteristics which we find in and associate with [Beethoven's] later works'.

The cantata was not published in Beethoven's lifetime; it first appeared in 1888 in a supplement to the complete edition issued by Breitkopf & Härtel.* Beethoven used material from one of the soprano arias in the last finale of all three versions of *Fidelio*.

Junker, Karl Ludwig (b. Kirchberg an der Jagst, 3 August 1748; d. Ruppertshofen, 30 May 1797). Pastor; composer and writer on music. In a long letter published in Bossler's* *Musikalische Korrespondenz* on 23 November 1791 he gave a glowing account of the musical performances which he had heard during a visit to Mergentheim on 11–12 October. Among the artists he singled out for special praise was Beethoven, whom he described as 'one of the greatest performers on the piano', as well as an amiable and unassuming man. He had heard him play, not at a public concert, but in private, and had been dazzled by his improvisations which he thought superior to those of the celebrated Abbé Vogler:* 'I have heard Vogler on the pianoforte . . . , I have often heard him, and for several hours at a time, and I have always admired his extraordinary technical mastery; but Beethoven, in addition to his technical mastery, plays with greater eloquence, greater profundity, greater expressiveness, in short, more to the heart.'

Beethoven never forgot. In a letter to Schott's Söhne* on 29 December 1824 (*Corr.* A1357/B1917) he wrote: 'I see from your periodical [*Cäcilia*] that Junker is still alive. He was one of the first to take note of me when I was still "young and innocent". Please give him my regards.' In fact, Junker had died long before. Beethoven evidently confused him with the Mainz writer Franz Wilhelm Jung (1757–1833) who had been among the contributors to *Cäcilia* in 1824.

(Wates[1,2])

Kanka, Johann [Jan] **Nepomuk** (b. Prague, 10 November 1772; d. Prague, 15 April 1863[?5]). Lawyer; composer and pianist. His father, likewise called Johann Nepomuk and also a distinguished lawyer (1744–98), was an excellent amateur cellist and well known in musical circles in Prague for the frequent concerts he gave at his house. Among his compositions was a set of dances, *Balli tedeschi*, on themes from Mozart's* *Le nozze di Figaro*. These dances have sometimes been wrongly ascribed to the son.

The younger Johann Nepomuk qualified as a lawyer in 1794. He was granted the title 'Hofrat' by the elector of Hesse-Kassel Wilhelm I in 1812, and was appointed dean of the law faculty of the University of Prague in 1815, and rector of the university in 1829. He was also a very fine pianist and the composer of some seventy musical works, most of which are preserved in manuscript in the library of Prague University. He composed mainly songs (in 1809 he set Heinrich von Collin's* *Lieder österreichischer Wehrmänner*) and pieces for the solo piano, but he also wrote some chamber music, cantatas, a symphony, and two piano concertos (one of which was published in Leipzig in 1804). In his *Jahrbuch der Tonkunst von Wien und Prag* (1796), J. F. von Schönfeld states that he played the piano 'with consummate skill, accuracy, and superb taste'; his sister Jeanette is said to play the same instrument 'with great expressiveness and skill'.

Beethoven is believed to have met Kanka in Vienna during the summer of 1814, but he may already have made the acquaintance of the family when he visited Prague in 1796. Kanka, who after the death of Prince Ferdinand Kinsky* was appointed curator of his son Joseph's estate, was a great admirer of Beethoven's music and also sympathetic to Beethoven's financial needs. He was able to bring about judicial decisions concerning the continued payment of the annuities which were satisfactory to the Kinsky family as well as to the composer (*see* Karolina Maria Kinsky von Wchinitz und Tettau*). Beethoven was conscious of the debt he owed to Kanka in this connection and expressed his profound gratitude to him in several letters. Thus he wrote on 24 February 1815 in a letter addressed to 'My most highly esteemed Kanka': 'I have repeatedly conveyed my thanks to you through Baron Pasqualati [a brother of Beethoven's Viennese friend and landlord Baron Johann Baptist Pasqualati*] and am now sending you a thousand thanks in my own hand . . . I shall always and for ever be appreciative of your friendly efforts on my behalf.' And on 6 September 1816 he wrote: 'I kiss you and press you to my heart.' In 1817 Kanka, at Beethoven's request, acted in proceedings involving Karl van Beethoven's* right of inheritance to a part of the estate of his great-grandfather Johann Paul Lamatsch who had resided at Retz in Lower Austria.

In 1814 Beethoven promised to dedicate a composition to Kanka, once the matter of the Kinsky annuity had been settled (*Corr.* A497/B737). While he never fulfilled this promise, he did send Kanka copies of several of his published works.

(Černý, Kratochvil, Nettl[1])

Kanne, Friedrich August (b. Delitzsch, Saxony, 8 March 1778; d. Vienna, 16 December 1833). Poet, composer, and writer on music. He was a person of great and varied knowledge, having studied medicine at Leipzig, theology at Wittenberg, and music at Dresden. In 1808 he settled in Vienna, where, supported by Prince Joseph Franz Maximilian Lobkowitz,* he earned his living as a music teacher, journalist, and composer. A well-known eccentric of fiercely independent character, he refused all permanent appointments and died destitute.

He was a regular contributor to the Vienna *Allgemeine musikalische Zeitung,* which he moreover edited from 1821 to 1824. He also wrote for various other journals, among them Adolf Bäuerle's *Theaterzeitung* and Johann Valentin Schickh's* *Zeitschrift für Kunst, Literatur, Theater und Mode.* His compositions include symphonies, piano sonatas, songs, and works for the stage—both operatic settings of his own librettos (the most successful: *Orpheus*, produced at the Kärntnertor-Theater on 10 November 1807), and music for more popular spectacles, such as Bäuerle's *Lindane, oder Die Fee und der Haarbeutelschneider* (produced at the Theater in der Leopoldstadt on 27 March 1824). He also contributed a number to Georg Friedrich Treitschke's* Singspiel *Die gute Nachricht,* for which Beethoven composed the final bass aria and chorus (WoO 94).

Kanne was introduced to Beethoven by Georg August von Griesinger* in 1804 while he was on a visit to Vienna (*see* Griesinger's letter to Breitkopf & Härtel* of 29 December 1804). When he later lived there permanently, they became friends and addressed each other with the familiar 'Du'. There are many mentions of Kanne in the conversation books, as well as entries in his hand. According to

Schindler* (who on occasion referred to him by the affectionate diminutive 'Kannerl'), he enjoyed engaging in lively discussions with Beethoven on musical matters, such as the theory of the distinctive character of different music keys, to which Beethoven subscribed but he did not. Above all, Beethoven was grateful for Kanne's profound understanding and fervent championship of his music. He moreover appreciated Kanne's literary talent; thus he sought his opinion on Karl Joseph Bernard's* libretto for the oratorio *Der Sieg des Kreuzes*. Kanne advised that the text should be shortened. In the spring of 1826 he considered adapting Goethe's* Singspiel *Claudine von Villa Bella* as a libretto for Beethoven, but in the end he had qualms about tinkering with Goethe's text. At about the same time, Louis Antoine Duport* sent Beethoven Kanne's opera libretto *Die Mainacht, oder Der Blocksberg*. Apart from the first act, Beethoven found the text excellent and felt not averse to setting it: 'I won't go so far as to say that it is the most suitable one *for me*, but if I can free myself from previous commitments, who knows what might happen—or can happen!' (*Corr.* A1246/B2155). In the end, nothing happened, and Kanne later set the text himself. (The opera was never produced in his lifetime, but may have been performed at the Königstädtisches Theater in Berlin in 1834.) There is no evidence of any contact between Kanne and Beethoven during the final months of the latter's life.

In his *Reisenovellen* (1834–7), mainly inspired by a journey to Italy in August–September 1833, during which he paid a brief first visit to Vienna, the German dramatist and novelist Heinrich Laube devotes a short chapter to Beethoven and Kanne. In it he offers the reader some superficial remarks about the former and a few banal anecdotes about the latter, and points out similarities in their physical appearance. Since certain passages from this chapter are sometimes quoted (for instance, in P. Nettl's *Beethoven Encyclopedia*), it should be stressed that not only had Laube, of course, never known Beethoven, but that it is far from certain that he ever set eyes on Kanne either during the few days he spent in Vienna. (In 1849 Laube was appointed director of the Burgtheater.)

(Branscombe[3], Fellinger[2], Griesinger, Ullrich[1])

Karl XIV Johan: *see* Bernadotte.*

Keglevics, Barbara: *see* Odescalchi.*

Kiesewetter von Wiesenbrunn, Raphael Georg (b. Holleschau [Holešov, Czech Republic], 29 August 1773; d. Baden, near Vienna, 1 January 1850). Civil servant; musicologist and singer. He became an official in the war department in Vienna in 1801, was accorded the title 'Hofrat' in 1807, and ennobled in 1843. He was an accomplished musician, having been taught the piano and singing in his youth and having later learned to play the flute, bassoon, and guitar; he furthermore studied theory with Albrechtsberger.* His interest in early music led him to collect a large number of scores and also to hold at his apartment concerts devoted to vocal compositions from the sixteenth to the eighteenth century. He published important studies on Greek, Egyptian, Arabic, Dutch, and medieval music. From 1818 to 1821 he was a member of the executive committee of the Gesellschaft der Musikfreunde,* and from 1821 until 1843 the society's vice-president. On 7 January 1816 he conducted a concert of the society which included Beethoven's Second Symphony.

Kiesewetter's name is occasionally mentioned in Beethoven's conversation books, but there is no record of any social contact between them. However, in January 1824, they exchanged letters concerning the oratorio which Beethoven had undertaken to compose for the society. (*See also* Gesellschaft der Musikfreunde.*)

(Clive², Kier, Wessely²,⁹)

Kinsky von Wchinitz und Tettau, Ferdinand Johann Nepomuk, Prince (b. Vienna, 4 December 1781; d. Weltrus [Veltrusy, Czech Republic], 3 November 1812; son of Prince Joseph Kinsky (1751–98) and Princess Maria Rosa Aloysia Kinsky (1758–1814), née Countess Harrach. He married Baroness Karolina Maria Kerpen (*see* Karolina Maria Kinsky von Wchinitz und Tettau*) on 8 June 1801. They had three children: Rudolph (1802–36), Hermann (1803–6), and Joseph (1806–62).

Nothing is known about any contacts between Kinsky and Beethoven prior to 1809, when the prince joined Archduke Rudolph* and Prince Lobkowitz* in pledging to provide Beethoven with an annuity of 4,000 florins, to which amount Kinsky was to contribute 1,800 florins. However, Kinsky left Vienna almost immediately afterwards for Bohemia, where he had recruited men from his estates to form a regiment which he subsequently commanded in various engagements against the French; thus he fought with it at Regensburg in April, at Aspern in May, and at Wagram in July. Because of these and subsequent military activities, it was not until 20 June 1810 that Kinsky got around to issuing instructions for the first payments to be made to Beethoven, who had been complaining bitterly about the delay to his correspondents.

The following year, the real value of the annuities declined as a result of inflation and their nominal value was reduced by the *Finanzpatent* of 20 February 1811 (effective from 15 March), which was subsequently modified by a court decree issued on 13 September 1811. As far as Kinsky's share of the annuity was concerned, this meant that the original 1,800 florins (Konventionsmünze) were to be replaced, first by 360 florins (Wiener Währung) and then, according to the September regulations, by 726 florins (Wiener Währung). Beethoven appealed to his three patrons to maintain the payments in the new currency at the original figure. Archduke Rudolph promptly agreed; Lobkowitz's position was more ambiguous (*see* Lobkowitz*). In Kinsky's case, it fell to Karl August Varnhagen von Ense* to raise the matter, at Beethoven's request, when he met the prince in Prague on 8 June 1812. Kinsky readily consented, and moreover undertook to apply the adjustment to both future and still outstanding payments (for none had then been made since August 1811); and when Beethoven himself called on the prince in Prague on his way to Teplitz [Teplice] the following month, he received a similar assurance. Since Beethoven was unable to remain in Prague long enough for arrangements to be completed for the full payment of the amount due to him, the prince gave him 60 ducats (as the equivalent of 600 florins Wiener Währung) on account. In September, when Beethoven had still not received the balance, he reminded Kinsky of his promise in a letter from Teplitz which was presented to the prince in Vienna by Franz Oliva* (*see Corr.* A393/B608). Once more, Kinsky confirmed his decision regarding the annuity, adding that he would issue ·the necessary instructions within a few days. But after he died on 3 November from injuries sustained in a riding accident while in Bohemia, it transpired that he had failed to do so. This omission was to cost Beethoven considerable vexation (*see* Karolina Maria Kinsky von Wchinitz und Tettau*).

The Mass in C (Op. 86), written for Prince Nikolaus Esterházy,* was published in October 1812 with a dedication to Kinsky. It is interesting that as late as October 1811 Beethoven was still undecided to whom to offer the work (he had at one time thought of Zmeskall* and then of a lady he did not name); not until May 1812 did he inform Breitkopf & Härtel* of the name of the eventual dedicatee (*Corr.* A370/B577). The decision was thus taken prior to Varnhagen's interview with Kinsky in June, and cannot therefore be regarded as a token of his gratitude for the prince's positive response to his request regarding the annuity. Moreover, it seems likely that Beethoven sought Kinsky's consent to the dedication before advising the publishers, or that, at least, he informed Kinsky of his intention. It is accordingly reasonable to assume that Kinsky was aware, at the time of the interview, that the Mass would be dedicated to him. In that case, the dedication can perhaps be viewed as a strategic move on Beethoven's part, designed to put the prince in a generous frame of mind.

(Kratochvil)

Kinsky von Wchinitz und Tettau, Karolina [Charlotte] **Maria**, Princess, née Baroness Kerpen (b. 4 March 1782; d. 2 November 1841); wife of Prince Ferdinand Kinsky von Wchinitz und Tettau.* In a letter to Breitkopf & Härtel* on 28 January 1812, Beethoven described her as 'one of prettiest and plumpest women in Vienna'. He dedicated to her the *Sechs Gesänge* (Op. 75) in October 1810, and the *Drei Gesänge* (Op. 83) in October 1811. After her husband's death (3 November 1812), she and her brother-in-law Count Franz Anton Kolowrat-Liebsteinsky (who was married to Ferdinand's sister Maria Rosa) were appointed joint guardians of her two young sons Rudolph (1802–36) and Joseph (1806–62).

Since Prince Kinsky had failed to settle the matter of Beethoven's annuity as he had promised (*see* preceding article), Beethoven addressed a petition on the subject to the princess on 30 December 1812 (*Corr.* A403/B607); she passed it on to Kolowrat. The affair dragged on for several years, and it was not until 18 January 1815 that a settlement was reached which was acceptable to both Beethoven and the Kinsky heirs and which received the approval of the Bohemian Landrecht, the ultimate authority in the matter. Under this settlement, which was negotiated with the help of Beethoven's admirer Johann Nepomuk Kanka,* his annuity was fixed at 1,200 florins (Wiener Währung), and he also received the outstanding arrears. The arrangement continued after Prince Rudolph took over the management of the Kinsky estates in 1823.

The grateful composer dedicated the song 'An die Hoffnung' (Op. 94) to Princess Kinsky in 1816.

(Kratochvil)

Kirchhoffer, Franz Christian (1785–1842). Cashier and accountant employed by the Viennese firm Hofmann & Goldstein, manufacturers of silk products. In 1823 he arranged on several occasions the transmission of correspondence and money between Beethoven and Ferdinand Ries* (who was then in London). He was also asked to help with the dispatch to London of copies of the *Missa solemnis* and the Ninth Symphony. On receiving the score of the symphony on 27 April 1824 he paid Beethoven the fee of £50 due to him from the London Philharmonic Society.* The score reached London later that year, and the work was given its first London performance under Sir George Smart* at a Philharmonic Society concert on 21 March 1825. (It is not known whether Kirchhoffer ever sent the manuscript of the Mass to England.) The tone of two extant notes from Beethoven to Kirchhoffer (*Corr.* A1239/B1708a, A1238/B1739) points to a very cordial relationship between the two men.

Kirnberger [Kernberg], **Johann Philipp** (bapt. Saalfeld, 24 April 1721; d. Berlin, 26/7 July 1783). Theorist and composer. His most important theoretical work was *Die Kunst des reinen Satzes in der Musik, aus sicheren Grundsätzen hergeleitet und mit deutlichen Beyspielen erläutert* (2 vols., Berlin, 1771–9). Beethoven began to study Kirnberger's writings before he left Bonn. Many years later he asked Tobias Haslinger* (*Corr.* A1104/B1102) to lend him his 'Kirnberger'—probably *Die Kunst des reinen Satzes*—because his own set was incomplete and he needed it for certain lessons in counterpoint (perhaps those he was giving to Archduke Rudolph*). The epigram 'Wir irren allesamt, nur jeder irret anderst' [We all err, but each one errs in a different way], which appears in the canon printed at the beginning of *Die Kunst des reinen Satzes*, was set by Beethoven in a short piece (WoO 198) which he included in a letter he sent to Karl Holz* in December 1826 (*Corr.* A1541/B2234). A six-volume edition of Kirnberger's writings published in Vienna in 1793 was among the items sold at the auction of Beethoven's effects in November 1827.

(Kramer², Serwer)

Kissow, Elisabeth von: *see* Bernhard.*

Klein, Franz (b. Vienna, 27 April 1777; d. Vienna, 30 August 1840). Sculptor; father of the landscape painter Eduard Klein and cousin of the painter Joseph Rebell. He studied at the Akademie der bildenden Künste from 1795 (but withdrew for financial reasons and served in the army from 1799 to 1803) and again from 1804, when his principal teacher was Johann Martin Fischer. He was also in contact with the anatomist and phrenologist Joseph Gall, for whose celebrated collection of skulls and busts he prepared anatomical models. In 1811 he was commissioned by Count Dietrichstein* to make a bust of Heinrich von Collin* who had recently died.

The following year he undertook what was to be his most famous work, a bust of Beethoven which the piano manufacturer Johann Andreas Streicher* had ordered for his new music room. As was to be his preferred method of working, Klein first took a life mask of his subject. Beethoven found the process so uncomfortable that he finally tore off the plaster mask and threw it on the floor. Fortunately, the pieces had sufficiently hardened for Klein to be able to fit them together again. He later gave the negative face-mask to Joseph Franz Danhauser,* who, in turn, passed it on to Anton Dietrich,* together with the death mask he had taken himself. After Dietrich's death, Klein's life mask came into the possession of Caspar von Zumbusch.* It is now at the Beethoven-Haus, Bonn. As for the sculpture for which the life mask had served as a preparatory study, it is thought probable that the bust which has been in the collection of the Historisches Museum der Stadt Wien since 1939 is the original one.

Among other subjects portrayed by Klein were two sisters of Tsar Alexander,* who were in Vienna at the time of the Congress, and various members of the Austrian imperial family, including the Emperor Franz II; he also made busts of Johann Andreas Streicher and his wife Nannette.

(Badura-Skoda⁵, Krasa-Florian, *ÖBL*, Steblin²)

Kleinheinz, Franz Xaver (b. Nassenbeuren, Allgäu, 1765; d. 1832). Composer, conductor, and pianist. Information concerning his life is sketchy. According to Schilling's *Enzyklopädie*, he received his early musical instruction from the monks at Memmingen and later was employed for a short time as a court secretary by the elector of Bavaria Karl Theodor at Munich. In 1799 he moved to Vienna, where he studied composition with Albrechtsberger* and became himself a popular teacher; among his pupils there was Julia [Giulietta] Guicciardi.* Through the Brunsviks he became acquainted with Beethoven, who succeeded him as

Giulietta's teacher. (Kleinheinz subsequently taught Countess Therese Brunsvik in Hungary.)

On 21 May 1803 Kaspar Karl van Beethoven* offered Breitkopf & Härtel* some arrangements for string quartet of several of his brother's piano pieces, as well as arrangements for piano and accompaniment of certain instrumental works, all of which had been made by Kleinheinz 'under my brother's direction' (*Corr.* B138). In offering the same arrangements to Nikolaus Simrock* on 25 May, Kaspar Karl describes the arranger (whom, this time, he does not name) as a 'competent composer' (*Corr.* B139). Beethoven himself stated, with reference to Opp. 41 and 42 (see below), that 'these arrangements were not made by me, but I have looked them over and have completely changed some passages' (letter to Hoffmeister* & Kühnel, *Corr.* A82/B157). In addition to other arrangements (*see also* Held*), Kleinheinz may be responsible for some or all of the following: the arrangement of the Trio Serenade (Op. 25) as the Serenade for piano and flute (Op. 41), published by Hoffmeister & Kühnel in December 1803; of the Serenade for string trio (Op. 8) as the Notturno for piano and viola (Op. 42), published by the same firm in January 1804; of the String Quintet (Op. 4) as the Piano Trio (Op. 63), published by Artaria & Co.* in July 1806; and of the String Trio (Op. 3) as the Cello Sonata (Op. 64), published, likewise by Artaria & Co., in May 1807.

In 1804 Kleinheinz was at St Petersburg; later he lived in Vienna, Brünn [Brno], and Pest [Budapest]. He was engaged as conductor at the German Theatre at Pest in 1814–15 and again in 1817–24. His opera *Harald* was produced there in 1814, and at the Theater an der Wien the following year. His secular works range from piano sonatas and chamber music to songs and works for the stage; he also composed masses and oratorios.

(Goldschmidt², Sandberger)

Kleinschmid, Friedrich August (b. Steinheim, Westphalia, 21 November 1749; d. Vienna, 18 March 1838). Senior police official; writer. He enrolled in law studies at Vienna University in 1776, and later occupied prominent positions in the Vienna police force; in 1810 he was appointed director of the Vienna prison. He was granted the title 'Regierungsrat' in 1812. Kleinschmid had wide cultural interests, owned a valuable collection of paintings, and was a contributor to Adolf Bäuerle's *Theaterzeitung*. In 1816 Beethoven set one of his poems in 'Der Mann von Wort' (Op. 99); the song was published that same year by S. A. Steiner & Co.*

(*ÖBL*, Slezak², Wurzbach¹)

Kloeber [Klöber], **August (Karl Friedrich) von** (b. Breslau [Wrocław], 21 August 1793; d. Belin, 31 December 1864). Painter. He studied architecture at Breslau (from 1808), and then painting in Berlin (from 1810) and later in Vienna.

Subsequently he settled in Berlin and, except for an extended stay in Italy (1821–8), he resided in that city until his death. In 1834 he was appointed to a professorship at the Preussische Akademie der Künste. He made a number of portraits, but preferred to depict mythological subjects; he also decorated the walls and ceilings of many public buildings in Berlin.

In 1818, while in Vienna, he painted a full-length oil portrait of Beethoven for his brother-in-law, Baron Skrbensky, a landowner residing in Austrian Silesia. Kloeber later stated that he owed his introduction to Beethoven to the cellist Johann Valentin Dont (the father of the future violinist virtuoso Jakob Dont). He was cordially received by Beethoven at his summer quarters at Mödling and granted several sittings. (Beethoven stayed at Mödling that year from 19 May until September.) On 19 November 1818 the *Wiener Zeitschrift für Kunst, Literatur, Theater und Mode* reported the 'recent' completion of this painting, which showed the composer 'at the supreme moment of artistic creativity', set against the countryside near Mödling; his young nephew Karl* also appeared in the picture. In November 1863 Kloeber himself wrote down a fairly detailed account of his contacts with Beethoven during that summer of 1818 for his friend Friedrich Wilhelm Jähns, a noted singing teacher and composer. The text was reproduced, with some alterations and omissions, in the Leipzig *Allgemeine musikalische Zeitung* in May 1864; many passages from Kloeber's account are also cited or paraphrased in A. C. Kalischer's *Beethoven und seine Zeitgenossen*.

The portrait, which presumably formed part of Baron Skrbensky's private collection, is now lost. However, the Beethoven-Haus, Bonn, possesses a pencil drawing and a charcoal sketch made by Kloeber of Beethoven's head. The pencil drawing, at any rate, is likely to have been a preliminary study for the missing portrait. A variant of the charcoal sketch was sold by Kloeber's widow in 1886 to the Leipzig music publishing firm C. F. Peters;* it also is lost. However, it had earlier served as the model for a lithograph made by Theodor Neu under Kloeber's supervision in 1841, which sold extremely well and was, in fact, instrumental in creating a certain Beethoven 'image'. Lastly, the Beethoven-Haus has in its collection a drawing by Kloeber of Beethoven's hands, no doubt another study done in preparation for the lost portrait.

Schindler,* in the 1860 edition of his Beethoven biography, writes scathingly about the lithograph, declaring that it presents 'the face of a worthy brewer, but not that of an artist' and that 'among the bad portrayals of [Beethoven], this is without any doubt the crudest'. Frimmel, though for different reasons, also regarded Kloeber's representation of Beethoven as a failure. Kloeber himself does not describe Beethoven's own reaction to the portrait as a whole, but he reports Beethoven's approval of the way he had painted his hair, which, he told Kloeber, 'other artists had until then always shown plastered down, the way he had to appear before the court officials, which was not at all his natural style'. Among the admirers of the lithograph was Franz Liszt* who kept it in a prominent place in his music room at Weimar. During his stay in Vienna, Kloeber also painted portraits of Grillparzer* and Karoline Pichler.

(Frimmel³, Kalischer, Schindler¹)

Klopstock, Friedrich Gottlob (b. Quedlinburg, 2 July 1724; d. Hamburg, 14 March 1803). Poet and dramatist. Beethoven left sketches for settings of Klopstock's poems 'Das Rosenband' and 'Edone'.

Klüpfell [?Klüpfeld]. First secretary at the Russian Embassy in Vienna. Frau von Bernhard* told Ludwig Nohl that Beethoven frequently visited Klüpfell's house and played the piano there when she was herself staying with the family in the later 1890s. One day, however, he displeased his host by his discourteous behaviour towards Franz Kommer while the latter was playing one of his own compositions. Klüpfell thereupon asked Nikolaus Zmeskall von Domanovecz* to tell his friend Beethoven that 'a young man who is still a nobody ought always to show respect when an older, well-established composer was performing'. Beethoven never set foot in Klüpfell's house again.

(Nohl⁴)

Koch (family). Bonn family with which the young Beethoven was on very friendly terms. The mother, **Anna Maria** (bapt. Bonn, 21 January 1749; d. Bonn, 11 June 1816), owned a house called 'Zum Zehrgarten' on the market square, which had been bought by her husband Michael (*c*.1736–83) in 1777. There the 'widow Koch' ran a restaurant which drew its customers from various circles of local society, including teachers from the university and young musicians and artists. She must have had wider cultural interests than the average restaurateur, for she also sold books. She had close contacts with the Beethoven family, as is shown by the fact that she was godmother to Ludwig's sister Anna Maria Franziska (b. and d. February 1779). She is believed to have sold the house and the business in 1802.

Her daughter **Barbara** [Babette] (bapt. Bonn, 18 June 1771; d. Bonn, 25 November 1807) was a beautiful and well-educated young lady who was reportedly much courted in Bonn. She sang, and probably also played the piano. Franz Gerhard Wegeler* later declared that 'of all the members of the female sex whom I have met in a rather active and long life, [she] came closest to my ideal of the perfect woman'. Barbara was a close friend of Eleonore von Breuning.* Beethoven knew her well; indeed, according to Gerhard von Breuning*—who presumably had been told by his father Stephan—he fell in love with her. It is worth noting that, of the various members of the Koch family, she alone did not write in the album which was presented to Beethoven on his departure for Vienna; nor did she reply to two letters he sent her from there. (The letters appear to be lost, but there is a reference to them in

Corr. A7/B11.) Perhaps she did not return his affectionate feelings for her, with the result that their relations became strained. If this was indeed the situation, Beethoven may have sought, but unavailingly, to smooth out matters once he had arrived in Vienna. (It is interesting that he, in his turn, made no entry in Barbara's own album which was in use from the spring of 1790.) In 1802 Barbara married Count Anton Belderbusch (1758–1820), whose uncle Count Kaspar Anton Belderbusch (1722–84) had been a celebrated minister under the Elector Maximilian Friedrich.*

Barbara had a younger sister, **Marianne** (bapt. Bonn, 15 April 1775; d. Potsdam, 1820), and a brother, **Matthias** (bapt. Bonn, 4 February 1773; d. ?Bonn, 27 September 1805). Matthias is said to have been a very close friend of Beethoven's (*see also* Degenhart*). He went to Vienna in late 1795 or early 1796, perhaps for the purpose of visiting Beethoven, and he stayed there for some time before returning to Germany. In 1801 he was engaged as a singer at the Frankfurt theatre; later he became librarian to Prince Isenburg-Birstein at Offenbach.

As already indicated, Anna Maria, Marianne, and Matthias Koch all wrote in Beethoven's album; so did Anna Maria's brother Jakob Klemmer.

(Braubach[2,7], Wegeler/Ries)

Körner, Karl Theodor (b. Dresden, 23 September 1791; d. Gadebusch, Mecklenburg, 26 August 1813). Poet and dramatist. In August 1811 he went to Vienna where he had considerable success with his comedies (*Die Braut, Der grüne Domino, Der Nachtwächter*) and tragedies (notably *Toni* and *Zriny*). As a result, he was appointed house dramatist [Hoftheaterdichter] at the Burgtheater in January 1813. But two months later he left Vienna and enlisted in Baron Adolf Lützow's Free Corps in order to fight against the French in the Wars of Liberation. He was killed at the battle of Gadebusch. While in Vienna, he had become engaged to the actress Antonie Adamberger.*

In a letter to Körner on 21 April 1812, Beethoven refers to an operatic subject which Körner had proposed to him some time before. Apologizing for his tardy acknowledgement, Beethoven invited Körner to visit him two days later to discuss the project, as well as another libretto which he wished Körner to write for him. The letter (the only extant written communication between them) evidently led to more frequent contacts, for on 6 June of that year Körner informed his parents that he was being 'constantly pestered' by several composers, Beethoven among them, to supply them with librettos. It is not known what subject Körner had initially suggested; but on 10 February 1813 he wrote to his parents: 'I have been asked to treat the return of Ulysses for Beethoven.' He only got as far as an outline for a 'grand opera in two acts' and the opening scenes. The outline and the textual fragment were first printed in Adolf Stern's edition of his works (3 vols., Stuttgart, 1890–1).

(Berger[2], Kalischer, Körner[1,2], Pečman)

Kotzebue, August von (b. Weimar, 3 May 1761; d. Mannheim, 23 March 1819). Prolific dramatist. In the course of a tumultuous life he was, at different times, employed as a lawyer at Weimar, a dramatist at the court theatre in Vienna (1798) and at St Petersburg, a high government official in the Russian province of Estonia, a political journalist, and a magazine editor. In 1816 he was attached to the Russian foreign ministry at St Petersburg; the following year he returned to Germany. Hated by the young German liberals, whose demands for greater freedom he ridiculed, he was assassinated by a theology student named Karl Ludwig Sand.

His plays attracted the attention of several composers, who either based entire operas on them (as did Lortzing in *Der Wildschütz*) or wrote incidental music for them. Beethoven fell into the second category. The new theatre at Pest [Budapest] was inaugurated on 9 February 1812 with two plays by Kotzebue, *Die Ruinen von Athen* and *Ungarns erster Wohltäter* [*König Stephan*], for both of which Beethoven had written a number of musical pieces (Opp. 113, 117).

Beethoven was impressed by the dramatic quality of Kotzebue's plays, and in a letter on 28 January 1812 he asked him for a libretto for an opera, to be performed at the Kärntnertor-Theater (which, since 30 September 1811, had been under the direction of Beethoven's great patron Prince Lobkowitz*). Beethoven indicated his preference for a historical subject, 'especially from the Dark Ages', such as Attila, but declared his readiness to accept any topic Kotzebue might wish to treat, whether serious or comic. In reply to Beethoven's request, Kotzebue, who was then living at Reval [Tallinn, Estonia], wrote twice, on 6 March and 20 April; between those dates he apparently received at least one further (now lost) letter from Beethoven. The first of Kotzebue's letters has itself been lost, but the second (*Corr.* B573) is preserved at the Beethoven-Haus, Bonn. In it he declared his readiness to write a libretto for a grand opera, as soon as he had worked out a suitable plot. In the meanwhile, he offered Beethoven (and Lobkowitz) five comic opera librettos, which were already available in manuscript, for 200 ducats. Evidently this offer was, for whatever reason, declined, and no further correspondence on the subject has come to light. On 24 September 1813 Kotzebue wrote a letter of introduction to Beethoven for Johann August Hagen, a singer in the chorus of the Dresden court theatre; the note (*Corr.* B669) makes no reference to the earlier exchange.

In 1822 the writer Karl Meisl* adapted Kotzebue's *Die Ruinen von Athen* to serve as a festival play at the opening of the new Theater in der Josefstadt in Vienna on 3 October (*see* Hensler*). The performance again featured Beethoven's music, though slightly modified (one of the original numbers was revised—*see* Op. 114), and with the addition of a new chorus (WoO 98) and a new overture (Op. 124).

One further aspect of Kotzebue's activities merits mention in connection with Beethoven. In 1803 he founded, together with Garlieb Merkel, a periodical named *Der Freimüthige* in Berlin. In addition to presenting articles on literature, which constituted its main function, the journal carried reports of musical events, at least some of which were probably written by Kotzebue himself. They contain generally positive, but by no means entirely uncritical, assessments of certain works by Beethoven.

Kozeluch [Kotzeluch, Koželuh], **Leopold** [Jan Antonín, Ioannes Antonius] (b. Welwarn [Velvary, Czech Republic], 26 June 1747; d. Vienna, 7 May 1818). Composer, pianist, teacher, and publisher. In 1778 he settled in Vienna, where his students included Maria Theresia von Paradis, Ignaz von Seyfried,* and Simon Sechter.* He was an enormously prolific composer of all types of vocal and instrumental music, from songs to operas and from pieces for the piano to symphonies: an incomplete list of his works occupies five small-print columns in *Musik in Geschichte und Gegenwart*. J. F. von Schönfeld, who allots no fewer than sixty-one lines to him in his *Jahrbuch der Tonkunst von Wien und Prag* (1796), asserts that he 'has for some ten years enjoyed an outstanding reputation throughout musical Europe'. In 1792 he was appointed Kammer Kapellmeister und Hofmusik Kompositor. (It has sometimes been stated—e.g. by P. Nettl in his *Beethoven Encyclopedia*—that he succeeded Mozart* as Kammer Kompositor to the Viennese court, but O. Wessely, in his article on Kozeluch in *MGG*, dismisses the statement as an error and stresses that this post was quite distinct from those occupied by Kozeluch.)

Kozeluch is said to have been of an extremely competitive nature and jealous of any potential rival. Indeed, Franz Xaver Niemetschek informed Breitkopf & Härtel* in 1799 that he had deliberately refrained from mentioning Kozeluch's name in his Mozart biography 'because of the petty jealousy with which he always pursued Mozart in Prague. At the time of the coronation of Emperor Leopold II, he calumniated him in the most villainous manner, and even maligned his character.' It may be assumed that he did not feel much more kindly towards Beethoven, once the latter's reputation as a pianist and composer was on the rise in Vienna. At the same time, his reported distaste for Beethoven's compositions was probably also a result of their difference in age and hence in musical taste. Jan Emanuel Doležálek told Otto Jahn in 1852 that when he played one of Beethoven's compositions to Kozeluch, the latter threw the music on the floor; and that Kozeluch once remarked to Haydn,* with reference to Beethoven's music: 'We would have done that differently, wouldn't we, Papa?' (to which Haydn is said to have replied, with a smile, 'Yes, we would have done that differently').

It must be added that Beethoven's estimation of Kozeluch's worth as a composer was equally unenthusiastic. In a letter to George Thomson* on 29 February 1812 concerning the fees due to him for his arrangements of Irish and Scottish songs, he wrote: 'Haydn himself assured me that he also received four gold ducats for each song . . . As for Herr Kozeluch, who delivers each of his songs with accompaniment to you for two ducats, I congratulate you very much and also the English and Scottish listeners if they enjoy them. But I esteem myself in this regard superior to Herr Kozeluch (Miserabilis), and believing you to possess a certain discrimination, I trust that it will prompt you to do me justice.'

In the circumstances it is amusing that three little piano duets in a manuscript at the British Library in London (Additional MS 31,748), which used to be attributed to Mozart and were later regarded as Beethoven *juvenilia*, should eventually have been identified as arrangements of three pieces from Kozeluch's ballet *La ritrovata figlia di Ottone II* (*see* O. E. Deutsch, 'Kozeluch *ritrovato*', *Music & Letters* (1945); also G. de Saint-Foix, 'About a Ballet by Leopold Kozeluch', ibid. (1946), and correspondence about Deutsch's identification, ibid. (1952)).

Kozeluch owned a music publishing firm from the mid-1780s, which was taken over by his brother Anton Thomas (1752–1805) in 1802 (*see* Maisch*).

(Deutsch[6], Poštolka[3], Wessely[2])

Kraft, Anton (b. Rokitzan [Rokycany, Czech Republic], 30 December 1749; d. Vienna, 28 August 1820). Cellist and composer. He received his musical instruction from Werner, the cellist at the Kreuzherren Church in Prague, and later from Haydn.* After studying philosophy and law at the University of Prague, he decided to make music his career and moved to Vienna. From 1778 until 1790 he was first cellist in Prince Nikolaus Esterházy's orchestra (which was dissolved following the prince's death in the latter year); he then joined the orchestra of the prince's son-in-law, Prince Anton Grassalkovics, at Pressburg [Bratislava], and later that of Prince Joseph Franz Maximilian Lobkowitz* in Vienna. He may also have performed at times with the Schuppanzigh* Quartet at Prince Karl Lichnowsky's.* He enjoyed a high reputation and often toured as a virtuoso, either alone or, from 1789, together with his son Nikolaus.* Haydn wrote his Cello Concerto for him, and Beethoven the cello part in his Triple Concerto. Kraft played in the first performances of Beethoven's Seventh Symphony and *Wellingtons Sieg* (8 December 1813).

After Lobkowitz's bankruptcy in the summer of 1813 Kraft received no further regular salary, and on 10 February 1814 he was ordered to vacate his free apartment at the prince's palace by 24 April. In his despair, he called on Beethoven and requested that he ask his patron the Archduke Rudolph* to grant him some accommodation at his palace, in return for which Kraft would be at the archduke's disposal whenever he required it. Beethoven duly wrote to Rudolph, pleading that 'the situation in which the poor, deserving old man finds himself is hard' (*Corr.* A445/B714). It is not known how Rudolph responded to the letter. On 1 December of that same year Kraft's position in Lobkowitz's service was formally terminated and he was awarded an annual pension of 666 florins.

(Macek[2], Wessely[4])

Kraft, Nikolaus (b. Eszterháza, Hungary, 14 December 1778; d. Eger [Cheb, Czech Republic], 18 May 1853. Cello virtuoso and composer. Son of Anton Kraft,* who was his principal teacher (but in 1801 Nikolaus went to Berlin for some advanced instruction from Jean-Pierre Duport*). In 1789, when he was only 11 years old, he accompanied his father on a concert tour which took them to Vienna, Pressburg [Bratislava], Berlin, and Dresden. After attending the Josefstädter Gymnasium (1792–5), he joined in 1796 Prince Lobkowitz's* orchestra, of which his father was also a member. In addition, Nikolaus was recruited as cellist for Schuppanzigh's* quartet which initially performed weekly at Prince Karl Lichnowsky's* house. In 1809 he became solo cellist at the Kärntnertor-Theater; he also frequently appeared at public concerts. After his employment in Lobkowitz's service had ended in October 1814, he spent the next twenty years as a chamber musician to the court at Stuttgart. He reportedly moved to Chemnitz in 1838; it is not known when he settled at Eger.

As a member of Schuppanzigh's original quartet, he became familiar with several of Beethoven's compositions, and he no doubt knew Beethoven himself quite well. On 5 March 1809 he and Baroness Ertmann* gave the first public performance of the Cello Sonata Op. 69. Like his father, he played in the first performances of the Seventh Symphony and *Wellingtons Sieg* on 8 December 1813.

Kraft, who, in the course of his career, gave numerous concerts not only in Vienna, but throughout Germany, was a brilliant virtuoso who gained the admiration even of his peers. Thus Bernhard Heinrich Romberg* praised his technical mastery and the clear, rich tone which he was able to draw from this 'difficult' instrument, and regarded his performances as models for other cellists, 'being free of the usual affectation, noble, and inspired by perfect taste'.

(Wessely[4])

Kreutzer [Kreuzer], **Conradin** [Conrad] (b. Messkirch, Baden, Germany, 22 November 1780; d. Riga, 14 December 1849). Composer and conductor. During his first stay in Vienna (1804–10) he probably studied with Albrechtsberger.* In the course of the next twelve years he undertook several concert tours, and held appointments as Kapellmeister at Stuttgart (1812–16) and Donaueschingen (1818–22). Following the successful première of his opera *Libussa* at the Kärntnertor-Theater on 4 December 1822 he was appointed Kapellmeister at that theatre, a position he held until 1827, and again from 1829 to 1832. After spending some time in Paris he moved back to Vienna, where he was employed as Kapellmeister at the Theater in der Josefstadt from 1833. On 13 January 1834 his comic opera *Das Nachtlager in Granada* was produced with great success there. He returned to the Kärntnertor-Theater in 1835, but left Vienna in 1840 and thereafter led a fairly peripatetic existence.

Very little is known about his relations with Beethoven, which were clearly not intimate. As Kapellmeister at the Kärntnertor-Theater he played a certain role in the rehearsals of the Ninth Symphony (*see BKh*6/159) and reportedly also took part in the actual performance on 7 May 1824; and Beethoven stated in a letter to Schott's Söhne* on 22 February 1827 that he had received their most recent communication through Kreutzer. That is the sum total of our knowledge of their contacts—except for a story later told by Schindler* to Robert Hornstein and related by the latter in his 'Memoiren' (published in *Süddeutsche Monatshefte* in 1907). According to Schindler, Beethoven had been furious when Kreutzer, in speaking to him at the theatre, had rather ostentatiously treated him as just another composer. Beethoven never forgave Kreutzer and thereafter avoided any further contact with him, and when, during Beethoven's final illness, Schindler acceded to Kreutzer's request and 'smuggled' him into the sickroom, Beethoven turned his back on Kreutzer ('who stammered some words of apology and sought to move him by his entreaties') and maintained that position until Kreutzer had left the room. However, like so many of Schindler's tales, this story needs no doubt to be regarded with some caution, not least because his alleged action suggests a certain cordiality on his own part towards Kreutzer, whereas the feelings he displays for Kreutzer in his Beethoven biography are far from friendly. There Schindler attributes what he describes as 'the wretched circumstances in which [Kreutzer] ended his life on earth, far from his homeland' directly to 'his bad temper, and more especially the conceit and the scheming nature which he displayed at a time of great and unmerited good fortune (between 1823 and 1830) and which led him to look down even on Beethoven with undisguised disdain'. Schindler's evident dislike of Kreutzer, which may well have been prompted, at least in part, by jealousy, also finds expression in certain snide remarks in the conversation books; and it is probably not without significance that among the 'forged' entries in those books is one (*BKh*3/92) which reads 'Der Geck Kreutzer' [That fop Kreutzer].

(Hornstein, Schindler[1])

Kreutzer, Rodolphe (b. Versailles, 16 November 1766; d. Geneva, 6 January 1831). Violinist, composer, and teacher. The son of a German wind player (who had moved to Versailles in *c*.1760) and a pupil of Anton Stamitz, he had an outstanding career. In addition to being an internationally renowned violinist, he was also a prolific composer (of some twenty violin concertos, as well as numerous operatic and ballet scores), taught for many years at the Paris Conservatoire, and was active at the Opéra as conductor and, later, director. In 1798 he spent some two months in Vienna as a member of the party accompanying the French ambassador, General Bernadotte.* While in Vienna, he met Beethoven who also had opportunities to hear and admire his violin playing. 'He is a dear kind fellow who gave me a great deal of pleasure during his stay here,' Beethoven wrote to the publisher Nikolaus Simrock* on 4 October 1804, after he had decided to dedicate the Violin Sonata in A (Op. 47) to Kreutzer. 'I prefer his unassuming and natural manner to that of most virtuosi who are all *exterior*, with no *interior*. As the sonata is composed for a thoroughly competent violinist, the dedication to him is particularly appropriate.' Beethoven added that they had been corresponding ('I write to him once a year'), but no letters have survived from the period 1798–1804. Beethoven further stated that once the date of publication had been fixed, he would send Simrock a note to be delivered to Kreutzer together with the printed sonata. This note, if it was ever written, is no longer extant. The sonata appeared in April 1805, with a dedication by Beethoven 'al suo amico R. Kreuzer [*sic*]'. If Kreutzer acknowledged receipt of the composition, his letter has been lost.

More intriguingly, there is no record of Kreutzer ever performing the work in public. The usual explanation (e.g. by Frimmel, P. Nettl) is that he must have been well aware that the sonata had not been written for him, but for the mulatto violinist George Polgreen Bridgetower*—in fact, Beethoven, who gave its first performance with Bridgetower on 24 May 1803, inscribed a partial autograph of the work to the latter. (For a possible reason for Beethoven's decision to dedicate the published sonata to someone else, *see* the article on Bridgetower.) If Kreutzer did indeed know that not he, but Bridgetower, had been Beethoven's 'first choice', he may well have resented the fact, especially since he had already been a highly regarded virtuoso and well-known composer when the 10-year-old Bridgetower had made his professional debut in Paris in 1789. But it is also possible that Kreutzer did not greatly care for the sonata. Michael D. Williams has pointed out that it requires short staccato and spiccato bowings which were alien to Kreutzer's own style of writing, and therefore likely to be techniques at which he was not very adept. In any case, he is known to have felt an aversion for German music in general, and for Beethoven's works, in particular, for he reportedly shut his ears with his hands the first time he attended a rehearsal of a Beethoven symphony, and fled from the concert hall during a performance of the Second Symphony, with his hands clamped over his ears.

Beethoven was presumably unaware of Kreutzer's attitude when, in November 1825, he furnished the flautist Johann Sedlaczek* with a letter of introduction to him, in which he referred to himself as 'votre ancien ami' (*Corr.* A App.E, 6/B2087).

(Charlton, Williams²)

Kriehuber, Joseph (b. Vienna, 14 December 1800; d. Vienna, 30 May 1876). Painter and lithographer. He concentrated increasingly on portraits, of which he lithographed some 3,000 in the course of a highly successful career which reached its most brilliant period in 1840–50. His subjects included members of the imperial family, noblemen, scholars, writers, musicians, actors, and artists. Among the musicians were Carl Czerny,* Diabelli,* Haslinger,* Lanner, Liszt,* Paganini, Rossini,* Schubert,* Sechter,* Johann Strauss the Younger, and Beethoven. Although, as far as is known, he never met Beethoven, he was to make at least six lithographs of him, all of them after his death. The earliest, which probably dates from 1827, is based on one of Anton Dietrich's* busts. The following year Kriehuber's name appears on a portrait featured in the Beethoven biography of Johann Aloys Schlosser (Prague, 1828); another lithograph, done in 1841, recreates Stieler's* portrait, while a third (1865) is based on Mähler's 1804/5 portrait. Particularly appreciated was the lithograph published by Haslinger in 1832. Rita Steblin believes that it was based on a drawing by Joseph Hochenecker,* but according to Sieghard Brandenburg a more likely model was the portrait executed by Johann Stephan Decker* in 1824 (*see* the article on Hochenecker). The same lithograph served as the frontispiece of Ignaz von Seyfried's* *Ludwig van Beethoven's Studien im Generalbasse, Contrapuncte und in der Compositionslehre*, which appeared in 1832, and was furthermore shown on the title page of Ignaz Castelli's* *Allgemeiner musikalischer Anzeiger* that year. The anonymous author of an article in the Leipzig *Allgemeine musikalische Zeitung* (14 January 1835) was to praise this lithograph as the 'best likeness' of Beethoven; but if Steblin is correct in surmising that the writer was none other than the publisher of the lithograph, Tobias Haslinger, the judgement may not be entirely objective.

(Krasa, Steblin[1], Wurzbach[2])

Krumpholtz, Wenzel [Václav] (?Budenitz, near Zlonitz [Budenice, near Zlonice, Czech Republic], c.1750; d. Vienna, 2 May 1817). Violinist and mandolinist; brother of the harp virtuoso Jean-Baptiste Krumpholtz (1742–90). After leaving Bohemia in the mid-1790s he played in Prince Nikolaus Esterházy's* orchestra, and in 1796 was engaged as a violinist in the court opera orchestra in Vienna. He soon made the acquaintance of Beethoven and, according to Ferdinand Ries,* gave him some instruction on the violin. Krumpholtz was among the first to recognize Beethoven's greatness as a composer and, in addition to being a fervent admirer, he became an intimate friend. It may have been for him that Beethoven composed two works for the mandolin, the Sonatina in C minor and the Adagio in E flat (WoO 43). Krumpholtz was also on friendly terms with Wenzel Czerny, and it was he who introduced the latter's son Carl* to Beethoven.

Krumpholtz died of apoplexy while walking on the Glacis. Beethoven is said to have been deeply moved by his death, and the next day (3 May 1817) he made a setting for three male voices (WoO 104) of the sombre words sung by the monks over Gessler's dead body in Schiller's* play *Wilhelm Tell* (IV. iii). On the autograph, which he presented to the musicologist Franz Sales Kandler, he wrote: 'In commemoration of the sudden and unexpected death of our Krumpholz [*sic*].'

(Pohl/Zingel, Schünemann, Wegeler/Ries, Zingel)

Kübeck von Kübau, Karl Friedrich, Baron (b. Iglau [Jihlava, Czech Republic], 28 October 1780; d. Hadersdorf, Lower Austria, 11 September 1855). Senior official; politician. After studying law in Prague and Vienna, he entered government service in 1800. He was to play an important role in the organization of the Austrian railways and the development of the national telegraph system. Ennobled in 1816, he was created a baron in 1825, and accorded the title 'Geheimer Rat' in 1836. He was a member of the Kremsier Reichstag (1848–9), and in 1850 was appointed president of the newly constituted Reichsrat.

In his posthumously published diaries (*Tagebücher*, Vienna, 1909), he described his contacts with Beethoven, which extended over the period 1796–1801. After meeting Beethoven at the house of a mutual acquaintance (whom Frimmel tentatively identifies as the bass Sebastian Mayer*), Kübeck played for him. Beethoven concluded that he lacked the talent for a musical career; but recognizing a certain competence in his playing and knowing that he needed money, Beethoven found him a position in the household of Italian aristocrats then living in Vienna, to whose daughter he was himself giving weekly lessons. Kübeck coached the young girl in the pieces set her by Beethoven, who then taught her their 'artistic interpretation'. The tuition continued for a while even after Beethoven had stopped his lessons in January 1797. This was, however, not the end of Kübeck's contacts with Beethoven, for on 20 February 1801 he records a conversation they had when they accidentally met in the street.

(Kübeck, *ÖBL*)

Kudlich, Johann Baptist (1786–1831). Director of an educational institute in the Landstrasse suburb of Vienna [95 Erdbergstrasse]. Karl van Beethoven* became a pupil there at the end of December 1818 or in January 1819; from March he was a boarder. At first Beethoven was satisfied with the conditions and teaching provided by Kudlich, but in June he was calling him 'either a scoundrel or a weak person' (*Corr.* A950/B1308) and looking for a new school. The reason for his displeasure appears to have been that Kudlich allowed Johanna van Beethoven* greater contact with her son than Beethoven wished her to enjoy. By the end of June Karl had been enrolled in Joseph Urban Blöchlinger's* school.

Kuffner, Christoph (Johann Anton) (b. Vienna, 28 June 1777; d. Vienna, 7 November 1846). Civil servant; poet, dramatist, narrative writer, and translator. A prolific writer, he published poems and stories (in various journals, as well as in volume form), wrote novels and numerous historical plays, and translated Plautus. According to C. von Wurzbach, he had studied singing and the violin with Anton Wranitzky.* He knew Haydn* well and wrote for him the text of an oratorio, *Die vier letzten Dinge*, but Haydn did not set it.

If Carl Czerny's* statement that Kuffner supplied the words for the last movement of the Choral Fantasia is correct, his association with Beethoven must go back at least to the year 1808. However, the statement has been questioned by certain scholars, on the grounds that the text does not appear in the 1845 edition of Kuffner's collected works. Gustav Nottebohm thought that it might have been written by Georg Friedrich Treitschke.* In 1813 Beethoven composed a march (WoO 2a) for Kuffner's tragedy *Tarpeja* which was presented at the Burgtheater for the first time on 26 March 1813 (and for the last time the next day). The 'Introduction to Act II' (WoO 2b) for a play not identified in the autograph was perhaps written for the same work.

Beethoven and Kuffner met frequently during the early part of the summer of 1817, when both were staying at Heiligenstadt. During a later visit to Beethoven, Kuffner reminisced about 'the fish restaurant near Nussdorf where we sat on the terrace, under a full moon, until close to midnight' (*BKh*9/216, *see also* n. 662). But it was in 1826 that they seem to have enjoyed their closest contact; certainly Kuffner's name appears on numerous occasions in the conversation books of that year. He visited Beethoven at the Schwarzspanierhaus, and also kept in touch with him through Karl Holz,* whom he saw regularly. Beethoven, who had undertaken to compose an oratorio for the Gesellschaft der Musikfreunde* and was looking for a text to use in place of Karl Joseph Bernard's* unsatisfactory *Der Sieg des Kreuzes*, became interested in Kuffner's offer to write a libretto on the subject of Saul. (Other subjects proposed by Kuffner were *Der Brand von Moskau* and *Die vier Elemente*.) In due course, Kuffner completed the first part of *Saul*, but Beethoven never got around to setting it. He nonetheless remained attached to the project, for Dr Wawruch* relates in his report on Beethoven's last illness (*Ärztlicher Rückblick auf Ludwig van Beethovens letzte Lebensepoche*) that when his condition temporarily improved at one stage, he 'even imagined that he might be able to complete his oratorio *Saul und David*' (*see also* Handel*). The partial text of the oratorio was found among Beethoven's papers and published by Kuffner in 1828 in the anthology *Libanon* under the title *Saul und David: Ein lyrisch-dramatisches Gedicht. Gewidmet den Manen Beethovens, für welchen die Dichtung bestimmt war* [Saul and David . . . Dedicated to the Memory of Beethoven, for whom the Poem was intended]. Kuffner later made use of the text in preparing the libretto for Ignaz Assmayr's oratorio *Saul und David; Sauls Tod* in 1841/2.

(Badstüber, Bankl/Jesserer, Fischer², *ÖBL*, Schünemann)

Kügelgen, Gerhard (bapt. Bacharach, 6 February 1772; d. near Dresden, 27 March 1820) and **Karl Ferdinand** (bapt. Bacharach, 6 February 1772; d. near Reval [Tallinn, Estonia], 9 January 1832). Painters. The brothers attended Bonn Gymnasium from 1786 to 1789. Gerhard then trained as a painter under Januarius Zick at Koblenz, returning in the spring of 1791 to Bonn, where he painted portraits of the Elector Maximilian Franz* and Count Waldstein.* Karl, in the meanwhile, had registered at Bonn University (on the same day in May 1789 as Beethoven and Antoine Reicha*) and in 1790–1 had worked under Christian Georg Schütz at Frankfurt and Christoph Fessel at Würzburg. In May 1791 the brothers were granted a stipend by the elector to complete their studies in Rome. Gerhard left Rome in early 1795, and was subsequently active as a portrait and historical painter at Riga, Reval, and St Petersburg; in 1805 he settled at Dresden. As for Karl, he remained in Italy until 1796. In the summer of that year he also moved to Riga, and later from there to Reval; from 1798 he lived mainly at St Petersburg. His forte was landscape painting.

Beethoven must have known the brothers very well at Bonn, for they were frequent visitors to the Breunings* and also belonged to the circle around Barbara Koch.* Karl probably saw Beethoven once more in 1796 while passing through Vienna.

(*ALBK*, Braubach[7], Neumann[2])

Kuhlau, (Daniel) Friedrich [Frederik] **(Rudolph)** (b. Uelzen, near Hanover, 11 September 1786; d. Copenhagen, 12 March 1832). Composer and pianist. On 2 September 1825, while on an extended visit to Vienna, he called on Beethoven at his lodgings at Baden, together with Conrad Graf,* Tobias Haslinger,* Karl Holz,* Joseph Sellner,* and others. They had an exceptionally merry time, their high spirits owing more than a little to the champagne they consumed with their meal in the Helenental and to the local red wine which Beethoven later served them in his rooms. Ignaz von Seyfried* gave a lengthy account of the occasion in the appendix to his book *Ludwig van Beethovens Studien* . . . At one point Kuhlau improvised a canon on the name B-A-C-H (in English notation: B flat-A-C-B), to which Beethoven responded with a canon of his own (WoO 191) on the same notes, to the words 'Kühl, nicht lau' [Cool, not tepid], a pun on Kuhlau's name. The next day Beethoven sent a copy of the canon to Kuhlau through Holz, together with a short note.

In *c.*1832 Johann Peter Spehr published at Brunswick three rondos ['rondelettos'] by Kuhlau based on the following songs by Beethoven: 'Das Glück der Freundschaft' (Op. 88), 'Der Jüngling in der Fremde' (WoO 138), and 'Lied aus der Ferne' (WoO 137). An arrangement by Kuhlau for four hands of the last song had previously been issued by A. Cranz in Hamburg in 1827.

(Seyfried)

Kunst- und Industrie-Comptoir [Bureau des arts et d'industrie, Bureau d'arts et d'industrie]. Firm of music publishers and dealers in maps and art prints, originally founded in 1801 by the painter Joseph Anton Kappeller and the lawyer Jakob Holer under the name 'Kunst- und Industrie-Comptoir Kappeller und Holer'. In March 1802, following Kappeller's departure, Holer formed a new partnership with Joseph Schreyvogel,* and at the same time Joseph Sonnleithner* and the latter's brother-in-law Johann Sigmund Rizy were taken on as silent partners; the firm's name was changed to 'Kunst- und Industrie-Comptoir zu Wien'. Some years later Holer also left, and Schreyvogel was from 1807 until 1813 in sole charge of the business. After he retired, the firm was taken over in 1814 by Joseph Riedl von Leuenstern* who had worked for it for some ten years and had become a silent partner in 1811; he henceforth ran it under his own name. (For its later history, *see* the article on Riedl von Leuernstern.)

The Kunst- und Industrie-Comptoir was Beethoven's principal publisher from 1802 to 1808, replacing Artaria & Co.* The first two of his works to be issued by the firm were his own arrangement for string quartet of the Piano Sonata Op. 14, No. 1, and the Piano Sonata in D major, Op. 28 (for which he had signed a contract with the original owners in October 1801). The year 1808 was a particularly significant one in Beethoven's association with the firm. It saw the publication of the first editions of the Fourth Symphony, the Fourth Piano Concerto, the Violin Concerto and Beethoven's arrangement of it as a piano concerto, the three 'Razumovsky' String Quartets, and the *Coriolan* Overture. Altogether, the firm published first editions of some forty compositions by Beethoven. These included, in addition to those already mentioned, the Second and Third Symphonies; the Third Piano Concerto; the Romance for violin Op. 50; the Triple Concerto; five piano sonatas (among them the 'Waldstein'); three sets of piano variations (WoO 78–80); the three Violin Sonatas, Op. 30; and a number of songs.

After 1808 Breitkopf & Härtel* became Beethoven's principal publishers; but in 1810 the Kunst- und Industrie-Comptoir issued an edition of Beethoven's four settings of Goethe's* 'Sehnsucht' (WoO 134). These settings were then being published for the first time, with the exception of No. 1 which had appeared as a supplement to the periodical *Prometheus* in May 1808.

(Slezak[4])

Lachner, Franz Paul (b. Rain am Lech, Bavaria, 2 April 1803; d. Munich, 20 January 1890). Organist, conductor, and composer; son of the organist Anton Lachner. After his father's death in 1822 he moved to Munich, and soon afterwards to Vienna where he became organist at the Lutheran church. In 1827 he was appointed deputy Kapellmeister at the Kärntnertor-Theater, and in 1829 Kapellmeister. He was an intimate friend of Franz Schubert. In 1834 he left Vienna for Mannheim, and two years later he moved to Munich. There he became conductor of the court opera and of the concerts of the Musikalische Akademie; in 1852 he was made Generalmusikdirektor. He was a prolific composer of sacred and secular works.

On 29 September 1824 Johann Andreas Streicher* informed Beethoven that Lachner was to make piano arrangements of the *Missa solemnis* for two and four hands, 'in a spirit of true devotion' (*Corr.* B1884). Streicher was probably planning to sell these arrangements by subscription. However, the project was never carried out, presumably because there was insufficient public interest for it.

(Leuchtmann, Würz)

Lappe, Karl Gottlieb (b. Wusterhausen, near Wolgast, Pomerania, 24 April 1773; d. Stralsund, 28 October 1843). Teacher; poet. In 1817 Beethoven set one of his poems in the song 'So oder so' (WoO 148). It was published as a music supplement to the *Wiener Modenzeitung* in February of that year.

Lessing, Gotthold Ephraim (b. Kamenz, 22 January 1729; d. Brunswick, 15 February 1781). Dramatist, poet, and critic. He was the author of the text set by Beethoven in his song 'Die Liebe', published in 1805 in *Acht Lieder* (Op. 52).

Letronne, Louis René (b. Paris, 1790; d. Paris, 1842). Painter of miniature portraits and graphic artist; brother of the archaeologist Jean Antoine Letronne (1787–1848). He studied with Jacques-Louis David and N. A. Monsiaux. From 1805 [?1809] on he spent several years in Vienna, and during the Congress of Vienna (1814–15) he painted portraits of many of the participants. In 1817 he settled in Warsaw, where he opened an art school. He returned to Paris in 1829, but reportedly also spent some time at Munich and Dresden.

In 1814 he made a pencil drawing of Beethoven which served as the basis for Blasius Höfel's* engraving.

(*ALBK*)

Lichnowsky, (Maria) Henriette (Cajetana), Countess (bapt. Vienna, 10 May 1769; d. after 1829). Sister of Prince Karl Lichnowsky* and Count Moritz Lichnowsky.* On 15 August 1810 she married General Franz Adrian de Carneville (d. 1816). After her wedding she reportedly moved to Paris; she is known to have been still living there in 1829.

Beethoven dedicated the Rondo in G major (Op. 51, No. 2) to her in 1802 (*see* Guicciardi*).

(Igálffy-Igály)

Lichnowsky, Karl (Alois Johann Nepomuk Vinzenz Leonhard), Prince (b. Vienna, 21 June 1761; d. Vienna, 15 April 1814). One of Beethoven's most generous patrons. Eldest son of Prince Johann Karl Amadeus Ferdinand Lichnowsky (1720–88) and his wife Karoline, née Countess Althann (1742–1800); brother of Countess Henriette Lichnowsky* and Count Moritz Lichnowsky.* He married Countess Maria Christiane Thun-Hohenstein (*see* Maria Christiane Lichnowsky*) on 24 November 1788.

Lichnowsky was a pupil and friend of Mozart* and a competent pianist, though not as accomplished as his wife or his brother Moritz. A great music lover, he had in his service a quartet of young string players who gave regular concerts at his house during the latter half of the 1790s. They were the violinists Ignaz Schuppanzigh* and Ludwig Sina,* the violist Franz Weiss,* and the cellist

Nikolaus Kraft.* (Nikolaus's father Anton* may also have taken part in some of the music sessions.)

The Trios of Op. 1 were first heard at a soirée at Lichnowsky's in late 1793 or early 1794. They were dedicated to the prince and published by subscription in 1795; he himself bought twenty copies, his wife three, and Moritz and Henriette two each. Some years later Lichnowsky presented Beethoven with a set of four excellent Italian string instruments which are now at the Beethoven-Haus in Bonn. The gift may have been made in connection with the composition—or publication—in 1801 of the String Quartets (Op. 18), Beethoven's first works for that combination. Lichnowsky also helped in many other significant ways, notably by offering Beethoven hospitality not long after his arrival in Vienna. In *Biographische Notizen* Franz Gerhard Wegeler* reports that he found Beethoven living as the prince's house guest when he arrived in Vienna in October 1794. The prince reportedly gave yet further proof of his generosity in 1800 by granting Beethoven an annuity of 600 florins until he could find a suitable position. (He is believed to have paid it until at least 1806, and may even have done so until 1808—see below.) He frequently visited Beethoven, taking particular care not to disturb him in his work, if certain anecdotes are to be believed, and he maintained a close interest in Beethoven's compositions and helped where he could. Thus he did his best to ensure that the oratorio *Christus am Ölberg* would be well performed at the concert on 5 April 1803, tried to arrange for the publication of certain compositions by Breitkopf & Härtel* in the spring of 1805, and in December of that year offered his apartment for the meeting at which the revision of the original *Fidelio* score was to be discussed (*see also* Maria Christiane Lichnowsky*). It is therefore not surprising that Beethoven should have paid special tribute to Lichnowsky in his Heiligenstadt Testament; and in a letter to Breitkopf & Härtel on 16 January 1805 Beethoven wrote: 'He really is—surely a rare thing for a person of his social class—one of my most faithful friends and one of the most loyal patrons of my music.' Beethoven expressed his gratitude in a series of dedications. In addition to the already mentioned Piano Trios (Op. 1), he dedicated to Lichnowsky the variations for piano on 'Quant' è piu bello' from Paisiello's opera *La molinara* (WoO 69), also in 1795; the *Sonate pathé-tique* in 1799; the Piano Sonata in A flat major (Op. 26) in 1802; and the Second Symphony in 1804.

Yet there is more than one allusion in Beethoven's correspondence to certain tensions in his relationship with Lichnowsky. Writing to Wegeler on 29 June 1801, he mentions some 'slight misunderstandings', which, however, 'have probably only strengthened our friendship'; and in a letter to Josephine Brunsvik*-Deym in April 1805 he writes, with reference to the imminent departure of his 'dear L.': 'Despite the many rough passages which have marked the path of our friendship, nonetheless, now that he is about to leave Vienna, I feel how dear he is to me —and how much I owe to him' (*Corr.* A125/B219). Clearly, his association with

Lichnowsky was more troubled than his friendship with the prince's brother Moritz, who was, in any case, much closer to him in age. Finally, in 1806, his relations with Lichnowsky suffered a breach which was probably never healed. It occurred while Beethoven was staying at the prince's estate at Grätz, near Troppau, in Silesia [now Hradec, near Opava, Czech Republic].

Prince Lichnowsky divided his time between Vienna and Prussia (Potsdam and Grätz); his title was, in fact, a Prussian one, bestowed on his father in 1773. (Not until 1824 was the then head of the family, Karl Lichnowsky's son Eduard (1789–1845), made an Austrian prince.) Beethoven's stay at Grätz from late August or the beginning of September until the latter half of October 1806 was a profitable one, inasmuch as he composed most of the Fourth Symphony during that period. (Some scholars have suggested that he had visited Grätz previously, but of that there is no proof.) His stay ended abruptly, however, as a result of an episode of which differing descriptions exist (none of them, unfortunately, by an eyewitness). His refusal to play before visiting French officers reportedly led to an angry scene with Lichnowsky, who may even have threatened him in some manner, whereupon, according to one version, Beethoven was only just prevented by Count Oppersdorff* from striking the prince. Beethoven then rushed out of the house and walked by night—according to nineteenth-century versions of the incident, to the town of Troppau, but according to a modern scholar, Jindřich Urbánek, to the village of Hirschdorf [Jelenice], the distance in each case being about 8 kilometres. On arriving back in Vienna, he is said to have smashed the bust of Lichnowsky which he had in his rooms; but this incident is more likely to have occurred between early August and the middle of October 1808, for Ludwig Tieck,* who was in contact with Beethoven during this latter period, later recalled that Beethoven had, in his presence, destroyed 'a small marble bust of a certain count . . . which had stood on his writing desk and in whose palace he had lived'. (Despite the mistake about the nobleman's rank, the remark clearly refers to Lichnowsky.) Yet another twist was added to the story by Ferdinand Ries* who stated, in a letter to Wegeler on 28 December 1837, that Beethoven not only remained at Troppau on the day following the dispute, but even attended a large party given there by Lichnowsky's brother, Count Moritz, at which 'he behaved as if he did not know Prince Lichnowsky' (who was evidently assumed to have been present). However, Ries's knowledge of the circumstances surrounding the quarrel was almost certainly based on hearsay (he had been absent from Vienna from late 1805 until the summer of 1808). If he had received his information from Beethoven himself, he would surely have said so. He claims to have 'tried everything' to bring about a reconciliation in 1809, but without success.

Johann Friedrich Reichardt,* who visited Beethoven in November 1808, reported that although he was then living in the same house [10 Krugerstrasse] as the prince, he had no contact with him. On the first day of that month, Beethoven wrote to Count Oppersdorff:* 'My circumstances are improving—

without my requiring for that the assistance of persons who threaten to beat their friends with flails' (*Corr.* A178/B340; some words in this sentence are underlined twice, others even three times). The latter part of the sentence evidently refers to the quarrel at Grätz, the earlier presumably to the cessation of the annuity. It is tempting to speculate that the payments had stopped only a relatively short time before Beethoven wrote this letter on 1 November 1808, and that the destruction of Lichnowsky's bust—which, as already noted, probably occurred between early August and mid-October of that year—was mainly provoked by Beethoven's anger at the prince's cancellation of the annuity. In this connection it is worth noting that in the summer of 1807, according to Alan Tyson, he decided to dedicate the String Quartets Op. 59 to Lichnowsky, instead of to Razumovsky.* This strongly suggests that the annuity payments had not yet ceased at that time. (Beethoven subsequently reverted to his original intention to dedicate them to Razumovsky, who had, in any case, already paid for them.) Jürgen May's suggestion that Lichnowsky's decision to stop the annuity may have been prompted by his very burdensome financial obligations and not by any desire to punish Beethoven has a certain plausibility.

There is no firm evidence that Beethoven and Lichnowsky ever renewed their friendship. It is true that Thayer*—basing himself on notes made by Otto Jahn, who had probably received the information from the musicologist Aloys Fuchs*—writes that after leaving Teplitz [Teplice] in September 1811 Beethoven made a wide detour on his return journey to Vienna in order to visit the prince at Grätz and that, on that occasion, he directed a performance of the Mass in C major at Troppau. But there is no solid evidence to substantiate these statements, which, moreover, appear to be contradicted by Beethoven's letter to Breitkopf & Härtel of 9 October 1811, accordingly to which he travelled from Teplitz directly and speedily to Vienna: 'flugs nach Vien [*sic*]'. It has further been suggested that he and Lichnowsky may have resumed their friendship when both stayed at Teplitz in July 1812. This speculation can be neither proved nor disproved. However, there is certainly no evidence of any subsequent contact between them. Moreover, on 21 September 1814, five months after the prince's death, he paid the following discreet tribute to his former great benefactor in a letter to Count Moritz Lichnowsky: 'I have never forgotten what I owe to all your family, even if an unfortunate incident gave rise to circumstances in which I could not show it as I would have wished.' It seems unlikely that Beethoven would have written this if a reconciliation had taken place two years earlier. It is, incidentally, interesting that despite the breach in his friendly relations with Lichnowsky, he remained on terms of intimacy with his brother.

(Igálffy-Igály, Kopitz, May, Racek[1], Tyson[11])

Lichnowsky, Maria Christiane, Princess, née Countess Thun-Hohenstein (bapt. Vienna, 27 May 1765; d. Vienna, 11 April 1841). Daughter of Countess

Wilhelmine Thun-Hohenstein;* wife of Prince Karl Lichnowsky.* Highly cultivated and an exceptionally fine pianist, she was very well disposed towards Beethoven who was very conscious of the debt he owed her. Schindler* quotes Beethoven as remarking later that she had 'sought to educate him with grandmotherly love' (even though the princess was only some five years older than Beethoven!), and was so concerned for his welfare that she practically kept him under glass in order to prevent anyone unworthy from touching him or breathing on him. She played an important role at the celebrated meeting which was held at Lichnowsky's apartment in December 1805 to discuss the possible abridgement of the original *Fidelio* score; for she not only played the music of the opera on the piano, but was also, according to Joseph August Röckel,* responsible for persuading a very reluctant Beethoven to accept certain cuts.

In 1797 Beethoven dedicated to her the variations for harpsichord or piano on a theme from Handel's* oratorio *Judas Maccabaeus* (WoO 45), and in 1801 the piano arrangement of the ballet music *Die Geschöpfe des Prometheus* (Op. 43).

(Igálffy-Igály, Kerst)

Lichnowsky, Moritz (Joseph Cajetan Gallus), Count (bapt. Vienna, 17 October 1771; d. Vienna, 17 March 1837). Brother of Prince Karl Lichnowsky* and of Countess Henriette Lichnowsky.* He married twice: on 31 January 1797, Countess Maria Anna Caramelli di Castiglione-Faleta (1774–1817); and on 25 May 1820, against his family's wishes, the actress and singer Josepha [Johanna] Stummer (1790–1849). In June 1814 she had borne him a daughter, Josepha Maria, who was not legitimated until 1832. Josepha [Johanna] Stummer is perhaps identical with the 'Jeanette' Stummer who was a member of the Gesellschaft der Musikfreunde,* sang Emmeline in Weigl's* *Die Schweizerfamilie* at the Kärntnertor-Theater in 1815, and appeared the following year as Donna Elvira in Mozart's* *Don Giovanni* and as the Princess of Navarre in Boieldieu's *Jean de Paris* at the Theater an der Wien.

The count was a fine pianist and, like his brother Karl, is said to have been taught by Mozart. In 1798 he published a set of variations for the piano on the duet 'Nel cor più non mi sento' from Paisiello's opera *La molinara* (Beethoven had published variations on the same theme (WoO 70) two years earlier). He appears to have been devoted to Beethoven; Schindler,* who knew him well, called him 'Beethoven's ever supportive, lifelong companion'. His name appears frequently in the conversation books, especially in the years 1823–4, and there are numerous entries in his hand. It is evident that Beethoven sought his advice and help in many matters. He urged Beethoven to compose another opera and tried to find a suitable subject for him (*see* Grillparzer*). He even offered to guarantee payment of whatever fee Beethoven might demand (*see* BKh4/209). He was also actively involved in the arrangements for Beethoven's concert on 7 May 1824, and it was he who persuaded the authorities to permit the performance of parts of the *Missa solemnis* on that occasion.

Beethoven dedicated the *Variations* for piano Op. 35 to the count in 1803, because, as he informed Breitkopf & Härtel* on 8 April of that year, 'he has quite recently done me an unexpected favour'. (The nature of the favour is not known.) Beethoven expressed his gratitude and affection in more than one letter to the count. 'I hope to see you soon and, as always, press you to my heart,' he wrote early in 1814 (*Corr.* A460/B695), and, later that year: 'I see that you are always showering kindnesses on me' (*Corr.* A498/B740); and in 1818 he sent the count his 'profound love and admiration' (*Corr.* A890/B1238). Of course, these no doubt very genuinely felt sentiments did not prevent the occasional outburst of anger, prompted by Beethoven's chronic suspiciousness and irritability. Thus he once fiercely denounced what he wrongly imagined to be the count's duplicity in a curt note: 'I despise falsehood. Do not visit me any more' (*Corr.* A1283/B1803); and on another occasion he gave vent to his exasperation at some opinion expressed by the count by composing, while seated in a coffee house, a short canon (WoO 183) to the words 'Bester Herr Graf, Sie sind ein Schaf' [Most worthy Count, you are a dunce]. He probably did not show this canon to the count, but it became generally known. It would hardly have mattered, for the count was remarkably forbearing.

On 21 September 1814 Beethoven informed him that, in gratitude for his many kindnesses, he was dedicating to him a sonata which would soon be published. This was the Piano Sonata in E minor (Op. 90), which was published in June 1815. If Schindler is to be believed, Beethoven told the count that the sonata described his love for Josepha Stummer and that its two movements could be entitled 'Conflict between Head and Heart' and 'Conversation with the Beloved'. Schindler's assertion, for which he does not cite a source, first appeared in his book *Beethoven in Paris*, which was published in 1842 and subsequently reproduced in its entirety as a supplement to the second edition (1845) of his Beethoven biography. The assertion reappears in a footnote in the third edition of the biography (1860), where its credibility is weakened by the clearly erroneous statements that Lichnowsky did not fall in love with Josepha—whom Schindler does not identify by name, but simply refers to as an operatic singer—until after the death of his first wife (their illegitimate daughter was born in 1814, three years before Maria Anna's death!) and that he was unable to overcome all obstacles to his remarriage until 1816 (when his first wife was, in fact, still alive!). The credibility of Schindler's story is further undermined by the fact that, in order to lend support to his assertion, he forged an appropriate entry in one of Beethoven's conversation books (*BKh3/65*). It is nevertheless worth pointing out that, from a chronological point of view, the idea of Beethoven having invented such a 'programme' for the sonata is not impossible; for the count must have started his affair with Josepha Stummer at the latest in the year 1813—the illegitimate daughter was baptized on 13 June 1814—and Beethoven did not begin work on the sonata until 1814. (Sketches for both movements exist in a sketchbook now owned by the Gesellschaft der Musikfreunde, which also contains sketches for the final version of *Fidelio* dating from the spring of that year.)

(Igálffy-Igály, Krones[2])

Liechtenstein, Josephine Sophie, Princess of, née Countess Fürstenberg-Weitra (b. 20 June 1776; d. 23 February 1848); daughter of Count Joachim Egon Fürstenberg-Weitra. On 12 April 1792 she married Prince Johann Joseph of Liechtenstein (1760–1836) who later distinguished himself in the wars against Napoleon and became a field marshal. The Liechtensteins, an old aristocratic family of great wealth, possessed mansions in Vienna and Vaduz (the capital of the principality of Liechtenstein) and various properties elsewhere. They also owned a celebrated collection of paintings (which was moved from Vienna to Vaduz in February 1945).

According to A. C. Kalischer and T. Frimmel, Beethoven became acquainted with the princess at Prince Karl Lichnowsky's;* Kalischer believes that she subsequently became his pupil. Both suppositions may be correct, but they must be regarded as no more than speculation. In 1802 Beethoven dedicated to her the Piano Sonata Op. 27, No. 1. He presumably remained in contact with her during the following years, for in 1805 he provided Ferdinand Ries* with a letter in which he appealed to her to grant Ries some financial assistance (*Corr.* A121/B240); however, Ries did not deliver the letter.

(Criste, Czeike, Kalischer)

Linke [Lincke], **Joseph** (b. Trachenberg, Prussian Silesia [Żmigród, Poland], 8 June 1783; d. Vienna, 26 March 1837). Cellist and composer. Following the death of his father, a musician who had been his first teacher, he became a choirboy at the Dominican monastery at Breslau [Wrocław] and, while there, studied the cello. He subsequently played in the theatre orchestra of that city. In June 1808 he moved to Vienna, where he was chosen by Ignaz Schuppanzigh* to become a member of Count Razumovsky's* private quartet. When the quartet was disbanded after the count's palace had burnt down in December 1814, Linke was for a time attached to the household of Countess Anna Maria Erdödy,* both in Vienna and at her family's estate in Croatia. In 1818 he was appointed first cellist at the Theater an der Wien. He also played in Joseph Böhm's* quartet, and, following Schuppanzigh's return from St Petersburg in 1823, became a member of his new quartet. In 1831 he joined the court opera orchestra.

Linke was well acquainted with Schubert* and took part in numerous performances of his works. He was also on friendly terms with Beethoven, who had a high opinion of his musicianship and very probably wrote his two Cello Sonatas Op. 102 for him. Linke, for his part, greatly admired Beethoven's compositions,

1. Beethoven; oil painting by Willibrord Joseph Mähler, 1804/5. *Reproduced by courtesy of the Historisches Museum der Stadt Wien*

2. Beethoven; oil painting by Joseph Stieler, 1820. *Reproduced by courtesy of the Beethoven-Haus, Bonn*

3. Heiligenstadt Testament, first page. *Reproduced by courtesy of the Österreichische Nationalbibliothek, Vienna*

4. Title page, Three Piano Sonatas WoO 47 (Bossler, Speyer, 1783); Beethoven's age is incorrectly given as 11 years. *Reproduced by courtesy of the Österreichische Nationalbibliothek, Vienna*

5. Title page, Piano Sonata Op. 90 (S. A. Steiner, Vienna, 1815). *Reproduced by courtesy of the Österreichische Nationalbibliothek, Vienna*

6. Première, *Fidelio,* first version, 20 November 1805. *Reproduced by courtesy of the Österreichische Nationalbibliothek, Vienna*

7. Première, *Fidelio,* third version, 23 May 1814. *Reproduced by courtesy of the Österreichische Nationalbibliothek, Vienna*

Three famous interpreters of the role of Leonore

8. Anna Milder-Hauptmann; engraving by David Weiss, after a drawing by Sigmund Perger. *Reproduced by courtesy of the Österreichische Nationalbibliothek, Vienna*

9. Wilhelmine Schröder-Devrient; engraving by Karl Mauer, after a painting by J.K. *Reproduced by courtesy of the Gesellschaft der Musikfreunde, Vienna*

10. Lotte Lehmann in the role of Leonore. *Reproduced by courtesy of the Österreichische Nationalbibliothek, Vienna*

11. Karl van Beethoven, in cadet's uniform; unsigned miniature on ivory.
Reproduced by courtesy of the Österreichische Nationalbibliothek, Vienna

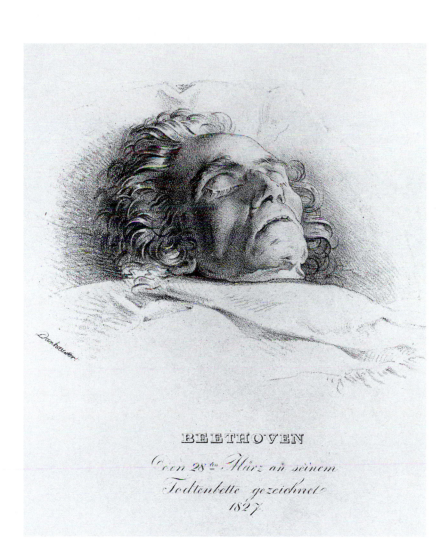

BEETHOVEN

Den 28ᵗᵉⁿ März an seinem Todtenbette gezeichnet 1827

12. Beethoven on his deathbed; drawing by Joseph Danhauser, 28 March 1827. *Reproduced by courtesy of the Österreichische Nationalbibliothek, Vienna*

13. Beethoven: statue by Ernst Julius Hähnel, in Bonn. *Reproduced by courtesy of the Österreichische Nationalbibliothek, Vienna*

14. Beethoven: statue by Caspar von Zumbusch, in Vienna; photograph by Charlotte Till-Borchardt. *Reproduced by courtesy of the Österreichische Nationalbibliothek, Vienna*

many of which he knew, of course, extremely well, both from his experience as a quartet player and from other private and public performances in which he participated. To mention a few important occasions: he was among the distinguished musicians who played in the first performance of *Wellingtons Sieg* on 8 December 1813; on 11 April 1814, at the hotel Zum römischen Kaiser, he gave the first performance of the 'Archduke' Trio with Schuppanzigh and Beethoven himself; he played in the orchestra at Beethoven's memorable concert on 7 May 1824 (and presumably also in the further one on 23 May); he took part in the earliest performances of the Quartet in E flat major (Op. 127), both the rather unsatisfactory first one directed by Schuppanzigh (6 March 1825) and the later, more successful ones, under Böhm; and he played in the private performances of the Quartet in A minor (Op. 132) at the hotel Zum wilden Mann on 9 and 11 September 1825, as well as in the first public performance of that work at his own benefit concert at the Musikverein on 6 November of the same year.

(Herrmann, *ÖBL*)

Liste, Anton (bapt. Hildesheim, 16 April 1772; d. Zurich, 30 July 1832). Conductor, pianist, teacher, and composer; son of the Hildesheim Cathedral organist Karl Joseph Liste. In 1789 his father sent him to Vienna where he studied with Albrechtsberger.* Afterwards he made a certain name for himself as a musician in Germany, and in 1804 he was invited to become music director of the Gesellschaft ab dem Musiksaal in Zurich. Although he relinquished that post three years later, Zurich remained his place of residence for the remainder of his life. There he founded the Liste-Gesangverein, a mixed choir which gave numerous performances of oratorios. He wrote a number of works for the piano, as well as choral compositions.

In 1805 Hans Georg Nägeli* published two piano sonatas by Liste, and in 1810 he brought out a further sonata which Liste dedicated to Beethoven. When Xaver Schnyder von Wartensee* went to Vienna the following year, Liste asked him to present a copy to Beethoven. Schnyder, who apparently thought highly of the sonata, was rather disconcerted when Beethoven, after examining it, expressed the opinion that it was 'a good school exercise'.

(Geiser, *SML*)

Liszt, Franz [Ferenc], (b. Raiding [Doborján] in Hungary [now in the Austrian province of Burgenland], 22 October 1811; d. Bayreuth, 31 July 1886). Composer, pianist, and teacher. In the spring of 1822 the family moved to Vienna, where the 10-year-old boy studied the piano with Carl Czerny* and composition with Salieri.* He gave two public concerts during his stay in the Austrian capital, on 1 December 1822 at the Landständischer Saal and on 13 April 1823 at the Kleiner Redoutensaal. (Between these dates he performed on 9 December and 12 January at concerts given by other artists.) His use in his 'free fantasy' of the Allegretto from Beethoven's Seventh Symphony at the first concert constitutes his earliest known public performance of music by Beethoven. Shortly before 13 April he visited Beethoven and, in an entry in the conversation books, requested him to attend his forthcoming concert (*BKh* 3/168). On the day preceding that event, Schindler* (whom Liszt had by then already met more than once) asked Beethoven on his behalf for a theme on which he could improvise at the concert (*BKh* 3/186–7), a request which Beethoven apparently refused.

For the rest of his life, Liszt was to speak with great emotion of the kiss which he claimed Beethoven had given him in recognition of the excellence of his playing. This kiss is usually referred to in Liszt literature as the 'Weihekuss' [kiss of consecration], since it came to assume a very particular significance for Liszt, in whose view it not only marked the beginning of his career as a performing artist, but also symbolized the special relationship which bound him to Beethoven. Yet the precise circumstances in which this accolade was bestowed—if it really was conferred—remain unclear. What renders the mystery particularly fascinating is the fact that its supposed recipient himself provided conflicting accounts of the incident, describing it in one version (told to his student August Göllerich, as well as to various acquaintances and biographers) as having taken place at the concert of 13 April, and in another version (reported by his student Ilka Horowitz-Barnay) as having occurred in Beethoven's rooms. The matter continues to intrigue Liszt scholars who—not surprisingly, given the ambiguity of the available material— tend to reach differing conclusions. Thus, among recent writers, Alan Walker, basing himself mainly on Horowitz-Barnay's recollections, unhesitatingly accepts the second version and firmly rejects any suggestion that Beethoven may have attended the concert; whereas Adrian Williams dismisses Horowitz-Barnay's account as a 'fable' and concludes that 'the *Weihekuss* was *either* bestowed at the public concert of 13 April, as stated so often by Liszt himself; *or* he afterwards genuinely confused Beethoven with some other imposing personage, such as King Maximilian I [i.e. Maximilian I Joseph*] of Bavaria, who likewise rewarded his playing with a kiss; *or*—least likely of all—it was a deliberate fabrication to which he stubbornly adhered until the very end of his life'. For Allan Keiler, on the other hand, the 'Weihekuss' was indeed an invention on Liszt's part, but rather than a 'deliberate fabrication', it constituted an essential feature of the 'personal and largely unconscious myth that Liszt constructed around the historic figure of Beethoven'.

Liszt was instrumental in making Beethoven's piano compositions better known. In 1872 he wrote to Franz Egger, the president of the Vienna Singakademie: 'Thirty, forty years ago, when Beethoven's piano works were only rarely performed, I clung to them with my soul and my fingers.' In due course, he became one of the foremost interpreters of Beethoven's piano compositions in the nineteenth century, but not until he had overcome widely held suspicions that he was liable to sacrifice the composer to the virtuoso pianist. (Among his severest critics was Schindler.) Liszt also served the cause of Beethoven's music in various other ways. Particularly noteworthy are his piano transcriptions of the nine symphonies, written over a period of close to thirty years. The complete set was published by Breitkopf & Härtel* in 1865. After hearing Liszt play his arrangements of the last three movements of the 'Pastoral' Symphony in Vienna in November 1839, Heinrich Adami declared in the *Allgemeine Theaterzeitung* that 'only an artist like Liszt, who, in addition to a limitless veneration of Beethoven, possesses the rare gift of understanding the great German composer, only such an artist was able, and could venture, to undertake so hazardous an undertaking'. Liszt furthermore composed (and published) a fantasia on the incidental music to *Die Ruinen von Athen* (Op. 113), and made and published transcriptions of the Septet (Op. 20) and of a number of the songs, including 'Adelaide' (Op. 46), the six Gellert* songs (Op. 48), several Goethe* settings (from Opp. 75, 83, and 84), and the cycle *An die ferne Geliebte* (Op. 98).

Lastly, Liszt provided striking proof of his admiration for Beethoven by his support for two projects designed to pay public homage to Beethoven, namely the erection of the Beethoven statues in Bonn in 1845 (*see* Hähnel*) and in Vienna in 1880 (*see* Zumbusch*). His role with regard to the Bonn project was particularly significant, for in addition to making a generous contribution to the costs (for details, *see* the article on Hähnel), he took a very active part in the music festival held at Bonn on the occasion of the unveiling ceremony. At a concert on 12 August 1845 he conducted Beethoven's Fifth Symphony and the quartet and finale from Act I of *Fidelio*, and he was also the soloist in the 'Emperor' Concerto. His Festival Cantata for soloists, chorus, and orchestra, to words by Oskar Ludwig Bernhard, was performed on the following day. It has, moreover, been repeatedly stated (for instance, in the printed catalogue to the *Monument für Beethoven* exhibition held at Bonn in 1995) that it was due to Liszt's objections that the original plans to hold the concerts in the riding arena (which had been specially adapted for the purpose) were abandoned and a special festival hall was built at the last moment, for the construction of which he paid out of his own pocket. However, these statements, which appear to go back to the period of the festival itself, are contrary to the account given by Heinrich Karl Breidenstein in his pamphlet *Zur Jahresfeier der Inauguration des Beethoven-Monuments: Eine actenmässige Darstellung dieses Ereignisses*, which was published at Bonn in 1846, i.e. at a time when the participants in those events, including Liszt, were still alive and able to confirm or deny the truth of his remarks. Breidenstein asserts categorically that Liszt had agreed, albeit reluctantly, to the original arrangement. According to Breidenstein, the decision to replace the chosen venue by a newly constructed hall had resulted from a proposal submitted to the committee on 25 July by a group of local artisans who had offered to build a suitable hall within the space of fourteen days, and to lease it subsequently, for the sum of 4,500 thaler, to the committee, which would be responsible for providing seating for the orchestra and the audience. This proposal, Breidenstein writes, was immediately accepted by the committee, notwithstanding the considerable expense it entailed and despite the fact that 'no one offered either to contribute to the cost of the festival or declared himself ready to cover the possible deficit, as has often been falsely alleged'.

In connection with the Viennese project, Liszt acceded to a request to take part in a concert on 16 March 1877 in aid of the monument fund. On this occasion, he was the soloist in the 'Emperor' Concerto and the Choral Fantasia, and also, together with Joseph Hellmesberger and Reinhold Hummel, accompanied the contralto Karoline von Gompertz-Bettelheim in some of Beethoven's settings of Scottish folk songs. The proceeds of this concert constituted the largest single contribution (some 10,000 florins) to the monument fund. In gratitude, the city of Vienna awarded Liszt the Salvator Medal, a distinction traditionally bestowed on persons who had rendered a signal service to the local community. In addition, the committee in due course presented him with a miniature copy of the statue, which had been specially made for him by Zumbusch himself. (For further evidence of Liszt's profound admiration for Beethoven, *see* Broadwood,* Danhauser,* and Kloeber.*)

(*Beethoven Statue*[1,2], Breidenstein[2], Keiler, Walker, Williams[1])

Lobkowitz, Joseph Franz Maximilian, Prince (b. Raudnitz [Roudnice nad Labem, Czech Republic], 7 December 1772; d. Wittingau [Třeboň, Czech Republic], 15 December 1816). Descendant of an old and wealthy Bohemian family; son of Prince Ferdinand Philipp Joseph (1724–84) and his wife Maria Gabriela, née duchess of Savoy-Carignano (1748–1828), a sister of Marie Antoinette's great friend, the hapless Princesse Marie Thérèse Louise de Lamballe. On 2 August 1792 Lobkowitz married Maria Karoline (1755–1816), a daughter of Prince Johann Anton Schwarzenberg; the couple had twelve children, of whom nine reached adulthood.

Several of Lobkowitz's ancestors displayed a prominent interest in music; his great-uncle Johann Georg Christian (1686–1755) and his father were patrons of Gluck. In Joseph Franz Maximilian's case, music and the theatre became veritable obsessions, which, coupled with a seemingly boundless generosity, ultimately caused his financial ruin. From 1799 he kept a private orchestra which played at his palatial house in Vienna [1 Lobkowitz Platz], where he usually stayed between mid-December and June, and at the family's Bohemian residences—in Prague [1 Jiřská], Raudnitz, and Eisenberg [Jezeří]—where he spent the rest of the year. This permanent orchestra was augmented, as occasion demanded, by outstanding instrumentalists and singers from Vienna, Prague, and elsewhere. It was directed by the composer and violinist Anton Wranitzky,* the composer Anton Kasimir Cartellieri,* and the composer Jan Josef Rösler. (Wranitzky had previously taught Lobkowitz, who became an excellent violinist and cellist; Cartellieri gave him singing lessons.) In order to create a suitable setting for the concerts, operas, and theatrical entertainment which he regularly presented, he had the largest room in his Viennese mansion turned into a concert hall. He furthermore made the house available to composers for rehearsals, in which they could try out their new works before deciding on the final version. Johann Friedrich Reichardt,* who described the house as 'the true residence and academy of music' and its owner as 'a true and insatiable music enthusiast', tells of several rehearsals taking place simultaneously in different parts of the building.

Lobkowitz actively promoted music in many different ways. He was a member of the Gesellschaft der Associierten Kavaliere (*see* Swieten*), and a founder member of the Gesellschaft der Musikfreunde* and of the Jednota pro Zvelebení Hudby v Čechách [Association for the Promotion of Music in Bohemia] which established the Prague Conservatoire. He was also one of the group of aristocrats who took over the management of the two Viennese court theatres and the Theater an der Wien in 1807; he himself assumed responsibility for the operatic performances. In July 1811 he acquired the Hoftheater-Musik-Verlag,* and on 30 September 1811 he took sole control of the court theatres, on which he expended considerable sums (see below). But of all the activities he undertook in the cause of music, and of all the countless instances of the financial support he so beneficently bestowed on musicians, it was his generosity towards Beethoven which was to bring him the most enduring fame.

The earliest example of his patronage of Beethoven dates from 1795. On 2 March of that year, Count Johann Karl Zinzendorf wrote in his diary about a concert given by Lobkowitz, at which 'un nommé Bethofen de Bon' had played, and later that year Lobkowitz was among the subscribers to the Piano Trios Op. 1. In 1801 Beethoven dedicated the String Quartets Op. 18 to him. Their relations became particularly close between 1803 and 1811, and during this period Beethoven dedicated the following further works to the prince: the 'Eroica' Symphony in 1806, the Triple Concerto in 1807, the Fifth and Sixth Symphonies (both of which he dedicated jointly to Lobkowitz and Count Razumovsky*) in 1809, and the String Quartet in E flat, Op. 74, in 1810. Several of his works were first performed at Lobkowitz's, including the Third and Fourth Symphonies, as well as the Triple Concerto—the last two of these works at his Viennese mansion, the 'Eroica' (according to W. Brauneis) at Eisenberg in August 1804 under the direction of Anton Wranitzky. (*See also* Louis Ferdinand.*) In Vienna, the first public performance of the 'Eroica' at the Theater an der Wien on 7 April 1805 was preceded by private performances at the house of the wholesale merchants and bankers Baron Andreas Fellner and his son-in-law Joseph Würth on 20 January, and at Lobkowitz's palace three days later. Finally, it is sometimes stated, though wrongly, that Beethoven also dedicated his song 'In questa tomba oscura' (WoO 133) to Lobkowitz; in fact, the entire collection of settings (including Beethoven's) of Giuseppe Carpani's* poem was dedicated to the prince in 1808, though not by Beethoven but presumably by Countess Constantia Rzewuska (*see* Rzewuski*). In 1809, Lobkowitz was one of the three patrons who pledged to provide Beethoven with an overall annuity of 4,000 florins (*see* Rudolph* and Ferdinand Kinsky von Wchinitz und Tettau*), of which Lobkowitz's share was to amount to 700 florins.

The year 1811 was to prove a turning point in Lobkowitz's relations with Beethoven, for it was in that year that he suspended payments of the annuity. His financial situation had been worsening for several years, and he was already quite heavily in debt. (Thus he had, by 1805, borrowed 70,000 florins from Count Ferdinand Pálffy,* to whom he would eventually owe 130,000 florins.) The effects of inflation and of the *Finanzpatent* which came into force in March 1811 must have made his position even more precarious. Yet he made little or no effort to change his extravagant lifestyle or curtail his lavish patronage of the arts: his total expenses for 1811 amounted to the staggering sum of 2,656,774 florins (old currency). Finally, in 1813, the orchestra personnel was greatly reduced, and the famous concerts in Vienna ceased; in 1814 he resigned from the direction of the theatres. As from 1 June 1813, the management of his affairs had been put in the care of a 'administration' headed by his brother-in-law Prince Joseph Schwarzenberg; the following year this was replaced by a new administration, again headed by Schwarzenberg, which operated under government supervision. Lobkowitz was henceforth deprived of all control of his affairs. He re-enlisted in the army, in which he had served in his youth, and after the Peace of Paris (30 May 1814) he returned to Bohemia, where he lived until his death.

One of the few economies he had practised concerned Beethoven's annuity. The initial series of payments covered the period up to 31 August 1811; thereafter Beethoven was to receive no further money until 1815. It has been remarked, evidently reproachfully, that Beethoven 'showed little understanding when financial difficulties obliged the prince to discontinue the annuity' (Milan Poštolka in *New Grove*), and it is true that he complained bitterly about Lobkowitz in his correspondence and even took legal steps to force him, or the administrators of his estate, to make up the arrears and to resume payments—and to do so, more-over, in the same amount in the new currency (Wiener Währung) as had been previously been paid in the old one (cf. Kinsky*). Beethoven even asserted that Prince Lobkowitz had agreed to this latter arrangement, a claim the prince disputed. It should, however, be pointed out in Beethoven's defence that he was for a considerable part of the period in question also deprived of Kinsky's annu-ity, with the result that the money at his disposal had shrunk significantly. Moreover, at the very time when Lobkowitz supposedly found it too burdensome to continue payment of the annuity, he organized brilliant and costly festivities at Raudnitz in celebration of the wedding of his daughter Maria Gabriela to Prince Vincenz Auersperg on 23 September 1811. For three weeks (12 September–3 October), the castle was the scene of splendid balls, plays, operas, and concerts.

The resident orchestra was augmented with leading musicians from Vienna and Prague, and Lobkowitz also invited a number of well-known singers and actors from those cities and elsewhere. The large Viennese contingent included Joseph Weigl,* who composed a special cantata (*Venere e Marte*) for the occasion, the violinist Joseph Mayseder,* and the singers Anna-Maria Sessi and Karoline and Anna Katharina Wranitzky. Altogether, the festivities, which were no doubt widely reported in Vienna, were rumoured to have cost the prince one million florins. Nor can it have remained a secret that Lobkowitz subsidized the Viennese court theatres more than generously during the next two years; in 1812, the Kärntnertor-Theater alone cost him over 157,000 florins. In these circumstances, it was surely not unreasonable for Beethoven to feel resentment at the suspension, from September 1811, of an annuity amounting to a mere 700 florins.

After Lobkowitz left Vienna in the spring of 1813 he does not appear to have met Beethoven again, but he continued to take an interest in his music, about which Anton Wranitzky kept him informed. On 29 December 1814 the prince wrote to Archduke Rudolph from Prague: 'Although I have cause to feel anything but pleased with Beethoven's conduct towards me, I nevertheless rejoice, as a passionate music lover, that his undoubtedly great compositions are now beginning to be properly appreciated. I have heard *Fidelio* here [*see* Weber*] and . . . I greatly enjoyed the music, with the exception of the two finales which I do not like very much. I find it most effective, and worthy of the man who composed it.' This generous tribute, written at a time when the prince and Beethoven were still in an adversarial legal situation, proves that his actions were never motivated by malice. The matter was, in fact, settled soon afterwards, for the decision reached by the Lower Austrian Landrecht in Beethoven's favour on 22 October 1813 (and which had been contested by the other party) became effective on 19 April 1815. Lobkowitz then agreed to resume his annuity and pay the arrears at the rate requested by Beethoven. The composer expressed his gratitude by dedicating the song cycle *An die ferne Geliebte* to Lobkowitz in 1816, but the prince died before the printed edition was ready, and Beethoven was obliged to send the dedication copies to his son, Prince Ferdinand (1797–1868). The annuity continued to be paid with scrupulous regularity until Beethoven's death, and a final instalment was paid on 6 October 1827 in respect of the period from 1 January to 26 March of that year. For Prince Ferdinand's birthday on 13 April 1823 Beethoven composed the so-called 'Lobkowitz' Cantata (WoO 106).

The Palais Lobkowitz still stands in Vienna to-day. For many years it was rented to foreign diplomatic or cultural missions—1869–1909 to the French embassy, 1919–38 to the Czech embassy, and 1947–79 to the Institut français de Vienne. In 1979 the building was sold by the Lobkowitz family to the Austrian Republic; since 1991 it has been the site of the national Theatermuseum.

(Brauneis, Czeike, Fojtíková/Volek, Gutiérrez, Macek[2], Schaal[2], Volek/Macek[1,2])

Löschenkohl, Hieronymus (bapt. Elberfeld, 18 March 1753; d. Vienna, 11 January 1807). Engraver and music publisher. He moved to Vienna in 1779, and in 1781 he received a licence to sell his silhouettes and copper engravings which proved very popular. He also published calendars and almanacs, and from 1788 musical compositions, mainly songs and dances from Singspiels and ballets. In 1803, as a gift to be offered on the feast day of St Teresa of Ávila on 15 October, he printed Beethoven's song 'Das Glück der Freundschaft' (Op. 88) on green paper in the shape of a sunflower.

Some time after his death, his business was taken over by the composer and art dealer Heinrich Friedrich Müller, who, however, did not register it in his own name until 1811.

(Slezak[4], Weinmann[15])

Louis Ferdinand [Ludwig Friedrich Christian], Prince of Prussia (b. Friedrichsfeld, 18 November 1772; d. Wöhlsdorf, Thuringia, 10 October 1806). Son of Prince August Ferdinand (1730–1813), the youngest brother of Frederick the Great, and his wife Luise von Brandenburg-Schwedt (d. 1820). Louis Ferdinand was a talented composer and a brilliant pianist. In fact, Beethoven, who made his acquaintance in Berlin in 1796, ranked him as a pianist above the Prussian court Kapellmeister Friedrich Heinrich Himmel.* Beethoven met the prince again when he visited Vienna in 1804 on his way to attending the autumn manœuvres of the Austrian army in Moravia. During his stay (8–13 September) he behaved particularly graciously towards Beethoven, and the latter was fond of relating how the prince had demonstratively seated him next to himself at a luncheon he was giving, after the composer had been slighted by an aristocratic hostess who, at her own dinner, had excluded him from her table.

Beethoven showed his admiration for Louis Ferdinand by dedicating the Third Piano Concerto to him. For his part, Louis Ferdinand is said to have been greatly impressed by Beethoven's compositions. When, after the aforementioned manœuvres, he visited Prince Lobkowitz* at Raudnitz [Roudnice] in Bohemia, his host reportedly entertained him with a performance by his private orchestra of the (as yet unpublished) 'Eroica' Symphony. It so moved Louis Ferdinand that he is said to have requested a second, and, after a break, even a third rendition. He himself wrote chamber music for different groups of instruments, but always involving the piano. According to A. B. Marx,* none of his compositions reflects his character more profoundly than the 'very beautiful F minor quartet in which blissful happiness exists side by side with painful longing'. If Baron Ledebur is to be believed, the prince purchased no fewer than thirteen English grand pianofortes. He also owned a Cremona violin which he took with him even on his military campaigns.

At the end of September 1806, on his way to rejoining the army, Louis Ferdinand once again visited Prince Lobkowitz, this time at Eisenberg [Jeseří].

Lobkowitz greatly admired the Prussian prince and had, indeed, urged him earlier that year to take control of what he termed the 'German chaos'—for, Lobkowitz had assured Louis Ferdinand, he alone possessed the necessary courage and vision to free the oppressed and restore order in Germany. But only two weeks after his brief stay at Eisenberg Louis Ferdinand was killed during the retreat from Saalfeld, where his forces had been defeated by a French army under the command of Marshal Lannes.

On 29 October (not 19, as stated in Kinsky/Halm), the *Wiener Zeitung* announced the publication by the Kunst- und Industrie-Comptoir* of Beethoven's Third Symphony. The work, which was dedicated to Prince Lobkowitz, was presented on the title page as a 'SINFONIA EROICA . . . composta per festeggiare il sovvenire di un gran Uomo'. Walther Brauneis has argued that the 'great man' whose memory the composition celebrated was in fact Louis Ferdinand, and that the replacement of the earlier heading 'Sinfonia grande' by the new title could only have been made by Prince Lobkowitz himself. He offers, however, no suggestion as to when the substitution might have been made ('Exactly when the symphony was . . . anonymously dedicated to Louis Ferdinand must at present remain an open question').

(Arnim[2], Brauneis, Klessmann, Ledebur, Wegeler/Ries)

Löwe, Ludwig (b. Rinteln, near Hanover, 29 January 1795; d. Vienna, 7 March 1871). Actor. As a child he performed with his father's theatrical company, and on 9 and 28 February 1811 he appeared at the Burgtheater in Vienna. That same year he was engaged at the German Theatre at Prague, from where he moved to Kassel in 1821. During the following years he made a number of guest appearances in various German cities and also in Vienna, where he performed in 1823 and again in June-July 1825. As a result of the latter engagement he was offered a permanent contract at the Burgtheater, of which he soon became one of the most admired and beloved actors.

In an article entitled 'Beethoven als Liebesbote', published in the Vienna *Neue freie Presse* in 1870, Eduard Hanslick described several meetings between Löwe and Beethoven at Teplitz [Teplice] in 1811, and told how Beethoven had acted as go-between for the young actor and the daughter of a local innkeeper who had caught his eye. The story had been told to Thayer* several years earlier by Marie von Breuning, and her brother Gerhard von Breuning* states in *Aus dem Schwarzspanierhaus* that he also had known it before Hanslick recounted it in print. It is plausible to think that it had come down to them through their father Stephan von Breuning.* It is therefore likely to be authentic, and all the more so since Hanslick's article appeared while Löwe was still alive and living in Vienna.

Löwe is said to have called on Beethoven when he was in Vienna in 1823 and to have spoken to him about the incident, which Beethoven had quite forgotten. There is no evidence in the conversation books of a visit by Löwe then, but his performances in Vienna two years later did leave a trace in the form of an entry by Karl van Beethoven,* who tells of having seen 'a very good visiting actor' in the role of Mortimer in Schiller's* *Maria Stuart* (*BKh*7/310). Löwe appeared in that role at the Burgtheater on 18 June 1825.

(*ÖBL*)

Lucchesi, Andrea (b. Motta di Livenza, near Treviso, 23 May 1741; d. Bonn, 21 March 1801). Composer and conductor. He arrived at Bonn late in 1771 as director of a travelling opera company. Among the spectacles presented by the troupe during the next three years were two operas by Lucchesi which had previously been performed at Venice, as well as several new works he had composed at Bonn. On 26 May 1774 he was appointed court Kapellmeister, in succession to Beethoven's grandfather Ludwig.*

Lucchesi is reported to have enjoyed good personal relations with the Beethoven family and to have repeatedly visited them. When he was granted a lengthy leave in April 1783, the young Ludwig benefited from his departure by being assigned some of his duties as organist, and by substituting at the cembalo during theatrical rehearsals for Christian Gottlob Neefe* who had to assume other responsibilities. The experience thus gained was extremely useful. (*See also* Cressener.*)

(Hansell)

Lyser, Johann Peter Theodor [really: Burmeister, Ludwig Peter August] (b. Flensburg [Denmark], 4 October 1803; d. Altona, 29 January 1870). Actor, writer, and graphic artist; son of the Saxon court actor Friedrich Burmeister. He was passionately fond of music, about which he wrote knowledgeably. Music and musicians played moreover an important part in his novellas; a collection of these, anonymously published at Leipzig in 1835 under the title *Kunstnovellen*, contained one dealing with Beethoven's youth. Lyser's enthusiasm for music was not affected by the at least partial deafness which afflicted him during most of his life.

Lyser's drawings of Beethoven enjoyed a wide distribution in the nineteenth century. A lithograph of two such drawings, made on a single sheet, is believed to have been first sold by the Hamburg music publisher August Heinrich Cranz in 1832; one shows Beethoven out walking, the other portrays only his head. A note by Lyser states that they were based on 'an original drawing', thus suggesting that they were done from life. If this is true, which is by no means certain, the original artist could not have been Lyser himself, for he never saw Beethoven; in fact, he did not visit Vienna until 1836. Nor is Beethoven's signature, which appears on the sheet together with Lyser's, authentic.

Two other small lithographed sketches of Beethoven by Lyser appeared in his almanac *Cäcilia* in Hamburg in 1833. One depicts Beethoven in the act of writing the 'Pastoral' Symphony. The other one shows him (to cite Lyser's accompanying explanation) 'as he bounded and ran, rather than walked, through the streets of Vienna in the last years of his life'. This drawing is very similar to one of those mentioned in the preceding paragraph: Beethoven is again portrayed striding along (though hardly bounding, let alone running), with his hands folded behind him and his hat tilted back at a slightly rakish angle. Lyser's biographer Friedrich Hirth claims that the Beethoven statue in the Heiligenstädter Park in Vienna (based on a model by Robert Weigl) was largely inspired by Lyser's drawings.

In 1834 Lyser published anonymously a novella describing Beethoven's early life, leading up to what is portrayed as his momentous meeting with Mozart, who instinctively recognizes the young man's genius ('Ludwig van Beethoven', *Neue Zeitschrift für Musik*, 17 July–7 August 1834; repr. in *Beethoven-Almanach der deutschen Musikbücherei*, Regensburg, 1927).

As already mentioned, Lyser was in Vienna in 1836. 'I visited Beethoven at Währing,' he afterwards reported to Robert Schumann—meaning that he visited Beethoven's grave at Währing Cemetery. Later, he lived in Vienna from April 1845 to September 1853, earning his living as a writer and, especially, as a journalist. On the occasion of the Beethoven Festival at Bonn in 1845 (*see* Hähnel* and Liszt*), he made a large commemorative drawing which was printed on 12 August as a supplement to the *Wiener Zeitschrift für Kunst, Literatur, Theater und Mode*, the journal in which most of his articles appeared.

(Bettermann, Frimmel[3], Hirth, Voss)

Mähler, Willibrord Joseph (b. Ehrenbreitstein, near Koblenz, 1778; d. Vienna, 20 June 1860). Civil servant; amateur portrait painter. A man of many talents, he was a competent singer, wrote poems which he himself set to music, and was also an accomplished painter, having studied with the well-known portraitist Anton Graff at Dresden and later at the Akademie der bildenden Künste in Vienna (where he settled in *c*.1803). Not long after his arrival there he was introduced to Beethoven by Stephan von Breuning,* and in 1804 or 1805 he executed what has since become one of the most celebrated portraits of the composer, who is shown almost at full length, seated, with his left hand resting on a lyre and his right hand extended 'as if he were beating time in a moment of musical exaltation' (according to the description of the pose which Mähler himself gave to Thayer* during an interview in 1860). The portrait remained in Beethoven's possession until his death, when it was inherited by his nephew Karl.* In 1960 it was acquired from the widow of the latter's grandson Raoul Heimler by the Historisches Museum der Stadt Wien. A copy once owned by Thayer is now at the New York Public Library.

Beethoven appears to have been on friendly terms with Mähler, who was a fellow Rhinelander and, more particularly, born in the same town as Beethoven's mother Maria Magdalene.* Some ten years after this first portrait of Beethoven, Mähler painted three more. He also painted a number of other musicians, among them Eybler, Gyrowetz,* Hummel,* Kozeluch,* Salieri,* Ignaz von Seyfried,* Michael Umlauf,* and Joseph Weigl.* This collection, including one of the new portraits of Beethoven, was later bequeathed to the Gesellschaft der Musikfreunde* by Joseph Sonnleithner* who presumably had either acquired them from Mähler or had commissioned some or all of them in the first place. Among Mähler's other portraits are two of Julie von Vering [later Julie von Breuning*], one of which is now also at the Historisches Museum der Stadt Wien.

Finally, Beethoven may be depicted in a partial view of the park of Laxenburg Castle which Mähler (according to *ALBK*) painted between 1818 and 1820. The present whereabouts of this painting, if indeed it still exists, are unknown.

(Czeike, Frimmel³, Glück², *ÖBL*)

Maisch, Ludwig (b. Nuremberg, 1776; d. Vienna, 18 April 1816). Music publisher. After moving to Austria in 1796 he worked for a number of firms, including from 1802 to 1808 for the Kunst- und Industrie-Comptoir.* In 1808 he went into partnership with Anna Kozeluch, the widow of Anton Kozeluch (1752–1805); the latter had taken over the music publishing business of his brother Leopold in 1802 (*see* Kozeluch*). When Anna remarried in late 1808 she automatically lost her licence and Maisch remained in sole control of the firm. In 1814 he published Beethoven's six German dances for piano and violin (WoO 42).

In 1818 Maisch's widow Anna Maria Carolina sold the firm to Daniel Sprenger; who died in September of the following year. In 1821 Sprenger's widow Karolina [Charlotte] married Mathias Artaria,* who officially registered the firm in his own name in 1822.

(Slezak⁴)

Malchus, Carl August, Baron (bapt. Mannheim, 27 September 1770; d. Heidelberg, 20 October 1840). In August 1792 the imperial ambassador to the Rhenish electoral courts, Count Clemens August Westphalen, whose secretary Malchus had become in January of that year, took up residence at Bonn. There Malchus was soon on friendly terms with the young Beethoven. In October he made an affectionate entry in the album which was presented to Beethoven on his departure for Vienna. A year later, in a letter to Eleonore von Breuning* on 2 November 1793, Beethoven complained that he had written three times to Malchus since arriving in Vienna, but had received no reply. Malchus was himself in Vienna in 1795/6. Later he was to hold senior government positions in Prussia, Westphalia, and Württemberg. He was created a baron in 1810. (In 1813 he was granted the title 'Count Marienrode', which he later renounced.)

(Braubach⁷,⁸)

Malfatti, Therese: *see* Malfatti von Rohrenbach zu Dezza.*

Malfatti von Montereggio, Johann [Giovanni Domenico Antonio] (b. Lucca, 12 June 1775; d. Hietzing, near Vienna, 12 September 1859). Physician; member of an old patrician family originally from Lucca. He trained under Aloysio Galvani at Bologna and Johann Peter Frank* at Pavia. In 1795 he followed Frank to Vienna and became his assistant at the Allgemeines Krankenhaus [General Hospital]; he completed his medical studies in 1797. By the time Frank left Vienna in 1804, Malfatti had set up in private practice. He was extremely successful and counted many prominent persons among his patients, including Archduchess Maria Beatrix d'Este; he also attended the duke of Reichstadt during his final illness. Malfatti was a highly intelligent and cultured man. Having been married to the Polish Countess Helena Ostrowska (1794–1826), he took a particular interest in the young Chopin during the latter's stay in Vienna in 1830–1 and was able to open many doors for him. Malfatti was ennobled in 1837. That same year he helped to found the Gesellschaft der Ärzte [Society of Physicians]; he served as its first president from December 1837 until March 1841.

It is stated in Frimmel's *Beethoven-Handbuch* and P. Nettl's *Beethoven Encyclopedia* that Ignaz von Gleichenstein,* who introduced Beethoven to Malfatti's cousin Jakob Friedrich and his family (*see* the next article), was also responsible for his acquaintance with Dr Malfatti. This is mere speculation. It should be noted, in any case, that while Beethoven did not meet Jakob Friedrich Malfatti until 1810, he was almost certainly acquainted with Dr Johann Malfatti by 1809 at the latest; for the 'Malfatti' to whom he sent his best regards in a letter to Ignaz Paul Vital Troxler* in the summer of 1809 (*Corr.* A225/B399) was most probably Dr Johann Malfatti. (Troxler had studied, and even lodged, with Malfatti during an earlier stay to Vienna in 1804–5, and he may safely be assumed to have contacted him again while he was in Vienna in 1807–9.) It is also worth remembering that Dr Johann Adam Schmidt,* who had been treating Beethoven for several years, died on 19 February 1809, so Beethoven may have sought professional advice from Malfatti already during the spring of that year; but their acquaintance could well go back even further.

Beethoven consulted Malfatti on various occasions over the next several years. It was Malfatti who strongly recommended Beethoven to take the cure at Teplitz [Teplice] in 1811, for he firmly believed in the curative powers of mineral springs and was indeed responsible for the development of certain Austrian spas (he was made an honorary citizen of Bad Ischl). Beethoven became quite friendly with Malfatti, and in 1814 he composed a short cantata (*Un lieto brindisi*, WoO 103) for the doctor's name day on 24 June (*see* Bertolini*). It was performed at the doctor's house in the Weinhaus suburb [79 Lacknergasse]; Beethoven probably played the piano accompaniment himself. However, Beethoven and Malfatti quarrelled in April 1817. According to Schindler,* Beethoven 'accused Dr Malfatti of having prescribed the wrong treatment and of much else . . . Malf[atti] at once broke off relations with him.' Beethoven, suspicious as ever, may not only have expressed doubts about Malfatti's professional competence, but also made some offensive remarks of a more personal nature. In a letter to Countess Erdödy* on 19 June 1817, he described Malfatti as 'a crafty Italian' who was lacking in both medical knowledge and honesty. Malfatti, by then a distinguished figure in Viennese society, was no doubt much too conscious of his position to tolerate such aspersions.

Some ten years later, when Beethoven was very ill and losing confidence in Dr Wawruch,* Malfatti agreed to take part in a doctors' conference on 11 January 1827. (The remedies he recommended—consumption of frozen fruit punch and rubbing the patient's abdomen with ice-cold water—were applied for a while.) A week later (19 January), Schindler arranged for him to be alone with Beethoven, and a reconciliation took place. Thereafter Malfatti visited Beethoven on several occasions and offered advice, but he was careful not to intrude on Dr Wawruch's position as the physician in charge of the case. At first, the frozen punch had a restorative effect on Beethoven's spirits, but when he began to absorb excessive amounts of it, Wawruch discontinued the treatment. At the end of February, Malfatti himself fell ill and sent his assistant.

(Albrecht[1], Brandenburg[2], Czeike)

Malfatti von Rohrenbach zu Dezza (family). The head of the family was **Jakob Friedrich** (1769–1829), a cousin of Johann Malfatti von Montereggio.* His father Johann Baptist [Giovanni Battista] and his uncle Franz [Francesco] settled in Vienna in *c.*1760, and in 1765 they were employed as bookkeepers in the bank and wholesale business Smitmer & Co.; later they were to become directors and eventually partners in the firm. They were ennobled in 1785. In 1797 Jakob Friedrich and his brother Johann Baptist (II) joined the firm, which they subsequently ran together after their father and uncle had retired. Jakob Friedrich himself withdrew from the firm in 1810, but he had other business interests which brought him a comfortable income. He was married, since 1791, to Therese von Velsern (1769–1829). They had two daughters, **Therese** (b. 1 January 1792; d. 27 April 1851) and **Anna** (b. 6 December 1792; d. 25 September 1869); a son, Johann Baptist Jakob (b. 1795), had died at a young age. In 1804 the couple had acquired a country estate at Walkersdorf am Kamp, near Krems in Lower Austria, where they usually spent the summer months.

Beethoven was introduced to the family by his friend Baron Ignaz von Gleichenstein,* probably soon after the latter's return to Vienna in February 1810. Beethoven found the Malfattis extremely congenial company and became a frequent visitor. To Gleichenstein he wrote: 'I am so happy when I am with them. I feel that they may be capable of healing the wounds with which wicked persons have torn my soul apart. I thank you, my dear G[leichenstein], for introducing me to them' (*Corr.* A235/B436). Beethoven seems to have been particularly attracted to Therese, and there are strong indications that he even contemplated marrying her. It was most probably for this reason that he requested Franz

Gerhard Wegeler* on 2 May 1810 to obtain his baptismal certificate and send it to him as soon as possible. But his contacts with the Malfattis were destined to be of short duration. A (lost) letter, in which Gleichenstein apparently informed him of the decision taken by certain friends not to receive him henceforth at their house except when there was to be music, almost certainly referred to the Malfattis. Gleichenstein's message is only known through Beethoven's reply. It devastated him. 'Your news has plunged me from the heights of the greatest ecstasy down into the depths . . . So, once again, it is only in my own heart that I can seek comfort, there is none for me outside of it. Friendship and kindred feelings have inflicted nothing but wounds on me . . . I ask you only to set my mind at rest and tell me that what has happened was not caused by anything I did yesterday. But if you cannot do so, then tell me the truth. I am as glad to hear it as I am to speak it' (*Corr.* A254/B445). The incident which prompted the Malfattis' decision probably occurred in early June, very likely at their estate at Walkersdorf. Beethoven had evidently been unaware, until he received Gleichenstein's note, that he had given offence. Perhaps he had declared his love; perhaps he had even proposed marriage; or perhaps he had simply treated Therese with a tenderness which reflected his feelings for her—and which had displeased her and alarmed his hosts. Whatever the reasons, his association with the Malfattis seems to have ceased at this time. A few weeks later Stephan von Breuning* wrote to Wegeler: 'I believe that [Beethoven's] marriage project has fallen through.' An entry in Beethoven's diary, apparently made in 1814—'Ask [Demand?] the return of *Rosamunda* by Alfieri and the edition of Gozzi . . . which I lent Theres [*sic*] Malfatti'—has been taken by Sieghard Brandenburg as evidence that Beethoven had by then re-established friendly relations with Therese. It is, however, by no means clear that she had received these books only recently, and not already four years earlier. Moreover, the verb here used by Beethoven—'zurückfordern' —tends to signify 'demand' rather than 'ask' and may reflect a less than friendly attitude.

An important link between Therese and Beethoven—to which biographers may, however, have attached greater significance than it merits—is constituted by the fact that she owned at the time of her death in 1851 the (now lost) autograph of the Bagatelle WoO 59. It was later owned by a certain Babette Bredl, who allowed L. Nohl to copy it in 1865. When he published the composition in *Neue Briefe Beethovens* in 1867, he stated that Beethoven had written on the autograph 'Für Elise am 27. April zur Erinnerung an L. v. Bthvn' [For Elise, on 27 April, as a memento of L. v. Bthvn]. Nohl accordingly concluded that the piece of music had been written for someone other than Therese. But Max Unger, in an article in the *Musical Quarterly* in 1825, maintained that it had indeed been composed for her and that Nohl had made a mistake, misreading 'Therese' as 'Elise'. Since the piece is, on the basis of other evidence, believed to have been composed in 1810, the identification of the dedicatee as Therese Malfatti is perfectly feasible as far as the dates are concerned, and Unger's conclusions have been widely accepted by Beethoven scholars. One may nevertheless wonder if Nohl could really have made such a mistake, especially as his natural expectation would have been to find Therese's name on the manuscript. On the other hand, the wording of Beethoven's dedication fits in well enough with idea that it may have been addressed to Therese, since the expression 'zur Erinnerung an' commonly implies the imminent separation of dedicator and dedicatee, and Therese appears to have left Vienna with her family for Walkersdorf not long after 27 April 1810 (*see Corr.* B442 n. 1). It should, in any case, be pointed out that even if the composition was indeed intended for Therese, Beethoven's inscription offers no clue as to his feelings for her. According to Kinsky/Halm, he probably also composed the songs 'Wonne der Wehmut' and 'Sehnsucht' (Op. 83, Nos. 1–2) for Therese in the spring of 1810.

Anna Malfatti married Baron Gleichenstein on 28 May 1811. Therese married Baron Johann Wilhelm Drossdick, a senior civil servant, on 14 June 1816.

(Beahrs², Brandenburg², Nohl¹, Unger⁵)

Mälzel [Maelzel], **Johann Nepomuk** (b. Regensburg, 15 August 1772; d. at sea, 21 July 1838). Inventor. One of his most celebrated mechanical creations was the Panharmonicon he perfected in 1812, which was capable of reproducing the sounds of many orchestral instruments. At his suggestion, Beethoven wrote for it a composition celebrating Wellington's defeat of the French at Vitoria, in northern Spain, on 21 June 1813. Subsequently, again at Mälzel's suggestion, Beethoven orchestrated this 'victory symphony'; at the same time, he composed a new section which was intended to precede it and which depicted the battle itself. The complete work, *Wellingtons Sieg, oder Die Schlacht bei Vittoria*, was first performed on 8 December 1813 at a public concert in the great hall of the University. Also on the programme was Beethoven's Seventh Symphony; in addition, the Mechanical Trumpeter, another famous invention of Mälzel's, played two marches by other composers. The concert, which had been arranged by Mälzel, was such a success that it was repeated four days later. It was a most notable event in Beethoven's career (Schindler* called it 'one of the most important moments in the life of the Master'), but it led to a lengthy and bitter quarrel between the two men over the question of the proprietorship of *Wellingtons Sieg*. A further concert at the Grosser Redoutensaal on 2 January 1814, at which the Seventh Symphony as well as *Wellingtons Sieg* were once more performed, was announced by Beethoven as being given for his own benefit, and the contributions previously made by the Mechanical Trumpeter were replaced by music drawn from Beethoven's *Die Ruinen von Athen*.

Beethoven was greatly incensed when he learned that Mälzel, who left Vienna soon after their quarrel, had taken with him copies of the orchestral parts of

Wellingtons Sieg, which were then used in performances of the work at Munich on 16 and 17 March 1814. Thayer* is, however, mistaken in believing that it was the receipt of this news which prompted Beethoven to send a copy of the score to the prince regent (*see* George IV*) in London 'in order at least to prevent any attempt by Mälzel to produce it there as a new work'. (Mälzel was known to be planning a visit to England; indeed, he and Beethoven had at one time intended to present jointly a performance of *Wellingtons Sieg* in London.) It is clear from a 'Deposition' which Beethoven later drafted for his lawyer Karl Schwabel von Adlersburg* (*Corr.* A485/B728) that the possibility of presenting a copy of the score to the prince regent had arisen while Mälzel was still in Vienna (*see also Corr.* B692 n. 1, where it is stated that the score was dispatched to England before 13 February 1814). On the other hand, Beethoven did react to Mälzel's activities in Germany by sending Ferdinand Ries* later that year a statement asserting that any performance of *Wellingtons Sieg* which Mälzel might arrange in London would be illegal and undoubtedly incomplete (*see Corr.* A499/B742). Ries was asked to circulate this statement among musicians in London, but it is not known whether he brought it to anyone's attention. The following year Beethoven was surprised to learn from a report in the Viennese press that Sir George Smart* had conducted the still unpublished work at Drury Lane Theatre on 10 and 13 February 1815. But Mälzel, though he is likely to have been in contact with Smart during his lengthy residence in London, appears to have had nothing to do with these performances, for Ries informed Beethoven that Smart had used the score which he had sent to the prince regent (*see Corr.* A1142/B1579).

Beethoven and Mälzel made up their differences when they met in Vienna in late 1817, and they even renewed their plans for a joint journey to London. To please Beethoven, Mälzel subsequently devised a hearing aid for his use while conducting—at any rate, so he informed Beethoven in a letter from Paris in April 1818 (*Corr.* B1253), but nothing else is known about it. (Years earlier he had fashioned several ear trumpets for Beethoven which had not proved particularly effective.) By now Mälzel had perfected his metronome, the principal feature of which had actually been developed by the Amsterdam mechanic Dietrich Nikolaus Winkel. Beethoven, after some hesitation, became convinced of its usefulness and prepared a table of tempos for his eight symphonies which was published in the Leipzig *Allgemeine musikalische Zeitung* on 17 December 1817. A joint endorsement of Mälzel's metronome by Beethoven and Salieri* appeared in the Viennese periodical of the same name on 14 February 1818.

The canon 'Ta ta ta . . . lieber, lieber Mälzel' (WoO 162), which, according to Schindler, was the origin of the Allegretto scherzando in the Eighth Symphony, was almost certainly composed by Schindler himself, who also forged two entries in the conversation books relating to it (*BKh*1/312 and 5/232–3).

(Goldschmidt[5], Howell, Küthen[1], Levin, Orel[4], Schindler[1], Ullrich[5])

Maria Theresia, empress of Austria (b. Naples, 6 June 1772; d. Vienna, 13 April 1807). Daughter of King Ferdinand I of the Two Sicilies (1751–1825); on 19 September 1790 she became the second wife of Emperor Franz II (1768–1835).

She was very musical and occasionally sang at concerts at court. Haydn* dedicated his Mass in B flat major (the so-called 'Theresienmesse') to her in 1799. Beethoven dedicated his Septet Op. 20 to her in 1802.

Marschner, Heinrich August (b. Zittau, 16 August 1795; d. Hanover, 14 December 1861). Composer, famous for his operas *Der Vampyr* (première: Leipzig, 29 March 1828), *Der Templer und die Jüdin* (Leipzig, 22 December 1829), and, especially, *Hans Heiling* (Berlin, 24 May 1833). In the *Niederrheinische Musikzeitung* in 1857, L. Bischoff told the story of Marschner's first meeting with Beethoven, as recounted by Marschner himself. It appears that he owed his introduction to Beethoven to Baron Thaddeus Amadée [Amade de Varkony], a well-known music lover whose acquaintance he had made at Karlsbad [Karlovy Vary] in 1815. In 1816 he settled at Pressburg [Bratislava], where he was engaged as music teacher by Count Johann Nepomuk Zichy. It is not clear exactly when he first presented himself and his compositions to Beethoven. According to his own account, as related by Bischoff, Beethoven 'received him cordially enough, looked quickly through the manuscripts, handed them back with a "Hm!", which expressed approval rather than the contrary, and said: "I don't have much time—don't come too often—but bring some more music." ' Marschner was greatly disappointed, having hoped for a detailed discussion of his scores, and was ready to renounce his plans for a career in music, until, having been told that Beethoven's manner was habitually rather gruff, he formed 'quite a different and truer impression' of his visit, and remembered that Beethoven had looked at him in a kindly fashion and had given him a friendly handshake when he left. During his later visits Beethoven was unfailingly kind and even occasionally offered a word of encouragement. (These later visits, and perhaps already the first, occurred while Marschner was living at Pressburg.) Marschner's contacts with Beethoven ceased when he moved to Dresden some time after his opera *Heinrich IV und d'Aubigné* had been produced there on 19 July 1820. It will be seen from the above that P. Nettl's statement, in his *Beethoven Encyclopedia*, that at their first meeting Beethoven 'did not receive the young man in a very friendly way' is, to say the least, misleading.

(Köhler[3])

Marx, Adolph Bernhard (b. Halle, 28 November ?1795; d. Berlin, 17 May 1866). Music theorist, author, and composer. A lawyer by training, he soon decided to devote his life to music; he studied thoroughbass with Daniel Gottlob Türk and composition with Carl Friedrich Zelter.* When Adolph Martin Schlesinger* founded the weekly *Berliner allgemeine musikalische Zeitung* in 1824, Marx was appointed its editor, and he retained that position throughout the seven years of its publication (1824–30). He was a fervent admirer of Beethoven's compositions and the periodical played a major role in promoting deeper understanding and greater appreciation of Beethoven's music in Germany. In its first year, it published articles on no fewer than eight of his recent compositions. 'Please arrange for [the *Berliner allgemeine musikalische Zeitung*] to be sent to me regularly in future,' Beethoven wrote to Schlesinger on 19 July 1825. 'On looking through it I noticed several articles which I immediately recognized as the work of the clever Herr Marx.' The following year Beethoven was asked to send a short piece of music for publication in the *Zeitung* and he promised to do so, but never got around to it.

In 1830 Marx was appointed professor of music at the University of Berlin. In 1850 he founded the Berliner Musikschule, together with Theodor Kullak and Julius Stern, and he taught there until 1856. (It was renamed the Sternsches Konservatorium in 1857.) His compositions, which comprise both sacred and secular works, many for single voice or choir, achieved only a modest success, except for the oratorio *Mose* which received numerous performances, including one by Liszt* at Weimar in 1853. His theoretical writings, on the other hand, brought him considerable renown, foremost among them *Die Lehre von der musikalischen Komposition, praktisch-theoretisch* (1837). In 1859 he published a book on Beethoven (*Ludwig van Beethoven: Leben und Schaffen*).

(Bauer[3], Burnham, Hahn[2], Moyer, Schmitz)

Matthisson, Friedrich von (b. Hohendodeleben, near Magdeburg, 23 January 1761; d. Wörlitz, near Dessau, 12 March 1831). Poet. His first volume of verse appeared in 1781 under the title *Lieder*, which he changed to *Gedichte* in the 1787 edition. His *Gesammelte Schriften* were published in eight volumes in Zurich in 1825–9, followed by the posthumous *Literarischer Nachlass* (4 vols., Berlin, 1832). His elegant poetry, tinged with a certain melancholy, was highly popular in his day and attracted a number of composers, among them Johann Friedrich Reichardt,* Zelter,* Zumsteeg, and especially Schubert.*

Matthisson's verse inspired Beethoven to compose the songs 'Adelaide' (Op. 46, published by Artaria & Co.* in 1797), 'Andenken' (WoO 136, published by Breitkopf & Härtel* in 1810), 'An Laura' (WoO 112, not published in Beethoven's lifetime), and 'Opferlied', of which a setting for single voice and piano appeared at Bonn in 1808 (WoO 126, Simrock*) and another for soprano and chorus, with orchestral accompaniment, at Mainz in 1825 (Op. 121b, Schott's Söhne*). In addition, Beethoven wrote out two canons to the words 'Das Schöne zum Guten' taken from the text of 'Opferlied', one for Marie Pachler* on 27 September 1823 (WoO 202) and the other for Ludwig Rellstab* on 3 May 1825 (WoO 203). He also left a sketch for another song, 'Wunsch'.

When Beethoven published 'Adelaide' in 1797, he dedicated the song to Matthisson. Three years later he sent a copy to the poet, together with a letter, from which it is clear that he had not sought Matthisson's permission for the dedication. Explaining that diffidence and doubts about the merit of the composition had prevented him from approaching Matthisson earlier, he wrote: 'My most ardent wish will be fulfilled if my musical setting of your heavenly "Adelaide" does not altogether displease you and if, as a result, you should be prompted to write another similar poem and to send it to me straightaway, if such a request does not appear presumptuous to you. I will then strive to compose a setting worthy of your beautiful poetry' (*Corr.* A40/B47). It is not known whether Matthisson replied to this letter. However, in an edition of his poems published at Tübingen in 1811, he characterized Beethoven's as the most profound setting of 'Adelaide' which had yet been composed. And 'Adelaide' soon became, and still remains, one of the most popular of Beethoven's songs. On 25 January 1815, during the Congress of Vienna, it was sung by Franz Wild,* accompanied by Beethoven himself, before an illustrious audience at a concert in honour of the Tsarina Elisabeth Alexievna's* birthday.

Max(imilian) Franz, Archduke (b. Vienna, 8 December 1756; d. Hetzendorf, near Vienna, 26/7 July 1801). Youngest son of Emperor Franz I and Empress Maria Theresa. In 1780 he was elected coadjutor to Maximilian Friedrich,* archbishop and elector of Cologne and bishop of Münster, and following Maximilian Friedrich's death on 15 April 1784 he succeeded him in those positions. He was also, from 1780 until his death, grand master of the Teutonic Order, which had its seat at Mergentheim. Kindly in character, honest, and well intentioned, he proved a popular ruler who was generally attentive to the interests of his subjects, even to the point of adopting at times a policy at odds with that pursued by the Austrian government. Though far from brilliant, he was surely not, at any rate in his later years, as foolish a man as Mozart* described in a famous letter (17 November 1781) to his father, soon after Maximilian had become a priest: 'Stupidity stares out of his eyes. He talks and pontificates incessantly, and always in falsetto.' Maximilian was passionately fond of music, of the theatre, and (despite his increasing corpulence) of dancing. He played the violin and viola, and in his youth participated with his brother Joseph II* in private chamber music performances. He had a particular admiration for Mozart (who wrongly believed that Maximilian would appoint him his court Kapellmeister once he had become elector of Cologne). Musical activities flourished at Bonn under Maximilian; it was also during his reign that the University of Bonn was established, in 1786.

Maximilian actively encouraged the studies of the young Beethoven, who became a court organist in 1784 at a salary of 150 florins. The formal appointment was made in June by the new ruler; but it had already been recommended by the court chamberlain Count Salm prior to Maximilian Friedrich's death. (Schiedermair interprets a memorandum expressing Salm's support, dated 29

February 1784, as a rejection of Beethoven's application, but other scholars such as Thayer* and Elliot Forbes correctly read it as signifying approval.) The elector evidently authorized Beethoven's journeys to Vienna to study with Mozart (in 1787) and Haydn* (in 1792), and he seems to have paid for the expenses, though the support he provided may not have been very generous, since Beethoven incurred debts on both occasions. When Haydn appealed for further financial help for his pupil (*Corr.* B13, 23 November 1793), Maximilian, in a tart response (of which only a draft survives (*Corr.* B14)), asserted that the funds granted to Beethoven were more than adequate and went on to suggest that it might be time for Beethoven to return to Bonn, 'for I greatly doubt that he will have made any really significant progress in composition and musical taste during his present stay [in Vienna] and I fear that, as was the case with his first journey to Vienna, he will bring back nothing but debts'. (On this letter, *see also* the article on Haydn.) Although Beethoven remained in Vienna, he continued to draw his Bonn salary until April 1794. Maximilian was himself in Vienna from mid-January until April that year, and some discussion of Beethoven's situation and future plans may well have taken place at this time. (After Haydn's departure for England on 19 January 1794, Beethoven continued his studies with Albrechtsberger.*)

During the second half of the 1790s, the Napoleonic wars obliged Maximilian to lead a precarious and peripatetic existence. From Bonn, which he left for good in October 1794, he went first to Münster, then to Frankfurt, and in December to Mergentheim. During the following years he had to move his court on several further occasions, until finally, a demoralized and very sick man, he reached Vienna in April 1800. But there is documentary evidence that in that very year, long after Beethoven had ceased to receive any salary, Maximilian still regarded him as a member of his court and that he foresaw the day when Beethoven would be called upon to resume his duties wherever that court might eventually be re-established—perhaps, Maximilian thought, at Münster. In the meanwhile, the archduke took up residence in May 1801 in a house owned by Count Christian August Seilern close to the emperor's mansion at Hetzendorf, near Vienna [now part of the twelfth district]; and there he died a few weeks later. By coincidence, Beethoven reportedly himself spent some time at Hetzendorf in the summer of 1801, but neither the dates of his stay there nor the location of his lodgings are known. In this context, it is difficult to decide what significance should be attached to the fact that Beethoven, who had not thought of dedicating any of his early works to Maximilian, informed the publisher Franz Anton Hoffmeister* in June 1801 that his First Symphony was to be dedicated to the archduke (*see Corr.* A50/B64). At the very least, the decision suggests that he had some contact with Maximilian after the latter's arrival in Vienna the previous year. Following Maximilian's death, the symphony was dedicated to Baron Gottfried van Swieten* instead; it was published in December 1801.

(Braubach[4], Schiedermair[1])

Maximilian Friedrich, Count **Königsegg-Rothenfels** (b. Cologne, 13 May 1708; d. Bonn, 15 April 1784). Member of an old Swabian family which in 1681 split into two lines, Königsegg-Aulendorf and Königsegg-Rothenfels; its members had been created imperial counts in 1629. On 6 April 1761, at which time he held the position of dean of Cologne Cathedral, he became archbishop and elector of Cologne and bishop of Münster, in succession to Clemens August von Wittelsbach, duke of Bavaria. Henry Swinburne, who met him in 1780, when the elector was in his early seventies, described him as 'a little, hale, black man, very merry and affable' and as being 'easy and agreeable, having lived all his life in ladies' company, which he is said to have liked better than his breviary'.

Although Maximilian Friedrich was forced to apply the brake to the extravagant expenditures indulged in by his predecessor, music continued to play an important role in the cultural life of the court. It benefited, moreover, from the establishment of a permanent theatre at Bonn in 1778, for while the repertoire naturally focused on plays, it did not exclude music drama. The Beethovens do not appear to have suffered as a result of the economies imposed by the new regime. In July 1761 the composer's grandfather (Ludwig van Beethoven*) was appointed court Kapellmeister, and since he was allowed to retain his position as a bass singer, his salary increased by a third; and in April 1764 Johann van Beethoven* was granted an increase in his own salary. The young Ludwig dedicated to the elector the three Piano Sonatas (WoO 47) which H. P. C. Bossler* published at Speyer in 1783. In February 1794, shortly before the elector's death, he applied successfully for an appointment as a court organist (*see* Maximilan Franz*).

(Braubach[3], Schiedermair[1])

Maximilian I Joseph, king of Bavaria (b. Mannheim, 27 May 1756; d. Munich, 13 October 1825). Prince elector of Bavaria, 1799–1805; from 1 January 1806 king of Bavaria. His daughter Sophie* married Archduke Franz Karl of Austria in 1824.

When Beethoven's Choral Fantasia was published in July 1811 by Breitkopf & Härtel,* the title page carried the composer's dedication of the work to the king. However, it is clear from Beethoven's letter to the publishers of 9 October 1811 that he had not been consulted concerning the dedication and was, in fact, far from pleased about it.

Mayer [Meyer, Meier], **(Friedrich) Sebastian** (b. Benediktbeuern, Bavaria, 5 April 1773; d. Vienna, 9 May 1835). Actor and singer (bass); according to his friend I. F. Castelli,* he was a better actor than singer. He was engaged at the Freihaus-Theater, Vienna, in 1793, making his debut as Sarastro in *Die Zauberflöte*. His contribution to the success of Schikaneder's* companies at that theatre and, later, at the Theater an der Wien went far beyond his appearances on the stage, for he was also partly responsible for choosing the repertoire. He favoured French works and, where necessary, arranged for their translation into

German; in addition, he frequently directed their ultimate production. He even wrote some texts himself (for instance, for the Zauberoper *Rosalinde, oder Die Macht der Feen*, which, with music by Franz Anton Hoffmeister,* was presented on 23 April 1796). A great admirer of Mozart,* his links with that composer assumed a personal nature when, on 23 December 1797, he married Josepha Hofer (née Weber), a sister of Mozart's widow Constanze and, incidentally, the original Queen of the Night. (Mayer and his wife were to sing together, in the roles of Publio and Servilia, in concert performances of *La clemenza di Tito* at the Freihaus-Theater on 8 September 1798 and 25 March 1799.)

Mayer helped to prepare the première of *Fidelio* on 20 November 1805, and, in addition, he created the role of Pizarro. The following month he took part in the meeting at Prince Lichnowsky's* apartment at which Beethoven was persuaded to make some cuts in the score. He sang Pizarro once more in the revised version on 29 March 1806. Although nothing is known about Beethoven's earlier contacts with him, these must clearly have gone back over several years, for in several notes written in 1805–6 Beethoven addresses him with the familiar 'Du', and in one of them (*Corr.* A129/B247) he alludes to 'the attachment and friendship which you have always shown me'. Beethoven was no doubt remembering, among other occasions, Mayer's benefit concert on 27 March 1804, which had opened with his Second Symphony and closed with his oratorio *Christus am Ölberg*, with Mayer himself taking the bass solo. (The programme of Mayer's benefit concert on 11 April 1808 included the 'Eroica' Symphony.) Their cordial relations were evidently not seriously troubled by an amusing incident which occurred during the rehearsals for *Fidelio* and was described by Schindler* in his Beethoven biography. Irked by Mayer's high opinion of his musical accomplishments, Beethoven devised a particularly tricky passage for Pizarro's 'Revenge' aria. Mayer duly came to grief, to the amusement of the orchestra, whereupon he flew into a rage and angrily shouted at Beethoven: 'My brother-in-law [i.e. Mozart] would never have written such damned nonsense!' Beethoven subsequently rewrote the aria.

(Castelli, Hess[8], *ÖBL*, Schindler[1])

Mayseder, Joseph (b. Vienna, 26 October 1789; d. Vienna, 21 November 1863). Violinist and composer. He studied the violin with Joseph Suche, Anton Wranitzky,* and Ignaz Schuppanzigh* (in whose string quartet he later played second violin), and piano and composition with Emanuel Aloys Förster.* He made a brilliant debut at the age of 10 at a concert in the Augarten in July 1800, and thereafter enjoyed an outstanding career both on the public concert platform and in performances at private houses; he frequently played in chamber music. Eduard Hanslick, who heard Mayseder when he was already well advanced in years, paid tribute in his *Geschichte des Concertlebens in Wien* (1869) to his 'sweet tone, pure as a bell' and recalled with pleasure 'the matchless precision of his technique and the noble elegance of his playing'. Mayseder was appointed leader of the court theatre orchestra in 1810, soloist in the court Kapelle in 1816, and its assistant director in 1836. He excelled in the music of Haydn* and Mozart;* his own compositions include violin concertos and string quartets. In 1815 Louis Letronne* drew his portrait which was subsequently engraved by Blasius Höfel.*

Mayseder, who probably met Beethoven through Schuppanzigh around 1800, played at some of his concerts (*see Corr.* A504/B758), and he participated in, and even led, performances of Beethoven's quartets (*see* Dembscher*). According to Hanslick, he preferred the early quartets to the later ones.

(Hanslick, Moser[1], *ÖBL*)

Mechetti, Pietro (b. Lucca, 20 April 1777; d. Vienna, 25 July 1850). Music publisher. Having moved to Vienna as a young man (perhaps in 1793), he entered the business of his uncle Carlo Mechetti (1747/8–1811), an art dealer, in 1798. In 1807 he was made a partner, and the firm was henceforth known as 'Carlo Mechetti e Nipote'; by then it was also publishing music. Following the uncle's death, the firm's name was changed to 'Pietro Mechetti quondam Carlo'. After Pietro died, his widow Theresia, née Rottmann (1788–1855), carried on the business with the help of Karl Schubert. Following her death, it was acquired by the firm C. A. Spina in 1856.

In 1815, Mechetti published the first editions of Beethoven's Polonaise in C major, Op. 89, and the song 'Des Kriegers Abschied', WoO 143 (*see* Reissig*). He also issued first editions of works by Mendelssohn, Moscheles,* Nicolai, Schubert,* Schumann, and Spohr,* and was the principal publisher of Joseph Lanner and Johann Strauss the Younger.

(Slezak[4], Weinmann[12])

Meisl, Karl (b. Laibach [Ljubljana, Slovenia], 30 June 1775; d. Vienna, 8 October 1853). Dramatist; civil servant. A prolific author, in the style of the popular Viennese theatre, he wrote some 200 plays, of which only about a fifth appeared in print. For the opening of the new Theater in der Josefstadt on 3 October 1822 (*see* Hensler*) he provided two festival pieces, *Die Weihe des Hauses* and *Das Bild des Fürsten*. The former was an adaptation of Kotzebue's* *Die Ruinen von Athen* which had been performed at the opening of the theatre at Pest [Budapest] on 9 February 1812, with music by Beethoven (Op. 113). For Meisl's version, Beethoven revised one of the original numbers (*see* Op. 114) and, in addition, composed a new chorus (WoO 98) and a new overture (Op. 124). The music for *Das Bild des Fürsten* was written by Josef Drechsler, who was a Kapellmeister at the theatre from 1822 to 1830.

(Czeike, *ÖBL*)

Meissner, August Gottlieb (b. Bautzen, 4 November 1753; d. Fulda, 18 February 1807). A versatile and popular writer, he published poems, biographies, novels, and stories (*Skizzen*—indeed, he became known as 'Skizzen-Meissner'). In 1785 he was appointed professor of aesthetics at the University of Prague; in 1805 he became director of the Lyceum at Fulda.

In 1803 Meissner offered to write the text of an oratorio for Beethoven. The proposal was conveyed to Beethoven in a (now lost) letter from the well-known painter Alexander Macco who had met him while staying in Vienna in 1802–3. In his reply to Macco on 2 November 1803, Beethoven welcomed the offer 'from one who is so highly esteemed as a writer', but explained that he was currently occupied with the composition of an opera (*Vestas Feuer*; *see* Schikaneder*). At the same time, he expressed great interest in the project: 'If the poem is not yet quite finished, I should be glad if M. did not hurry too much to complete it. I could come to Prague shortly before or after Easter [1804] and let him hear some of my most recent works. They would familiarize him with my style of composing, and either make him more enthusiastic—or, maybe, lead him to abandon his text.'

Meissner's grandson, the physician and writer Alfred Meissner (1822–85), explains in his *Rococobilder* (1871) that his grandfather's oratorio text had for its subject the persecution of the early Christians, and for its chief protagonists the Emperor Nero and the apostle Paul. Also according to Alfred Meissner, Beethoven had originally requested his grandfather to let him know if he ever had a plan for an opera libretto, but his grandfather had considered that Beethoven's genius was even better suited to the composition of oratorios. Nothing came of Meissner's proposal.

(Fürst, Meissner, Weber[2])

Mereau, Sophie, née Schubert [or Schubart] (b. Altenburg, 28 March 1770; d. Heidelberg, 31 October 1806). Novelist and poet. She is usually known by the name of her first husband, F. E. K. Mereau, whom she married in 1793 and from whom she was divorced in 1801. In 1803 she married Clemens Brentano.* Her novels include *Das Blütenalter der Empfindung* (1794) and *Amanda und Eduard* (1803); her poems were collected in two volumes as *Gedichte* (1800–2). Beethoven set her poem 'Feuerfarb' in 1792; it was published by the Kunst- und Industrie-Comptoir* in 1805 in the collection *Acht Lieder* (Op. 52).

Metastasio, Pietro [real name: Trapassi, Antonio Domenico Bonaventura] (b. Rome, 3 January 1698; d. Vienna, 12 April 1782). Poet and librettist. He wrote texts for some thirty three-act heroic operas, for several shorter dramatic works of the *azione teatrale* type, for eight oratorios, and for numerous serenatas. His librettos were set more than 800 times in the eighteenth and nineteenth centuries.

Beethoven used texts by Metastasio in the following compositions: *Ah! perfido* (Op. 65, first part), 'Liebes-Klage' (Op. 82, No. 2), 'Arietta buffa: L'amante impaziente' (Op. 82, No. 3), 'Arietta assai seriosa: L'amante impaziente' (Op. 82, No. 4), 'Lebens-Genuss' (Op. 82, No. 5), 'No, non turbati' (WoO 92a), 'Nei giorni tuoi felici' (WoO 93), 'O care selve' (WoO 119), 'La partenza' (WoO 124), and 'Te solo adoro' (WoO 186). In addition, Beethoven made a number of *a capella* settings (WoO 99) of texts by Metastasio during his studies with Salieri.*

(Hess[1], Nottebohm[1])

Meyerbeer, Giacomo (b. Vogelsdorf, near Berlin, 5 September 1791; d. Paris, 2 May 1864). Composer and pianist. He spent some eighteen months in Vienna in 1813–14, and, while there, performed repeatedly and to great acclaim at private houses, but he did not appear at any public concert as a pianist. He did, however, like many local and visiting musicians, take part in the first performance of Beethoven's *Wellingtons Sieg* on 8 December 1813, at which he played the bass drum. On 20 October 1814 his opera *Die beyden Kalifen*, a revised version of *Wirth und Gast* which had failed at its première at Stuttgart on 6 January 1813, was produced at the Kärntnertor-Theater, equally unsuccessfully. (It did not receive a second performance.) Shortly afterwards, Meyerbeer left for Paris.

Beethoven told Václav Tomášek* in September 1814 that he not been at all satisfied with Meyerbeer's performance in *Wellingtons Sieg*, as he consistently came in too late; he had been obliged to give him 'a thorough scolding', which had probably annoyed Meyerbeer.

(Tomášek)

Milder-Hauptmann, (Pauline) Anna (b. Constantinople, 13 December 1785; d. Berlin, 29 May 1838). Soprano. Her father Felix Milder worked at Constantinople as a confectioner for the Austrian ambassador, and later as an interpreter at Bucharest; he returned to Austria in *c.*1800, settling at Hütteldorf near Vienna.

Anna studied singing with Sigismund von Neukomm and Antonio Salieri.* According to a frequently told story, Haydn,* on first hearing her, was so impressed by the sheer volume of her voice that he said to her: 'My dear child, you have a voice like a house.' She made a very successful debut at the Theater an der Wien in 1803 as Juno in Süssmayr's comic opera *Der Spiegel von Arkadien*. On 20 November 1805, at the same theatre, she created Leonore in *Fidelio*. (She was also to sing in the first performances of the two later versions of the opera, presented at the Theater an der Wien on 29 March 1806 and at the Kärntnertor-Theater on 23 May 1814 respectively.) She quickly established a reputation as an exceptionally gifted singer, with an imposing stage presence. Cherubini* composed for her the title role in *Faniska* (Kärntnertor-Theater, 25 February 1806) and Joseph Weigl* the part of Emmeline in *Die Schweizerfamilie* (Kärntnertor-Theater, 14 March 1809). Johann Friedrich Reichardt* wrote in November 1808, after attending a performance of Weigl's *Das Waisenhaus*: 'Her voice is one of the most ravishing and strong ones I have ever heard—exceptionally rich, exceptionally pure and even; and she sings with very great intelligence.' And the tenor Franz

Wild* wrote in his memoirs that she possessed the most beautiful soprano voice he had heard during his long career. In 1809 she captivated Napoleon when she sang before him at Schönbrunn. As a result, she was offered a generous contract to sing in Paris, but she declined it, perhaps because of her attachment to the Viennese court jeweller Peter Hauptmann whom she married the following year. (The marriage ended in separation.)

For Beethoven she had, by 1814, become 'Unsre einzige Milder' [Our one and only Milder] (*Corr.* A464/B702). His great admiration for her explains no doubt why he agreed to alter certain passages in the adagio section of Leonore's 'Abscheulicher!' aria in the final version of *Fidelio*, because she found them unsuitable for her voice. (In 1836 she told Schindler* that she had refused to perform unless the changes were made.) Also in 1814, she sang in the first public performances of the trio 'Tremate, empi, tremati' (Op. 116) on 27 February and of the oratorio *Der glorreiche Augenblick* on 29 November. Of the various operatic roles in which she appeared in Vienna, it was her interpretation of Gluck's heroines which made the greatest impact. Indeed, she was responsible for Gluck revivals in Vienna and, later, in Berlin, where she was permanently engaged in 1816 following some highly acclaimed guest appearances which had included eleven triumphant Leonores. (At the Berlin première of *Fidelio* on 11 October 1815 the role had been sung by Josephine Schulz-Killitschky, Schuppanzigh's* sister-in-law; Milder took it over at the second performance on 14 October.) News of the success of her guest appearances soon reached Vienna and led Beethoven to write to her on 6 January 1816. Addressing her as 'My greatly esteemed and peerless Milder, my dear friend', he thanked her for 'having remained so faithful to my *Fidelio*'. He furthermore asked her to invite Baron de La Motte Fouqué* to devise a plot for a grand opera for him, which would, at the same time, have a suitable part for her. It is not known, however, whether Milder ever contacted Fouqué. Beethoven's warm feelings for her were further expressed in the same letter in a puzzle canon to the words 'Ich küsse Sie, drücke Sie an mein Herz' [I kiss you and press you to my heart] (WoO 169). In July 1816 he told Karl von Bursy* that none of the singers then in Vienna could replace her in her repertoire.

Milder performed with great distinction in Berlin until about 1829 and subsequently sang in Russia and Scandinavia, as well as in various German cities. Her last public appearance was probably at a concert in Vienna in 1836.

(Eisenberg, Kalischer, Kühner[2], Kutsch/Riemens)

Mittag, Karl August (b. Kreischa, near Dresden, 1795; d. Vienna, 21 November 1867). Bassoonist. He became a bandmaster in a Saxon regiment. In 1820 he moved to Vienna, and the following year he joined the faculty of the Conservatoire, where he taught the bassoon until 1839. He furthermore became a member of the Burgtheater orchestra and, in 1824, of the court Kapelle.

In his *Beethoven Encyclopedia*, P. Nettl states that Mittag 'appears many times in Conversation-books, discussing improvements'. This is incorrect. According to the published conversation books, he called on Beethoven only once, on 2 April 1826, on which occasion he was introduced by Karl Holz* (*see BKh*9/130, 133, and especially 138–41); but already seven months earlier, on 2 September 1825, Holz reported having spoken to Mittag, whom he called a 'very good fellow' (*BKh*8/84). The subject of that first conversation in 1825, and also the reason for Beethoven's wishing to meet Mittag in 1826, was the series of improvements which had been made in the design of the bassoon by Carl Almenräder, on the basis of Gottfried Weber's *Akustik der Blasinstrumente* (1816). Almenräder himself had published a *Traité sur le perfectionnement du basson* in *c.*1819–20, and Weber had written on the subject in the Mainz periodical *Cäcilia* in 1825. Beethoven was keen to have Mittag's expert assessment of the changes made by Almenräder, and the matter formed the most important subject of their discussion on 2 April 1826; but Mittag also spoke more generally about music making at Dresden. (Mittag did not actually make any entries in the conversation books; it was Holz who wrote down his remarks.) Afterwards he asked Holz to tell Beethoven that the hour he had spent in his company had been the happiest in his whole life (*BKh*9/151). The conversation offers, however, no grounds for Nettl's statement that 'Beethoven seemed to have a great liking for the man'.

Mollo, Tranquillo (b. Bellinzona, 10 August 1767; d. Bellinzona, 29 March 1837). Music publisher. In 1793 he became a partner in Artaria & Co.,* having worked for the firm since the previous year. He left in 1798 to set up in business with Franz Bernardini, under the name 'T. Mollo and Co.'; however, his connection with Bernardini ceased the following year. In October 1801 he entered into an agreement with Domenico (III) Artaria, and after Carlo Artaria had sold his business to them in 1802, Mollo managed T. Mollo & Co. and Domenico Artaria ran Artaria & Co., at the separate locations at which the firms had hitherto been operating. In 1805 Mollo and Domenico Artaria put an end to their association, but it was not until 1808 that Mollo registered the firm as 'Tranquillo Mollo'. In addition to music, he sold maps, globes, and views of Vienna and its surroundings; he also became a well-known printer. In 1832 he withdrew from the business which was then taken over by his sons Eduard (1797–1842) and Florian Dominikus (1803–69), but the new partnership lasted only until the following year when Florian left to found his own firm.

   T. Mollo & Co. published first editions of the following works by Beethoven: the Trio for piano, clarinet, and cello, Op. 11, in 1798; the Piano Sonatas Op. 14, and variations for piano on the quartet 'Kind, willst du ruhig schlafen' from Peter Winter's opera *Das unterbrochene Opferfest*, WoO 75, in 1799; the First Piano Concerto, the Piano Quintet Op. 16, the Horn Sonata Op. 17, the String Quartets Op. 18, and the Violin Sonatas Opp. 23–4, in 1801; *Contredanses* for orchestra, WoO 14, and variations for piano and cello on the duet 'Bei Männern, welche Liebe fühlen' from Mozart's *Die Zauberflöte*, WoO 46, in 1802. Finally, the collective work 'In questa tomba oscura' by a number of composers, including Beethoven (WoO 133, *see* Carpani*), appeared in 1808 under the imprint 'T. Mollo'.

(Slezak[4], Weinmann[16])

Molt, Theodor Friedrich [Theodore Frederic] (b. Gschwend, Baden-Württemberg, 13 February 1795; d. Burlington, Vermont, 16 November 1856). Pianist, organist, and music teacher. His own teachers were his father, a schoolmaster and organist, and an older brother. He probably settled in the Philadelphia region in the early 1820s; by 1823 he was teaching music in Quebec. He returned to Europe in 1825, and on or soon after 11 December of that year he called on Beethoven in Vienna. On 26 December, in response to a request from Molt for a contribution to his private album (*Corr.* B2099), Beethoven wrote out the eight-bar canon 'Freu dich des Lebens' (WoO 195, *see* Usteri*). The autograph is now at McGill University, Montreal.

Following his return to North America, Molt taught at Quebec City and Montreal, and also at Burlington, Vermont (1833–*c*.1837 and, again, from 1849). At Burlington he was employed, from 1835, as an instructor at the Burlington Female Seminary, and he also taught at the Young Ladies' School. From 1840 to 1849 he held the post of organist and choirmaster at the Roman Catholic cathedral in Quebec City. He was the author of manuals for teaching singing and the piano, and he is also remembered for having composed one of the first patriotic Canadian songs, 'Sol canadien, terre chérie', to a text by Isidore Bédard.

(*Beethoven and Quebec*, Converse, Kallmann)

Moscheles, Ignaz (b. Prague, 23 May 1794; d. Leipzig, 10 March 1870). Pianist, conductor, and composer. From 1804 to 1808 he studied with Bedřich Diviš Weber, who insisted that he play only music by Mozart,* Clementi,* and Bach during the first three years under his tuition. Nonetheless, Moscheles early on discovered Beethoven's piano sonatas, and from then until his death he was a ardent admirer of Beethoven's music. In 1808 he went to Vienna—above all, as he was to explain in his preface to the English edition of Schindler's* Beethoven biography (see below), because 'I longed to see and become acquainted with *that man* who had exercised so powerful an influence over my whole being; whom, though I scarcely understood, I blindly worshipped.' In Vienna he received instruction from Albrechtsberger* and Salieri.* It was not until 1810 that he became personally acquainted with Beethoven, thanks to Domenico Artaria who one day introduced Moscheles to Beethoven in his music shop. Moscheles states that he subsequently met Beethoven occasionally at the apartments of Johann

Nepomuk Zizius* and Nikolaus Zmeskall von Domanovecz,* but otherwise had little personal contact with him. When, however, he prepared a piano reduction of *Fidelio* in 1814 at Artaria's suggestion and with Beethoven's approval, he at last enjoyed a closer contact with the latter: 'During my frequent visits, the number of which I tried to multiply by all possible excuses, he treated me with the kindest indulgence.' Beethoven insisted on being shown each number and made various changes in Moscheles's arrangement. The piano score, accompanied by the text, was published by Artaria & Co.* in August 1816, without Moscheles's name; but he was duly identified as the arranger in another edition (published without the text) which appeared that same year.

By that time Moscheles had become a highly acclaimed pianist in Vienna. His own composition 'La Marche d'Alexandre', a bravura piece which he first performed on 8 February 1815 at a charity concert attended by the allied monarchs, became a celebrated item in his recitals for many years to come. His career as a travelling virtuoso began in 1816 and during the following years he played with great success in his native Prague and in various German cities, as well as in Paris and London. He also continued to appear in Vienna, though much less frequently. At the Landständischer Saal on 10 May 1818 he performed the Overture *Zur Namensfeier* (Op. 115) together with Joseph Mayseder* and the guitarist Mauro Giuliani; on 12 December 1819 he gave a concert at the Grosser Redoutensaal; and in late 1823 he gave four concerts in Vienna. At the third of these, on 15 December, he played part of the programme on Beethoven's Broadwood* piano which Beethoven had lent him for the occasion, and he probably used the same instrument at his final concert two days later. In 1825 he settled in London, where he taught at the Royal Academy of Music. He remained in London until 1846, when he took up an appointment as professor of piano at the Leipzig Conservatoire.

Despite his considerable international reputation, he was not very highly regarded as a pianist in Beethoven's circle. Cipriani Potter* told Thayer* that Beethoven himself, in the course of a conversation they had in 1817–18, had ranked Moscheles no higher than a mere 'player of passages'. The conversation books contain similarly unflattering remarks by Franz Oliva* (*BKh*1/147, 154) and Schuppanzigh* (*BKh*3/225). As for Moscheles, he never wavered in his reverence for Beethoven, and when the latter, during his final illness, appealed to him for financial assistance, as he also did to other friends in London, Moscheles was happy to inform him on 1 March 1827 that the Philharmonic Society* had decided to present him with £100, and he arranged the transfer of the gift to Vienna (*Corr.* B2268; *see also* Stumpff*). In a letter on 14 March, Beethoven assured Moscheles that he would never forget his 'noble behaviour' and expressed his profound gratitude to the society (for the ultimate fate of the gift, *see* Philharmonic Society*). On 24 March Schindler informed Moscheles of Beethoven's death and sent him a lock of Beethoven's hair (*Corr.* B2286). Finally, on 14 September of that year, in response to a request for an autograph, Schindler sent him two pages from an autograph of the Ninth Symphony and an exercise book containing some sketches for the Quartet Op. 131. On 24 December 1832 Moscheles conducted the first complete London performance of the *Missa solemnis*. Later he was to edit many of Beethoven's works for Cramer & Co. (*see* Cramer*).

In 1841 Moscheles published in London his edition (*The Life of Beethoven*) of Schindler's biography which had appeared at Münster the previous year. Curiously, Schindler's name does not appear on the title page of the translation, although it is duly mentioned in Moscheles's preface. (Sir George Smart,* in his personal diary, writes of Moscheles 'pirating' Schindler's book, but this statement seems groundless, for Moscheles refers in the preface to the agreement which had been concluded in this connection between Schindler and Henry Colburn, the publisher of the translation.) The English text was accompanied by Moscheles's notes and was followed by an ample supplement which contained, among other items, a number of Beethoven's letters.

In the preface, Moscheles gave an account of his first meeting and his subsequent cordial contacts with Beethoven. This account infuriated Schindler (as did similar remarks later made by Moscheles about his acquaintance with Beethoven in a foreword to an edition of the piano sonatas, published at Stuttgart). Until 1841, Moscheles and Schindler, who had known each other since 1815, had enjoyed a pleasant relationship. In a letter on 22 February 1827 (*Corr.* B2261) Schindler had even gone so far as to address his correspondent as 'Mein herrlicher Moscheles' [My magnificent Moscheles], and as recently as 5 October 1840 Schindler had 'embraced' Moscheles when they met at Aix-la-Chapelle (according to Moscheles's letter to his wife written later that day). But in *Beethoven in Paris* (Münster, 1842), Schindler, while still referring to Moscheles as a 'revered friend', comments scathingly on his remarks about his friendship with Beethoven. Dismissing Moscheles's statement (in a note to his English edition) that Carl Maria von Weber had enjoyed a friendly relationship with Beethoven, Schindler writes: 'C. M. v. Weber was never on terms of personal friendship with Beethoven any more than Moscheles was.' And in support of this assertion, Schindler claims that when Moscheles called on Beethoven with his brother (in 1823)—an incident described by Moscheles in another note to his English version of Schindler's biography—it was he who had presented Moscheles to Beethoven, and that it was indeed entirely due to him that Beethoven had agreed to receive Moscheles on that occasion. It is characteristic of Schindler that he then inserted a false entry in the conversation book used on the day of the visit, which begins: 'Hier, theurer Meister, stelle ich Ihnen Moscheles vor' [Dearest Master, may I present Moscheles to you] (*BKh4*/292); Schindler was presumably unaware that Beethoven already knew Moscheles quite well. Ultimately, in the third, largely revised edition of his Beethoven biography (Münster, 1860), Schindler gave vent to his animosity towards Moscheles in an extraordinarily violent diatribe. Having once more strongly denied that Moscheles had enjoyed a friendly personal relationship with Beethoven, he declares that such an association would, in any case, have been quite impossible in view of 'Beethoven's hatred for the children of Israel who were active in the arts, since he saw how they all espoused the latest innovations, intent on deriving the most lucrative gain from them'. Donald W. MacArdle's comment that 'Schindler's charge probably reflects his own attitude more accurately than that of Beethoven' (*Beethoven as I knew him* . . . , 391) is a persuasive one.

(Moscheles, Roche, Smidak, Schindler[1a–c])

Mosel, Ignaz Franz von (b. Vienna, 1 April 1772; d. Vienna, 8 April 1844). Composer, conductor, and writer on music. A competent violinist, violist, and cellist, he took an active part in the foundation of the Gesellschaft der Musikfreunde.* He was the author of a life of Salieri* (*Ueber das Leben und die Werke des Anton Salieri*, 1827) and of numerous articles on musical matters. His own compositions include Masses, the Singspiel *Die Feuerprobe* (Kärntnertor-Theater, 28 April 1811), and the heroic opera *Cyrus und Astyages* (13 June 1818). In government service since 1788, he was ennobled in 1818 and awarded the title 'Hofrat' in 1821. In the latter year he was appointed deputy director of the court theatres, a post he held until 1829 when he became principal curator of the court library.

He must have been well acquainted with Beethoven, but was never a close friend; in his only known communication to Mosel, in November 1817 (*Corr.* 845/B1196), Beethoven addresses him as 'Euer Wohlgeboren' [Your Excellency]. Although Mosel signed the flattering letter sent to Beethoven by a number of Viennese music lovers in February 1824, it is evident from his article 'Die Tonkunst in Wien während der letzten fünf Decennien' that while he greatly admired Beethoven's earlier works, he found the later ones altogether incomprehensible. Indeed, he characterized them as 'aberrations' ['Verirrungen'], created by the deaf and sick composer as an act of defiance against his cruel fate and with the deliberate intention of composing, in a spirit of irony, as no one had ever composed before, nor would have wished to compose. As particularly striking examples of Beethoven's bizarre style he cited the String Quartet Op. 127 (*see also* BKh8/301) and the 'grotesque recitative of the basses' in the Ninth Symphony. (The article first appeared in *Jahrbücher des deutschen National-Vereins für Musik und ihre Wissenschaft* in 1841 and was reprinted in a revised form in the *Allgemeine Wiener Musikzeitung* on 9 November 1843.)

(Antonicek[3,6], *ÖBL*, Kerst, Wurzbach[1])

Mozart, Wolfgang Amadeus (b. Salzburg, 27 January 1756; d. Vienna, 5 December 1791). Composer. Beethoven's lifelong reverence for Mozart's music is well documented—'I have always counted myself among the greatest admirers of Mozart and shall remain so until my last breath,' he wrote to the Abbé Maximilian Stadler* on 6 February 1826. No less well established is the fact that Mozart was the dominant influence on his compositions until at least the year 1800. Mozart was, of course, held in high regard at Bonn, not least by the elector, Maximilian Franz,* who, Mozart wrote to his father on 23 January 1782, 'thinks the world of me'; and he added: 'He is always singing my praises, and I am almost certain that if he were already Prince Elector of Cologne, I would be his Kapellmeister by now.' The thought that Mozart might have directed the Bonn court orchestra, with the young Beethoven as one of its members, is a tantalizing one.

In addition to the influence which Mozart's music exercised on several of Beethoven's early compositions, the latter's fascination with the operas, in particular, is evidenced by the following sets of variations written during his early years in Vienna: on 'Se vuol ballare' from *Le nozze di Figaro* (WoO 40, for violin and piano, published 1793); on 'Là ci darem la mano' from *Don Giovanni* (WoO 28, for two oboes and English horn, performed in Vienna on 23 December 1797, but not published in Beethoven's lifetime); on 'Ein Mädchen oder Weibchen' from *Die Zauberflöte* (Op. 66, published 1798); and on 'Bei Männern, welche Liebe fühlen', likewise from *Die Zauberflöte* (WoO 46, published 1802). Many years later, he was to quote Leporello's 'Notte e giorno faticar' in Variation 22 of his *Diabelli Variations*. He is said to have considered *Die Zauberflöte* the greatest of all Mozart operas.

Beethoven also wrote cadenzas (WoO 58) for the first and third movements of the Piano Concerto in D minor (K466) for Ferdinand Ries.* It was probably this concerto, reportedly a favourite of his, which Beethoven played between the acts of *La clemenza di Tito* at a performance of that opera arranged by Constanze Mozart at the Burgtheater on 31 March 1795. Further proof of his great interest in Mozart's works is provided by the copies which he made, by way of study, of some of the chamber music, of a number of operatic excerpts, and of certain contrapuntal works and passages. There is thus no doubt that he was familiar with a great part of Mozart's vast output.

Information about his personal acquaintance with Mozart is, on the other hand, extremely sketchy and not necessarily reliable. In fact, nothing definite is known about his activities during his short stay in Vienna in the spring of 1787 (from about 7 to about 20 April). It is, however, highly probable that he called on Mozart, and he may well have been given some tuition by him; it is furthermore very likely that he heard him play, if not during those lessons, then either at a private house or in public. The principal contemporary sources for these conclusions are the following: Ferdinand Ries's statement (in *Biographische Notizen*) that Mozart gave Beethoven some instruction, but did not, to Beethoven's regret, ever play for him (presumably meaning during the lessons); Ignaz von Seyfried's* description in *Ludwig van Beethovens Studien* of Beethoven's first visit to Mozart and of the powerful impression which his improvisation made on his host (even if the account were essentially correct, which is not certain, it is likely to present a romanticized version of what happened); and Carl Czerny's* recollection (in his memoirs) of Beethoven declaring that he had heard Mozart play on several occasions, and the statement made by Czerny some years later to Otto Jahn that Beethoven had described Mozart's style of playing to him ('ein feines, aber zerhacktes [jerky] Spiel . . . , kein *ligato*'). Two successive questions written by Beethoven's nephew Karl* in a conversation book (*BKh3/333*) in 1823—'You knew Mozart? . . . Where did you see him?'—are surely also of some significance, inasmuch as the second suggests a positive reply to the first.

Following Beethoven's death, Mozart's Requiem was performed at the Augustinerkirche on 3 April 1827.

(Churgin, Schünemann, Seyfried)

Müller, Wilhelm Christian (b. Wasungen, near Meiningen, 1752; d. Bremen, 1831). Teacher; writer on music. After his theological studies at Göttingen he spent some time at Kiel and Altona. In 1788 he was appointed headmaster of a school at Bremen, and in 1784 became director of music at Bremen Cathedral and a teacher at the school attached to the cathedral. Following his official retirement in 1817 he travelled extensively, together with his daughter Elise (b. 1782) who was a competent pianist. On their way to Italy they reached Vienna in October 1820, and there they twice called on Beethoven. Later Müller described these visits in his *Briefe an deutsche Freunde, von einer Reise durch Italien über Sachsen, Böhmen und Oestreich [sic]* . . . (Altona, 1824). After Beethoven's death he published a long obituary in the Leipzig *Allgemeine musikalische Zeitung* on 23 May 1827. Both texts contain some factual errors.

Friedrich Kerst, who reprints the relevant passage from the book and some extracts from the obituary in *Die Erinnerungen an Beethoven*, also quotes from a letter written by Müller on 22 April 1827 to an unidentified correspondent which is not without interest. In his book Müller had explained that he and his daughter had been in correspondence with Beethoven for several years prior to meeting him in Vienna. In the letter he mentioned that they had once asked Beethoven to let them know the date of his birthday, so that they might celebrate it (his daughter wished to send him a ring). Beethoven had replied that he knew neither on which day nor in which year he was born. Elise had thereupon contacted an acquaintance living at Bonn, who procured and sent her a certificate attesting that Beethoven was born on 17 December 1770. It was thus through Elise and himself, Müller asserts in his letter, that Beethoven learnt the true date of his birth. (The document in question was almost certainly not a birth certificate, as Müller states, but a baptismal certificate.) Müller adds that the matter came up again during their conversation in Vienna in 1820, on which occasion Beethoven said jokingly that he had not thought that he was such an old fellow. The remark may seem surprising, if only because his friend Franz Gerhard Wegeler* had already in 1810, at his request, sent him his baptismal certificate, on which the correct information had appeared. But a note made by Beethoven on the back of the certificate shows that he had even then doubted the accuracy of the information, believing that he might have been confused with his elder brother, also called Ludwig (who had, in fact, been born and had died in 1769).

It is not possible to date the beginning of the correspondence between the Müllers and Beethoven. None of their letters has survived, apart from a brief note written by Beethoven during the Müllers' stay in Vienna (*Corr.* A1035/B1413). A statement in Fanny Giannattasio's* diary on 31 January 1817 that Beethoven had received letters and a gift from a lady in Bremen almost certainly refers to Elise, in which case this would be the earliest known evidence of their relations. In 1822 Beethoven arranged for Adolph Martin Schlesinger* to send Müller a copy of the recently published Piano Sonata Op. 109 (*see Corr.* B1458, B1474).

(Müller[2,3])

Nägeli, Hans Georg (b. Wetzikon, near Zurich, 26 May 1773; d. Zurich, 26 December 1836). Composer, educator, music publisher, and writer on music. In the spring of 1802 he invited Beethoven to contribute to a series of contemporary compositions which he was planning to publish under the title *Répertoire des clavecinistes*. In due course, Beethoven sent him three as yet unpublished piano sonatas (Op. 31). The first two appeared in 1803 as Book 5 of the series, the third in 1804 in Book 11 which also included a reprint of the *Sonate pathétique*. Nägeli would have liked Beethoven to provide him with a fourth new sonata, but Beethoven was not willing to do so, mainly because he was working on other compositions (*see* Ferdinand Ries's* letter to Nikolaus Simrock* of 6 August 1803, *Corr.* B152), but no doubt also because of his dissatisfaction with the quality of Nägeli's edition of the Sonatas Op. 31, Nos. 1–2. What angered him even more than its numerous errors was the fact that Nägeli had taken it upon himself to add four bars to the final movement of the first sonata. Beethoven expressed his annoyance in a furious letter to Nägeli (the letter has not survived); he furthermore asked Simrock, whom he provided with a full list of the mistakes, to publish a fresh edition of the two sonatas and clearly indicate that it alone contained the correct versions of those compositions (*see Corr.* B145). The new edition was labelled 'Édition très correcte' by Simrock, who, in due course, also brought out a further, similarly designated, edition of Op. 31, No. 3. (The *Répertoire des clavecinistes* continued to appear until 1810 and offered, in its final volume, a piano sonata by Anton Liste* dedicated to Beethoven.)

There seems to have been no further contact between Nägeli and Beethoven until August 1817, when Beethoven gave his friend Johann Bihler,* who was about to depart for Switzerland, a letter of introduction to Nägeli (*see also* Schnyder von Wartensee*). Later he assisted in finding subscribers, including Archduke

Rudolph,* for Nägeli's volume of poems *Liederkränze* (Zurich, 1825). It contained a poem in praise of Beethoven, and Nägeli's admiration for his music was further expressed in lectures which he gave in several German cities in 1824 and later published in book form (*Vorlesungen über Musik mit Berücksichtigung der Dilettanten*, Stuttgart, 1826). This book he dedicated, at Beethoven's suggestion, to the archduke.

(Hunziker, Schattner, Staehelin³)

Napoleon I [Bonaparte, Napoleon] (b. Ajaccio, 15 August 1769; d. St Helena, 5 May 1821). Beethoven's ambivalent attitude towards Napoleon has intrigued his biographers. They have focused their attention primarily on the Third Symphony, in which Beethoven originally set out to portray the heroic figure of Napoleon, whom he then regarded as the epitome of the enlightened ruler. Schindler* states that Beethoven told him that the idea of thus doing homage to Napoleon had been suggested to him by General Bernadotte,* while he was ambassador to Austria. In a letter to Nikolaus Simrock* on 22 October 1803, Ferdinand Ries* wrote that Beethoven was very much inclined to dedicate the symphony, which he considered 'the greatest work he has so far composed', to Napoleon; if he should in the end decide not to do so—for Prince Lobkowitz* had offered him 400 gulden for the rights to it for half a year—he intended, at any rate, to give it the title 'Bonaparte' (*Corr.* B165). On a copy now owned by the Gesellschaft der Musikfreunde* the title initially read 'Sinfonia grande titolata Bonaparte' ('titolata' was subsequently amended to 'intitolata').

However, when Beethoven learned that Napoleon was no longer content to be just a consul but had himself proclaimed emperor, he flew into a rage, convinced that Napoleon's overweening ambition would henceforth cause him to trample on the rights of his subjects and become a tyrant; he tore up the title page and threw it on the floor. This famous incident, so dramatically described by Ries, must have occurred either shortly after Napoleon was proclaimed emperor on 18 May 1804, or, which seems more likely, when news of his coronation on 2 December of that year reached Beethoven. The first edition of the symphony, published in October 1806, was dedicated to Prince Lobkowitz and bore the title 'SINFONIA EROICA . . . composta per festeggiare il sovvenire di un gran Uomo' (*see* Louis Ferdinand*).

With the resumption of the war against France in 1805, which resulted in several defeats of the Austrian army and in the temporary occupation of Vienna in 1805 and again in 1809, Beethoven had good cause to feel hostile towards the French, and particularly towards Napoleon. Speaking to Wenzel Krumpholtz* about the French victory over the Prussians at Jena in October 1806, he reportedly said: 'It *is* a pity that I do not understand the art of war as well as I do the art of music—I would certainly defeat him!' There is no record of Beethoven being received by Napoleon during the latter's residence in Vienna in 1809.

There are indications that Beethoven's attitude towards Napoleon changed again later. In October 1810—by which time, of course, Austria was at peace with France and Napoleon was married to the Austrian Archduchess Marie Louise— he seems to have at least briefly considered the possibility of dedicating the Mass Op. 86 to Napoleon. And many years later, in 1824, he reportedly told Carl Czerny:* 'I used to detest him; but now I think quite differently.' (*See also* Trémont.*)

(Beahrs, Prod'homme[1], Wegeler/Ries)

Neate, Charles (b. London, 28 March 1784; d. Brighton, 30 March 1877). Pianist, cellist, and composer. He studied the piano with John Field, the cello with William Sharp, and composition with Joseph Wölfl.* His concert debut as a pianist took place at Covent Garden in 1800; his first publication, a piano sonata, appeared in 1808. Though already a well-established musician, he travelled to the Continent in 1814 to study, first with the composer and Bavarian court Kapellmeister Peter Winter in Munich and subsequently with Beethoven. He arrived in Vienna in May 1815 and was introduced to Beethoven by Johann von Häring,* whom he had previously met in London. However, Beethoven was not willing to give him lessons and instead recommended him to his own former teacher Emanuel Aloys Förster;* but he agreed to examine Neate's compositions. As a result, Neate saw him regularly that summer, which, so Neate told Thayer* in 1861, they both spent at Baden near Vienna. (Beethoven may also have stayed for a time at Döbling.) When Neate eventually left Vienna early in February 1816, Beethoven presented a manuscript copy of his Violin Concerto to him as a parting gift; he furthermore wrote the two canons 'Das Schweigen' and 'Das Reden' (WoO 168) in his album, together with an affectionate dedication. In a note to Antonie Brentano* (on whom Neate was to call at Frankfurt, on his journey back to England) Beethoven described him as an excellent musician and a charming man (*Corr.* A607/B897).

In Vienna, Neate bought from Beethoven, on behalf of the Philharmonic Society,* the Overtures to *Die Ruinen von Athen* and *König Stephan* and the Overture *Zur Namensfeier* for 75 guineas. In addition, Beethoven gave him the scores of several unpublished works to sell to English publishers. However, for various reasons—one of which was the general disappointment felt at the quality of the three overtures—Neate was unable, either then or in later years, to find a buyer for any of these compositions (on this matter, including the purchase of the overtures, *see* Philharmonic Society*). Beethoven laid the blame squarely on Neate. 'I swear', he chastised him on 19 April 1817, 'that you have done nothing for me, are doing nothing, and will also do nothing for me—*summa summarum*. Nothing! Nothing! Nothing!' There had been some talk of Beethoven dedicating the Cello Sonatas Op. 102 to Neate, but no more was heard of that idea, even though relations between the two men improved and several letters were exchanged by them during the following years. Neate, who was a founding member of the Philharmonic Society and had again become a director in 1817, was probably largely responsible for the society inviting Beethoven to come to England and, while there, compose and conduct for it. 'Neate and I are absolutely delighted at the thought of seeing you here,' Ferdinand Ries* wrote to Beethoven on 9 June 1817 (*Corr.* B1129). The offer was renewed in 1824; on that occasion, Beethoven was to conduct the first English performance of the Ninth Symphony at the opening concert of the 1825 season. Nothing came of either project. On the other hand, Neate was finally able to render Beethoven a significant service in 1827; for it was at his suggestion—and that of Francis Tatton Latour, formerly a partner in the music-publishing firm of Chappell & Co.* and, like Neate, a member of the executive committee—that the society decided at its meeting of 28 February 1827 to send Beethoven a gift of £100.

There is an interesting later link between Beethoven and Neate. In June 1845 Neate, acting on behalf of the director of the British Museum, visited Schindler* at Aix-la-Chapelle, with the intention of buying his considerable collection of Beethoven manuscripts, which included musical scores, autograph letters, sketches, and conversation books. Having spent some three weeks examining and cataloguing the material, Neate proposed a purchasing price of £1,500, which Schindler was ready to accept. At the beginning of August, Neate informed Schindler that there was no objection in London to the transaction, but that the contract could not be concluded immediately owing to the absence of some of the directors. However, news of the proposed sale reached David Hansemann, a wealthy Prussian businessman and a prominent politician (and a future minister of finance), who had previously tried, without success, to arrange for the purchase of the material by the Königlich-Preussische Bibliothek in Berlin. Hansemann thereupon appealed to King Friedrich Wilhelm IV* not to allow the collection to leave Germany, and as a result of the king's intervention it was acquired by the Berlin library.

(Anderson[3], Hüffer, Husk/Carr)

Neberich, Adam (1765–1822). Wine merchant at Mainz who visited Vienna more than once. Beethoven, who had made his acquaintance by March 1816, recommended him as the 'finest artist in wines in Europe' in a humorous note to Franz Brentano* (*Corr.* A619/B914). Neberich, he declared, was qualified to act as high priest at any sacrifice offered to Bacchus.

Neberich was again in Vienna from 17 January to 26 March 1820, and he repeatedly visited Beethoven and also dined out with him during that period; the conversation books contain numerous entries in his hand. He spoke to Beethoven about E. T. A. Hoffmann,* and when he left Vienna for Dresden and Berlin, he took with him a letter from Beethoven to Hoffmann (*Corr.* A1014/B1373).

Neefe, Christian Gottlob (b. Chemnitz, 5 February 1748; d. Dessau, 26 January 1798). Composer. When he first came to Bonn in October 1779 to join the Grossmann-Hellmuth theatrical company as its Kapellmeister, he had already written a considerable number of works, among them songs, piano sonatas, and operas (but the most popular of his stage works, the Singspiel *Adelheit von Veltheim*, was composed largely or entirely at Bonn; it was first produced at Frankfurt am Main in September 1780). In 1782 Neefe succeeded Gilles van den Eeden* as court organist. By that time he was probably already giving some tuition to the young Beethoven, who was to assist him in his duties on various occasions over the next two years before being officially appointed assistant organist in 1784.

Neefe was to prove a very supportive teacher for Beethoven. In his account of musical life at Bonn which appeared in Carl Friedrich Cramer's *Magazin der Musik* on 2 March 1783, he describes Beethoven as already a highly skilled and powerful pianist, and states that he has been giving him instruction not only in pianoforte playing (using mainly Bach's *Das wohltemperirte Clavier*), but also in thoroughbass and composition. He concludes with the following, frequently cited, statement: 'This young genius deserves support to enable him to travel. He will assuredly become another Wolfgang Amadeus Mozart, if he continues as he has begun.' Ten years later, in Johann Gottlieb Karl Spazier's *Berlinische musikalische Zeitung* (26 October 1793), he reported that Beethoven, 'assistant court organist and unquestionably now one of the foremost pianists', had gone to Vienna to perfect himself in the art of composition under Haydn's* guidance; and he went on to quote with evident satisfaction and pride the following passage from a letter addressed to him by Beethoven (it is not clear whether before or after his departure from Bonn): 'I thank you for the advice which you have so often given me during my progress in the divine art of music. Should I ever become a great man, a part of the credit will be yours.' (*See also* Dressler.*)

(Hoffmann-Erbrecht, Kaden, Kahl[5], Leux[1,2], Nettl[2])

Neidl, Johann Joseph (bapt. Graz, 20 March 1776; d. Pest [Budapest], 31 August 1832). Copperplate engraver. He studied with J. G. Prestel at Frankfurt am Main, J. Glauber at Augsburg, and F. John in Munich. In *c.*1800 he arrived in Vienna where he worked as an engraver and also opened an art shop. He produced numerous engravings of views of the city and its surroundings, as well as of portraits of well-known persons, including Clementi,* Haydn,* and Ignace Pleyel.*

In 1801 he made an engraving of Stainhauser von Treuberg's* portrait of Beethoven. The engraving was published by Giovanni Cappi*—and not by Artaria & Co.,* as Beethoven stated in a letter to Franz Gerhard Wegeler* on 29 June of that year (*see Corr.* A51/B65; see also n. 12 to B65). On 26 August, before Neidl's engraving was published in Vienna, Franz Anton Hoffmeister* sent a copy of it to Hoffmeister & Kühnel in Leipzig, with the suggestion that a fresh engraving be made from it, omitting the names of the original artist and engraver and with a different border, 'so that the new engraving would look different from the original one'. This task was carried out by Karl Traugott Riedel, and the new engraving was duly offered for sale by the Leipzig firm.

(*ALBK, ÖBL*)

Neugass, Isidor (b. Berlin, *c*.1780; d. ?Hungary, after 1847). Painter, best known today for his portraits of Haydn* and Beethoven. Little information is available about his life. According to *ALBK,* he studied at the Berlin Academy in 1800–2, spent some time in Vienna, moved soon after 1806 to Budapest, travelled to Italy and to Russia sometime after 1811, returned to Budapest in 1841, and was at Temesvár [then in Hungary, now Timisoara in Romania] in 1847.

The portrait of Beethoven, which dates from 1806, was probably commissioned by Prince Karl Lichnowsky;* it is now exhibited at the Beethoven-Haus in Bonn. A copy was made for the Brunsvik* family, perhaps by Neugass himself, and probably shortly after the original was painted; a photograph of this copy can likewise be seen at the Beethoven-Haus. Lastly, the Brunsvik copy was itself copied, by Frau von Ostergarden-Festetics, not earlier than 1860; her painting was acquired by the Beethoven-Haus in 1976.

In an article in *Zeitschrift für Musik* in 1935, Max Unger asserted that the Brunsvik portrait was clearly superior in quality to the Lichnowsky portrait and that it should therefore be regarded as the original painting. His conclusion has, however, been rejected by Ulrike von Hase-Schmundt, who argues that it is the Lichnowsky portrait which must be the original one, since it is signed, whereas the other one is not. According to Frimmel, the Lichnowsky portrait bore on the back the inscription 'peint par Neugass Wienne 1806'. When the picture was restored after the Second World War and the back of the canvas strengthened, this inscription, which would henceforth be hidden, was transferred to the frame as 'Peint par Neugast à Vienne 1806'. The painting was once more restored in 1980.

(Frimmel[3], Hase[3], Unger[7], Wackernagel)

Nickelsberg [Nicklsberg], **Karl** [Carl] **Nickl** [Nikl] **von** (b. Bohemia, *c*.1738; d. Vienna, 15 March 1805). Treasury official. He was probably the son of Johann Wolf(gang) Nickl [Nickhel] (?1691–1751), a government accountant; in 1763 he married Regina Dietmay(e)r von Dietmannsdorf (1738–1812). He was ennobled in 1787, at which time he was a secretary at the Austro-Bohemian court chancellery; ten years later, when he was a senior court secretary at the treasury, he was accorded the title 'Hofrat'.

The Nickelsbergs were evidently a musical family, for J. F. von Schönfeld, in his *Jahrbuch der Tonkunst von Wien und Prag* (1796), mentions two of the children: the son Heinrich (1766–1822) 'is a good pianist and also plays the cello', whilst one of the daughters, 'a pupil of Herr Stephan, plays the piano very nicely'. The

'Stephan' referred to was presumably the Czech composer, pianist, and teacher Josef Antonín Štěpán who counted the Archduchesses Maria Karolina (later queen of Naples, and of the Two Sicilies) and Marie Antoinette (future queen of France) among his pupils.

Beethoven dedicated the Second Piano Concerto, published by Hoffmeister* & Co. in 1801, to Nickelsberg.

(Slezak[2])

Niemetz, Joseph (b. 20 January 1808). A close friend of Karl van Beethoven,* who had made his acquaintance at Blöchlinger's* school. He formed the subject of a long argument between Beethoven and Karl which took place at Baden in September 1823 and is recorded in Beethoven's conversations books (*BKh4*/137–9). The exchange is particularly interesting, because Beethoven, for once, wrote down his remarks (probably because Niemetz, who had accompanied Karl to Baden, was nearby at the time and Beethoven did not wish him to overhear his derogatory observations). He considered Niemetz an unwelcome guest who disturbed the quiet he needed for his work, and who was, moreover, coarse and totally lacking in decency and good manners, and thus altogether an unsuitable friend for Karl. To this his nephew replied, politely but with impressive firmness, that Beethoven was mistaken about Niemetz's character, which he himself had had ample opportunity to appreciate at its true worth in the course of the past four years, and that he would go on loving him as he would love a brother, if he had one.

When Beethoven took the matter up again, probably on Karl's next visit, Karl reiterated his belief in Niemetz's excellent character and made it clear that he would not cease his association with him; there would, however, be no further occasion for irritation or quarrelling, since he did not intend to bring Niemetz to the house again (*BKh4*/143–4). This time Beethoven did not write down his remarks, presumably because Niemetz had not accompanied Karl on this occasion.

Karl evidently continued to associate with Niemetz, over his uncle's objections, for when he wrote some letters, including one to Beethoven, before attempting suicide in the summer of 1826, he sent them to Niemetz (who delivered them to Mathias Schlemmer,* with whom Karl was lodging at the time).

Obermayer, Leopold (1784–1841). Baker. His sister Therese was married to Nikolaus Johann van Beethoven.* Obermayer owned a house in the Windmühle suburb of Vienna. (The suburb was incorporated in 1850 in the newly formed fifth district Mariahilf, which was renumbered sixth in 1861.) The site of the house corresponds to the modern 20 Laimgrubengasse/22 Gumpendorferstrasse. Johann had a flat in that house, which he usually occupied with his family during the winter months. P. Nettl, following Frimmel's *Beethoven-Handbuch*, states incorrectly in his *Beethoven Encyclopedia* that 'in 1822 Beethoven lived at the

Obermayer's [*sic*] in the same house with Johann von [*sic*] Beethoven and his family'. In fact, Beethoven rented rooms from July 1822 until the following summer in a house [now 22 Laimgrubengasse] which adjoined Obermayer's. Subsequently Johann placed a room in his flat at his brother's disposal, for occasional use during the summer months.

After Johann once visited Beethoven at Baden together with Obermayer (on 13 July 1825), Beethoven wrote to his nephew Karl:* 'The day before yesterday *Signor Fratello* was here with his brother-in-law—what a wretched fellow' (*Corr.* A1396/B2007).

Odescalchi [Erba-Odescalchi], **(Anna Luise) Barbara** [Babette], Princess, née Countess Keglevics [Keglevich] von Buzin (b. *c*.1780; d. Vienna, 13 April 1813 (according to F. Slezak, and not 3 April, as stated in Kinsky/Halm, or 18 April, as indicated by Nováček). Daughter of Count Karl Keglevics von Buzin (1739–1804) and his wife Katharina Maria Josepha, née Countess Zichy (b. 1752). While the Keglevics' principal mansion was at Pressburg [Bratislava], they maintained a secondary residence in Vienna. There, by 1797 at the latest, Babette had become Beethoven's pupil. A nephew of hers later told Gustav Nottebohm that Beethoven, who lived right across the street from her, used to present himself for the lessons in his dressing-gown, slippers, and nightcap, but the story may well be apocryphal. On 10 February 1801, at Pressburg, Babette married Prince Innocenz d'Erba-Odescalchi (1778–1831), a son of Prince J. Balthasar Odescalchi and Katharina, née Princess Giustiani.

Beethoven dedicated to Babette the Piano Sonata in E flat, Op. 7 (published in 1797); the *Ten Variations* on the duet 'La stessa, la stessima' from Salieri's* opera *Falstaff*, WoO 73 (1799), the First Piano Concerto (1801), and *Six Variations* Op. 34 (1803).

Prince Odescalchi was an imperial chamberlain. He held musical soirées, at one of which, probably in about 1801, Beethoven's Septet Op. 20 was performed (*see Corr.* A56/B52). From 1818 until 1821 he served as vice-president of the Gesellschaft der Musikfreunde.* In that capacity he wrote in 1819 to enquire about the oratorio which Beethoven had undertaken to compose for the society. In his reply, Beethoven promised to honour his commitment (*Corr.* A981/B1356); but he never did.

In 1831 Odescalchi married Countess Henriette Zichy-Ferraris (whose sister Melanie became Prince Clemens Wenzel Lothar Metternich's third wife that same year).

(Nováček, Slezak²)

Oliva, Franz (b. Vienna, 24 November 1786; d. St Petersburg, 1848). Only child of Adam Oliva (*c*.1753–1808), an official in the censorship department, and his wife Elisabeth, née Bücklin. Information about Oliva's life is scant; nothing is known about his education, but he is believed to have attended the Akademisches Gymnasium. Some of his entries in Beethoven's conversation books indicate a certain acquaintance with German and foreign literature, and his later appointment as a teacher of German literature testifies to a cultured mind. He also played the piano, and must have done so competently enough, since he ventured to perform in front of Goethe* and his guests (see below). At the time of his father's death, he was employed as a clerk by the wholesalers and bankers Offenheimer & Herz; after the firm was dissolved in 1810, he worked for a time for its successors, Gebrüder Offenheimer and Leopold Herz & Co. In 1813 he left Austria to spend several years in Hungary, but he was back in Vienna by the spring of 1819 at the latest. At the end of that year he was working for the silk merchants Nathan Mayer & J. G. Landauer, and by the following summer for the wholesale firm of J. Biedermann und Bruder. In December 1820 he received a passport for Moscow, where he appears to have travelled together with the head of the company, Joseph Biedermann. He was to spend the rest of his days in Russia. From 1821 he taught German literature at the Lyceum at Tsarskoye Selo [Pushkin], near St Petersburg. He married while he was in Russia, and had a daughter. He died from cholera in 1848.

Oliva is likely to have met Beethoven before 1810, for the phrase 'a friend of mine who is familiar with bills of exchange' in Beethoven's letter to Breitkopf & Härtel* on 2 January of that year very probably refers to him. That summer he was helping Beethoven with his correspondence, and throughout their association he was to act as a kind of—no doubt unpaid—secretary. For his part, Beethoven must have appreciated the young man's help, for his *Variations* Op. 76 were published in October 1810 with a dedication 'à son ami Oliva'. When Oliva set out on a business trip to Saxony and northern Bohemia in April 1811, Beethoven empowered him to negotiate with Breitkopf & Härtel regarding the possible publication of the 'Archduke' Trio (which was eventually issued by S. A. Steiner & Co.*), and he furthermore entrusted him with a letter to Goethe, which Oliva duly delivered at Weimar on 2 May. The art collector Sulpiz Boisserée, a great friend of the poet, who observed his arrival at Goethe's residence, described him to his brother Melchior as a 'short, thin little man clad in black and wearing silk stockings'. Oliva was invited back to Goethe's house on 4 May, on which occasion he played some music by Beethoven—'Clärchen's song, I believe', Boisserée noted in his diary, without indicating which one (for the quotations from Boisserée, see *Corr.* B509 n. 2). Oliva visited Goethe once more on 6 May.

In late July 1811 Oliva was at Reichenberg [Liberec, Czech Republic]. From there he travelled to Teplitz [Teplice] where he kept Beethoven company for several weeks. During his stay at the Bohemian spa he struck up a friendship with Karl August Varnhagen von Ense* and his future wife Rahel Levin, and he introduced both to Beethoven. The summer ended badly, however, with a violent altercation between Beethoven and Oliva which resulted in their returning to Vienna separately. They did not resume cordial relations until the following spring. In a letter to Varnhagen von Ense in June 1812, Oliva laid the blame for their lengthy estrangement on Joseph Ludwig Stoll,* who 'has deceived me in the most despicable manner and even tried to break up my friendship with Beethoven, in which he almost succeeded' (*Corr.* B578). Though the quarrel was superficially patched up, Beethoven continued to feel great rancour, as is evident from a letter written by him to Count Franz Brunsvik* in the summer of 1813: 'That scoundrel Oliva . . . is going to Hungary. Don't have much to do with him. I am delighted that our association, which was brought about solely by necessity, will thus be completely terminated' (*Corr.* A427/B665).

These ill feelings were evidently forgotten by the time Oliva returned from Hungary a few years later. His numerous entries in the conversation books show very clearly the important position he then occupied in Beethoven's immediate circle, for not only did he take up his secretarial duties once more—various letters were written out (and perhaps drafted) by him and merely signed by Beethoven—but his advice was frequently sought in connection with the legal proceedings undertaken by Beethoven and also regarding Karl's* education. Beethoven's trust in his judgement and probity was demonstrated by his insistence that only Karl Joseph Bernard,* Magistratsrat Franz Xaver Piuk,* and Oliva were to have free access to his nephew while he was at Joseph Blöchlinger's* school (letter to Blöchlinger of 14 September 1819).

In 1854 Oliva's daughter Elisabeth informed Otto Jahn that whatever letters from Beethoven had been in the family's possession were lost in a fire and as a result of her father's death. They would no doubt have thrown light on many aspects of his relationship with Beethoven which remain obscure. As it is, Beethoven's published correspondence contains not a single written communication between them, apart perhaps from a very brief note by Beethoven which, it is thought, may have been meant for Oliva (*Corr.* A1065/B1412).

(Ullrich³)

Oppersdorff, Franz Joachim Wenzel, Imperial Count (b. Kopetzen, 29 September 1778; d. Berlin, 21 January 1818). Son of Imperial Count Franz Philipp Oppersdorff and his wife Anna Maria, née Baroness Schirndinger von Schirnding. A great music lover, he maintained his own orchestra at his castle at Oberglogau in Upper Silesia [Głogówec, Poland]; reportedly all officials in his household were expected to be able to play an instrument. While Beethoven was staying with Prince Lichnowsky* at Grätz [Hradec, Czech Republic] in 1806, he and his host one day visited Oppersdorff, who lived some 50 kilometres away. On this occasion, the count's orchestra performed Beethoven's Second Symphony. Some time later, Oppersdorff was present at the fierce quarrel between Lichnowsky and Beethoven (*see* the article on Karl Lichnowsky*).

Beethoven became very friendly with the count, as is evident from his addressing him as 'my beloved friend' in a letter probably written in March 1808 (see below) and from which it appears that Beethoven had met him in Vienna not very long before. Oppersdorff's name is connected with two of Beethoven's symphonies (the Fourth and the Fifth), but the circumstances linking the count to the two works remain somewhat obscure. Two letters from Beethoven to Oppersdorff have survived, the first undated but believed to have been written in March 1808 (*Corr.* A166/B325), the other written on 1 November 1808 (*Corr.* A178/B340). Thayer* reproduces, moreover, the text of several receipts signed by Beethoven for payments made to him by the count. The earliest of these receipts is dated 3 February 1807, the last 25 November 1808 (acknowledging a sum received in June of that year); the payments total 850 florins.

From these various documents it appears that Oppersdorff commissioned two symphonies and paid most of the fees for them in advance, but that in the end he had to be content with just the dedication of one. In March 1808 Beethoven told the count that 'his symphony' had been ready for some time and would be dispatched by the next mail (from a reference to the orchestration of the final movement it is clear that he was speaking of the Fifth Symphony). In November 1808, however, he informed Oppersdorff that he had been compelled by necessity to sell 'the symphony which was written for you' to someone else, at the same time as another one. (Both the Fifth and Sixth Symphonies had, in fact, been bought by Breitkopf & Härtel* on 14 September.) But Beethoven went on to assure the count, somewhat enigmatically, that he would soon receive 'the one which is intended for you'. This turned out to be the Fourth (composed in 1806), of which the orchestral parts had either recently been published, or were shortly to be published, by the Kunst- und Industrie-Comptoir,* with a dedication to Oppersdorff. In his *Thematisches Verzeichniss* (1868), Gustav Nottebohm states that this edition, which bears no date, appeared in March 1809, but modern scholars (e.g. Kinsky/Halm and Friedrich Slezak) firmly assign it to the year 1808. It had first been performed at Prince Lobkowitz's in March 1808.

Thus, if Oppersdorff had expected an entirely new work, he must have been disappointed. The fact that there is no record of any further contact between him and Beethoven after November 1808 has been interpreted as an indication that he was probably displeased with Beethoven's comportment in the matter.

(Kinsky/Halm, Oppersdorff, Reimann, Slezak[4])

Pachler, Marie Leopoldine, née Koschak (b. Graz, 2 February 1794; d. Graz, 10 April 1855). Amateur pianist; daughter of Aldobrand Koschak (1759–1814), a lawyer. She soon made a name for herself in Graz as a highly skilled pianist and a talented composer. At a concert on 3 March 1808 she played a concerto by Daniel Steibelt;* on 22 December 1811 she was the soloist in a performance of Beethoven's

Choral Fantasia, having been recommended by the composer himself who had been told of her accomplishments by Julius Schneller* (*see Corr.* A334/B531). She subsequently abandoned her plans for a professional career for family reasons. On 12 May 1816 she married the lawyer Karl Pachler (1789–1850). At their house in Graz they received numerous visitors, including actors, writers, poets, and musicians; Schubert stayed with them in September 1827.

Marie was a very great admirer of Beethoven's music. Her wish to make his acquaintance was fulfilled in 1817 when, during a visit to Vienna, she was introduced to him by her brother-in-law Anton who practised law there and already knew Beethoven. (The previous year he had, at her request, shown Beethoven a fantasia she had written, but without revealing the composer's identity; Beethoven had pronounced it a praiseworthy effort for someone who had not studied composition, but not without faults.) After Beethoven's death, Marie was to write to a friend, Anton Prokesch [later Count Prokesch von Osten]: 'I don't know whether you are aware how greatly I venerated him also as a man. I made his acquaintance during my first visit to Vienna; we were often together.' Marie was not only very musical, she was also an intelligent and beautiful young woman, and Beethoven is likely to have enjoyed her company. But Schindler's* statement that she was his 'autumnal love' is almost certainly incorrect, and the dates and chronology on which he based it are manifestly wrong. In 1866 Marie's son Faust published *Beethoven und Marie Pachler-Koschak: Beiträge und Berichtigungen*, a study of his mother's contacts with Beethoven which had previously appeared in the *Neue Berliner Musikzeitung*. It contains the text of a short letter which, the author explains, was written by Beethoven to Marie during her stay in Vienna and afterwards piously preserved by her. In it Beethoven warmly compliments Marie on her interpretation of his sonatas, which he judges superior to that achieved by any other pianist, and he salutes her as 'the true nurturer of my spiritual children'. The letter was later repeatedly reproduced (e.g. by O. E. Deutsch and in Emily Anderson's translation of Beethoven's letters (*Corr.* A815)), but it has since been recognized as a forgery (*see Corr.* B2031 n. 1).

Beethoven was invited by Karl (or perhaps Anton) Pachler to visit Graz, and considered the idea favourably (*see Corr.* A823/B1124), but in the end did not go there. He met Marie again in September 1823, on which occasion he presented her, at Vöslau, with a setting of 'Das Schöne zum Guten' (WoO 202), the concluding words of Matthisson's* 'Opferlied'. After Beethoven's death, her friend Johann Baptist Jenger* sent her a lock which he had cut from Beethoven's hair (she presented one half of it to Schneller). He also bought for her, at the sale of Beethoven's personal effects on 5 May 1827, two silver spoons, a silver salt and pepper pot, and a metronome made by Mälzel, which, according to Jenger, was still in excellent working order.

(Deutsch[1], Lohberger, Pachler)

Pacini, Antonio Francesco Gaetano Saverio (b. Naples, 7 July 1778; d. Paris, 10 March 1866). Parisian music publisher; composer. From Nîmes, where he was leader of a theatre orchestra, he moved to Paris in 1804. There he was active as a singing teacher and, from 1806, as a publisher. He issued numerous piano-vocal scores of Italian operas, including works by Mercadante, Bellini, Donizetti, and Rossini.* In *c*.1846 Bonoldi Frères became his successors, but he resumed publishing in 1852. He was also the composer of several *opéras comiques* and of many songs.

In June 1822 Pacini wrote to Beethoven requesting some as yet unpublished quartets or quintets. In his reply of 22 December (*Corr*. B1518), Nikolaus Johann van Beethoven* explained that his brother was unable to undertake the desired compositions, as he was currently working on several major projects; but he offered to send Pacini a 'new trio' (probably the re-scored *Variations on 'Là ci darem la mano' from 'Don Giovanni'*, WoO 28), a 'grand overture' (*Die Weihe des Hauses*, Op. 124), and six Bagatelles (Op. 119, Nos. 1–6). Pacini was willing to buy the Trio and the Bagatelles. However, Beethoven then decided not to sell him the Trio after all, but on 5 May 1823 offered him the *Thirty-Three Variations on a Waltz by Diabelli* (Op. 120), the previously mentioned six Bagatelles, and the songs 'Bundeslied' (Op. 122) and 'Opferlied' (Op. 121b). In the end, Pacini published none of these compositions.

(Macnutt[1])

Paer, Ferdinando (b. Parma, 1 June 1771; d. Paris, 3 May 1839). Composer, especially of operas. From Parma, to whose court he had been attached for some time, he moved in late 1797 to Vienna, where, for the next four years, he was employed as music director at the Kärntnertor-Theater. During that period several of his operas had their première there, notably *Camilla, ossia Il sotterraneo* (28 February 1799) and *Achille* (6 June 1801). During his stay in Vienna he became acquainted with Beethoven. Two instances of their contacts are known: both participated in a concert at the Grosser Redoutensaal on 30 January 1801, Beethoven performing his Horn Sonata Op. 17 with Giovanni Punto* and Paer conducting the orchestra for the vocal pieces; and on 15 August of that year Paer was among the guests present at a musical entertainment offered by Beethoven in his own rooms. They undoubtedly met also on other occasions. In 1802 Paer accepted an engagement at Dresden, but it was not until 1804 that he signed a contract for the position of full-time Kapellmeister in that city. In 1807 Napoleon made him his *maître de chapelle*, and Paris was to remain his principal place of residence for the rest of his life. From 1812 to 1826 he was director of the Théâtre Italien.

Paer's opera *Leonora, ossia L'amore coniugale* had its première at Dresden on 3 October 1804. The Italian text was, like that of Beethoven's *Fidelio*, based on Jean-Nicolas Bouilly's* libretto for Pierre Gaveaux's opera *Léonore, ou L'Amour conjugal* (first produced at the Théâtre Feydeau in Paris on 19 February 1798).

Richard Engländer, in a comparative study of Paer's and Beethoven's operas published in 1930, identified what he regarded as certain common elements in their text, dramatic structure, and music, none of which existed in the Bouilly –Gaveaux opera. He came to the conclusion that Paer's opera had exercised some influence on all the different versions of Beethoven's. His arguments, especially insofar as they concern the 1805–6 versions, have been treated with great caution by other scholars, including Willy Hess in his comprehensive study of Beethoven's opera (*Das Fidelio-Buch*, Winterthur, 1986). The fact that a manuscript copy of Paer's score was found among Beethoven's personal effects after his death is obviously of some interest, but there is no way of determining when it had come into his possession. (In his article on Paer in *New Grove*, J. Budden gives 1805, with a question mark, as the year when excerpts and the vocal score were published at Leipzig.)

As to the possibility that Beethoven was familiar with Paer's treatment of Bouilly's plot when he embarked on the composition of *Fidelio*, it has been suggested (in the first place, by Leopold von Sonnleithner,* the nephew of the original librettist of *Fidelio*, Joseph Sonnleithner) that when Paer visited Vienna in early 1803 for the purpose of composing and conducting his cantata *Il San Sepolcro*, he told Beethoven about the opera on which he was then working, and that Beethoven was so fascinated by the story that he resolved to write an opera on the same subject. (Paer's cantata was performed at the Burgtheater on 3 and 4 April 1803.) The Italian text of Paer's opera was published at Dresden in 1804, together with a German translation. It is, furthermore, interesting to note that Beethoven had an opportunity to acquaint himself with Paer's finished opera while he was preparing the revised version of *Fidelio* early in 1806. For, although Paer's *Leonora* was not publicly produced in Vienna until 8 February 1809, when it was presented at the Kärntnertor-Theater with a German text by J. F. Rochlitz,* the opera was performed, most probably in the original Italian version, at Prince Lobkowitz's palace shortly before the new version of *Fidelio* was produced at the Theater an der Wien on 29 March 1806. A brief report on this private performance of *Leonora* was published in the Weimar journal *Journal des Luxus und der Moden*; it specially mentioned the excellent singing of 'Brizzi'—perhaps the well-known amateur tenor Giuseppe Antonio Bridi, who may have taken the part of Florestano. Beethoven could well have attended this performance of *Leonora*, and he may even have been present at some of the rehearsals. Incidentally, neither Engländer nor Hess appears to have known about this private performance; the report which appeared in the Weimar journal is reprinted in S. Kunze's *Ludwig van Beethoven: Die Werke im Spiegel seiner Zeit*. (Bridi, who was a partner in the Viennese firm Bridi, Parisi, & Co., later arranged for the transportation from Trieste to Vienna of the piano which Thomas Broadwood* presented to Beethoven—*see Corr.* A890/B1238 and B1243.)

(Engländer[1,2], Frimmel[5], Hess[8], Kunze)

Pálffy von Erdöd, Ferdinand, Count (b. Vienna, 1 February 1774; d. Vienna, 4 February 1840). Mining engineer; theatre manager. Son of Count Leopold Pálffy (1739–99) and Maria Theresia, née Countess Daun (d. 1777). He was a member of the Gesellschaft der Kavaliere [Association of Noblemen] which, in 1807, acquired the Theater an der Wien and, at the same time, leased the Burgtheater and the Kärntnertor-Theater. In 1810 he became fully responsible for the management of the two court theatres, and during most of the period between March 1814 and April 1817 he was their sole lessee. He furthermore bought the Theater an der Wien in 1813 and remained its proprietor until 1826. By then his efforts to attract a wide public by ever more lavish spectacles had cost him his not inconsiderable private fortune, and he was forced to sell the theatre at auction. Fearing arrest, he fled to his estate at Pressburg [Bratislava]; he did not return to Vienna until 1830.

Pálffy is not ranked by Beethoven scholars among the composer's greatest admirers, let alone his major patrons. If he did indeed, as has been suggested, feel some hostility towards him, the initial reason may lie in an incident described by Ferdinand Ries:* while playing duets with Ries at Count Browne's* one evening, Beethoven was so incensed by the behaviour of the 'young Count P . . .', who, despite several attempts to silence him, persisted in carrying on a loud conversation with a lady, that he stopped playing, exclaiming 'I will not play for such pigs'; the young nobleman in question was probably Pálffy. Nor did Beethoven behave more circumspectly later when he was in professional contact with the count. Spohr,* who was leader of the orchestra at the Theater an der Wien in 1813–15, relates meeting Beethoven occasionally at the theatre (where Pálffy had given him a free seat just behind the orchestra) and taking him back to his apartment after the performance. Before they had even left the building, Beethoven would begin a loud tirade against Pálffy—loud enough to be heard not only by the rest of the audience, but also by the count in his office. Thus Pálffy may well have felt some animosity towards Beethoven. When Beethoven was preparing the concert which, after several postponements, took place on 29 November 1814 at the Grosser Redoutensaal, Pálffy stipulated that the court opera was to receive one half of the receipts. He was subsequently obliged to withdraw this demand after receiving a protest from Prince Ferdinand Trauttmansdorff, the court official responsible for entertainments during the Congress of Vienna, to whom Beethoven had complained and who pointed out to Pálffy the desirability of supporting 'an outstanding artist, of whose presence in Vienna the city has reason to be proud' (*Corr.* B756). Beethoven recalled the occasion with glee during a conversation in 1816 with Karl von Bursy,* who noted in his diary: 'He is particularly ill disposed towards him [i.e. Pálffy].'

It should not be forgotten, however, that it was Pálffy who put on the successful production of the final version of *Fidelio* (23 May 1814). Furthermore, he signed the celebrated memorial addressed to Beethoven by a number of Viennese music lovers in February 1824 (*Corr.* B1784). And finally, he appears to have acted with propriety during the delicate and rather tedious discussions preceding Beethoven's concert of 7 May 1824, which was originally to be held at the Theater an der Wien. There is little doubt that, whether for reasons of profit or prestige, he genuinely wished to present it at his theatre; he even told Schindler* at a late stage of the negotiations that he would sooner lose the stated fee of 1,000 florins for the hall, orchestra, and lights, than forgo the honour of having the concert there. Nevertheless, it eventually took place at the Kärntnertor-Theater (*see* Clement* and Louis Antoine Duport*).

Pasqualati von Osterberg, Johann Baptist, Baron (b. Vienna, 2 March 1777; d. Vienna, 30 April 1830). Wholesale merchant; son of Johann Benedikt Pasqualati von Osterberg (1733–99), an eminent physician who was ennobled in 1777 and created a baron in 1798. In 1804 the so-called 'Pasqualatihaus' [8 Mölkerbastei], which had been built for Johann Benedikt in 1786–8, was owned, in equal portions, by his four surviving children Johann Baptist, Josepha, Joseph Andreas, and Johanna. It was in that year that Beethoven first took rooms in the house, and he was to live there until early 1814, with some interruptions (notably from the autumn of 1808 to the spring of 1810). During that overall period, the proprietorship of the building changed on several occasions. Thus, when Beethoven wished to move back there in 1810, Baron Johann Baptist no longer had a share in the house, and Beethoven had to deal with Peter von Leber, who together with his wife Josepha (Johann Baptist's sister) then owned two-thirds of the 'Pasqualatihaus'. (In early 1814 Beethoven moved from the 'Pasqualatihaus' to a smaller adjoining house [10 Mölkerbastei] which had been built for Johann Benedikt in 1791. He sold the house the following year to Desideria Grahowska who, in her turn, sold it in 1793 to Regina Bartenstein; in 1813 it was acquired by Anton von Rachowin. It was thus Rachowin who was Beethoven's landlord when he stayed there in 1814–15. The house was sometimes referred to as the 'little Pasqualatihaus', and more generally as the 'Bartensteinisches [or Bartensteinsches] Haus). Beethoven maintained his personal and friendly contacts with Johann Baptist Pasqualati until his death.

Pasqualati, a great music lover and himself a good pianist, was among the original fifty *Repräsentanten* [representatives] of the Gesellschaft der Musikfreunde.* He was also a composer; Frimmel mentions some waltzes and a polonaise for the piano. It is therefore not surprising that Beethoven should have presented him with suitably inscribed copies of several of his compositions. (One such inscribed copy of Artaria & Co.'s* 1814 edition of the piano reduction of *Fidelio* was presented by the Austrian government to Arturo Toscanini in 1934.) Moreover, in commemoration of the third anniversary of the death of Pasqualati's second wife Eleonore (1787–1811), Beethoven composed the *Elegischer Gesang* (Op. 118) in 1814; the first edition, published in Vienna in 1826, was dedicated to Pasqualati.

For New Year 1815 Beethoven sent his good wishes to the baron in the form of a canon (WoO 165).

Beethoven had cause to feel grateful to Pasqualati, who helped with the preparations for some of his concerts, lent him money on at least one occasion, and advised and assisted him in several matters, above all in his efforts to obtain an adequate annuity from Prince Kinsky's* heirs in 1814/15. In this connection, a useful role was also played by Pasqualati's brother Baron Joseph Andreas (1784–1864), who was in Prague at the time and in contact with Dr Johann Nepomuk Kanka.* It was he who accepted the first payment under the new agreement with the Kinsky family on Beethoven's behalf (2,479 florins for all annuity payments covering the period up to 31 March 1815).

Pasqualati remained a good friend to the end, sending Beethoven food and drink during his final illness. 'How can I thank you enough for the superb champagne which has so greatly refreshed me and will continue to do so,' Beethoven wrote not long before his death. 'May Heaven bless you for everything, and especially for your affectionate sympathy with your respectful and ailing Beethoven' (*Corr.* A1570/B2275).

(Frimmel[1], Klein[1], Smolle, Wurzbach[1])

Payne, Sarah Burney (b. *c.*1793). Daughter of Rear-Admiral James Burney (1750–1821) and his wife Sally, née Payne; granddaughter of the composer and music historian Charles Burney (1726–1814). She was musically gifted and is said to have 'played classic music in a professional manner'. In 1821 she married her cousin, the bookseller John Payne (who, from 1825, ran the firm Payne & Foss in partnership with Henry Foss). After her husband's business closed down in 1850 the couple lived in Rome, where they reportedly counted the prominent statesman Cardinal Giacomo Antonelli among their intimate friends.

Sarah visited Vienna with her husband from 22 September to 2 October 1825. On 27 September she called on Beethoven at Baden; to mark the occasion, he composed the *Klavierstück* (WoO 61a) for her. Sarah published an account of their meeting, anonymously, in the London periodical *Harmonicon* later that year. In 1826 she sent Beethoven a copy of her grandfather's *A General History of Music*.

(*DNB*, Payne, Scholes)

Pecháček [Pechaczek, Pechatschek], **Franz Xaver** (b. Vienna, 4 July 1793; d. Karlsruhe, 15 September 1840). Composer and violinist. He was taught by his father Franz Martin Pecháček (1763–1816), a Bohemian-born composer and violinist, and later by Schuppanzigh.* From 1803 he studied composition with Emanuel Aloys Förster.* He frequently appeared at concerts in Vienna, especially during the decade 1810–1820. Leopold von Sonnleithner* lists him among the string players who took part in the musical soirées given by his father Ignaz von

Sonnleithner* (but places him, rather puzzlingly, among the cellists; he gives his date of death as 29 January 1840). Pecháček also became a member of the Theater an der Wien orchestra (1809–22). In 1820 he conducted two concerts of the Gesellschaft der Musikfreunde.* The programme of the first (20 February) included Beethoven's Third Symphony, that of the second (9 April) his Second Symphony and a chorus from the oratorio *Christus am Ölberg*. In October 1822 Pecháček became Konzertmeister of the Württemberg court Kapelle at Stuttgart, but he later returned to Vienna and the Theater an der Wien. From 1826 until 1840 he led the orchestra of Grand Dukes Ludwig I and Leopold of Baden at Karlsruhe. His own compositions were almost entirely written for the solo violin, with accompaniment.

Although Pecháček is likely to have met Beethoven on various occasions, only one instance of their personal contacts is documented. It occurred on 12 July 1825 (for details, *see* Clement*).

(Haas³, Hanslick, *ÖBL*, Sonnleithner, Wurzbach¹)

Peters, Carl Friedrich (b. Leipzig, 30 March 1779; d. Sonnenstein, Bavaria, 20 November 1827). Music publisher at Leipzig. On 1 April 1814 he became the owner of the Bureau de musique, which had been founded by Franz Anton Hoffmeister* and Ambrosius Kühnel in 1800 and managed by Kühnel alone from 1805 until his death in 1813.

In April 1818 Peters sounded out his friend Johann Andreas Streicher* about the possibility of buying some of Beethoven's compositions, but it was not until 18 May 1822 that he wrote directly to Beethoven himself (*Corr.* B1465). There then ensued protracted negotiations which extended over more than three years and focused principally on a Mass which Beethoven offered and Peters was willing to buy, but which Beethoven never delivered. (Originally he presumably had the *Missa solemnis* in mind, though he later spoke of his intention of writing two other Masses.) In addition, Peters wished to purchase various other kinds of works, but he was so disappointed by what he considered the unsatisfactory quality of the songs and the trifling nature of the Bagatelles which he had received from Beethoven that he sent these compositions back. In the end, Beethoven returned in December 1825 the sum which Peters had paid in advance in August 1822, and thereupon their contacts ceased. (*See also* Kloeber* and Streicher.*)

Peters, Karl (b. Prague, 16 April 1782; d. Vienna, 9 November 1849). Tutor and estate manager, in the service of the Lobkowitz family; son of Joseph Peters, cook to Count Salm-Reifferscheid. He was engaged by Prince Joseph Franz Maximilian Lobkowitz* in April 1810 as tutor to his sons Ferdinand, Joseph, and Johann Karl. A well-educated man, he spoke Italian and French in addition to Czech and German, knew classical Greek, and was a talented painter. The prince, in appreciation of the manner in which he carried out his duties, granted him the title 'Hofrat'.

On 5 May 1814, in Vienna, Peters married Josephine Hochsinger (1790–1866); she was a highly regarded amateur singer, with a pleasing, if rather weak, voice. The couple was assigned an apartment in the prince's summer palace in Ungargasse, which they occupied until they left Vienna in 1825. There Josephine regularly received a number of persons attracted to literature and the arts. They included Karl Joseph Bernard,* Joseph Czerny,* Franz Oliva,* and Johann Baptist Bach.* Peters himself was in contact with the folk music collector Julius Max(imilian) Schottky and with the composer and violinist Paul Wranitzky.*

Beethoven's first extant letter to Peters dates from January 1817, but he had probably made Peters's acquaintance shortly after the latter had taken up his post in the Lobkowitz household. Beethoven also knew Josephine quite well and reportedly accompanied her occasionally at concerts at the Palais Lobkowitz. In January 1817 he presented her with a copy of his song cycle *An die ferne Geliebte*. For several years he was in regular contact with Peters, who took a close interest in Karl van Beethoven's* education. The conversation books for the winter of 1819–20 contain very numerous entries in Peters's hand. In his submission of 7 January 1820 to the Lower Austrian Court of Appeal (*Corr.* A App.C, 14/B1363), Beethoven requested that Karl's mother Johanna van Beethoven* be excluded from the guardianship, and that instead he himself and Peters—'a man . . . who is universally esteemed for his great knowledge and his excellent moral character' —should be appointed joint guardians of the boy. In a letter written during the same period, probably to Bernard, Beethoven again expressed his confidence in Peters's judgement and integrity: 'How could I have made a better choice for my nephew's welfare than to have as joint guardian Herr von Peters, who not only has a full understanding of the situation but will also always show true devotion to and love for the good cause . . . ?' (*Corr.* A1008/B1362). On 20 April 1820 the Magistracy of the City of Vienna advised Beethoven that his request had been granted. In actual fact, though, Peters, who had left Vienna with Prince Ferdinand Lobkowitz in March on an extended trip to Switzerland and Italy, was unable to assume his duties as joint guardian until October of that year. He exercised this function until he moved to Prague in April 1825 on being appointed chief admin-istrator of Prince Ferdinand Lobkowitz's estates. His position as joint guardian was then taken over by the vice-principal of the Polytechnisches Institut, Franz de Paula Michael Reisser.* Peters and his wife remained in Prague until 1848.

Beethoven's close association with Peters was facilitated by the fact that they lived at various times not far from one another in the Landstrasse suburb, especially after Beethoven had moved to the house 'Zur schönen Sklavin' [now 5 Ungargasse] in the autumn of 1823. His favourable view of Peters was supported by the testimony of others. Thus Bernard, who first suggested to Beethoven that he make Peters his co-guardian, assured him that Peters was 'too honourable to be motivated by petty considerations' (*BKh1*/89). And Joseph Czerny described him as 'an intelligent and honourable man' and as 'one of the noblest of men' (*BKh1*/134, 314). Even Schindler* later claimed to have been impressed by Peters: 'It is true that Hofrath Peters chatters a great deal,' he observed in a forged (!) entry, 'but he has your best interests at heart' (*BKh1*/142). Whether one really believes, as Maynard Solomon asserts in his biography of Beethoven, that Peters's concern for Beethoven's well-being was so profound that 'on several . . . occasions documented in the Conversation Books, [he] offered a girl to Beethoven' depends on how one chooses to interpret certain remarks. Solomon even states that on one occasion Peters 'generously offered his wife to Beethoven for a night'—but this bizarre allegation is based on his mistranslation of the relevant entry. It is interesting to note that Beethoven's relations with Peters remained in fact quite formal till the end, for in his last known letter to Peters, written in March or April 1825 (*Corr.* A1360/B1956), he addressed Peters as 'Verehrter Freund!' [Esteemed friend] and signed himself 'Hochachtungsvoll ihr Freund Beethoven' [Yours faithfully, your friend Beethoven].

The friendship produced two small pieces of music. While visiting Peters one day (12 April 1823), Beethoven learned that the following day would be Prince Ferdinand Lobkowitz's birthday, so he quickly composed the so-called 'Lobkowitz' Cantata for soprano solo, chorus, and piano (WoO 106), which was to be sung to the prince the next day. Some years earlier (in late 1819, according to Kinsky/Halm), he had written a puzzle canon (WoO 175) to the words 'Sankt Petrus war ein Fels, Bernardus war ein Sankt' (an amusing reference to Karl Peters and Karl Joseph Bernard).

Peters having expressed the wish to be buried near Schubert and Beethoven, Prince Ferdinand arranged for him to be interred at Währing Cemetery.

(Macek[1], Solomon[2])

Petrarch [Petrarca, Francesco] (b. Arezzo, 20 July 1304; d. Arquà, 18 July 1374). Poet. Beethoven left sketches for settings of Karl Streckfuss's* German versions of the sonnets 'Quando fra l'altre donne ad ora ad ora' and 'Ove ch'i posi gli occhi lassi o giri'.

(Schürmann, Virneisel)

Pfeffel, Gottlieb Conrad (b. Colmar, 28 June 1736; d. Colmar, 1 May 1809). Translator, dramatist, and poet. Although blind from 1758, he pursued an active literary career. In 1761 he published a three-volume collection of verse, *Poetische Versuche*; three further, augmented, editions were to follow, the last in ten volumes (1802–10). A ten-volume edition of his prose writings, *Prosaische Versuche*, appeared posthumously (1810–12).

Beethoven set one of his poems in 'Der freie Mann' (WoO 117). The composition exists in two versions. One was published by Simrock* at Bonn in 1808 as one of Beethoven's *Drei deutsche Lieder*. The other, presumably earlier one, did not appear in print in Beethoven's lifetime; it was published by Willy Hess in *Musica* in 1956.

(Guhde)

Pfeifer, Tobias Friedrich. Actor, pianist, oboist, and flautist. He arrived at Bonn in 1779 as a member of the theatrical company led by Gustav Friedrich Wilhelm Grossmann, and reportedly left at Easter 1780. During his stay he lodged with the Beethovens, who were themselves then living as tenants in a house owned by Gottfried Fischer's* family. In his notes on the Beethoven family, Fischer draws an amusing portrait of Pfeifer, who was evidently a gifted but rather eccentric individual. According to Fischer, he gave the young Ludwig instruction in piano playing (sometimes in the middle of the night) and occasionally played the flute to Ludwig's accompaniment. At other times they made music with the violinist Franz Georg Rovantini* who was living in the same house. Their performance was so pleasing, Fischer wrote, that passers-by would stop in the street to enjoy it, declaring that 'one could listen to them all day and all night'.

Franz Gerhard Wegeler,* who probably attached greater importance to the benefit Beethoven received from Pfeifer's instruction than was merited, recalled in *Biographische Notizen* that Beethoven later sent a gift of money to him from Vienna through Nikolaus Simrock.* Little is known about Pfeifer's life after he left Bonn. For several years he apparently pursued his stage career in various German towns; in 1794 he was active as a music teacher at Düsseldorf.

(Fischer[4])

Philharmonic Society [from 1912, 'Royal Philharmonic Society'] (London). It was formed in 1813 with thirty members and an unlimited number of associate members; from among the members, seven directors were chosen each year 'for the management of the concerts', the number of which was fixed at eight annually. The original members and associate members included Bridgetower,* Clementi,* Cramer,* Neate,* Salomon,* and Smart.* Beethoven was represented at the inaugural concert at the Argyll Rooms on 8 March 1813 by an (unidentified) symphony, and his music regularly figured on the programme of later concerts. Thus, out of the eighty concerts given during the society's first decade (1813–22), only twelve did not contain at least one of Beethoven's works. Moreover, two of the symphonies are known to have received their first London performances at concerts of the society—No. 5 on 15 April 1816 and No. 9 on 21 March 1825; others may well have done so too.

Beethoven's dealings with the society can be traced back to a letter to Smart, written on his behalf on 16–19 March 1815 by Johann Baptist von Häring,* who was personally acquainted with Smart. The purpose of the letter was to ask Smart to find English publishers for a number of compositions listed by Häring, which had not yet been printed anywhere, although five of them were described by Häring as having already been performed 'to very great applause'. It is probable that Charles Neate, who arrived in Vienna in May 1815, reviewed the music on offer and then recommended purchase of the following three overtures to Smart: *Die Ruinen von Athen* (Op. 113), *Zur Namensfeier* (Op. 115), *König Stephan* (Op. 117). At any rate, Smart proposed at the general meeting on 11 July 1815 that the society should buy these overtures for 75 guineas, and his motion was approved. The overtures had appeared on Häring's list, where all three were included among those identified as having been previously performed. There are thus no grounds for the allegations made by certain scholars that Beethoven had deceived the society, which thought it was acquiring works specially written for it. There is, however, evidence that considerable disappointment was felt in London regarding the quality of the compositions, and that this was a major reason for the reluctance shown by London publishers to buy any of the other compositions by Beethoven which Neate had brought back from Vienna. In October 1816 Beethoven wrote to Smart (in English): 'I own that the three overtures do not belong to my best and great works, they being all occasional pieces composed for the Theatre . . . Mr Neate had in his possession other more essential works, he chose those three' (*Corr.* A664/B983). Only one of the three overtures—probably *Zur Namensfeier*—was actually performed at a concert of the society at the time (25 March 1816); the other two were apparently only tried out at rehearsal. (Beethoven held Neate responsible for the failure to find publishers for his works in London.)

Beethoven more than once entertained the idea of visiting England, and the Philharmonic Society naturally assumed an important part in his plans. Indeed, the society made him some tempting proposals. On 9 June 1817 his friend and former pupil Ferdinand Ries* informed him that he and Neate (both were then directors of the society) had been instructed to offer him 300 guineas—of which 100 guineas would be paid in advance—if he would come to London during the following winter and compose two symphonies for the society (*Corr.* B1129). In his reply of 9 July Beethoven agreed to the other conditions, but asked for a further 100 guineas for travelling expenses and an advance of 150 guineas. At a directors' meeting on 19 August it was decided not to accept these terms, but to repeat the first offer. It may be assumed that Ries promptly contacted Beethoven again; but it was not until 5 March 1818 that Beethoven informed him that ill health had prevented him from going to London that winter; he hoped, however, to be fit enough to take up the society's offer later that year. If he seriously entertained such an idea at the time, he dropped it before long. Yet a letter to Ries four years later (6 July 1822) indicates that he never entirely abandoned the hope of visiting London one day ('if my health will allow it, perhaps next spring?!'). In the meanwhile, he wished to know how much the society would be willing to pay for a grand symphony. The directors decided on 10 November 1822 to offer £50,

provided they received it by the following March and had the sole right to its performance for a period of eighteen months. On 15 November (*see Corr.* B1510) Ries
transmitted the offer to Beethoven, who accepted it on 20 December. While
awaiting the delivery of the symphony, the society agreed at a directors' meeting
on 25 January 1823 to buy the Overture *Die Weihe des Hauses* (Op. 124) for £25.
The score of the overture was dispatched from Vienna on 25 February, and performed at a concert of the society on 21 April. As for the symphony, it was far from
finished at the stipulated date, and it was not until 27 April 1824 that the score
(Op. 125) was handed to Franz Christian Kirchhoffer,* a cashier and bookkeeper
employed by the Viennese silk merchants Hofmann & Goldstein, who was to
send it to London; only then did Beethoven receive his fee of £50. (The first performance of the Ninth Symphony took place in Vienna on 7 May.)

Meanwhile Beethoven had resurrected the idea of a trip to London. On 25
February 1823 he had written to Neate: 'If my health, which has been very bad
these past three years, should improve, I hope to come to London in 1824 . . .
Whatever the Philharmonic Society should require, I would be glad to compose
for it.' However, he did not travel to London in 1824 either. Undaunted, the directors of the society decided, at their meeting of 19 December 1824, to invite him
for the forthcoming concert season (which was to run from mid-February to
June 1825) at a fee of 300 guineas, 'under the stipulation that he should write a
Symphony and a Concertante for the use of the society exclusively during his residence in England, and that he shall preside at the performance of his own works'.
The next day, Neate wrote to inform Beethoven of the new offer, and at the same
time pointed out that during his visit Beethoven would also have other opportunities of earning substantial fees (*Corr.* B1914). From this point on, negotiations
followed more or less the same pattern as in 1817: Beethoven, while accepting all
other conditions, demanded travelling expenses amounting to 100 guineas (letters
to Neate of 15 and 27 January 1825); these the society refused (*see* Neate's letter
of 1 February, *Corr.* B1930). Finally, Beethoven informed Neate on 19 March
that he would be unable to come that spring, but held out the vague possibility of
a visit in the autumn. Two days after he wrote this letter, the Ninth Symphony
was given its first performance in London—not, as the society had hoped, under
the direction of the composer himself, but under that of Sir George Smart. (In
September of that year Smart would travel to Vienna, principally in order 'to
ascertain from Beethoven personally the exact times of the movements of his
characteristic [i.e. the Ninth]—and some of his other—Sinfonias'.)

Beethoven's contacts with the Philharmonic Society continued until the very
end of his life, for during his final illness he turned to his English friends for financial assistance and they did not fail him (*see* especially Moscheles,* Smart,* and
Stumpff*). While the society did not, as he requested, arrange a special concert
for his benefit, its directors decided, at their meeting of 28 February 1827, to make
him a gift of £100 'to be applied to his comforts and necessities during his illness'.

The money was sent by Moscheles to his friend Sebastian Rau,* a tutor in the household of Baron Bernhard Eskeles,* and Rau handed the equivalent sum, 1,000 florins, to Beethoven—who expressed his profound gratitude in a letter to Moscheles on 18 March.

When, after Beethoven's death, an inventory was taken of his possessions—on which occasion Rau was present—the 1,000 florins were found untouched. Rau immediately reclaimed the money on behalf of the Philharmonic Society; pending receipt of precise instructions from the society, it was temporarily held by the Vienna Magistracy. Subsequently, Rau was involved in a protracted debate concerning its ultimate fate, and, as indicated below, his advice was at least partly responsible for the final decision taken by the society in the matter. Various proposals were made by persons who would have liked the money to remain in Vienna; Schindler* even let it be known that he would not be averse to receiving a small portion of it as an 'indirect' legacy from Beethoven. Finally, on 10 February 1828, Jakob Hotschevar,* who had been appointed Karl van Beethoven's* guardian following the death of Stephan von Breuning* on 4 June, addressed a long letter to Moscheles, in which he described the precarious financial situation in which his ward found himself in consequence of the modest sum left by his uncle, that sum having moreover been substantially diminished by the heavy cost of the funeral. He therefore expressed the fervent wish that the society would not press its claim for the return of the gift. It might even, he suggested, wish to give additional proof of its generosity by donating, together with certain old admirers of the composer, a further sum to assist Karl's future living expenses. This letter was forwarded to Moscheles by Rau, who, in a covering note, advised the society not to insist on the repayment of the gift, since it might otherwise encounter much unpleasantness and perhaps be drawn into legal proceedings, the costs of which could well swallow up the total of the money involved. He pointed out, furthermore, that it might be extremely difficult to prove that the recovered banknotes were indeed identical with those he had handed to Beethoven. After perusal of these two communications, the directors of the society decided to take no further action, and on 10 April 1828 Rau, in a letter to the Magistracy, formally withdrew the society's claim to the money. (Hotschevar's and Rau's letters of 10 February 1828, as well as certain others relating to this matter, were printed by Charlotte Moscheles in her book *Aus Moscheles' Leben nach Briefen und Tagebüchern* (1872).)

On the occasion of the centenary of Beethoven's birth, the society was presented, as a token of gratitude for the generosity it had shown him, with a bust of the composer which had been made, probably shortly after his death, by the Austrian sculptor Johann Nepomuk Schaller for Karl Holz.* The donor was Fanny Linzbauer, the wife of a well-known physician, Franz Xaver Linzbauer, who was on the faculty of the University of Pest [Budapest] at the time. William [later Sir William] George Cusins, a distinguished musician and, from 1867 to

1883, conductor-in-chief of the Philharmonic concerts, travelled to Budapest to take possession of the bust in January 1871. It was displayed at the society's first concert in 1871, and a copy of it has ever since been placed on the platform at all Royal Philharmonic Society concerts. Schaller's bust served, furthermore, as the model for Beethoven's head shown on the gold medal which was designed and struck, also in 1871, for presentation to eminent persons who had rendered notable services to the society, or might do so in the future. Among its first recipients was Fanny Linzbauer.

(Craig, Elkin, Hadley, Levien, MacArdle[7], Moscheles)

Pinterics, Karl (b. *c.*1780; d. 6 March 1831). Private secretary of Prince Joseph Franz Pálffy von Erdöd, and after his death in 1827, of his son Prince Anton Karl. He had an office at the Pálffys' residence [6 Josefsplatz]. Highly musical, he played the piano very well and had a pleasing bass voice. He was a close friend of Franz Schubert.*

Schindler* states that in 1815, when he himself came to know Beethoven better, Pinterics and Beethoven used to meet frequently at the Zum Blumenstöckl tavern [3 Ballgasse]. That they were still in close contact in 1820 is attested by a letter from Beethoven (26 April 1820), in which he informs Pinterics of the decision in his favour which had just been handed down by the Lower Austrian Court of Appeal in the matter of Karl's* guardianship. On the other hand, P. Nettl is mistaken in stating, in his *Beethoven Encyclopedia*, that 'numerous letters from Beethoven to Pinterics are preserved'. The letter of 26 April 1820 is the only extant one. Incidentally, an entry in the conversation books in early 1820 (*BKh*1/312), in which reference is made to an occasion when Pinterics is said to have joined others in singing the 'Mälzel' canon (WoO 162), has been shown to be one of Schindler's forgeries, like the canon itself (*see* Mälzel*).

(Clive[2])

Piringer, Ferdinand (b. Unterretzbach, Lower Austria, 18 October 1780; d. Vienna, 11 November 1829). Government official; musician. The son of a schoolteacher and choirmaster, he studied the humanities and law at Vienna University and subsequently entered government service. At the same time he must have received extensive musical training, for he was a competent violinist, conductor, and bass singer. He became assistant conductor to Franz Xaver Gebauer* at the Concerts spirituels, and in March 1824, with the help of Johann Geissler, he revived these concerts which had been discontinued following Gebauer's death in December 1822. He also played the violin at concerts of the Gesellschaft der Musikfreunde* (he was elected to its executive committee in 1826), and took part in chamber music concerts directed by Schuppanzigh* and Joseph Böhm.* He was thus familiar with many of Beethoven's works, either as an instrumentalist or conductor.

The Allegretto for piano (WoO 61) which Beethoven wrote out for Piringer's album and dated 18 February 1821 constitutes the first known contact between them. The earliest extant letter was sent by Beethoven on 6 November of the same year, and signed 'Your amicus Beethoven Bonnensis'. Its bantering tone already suggests a less than formal association. Schindler* describes Piringer as 'an extremely amusing fellow who, just by his facial expressions, could often put Beethoven in a good mood'. Piringer called Mozart* the 'king of musicians' and Beethoven his 'Generalissimus', and he frequently addressed Beethoven by that term (see Corr. B1792 n.). In an entry in the conversation books (BKh4/202), Beethoven's nephew Karl* describes him as 'beschränkt aber gutmütig' [not very intelligent, but good-natured']. Piringer's name appears frequently in the conversation books from 1823 onwards; several entries are in his own writing. In addition to performing Beethoven's music, he rendered him other services. Thus it was he who selected the musicians for Beethoven's concert of 7 May 1824; and in 1825 he checked a copy of the Missa solemnis for him. He was among those friends who visited Beethoven during his final illness. At the funeral he was one of the torchbearers.

(ÖBL)

Piuk, Franz Xaver (c.1753–1826). Magistratsrat [magisterial councillor]. In May 1819 he took over responsibility for matters relating to the guardianship of Karl van Beethoven* from Magistratsrat Leopold Joseph Pianta. One of his first actions, on 7 May, was to deny Beethoven's application for a passport for Karl (see Sailer*), following Johanna van Beethoven's* objections. On 19 July Beethoven addressed a long letter to Piuk, in which he set out his views regarding the guardianship. On 14 September he instructed Joseph Blöchlinger* that only Karl Joseph Bernard,* Franz Oliva,* and Piuk were to be granted free access to Karl. (Beethoven would no doubt have preferred that Karl should not be interviewed by Piuk, and especially not without himself being present, but he could hardly deny access to an official appointed by the Magistracy.) Piuk appears to have been generally sympathetic to Johanna's arguments, for it must have been largely on his recommendation that the Magistracy decided on 17 September 1819 to award the guardianship jointly to her and Leopold Nussböck. (This decision was ultimately overturned by the Lower Austrian Court of Appeal in April 1820.)

Pleyel, Ignace [Ignaz] **Joseph** (b. Ruppersthal, Austria, 18 June 1757; d. Paris, 14 November 1831). Composer, music publisher, and piano manufacturer, active in France. He founded his firm in Paris in 1795; in 1805 he travelled to Vienna, probably together with his son Camille (1788–1855), with the intention of setting up a branch of the firm there, but in this he was unsuccessful. During his stay his latest quartets were performed at Prince Lobkowitz's* palace before a select audience. Carl Czerny* relates that afterwards Beethoven, who was among those present, was asked to improvise, and that, basing his extemporization on a passage from the second violin part in one of Pleyel's quartets, he played so brilliantly that Pleyel was moved to kiss his hands in admiration.

In 1807 Beethoven offered Pleyel, for publication in Paris, 'six new works' which, he wrote, he was simultaneously offering for publication in London and Vienna (*Corr.* A140/B277). The compositions in question were the Fourth Symphony, the Overture to *Coriolan*, the Violin Concerto and its arrangement as a piano concerto, three String Quartets (Op. 59), and the Fourth Piano Concerto—in fact, a total of eight works. The offer was not taken up by Pleyel, whose reply has not survived.

In addition to his numerous compositions, Pleyel published a piano manual which enjoyed widespread success; but when Beethoven learned that the young Gerhard von Breuning* was being taught according to it, he recommended Clementi's* *Introduction to the Art of Playing on the Piano Forte* instead, which he regarded as the best of all.

(Schünemann)

Polledro, Giovanni Battista (b. Piovà, Casale Monferrato, near Turin, 10 June 1781; d. Piovà, 15 August 1853). Violinist and composer. During his career he held appointments in Turin, Bergamo (1804), Moscow, Dresden (from 1814), and finally again at Turin (1824–44). In March 1812 he performed with great success in Vienna. On 6 August of that same year he gave a concert at Karlsbad [Karlovy Vary] together with Beethoven, for the benefit of the victims of the fire which had destroyed a large part of Baden, near Vienna, on 26 July. The programme consisted of a violin sonata by Beethoven, a *Grand Trio* and a set of variations composed and played by Polledro, and a *Fantaisie* (probably an improvisation) performed by Beethoven. 'Signor Polledro helped me with the concert and played well, once he had overcome his customary nervousness,' Beethoven informed Breitkopf & Härtel* on 9 August.

(Hanslick, Schwarz[5])

Potter, (Philip) Cipriani (Hambly) (b. London, 3 October 1792; d. London, 26 September 1871). Composer, pianist, and teacher; son of the flautist and violist Richard Huddleston Potter (1755–1821), a founder member of the Philharmonic Society.* By 1817 Potter was already an established pianist (he had made his public debut at a Philharmonic Society concert on 29 April of the previous year) and had begun to compose. But he decided to study composition further on the Continent, and Johann Baptist Cramer's* enthusiastic remarks about Beethoven prompted him to travel to Vienna, in the hope of making Beethoven's acquaintance and, if possible, becoming his pupil. He arrived in Vienna on 19 December 1817 and remained there until the following summer.

Beethoven received him cordially, but was unwilling to give him lessons himself and instead recommended him to study counterpoint with Emanuel Aloys Förster,* which he did. Beethoven agreed, however, to review Potter's compositions with him. Potter called on him several times and also accompanied him on his walks. They conversed mainly in Italian, which, Potter later told Thayer,* Beethoven spoke fluently. Beethoven took a liking to him and judged that he possessed a certain talent for composition (*see* his letter of 5 March 1818 to Ferdinand Ries*).

On 29 April 1836 Potter published an article in the *Musical Times* under the title 'Recollections of Beethoven, with Remarks on his Style'. In it he dismissed the popular notion that Beethoven had been a morose and ill-tempered man: 'This opinion is perfectly erroneous. He *was* irritable, passionate, and of a melancholy turn of mind—all which affectations arose from the deafness which, in his latter days, increased to an alarming extent. Opposed to these peculiarities in his temperament, he possessed a kind heart, and most acute feelings.' Potter's observations on Beethoven's compositions include the following: 'The most prominent feature in Beethoven's music is the *originality* of his ideas, even in his mode of treating a subject, and in the conduct throughout of a composition. No author is so free from the charge of *mannerism* as Beethoven.' This article was reprinted in the *Musical Times* on 1 December 1861. In the latter year Thayer had an occasion to record Potter's recollections of Beethoven. They contain much interesting information, not least Beethoven's statement that among living composers Cherubini* was his favourite, whilst he placed Handel* first among the others, and Mozart second.

Potter had a very successful career as a pianist and teacher. He gave the first performances in England of many Mozart piano concertos, as well as of Beethoven's Third Concerto (on 8 March 1824) and Fourth Concerto (on 7 March 1825). He was a member of the Philharmonic Society, and became principal of the Royal Academy of Music (1832–59).

(Potter)

Preindl, Joseph (b. Marbach, Lower Austria, 30 January 1756; d. Vienna, 26 October 1823). Composer, organist, and theorist. From 1772 he held appointments as organist at various Viennese churches; in 1793 he became Kapellmeister at St Peter's, and in 1809 he succeeded his former teacher Johann Georg Albrechtsberger* as Kapellmeister at St Stephen's Cathedral. He was also a highly regarded piano teacher; among his pupils was Countess Therese Brunsvik* when she was a child.

Beethoven had some contact with Preindl, at least during his earlier years in Vienna. On 15 August 1801 Preindl was present at a musical soirée in Beethoven's rooms. But, according to Schindler,* Preindl was among the traditionalist theoreticians who never forgave Beethoven for opening his *Prometheus* Overture with a dissonant chord. Schindler is, however, probably mistaken in stating that Beethoven—who is well known for having had little patience with these musical 'die-hards'—administered countless 'whiplashings' ['Geisselhiebe'] to Preindl's composition manual *Wiener Tonschule,* for it did not appear in print until after Beethoven's death (in 1827, in an edition by Ignaz von Seyfried*). Perhaps Beethoven had seen the text in manuscript.

(Harten)

Probst, Heinrich Albert (b. Dresden, 1791; d. Leipzig, 24 May 1846). Music publisher active in Leipzig and Paris. He owned a leather goods shop in Leipzig (1817–23) before setting up as a music publisher in May 1823. While his list included numerous composers from different countries, pride of place was given to the works of Frédéric Kalkbrenner, of which more than a hundred were published between 1823 and 1839 by Probst and his successor Carl Friedrich Kistner (1797–1844). After selling the business to Kistner on 28 May 1831, Probst left Leipzig to join the Maison Pleyel* in Paris, but he later returned to Germany.

Probst was eager to publish some new works by Beethoven and was in negotiation with him throughout the year 1824. On 25 February Beethoven offered him 'Opferlied' (Op. 121b), 'Bundeslied' (Op. 122), and 'Der Kuss' (Op. 128), the Overture *Die Weihe des Hauses* (Op. 124), and the six Bagatelles for piano (Op. 126), for a combined fee of 104 gold ducats. The offer was accepted by Probst on 1 March, but for a reduced fee of 100 ducats, which was to cover also piano arrangements of the overture for two and four hands (*Corr.* B1785). Beethoven raised no objection to these modified terms. When, in due course, he notified Probst that the manuscripts were ready, Probst sent the fee to his Viennese trading partner, the leather goods store Joseph Loydl & Co., on 10 July 1824, with instructions that it be handed to Beethoven upon receipt of the music. But on 28 August Beethoven, writing from Baden, informed Probst that he would not be able to deliver the manuscripts until after his return to Vienna a week later.

In fact, he did not move back to Vienna until November, and the manuscripts remained undelivered even then. Instead, soon after his return, he offered the selfsame works to Schott's Söhne* for 130 gold ducats, in the name of his brother Nikolaus Johann,* to whom, he explained, he had ceded the rights in exchange for a loan (*Corr.* A1321/B1901). The terms were accepted by the Mainz firm on 30 November 1824 (*Corr.* B1903); yet it was not until 26 January 1825 that Beethoven supplied Probst with an explanation for not having respected their earlier arrangement. In his letter he somewhat disingenuously laid almost the entire responsibility on his brother, whose rights to the works he now disclosed to Probst for the first time. Johann, he alleged, had been offended by certain remarks made by Herr Loydl, and especially by the latter's assertion that Probst wished to have the compositions appraised before he would pay the fee; furthermore, Johann had received more advantageous offers from other publishers which had convinced him that the works had been priced too low. Beethoven claimed to have tried his best to change Johann's mind, but in vain. By way of an olive branch, he offered to sell Probst one or two of the quartets which he was then in the process of composing (i.e. those commissioned by Prince Golitsïn*). Probst did not, however, accept this new proposal, nor did anything come of Beethoven's further offer of a new quartet (presumably Op. 131) on 3 June 1826.

If Probst was unable to bring out any new works by Beethoven, he showed his evident admiration for him by publishing, over the years, a number of piano transcriptions, notably Carl Czerny's* arrangements for four hands of all the nine symphonies (1827–9). It appears, moreover, from Czerny's correspondence with Probst that the latter was in Vienna during Beethoven's final illness in 1827 and called on him together with Czerny. Whether he actually saw Beethoven is not known, but he received, as a souvenir of his visit, a metronome by Mälzel* which was then in Beethoven's possession and which Probst was to treasure for the rest of his life.

(Linnemann, Neumann[1])

Prónay (von Tót-Próna und Blatnica), Sigismund, Baron (1780–1848). In 1817 Peónay acquired a villa at Hetzendorf, then a suburb of Vienna [since 1890/2 part of the twelfth district, Meidling]. A keen botanist and horticulturist—in 1837 he would become a vice-president of the newly founded Gartenbaugesellschaft [Horticultural Society]—he laid out a splendid garden which became famous [75 Hetzendorfer Strasse]. In 1839 he sold the property to Count Dominicus Bethlen von der Iktar. The villa was demolished in 1915.

Beethoven rented some rooms in the house from 17 May until 13 August 1823. When his *Thirty-three Variations on a Waltz by Diabelli** were published in June of that year, he presented a personally inscribed copy to the baron. However, in August he suddenly decided to leave the villa and move to Baden, because, according to Schindler,* 'the baron made deep bows to him whenever they met'. Schindler links this decision with the phrase 'Humility of one man towards another—it pains me' which occurs in Beethoven's second letter to the 'Immortal Beloved'.

(Auer, Czeike, Schindler[1], Smolle)

Punto, Giovanni [real name: Stich, Jan Vacláv [Johann Wenzel]] (b. Schuschitz [Zehušice, near Čáslav, Czech Republic], 28 September 1746; d. Prague, 16 February 1803). Horn virtuoso, violinist, and composer. He was a bondman of Count Johann Joseph Anton Thun-Hohenstein, a wealthy patron of music, who, recognizing his talent, arranged for him to study the horn, first with Josef Matiegka in Prague, and later with Schindelarž in Munich and Anton Joseph Hampel at Dresden. From 1763 to 1766 he played in the private orchestra which the count maintained at his palace in Prague, but subsequently he fled from

Bohemia, together with several other musicians, and to cover his tracks he Italianized his name to 'Giovanni Punto'. He was a member of the Mainz court orchestra from 1769 to 1774, and later performed as a much admired virtuoso in many of the leading European music centres. After Mozart* heard him in Paris in 1778, he informed his father that 'Punto blows magnifique' (letter of 5 April 1778), and he composed for him the horn part in the (lost) *Sinfonia concertante* for flute, oboe, horn, and bassoon (KAnh.9/297B). The well-known German conductor, theorist, and critic Joseph Fröhlich wrote in the *Allgemeine Encyclopädie* (Leipzig, 1818–89) that Punto 'was remarkable no less for the purity of his interpretation and the delicacy of his taste than for his dynamic control, variety of tone-colour, and amazing articulation'.

In the spring of 1800 Punto arrived in Vienna from Munich, where he had been greatly acclaimed. It is not known how he became acquainted with Beethoven, but the latter promised to write a piece of music for him. The resulting composition, the Sonata for horn and piano in F major (Op. 17), was given its first performance by Beethoven and Punto at the latter's concert at the Burgtheater on 18 April. Ferdinand Ries's* statement (in *Biographische Notizen*) that Beethoven only began working on it the day before the concert has been treated with some scepticism. The sonata was received so enthusiastically that it was immediately played a second time. It was probably also on the programme of a concert at which Beethoven and Punto performed together in Budapest on 7 May. (The concert formed part of the celebrations of the birthday of Alexandra Pavlovna, the former Russian grand duchess who had married Joseph Anton, palatine of Hungary, the previous year.) Yet another public performance of the sonata by Beethoven and Punto is documented on 30 January 1801, at a charity concert arranged by Christine Gerhardi* at the Grosser Redoutensaal in Vienna. The work was published by T. Mollo* & Co. in Vienna in March of that year, with a dedication to Baroness Braun.* Punto himself composed a number of horn concertos and also much chamber music featuring the horn.

(Morley/Fitzpatrick, Wegeler/Ries)

Puthon, Johann Baptist, Baron (1773/6–1839). Owner, together with his brother Baron Karl Puthon (1780–1863), of the firm J. G. Schuller & Co.; he was also a director of the Austrian Nationalbank. His wife **Antonie** (c.1782–1824) was a daughter of Baron Lilien. Beethoven's conversation books provide evidence of his acquaintance with the couple by early 1820, but their contacts very likely go back further. (Beethoven had known Johann Bihler,* who worked as tutor in their household, since 1817 at the latest.) Karl Peters* told Beethoven in late January or early February 1820 that Puthon would very much like to see him (*BKh*1/235); and shortly afterwards Karl Joseph Bernard* reminded Beethoven that he had promised to visit the baroness, adding 'she is longing to see you' (*BKh*1/244). Antonie was interested in music, and had taken piano lessons with Muzio

Clementi.* Johann Friedrich Reichardt,* who met her in 1809, thought that she was very pretty and highly cultured, and that she played the piano most agreeably. Like Beethoven, she suffered from a hearing disability.

There are more references to the Puthons in the later conversation books. An entry by Karl van Beethoven* in April 1824 indicates that Beethoven had met them (or perhaps only the baroness) at Baden the previous year (*BKh*6/24). At the same time, Karl's remark that they ought to pay the baroness another visit, as she was in a pitiful condition, shows that they had not been in contact with her very recently, for she had in fact died on 14 February 1824. It was not until September that Karl learned of her death (*see BKh*6/346).

(*ÖBL*, Reichardt)

Radicati, Felice Alessandro (b. Turin, 1775; d. Bologna, 19 March 1820). Composer and violinist, a pupil of Gaetano Pugnani. He was married to the operatic soprano Teresa Bertinotti (1776–1854). The couple travelled widely in Europe, spending, in particular, lengthy periods in Germany and Austria (1805–8), England (1810–12), and Lisbon (1812–14), before returning to Italy. They settled first at Turin and, in 1815, at Bologna where Felice became leader and director of the orchestra, as well as a professor at the Conservatoire. (The above information about their peregrinations is taken from A. Mell; F. Göthel provides somewhat different details and dates.) Radicati was highly regarded as a violinist and had some success as a composer of chamber music (especially quartets) and operas.

Thayer* relates an anecdote about Radicati which he was told in England by Samuel Appleby, a fervent admirer of Beethoven's music. Visiting Samuel's father Thomas Appleby in Manchester, Radicati had caught sight of a copy of some quartets by Beethoven. The discovery drew the following comments from him: 'Beethoven, as the world says and I myself believe, is a musical madman; this is not music. He showed it to me in manuscript, and at his request I wrote in some fingering. I said to him that he surely could not consider these compositions to be music, to which he replied: "Oh, they are not for you, but for a later age!" '

(Göthel², Mell)

Radicchi [Radichi], **Giulio** [Julius] (b. Italy, 1763; d. Vienna, 16 September 1846). Singer (tenor). He settled in Vienna in 1810. Initially he sang only in Italian opera, but later he appeared also in German works; at the première of the final version of *Fidelio* at the Kärntnertor-Theater on 23 May 1814 he sang Florestan. In addition to his operatic career, Radicchi was highly regarded as an oratorio singer, regularly taking the tenor parts in Haydn's* *Die Schöpfung* and *Die Jahreszeiten*. Some time after retiring from the stage, he gave a farewell concert on 22 March 1829.

(Wurzbach¹)

Radziwill, Antoni Henryk [Anton Heinrich], Prince (b. near Vilna [Vilnius, Lithuania], 13 June 1775; d. Berlin, 7 April 1833). Member of an old, distinguished Lithuanian family; son of Prince Michael Radziwill (1744–1831), governor of Vilna. On 17 March 1796, in Berlin, he married Princess Luise of Prussia (1770–1836), who was a sister of Prince Louis Ferdinand,* a niece of Frederick the Great, and a cousin (not, as stated in *New Grove*, a sister) of King Friedrich Wilhelm II.* In 1815 Radziwill was appointed governor of the grand duchy of Posen [Posnań] which had been created at the Congress of Vienna and formed part of Prussia; he was to hold the position until 1828. He normally spent summer and autumn at his estates in Posen or Silesia, and in winter resided in Berlin in the mansion [75 Wilhelmstrasse] which his father had presented to him and his wife as a wedding present. There Radziwill, who was a highly accomplished musician—he was an excellent cellist, guitarist, singer, and composer—regularly arranged concerts of chamber music by contemporary composers, including Beethoven. He himself frequently took part in these concerts. His own *magnum opus* was his music to Goethe's* *Faust*, which he began to write in *c*.1808 and on which he continued to work for the remainder of his life. Portions of the music were performed at the Palais Radziwill in 1816 and at Monbijou Palace in 1819. The entire composition, reportedly completed by another hand, was performed at a concert of the Berliner Singakademie in October 1835; the score was published that same year. Radziwill also composed some songs and choral pieces. He was made an honorary member of Zelter's* *Liedertafel* in 1821. (The Palais Radziwill was purchased by the state in 1876 and subsequently housed the Reichskanzlei [chancellery].)

There is no record of a meeting with Beethoven in Berlin in 1796, but when Radziwill was in Vienna for the Congress in 1814–15 he called on Beethoven, together with Karl August Varnhagen von Ense.* However, the visit did not lead to regular contact between them. Nonetheless Beethoven dedicated the English–German edition of his settings of twenty-five Scottish airs (Op. 108) to Radziwill when it was published in Vienna in 1822. (In the original edition of 1818, George Thomson* had printed the English text only.) In early February 1823 Beethoven asked Radziwill to persuade King Friedrich Wilhelm III* to subscribe to the *Missa solemnis* (*Corr.* B1558); eventually both the king and Radziwill himself were among the subscribers. By chance or design, Radziwill was in St Petersburg when the Mass received its first performance on 7 April 1824 (NS). As Prince Golitsïn* informed Beethoven, 'il en a été ravi comme moi, et comme tous les assistans'. The work was then still entirely new to Radziwill, for he was not to receive his manuscript copy until 1825, probably at the same time as a (printed) copy of the Overture *Zur Namensfeier* (Op. 115) which Beethoven dedicated to him that same year. Among other well-known composers who dedicated compositions to him were Chopin (Piano Trio in G minor, Op. 8) and Mendelssohn (Piano Quartet in C minor, Op. 1).

(Ledebur, Luise, Nowak-Romanowicz, Parthey[1], Sietz[3])

Rampl [Rampel], **Wenzel** (b. 1783 (*see BKh*4 n. 197); d. after 1830). Music copyist at the court theatre. Son of Peter Rampl, likewise a copyist at the court theatre who also frequently worked for Haydn.* Wenzel Rampl appears to have been Beethoven's most important copyist after Wenzel Schlemmer.* He evidently became well acquainted with the latter early in his life, since Schlemmer was a witness to his marriage to Anna Ettmann in 1811. Alan Tyson, who regards Rampl as the 'most plausible candidate' for the copyist he calls Beethoven's 'Copyist B', conjectures that the close similarity between 'Copyist A' (whom he tentatively identifies as Schlemmer) and 'Copyist B' may result from 'B' having been a pupil or apprentice of 'A'. Rampl is known to have done work for Schlemmer in 1822, for in February 1823 he complained that Schlemmer had only recently paid him money he had owed him for over half a year (*BKh*3/40). He may well have worked for Schlemmer on other occasions as well.

Tyson recognizes the handwriting of 'Copyist B' in a score written in 1809, in three scores of Beethoven's music dating from 1815–16, in one written in 1818, and in seven manuscripts executed between 1822 and 1826, including the presentation copy of the Ninth Symphony for King Friedrich Wilhelm III* ('almost entirely in the hand of Copyist B'). Tyson adds that this list 'could be considerably extended' and explains that the dates assigned by him to specific scores are only 'approximate'; and, in fact, the copy of *Fidelio* 'in the hand of several copyists, predominantly Copyist B', to which he ascribes the date 1823, was almost certainly not completed until May 1826 (*see BKh*9 n. 246; it is now at the Deutsche Staatsbibliothek, Berlin (Artaria 158)).

There are several references to Rampl in Beethoven's extant correspondence, the earliest in a note to Johann Baptist Pasqualati* which was probably written in 1815–16, and, more precisely, perhaps in February of the latter year (*Corr.* A678/B892). In it Beethoven asks Pasqualati to lend his score of the String Quartet in F minor (Op. 95) to Rampl for copying; however, no copy of the quartet in Rampl's handwriting has been found. The next mention of Rampl in Beethoven's correspondence does not occur until May 1823, in connection with his work on a copy of the *Diabelli Variations* (*Corr.* A1180/B1650). In the surviving conversation books his name appears for the first time in January 1823.

The only known letter from Beethoven to Rampl (undated, perhaps written in late November 1823) throws an interesting light on their relations, for in it Beethoven addresses him affectionately as 'Bestes Ramperl' and uses the familar 'Du' (*Corr.* A1335/B1753). At a later period Rampl, possibly stung by some critical remark, must have refused to struggle any more with Beethoven's notoriously difficult handwriting, for on 18 July 1825 Beethoven asked his nephew Karl* to tell Rampl, whom he wished to copy the String Quartet in A minor (Op. 132), that he now wrote 'quite differently, more legibly'. In due course Rampl produced copies of the parts of the quartet (which were sent to Prince Golitsïn*), but instead of using Beethoven's autograph for this purpose he based himself on copies previously made by Karl Holz* and Joseph Linke.*

(Tyson[7])

Rau, Sebastian (1782–1846). Tutor in the household of Baron Bernard Eskeles.* When Ignaz Moscheles* arranged in 1827 for the Philharmonic Society's* gift of £100 (equivalent to 1,000 Viennese florins) to be sent to Beethoven, Rau was asked to take charge of the sum and to pay it, in part or in full, to the composer. (Moscheles and Rau were evidently on intimate terms, for they addressed each other with the familiar 'Du'.) Rau duly called on Beethoven and, at the latter's request, he handed over the full amount to him. In expressing his deep gratitude to the society and to Moscheles in his letter of 18 March, Beethoven wrote: 'I thank the Philharmonic Society and yourself for providing me with a new friend in Herr Rau.' Rau had been much distressed to find Beethoven so ill: 'I found poor Beethoven in the most wretched condition, looking more like a skeleton than a living person,' he wrote to Moscheles on 17 March (*Corr.* B2283). (On the ultimate fate of the society's gift and on Rau's role in the discussions, *see* Philharmonic Society.*)

Frimmel (in *Beethoven-Handbuch*) and P. Nettl (in *The Beethoven Encyclopedia*) confuse Sebastian Rau with the writer Heribert Rau (1813–76) who published books about Mozart,* Weber,* and Beethoven (*Beethoven: Ein Künstlerleben, kulturhistorisch-biographisch geschildert*, Leipzig, 1859).

Razumovsky, Andrey Kyrillovich, Count [from 24 November 1814, Prince] (b. St Petersburg, 2 November 1752 (NS); d. Vienna, 23 September 1836). Diplomat; art collector and music lover; son of a wealthy Russian landowner, Field Marshal Count Kyril Grigorievitz Razumovsky (1728–1803), and his wife Catharina Ivanovna, née Narishkin (1731–77). After serving in the navy, Razumovsky became a diplomat and in 1779 took up the post of ambassador in Naples. From there he was transferred to Copenhagen (1785/6), and later to Stockholm (1786–8). In 1792 he was appointed Russian ambassador to the Austrian court, a post he held, except for a relatively brief interruption (1799–1801), until 1807. Admired for his diplomatic skills, he was later called upon to represent his country at several international meetings, including the Congress of Vienna. He continued to reside in Vienna until his death. He married twice: on 4 November 1788 Countess Maria Elisabeth Thun-Hohenstein (1764–1806), and on 10 February 1816 Countess Constanze Thürheim (1785–1867).

Having inherited great riches, he indulged to the full his love of luxury and his passion for art, music, and literature. The palatial residence which he built in Vienna [23–5 Rasumofskygasse] housed a magnificent library and a fabulous art collection. In addition, he maintained for a number of years (1808–16) his own string orchestra, consisting of Ignaz Schuppanzigh,* Ludwig Sina,* Franz Weiss,* and Joseph Linke;* he frequently took the second violin part himself. He was without doubt one of the most influential figures in the social and musical life of Vienna. His parties and musical soirées were famous; during the Congress, the palace was used by Tsar Alexander* for official receptions. But most of Razumovsky's treasures and, with them, much of his wealth literally went up in smoke when a fire destroyed a large portion of the palace in late December 1814. It was rebuilt, though on a less lavish scale, with the aid of a loan granted him by the tsar; but he never recovered from the disaster, and his last years were troubled by financial problems. The Razumovsky Quartet was dissolved soon after the fire, and Schuppanzigh left Vienna for several years in 1816.

Beethoven benefited greatly from the interest which Razumovsky took in his music from the very outset. Count Johann Karl Zinzendorf reports in his diary that Beethoven played at Razumovsky's on 23 April 1795. Razumovsky was also among the subscribers to the Trios Op. 1 published that same year. Beethoven's compositions were no doubt frequently performed at his residence, especially once the Razumovsky Quartet had been formed. At one time Razumovsky asked Beethoven to teach him musical theory and quartet composition, but Beethoven, ever reluctant to undertake tuition, recommended Emanuel Aloys Förster* in his place. In 1808 he dedicated the three String Quartets Op. 59 to Razumovsky, and the following year he dedicated the Fifth and Sixth Symphonies jointly to Razumovsky and Prince Lobkowitz.* In 1814, Razumovsky arranged for the dispatch to the prince regent in London of the manuscript score of *Wellingtons Sieg* (*see* under George IV*).

(Federhofer-Königs¹, Thürheim)

Recke, Elisabeth [Elisa] **Charlotte Constantia von der** (b. Schönberg, Courland, 1 June 1754 (NS); d. Dresden, 13 April 1833). Writer and poetess. Daughter of Count Johann Friedrich Medem (1722–85); half-sister of Dorothea, duchess of Courland (1761–1821). She married George Peter Magnus von der Recke on 20 May 1771; the couple separated in 1776 and divorced in 1781. In 1797 she moved to Germany; from 1803 until her death she lived with Christoph August Tiedge.*

Her first book of poems, a collection of hymns (*Geistliche Lieder*), appeared anonymously at Leipzig in 1780; they were provided with musical settings by Johann Adam Hiller. Her other publications included a volume of her poetry (*Gedichte*) in 1806, and a diary kept during her travels through Germany and Italy (4 vols., 1815–17). But she was probably best known for her book on Cagliostro, whose charlatanism she had experienced at first hand (*Nachricht von des berüch-tigen Cagliostro Aufenthalte in Mitau, im Jahre 1779 . . .*, Berlin, 1787).

She made Beethoven's acquaintance in the summer of 1811 at Teplitz [Teplice], where she was staying with Tiedge. In December of that year she sent him some of her poems (*see Corr.* B532). Beethoven had already, in a letter to her on

11 October, expressed the intention of setting one of them, but, as far as is known, he never did.

(Eschenhagen)

Regent's Harmonic Institution. The Institution was set up in *c*.1819 by a group of music teachers for the purpose of selling and publishing music on a cooperative basis, as well as for the performance of concerts; its premises were at the Argyll Rooms, Regent Street, London. It continued under the name 'Royal Harmonic Institution' from *c*.1820 until *c*.1825, when it was taken over by two of the teachers, William Hawes and Thomas Welsh. The latter was solely responsible for it from *c*.1828 until 1830. The institution published compositions by its members, as well as by other musicians. According to F. Kidson, it was never a success: 'From the first conception of the Royal Harmonic Institution, the thing had been an utter failure, and a fire which occurred in February, 1830, put a stop to its continuance.'

On or shortly before 19 May 1818 (*Corr.* A898/B1258), Beethoven requested Ferdinand Ries,* who was then living in London, to find a publisher for English editions of the String Quintet in C minor (Op. 104) and the Piano Sonata in B flat major (Op. 106). The quintet was published by Elizabeth Lavenu (according to Kinsky/Halm in 1820, but A. Tyson believes it may have appeared shortly after the first edition had been issued by Artaria & Co.* in Vienna in February 1819). As for the 'Hammerklavier' Sonata, it was published—soon after the first edition, issued by Artaria in September 1819—by the Regent's Harmonic Institution without opus number and in two parts, one containing the first, third, and second movements (in that order), the other consisting of the final movement, with no indication that the music came from the same composition. The institution should not, however, be condemned for taking such liberties, for it was merely following suggestions made by Beethoven himself in a letter to Ries on 19 March 1819: 'Should the sonata not be suitable for London, I could send another one; or you could omit the Largo [the slow introduction to the finale] and begin the last movement directly with the fugue; or you could have the first movement, then the Adagio [i.e. the third movement], and in third place the Scherzo [the second movement], and omit the Largo and the Allegro risoluto altogether; or you could simply use the first movement and the Scherzo together as a whole sonata.' Thus the manner in which the sonata was printed by the institution may in fact have been determined by Ries, to whom Beethoven had clearly given a free hand in the matter. (Some years later the Royal Harmonic Institution reissued the sonata, this time with an indication that the two parts together formed Op. 106.)

(Humphries/Smith, Kidson, Tyson[3])

Reicha [Rejcha], **Antoine(-Joseph)** [Antonín, Anton] (b. Prague, 26 February 1770; d. Paris, 28 May 1836). Composer, theorist, and teacher. When he was 11 he went to live at Harburg, Swabia, with his uncle Josef Reicha (1752–95) who was principal cellist in the orchestra of Prince Kraft Ernst von Oettingen-Wallerstein; in 1785 both uncle and nephew moved to Bonn, where Josef Reicha had been appointed cellist and leader of the court orchestra (in 1789 he became director of the new theatre orchestra, and in 1790 director of instrumental music and opera).

At Bonn Antoine Reicha soon became acquainted with Beethoven: 'Like Orestes and Pylades, we were constant companions during fourteen years of our youth,' he later recalled. (The 'fourteen years' evidently include the time he spent in Vienna—see below.) On 14 May 1789 both he and Beethoven enrolled at the university to attend lectures in philosophy. From 1790 Reicha, who had been taught mainly by his uncle, played the violin and flute in the court Kapelle. In 1794 he moved to Hamburg, and five years later to Paris. In the autumn of 1802 he arrived in Vienna, where he quickly contacted Beethoven: 'After a separation of eight [really: ten] years, we met again in Vienna where we discussed all the things we were doing.' (This remark, taken from Reicha's autobiographical notes, was mistakenly attributed by Frimmel to Beethoven in his *Beethoven-Handbuch*.) While in Vienna, Reicha (who was studying with Albrechtsberger* and Salieri,* saw a good deal of his old friend Beethoven, and he presumably had Beethoven in mind when he wrote to Breitkopf & Härtel* on 5 January 1804: 'I have until now (i.e. during the past fourteen months) met only one person with whom I could hold an intelligent conversation about music.' Paul Nettl's statement, in his *Beethoven Encyclopedia*, that Reicha 'was frequently mentioned in Beethoven's correspondence' is, however, something of an exaggeration. Moreover, one of the two instances he cites in support, namely a letter to Breitkopf & Härtel dated 22 January 1803 in which the writer offers the publishers some compositions by Reicha (which he describes as 'very fine'), was not written by Beethoven but by his brother Kaspar Karl,* who explained that he was making the offer at Reicha's request, 'since I have known him for a long time' (*Corr.* B125).

From 1808 until the end of his life Reicha lived in Paris. While he never achieved his ambition of gaining fame as a composer, he was highly regarded for his theoretical writings about music. He also became a much sought after teacher, whose pupils included Berlioz, Liszt,* Gounod, and César Franck; in 1818 he was appointed professor of counterpoint and fugue at the Conservatoire. According to Berlioz, Reicha spoke disparagingly of Beethoven's compositions to his pupils and made ironic remarks about the enthusiastic response which they evoked.

(Berlioz, Lütge², Prod'homme³, Simpson¹, Stone)

Reichardt, Johann Friedrich (b. Königsberg [Kaliningrad, Russia], 25 November 1752; d. Giebichenstein, near Halle, 27 June 1814). Composer and writer on music. Reichardt visited Vienna from late November 1808 until the following spring. His travel journal *Vertraute Briefe geschrieben auf einer Reise nach Wien* . . . (2 vols., Amsterdam, 1809–10) offers a host of information about musical life in Vienna, with numerous observations on prominent musicians, both amateur and professional, including several closely associated with Beethoven's works, such as Marie Bigot,* Dorothea von Ertmann,* and Ignaz Schuppanzigh.* There are also a number of laudatory comments on the works of the composer whom, more than once, he calls 'der brave [worthy] Beethoven'.

While their relations were cordial, Beethoven's attitude towards Reichardt was marked by a certain wariness. For one thing, he was clearly peeved when Reichardt undertook to set Heinrich von Collin's* libretto for *Bradamante*. For another, he became suspicious when Reichardt, on learning that he had recently been offered the post of Kapellmeister at Kassel (*see* Jérôme Bonaparte*)—a post previously held by Reichardt himself—strongly advised him not to accept it. His suspicions were strengthened by a report in the *Allgemeine musikalische Zeitung* on 22 March 1809 that it was Reichardt who had communicated to him the offer from the Westphalian court. He promptly asked Breitkopf & Härtel,* the publishers of the journal, to correct the statement in a future number: 'I was most certainly not engaged by Reichardt. On the contrary, it was the chief chamberlain of His Majesty the King of Westphalia, Count Waldburg, who arranged for the offer to be made to me, namely, of the post of first Kapellmeister of H.M. of Westphalia. This offer was made to me before Reichardt's arrival in Vienna, and he was himself, as he told me, surprised that no news of the matter had reached him. R. did all he could to dissuade me from going there. As I have, in any case, good cause to distrust Herr R.'s character and since he has perhaps, for various political reasons, even given you this information himself, I really think that I deserve to be believed more than he does' (*Corr.* A209/B375).

The *Vertraute Briefe* were generally accorded a cool reception; even in Vienna, where the myriad complimentary remarks about everybody and everything Reichardt had encountered in that city could not fail to give a certain pleasure, reviewers were critical of the fulsomeness of the praise and the general triteness of the account. As for Beethoven, he was far from impressed. 'What do you think of the silly twaddle of Reichardt's letters?', he enquired of Breitkopf & Härtel, after reading a few passages from the first volume (*Corr.* A232/B424).

(Fischer-Dieskau, Helm)

Reisser, Franz de Paula Michael (b. Vienna, 2 April 1769; d. Vienna, 7 January 1835). Teacher and writer. The son of a grocer, he studied philosophy at the university (?1785–92, 1815–17) and in 1817 obtained the degree of doctor of philosophy. He taught history and geography at a school for the emperor's guards (1794–1815), at St Anna's School (1808–15), and from 1816 until 1832 at the Polytechnisches Institut, of which he became vice-principal in 1820. In 1821–2, 1827–8, and 1834–5 he held the position of dean of the philosophical faculty at the university. He was the author of a number of textbooks on history and trade.

At Beethoven's request, Reisser assumed the co-guardianship of his nephew Karl van Beethoven* after Karl Peters* had left for Prague in April 1825 (*see* Beethoven's letter to Joseph Karl Bernard* of 10 June 1825). In May 1825 Reisser borrowed the score of the *Missa solemnis* in order to have it copied; it was still in his possession in November when Beethoven, who was then making plans for some concerts, asked for its return. Reisser laid down his co-guardianship after Karl's attempted suicide in 1826.

(*ÖBL*)

Reissig, Christian Ludwig (von) (b. Kassel, 24 July 1784; d. Steinamanger [Szombethely], Hungary, 5 December 1847). Poet. Arriving in Vienna in February 1809 while on his way to Italy, he volunteered to serve in the Austrian army against Napoleon. He was seriously wounded at the Battle of Aspern and Esslingen (21–2 May 1809), but later fought in the Peninsular War. In 1822 he was obliged, as a result of financial problems, to sell his house at Hietzing, on the outskirts of Vienna. Soon afterwards he moved to Hungary, where his fortunes reportedly improved.

In July 1809 Reissig published a collection of poems, *Blümchen der Einsamkeit* (an augmented edition appeared in 1815). It was his practice to request well-known musicians to set his verse, frequently without a fee; and between 1810 and 1826, some fifty of his poems were thus set to music by more than forty different composers, among them Gyrowetz,* Conradin Kreutzer,* Wenzel Müller, Salieri,* Ignaz von Seyfried,* Joseph Weigl,* and Zelter.* Reissig would publish the songs, sometimes without the composer's consent, and dedicate them to eminent persons who might be expected to show their appreciation in a suitable manner. When Beethoven, who set five of Reissig's poems in 1809, learned that Reissig had, without his knowledge, arranged for one of the songs, 'Lied aus der Ferne' (WoO 137), to be printed by Artaria & Co.,* he was furious, especially as he wished it to be published by Breitkopf & Härtel.* In his communications to the Leipzig publishers he railed against 'that scoundrel of a captain' and urged them to lose no time in printing the song, so as to forestall the competition. In his letter of 15 October 1810 he wrote: 'It is an abominable lie that Rittmeister Reissig has ever paid me for my compositions. I wrote them for him as a favour, out of friendship, because he was an invalid at the time and aroused my compassion.' (Despite his denial, Beethoven may have received some payment for these songs—*see Corr.* B474 n. 29.) Spurred on by Beethoven, Breitkopf & Härtel brought out 'Lied aus der Ferne' in February 1810, some five months before it appeared in Artaria's set of eighteen Reissig songs. The latter publication did, however, include the first printing of two other settings by Beethoven, 'Der Jüngling in der Fremde' (WoO 138), and 'Der Liebende' (WoO 139). The remaining two settings made in 1809, 'An den fernen Geliebten' and 'Der Zufriedene'

(Op. 75, Nos. 5 and 6), were among the *Sechs Gesänge* which Breitkopf & Härtel published in October 1810.

In view of Beethoven's fulminations against Reissig in 1810, it is somewhat surprising that he should later have set two more of his poems: 'Des Kriegers Abschied' (WoO 143) in 1814 (published by Mechetti* in June 1815 as one of *Sechs deutsche Gedichte*, a set of six songs by different composers to texts by Reissig), and 'Sehnsucht' (WoO 146) in 1815–16 (published by Artaria & Co. in June 1816 as one of *Drey deutsche Gedichte*, a collection which brought together settings of Reissig poems by Beethoven, Gyrowetz, and Seyfried).

(Deutsch[4,5])

Rellstab, (Heinrich Friedrich) Ludwig (b. Berlin, 13 April 1799; d. Berlin, 28 November 1860). Poet, novelist, and music critic. When he set out for Vienna in March 1825, his greatest wish was to meet Beethoven, for whose music he felt profound admiration. He arrived in Vienna on 30 March and, except for a short journey into Hungary, spent the next five weeks there. Thanks to a letter of introduction from Carl Friedrich Zelter,* he was very cordially received by Beethoven, whom he visited more than once. On 3 May, the day before Rellstab left Vienna, Beethoven sent him a brief farewell note in which he included a short canon to the words 'Das Schöne zu dem Guten' (WoO 203—*see* Matthisson*).

Rellstab later described his visits to Beethoven in several of his publications. The most comprehensive account is to be found in his posthumously published memoirs *Aus meinem Leben* (Berlin, 1861). Though interesting in part, it is spoilt overall by an excess of detail and a gushing style. By his own admission, the verbatim recollection of their conversations is unlikely to be completely accurate, but it presumably offers the reader the gist of what was actually said. The principal topic discussed appears to have been the choice of a suitable operatic subject for Beethoven. Rellstab, who was not without experience in the matter, having supplied the text for Bernhard Klein's *Dido* (produced in Berlin on 15 October 1823), promised to prepare a libretto for Beethoven and proposed as its subject a historical figure such as Attila, Antigone, Belisarius, or Orestes.

Some time after his visit to Vienna, Rellstab sent Beethoven copies of a number of his poems, in the evident hope that Beethoven might set them to music. He probably intended to publish these compositions in Berlin where he was a partner in the publishing house recently founded by Friedrich Laue. When the poems were returned to him by Schindler* after Beethoven's death, 'some had pencil marks in Beethoven's own hand; those were the ones he liked best and which, at the time, he had passed on to Schubert* to set, for he felt too unwell to do so himself'. It is, however, more likely that they were handed to Schubert by Schindler after Beethoven had died. Rellstab does not specify which poems he had given to Beethoven. (Schubert was to set altogether ten poems by Rellstab, all in 1828. It is worth noting that by the time he composed these ten Lieder, the text of all of them was available in print, having been published in Rellstab's *Gedichte* in 1827.)

It was Rellstab's remark that the first movement of the Piano Sonata Op. 27, No. 2, reminded him of moonlight on Lake Lucerne which led to that composition being nicknamed the 'Mondscheinsonate' [Moonlight Sonata].

(Franke, Rellstab)

Riedl von Leuenstern, Joseph (b. Vienna, 7 November 1786; d. Vienna, 30 November 1856). Art dealer, music publisher, mathematician, and civil servant. Son of Johann Michael Riedl von Leuerstern (1763–1850), a court official who became commandant of the palaces at Laxenburg, Schönbrunn, and Hetzendorf, and was ennobled in 1835.

After completing his university studies (1800–3) Riedl was employed at the Kunst- und Industrie-Comptoir,* in which he became a silent partner in 1811. When Joseph Schreyvogel* retired, he took over the firm in 1814 and ran it under his own name until 1830.

In 1816 he issued a collection of previously published Beethoven songs to poems by Goethe* and Matthisson,* to which he added, as a supplement, the first edition of the canon 'Glück zum neuen Jahr' (WoO 165). However, by then the music side of the business was becoming less important, as Riedl concentrated increasingly on the production of maps and globes. The last musical publication was a reprint, in *c*.1820, of an arrangement (originally issued by Breitkopf & Härtel* in 1812) of the Choral Fantasia, in which the orchestra was reduced to a few instruments. Riedl's stock of music was acquired by S. A. Steiner & Co.* in 1822–3, and the plates by Tobias Haslinger* in *c*.1826.

From 1821, when profits were declining, Riedl supplemented his income with the help of some work in the civil service. Eventually he obtained a modest, but stable, post in the central map department of the land registry, and in 1830 he handed in his trade licence.

(*ÖBL*, Slezak[1])

Ries, Ferdinand (bapt. Bonn, 28 November 1784; d. Frankfurt am Main, 13 January 1838). Pianist and composer; eldest son of Franz Ries.* He received his first musical instruction from his father and later studied with the cellist Bernhard Romberg.* In 1797 he spent some nine months at Arnsberg, in Westphalia, where he was supposed to learn thoroughbass and composition from a well-known organist, but instead ended up teaching the man to play the violin. He then lived at Bonn until the end of the decade, studying and composing. In 1800 he went to Munich, where he earned some money by copying music. In late 1801 or perhaps early 1802 he moved to Vienna, armed with a letter of introduction from his father to Beethoven. The precise date when he settled there is not known.

Maynard Solomon even affirms in his Beethoven biography that Ries had already previously visited Vienna in 1800. (Solomon states that, in reaching this conclusion, he is following Ries's biographer Ludwig Ueberfeldt. In actual fact, Ueberfeldt explicitly rejects the idea that Ries may have been in Vienna any earlier than the autumn of 1801.)

For the next four years Ries lived in Vienna. Beethoven accepted him as a pupil, but sent him to Johann Georg Albrechtsberger* for instruction in theory. The piano lessons no doubt varied in frequency in accordance with Beethoven's other commitments and were, in any case, presumably limited to the periods when Beethoven was living in Vienna. Yet he did not take his responsibility lightly. 'Beethoven takes more pains with me than I would ever have believed possible,' Ries wrote to Nikolaus Simrock* on 6 May 1803. 'I have three lessons a week, usually from one o'clock till half past two. I shall soon be able to play his *Sonate pathétique* in a manner that will please you, for the accuracy on which he insists passes belief' (*Corr.* B136). In addition to teaching him, Beethoven entrusted various secretarial duties to Ries and he also used him for copying music. Knowing him to be short of funds, Beethoven obtained for him the post of pianist to Count Browne* in 1802, and he secured similar employment for him with Prince Lichnowsky* in 1805. Ries made his public debut at a concert in the Augarten in 1804, on which occasion he played Beethoven's Third Piano Concerto with his own cadenza.

He left Vienna in late 1805—probably at the beginning of November—in order to return to Bonn where he was due to be conscripted into the French army. (Under the Treaty of Campo Formio of October 1797, the Austrian emperor had agreed to the cession of the left bank of the Rhine to the French.) Ries was, however, considered unsuitable for service owing to his poor eyesight. In 1806 Simrock published his two Piano Sonatas Op. 1 which Ries dedicated to Beethoven. That same year, Simrock also brought out his arrangements for piano trio of Beethoven's six String Quartets Op. 18 and of the three String Trios Op. 9; in 1807 Simrock published Ries's arrangement for string quintet and double bass, flute, and two horns *ad lib.* of Beethoven's Second Symphony. (Years later, Ries was to publish also his arrangements for string quartet of the Violin Sonata Op. 30, No. 2, and of the piano sonatas Op. 10, No. 3, Op. 28, and Op. 31, No. 3.)

Ries lived in Paris from early 1807 to the summer of 1808, but his stay there appears to have brought him little success. By late August 1808 he was once more in Vienna, and he remained there until July 1809. His relations with Beethoven were temporarily troubled by the latter's unfounded suspicions that Ries was intriguing behind his back to obtain the post of Kapellmeister at Kassel, in which he had himself been interested for a time (*see* Jérôme Bonaparte*). When the misunderstanding was cleared up, Beethoven offered to help Ries obtain the appointment, but by then it was too late. Ries spent the four years following his departure from Vienna mainly on tour, visiting Marburg, Kassel, Hamburg, Copenhagen, Stockholm, and St Petersburg, among other cities. In April 1813 he arrived in England, and there, over the next eleven years, he was to enjoy the most successful and profitable period of his career, not only as a pianist and composer, but also as a teacher. On 25 July 1814 he married a girl of French descent named Harriet Mangeon (1796–1863), by whom he had two daughters.

Ries was elected a member of the Philharmonic Society* in 1815, and from then until 1821 served as one of its directors. During his stay in London he was in frequent contact with Beethoven, for whom he acted as a faithful though unpaid agent in his dealings with publishers. The extent to which Beethoven came to rely on Ries's assistance is proved by his statement in a letter to Adolph Martin Schlesinger* on 19 July 1825 that 'since my friend Ries left England I have not sent anything there, for the correspondence and arrangements involved take up too much of my time'. On 9 June 1817 Ries conveyed to Beethoven the Philharmonic Society's invitation and terms for a visit to London the following year, but nothing ever came of the offer, even though it was repeated in later years. In 1818 Ries dedicated his Second Symphony to Beethoven. The compliment was not returned, even though in May 1823 Beethoven promised to dedicate his Ninth Symphony to Ries. The closest Ries came to actually seeing a dedication was one which Beethoven wrote to his wife on a copy of his *Diabelli Variations* on 30 April 1823. (The edition itself was dedicated to Antonie Brentano.*)

Ries did so well for himself in London that he was able to retire in July 1824 to Godesberg, near Bonn, where he bought a house belonging to his father. In 1827 he moved to Frankfurt. While he occupied no official position in the world of music—he declined invitations to head conservatoires at Liège (1826) and Brussels (1832)—he remained active. He was, in particular, closely associated from 1825 to 1837 with the Niederrheinisches Musikfest, an annual music festival established in 1817. At the 1825 festival, which was held at Aix-la-Chapelle on 22–3 May, he conducted Beethoven's Ninth Symphony and the oratorio *Christus am Ölberg*. On 9 June he informed Beethoven of the outstanding success of the two-day event and sent him a fee of 40 louis d'or. About the symphony (which he described as 'a hard nut to crack') he wrote: 'It is a work which is without its equal; had you never written another one, you would have assured your immortality by it. Where will you lead us yet??' (*Corr.* B1987).

Ries himself continued to compose until the very end of his life. His very considerable output includes operas, sacred and secular songs, chamber music, and numerous works for the piano. Nevertheless, Ries is remembered today not so much as a composer than as the co-author, with Franz Gerhard Wegeler,* of *Biographische Notizen über Ludwig van Beethoven* (Koblenz, 1838). His contribution, which occupies the major part of the book, consists of various anecdotes and recollections, as well as letters addressed to him by Beethoven. Despite a few factual errors, it is justly regarded as an invaluable and generally reliable source of information by modern Beethoven scholars. Schindler's* critical remarks were, like his attacks on some other contemporaries of Beethoven, inspired primarily by his desire to eliminate all possible rivals to his claim to be the supreme authority on Beethoven's life and works. Ries's recollections are illuminated throughout by a profound admiration for both the man and his music, and while he is not blind to certain less endearing idiosyncrasies of Beethoven's character to which he was himself at times exposed, he portrays them with tolerance and good humour. In Alan Tyson's words, his 'portrait of Beethoven in the years 1801–05 and 1808–09 is his priceless legacy to us'.

(MacArdle[13], Ries, Schindler[1], Sietz[4], Solomon[2], Tyson[12], Ueberfeldt)

Ries, Franz (Anton) (b. Bonn, 10 November 1755; d. Godesberg, 1 November 1846). Violinist; son of Johann Ries (1723–84), a trumpeter and violinist and for many years a member of the court Kapelle at Bonn; father of Ferdinand Ries.* He studied with Johann Peter Salomon,* and entered the elector's service in 1774. In 1778–80 he was in Vienna, where he had considerable success as a soloist and quartet player. Once back in Bonn, he joined the court Kapelle. A report in 1784 described him as its best violinist, and, moreover, as a person of excellent moral conduct; in 1791 he was appointed Konzertmeister.

After his return from Vienna, he is believed to have given Beethoven violin lessons, but no details or dates of his tuition are known. The two families were on friendly terms, and Ries was particularly supportive during the difficult years which preceded Beethoven's departure from Bonn. Beethoven always remembered his kindness; when Ferdinand first called on him in Vienna in 1801/2, bearing a letter from his father, Beethoven said to him: 'I cannot reply to your father just now, but write and tell him that I have not forgotten what he did when my mother died. He will be content with that.' And he readily accepted to teach Ferdinand, as his father had requested. In later years, Beethoven repeatedly took advantage of opportunities to send greetings to Franz Ries. After the occupation of Bonn by the French in 1794, Ries fell on hard times, but his fortunes appear to have improved in later years. In 1845 he attended the festivities held in Bonn to celebrate the unveiling of Beethoven's statue. Sir George Smart,* who met him there, described him in his journal as 'a very fine, agreeable old man'. On that occasion the university bestowed an honorary doctorate upon him.

Ries had married Anna Horst in 1783. They had eleven children, two of whom—Ferdinand (*see* separate article) and Hubert (1802–86), a violinist and composer—had distinguished careers in music. Another son, Joseph Franz (1792–*c*.1860), became a piano teacher and piano manufacturer in Vienna. Ries's sister Anna Maria (b. 1751), a very good soprano, was also a member of the court Kapelle (1765–94); she was married to the violinist Ferdinand Drewer.

(Braubach[5], Wegeler/Ries)

Rochlitz, (Johann) Friedrich (b. Leipzig, 12 February 1769; d. Leipzig, 16 December 1842). Writer, composer, critic, and editor. In his time he enjoyed some success with his comedies, novels, and stories, but today he is best remembered for having edited Breitkopf & Härtel's* famous journal *Allgemeine musikalische Zeitung* from 1798 (the year it was founded) until 1818; he remained a contributor until 1835. He had a very sound grounding in music, having studied composition and counterpoint with Johann Friedrich Doles, Kantor at the Thomaskirche in Leipzig; he was, moreover, himself the composer of a number of works, including the cantata *Die Vollendung des Erlösers*.

He was a fervent, though not entirely uncritical, admirer of Beethoven. By no means all the remarks which appeared in the *Allgemeine musikalische Zeitung* concerning Beethoven's works and their performance were welcomed by the composer, who held Rochlitz as its editor responsible for their insertion and did not fail, on occasion, to inform the journal's publishers of his displeasure. As a result, they thought that he was joking when, in July 1806, he followed one such complaint with the request that they convey his greetings to Rochlitz ('I hope that his animosity towards me has abated. Tell him that I am not so ignorant about foreign literature as not to know that Herr Rochlitz has written some excellent things'). Beethoven had to explain that he had been quite sincere. In fact, he had already been in direct contact with Rochlitz two years earlier, when he had politely declined to set a (still incomplete) libretto Rochlitz had sent him, on the grounds that 'Zauberopern' [magic operas] were no longer in favour in Vienna (*Corr.* A87a/B176).

Rochlitz visited Vienna from late May until early August 1822. On 2 January 1828 the *Allgemeine musikalische Zeitung* printed a letter which he had addressed jointly to his wife Henriette and Gottfried Christoph Härtel from Baden, near Vienna, on 9 July 1822. (Its text also appears in Rochlitz's *Für ruhige Stunden* (1828) and in vol. iv (1832) of *Für Freunde der Tonkunst* (1824–32)). This letter contains a detailed account of three meetings with Beethoven. At the first meeting, which probably took place at Sigmund Anton Steiner's* music shop, Rochlitz was introduced to Beethoven, very likely by Tobias Haslinger;* the second took place at a Viennese restaurant, and the third at Baden. In his Beethoven biography, Maynard Solomon dismisses Rochlitz's account of these meetings as 'almost certainly invented' and asserts that 'at best, he met the composer on only one occasion, and did not receive a hearty welcome'. These statements constitute a pithy summary of the conclusions reached by Solomon in his article 'On Beethoven's Creative Process: A Two-Part Invention', first published in *Music & Letters* in 1980 and reprinted in his *Beethoven Essays* (1988). While there are one or two evident errors in the remarks Rochlitz attributes to Beethoven, which might point to misguided efforts on his part to embroider the story, it must be stressed that Solomon's conclusions are entirely speculative and based, moreover, on a sometimes faulty or highly tendentious interpretation of the text. Thus he writes

that 'Rochlitz admitted that he approached the composer with great trepidation [because, Solomon contends, some recent observations in the *Allgemeine
musikalische Zeitung* were certain to have displeased him] through an unnamed
intermediary, and that their first meeting was a fiasco, for Beethoven spoke not a
word'. In fact, Rochlitz does not 'admit' anything of the kind (Solomon's choice
of the verb 'admit' is in itself significant); and he says not one word about feeling
apprehensive, nor did he go out of his way to find an 'intermediary', as Solomon
implies. He simply states that when he spoke about his desire to visit Beethoven
to an intimate friend of the composer (probably Haslinger), that person offered
to arrange the meeting. Furthermore, according to Rochlitz's account, Beethoven
seemed pleased to see him and, far from preserving a stiff silence, he made a few
'friendly, affable remarks'; only later, as he listened to Rochlitz's observations
without, it subsequently turned out, understanding any of them owing to his
deafness, is he said to have refrained from speaking. As for Solomon's suggestion
that Rochlitz's placing of the third meeting at Baden is evidence that it never really
occurred, because at that time 'Beethoven was spending his holiday elsewhere—
in Döbling' and did not move to Baden until later that summer, it also is open
to serious challenge, for Rochlitz never said that Beethoven was then staying at
Baden. On the contrary, he states clearly that it was Beethoven who travelled out
to Baden that day, accompanied by the aforementioned friend (?Haslinger) and
Franz Xaver Gebauer,* in order to spend a few hours with Rochlitz ('he remained
from approximately ten in the morning until six o'clock in the afternoon'). As
the text plainly indicates, it was Rochlitz, not Beethoven, who was staying at
Baden at the time; in fact, Rochlitz's aforementioned letter to his wife and Härtel
is dated 'Baden, 9 July'.

To sum up: while it is impossible to verify the accuracy of Rochlitz's account
of these meetings, there does not appear to be sufficient internal evidence to
justify the assertion that they were 'almost certainly invented'. The probability
that they did take place is, in any case, strengthened by a letter which Rochlitz
wrote to Schindler* on 18 September 1827 and from which the latter quoted in
his Beethoven biography in 1840 (i.e. at a time when Rochlitz was still alive, so its
authenticity is beyond question). The passage reproduced by Schindler contains
the following sentence: 'If during my stay in Vienna in the year 1822 I met
[Beethoven] only a few times . . . this was due solely to the affliction from which
he suffered and which made any conversation extremely difficult.' It is surely
unlikely that Rochlitz would have written this to Schindler if it had not been true.
Schindler, moreover, stated in the third edition of his biography (1860) that he
was present at two of the three meetings mentioned by Rochlitz.

Rochlitz did not give up hope that Beethoven might yet set some of his texts,
and in a letter to Haslinger in late 1822 he proposed the poem 'Der erste Ton'
as particularly suitable for the composer he called 'der herrliche Beethoven' [the
sublime Beethoven]. He was to be disappointed (as he would be again five years

later, when he offered the same poem to Schubert*). Ironically, he was to realize his desire for collaboration only after Beethoven's death, and then not in the way he had envisaged. In 1837 Haslinger issued two parallel editions of the cantata *Der glorreiche Augenblick*: one, which bore the original title, presented Aloys Weissenbach's* text (as revised, at Beethoven's request, by Joseph Karl Bernard*); the other one, entitled *Preis der Tonkunst*, carried a completely new text specially written for Haslinger by Rochlitz, the aim being evidently to make suitable for general performance in 1837 a work conceived twenty-three years earlier in honour of the Congress of Vienna. Rochlitz's name was not mentioned either on the title page or in the preface.

Despite Beethoven's irritation with certain statements published in the *Allgemeine musikalische Zeitung* under Rochlitz's editorship, one would assume that he must have formed a high opinion of his musical judgement and overall ability as a writer, if Schindler was correct in stating that Beethoven had shortly before his death expressed the wish that Rochlitz should write his biography. However, as Clemens Brenneis has persuasively argued, this was most likely an invention on Schindler's part. In the event, Rochlitz, when approached by Schindler in September 1827, declined the invitation on the grounds of his poor health. Thereupon Schindler undertook the task himself.

(Brenneis[1], Ehinger[3], Rochlitz[1-4], Solomon[1])

Röckel, Joseph (August) (b. Neunburg vorm Wald, Bavaria, 28 August 1783; d. Köthen, 19 September 1870). Tenor. In 1805, while secretary to the Bavarian chargé d'affaires at Salzburg, where he was known as a promising amateur singer, he was discovered by an agent of Baron Braun* and offered an engagement at the Theater an der Wien in Vienna. Soon after his arrival there he was taken by Sebastian Mayer* to the meeting at Prince Karl Lichnowsky's* apartment, at which the possibility of shortening the score of *Fidelio* was to be discussed. At the run-through of the opera that evening he was asked to sing the part of Florestan, and his rendition so pleased Beethoven that the role was assigned to him when the new version was produced at the Theater an der Wien on 29 March 1806. Beethoven, moreover, took a personal liking to him, and he became for a time a frequent visitor and a favourite companion during walks and at meals. He was to give an interesting account of his contacts with Beethoven in conversation and correspondence with Thayer* in 1861. Some further details can be found in Rudolph Bunge's account of a conversation with Röckel which appeared in the Leipzig periodical *Die Gartenlaube* in 1868, but not all the statements in this article are correct.

Röckel later taught at the singing school attached to the court opera. After various travels inside and outside Germany he successfully led a company which performed German opera in Paris in 1830–2; subsequently he went to London where, at the King's Theatre, he presented performances of *Fidelio*, *Der Freischütz*, and other German operas. According to Kutsch-Riemens, he was principal of a music school in New York from 1846 to 1853. After his return to Germany he lived mainly at Dresden.

His sister Elisabeth (1793–1883) married Johann Nepomuk Hummel* in 1813; his son August (1814–76), a composer and, at different times, director of music at Bamberg, Weimar, and Dresden, became a close friend of Richard Wagner.

(Bunge, Kutsch/Riemens, Sietz[5])

Rode, (Jacques) Pierre (Joseph) (b. Bordeaux, 16 February 1774; d. Château de Bourbon, near Damazon, 25 November 1830). Violinist and composer. A pupil of André-Joseph Fauvel and, from 1787, of Viotti, he made his Paris debut at the Théâtre de Monsieur in 1790; five years later he was appointed a professor at the Conservatoire. In 1800 he became solo violinist to Napoleon* Bonaparte, and from 1804 to 1808 he held a similar position under Tsar Alexander I* at St Petersburg. He toured in Europe at various times during his career; in December 1812 he arrived in Vienna. By then his skill was on the decline. Louis Spohr,* who had been thrilled by his playing ten years earlier at Brunswick, now found it wanting in several respects. Nevertheless Beethoven, perhaps at the request of Archduke Rudolph,* set about completing his Violin Sonata in G major (Op. 96) for him. In so doing, Beethoven took account, especially in the finale, of Rode's particular style, for, as he explained to the archduke (*Corr.* A392/B606), 'in the finales we like to have rather boisterous passages, but these do not appeal to Rode'. (Boris Schwarz considers that Rode's own thirteen concertos 'represent, to a greater degree than those of Viotti, the model of the French violin concerto'.)

Beethoven's new sonata was given its first performance by Rode and the archduke at an evening concert at Prince Lobkowitz's* on 29 December 1812. In reporting the event in the *Musikalische Zeitung für die oesterreichischen Staaten* (28 January 1813), Franz Glöggl* stated that 'the piano part was executed far more excellently, in a manner more closely suited to the spirit of the piece, and with greater feeling, than the part assigned to the violin'. Beethoven and Rudolph seem to have shared Glöggl's dissatisfaction with Rode's performance (*see Corr.* A402/B615). Nevertheless Rode and Rudolph played the sonata again at Lobkowitz's on 7 January 1813. It was published by S. A. Steiner & Co.* in July 1816, with a dedication to Rudolph.

(Pougin, Schwarz[6])

Romberg, Andreas Jakob (b. Vechta, near Münster, 27 April 1767; d. Gotha, 10 November 1821). Violinist. He and his cousin **Bernhard Heinrich Romberg** (b. Dinklage, Oldenburg, ?11 November 1767; d. Hamburg, 13 August 1841), a cellist, made their joint debut at Münster at the age of 7, and thereafter had largely similar careers, at least until about 1800. From 1790 until 1793 both played in the electoral orchestra at Bonn, as a result of which they must have become well acquainted with Beethoven. After leaving Bonn they joined the opera orchestra of the Ackermann Theatre at Hamburg, which they left in 1795 to undertake a lengthy concert tour of Italy. In December 1796 they gave a concert in Vienna, in which Beethoven took part. They eventually returned to Hamburg, where they lived until 1800. Later Andreas became court Kapellmeister at Gotha, whilst Bernhard held a similar appointment in Berlin (1816–19). Both were highly productive and successful composers.

In January and February 1822 Bernhard Romberg gave six concerts in Vienna together with his son Karl (1811–97), also a cellist, and his daughter Bernhardine (1803–78), who was a singer. A letter from Beethoven to Bernhard has survived, dated 12 February 1822, in which he explains that he cannot attend that day's concert owing to persistent earache. Beethoven uses the familiar 'Du', and the general tone of the letter is a very friendly one. Presumably they had already met earlier during Romberg's current visit to Vienna. One other point of contact between them may be mentioned. In the course of yet another concert tour, Bernhard visited St Petersburg in 1825. On 29 April of that year, Prince Golitsïn informed Beethoven that Bernhard would shortly take part in a performance of his 'new quartet'—i.e. Op. 127, commissioned by the prince and of which he had just received a manuscript copy (*Corr.* B1962).

(Stephenson[2,3])

Rossini, Gioachino (Antonio) (b. Pesaro, 29 February 1792; d. Paris, 13 November 1868). Composer. Invited by Domenico Barbaia, the recently appointed manager of the Kärntnertor-Theater, he arrived in Vienna in late March 1822 for what turned out to be a triumphant three-month season of his operas. The brilliant Neapolitan company imported by Barbaia for the occasion included Rossini's wife Isabella Colbran.

Schindler* asserts that Beethoven would not receive Rossini, even though the latter twice called on him—the implication being that Beethoven deliberately slighted the Italian composer. However, Schindler's assertion is contradicted by statements made by Rossini himself. What apparently happened was that Rossini was taken by Domenico Artaria* to see Beethoven, but Artaria was told that Beethoven was ill and could not receive anybody that day. Rossini was more fortunate at the second attempt. Both Eduard Hanslick, in an article in the Viennese newspaper *Neue freie Presse* on 21 July 1867 (reprinted in his book *Aus dem Concertsaal*, 1870) and Ferdinand Hiller* in *Aus dem Tonleben unserer Zeit* (Leipzig, 1868) reported that Rossini had told them that he had been presented to Beethoven by the poet Carpani.* He had been very cordially received, he assured Hanslick, but Beethoven's deafness had made conversation most difficult, and the visit had been a short one. Both accounts appear trustworthy, especially that of Hanslick who was relating a conversation which had taken place in Paris only a few days earlier, and moreover in the presence of two other persons; Hiller had spoken to Rossini at Trouville-sur-Mer in 1855.

Another writer whose testimony refutes Schindler's allegation is Edmond Michotte who accompanied Richard Wagner on his visit to Rossini in Paris in 1860. Michotte's description of the meeting, published in 1906, more than forty-five years after the event (*Souvenirs personnels: La Visite de R. Wagner à Rossini (Paris 1860)* . . .), contains a very detailed account of the conversation, apparently based on notes he had made at the time. In reply to a question from Wagner, Rossini once again credited Carpani with having introduced him to Beethoven, for whose music he had then already felt the greatest admiration. (Rossini had heard some of the quartets and piano sonatas in Italy and had attended a performance of the 'Eroica' Symphony in Vienna.) Beethoven had congratulated him on having composed *Il barbiere di Siviglia* and urged him to stick to writing *opera buffa* which was the ideal genre for Italians, whereas they were not qualified, either by temperament or musical training, to treat really dramatic subjects. (The last remark, if true, can hardly have pleased Rossini, for Beethoven had just before acknowledged that he had looked through the scores of *Tancredi*, *Otello*, and *Mosè in Egitto* which Carpani had sent him.) The visit, which was a short one, concluded with Beethoven advising Rossini, by way of a valedictory counsel, to 'write many more *Barbieri*'. But what made the greatest impression on Rossini, according to Michotte's account, was not anything Beethoven said but the sight of the wretched conditions in which he lived. These so moved Rossini that he wept after leaving Beethoven, and at a dinner at Prince Metternich's that evening he appealed to the Viennese aristocrats to provide 'the greatest genius of the age' with an income adequate for his needs. The response was cool, it being the general opinion that Beethoven, with his misanthropic and surly character, was the architect of his own misery.

The works by Rossini performed in Vienna during the 1822 season, which opened on 13 April, included, in addition to his latest opera *Zelmira* (first produced at Naples on 16 February), *La Cenerentola*, *Elisabetta, regina d'Inghilterra*, *La gazza ladra*, *Matilde di Shabran*, and *Ricciardo e Zoraide*. The Viennese audiences were generally entranced by the music, and the city was gripped by a veritable 'Rossini fever'; in consequence, this first Italian season was followed by others in subsequent years. In Beethoven's circle, not surprisingly, Rossini's operas were less warmly received. (The rather tactless advice Beethoven reportedly gave Rossini to keep away from *opera seria* has already been mentioned.) Some entries in the conversation books reflect a certain disdain for the Italian composer's music, which finds expression in the pejorative terms 'dudeln' and 'Dudelei' [literally 'tootle, 'tootling' on a woodwind instrument]. Thus Johann Baptist Bach,* who nevertheless declares that he is not an enemy of Rossini, writes in January 1823: 'When, after so much tootling, one hears once more something powerful [such as *Fidelio*], it is like a refreshing breeze in a hot and sultry atmosphere'

(*BKh*2/322). And the performance of a Rossini aria at Beethoven's concert on 23 May 1824 prompted his nephew Karl* to remark: 'A number of persons stayed away because they felt indignant at the inclusion of the [Rossini] aria . . . To you it can do no harm; except that people may be outraged that your compositions should be profaned by being placed, as it were, in the same category as Rossini's tootlings' (*BKh*6/228). The decision to make the concert, which featured performances of the Ninth Symphony and the Kyrie from the *Missa solemnis*, more attractive by adding two 'Italian' pieces, sung by members of the Italian company at the Kärntnertor-Theater, had in fact not been taken by Beethoven, but by Louis Antoine Duport,* the manager of the theatre. As a result, Beethoven's trio 'Tremate, empi, tremate' was inserted between the Overture *Die Weihe des Hauses* and the Kyrie, and the aria 'Di tanti palpiti' from Rossini's *Tancredi* was sung by the celebrated tenor Giovanni Davide between the Kyrie and the symphony. (Interestingly enough, Davide would have liked Beethoven to compose a grand aria for him for the occasion.) The disappointingly low receipts from the concert did nothing to increase Beethoven's respect for Duport's judgement, nor, one suspects, for Rossini's music. 'He can be proud', Karl told his uncle, 'that you have presented one of his arias at your concert' (*BKh*6/228). In 1825 Beethoven reportedly observed to Karl Gottlieb Freudenberg that Rossini was a talented and melodious composer whose music suited the frivolous and sensuous spirit of the times.

(Jacobs[2], Kalischer)

Rousseau, Jean-Jacques (b. Geneva, 28 June 1712; d. Ermenonville, 2 July 1778). Philosopher, writer, and composer. In 1792/3 Beethoven sketched out two different settings of Rousseau's poem 'Que le jour me dure'; in these compositions, the word 'jour' has been replaced by 'temps' (WoO 116). The first version was published in *Die Musik* in 1902, and both were printed in *Zeitschrift für Musik* in 1935. Rousseau had himself set the text to music.

Rovantini, Franz Georg (b. Ehrenbreitstein, near Koblenz, 7 May 1757; d. Bonn, 9 August 1781). Violinist; relative and teacher of Beethoven. His father Johann Konrad Rovantini, a violinist at the court of the Prince Elector of Trier at Koblenz, joined the court Kapelle at Bonn in August 1765; he died at Bonn on 21 November 1766. The Rovantini and Beethoven families were linked through marriage, for Franz Georg Rovantini's maternal grandmother, Maria Magdalena Daubach (1699–1762), and Ludwig van Beethoven's maternal grandmother, Anna Klara Keverich (1704–68), were both daughters of Jakob Wistorff [Westorff] (1667–1727) and his wife Maria Magdalena (b. 1680).

Franz Georg Rovantini was accepted into the Bonn court Kapelle in March 1771, at the age of 13. From 1773 until 1775 he studied with Johann Peter Salomon,* who was then in the service of Prince Heinrich of Prussia at Rheinsberg, but had himself previously played in the Bonn Kapelle. (His father Philipp Salomon, an oboist and violinist, was still a member of the Kapelle.) From 1778 until his death in 1781 Rovantini was a court musician at Bonn. He was on intimate terms with Beethoven's parents, as is evident from the fact that he was godfather to the two children born to them during this period, Anna Maria Franziska (23 February 1779) and Franz Georg (17 January 1781); the latter's names had evidently been chosen in Rovantini's honour. He furthermore gave the young Ludwig violin and viola lessons (*see also* Pfeifer*).

(Braubach[5], Krauthausen, Schiedermair[1], Schmidt-Görg[4])

Rudolph (Johann Joseph Rainer), Archduke (b. Florence, 8 January 1788; d. Baden, near Vienna, 24 July 1831). Patron of music and amateur composer. Youngest son of Leopold (1747–92), grand duke of Tuscany [from 1790, Emperor Leopold II], and his wife Maria Ludovica [Maria Luisa] (1745–92). He moved to Vienna when his father became emperor. Prevented by poor health from following the military career for which he was intended, he turned instead to the Church and in 1805 took minor vows. He received musical instruction from the court composer Anton Tayber and became an excellent pianist; in due course Tayber was replaced as his teacher by Beethoven. It used to be thought that the latter became his instructor as early as the winter of 1803–4, solely because of the—perhaps erroneous—statement by Schindler* that the piano part of the Triple Concerto in C major (Op. 56) was written for him. However, the fact that in 1806 Rudolph still had relatively few of Beethoven's works in his music collection, lacking notably all of the early piano sonatas and most of the sets of variations, would seem to indicate that they were not yet in close personal contact at that time.

The first formal evidence of such contact dates from 1808, in which year Beethoven dedicated his Fourth Piano Concerto to Rudolph. It is quite possible that they first met or, at any rate, became better acquainted, at the brilliant concerts given by Prince Lobkowitz,* in which Beethoven often participated and at which the archduke himself was a regular performer. Johann Friedrich Reichardt* heard him play there 'several of the most difficult compositions by Prince Louis Ferdinand* and Beethoven with great skill, accuracy, and refinement', and also had occasion to admire his performance in renditions of the same composers' 'very difficult' trios, in which Rudolph was partnered by the violinist Karl August Seidler and the cellist Anton Kraft* (*Vertraute Briefe . . .* , letters of 8 January and 1 March 1809).

Rudolph was to help Beethoven in various ways. His most celebrated and enlightened act of generosity was his (probably leading) role in the arrangement —set out in a contract ratified by the parties on 1 March 1809—under which the composer was granted an overall annuity of 4,000 florins, provided that he pledged to make his domicile in Vienna 'or some other town situated in the hereditary lands of His Austrian Imperial Majesty' (the latter part of the stipulation is usually forgotten). To this sum Rudolph undertook to contribute 1,500 florins, while Prince Lobkowitz was to pay 700 florins and Prince Kinsky* 1,800 florins. Rudolph's annuity was paid to Beethoven with scrupulous regularity; he acceded, moreover, very readily to Beethoven's request, following the financial crisis of 1811, that the annuity should be paid in the new notes of redemption ('Einlösungsscheine') at the original figure, rather than at the officially sanctioned reduced figure.

For many years, at least until late 1824, Beethoven gave Rudolph instruction in theory and composition, and at first probably also in the interpretation of his own compositions, even though, as indicated above, Rudolph was already an accomplished performer by the time the lessons are likely to have started; by 1814 he found it increasingly painful to play the piano, due to gout. While the precise date at which the instruction commenced is not known, S. Brandenburg's suggestion that Beethoven committed himself to providing it when he accepted the 1809 annuity arrangement is a persuasive one. He was to find it at times a burdensome duty, and while he appears, on the whole, to have fulfilled his obligations conscientiously, he not infrequently found good reasons and excuses to explain why he was unable to present himself at the palace on certain days. (Schnyder von Wartensee* quotes Beethoven as saying to him in 1811: 'I have only one pupil and I cannot get rid of *him*, much as I should like to.') Of course, Rudolph was away from Vienna for long periods in later years, but as soon as he returned he would summon Beethoven for regular, lengthy sessions. On 25 April 1823, Beethoven complained to Ferdinand Ries:* 'The four-week stay of the Cardinal (Archduke Rudolph) in Vienna, during which I was obliged to give him daily lessons of two and a half or even three hours, robbed me of a great deal of time. After such lessons one is scarcely capable, the next day, of thinking, let alone composing.' And in November 1824 he wrote to Schott's Söhne:* 'I must now give His Imperial Highness the Archduke Rudolph a two-hour lesson every day. This takes so much out of me that it makes me almost unfit for any other work' (*Corr.* A1321/B1901). Beethoven was careful, however, not to let his occasional exasperation show in his letters to the archduke which were almost uniformly servile and even fawning in tone.

In 1818 Rudolph composed forty variations on a theme set him by Beethoven (WoO 200). They were published by S. A. Steiner* in 1819, with a dedication to Beethoven. Among Rudolph's other compositions was a contribution to the *Diabelli* Variations*. Beethoven himself dedicated a greater number of his works to Rudolph than to any other person; nearly all of them, understandably, were written for the piano, or contained an important part for it. Mention has already been made of the dedication of the Fourth Piano Concerto to Rudolph in 1808. In 1811 Beethoven dedicated to Rudolph the Fifth Piano Concerto and the Piano Sonata in E flat major, Op. 81a. The three movements of the sonata commemorated the departure, absence, and return of the archduke who, with his family, had sought refuge from the approaching French army at Ofen [Budapest] from May 1809 to January 1810. After 1811, Beethoven was to dedicate the following further works to Rudolph: in 1814, Ignaz Moscheles's* piano arrangement of the final version of *Fidelio*; in 1816, the Violin Sonata in G major (Op. 96) and the Piano Trio in B flat major (Op. 97); in 1819, the 'Hammerklavier' Piano Sonata (Op. 106); in 1823, the Piano Sonata in C minor (Op. 111); and in 1827, the *Grosse Fuge* for string quartet (Op. 133) and his own arrangement of it for piano duet (Op. 134), as well as the *Missa solemnis* (Op. 123), a work closely associated with the archduke from its inception (see below). In addition, the canon 'Seiner kaiserlichen Hoheit ... Alles Gute, alles Schöne' (WoO 179) was written for Rudolph, as was the previously mentioned theme WoO 200 and its short parody WoO 205e.

In 1805 Rudolph was appointed coadjutor of the archbishopric of Olmütz [Olomuc, Czech Republic]. He did not claim his right to succession when Archbishop Anton Theodor von Colloredo died in 1811, but following the death on 20 January 1819 of the latter's successor, Count Maria Thaddäus Trauttmansdorff, he was elected archbishop of Olmütz on 4 June 1819 (he had been made a cardinal on 24 April). It was for Rudolph's installation as archbishop of Olmütz on 9 March 1820 that Beethoven set about composing his *Missa solemnis*; however, the work was not completed in time.

Beethoven, though the most illustrious, was by no means the only contemporary composer with whom Rudolph was in contact and who dedicated compositions to him. He assembled a splendid music collection which was housed in the archiepiscopal palace at Kremsier [Kroměříž], near Olmütz. It contained almost all the first editions of Beethoven's works from about 1805 onwards, as well as manuscripts, including some autographs. (*See also* Haslinger.*) In his will Rudolph bequeathed his collection to the Gesellschaft der Musikfreunde* in Vienna, whose 'Protektor' he had been from the outset. That society also has in its archives almost all the letters and notes which Rudolph received from Beethoven.

(Brandenburg[5], Federhofer-Königs[2], Kagan, MacArdle[10])

Rupprecht, Johann Baptist (b. Wölfelsdorf, near Glatz, Silesia [Wilkanów, near Kładzko, Poland], 24 June 1776; d. Vienna, 15 September 1846). Merchant; writer, and botanist. He arrived in Vienna in 1804 and soon ran a successful business cultivating madder. However, the adverse conditions created by the French invasion of 1809 led to the collapse of his firm, and he thereafter devoted himself to horticulture and to writing. In 1811 he bought a house and garden at Gumpendorf, near Vienna. The garden, famous especially for its regular chrysanthemum shows, attracted many visitors. As a writer, Rupprecht published articles on a wide range of subjects, as well as numerous poems, in various journals and almanacs. In 1819 he was appointed a book censor.

In 1814–15, at his request, Beethoven set his poem 'Merkenstein'. (This was the name of an old castle near Baden, of which only ruins survived.) Beethoven made two versions: one for single voice (WoO 144), which appeared in late 1815 as a supplement to I. F. Castelli's* almanac *Selam*; the other for duet (Op. 100), which was published in September 1816 by S. A. Steiner & Co.* Beethoven evidently liked the poem, for he asked Rupprecht for six more, as yet unpublished, texts (*Corr.* A553/B870), but no other settings by him of Rupprecht poems are known. In 1817 Rupprecht, who had published metrical German translations of a number of English poems in 1812, undertook to provide German texts for Beethoven's arrangements of certain Scottish songs, which had originally been published by George Thomson* and of which Beethoven had sold the non-British rights to Steiner. But nothing came of this project either, because Rupprecht failed to produce the promised translations. Beethoven probably also had Rupprecht in mind when, in his letter of 30 April 1820 to Adolph Martin Schlesinger* concerning a projected bilingual edition of twenty-five Scottish songs (Op. 108), he offered to provide a competent translator 'who has already distinguished himself in similar work, and who is quick and not too expensive'; but in the end the translation was made in Berlin by Samuel Heinrich Spiker.*

If Rupprecht does not appear to have been greatly interested in translating English texts for Beethoven, there is some indication in the conversation books that he would have liked to collaborate with Beethoven in a more ambitious project. In January 1820, a visitor, Franz Janschikh [Janschig, Janschek], made the following entry: 'Ruprecht [*sic*] has made a marvellous sketch for an opera. Its title is *Die Begründung von Pensilvanien oder die Ankunft der Pen [silvanier] in Amerika*. He was planning to give it to you to set to music' (*BKh*1/213). There is no evidence that Beethoven ever saw the libretto.

(Czeike, *ÖBL*, Pečman)

Russell, John. Author of *A Tour in Germany and Some of the Southern Provinces of the Austrian Empire, in 1820, 1821, 1822*, published anonymously in Edinburgh in 1824, and under his name in the same city in 1825; a German translation appeared in 1826. Frimmel, who misspells the surname as 'Russel' (as does P. Nettl in his *Beethoven Encyclopedia*), identifies him in his *Beethoven-Handbuch* as the 'Earl of Russel'—presumably meaning Lord John Russell, first Earl Russell (1792–1878). But that identification is almost certainly incorrect, for there is no mention of such a journey or of such a publication in the biographies of that English statesman. According to the British Library catalogue, the author of the book was an 'advocate' (i.e. lawyer), and the entry relating to him also includes the following item: 'Bill of Advocation [signed, John Russell]. Mrs. Stewart-Nicolson against H. Stewart-Nicolson, Esq. Edinburgh, 1770.' If the catalogue is correct, Russell must have been a remarkably robust old gentleman when he set out on the journeys described in the book.

There are two long chapters on Vienna, which he probably reached in late 1821. Several pages are devoted to Beethoven, but it is plain that many of Russell's remarks are not based on personal observation, but on information supplied to him by others. Nor is there any indication that he visited Beethoven, as Frimmel states; in fact, nothing in his account suggests that he ever held a conversation, oral or in writing, with Beethoven. Russell did, however, attend at least one party at which Beethoven was present and persuaded to improvise on the piano, and there may well have been other occasions when they found themselves in the same company. Russell gives a striking account of Beethoven's appearance: 'His features are strong and prominent; his eye is full of rude energy; his hair, which neither comb nor scissors seem to have visited for years, overshadows his broad brow in a quantity and confusion to which only the snakes round a Gorgon's head offer a parallel.' No less dramatic is his description of the manner in which 'the music of the man's soul passed over his countenance' while he was improvising: 'He seems to feel the bold, the commanding, and the impetuous, more than what is soothing or gentle. The muscles of the face swell, and its veins start out; the wild eye rolls doubly wild; the mouth quivers, and Beethoven looks like a wizard, overpowered by the demons whom he himself has called up.' On one occasion he heard Beethoven declare that 'he found no piano so good as those made in London'. (Nettl's account of an anecdote related by Russell, describing Beethoven's bizarre behaviour at a tavern, is far from accurate.)

Rzewuski (family). Polish aristocratic family. Of particular interest to Beethoven scholars are the following two ladies: Countess **Constantia Rzewuska**, née Princess Lubomirska (b. 1763), who had married Count Seweryn [Severin] Rzewuski (1743–1811) in *c.*1783 and was a prominent figure in Viennese society in the early nineteenth century; and her great-niece Countess **(Alexandra) Rosalia Rzewuska** (b. Paris, 3 September 1788; d. Warsaw, 1 January 1865), née Princess Lubomirska, the daughter of Prince Alexander Lubomirski (d. Vienna, 1804) and Princess Rosalia Lubomirska, née Countess Chodkiewicz (guillotined in Paris in 1794). After her father's death, Rosalia lived for some time with Constantia and her husband. On 17 August 1805 she married their son Wacław Seweryn [Wenzel Severin] (1784–1831); the couple's first child, Stanislaw, was born on 24 June 1806 (d. Cracow, 1831).

In her memoirs—later published by her great-granddaughter Giovanelli Caetani Grenier (3 vols., Rome, 1939–50)—Rosalia, who resided in Vienna at different periods in her life, devotes many pages to describing the activities of the local society. But although she is known to have been a great music lover, remarks about music and musicians are extremely rare in the memoirs. Thus the only mention of Beethoven occurs in a reference to the dramatic effect produced by *Wellingtons Sieg*. Beethoven scholars have nevertheless assigned to her an important place in the history of the composition of 'In questa tomba oscura' (WoO 133). The arietta first appeared in a collection, published by Tranquillo Mollo* in 1808, of sixty-three settings by forty-six different composers of this poem by Giuseppe

Carpani.* The publication reportedly resulted from an incident which took place at Baden, near Vienna. The Weimar periodical *Journal des Luxus und der Moden* informed its readers about it in November 1806 (a similar report may also have appeared in other periodicals): 'Countess Rzewuska improvised an air on the piano, and the poet Carpani promptly improvised words to the music.' Since then, the writer adds, the text has been set by a number of amateur and professional musicians, whose compositions Carpani was planning to publish in a collective volume. A rather similar story (but without any mention of the persons involved) is told in the 'Avvertimento degli editori' (preceding the collection) which was printed as an introduction to the musical settings and was most probably written by Carpani himself. The writer explains that several of those present liked the poem so much that they also tried their hand at setting it to music, and later a number of well-known composers were invited to do the same. The first fourteen printed settings include two by Countess Rosalia, two by Count Wenzel, one by Countess Constantia, and two by Carpani himself. Among the 'professional' composers are Carl Czerny,* Danzi, Gelinek,* Gyrowetz,* Kozeluch,* Paer,* Salieri,* Tomášek,* Vanhal, Joseph Weigl,* Zelter,* Zingarelli (who contributed no fewer than ten settings!)—and Beethoven, whose setting stands last, presumably because it was the last to be received by the editors. The settings are followed by a burlesque engraving and by a musical parody in the style of one of Lully's minuets composed by the principal editor, Johann Jakob Heckel (*see* Heckel*). These two items offended some of the composers represented in the collection and, according to Schindler,* made Beethoven determined not to participate again in a collective volume.

It seems likely that the incident took place during the summer of 1805. (Carpani stayed at Baden from July until early September that year; as far as is known, he did not visit the town in 1806.) Beethoven scholars state unanimously that it was Countess Rosalia who provided the initial musical improvisation, that the incident occurred in her salon at Baden, and that she was the 'initiator' of the entire collection; and the fact that one of her settings opens the printed collection might be regarded as justifying these assertions. Yet there are indications that the person responsible for the 'musical joke' and for the publication to which it gave rise was not Countess Rosalia, but her great-aunt and mother-in-law Constantia. It seems, after all, rather unlikely that the then 16- or 17-year-old girl had her own salon at Baden. (It has, in any case, not been established whether the incident took place before or after her marriage in August.) On the other hand, Countess Constantia was a very prominent hostess in Vienna, and Carpani was, according to Rosalia's memoirs, 'un des habitués les plus fidèles' of her salon.

Johann Friedrich Reichardt's* *Vertraute Briefe* provide further arguments for identifying the 'initiator' of the collection as Constantia rather than Rosalia. In his letter of 30 November 1808 he describes meeting Carpani and singing his own setting of 'In questa tomba oscura' to him. Carpani, he reports, 'made me sing [my composition] several times and asked me for a copy for the Polish Countess Rzewuska, who was, in fact, the person responsible for arranging that unusual collection and who had had it printed at her own expense, and who was a very charming lady and an enthusiastic music lover'. Carpani promised to present Reichardt to the countess in the near future, but it was some time before Reichardt actually made her acquaintance at a musical soirée. After being invited to dinner at her house, Reichardt writes on 20 February 1809: 'The countess [i.e. Constantia] is a delightful, cultivated, and sensitive lady who lives only for music . . . The countess and her daughter-in-law [i.e. Rosalia] are both highly musical, play and sing from music, and no doubt also compose.' From this it seems fairly clear that during his initial conversation with Reichardt Carpani had been referring to Constantia and not Rosalia. It may also be significant that Johann Jakob Heckel, who, as indicated above, acted as principal editor of the collection, was described in the official list of visitors to Baden that year as 'Kapellmeister Sr. Excellenz der Frau Gräfin Constanzia v. Rzewaska [*sic*]'. Lastly, the absence of any reference to the whole matter in Rosalia's memoirs could plausibly be regarded as an additional indication that she was not the person responsible for what must have been quite a noteworthy event at the time.

A curious link exists between Rosalia's own daughter Caliste (1810–42) and Beethoven, which is has not been possible to explain so far. She appears to have had in her possession in 1832 what is now known as the 'Wielhorsky' sketchbook (so called because when it was first described in print in 1860 it was owned by Count Mikhail Yurevich Wielhorsky). The book, which is today at the Glinka Museum for Musical Culture in Moscow, contains sketches made by Beethoven for, among other works, the Piano Sonata in E flat major (Op. 31, No. 3), the *Variations* for piano (Op. 35), the 'Eroica' Symphony, the oratorio *Christus am Ölberg*, and the 'Kreutzer' Violin Sonata. It is not known how Caliste (who married Prince Michelangelo Teano in 1840) came to acquire the book.

(Jacobs[2], Johnson/Tyson/Winter, Litschauer, *Polski słownik*, Reichardt, Rzewuska)

Sailer, Johann Michael (b. Aresing, Bavaria, 17 November 1751; d. Regensburg, 20 May 1832). Catholic theologian. He was ordained in 1775, and subsequently taught theology at the universities of Ingolstadt (1780–1) and Dillingen (1784–94). In 1799 he rejoined the University of Ingolstadt, which, in 1800, moved to Landshut; he remained on its faculty until 1821. In that year he was appointed a canon at Regensburg Cathedral, and, after holding various other ecclesiastic offices, he became bishop of Regensburg in 1829. He enjoyed a considerable reputation as a teacher and theologian, but he also had his critics within the Church who accused him of being a crypto-Protestant, of leaning towards mysticism, and even of having links with the Illuminati. In 1817 Klemens Maria Hofbauer, the influential Redemptorist priest who was active in Vienna, declared Sailer to be unsuitable for the episcopate.

When Beethoven was considering the possibility of having his nephew Karl* educated outside Vienna, principally in order to remove him from his mother's influence, he conceived the idea of entrusting him to Sailer. Upon learning that Antonie Brentano* knew Sailer, he asked her in February 1819 to write to the latter on his behalf, which she did on 22 February (*Corr.* B1289). Sailer thereupon contacted Beethoven, offering to accept Karl as a pupil at a modest fee. (Neither Beethoven's letter to Antonie, nor Sailer's to Beethoven has been preserved.) Beethoven and his advisers regarded the arrangement as an excellent solution to the problem, and the wisdom of his choice was confirmed by Don Ignatius Thomas, the provost of the Michaelerkirche in Vienna, who assured Karl Joseph Bernard* that 'nothing could be more beneficial for the boy than to spend a few years under [Professor Sailer's] supervision' (*see BKh*1/68). The boy's guardian, Mathias von Tuscher,* also agreed to the idea. Beethoven applied on 23 April 1819 for a passport for Karl, but Johanna van Beethoven* protested to the authorities against the proposal to send her son out of the country, and the application was refused on 7 May (*see* Piuk*).

(Sandberger, Schiel², Schwaiger, Taddey)

Salieri, Antonio (b. Legnago, 18 August 1750; d. Vienna, 7 May 1825). Composer and teacher. When Beethoven arrived in Vienna in 1792, Salieri was a dominant figure on its musical scene: court composer since 1774, court Kapellmeister since 1788, and vice-president of the Tonkünstler-Societät (he had been its president from 1788 until 1791); in addition, he was a highly successful operatic composer and a prominent teacher. It is not surprising then that Beethoven should have turned to him for instruction in vocal composition. He probably did not receive regular tuition, but rather took advantage of Salieri's generous habit of giving free instruction to talented young musicians and singers on a rather informal basis. (According to his biographer Ignaz Franz von Mosel,* Salieri set aside three mornings a week for this purpose in his later years.) In *Beethoven's Unterricht bei J. Haydn, Albrechtsberger und Salieri* (Leipzig, 1873), Gustav Nottebohm analysed Salieri's corrections of certain settings made by Beethoven of Italian texts. Nottebohm ascribed these settings to the period 1792–1803; but Richard A. Kramer has argued that 'Beethoven's studies with Salieri were concentrated over a few years, presumably from 1799 through 1801'. Beethoven dedicated the Violin Sonatas Op. 12 to Salieri in 1798/9. In February 1799 he published a set of variations, WoO 73, on the duettino 'La stessa, la stessima' from Salieri's opera *Falstaff* (first produced on 3 January 1799). Incidentally, it was at one of the concerts of the Tonkünstler-Societät, which were regularly conducted by Salieri between 1788 and 1818, that Beethoven made his first public appearance in Vienna as pianist and composer on 29 March 1795, playing one of his first two piano concertos. When Beethoven gave a musical soirée in his rooms on 15 August 1801, Salieri was among the guests.

Beethoven reportedly sought Salieri's advice on later occasions, even regarding *Fidelio*—which is rather surprising, since Salieri had little respect for German opera. At any rate, Anselm Hüttenbrenner* recalled in a letter to Ferdinand Luib, a Viennese writer on music, on 21 February 1858 that Salieri had told him that Beethoven had asked for his opinion on *Fidelio*. Salieri added that he had expressed some criticism and suggested several changes, but that Beethoven had ignored his recommendations—and had never visited him again. Beethoven may well have felt irritated by Salieri's comments, but the last statement seems to have been an exaggeration (see below). It is nevertheless true that, in a letter to Breitkopf & Härtel* on 7 January 1809, he went as far as describing Salieri as his enemy: 'The promoters of the widows' benefit concert [i.e. the Tonkünstler-Societät], out of hatred for me, and Herr Salieri foremost among them, played an abominable trick on me: they threatened to expel any musician who played in my concert and was a member of their society.' Beethoven was here referring to his important concert on 22 December 1808 which had clashed with one given by the society on the same day. But, as Volkmar Braunbehrens points out in his biography of Salieri, the society had for years given one of its semi-annual concerts on that day. Thus, if anyone had cause to feel vexed it was Salieri, especially since Beethoven, in addition to choosing a date traditionally favoured by the society, had tried to 'poach' some of its musicians for his own concert. In any case, Beethoven's resentment did not last long, for Ignaz Moscheles* relates, in a letter to Luib on 28 February 1858, that he had seen a piece of paper on Salieri's table in 1809 on which Beethoven had written, in large letters: 'The pupil Beethoven was here.' Perhaps Beethoven had wished to show Salieri the settings of Italian texts (Op. 82) which he subsequently offered to Breitkopf & Härtel on 4 February 1810 (some of the settings may even have originally been made while Beethoven was studying with Salieri).

There is also evidence of some later contacts. On 8 and 12 December 1813, Salieri was in charge of the canons and drums at the performances of *Wellingtons Sieg*; and on 14 February 1818 Salieri and Beethoven issued a joint declaration in the Vienna *Allgemeine musikalische Zeitung* in praise of Mälzel's metronome. After Salieri was hospitalized in October 1823, there are several references to his illness in Beethoven's conversation books, as well as to his rumoured confession of having poisoned Mozart.* Beethoven's own remarks on the subject are unfortunately not recorded. No particular significance need be attached to Beethoven's absence from Salieri's funeral; on the very day of Salieri's death (7 May 1825) he had left Vienna for Baden, enfeebled by the effects of a stomach ailment.

(Angermüller[1], Braunbehrens, Kramer[2], Nottebohm[1], Pohl[2])

Salomon, Johann Peter (bapt. Bonn, 20 February 1745; d. London, 28 November 1815). Violinist, composer, and impresario. He was a court musician at Bonn (1758–65), subsequently became music director to Frederick the Great's brother

Prince Heinrich of Prussia at the latter's residence at Rheinsberg, and in 1780/1 went to London, where he made his first public appearance at Covent Garden on 23 March 1781. Apart from several journeys to the Continent, he spent the remainder of his life in England. His fame was founded primarily on his brilliance as a violinist; but he turned increasingly to conducting and promoting concerts. In particular, he was responsible for bringing Joseph Haydn* to London in 1790–1 and 1794–5. (At a farewell dinner for Haydn held in Vienna on 14 December 1790, he reportedly offered Mozart* a similar contract for London for the following year.)

Salomon's father Philipp (before or *c.*1720–1780), an oboist and violinist, and Salomon's sisters Anna Jacobina and Anna Maria, both singers, also took an active part in the musical life at Bonn; in 1765 all three were appointed members of the court Kapelle. At a performance of Grétry's opera *Silvain* in 1771, the cast included both sisters, as well as Beethoven's grandfather and father. The contacts between the two families moreover transcended the professional level: Philipp Salomon was a witness to Johann van Beethoven's* marriage in 1767.

Beethoven met Johann Peter Salomon during some of the latter's several visits to Bonn. (In December 1790, for instance, Salomon stayed there together with Haydn during their journey to London.) On 28 February 1816 Beethoven wrote to Ferdinand Ries:* 'Salomon's death saddens me greatly. He was a noble man, whom I remember well from my childhood.' The previous June Beethoven had asked Salomon to help him find a London publisher (*Corr.* A544/B809), and Salomon had obliged by arranging for Robert Birchall* to purchase the Violin Sonata in G major (Op. 96) and the 'Archduke' Trio (Op. 97), as well as piano reductions of *Wellingtons Sieg* and the Seventh Symphony.

(Braubach[5], Unverricht[1,2])

Sauer & Leidesdorf. Firm of art dealers and music publishers, established by **Ignaz Sauer** and **Marcus (Maximilian) Leidesdorf** in July 1822. Sauer (b. Triebsch [Třebušín, Czech Republic], 1 April 1759; d. Vienna, 2 December 1833) was a composer, and also choirmaster and organist at the imperial orphanage in Vienna. Leidesdorf (b. Vienna, 5 July 1787; d. Florence, 27 September 1840) was a virtuoso pianist and a prolific composer; he had studied with Albrechtsberger,* Förster,* and Salieri.*

From the outset, the business was almost entirely run by Leidesdorf, who alone had signatory powers. It was he who represented the firm in its dealings with Beethoven; in one letter (*Corr.* A120/B1777) Beethoven addressed him punningly as 'Dorf des Leides' [Village of sorrow]. The firm was not responsible for the first editions of any of Beethoven's works, although it negotiated for the purchase of several compositions in 1824 which were ultimately published by Schott's Söhne* (Opp. 121b, 122, 124, 126, 128). It did, however, issue later editions of certain works. Thus it published in 1823 the four songs 'Das Geheimnis' (WoO 145),

'So oder so' (WoO 148), 'Resignation' (WoO 149), and 'Abendlied unterm gestirten Himmel' (WoO 150) under the overall title of *Vier deutsche Gedichte*. It also brought out editions of the Piano Sonatas Opp. 110–11 and of the Bagatelles Op. 119. At one time Leidesdorf drew up a plan for a collective edition of Beethoven's works.

The partnership between Sauer and Leidesdorf was renewed in 1824, but finally dissolved in February 1826. The following year Leidesdorf registered a new firm in his own name, which he ran until 1833; by that time he had settled at Florence, where he taught at the Conservatoire attached to the church of Santa Croce.

(*ÖBL*, Schmutzenhofer, Slezak[4], Weinmann[3])

Sauter, Samuel Friedrich (b. Flehingen, Baden, Germany, 10 November 1766; d. Flehingen, 14 July 1846). Poet. A schoolteacher by profession, he became known for his charming, if rather naïve poems. These achieved a certain popularity in his day, but were later ridiculed by Ludwig Eichrodt and Adolph Kussmaul, who presented some of them—together with others deliberately written in the same vein by Eichrodt—in the Munich weekly *Fliegende Blätter* as the work of 'the Swabian schoolmaster Gottlieb Biedermaier [*sic*] and his friend Horatius Treuherz'. Sauter was thus posthumously associated with the coining of the term 'Biedermeier' and its pejorative connotations.

In 1803 Beethoven set Sauter's poem 'Der Wachtelschlag' (WoO 129); the song was published by the Kunst- und Industrie-Comptoir* the following year. Schubert's* setting of the same poem appeared in 1822.

(Siegert)

Schaden, Joseph Wilhelm von (b. Wallerstein, 1752; d. Munich, 29 September 1813). A lawyer active at Augsburg, he owed his title 'Hofrat' to his connection with the court of Prince Kraft Ernst von Oettingen-Wallerstein. On 4 November 1779, in Vienna, he married **Nanette** [Anna] **von Stadler** (b. Ebelsberg, near Linz, 2 June 1763; d. Regensburg, 17 January 1834), who was an illegitimate daughter of the director of the Salzburg court war department, Count Leopold Pranck. She had studied the piano with Ignaz von Beeke in Vienna and later received instruction in composition from Antonio Rosetti at Wallerstein. She was an excellent pianist and an accomplished singer. Johann Friedrich Reichardt,* who heard her play at Augsburg in 1790, asserted that her technical skill equalled that of any virtuoso. Her husband was himself a knowledgeable music lover. (The couple later divorced, and on 22 September 1803 Schaden married Friedericke Zehler (d. 1863).)

Schaden was the recipient of the earliest known letter written by Beethoven (apart from the formal letter of dedication of the Piano Sonatas WoO 47 to the Elector Maximilian Friedrich*). Beethoven made the acquaintance of the

Schadens at Wallerstein (or possibly at Augsburg) in March 1787, and he travelled in their company to Munich, where all three lodged at the hotel Zum schwarzen Adler. From Munich Beethoven continued alone to Vienna. On his return journey he visited the Schadens at Augsburg at the end of April, and on that occasion Schaden lent him 3 carolins (about 27 gulden). The purpose of Beethoven's letter, which is dated 15 September 1787, was to apologize for not having written since his departure from Augsburg. He described, in moving terms, his mother's death and what her disappearance meant to him, and went on to explain that his circumstances made it impossible for him to repay the loan at that time. (*See also* Stein (family).*)

(Panzerbieter[1], Schenk[2], Staehelin[2])

Schechner [Schechner-Waagen], **Nanette** [Anna] (b. Munich, 1806; d. 29 April 1860). Soprano. After studying at Munich and in Italy, she quickly established herself as a leading singer in both the German and Italian repertoire at the Munich opera. In 1826 she took up an engagement at the Kärntnertor-Theater in Vienna, where she made a brilliant debut as Emmeline in Joseph Weigl's* *Die Schweizerfamilie* on 22 May. Her first appearance in Italian opera occurred on 3 June, when she sang Ninetta in Rossini's* *La gazza ladra*. The Viennese audiences were enchanted with her performances. Many, including Schubert,* compared her to Anna Milder,* but Karl Holz* thought that her voice showed even greater flexibility (*BKh*9/262). Schindler* was particularly lavish in his praise: Vienna had never heard her equal before, he informed Beethoven, and if she only bore an Italian name she would be the most celebrated singer in the world (*BKh*9/295). Schechner had arrived with the reputation of being a very fine interpreter of the role of Leonore, and there was soon talk of reviving *Fidelio*, which had not been heard in Vienna for over three years. However, nothing came of that idea, and the opera would not be given there again in the composer's lifetime. (In fact, there was to be no further performance of it until 1831.) Schindler sought Beethoven's permission on more than one occasion to bring Schechner to see him, as she was very eager to make his acquaintance; but it was not until February 1827 that she finally visited him, together with her fiancé, the tenor Ludwig Cramolini.*

From May to September 1827 Schechner sang in Berlin, where she scored an equally great personal triumph. The performances began once more with *Die Schweizerfamilie*, and concluded with Gluck's *Iphigénie en Tauride*, in which she sang the title role. After hearing her as Leonore on 25 June, Ludwig Rellstab* described her performance as an 'unforgettable' operatic experience. Her 'extraordinary talent', he declared, was 'a divine gift, such as is bestowed scarcely more than once in a hundred years'.

Subsequent to her Berlin engagement, Schechner was appointed a court singer in Munich, but her career was increasingly hampered by a chest disease which eventually forced her to retire in 1835. During the final years she had appeared under the name 'Schechner-Waagen', following her marriage in 1832 to the painter Kurt Waagen.

(Clive[2], Kutsch/Riemens, Schletterer)

Schenk, Johann Baptist (b. Wiener Neustadt, 30 November 1753; d. Vienna, 29 December 1836). Composer and music teacher. He studied counterpoint and composition with Georg Christoph Wagenseil (1774–7). At the time he met Beethoven—probably in early 1793—he had already made a name for himself with his instrumental music and his stage works (but his best and most popular opera, *Der Dorfbarbier*, was not produced until 1796).

When he heard Beethoven play at the Abbé Gelinek's* lodgings, Schenk was immensely impressed, not only by his technical virtuosity, but also by the beauty of his improvisation: 'This unforgettable fantasy, in which he enthralled the ear and the heart and charmed the musical palate, still remains fully alive in my soul,' he wrote in 1830 in an autobiographical sketch which was not published until nearly a hundred years later. Schenk alleges that Beethoven became dissatisfied with the slow pace of Haydn's* tuition and he claims that he himself began to give Beethoven instruction in counterpoint after discovering numerous errors in exercises which Haydn had supposedly corrected. Henceforth, according to Schenk, Beethoven would first show his exercises to him and subsequently copy out the corrected version for Haydn, who thus saw only his pupil's handwriting, for Schenk wished to keep the matter secret. Eventually it was revealed to Haydn by Gelinek. The period of Schenk's tuition probably extended over several months and came to an end when Beethoven left for Eisenstadt in mid-June 1793. (The starting date of August 1792 given by Schenk himself is manifestly incorrect, since Beethoven did not arrive in Vienna until November of that year.)

Schenk's statements concerning his role in the musical education of the young Beethoven used to be fully accepted by the latter's biographers, but they have been challenged by a modern scholar, James Webster, who argues that Schenk exaggerated whatever help he may have given Beethoven and, more specifically, that 'the story of Schenk's having corrected Beethoven's counterpoint exercises for Haydn is most likely a pure fabrication'. Given this conclusion, it is not surprising that Webster is also sceptical about the authenticity of an anecdote related by Schindler,* which, if true, would largely bear out Schenk's claims of having played an important part in Beethoven's life. According to Schindler, he and Beethoven happened to meet Schenk one day in 1824 while walking along the Graben. Beethoven was 'overjoyed at seeing once more this old friend, from whom he had heard nothing for many years' and led him to the nearby Zum Jägerhorn restaurant. There the conversation soon turned to their association in the distant 1790s, and Beethoven expressed his profound gratitude for Schenk's kindness and broke into loud laughter at the recollection of how 'they had both deceived Papa Haydn'. Their leave-taking was moving, 'as if they were saying farewell for ever—

and, indeed, Beethoven and Schenk never saw one another again after that day'. Webster comments: 'Given Schindler's general lack of reliability . . . we can hardly accept this as sole support for Schenk's story as a whole.'

It may be noted that Eduard von Bauernfeld,* who was Schenk's pupil and later his friend, gives in his memoirs an account of Schenk's tuition of Beethoven which corresponds closely to the story told by Schenk himself. This is, however, not necessarily significant, since he had probably received his information directly from Schenk.

(Bauernfeld, Branscombe[4], Federhofer[3], Schenk[1], Schindler[1], Webster[1])

Schickh, Johann Valentin (b. Vienna, 6 January 1770; d. Badgastein, 1 August 1835). Merchant and newspaper editor. After working for many years in the textile industry at Linz, he opened a haberdashery store in Vienna in 1814. Two years later he founded the *Wiener Moden-Zeitung und Zeitschrift für Kunst, schöne Literatur und Theater*, which in June 1817 was renamed *Wiener Zeitschrift für Kunst, Literatur, Theater und Mode*. After the departure of his co-editors Wilhelm Hebenstreit* (in 1818) and Karl Joseph Bernard* (in 1820), he remained in sole charge of the journal which achieved considerable success and proved a worthy rival in the field of cultural matters to Adolf Bäuerle's *Theater-Zeitung*.

A notable feature of Schickh's periodical, which appeared three times weekly, was the publication, in the form of supplements, of engraved fashion-plates and new music, generally songs. Twelve of Schubert's* songs first appeared there, including 'Die Forelle'. In Beethoven's case, Schickh was responsible for the first publication of the songs 'Das Geheimnis', WoO 145 (29 February 1816), 'So oder so', WoO 148 (15 February 1817), 'Resignation', WoO 149 (31 March 1818), and 'Abendlied unterm gestirnten Himmel', WoO 150 (28 March 1820), and of the canon 'Edel sei der Mensch, hülfreich und gut', WoO 185 (21 June 1823). The numerous references to Schickh in the conversation books, as well as the entries in his own hand, indicate that Beethoven was in frequent contact with him in the 1820s.

After Schickh's death, the journal continued to appear until 1849 under various editors and different titles.

(*ÖBL*)

Schikaneder, Emanuel [real name: Schickeneder, Johann Joseph] (b. Straubing, 1 September 1751; d. Vienna, 21 September 1812). Dramatist, theatre director, actor, and composer. At the beginning of 1803, in his capacity of artistic director of the Theater an der Wien (then owned by Bartholomäus Zitterbarth), he engaged Beethoven who undertook to write an opera for the company. A service flat in the theatre complex was placed at his disposal. It was, however, not until November of that year that Beethoven could give his full attention to the task; but any enthusiasm he may have felt for the libretto *Vestas Feuer* which Schikaneder himself had finally provided soon evaporated, and he refused to continue with the project. On 4 January 1804 he complained in a letter to Johann Friedrich Rochlitz* that Schikaneder had made him waste half a year: 'I allowed myself to be deceived, because I was hoping that, given his well-known ability to create stage effects, he would produce something more intelligent than usual. How wrong I was! I had at least hoped that he would get someone to improve and polish the verses and the plot, but no, this conceited man could not be persuaded to do so. I have withdrawn from my arrangement with him, even though I had already composed several numbers. Imagine a Roman subject . . . and language and verses such as one might expect from Viennese "Äpfelweiber" [women apple vendors].' Beethoven added that he had now begun work on a libretto which had been adapted for him from a French text (i.e. Bouilly's* *Léonore*).

In February 1804 Zitterbarth sold the Theater an der Wien to Baron Braun,* who promptly replaced Schikaneder as artistic director with Joseph Sonnleithner;* but when Sonnleithner relinquished the post at the end of August in order to become secretary of the court theatres, Braun reappointed Schikaneder, and he held that position until the end of 1806. It was, however, (Friedrich) Sebastian Mayer,* his assistant in operatic productions, who appears to have been mainly responsible for preparing the première of *Fidelio* in November 1805; he also sang the part of Pizarro.

Vestas Feuer was set to music by Joseph Weigl,* and the opera had its première on 10 August 1805; according to A. Bauer, it achieved twenty-six further performances, the final one on 17 July 1806. As for Beethoven's preliminary work on the text, this was not entirely wasted; for as Gustav Nottebohm was the first to demonstrate, the sketch for the trio Volivia–Sartagones–Porus, with which the opening scene concludes, closely foreshadowed the original version of the great Leonore–Florestan duet 'O namenlose Freude!'

(Bauer[1], Biberhofer, Nottebohm[2], Pečman)

Schiller, (Johann Christoph) Friedrich (b. Marbach am Neckar, 10 November 1759; d. Weimar, 9 May 1805). Poet, dramatist, and philosopher. Beethoven was a great admirer of Schiller and referred to him on more than one occasion as one of his favourite poets (e.g. in a letter to Breitkopf & Härtel* on 8 August 1809). He evidently knew several of the plays and poems very well, and he quoted lines from them in speech, correspondence, and entries in friends' albums, as well as using them in canons. Carl Czerny* recalled that when Beethoven and Gyrowetz* were chosen to write music for performances of Schiller's *Wilhelm Tell* and Goethe's* *Egmont*, Beethoven would have preferred to compose for the former play, but was assigned the latter. (In actual fact, though, there was no production of *Wilhelm Tell* at the Burgtheater until 1827, so perhaps Czerny was confusing the play with a ballet of that name which is reported to have been performed in Vienna in 1810, to music by Gyrowetz.)

At the same time, Beethoven was well aware of the problems which Schiller's poems present to a composer. In this connection, Czerny attributes the following statement to him: 'Schiller's poems are extremely difficult to set to music. The composer must be able to raise himself far above the poet, but who can do that in Schiller's case?' It is therefore not surprising that Beethoven made very few settings of Schiller's texts. In 1810 he wrote out a sketch for a stanza from 'Das Mädchen aus der Fremde'; in November 1813 and in March 1815 he used the final line from *Die Jungfrau von Orleans*, 'Kurz ist der Schmerz, und ewig ist die Freude!', in canons for Johann Friedrich Naue (WoO 163) and Louis Spohr* (WoO 166); on 3 May 1817 he wrote a short setting of the 'Gesang der Mönche' from *Wilhelm Tell* in Franz Sales Kandler's album (WoO 104; the piece also commemorated the sudden death, on the previous day, of Beethoven's friend Wenzel Krumpholtz*); and, finally, towering over these very modest attempts, there is the magnificent partial setting of 'An die Freude' in the last movement of the Ninth Symphony. Beethoven had long been fascinated with the poem, which was written in 1785 and first published in Schiller's periodical *Die Thalia* the following year. Schiller subsequently deleted the last strophe and chorus of the original nine strophes and nine choruses (he also slightly modified the text). It appears from a letter which Bartholomäus Ludwig Fischenich,* a professor of law at the University of Bonn, addressed to Schiller's wife Charlotte on 26 January 1793 that Beethoven was already at that time contemplating setting the poem to music, 'strophe by strophe'. He did not do so then, but the idea of making some setting of the ode recurred to him more than once during the next thirty years, before the plan finally bore fruition in the early 1820s. In the Ninth Symphony he was to use only the first three strophes and the first, third, and fourth choruses. (*See also* Sonnleithner.*)

(Kalischer, Parsons, Schünemann, Solomon[5])

Schimon, Ferdinand (b. Pest [Budapest], 6 April 1797; d. Munich, 29 August 1852). Singer (tenor) and painter. He studied painting with the younger Johann Baptist Lampi before deciding, reportedly on Franz Schubert's* advice, to make music his career. On 19 August 1820 he took the part of Palmerin at the première of Schubert's *Die Zauberharfe* at the Theater an der Wien. The following year he was engaged at the Munich court theatre, from which he retired in 1840. He appeared there in various secondary roles, such as Basilio in Mozart's* *Le nozze di Figaro*, Rodolphe in Rossini's *Guillaume Tell*, and Lorenzo in Auber's *La Muette de Portici*. On 1 July 1821 he sang Jacquino in the first Munich production of *Fidelio*.

Schimon continued to paint while pursuing his musical career, and after his retirement from the stage he devoted all his time to that art. He executed a number of portraits of royal and aristocratic persons, as well as of such well-known actors as Ferdinand Esslair and Joseph Koberwein; he also excelled at painting female subjects. His portraits of Beethoven (now at the Beethoven-Haus, Bonn) and Weber* (now at the Carl-Maria-von-Weber-Gedenkstätte, Dresden-Hosterwitz) were judged particularly good.

Schindler* states in his Beethoven biography that Schimon painted Beethoven in the autumn of 1819, that it was he himself who had introduced him to Beethoven, and that the latter, busily engaged in the composition of the *Missa solemnis*, did not grant the young artist a formal sitting, but allowed him to set up an easel next to his study. Schindler goes on to explain that since Schimon had already made a few sketches while observing Beethoven during his walks, he was able to complete the painting under those rather unfavourable conditions, except for the expression of Beethoven's eyes, which he was finally able to study when the composer invited him one day to coffee. The aforementioned date indicated by Schindler was challenged by Theodor Frimmel who, in *Beethovens äussere Erscheinung* (1905), confidently corrects it to late 1818, whereas in his *Beethoven im zeitgenössischen Bildnis* (1923) and his *Beethoven-Handbuch* (1926) he ascribes the portrait less dogmatically to 'the period 1818 to 1819'. This latter dating appears to have been generally accepted (*see*, for instance, *The Beethoven Compendium* and the article on Schimon in *ÖBL*). Unfortunately, in opting for 1818 as the correct, or at any rate a possible, date, Frimmel was basing himself on an entry by Schindler in the conversation books (*BKh1*/376–7) which has since been revealed as a forgery; it must therefore be regarded as unreliable. Moreover, if Schindler is correct in stating in the biography that Beethoven was working on the *Missa solemnis* at the time Schimon painted his portrait, it would be difficult to place that event in the year 1818, for the Mass was written for the installation of Archduke Rudolph* as archbishop of Olomuc [Olmütz], in succession to Count Maria Thaddäus Trauttmansdorff who had died on 20 January 1819. While it may have been considered a foregone conclusion that, after the count's death, the coadjutor Rudolph would be elected to succeed him and Beethoven might accordingly have started the composition of the Mass well before the formal election on 4 June 1819, it seems rather unlikely that he commenced it while the count was still alive. Perhaps Schindler, in ascribing the portrait to the autumn of 1819, is for once a trustworthy witness; or perhaps he is wrong in linking Beethoven's unwillingness to sit for Schimon to his work on the Mass. (As so often, he muddies the waters still more by asserting elsewhere in his biography that he saw Beethoven start work on the score of the Mass in the late autumn of 1818.)

Schindler appears to be on firmer ground in stating that the painting (though 'not a significant work of art') is an excellent likeness of the composer and faithfully conveys his character. (When Louis Schlösser* met Beethoven in 1823, he assured him that he would instantly have recognized him from a portrait—perhaps a copy of the above or one of the earlier sketches—which he had seen in Schimon's rooms in Munich.) Schindler proved the sincerity of his favourable judgement by using as the frontispiece of his Beethoven biography an etching made from Schimon's portrait by the Berlin engraver Eduard Eichens. Schindler had kept the portrait after Beethoven's death, and he even took it to Paris with him in 1841. In *Beethoven in Paris* he describes the excitement and reverence it inspired in members of the Conservatoire orchestra. Some knelt down before it, while others climbed on to tables and chairs to get a better view; finally, all contemplated it in utter silence for a long while. The portrait was acquired by the Königlich-Preussische Bibliothek in Berlin in 1846, at the same time as other items in Schindler's possession; before parting with it, Schindler had a copy made at Aix-la-Chapelle. Eventually the portrait entered the collection of the Beethoven-Haus.

(Frimmel[1], *ÖBL*, Schindler[1,2])

Schindler, Anton Felix (b. Meedl [Medlov, Czech Republic], near Olmütz [Olomuc], 13 June 1795; d. Bockenheim, near Frankfurt am Main, 16 January 1864). Violinist, conductor, and writer on music. Son of Joseph Schindler (1758–1835), a schoolteacher and choirmaster, who taught him to play the violin when he was still a child. He was educated at Olmütz (1811–13) and subsequently at the University of Vienna, where he studied philosophy and probably also law. He did not, however, neglect music altogether, and, by his own account, it was his participation in some amateur concerts which led to his first meeting with Beethoven in March 1814, when another musician asked him to deliver a note from Ignaz Schuppanzigh* to the composer. He spoke to Beethoven again at the concert on 11 April, at which Beethoven, Schuppanzigh, and Joseph Linke* gave the first performance of the Trio Op. 97. During the following years, he had further occasional meetings with Beethoven.

For some years from 1817 onwards Schindler worked part-time in the office of Johann Baptist Bach,* who became Beethoven's lawyer in 1819. But in late 1822 Schindler switched to a career in music, when he was appointed leader of the violins and conductor at the new Theater in der Josefstadt. It is at this time that his close association with Beethoven began. His first genuine entry in the conversation books dates from November 1822; all earlier entries, going back as far as 1819, have been identified as forgeries. Schindler soon came to assume the functions of an (unpaid) general factotum, carrying out a multitude of tasks and errands, apparently with efficiency and devotion. Yet he was never on intimate terms with Beethoven. The reason for this must lie with his character rather than with the difference in age, for Beethoven later treated his successor, the even younger Karl Holz,* with an affection he clearly never felt for Schindler. In fact, by the summer of 1823 Schindler was already out of favour: in a letter to his brother Nikolaus Johann* on 19 August, Beethoven calls him a 'miserable scoundrel' and 'a vile, contemptible creature'. The cause of his anger is not known, but it is evident from later correspondence that Schindler's rather sycophantic manner had by then become distasteful to him: 'As you must have noticed at Hetzendorf [where Beethoven had stayed in May–August 1823], I have long found this importunate hanger-on Schindler most repulsive,' he wrote to Grillparzer* in late 1823 or early1824 (*Corr.* A1242/B1759).

Beethoven nevertheless continued to use Schindler's services in various different ways, notably in the preparation of the 'grand musical concert' of 7 May 1824, at which the Ninth Symphony was first performed. But when he accused Schindler, no doubt unjustly, of cheating him over the receipts from that concert, their relations suffered a temporary break, and in 1825 Holz became his secretary. It was not until the spring of 1826 that Schindler managed to renew contact with Beethoven (but he later forged a number of entries in the conversation books relating to the intervening period). However, they did not resume their closer association until after Beethoven's return from Gneixendorf in December 1826. Thereafter Schindler was in close attendance until the end. After Beethoven's death, he took possession of the conversation books and of a quantity of letters and manuscripts. In 1846 he sold a major part of this material, to the ownership of which he had a dubious claim, to the Königlich-Preussische Bibliothek [now Staatsbibliothek] in Berlin, in exchange for a lump payment and a life annuity (*see also* Neate*); the library eventually received further items from his sister Marie.

Since 1825 Schindler had been a conductor at the Kärtnertor-Theater. In September 1827 he moved to Pest [Budapest], where Marie, a professional actress and singer, performed at the local theatre. He returned to Vienna in 1829 to teach aesthetics at the singing school attached to the Kärntnertor-Theater. In 1831 he was appointed director of music at Münster, and from 1835 he occupied a similar position at Aix-la-Chapelle. After a further stay at Münster (from 1846) he settled in 1848 at Frankfurt am Main, where he was active as a teacher and writer. From 1856 until his death he resided at nearby Bockenheim.

Schindler is best known today for two reasons: as the author of the first important biography of Beethoven, and as the man who falsified Beethoven's conversation books. The book, *Biographie von Ludwig van Beethoven*, first appeared at Münster in 1840. Two years later he published *Beethoven in Paris*. The latter volume takes its title from the first item, a record of Schindler's musical experiences during a visit to Paris in January–April 1841; but at the same time it constitutes a supplement to the biography, inasmuch as it also presents some new material, as well as a response to certain criticisms. In 1845, a further edition of the biography was published, identical with the original one, except for two annexes, of which the first offered extracts from the conversation books (including several fictitious remarks attributed to Schindler himself), while the second reproduced the text of *Beethoven in Paris*. A third, completely revised and greatly expanded, edition was issued in 1860.

Already in his lifetime, Schindler's pretentious and arrogant character and, especially, the position he arrogated to himself as the supreme authority on

Beethoven's life and on the performance of his works aroused hostility and ridicule. The most notorious reaction is that of Heinrich Heine, who, after meeting him in Paris, drew a devastating portrait of him in the *Augsburger allgemeine Zeitung* (29 April 1841), in which he described him as 'a black beanpole with a horrible white tie and a funereal expression' who presented himself everywhere as 'l'ami de Beethoven' and bored everyone to death with his fatuous chatter. (Heine even suggested, maliciously, that Schindler had the words 'L'ami de Beethoven' engraved on his visiting card.) It must be said that Schindler went out of his way to make enemies by publicly attacking, often in the most vitriolic language, anyone who disagreed with him or offered an interpretation of Beethoven's life and music contrary to the 'official' one he himself championed. One favourite target for his attacks was Liszt,* whom he branded as a 'musical vandal'. On 2 July 1845 he protested in the *Kölnische Zeitung* ('*Ad vocem* Beethoven-Fest-Polemik') against the important role assigned to Liszt at the Beethoven Festival which was shortly to take place at Bonn on the occasion of the unveiling of the composer's statue (for particulars of Liszt's participation, *see* the article devoted to him). He moreover brusquely refused an invitation from the organizing committee to be present at the festivities, adding, for good measure, that no notice was to be taken of him, should he decide to attend after all—which he did.

Schindler himself acknowledged that his biography, at any rate in the early editions, contained various errors and chronological inaccuracies. These he attributed to the fact that he had been writing mostly from memory; and even the third edition is by no means free of such blemishes. These errors pose few problems for to-day's reader, since modern research has detected and corrected most of them. More insidious, because less immediately obvious, is the personal bias which colours his portrait of certain persons, such as Karl Holz, Beethoven's brother Nikolaus Johann,* and Beethoven's nephew Karl,* towards whom he felt a strong antipathy.

On the whole, Schindler's credibility, though somewhat eroded, survived largely intact until the 1970s, when it was dealt a fatal blow by the discovery that more than 150 of his entries in the surviving conversation books had been made after Beethoven's death. The purpose of these falsifications has been shown to be essentially self-serving: to bolster his claim of having enjoyed a relationship with Beethoven that was both intimate and mutually respectful; to lend authenticity to his pronouncements concerning Beethoven's intentions regarding certain compositions; and to obtain ammunition for use in his personal feuds. As a result, scholars now hesitate to accept any of his observations unless they are supported by other evidence. (*See also* Cramer.*)

(Badura-Skoda[4], Beck/Herre[1,2], Hüffer, Klein[9], MacArdle[11], Stadlen[2,3,5])

Schlemmer, Mathias (b. *c.*1783; d. Vienna, 8 February 1827). Civil servant. Karl van Beethoven* lodged with him and his wife Rosalia (b. 1790) from early

May 1825, while attending the Polytechnisches Institut [now the Technische Hochschule, 13 Karlsplatz]. They lived in Alleegasse in the Wieden suburb, not far from the institute. Beethoven's conversation books for 1825–6 contain numerous references to the Schlemmers, especially in connection with Karl's attempted suicide; for it was Schlemmer who, after learning of his intentions and finding a loaded revolver in his room, alerted Beethoven. There are also several entries in Schlemmer's writing.

Schlemmer, Wenzel (b. Bohemia, 1760; d. Vienna, 6 August 1823). Beethoven's favourite music copyist, who himself employed a number of clerks. After his death his widow Josepha, née Seidemann (1781–1828), whom he had married in 1808 as his second wife, accepted some further orders from Beethoven.

In an important article on Beethoven's copyists published in the *Journal of the American Musicological Society* in 1970, Alan Tyson tentatively identifies Schlemmer as the 'Copyist A' (whose work he believes can be traced back as far as the year 1799). He bases this identification on a letter written by Beethoven to Hofrat János Karner, an official of Prince Nikolaus Esterházy's* household at Eisenstadt, on 22 September 1807. Together with his letter, Beethoven forwarded the bills submitted by the two persons who, between them, had been responsible for copying the Mass in C major (Op. 86) which Beethoven had composed for the prince. Portions of the letter run as follows: 'One account, in which the charge per sheet is ten kreuzer, has been presented by my own copyist, whom I am paying at the same rate when he works for me; the second account has been presented by another copyist whom I do not know and whose charges, as you can see, are higher . . . I should like the drafts to be made out in the names of the two copyists and payable in Vienna, so that each may collect the amount due to him at the Prince's palace.' Tyson assumes that the person to whom Beethoven refers as 'my own copyist' was Schlemmer, and he accordingly concludes that 'by 1807, therefore, Schlemmer and his team of clerks evidently copied regularly for Beethoven'. He goes on to speculate further, on the strength of two letters dating from 1805 (*Corr.* A108/B209 and A116/B222)—in which, however, no specific copyist is named—that Schlemmer may have been 'one of two copyists who were working regularly for Beethoven in the years 1804–1805'. Lastly, recognizing the hand of 'Copyist A' in parts of the early version of the String Quartet in F, Op. 18, No. 1, on which Beethoven inscribed a dedication to Karl Amenda* on 25 June 1799, Tyson surmises that 'Schlemmer was probably in charge of the copying, since he was responsible for the first movement and for the title-pages'.

Emily Anderson's edition of Beethoven's correspondence, which Tyson consulted for his 1970 article and which, though in English, was the most authoritative and comprehensive one then available, contained Beethoven's above-mentioned letter to Karner, but not the text of the copyists' bills which were attached to it. These bills, which also bear the copyists' subsequent endorsements confirming receipt of the payments, have now been printed in full in Sieghard Brandenburg's new German edition of the correspondence. They reveal that it was, in fact, Schlemmer who was charging the higher rate (12 kreuzer per sheet) and that, in consequence, Beethoven's 'own', regular copyist at that time was not Schlemmer, but the copyist who signed himself 'Jos. Klumpar' and who was charging only 10 kreuzer. It follows that Schlemmer was the person referred to by Beethoven as 'the copyist whom I do not know', and that, accordingly, he was not, as Tyson surmises, employed by Beethoven before 1807 and cannot therefore be associated with any of the pre-1807 copies attributed to him by Tyson. Within a few years he had, however, become Beethoven's most trusted copyist, and he was to remain so until his death. 'The greatest impediment is the illness of my copyist, for I cannot entrust my works to anyone else,' Beethoven wrote to Joseph von Varena* in March 1812, explaining the delay in dispatching certain compositions which were to be performed at a charity concert in Graz (*Corr.* A359/B564). That the copyist referred to here is indeed Schlemmer is proved by a statement signed by him, promising to complete his work by a specified date.

Schlemmer's name occurs frequently in Beethoven's letters, although Beethoven's published correspondence contains only one brief note directly addressed to him (*Corr.* A973/B1334). Among the compositions, on copies of which he or his of clerks appear to have worked are, according to Tyson, the Seventh Symphony, the 'Hammerklavier' Sonata, the *Missa solemnis*, and the *Diabelli Variations*. Towards the end of his life Schlemmer's eyesight deteriorated; but Beethoven's remark 'mein alter Copist sieht nicht mehr' in a letter to C. F. Peters* on 20 February 1823 (*Corr.* A1158/B1575) evidently signifies—if, as is probable, it refers to Schlemmer—that he could no longer see very well rather than that he was blind, as Emily Anderson translates, for it is evident from later correspondence that he was subsequently still employed by Beethoven in the copying and checking of music. His death was a considerable loss to Beethoven which added greatly to the problems he faced in his final years. On 17 December 1824 he wrote to Schott's Söhne:* 'I lack a competent copyist. The one I used to have has been in his grave these past eighteen months; on him I could rely.' And on 9 April 1825 he complained to Ferdinand Ries,* to whom he had been obliged to send a second, corrected, copy of a song because the first one had been full of errors: 'Here you have an sample of the work of the wretched copyists I have had since Schlemmer's death—one can hardly rely on a single note.'

(Tyson[7])

Schlesinger. Music publishers. The well-known Berlin firm was founded by **Adolph Martin Schlesinger** (b. Sülz, Silesia, 4 October 1769; d. Berlin, 11 October 1838) in 1810. His oldest son **Maurice** [Moritz Adolph] (b. Berlin, 30 October 1798; d. Baden-Baden, 25 February 1871) went to work in the firm when still quite young. While staying in Vienna in 1819, he was introduced to Beethoven by Tobias Haslinger* at Steiner's* music shop, and he subsequently called on him at Mödling. According to the account of his early contacts with Beethoven which Schlesinger gave to Adolph Bernhard Marx* in 1859, he endeared himself to Beethoven by sending him a dish of roast veal after Beethoven, to his great annoyance, had been unable to get one at a restaurant. In 1822, Maurice wrote to Beethoven: 'I shall always remember the hours which I had the good fortune to spend in your company. The opening bars of a canon [WoO 194] which you gave me on that occasion I revere like a holy treasure' (*Corr.* B1476).

Shortly after leaving Vienna, Maurice settled in Paris, where he was at first employed by the bookseller Bossange Père. But by 1821 he had established his own music publishing business, which, though independent, worked closely with the Berlin firm; many works were issued simultaneously by both, or appeared in Paris very soon after their publication in Berlin. In August–September 1825 Maurice once again visited Vienna. On this occasion he bought the recently completed String Quartet in A minor, Op. 132, and arranged to purchase also the next quartet which Beethoven would write (Op. 135). He furthermore attended two private performances of Op. 132 (*see also* Smart*). The second one was followed by a meal, at which about a dozen persons were present, including the four performers (Schuppanzigh,* Holz,* Weiss,* Linke*), Beethoven, his nephew Karl,* and Sir George Smart. As a souvenir of their meetings in 1825, Beethoven presented Maurice Schlesinger with the canon 'Si non per portas, per muros' (WoO 194). In 1826, the older Schlesinger made Beethoven's acquaintance during a visit to Vienna.

The following compositions by Beethoven first appeared under the Schlesinger imprint: the Piano Sonata Op. 109 (published in Berlin in November 1821 and in Paris not later than February 1822); *Schottische Lieder*, containing the English and German texts of Op. 108 (July 1822); the Piano Sonata Op. 110 (the first edition—prepared, according to Alan Tyson, in Paris—was intended for simultaneous publication in Paris and Berlin and appeared in July/August 1822); the Piano Sonata Op. 111 (the first edition—according to Tyson, likewise prepared in Paris—was published there in about April 1823, and was followed by a slightly corrected version issued in Berlin); and the String Quartets Opp. 132 and 135 (which appeared almost simultaneously in Paris and Berlin, in September 1827). As for the Bagatelles Op. 119, Tyson has argued that Maurice Schlesinger's Paris edition of 1823 is 'nothing more than a rather inaccurate reprint' of the one which Muzio Clementi* had published in London in June of that year. Finally, mention should be made of the edition of Beethoven's collected works for string trios, quartets, and quintets, which Maurice Schlesinger published in the autumn of 1827.

Given Beethoven's often quarrelsome and suspicious character, it is not surprising that his remarks about the Schlesingers were at times somewhat acerbic in nature. It is, however, clear that he valued his association with them. He had, in any case, a particular reason for feeling kindly disposed towards them (*see* Marx*).

(Bauer[3], Elvers[1], Macnutt[2], Tyson[1], Unger[3])

Schlösser, Louis (b. Darmstadt, 17 November 1800; d. Darmstadt, 17 November 1886). Composer, violinist, Kapellmeister, and teacher. From spring 1822 until May 1823 he lived in Vienna, where he studied with Joseph Mayseder,* Salieri,* and Ignaz von Seyfried.* In 1846 he became Konzertmeister of the court Kapelle at Darmstadt, and in 1858 its Kapellmeister. He wrote several operas and much orchestral and chamber music, as well as compositions for the violin.

During his stay in Vienna he met Beethoven, and many years later he published his recollections of his contacts and conversations with him (in the *Allgemeine deutsche Musik-Zeitung* in 1880 and, in a revised version, in the Hildburghausen journal *Halleluja* in 1885). His reminiscences are viewed with some caution, not to say suspicion, by scholars, especially his verbatim account of certain remarks supposedly made by Beethoven. Schlösser states that he first caught sight of Beethoven after the performance of *Fidelio* on 4 November 1822; but he did not make Beethoven's acquaintance until early the following year when the Hessian ambassador in Vienna, Baron Anton Türckheim, asked him to deliver an official letter advising Beethoven that Grand Duke Ludewig I of Hesse-Darmstadt had accepted his invitation to subscribe to the *Missa solemnis*. This was presumably the letter from the grand duke's secretary Ernst Christian Schleiermacher (*Corr.* 1584, dated 26 February 1823) to which Beethoven replied on 24 March.

Schlösser met Beethoven several more times, in Vienna and at Baden. When he left for Paris (where he received further instruction from Jean-François Le Sueur and Rodolphe Kreutzer*), Beethoven gave him letters of introduction to Cherubini* and Maurice Schlesinger,* and also presented him with a canon on the words 'Edel sei der Mensch, hülfreich und gut' (WoO 185). Altogether, Beethoven seems to have taken a liking to Schlösser and to have treated him with great kindness. 'Herr Schlösser . . . will not fail to inform you in what a cordial and friendly manner I received him as a young and talented artist,' he wrote to Schleiermacher on 2 August 1823; and to Maurice Schlesinger, on 25 February 1824: 'My greetings to Schlösser; I wish him all success. Only lack of time prevents me from writing to him myself.'

(Noack)

Schmidt, Johann Adam (b. Aub, near Würzburg, 12 October 1759; d. Vienna, 19 February 1809). Ophthalmologist, pharmacognosist, army doctor. He studied medicine at Würzburg and, after service in a military hospital, underwent further training at the Josefs-Akademie [Josefinum] in Vienna, where he qualified as a doctor of surgery in 1789. Subsequently he studied ophthalmology under the famous specialist Joseph Barth. He taught anatomy and later also pathology, therapy, and *materia medica* at the Akademie, and he was also the author of numerous scientific publications, particularly in the area of ophthalmology.

On 16 November 1801 Beethoven, who was becoming dissatisfied with his current physician, Dr Gerhard von Vering,* wrote to Franz Gerhard Wegeler* in Bonn: 'What is your opinion of Schmidt? I am not really eager to change doctors, but I believe that V[ering] is too much a "practical" physician to derive many new ideas from reading. S[chmidt] seems to me a very different person in that respect and he might, moreover, not be quite so casual. People speak of miraculous cures through *galvanism*—what do you think of it? A doctor has told me that *in Berlin* he saw a deaf and dumb child recover his hearing and also a man who had been deaf for seven years recover his. I have recently heard that *your Schmidt* is experimenting with it.' (Galvanism, named after the Italian physiologist Luigi Galvani, consists in the exposure of the affected part of the body to an electrical current.)

It is not known whether Wegeler, who had made Schmidt's acquaintance during his stay in Vienna in 1794–6 and remained in friendly contact with him after returning to Bonn, replied to Beethoven's questions, but if he did so, his response must have been positive, for Beethoven did indeed switch to Schmidt during the winter of 1801–2. There is no evidence, however, that Schmidt ever resorted to galvanism in his treatment of Beethoven's hearing difficulties, as Anton Neumayr states in *Musik und Medezin*. In any case, the pathetic Heiligenstadt Testament, written in October 1802, is proof that Schmidt was no more able to cure Beethoven's condition than his previous medical advisers. Yet the Testament also indicates that Beethoven had nonetheless a high regard for his new doctor's competence and that he had, moreover, established a warm personal relationship with him; for in expressing his gratitude to his friends, he made particular mention of Prince Karl Lichnowsky* and of Schmidt. Beethoven furthermore requested his brothers 'as soon as I am dead and if Professor Schmid [*sic*] is still alive', to ask the doctor, on his behalf, to write down a description of his ailment, to which the Testament should then be attached, 'so that the world may, as far as is possible, become reconciled with me at least after my death'. Beethoven continued to consult Schmidt at different times over the following years.

As a token of his friendship and gratitude, Beethoven dedicated to Schmidt the arrangement for piano trio (Op. 38) which he had made of the Septet Op. 20. Schmidt was an amateur violinist and his daughter played the piano. The trio was published by the Kunst- und Industrie-Comptoir* in January 1805.

(Bankl/Jesserer, Czeike, Franken, Neumayr)

Schmidt, Klamer Eberhard Karl (b. Halberstadt, 29 December 1746; d. Halberstadt, 12 November 1824). Poet and translator. He was a member of

Johann Wilhelm Ludwig Gleim's circle and, despite the considerable difference in their ages, enjoyed a close friendship with Gleim himself. Like his mentor, he wrote much anacreontic verse. Between 1769 and 1776 he published ten volumes of poetry; later he prepared a translation of Horace.

While still at Bonn, Beethoven set Schmidt's poem 'Prüfung des Küssens' to music (WoO 89). The composition was probably among those he offered Carl Friedrich Peters* in his letter of 5 June 1822; but it did not appear in print until 1888 when it was published in the supplement to the edition of his collected works issued by Breitkopf & Härtel.*

(Richter, Schürmann)

Schneider, Eulogius [really: Johann Georg] (b. Wipfeld, near Würzburg, 20 October 1756; d. Paris, 1 April 1794). Monk; political activist; poet. He entered the Franciscan monastery at Bamberg in April 1777, and was ordained at Salzburg on 23 December 1780. From 1785 to 1789 he was the court preacher of Duke Karl Eugen of Württemberg. In March 1789, by which time he had left the order and become a secular priest, he was appointed professor of literature at the University of Bonn. A fervent champion of the Enlightenment, he had almost from the beginning of his career attracted admiration, but also, increasingly, hostility and censure for his outspoken and often vitriolic attacks on certain traditional beliefs and practices of the Catholic Church. As a result, he was forced to leave Bonn in June 1791. He settled at Strasbourg, and, long an ardent supporter of the French Revolution (he was the first translator of the 'Marseillaise' into German), he became before long the leader of the German-speaking Jacobins in Alsace; in 1793 he even assumed the position of public prosecutor. Eventually, however, he was himself caught up in the shifting currents of the Reign of Terror. He was arrested and transferred to Paris, where he was tried as a counter-revolutionary, condemned, and guillotined.

In his first year at Bonn, in 1789, Schneider lectured on Greek literature; among his students was the young Beethoven, who had enrolled at the university on 14 May. Later that year Beethoven subscribed to the volume of poetry which Schneider was about to publish and which appeared early in 1790. It is quite possible that Beethoven was personally acquainted with Schneider by that time—but L. Schiedermair's argument that his presence among the subscribers actually *proves* such acquaintance is surely open to question. Nor is it certain that 'it was Schneider who was responsible for Beethoven's composition of the funeral cantata on the death of Joseph II*', as P. Nettl states in his *Beethoven Encyclopedia*.

After news of the emperor's death on 20 February 1790 had reached Bonn, the members of the *Lesegesellschaft* [Reading Society] decided to hold a commemorative ceremony on 19 March, at which Schneider, who had quickly become a prominent figure in the society, was to give the oration. Schneider then suggested that his speech should be preceded or followed by a musical composition such as a cantata, and he mentioned that a young local poet (evidently Severin Anton Averdonk*) had just that day (28 February) shown him a text which would be eminently suitable. He continued: 'All that is required, therefore, is that one of the excellent composers who are members of our society, or perhaps a composer from outside the society, should take the trouble to set the text.' Schiedermair believes that in referring to composers who were members of the *Lesegesellschaft*, Schneider 'was in the first place . . . thinking of Neefe* or Josef Reicha [Antoine Reicha's* uncle]'. He goes on to speculate that Neefe or another member of the society, such as Count Waldstein* or one of the Breunings,* then suggested that Beethoven (who was not a member) should be invited to undertake the task. And this speculation leads Schiedermair somewhat surprisingly to the conclusion that 'Beethoven was therefore the "composer from outside the society" whom Schneider had in mind'. If Beethoven's selection was indeed the result of a proposal by Neefe or Waldstein or one of the Breunings, it is difficult to see why Schneider should be given the credit for it.

(Braubach[1], Grab, Schiedermair[1])

Schneller, Julius Franz Borgias [pseud. Julius Velox] (b. Strasbourg, 3 March 1777; d. Freiburg im Breisgau, 12 May 1833). Historian, philosopher, dramatist, and poet. After studying philosophy, history, and law at the University of Freiburg, he completed his legal studies in Vienna (1796–8). He first worked as a private tutor and, in 1804–5, was employed at the censorship office. In 1804 he was introduced to Karoline Pichler, of whose circle he became a popular member; that same year he had two plays produced at the Burgtheater, the tragedy *Vitellia* and the comedy *Gefangenschaft aus Liebe*. In 1805 he was appointed an instructor in history at the Lyceum at Linz, and the following year took up a similar post at the Lyceum at Graz. He assumed an important role in the intellectual and cultural life of the latter city, where his circle included three persons listed in this dictionary: his pupil Marie Koschak [later Pachler*], on whom he exercised a considerable influence, Johann Baptist Jenger,* and Joseph von Varena.* Like the last named, he was active in arranging concerts for charitable purposes. Although he established a solid reputation as a scholar, particularly as a result of several important works on historical subjects, he was unable to obtain a teaching post in Vienna because his liberal political views displeased the authorities. In 1823 he accepted a professorship in philosophy and history at the University of Freiburg.

Schneller was very friendly with Baron Ignaz von Gleichenstein,* and may have made Beethoven's acquaintance through him. It is not known when Schneller first met Beethoven, but it was no doubt some time before he left Vienna for Linz. In a letter on 19 March 1807 he asked Gleichenstein to find out whether 'our friend Beethoven' might be interested in setting a libretto for a comic opera, which, in his view, had some merit. Beethoven's reply has not been preserved. It was from Schneller that Beethoven first heard about Marie Koschak's musical talent—at any rate, it appears almost certain that the reference, in a letter to Varena in late 1811, to a female amateur pianist in Graz 'about whom Professor Schneller spoke when he was here' was to the then 17-year-old Marie (*Corr.* A334/B531). Beethoven suggested to Varena that this amateur might be capable of taking part in a forthcoming performance of the Choral Fantasia, and Marie duly performed the piano part of that work at the concert of 22 December 1811. Apart from its reference to Marie Koschak, the letter to Varena is of some interest inasmuch as it attests to the continuation of Beethoven's direct contact with Schneller even after the latter had assumed professional responsibilities outside Vienna. There is, however, no record of any correspondence between them.

Schneller was known to be a great admirer of Beethoven's music and, like Varena, he did his best to acquaint Graz audiences with it. According to his biographer E. Münch, he particularly loved *Fidelio*, the Piano Sonata in F minor (Op. 57), and the Seventh Symphony. A concert given on 25 July 1811 to celebrate his recovery from illness included performances of the 'Pastoral' Symphony and of a quintet by Beethoven. He was reportedly working on a biography of Beethoven in 1828; but he did not complete it.

(Deutsch², Münch)

Schnorr von Carolsfeld, Ludwig Ferdinand (b. Königsberg, Prussia [Kaliningrad, Russia], 11 October 1788; d. Vienna, 13 April 1853). Painter, etcher, and lithographer; son of the well-known painter Johann Veit Schnorr von Carolsfeld (1764–1841). Probably in early 1810, he executed a set of pencil drawings—perhaps based on silhouettes—of members and friends of the Malfatti* family. In 1985, when Sieghard Brandenburg published an important study of these drawings, twelve of them were still in the possession of the descendants of Baron Ignaz von Gleichenstein* and his wife Anna, a daughter of Jakob Friedrich Malfatti. There is no doubt, however, that the original set had been larger. Among the now missing drawings is one of Beethoven; but although the original is lost, the drawing has survived in copies and photographic reproductions. Like all the subjects in the series, Beethoven is shown in profile.

(Brandenburg²)

Schnyder von Wartensee, (Franz) Xaver (b. Lucerne, 18 April 1786; d. Frankfurt am Main, 27 August 1868). Composer. In 1811 he travelled to Vienna, where, armed with a letter of introduction from Ignaz Paul Vital Troxler,* he called on Beethoven, with whom he hoped to study composition. Beethoven declined to take him on as a pupil, but offered to examine his compositions. On 17 December 1811 Schnyder wrote to his friend Hans Georg Nägeli:* 'I was most cordially received by Beethoven and have already visited him several times. He is a very strange man. His soul is filled with elevated thoughts, which, however, he is incapable of expressing other than through his music; he has little command over words . . . His whole education has been neglected and, except in his art, he is coarse, but honourable and without falsehood.' Schnyder studied with Johann Christoph Kienlen instead and, when the latter was appointed music director to Baron Zinnicq who ran a private theatre at Baden, near Vienna, Schnyder followed him there. After losing all his possessions, including his musical manuscripts, in the fire which ravaged Baden in July 1812, he returned to Lucerne. Later he taught singing at Johann Heinrich Pestalozzi's school at Yverdon (1816–17). In 1817 he moved to Frankfurt. He wrote some works for the stage, as well as orchestral music, choral compositions, and numerous songs.

Schnyder's account of his visits to Beethoven was first published by Gustav Weber in the Zurich periodical *Schweizerische Musikzeitung und Sängerblatt* in 1884, and later in Schnyder's memoirs, *Lebenserinnerungen*, in 1887. Although he did not meet Beethoven again after he left Austria in 1812, he did not entirely lose contact with him. In 1816 his friend Leonhard Ziegler delivered a letter from him to Beethoven while visiting Vienna, and the following year Beethoven returned the compliment when he sent a letter (*Corr.* A803/B1159) to Schnyder through Johann Bihler.* Lastly, Schnyder wrote to Beethoven from Frankfurt on 12 December 1826 (*Corr.* B2240). In his letter he expressed his enduring admiration for Beethoven's works, sought advice regarding the execution of certain passages in the Piano Sonata in C minor, Op. 111, and stated that he had arranged for the Frankfurt publisher E. Pichler to issue a new edition of Beethoven's own piano transcription of his music to the ballet *Die Geschöpfe des Prometheus* (this project seems to have been subsequently abandoned). According to a note made on Schnyder's letter by Schindler,* Beethoven never replied to it. In later years, Schnyder was in personal contact with Schindler after the latter had moved to Frankfurt.

(Geiser, Marretta-Schär, *SML*, Weber[1], Ziegler)

Scholl, Karl Hieronymus Nikolaus (b. Zolkiew, Galicia [now Ukraine], 8/12 January 1778; d. Vienna, 12 February 1854). Composer and flautist. He was taught singing, the violin, and the flute by his father, and later also studied the flute with Karl Kreith. In 1797 he was engaged as a flautist at the Burgtheater, and in 1813 transferred to the Kärntnertor-Theater. He wrote numerous compositions for his favourite instrument and was also sought after as a teacher. In his Beethoven biography Schindler* states that Scholl 'was Beethoven's constant instructor in the mechanics of the flute, which underwent so many changes in design during the first decades of the [nineteenth] century'.

(Wurzbach[1])

Scholz, Benedict (b. Ullersdorf, Silesia, *c.*1760; d. 1824). Violinist; from 1794 director of music at Warmbrunn [Cieplice, Poland]. He wrote a new German text for Beethoven's Mass in C major (Op. 86), which was delivered to the composer by Countess Johanna Nepomucena Schaffgotsch in May 1823 and which Beethoven considered a considerable improvement over that prepared by Christian Schreiber.* Beethoven probably had Scholz's text in mind when he wrote to Schott's Söhne on 7 May 1825: 'Someone has written an excellent German text to my Mass in C, quite different from the Leipzig one [i.e. Schreiber's, which was printed in the edition of the Mass published by Breitkopf & Härtel* in 1812]. Would you like to bring out a new edition of the Mass with the new text?' The suggestion was not taken up by Schott. Scholz's copy of the vocal score with his own German text is now at the Beethoven-Haus in Bonn.

According to Schindler,* Beethoven was so impressed by Scholz's version that he wanted him to prepare a German text for the *Missa solemnis*; but Scholz died before Beethoven could ask him.

(Schindler[1])

Schott [B. Schott's Söhne]. Firm of music publishers in Mainz, founded by Bernhard Schott (b. Eltville, 10 August 1748; d. Sandhof, near Heidesheim, 26 April 1809) and carried on under the name 'B. Schott's Söhne' by his sons Johann Andreas (1781–1840) and Johann Joseph (1782–1855). While Schott was active in the music business by 1770, the publishing house may not have been founded until 1780.

The firm's association with Beethoven goes back to 1791, when Schott published his variations on Righini's arietta 'Venni Amore', WoO 65 (*see also* Götz* and Träg*). Contacts do not appear to have been resumed until 1824 when Beethoven received a letter (now lost) expressing the firm's desire to publish some of his latest compositions; at the same time he was invited to contribute to the periodical *Cäcilia* which Schott's Söhne launched that year. In his reply of 10 March 1824 he politely declined to write for *Cäcilia*, but expressed his readiness to let the firm have his new Mass (Op. 123—'difficult though I find it to speak about myself, I nevertheless regard it as my greatest work'), a 'new grand symphony' (Op. 125), and a string quartet (evidently one of the three he was planning to compose for Prince Golitsïn).

The renewed association was to prove very fruitful. Between 1825 and 1827, Schott's Söhne published the first editions of Opp. 121b, 122–8, and 131, which, in addition to the *Missa solemnis* and the Ninth Symphony, include the Overture *Die Weihe des Hauses* and the String Quartets Opp. 127 and 131.

(Laaff, Müller/Daunton)

Schreiber, Christian (b. Eisenach, 15 April 1781; d. Ostheim, 15 August 1857). Doctor of theology, church councillor; contributor to the Leipzig *Allgemeine musikalische Zeitung*. He was entrusted by Breitkopf & Härtel* with the preparation of the German texts of *Vier Arietten und ein Duett* (Op. 82) and the Mass in C major, Op. 86. (*See also* Scholz.*)

(Schürmann)

Schreyvogel, Joseph [pseud. Thomas West, Karl August West] (b. Vienna, 27 March 1768; d. Vienna, 28 July 1832). Journalist, theatre secretary. Through his journalistic activities and in other important ways he played a prominent part in the cultural life of Vienna. In 1802 he became a partner in the Kunst- und Industrie-Comptoir,* and he was responsible for running the firm from 1807 until 1813. From 1814 to 1832 he was employed as secretary of the court theatres.

It is evident from Beethoven's correspondence that he was at various times in contact with Schreyvogel. 'Rest assured that I esteem you very highly,' he wrote to Schreyvogel on 29 November 1822 (*Corr.* A908/B1513).

(*ÖBL*)

Schröder-Devrient, Wilhelmine (b. Hamburg, 6 December 1804; d. Coburg, 26 January 1860). Soprano. Daughter of the singer and actor Friedrich Schröder (1759–1818) and the celebrated actress Sophie Schröder (1781–1868). The latter, who had previously appeared in Vienna in 1798 without making a great impression, returned there in 1815 with an outstanding reputation as a tragedienne, following highly successful engagements at Hamburg (1801–13) and Prague (1813–15). With her came her three daughters, who were all to have stage careers: Elisabeth [Betty] (1806–87) and Auguste (1810–74) as actresses, Wilhelmine above all as a singer.

Actually, Wilhelmine's first public performances in Vienna were with Friedrich Horschelt's famous children's ballet company at the Theater an der Wien in 1815–16, and from 1819 to 1821 she was engaged at the Burgtheater, where she made her acting debut on 13 October 1819 as Aricia in Schiller's* German version of Racine's *Phèdre*. She subsequently appeared with some success as Louise in *Kabale und Liebe*, Beatrice in *Die Braut von Messina* (both by Schiller), and Ophelia in Shakespeare's* *Hamlet*. However, after studying singing with Therese Grünbaum, Giulio Radicchi,* and Joseph Mozatti, she switched from drama to opera, and accordingly from the Burgtheater to the Kärntnertor-Theater. On 20 January 1821 she appeared there as Pamina in *Die Zauberflöte*. The following year was to prove of pivotal importance to her career. In March she sang Agathe in *Der Freischütz* under the direction of Weber* himself, who was reportedly delighted with her performance. Later in the year she visited Dresden, where Weber held the post of Royal Saxon Kapellmeister, and scored a great triumph as Emmeline in Weigl's* *Die Schweizerfamilie*. Finally, she sang Leonore in the new production of *Fidelio* at the Kärntnertor-Theater on 3 November. Her dramatic and impassioned performance won her universal plaudits. As the *Wiener allgemeine Theaterzeitung* reported on 9 November: 'It is not too much to say that Demoiselle Schröder not only surpassed herself, but also surpassed all the expectations of her audience.' Describing the occasion many years later, Schröder recalled that Beethoven had called on her on the day after the performance to express his gratitude and congratulations, and had even promised to write an opera for her. At the same time, she acknowledged that at 17 she had not yet been capable of doing justice, either vocally or intellectually, to all the demands of the role. It was to become one of her greatest.

In 1823 she moved to Dresden, and there, at her debut on 29 April, she triumphed once more as Leonore, in a performance conducted by Weber (on 22 July she sang the same role in Berlin). She appeared with equal success in German and Italian opera, and among other roles with which she became particularly closely identified were Donna Anna (*Don Giovanni*), Euryanthe, Norma, Romeo (in Bellini's *I Capuleti e i Montecchi*), Valentine (in Meyerbeer's* *Les Huguenots*), and Desdemona (in Rossini's* *Otello*). She also created three Wagner roles while she was at Dresden: Adriano in *Rienzi* (20 October 1842), Senta in *Der fliegende Holländer* (2 January 1843), and Venus in *Tannhäuser* (19 October 1845). While she remained principally associated with Dresden until her retirement from the stage in 1847, she also made very successful appearances in Berlin (1828), Paris (1830–2), and London (especially in 1832–3). On 18 May 1832, at the King's Theatre, she sang Leonore at the first London performance of *Fidelio*. On 19 July 1837 she took part in a concert in London which had been arranged for the purpose of raising money for the proposed Beethoven statue at Bonn; the programme included excerpts from *Fidelio*.

A most interesting account of Schröder's Leonore was given by the famous English critic Henry Chorley in his *Thirty Years' Musical Recollections* (1862). He was not greatly impressed by her vocal abilities, which, in his view, showed a lack of formal training: 'Her tones were delivered without any care, save to give them due force. Her execution was bad and heavy. There was an air of strain and spasm throughout her performances, of that struggle for victory which never conquers.' But he was deeply moved by the dramatic force of her interpretation of the role and the way she exhibited 'all her passion of by-play, in judicious interpretation of the situation'. He singled out for special praise her acting during the 'Prisoners' Chorus' and her reunion with Florestan. 'It was impossible . . . to see the eager woman as she unclosed cell after cell, and ushered its ghastly tenants into the fresh air, questioning face after face, all in vain,—without tears. Nor less earnestly wrought up was her scene in the vault, ending with her rapturous embrace of the rescued captive, for whom she had waited so long and dared so much. By no one has Madame Schroeder-Devrient been equalled in this opera.'

Schröder-Devrient was married three times: in 1823 to the actor Karl Devrient (1797–1872), in 1847 to David Oskar von Döring, an officer in the Saxon army, and in 1850 to Heinrich von Bock.

(Bab, Eisenberg, Kühner³, Lewald)

Schubert, Franz (Peter) (b. Vienna, 31 January 1797; d. Vienna, 19 November 1828). Composer. Given Schubert's profound admiration for Beethoven, it is not surprising that some of his compositions were influenced by Beethoven's music, especially in the earlier years. The question of his deliberate or unconscious musical imitation of Beethoven has been repeatedly discussed—for instance by E. Cone and N. Nettheim with regard to specific instances, and by W. Dürr within the more general context of his gradual abandonment of traditional forms in his pursuit of a more individual course. Dürr concludes that 'in some respects this course runs parallel to Beethoven's, in others Schubert adopts a new direction—but at no time does he regard the older composer as a model to be imitated; he sees in him rather an authority who confirms that he has chosen the right path for himself'. In April 1822 Schubert dedicated his *Eight Variations on a French Song* for piano duet (D624) to Beethoven.

It has not been possible to determine with certainty whether Schubert ever met Beethoven. Schindler* later stated that Schubert had called on Beethoven with the publisher Anton Diabelli* in 1822 to present a copy of the above-mentioned *Variations*, that he had completely lost his composure when Beethoven gently pointed out a mistake in harmony, and that he had never again summoned up the courage for a further visit. On the other hand, Joseph Hüttenbrenner, who had known Schubert well, told Ferdinand Luib (when the latter was gathering material for a biography of Schubert in 1857–8) that Beethoven was out when Schubert called with the *Variations*, but that Schubert eventually visited Beethoven shortly before his death, together with himself, his brother Anselm,* Schindler, and Joseph Teltscher.* Anselm likewise described this visit to Luib (though without mentioning his brother or Teltscher), dating it to about a week before Beethoven's death.

Schindler, rightly or wrongly, also claimed credit for having brought Schubert's songs to Beethoven's attention when, to keep him entertained during his final illness, he had shown him some sixty Schubert Lieder and partsongs, many still in manuscript. According to Schindler, Beethoven 'who until then did not know five songs by Schubert' was so astounded by their quality that he repeatedly exclaimed 'Truly, there is a divine spark in this Schubert.'

Schubert was a torchbearer at Beethoven's funeral. The following year, as he lay on his sick-bed in his brother Ferdinand's flat, he is said to have expressed a fervent desire to hear Beethoven's String Quartet in C sharp minor (Op. 131), and the work was reportedly performed in the flat five days before he died by Karl Holz* and others. It was no accident that his family decided to bury him at Währing district cemetery, where he could lie close to the composer he so greatly venerated.

(Clive[2], Cone, Dürr[1,2], Nettheim)

Schultz, Johann Reinhold. Schultz has been identified by Alan Tyson as the author of the article 'A Day with Beethoven' which appeared in the London periodical *Harmonicon* in January 1824, signed with the Greek letter sigma (which had earlier been wrongly believed to stand for Johann Andreas Stumpff* or for

'Edward Schulz'). Schultz, who had already met Beethoven in 1816, had on this occasion visited him at Baden on 28 September 1823, in the company of Tobias Haslinger* and Joseph Blahetka.* His article is quoted at length in the standard Beethoven biographies.

While in Vienna, in 1823, he seems to have acquired the English publishing rights to a number of compositions, including Beethoven's 'Kakadu' Variations for piano trio (Op. 121a). He arranged to have these variations published by Chappell & Co.* and Goulding & Co.,* and they appeared at about the same time as the edition issued by S. A. Steiner & Co.* in Vienna in May 1824. Schultz's experiences in the matter proved unexpectedly disagreeable: 'After I had so much misfortune with Beethoven's trio, I did not feel at all inclined to risk having the sonatas printed that you gave me to take away with me,' he wrote on 10 December 1824 to Haslinger, Steiner's partner, whom he addresses as 'best, most honest, and excellent old friend'. (It is not known to which sonatas Schultz was referring.) The edition of the variations was not entered at Stationers Hall, nor does Schultz's name appear on the title page of the edition, where it is merely stated that it was being 'published for the proprietor'. The same phrase occurs in certain other editions of continental music published in London in 1824–5, such as Moscheles's* arrangement of the *Egmont* Overture and Hummel's* arrangements of Mozart* and Beethoven symphonies, and some of that music was, in fact, entered at Stationers Hall in the name of 'J. R. Schultz'.

In the above-mentioned letter to Haslinger, Schultz asked the publisher to procure for him the music of Conradin Kreutzer's* opera *Libussa* (with which he proposed to 'speculate'), and also of Beethoven's 'beautiful overture for the opening of the Josefstadt Theatre [i.e. *Die Weihe des Hauses*, Op. 124], provided the publication rights to it have not already been sold to London or elsewhere'. (Neither composition was published by Schultz in London; the first edition of the overture was issued by Schott's Söhne* at Mainz in December 1825.) Further evidence of Schultz's interest in Viennese musicians is provided by the letters which he asked Sir George Smart* to deliver to several of them during Smart's visit to Vienna in September 1825. They include Joseph Böhm,* Joseph Mayseder,* and Ignaz Schuppanzigh.* There was to be one further link with Beethoven: the May 1827 issue of *Harmonicon* contained Schultz's article 'Beethoven's Last Illness and Death'.

The above represents almost all that is known about Johann Reinhold Schultz's life. His name points to a German origin, and that he did indeed have a command of that language is proved by a book, *A Key to Dr Noehden's Exercises for Writing German*, which he published in London in 1817 under the name 'John R. Schultz'. Finally, an entry in Beethoven's conversations books by his nephew Karl,* written shortly after Schultz's visit in September 1823, probably refers to him: 'The man is very well educated. We spoke about literature, art, etc., and he showed great understanding. He knows Greek and Latin well . . . His greatest wish is that you should come to London, where his house and all possible comforts would be placed at your disposal' (*BKh*4/195).

(Tyson[11])

Schuppanzigh, Ignaz (b. Vienna, 20 November 1776; d. Vienna, 2 March 1830). Violinist and conductor. He learned to play the viola before the violin, but made the latter his principal instrument when he decided to become a professional musician. From 1794 to 1799 he led a quartet which regularly performed at the residence of Prince Karl Lichnowsky;* the other members were Ludwig Sina,* Franz Weiss,* and Nikolaus Kraft,* and perhaps also occasionally Kraft's father Anton.* In addition, Schuppanzigh became associated, as conductor and from c.1798 also as manager, with the popular concerts given in the Augarten. He rapidly made a reputation for himself. J. F. von Schönfeld, in his *Jahrbuch der Tonkunst von Wien und Prag* (1796), hailed him as an excellent violinist, violist, and conductor, who was well known and much sought after in musical circles; in addition, Schönfeld describes him as a very pleasant young man. His association with Beethoven's music, to which he remained devoted all his life, dates from this early period. Occasionally he and Beethoven performed together, as in the first performance of the Piano Quintet Op. 16, at Jahn's* concert hall on 6 April 1797; on 29 March 1798 they played one of Beethoven's violin sonatas (probably one from Op. 12) there.

In the winter of 1804/5 Schuppanzigh formed a new quartet, in which his pupil Joseph Mayseder* played second violin. According to Eduard Hanslick, they were the first musicians to give regular subscription concerts of chamber music in Vienna. In 1805 Schuppanzigh directed the first performance of Beethoven's Sextet (Op. 71). When, in 1808, Schuppanzigh was asked by Lichnowsky's brother-in-law, Count Razumovsky,* to assemble a fine string quartet for him, he chose Sina, Weiss, and Joseph Linke* as his partners. At the same time he continued to appear at concerts elsewhere as violinist and conductor, frequently in music by Beethoven. Thus Johann Friedrich Reichardt* heard him play the Piano Trios Op. 70 with the composer and Linke at Countess Erdödy's* in December 1808; in May 1811, at a concert given by Linke, he directed performances of the *Egmont* Overture and the Sixth Symphony, on 16 April 1812 he conducted the *Coriolan* Overture, on 5 May 1812 the *Prometheus* Overture and the Fifth Symphony, on 1 May 1813 the March from *Tarpeja* and again the Fifth Symphony (in 1820 Franz Oliva* mentioned that Schuppanzigh had conducted several excellent performances of this work—'he understood it well' (*BKh*2/47)); on 11 April 1814 he took part with Beethoven and Linke in the first performance of the 'Archduke' Trio Op. 97; and in May 1814 his quartet gave the first performance of the String Quartet Op. 95. He furthermore led the violin section at Beethoven's highly successful concert of 8 December 1813, which featured performances of *Wellingtons Sieg* and the Seventh Symphony.

The Razumovsky Quartet was dissolved some time after the count's palace was destroyed by fire at the end of 1814. Schuppanzigh himself left Vienna after giving a farewell concert entirely devoted to Beethoven (the Quartet Op. 59, No. 3, the Quintet Op. 16 (with Carl Czerny*), and the Septet Op. 20) on 11 February 1816. During the following years he performed in Germany, Poland, and Russia, where he was instrumental in gaining a wider audience for Beethoven's music.

When he finally returned to Vienna in April 1823, he at once plunged back into the city's musical life, presenting his first concert on 4 May (the programme included the *Coriolan* Overture). He also became a member of the court Kapelle, and later conductor of the court opera orchestra. Most significantly, from Beethoven's point of view, he wasted no time in forming a new quartet, together with Karl Holz,* Weiss, and Linke. Their first series, consisting of six concerts, ran from 12 June to 17 July 1823; Beethoven's music was on the programme of five of the concerts. Among the many performances of Beethoven's chamber music which Schuppanzigh was to direct over the following years were the first renditions of the Quartets Op. 127 (6 March 1825, *see also* Joseph Michael Böhm*), Op. 132 (6 November 1825), and Op. 130 (with the fugue on 21 March 1826, and with the new finale on 22 April 1827). In addition, he was Konzertmeister of the orchestra at the first and second performances of the Ninth Symphony on 7 and 23 May 1824. Indeed, the choice of the Kärntnertor-Theater as the venue for the concert was determined by Beethoven's desire that Schuppanzigh rather than Franz Clement,* the Konzertmeister at the Theater an der Wien, should assume that position.

It is evident that Beethoven thought very highly of Schuppanzigh as a musician. The conversation books contain numerous references to him and also quite a few entries in his hand. He visited Beethoven during his final illness, and was a torchbearer at the funeral. Their relationship was cordial, but never intimate; a curious feature was their use of the third person in addressing each other, a formal practice which had already become old-fashioned by that time. Beethoven did not hesitate to allude humorously to Schuppanzigh's formidable girth. Thus he composed, in 1801, a musical joke for three solo voices and chorus, *Lob auf den Dicken* [In Praise of the Fat Man], WoO 100; and, many years later, on Schuppanzigh's return to Vienna in 1823, he greeted him with the comic canon 'Falstafferel, lass' dich sehen' [My dear Falstaff, show yourself], WoO 184, which he signed 'amici amicus'. Presumably, since there was no malice and even a hint of affection in the choice of the sobriquet (variants: 'Mylord Falstaff', or simply 'Mylord'), Schuppanzigh, by all accounts a good-natured man, did not take offence. Frimmel suggests that Beethoven may have taken the nickname either directly from Shakespeare,* or from Salieri's* opera *Falstaff.* (Salieri's opera had its première at the Kärntnertor-Theater on 3 January 1799 and received several further performances at the court theatres during the following three years; Beethoven wrote variations on the duet 'La stessa, la stessima' (WoO 73).) The above-mentioned canon WoO 184 was addressed 'To His Highness H[err] v. Schuppanzig[h], scion of the old English noble family of Milord Fallstaf[f]', to which Beethoven added: 'See Shakespeare's portrait of Mylord Falstaf[f]'.

In 1807 Schuppanzigh married Barbara Killitschky (b. 1776). She was a sister of the soprano Josephine Killitschky [later Schulz] who sang the aria *Ah! perfido* (Op. 65) at Beethoven's concert on 22 December 1808 and took the part of Leonore at the first performance of *Fidelio* in Berlin, on 11 October 1815.

(Forbes², Hanslick, Hellsberg, MacArdle[14])

Schwarzenberg, Joseph Johann Nepomuk, Prince (b. Vienna, 27 June 1769; d. Frauenberg [Hluboká, Czech Republic], 19 December 1833). Son of Prince Johann Nepomuk Schwarzenberg (1742–89) and Marie Eleonore, née Countess Oettingen-Wallerstein (1741–97); he married Princess Pauline Karolina Arenberg (1774–1810). A noted music lover, he maintained his own orchestra and regularly arranged performances of oratorios and chamber music at his palace in Mehlmarkt [Neuer Markt] in Vienna. It was there that Haydn's* oratorios *Die Schöpfung* and *Die Jahreszeiten* were first performed, in 1798 and 1801 respectively.

Beethoven dedicated his Piano Quintet Op. 16 to Schwarzenberg in 1801.

(Berger¹)

Schwind, Moritz von (b. Vienna, 21 January 1804; d. Munich, 8 February 1871). Painter. While he probably knew Beethoven by sight, there is no evidence that he was ever introduced to him. However, an interesting link connects one of his early works with Beethoven. In 1825 Schwind, a great music lover, made thirty pen-and-ink drawings showing Figaro's wedding procession. While the series is, of course, inspired by Act III of Mozart's* *Le nozze di Figaro*, it is not an illustration of the plot but rather a free composition in the spirit of the music. Each drawing depicts three or four members of the procession, which is led by Figaro and Susanna and Dr Bartolo and Marcellina, and includes other persons from that opera, as well as a Papageno in love, the four seasons, characters from Friedrich von Schlegel's novel *Lucinde*, and an assortment of musicians, dancers, soldiers, servants, and other folk; altogether there are over a hundred figures. Schwind showed the drawings to Franz Grillparzer,* who, as Schwind informed his friend Schubert* on 25 July 1825, was delighted with them. In due course they were passed on to Beethoven, probably by Grillparzer. Schwind later wrote on them: 'Beethoven had these drawings in his possession in his old age, during his last illness. They were returned to me only after his death.' The set was eventually published in 1905.

Schwind portrayed Beethoven more than once after his death. In the *Gazette des beaux-arts* in 1896, Frimmel published a drawing of Beethoven's head which he had discovered in a sketchbook in the possession of Schwind's daughter Marie Baurnfeind; he also reproduced it in *Beethoven im zeitgenössischen Bildnis* (1823).

In Schwind's *Symphony* (1852), a large oil painting in four 'movements', a bust of Beethoven presides over a rehearsal of his Choral Fantasia (*see also* Brentano*). Beethoven appears furthermore in the so-called *Lachner-Rolle*, a series of drawings done by Schwind in 1862 on a single roll of paper, which humorously depicts several episodes from the life of his friend Franz Paul Lachner,* who was then celebrating the twenty-fifth anniversary of his appointment as conductor of the Munich court opera.

(Frimmel[3], Kalkschmidt, Trost, Weigmann)

Sebald, Amalie (b. Berlin, 24 August 1787; d. Berlin, 4 January 1846). Daughter of Justizrat Sebald (b. 1754) and his wife Wilhelmine, née Schwadtke (d. 1844). Her mother was one of the original members of the Berlin Singakademie, and various other relatives also belonged to it. Amalie and her sister Auguste (1792–1861) were both extremely gifted singers and between 1803 and 1827 frequently appeared as soloists in works performed by the Singakademie. Gustav Parthey, whose family was on very friendly terms with them, states in his memoirs that Auguste 'enraptured all hearts with her radiant, youthful soprano, which was clear as a bell', while Amalie 'enchanted the listener with the silvery sound of her rich contralto voice'.

In August 1811 Amalie made Beethoven's acquaintance at Teplitz [Teplice], where she had travelled with Christoph August Tiedge* and Elisabeth von der Recke.* He was obviously attracted to her, though probably not too much should be read into his oft-quoted note 'Ludwig van Beethoven, whom, even should you wish it, you ought not to forget', for it was written only a day or two after he had met her. More significant might be the statement, in a letter to Tiedge the following month, that he was sending her 'a very ardent kiss, if no one can see us' (*Corr.* A324/B521). On 17 July 1812, writing from Teplitz, he asked Breitkopf & Härtel* to send the score of his *Christus am Ölberg* and some Goethe* songs in his name to her Berlin address ('a charming lady . . . a pupil of Zelter,* and we are very fond of her'). Later that summer both were in Teplitz during the same fortnight (10–23 September 1812). Since Beethoven was confined to bed for several days, he wrote a number of short notes to Amalie which have survived. They reflect a certain intimacy and even affection ('How could you ever imagine that you may mean nothing to me? . . . It has always been my wish that my presence would inspire in you feelings of serenity and peace, and that you would come to trust me'). But the emotions expressed seem a far cry from the passion which fills the letter to the 'Immortal Beloved' written just a few weeks earlier, and no Beethoven scholar now accepts the claim once made by Wolfgang A. Thomas-San-Galli that the letter was addressed to Amalie Sebald.

On 17 October 1815 she married Justizkommissar [later Justizrat] Ludewig Krause (*c*.1781–1825), who was to write to Beethoven in 1824 concerning Prince Radziwill's* subscription to the *Missa solemnis* (*Corr.* B1806, B1847). There is no evidence of any further communications between Beethoven and Amalie herself after 1812, but she did not forget her meetings with him. Her friend Lili Parthey records in her diary on 24 September 1823, with tantalizing brevity, that Amalie 'spoke in a very interesting manner about Teplitz and Beethoven'. Auguste's son Albrecht Ritschl even let it be known later that Beethoven would have liked to marry Amalie, but that the idea held no appeal for her, first because he was a Catholic, and secondly, because she did not feel attracted to a man of such unkempt appearance. It is difficult to know how seriously this statement should be taken.

(Kalischer, Parthey[1,2], Thomas-San-Galli[1,2])

Sechter, Simon (b. Friedberg [Frymburk, Czech Republic], 11 October 1788; d. Vienna, 10 September 1867). Theorist, composer, pianist, and organist. After completing his musical education in Vienna where he had moved in 1804, he was employed as a piano and singing teacher at the School for the Blind (1810–25). After the death of Johann Georg Albrechtsberger* he was regarded as the leading musical theorist in Vienna. In 1824 he was appointed assistant court organist, becoming principal organist the following year. From 1851 until his death he taught thoroughbass and counterpoint at the Conservatoire. He is believed to have composed some 8,000 works, of which, however, only a small number ever appeared in print. Of his theoretical writings, the three-volume *Die Grundsätze der musikalischen Komposition* (Leipzig, 1853–4) attracted the greatest attention.

Nothing is known about Sechter's personal contacts with Beethoven, nor is he mentioned in the latter's correspondence. However, he dedicated his Op. 5, a set of four fugues for the piano, to Beethoven. And following Beethoven's death, he reportedly set to music a poem written by I. F. Castelli* about the funeral ('Bei dem Leichenbegängnisse des Ludwig van Beethoven').

(Brown, Clive[2])

Sedlaczek, Johann (b. Oberglogau, Silesia [Głogówec, Poland], 6 December 1789; d. Vienna, 11 April 1866). Flautist. The son of a tailor, he was trained to exercise the same trade as his father, but also learned to play the flute. Eventually, some time after settling in Vienna in *c*.1810, he decided to devote himself entirely to music. He played in an orchestra, and, according to C. von Wurzbach, first performed in public in 1816. Thereafter he frequently played at concerts. In addition, he toured abroad, in Germany, Switzerland, and especially Italy where he spent several years; later he also performed in Paris. In 1826 he settled in London, and he lived there for some twenty years before returning to Austria.

Sedlaczek was personally acquainted with Beethoven, but information about their contacts is very scarce. The programme of his concert on 13 April 1818 is known to have included Beethoven's Choral Fantasia. On 11 September 1825 he was among the audience at the private performance of the Quartet in A minor, Op. 132, at the hotel Zum wilden Mann (*see* Schlesinger* and Smart*). According to Karl van Beethoven,* he spoke particularly enthusiastically about Beethoven's improvisation on that occasion (*see BKh8/141*). Finally, shortly before his departure for Paris in November of that year, Beethoven provided him, at his request, with letters of introduction to Cherubini* and Rodolphe Kreutzer* (*Corr.* A App.E, 5–6/B2086–7).

The quality of Sedlaczek's playing was apparently not always equally high. In an entry in the conversation books in March 1826, Karl Holz* reported that since Sedlaczek had arrived at Dresden with such high recommendations and had played so badly, the reputation of Viennese virtuosi had sharply declined at the Saxon court (*BKh9/121*).

(Hanslick, Smart, Wurzbach[1])

Seibert, Johann (1782–1846). Surgeon at the Allgemeines Krankenhaus [General Hospital]. During Beethoven's last illness, he performed four operations to remove fluid from his abdomen (on 20 December 1826, and 8 January, 2 February, and 27 February 1827).

Sellner, Joseph (b. Landau, Alsace, 13/15 May 1787; d. Vienna, 17 May 1843). An extremely versatile musician, he mastered a variety of instruments, eventually specializing as an oboist. In 1813 he was engaged by Carl Maria von Weber* for the Estates Theatre orchestra in Prague. Four years later he moved to Vienna. There he joined the court opera orchestra, appeared at concerts, and eventually also became a member of the court Kapelle. He was, furthermore, appointed to the faculty of the Conservatoire of the Gesellschaft der Musikfreunde,* where, in addition to his teaching, he conducted the students' concerts until 1838. Lastly, he made a significant contribution to the development of the oboe: 'By 1825, [he] had added some duplicate touchpieces and thus created his so-called "13-key oboe", the most advanced of its time . . . This still remains the basis of the Vienna-style instrument as used to-day' (P. Bate, article 'Oboe' in *New Grove*).

P. Nettl states in his *Beethoven Encyclopedia* that Sellner 'was a member of the Beethoven circle', but there seem to be no valid grounds for such an assertion, which suggests fairly close contact of a certain duration. In fact, there is firm evidence of only one meeting between him and Beethoven, on 2 September 1825. On that day, according to Ignaz von Seyfried,* Sellner was one of a group of persons who travelled from Vienna to spend the day with Beethoven at Baden (*see* Kuhlau*). Frimmel, in his *Beethoven-Handbuch*, suggests that Sellner joined the excursion with the intention of making Beethoven's personal acquaintance, and his conjecture that Beethoven had not previously met Sellner draws support from certain entries by Haslinger* and Holz* in the conversation books ('Sellner is a professor at the Gesellschaft der Musikfreunde', 'The professor's name is Sellner', *BKh8/79*, 83). There are no entries by Sellner himself.

(Seyfried, Wurzbach[1])

Seyfried, Ignaz (Xaver) von (b. Vienna, 15 August 1776; d. Vienna, 27 August 1841). Composer, conductor, teacher, and writer on music. He reportedly studied the piano with Mozart* and Leopold Kozeluch,* and composition with Albrechtsberger* and Peter Winter. In 1797 he became a conductor at Schikaneder's* Freihaus-Theater, and he subsequently occupied a similar post at the Theater an der Wien until 1826. Over the years he composed a vast number of operas and Singspiels; some 1,700 performances of his works were given at the Theater an der Wien alone. He was also a prolific composer of other kinds of music, such as orchestral works and Masses. He furthermore wrote for various musical journals, and also contributed articles to Gustav Schilling's *Encyclopädie* (1838), among others those on Franz Schubert* and his brother Ferdinand.

Seyfried was well acquainted with Beethoven by 1803 at the latest. In the Mainz periodical *Cäcilia*, in 1828, he stated that he had been responsible for rehearsing the orchestra and singers, in accordance with Beethoven's instructions, in the symphonies, concertos, and the oratorio (*Christus am Ölberg*) which had received their first performance at Beethoven's benefit concerts at the Theater an der Wien in 1803 and 1808, and that he had moreover himself conducted those performances. (The symphonies in question were the Second, Fifth, and Sixth, the piano concertos the Third and Fourth.) He furthermore rehearsed and conducted *Fidelio* in 1805, and probably also directed the second (and last) performance of the revised version on 10 April 1806 (*see Corr.* A130/B248).

If certain of Seyfried's other statements in the *Cäcilia* article are to be believed, he and Beethoven enjoyed a close personal friendship during those years, dining together almost daily and freely discussing each of Beethoven's new compositions, which Beethoven would play for Seyfried on his piano. Little is known about their later contacts, but in December 1824 Beethoven wrote to thank Seyfried for conducting his Overture *Die Weihe des Hauses* at a charity concert (*Corr.* A1109/B1915).

On 29 March 1827, Seyfried was one of the pallbearers at Beethoven's funeral. During the procession, two of the Equale (WoO 30) were performed; at Tobias Haslinger's* suggestion, Seyfried had arranged them for the occasion for male voices (No. 1 to the words 'Miserere mei . . .', No. 3 to 'Amplius lava me . . .'). During the funeral service at the Trinitarierkirche, Seyfried's setting of the responsory 'Libera me, Domine' from the Requiem Mass was sung. The 'Miserere' and 'Libera me' were again performed at the Augustinerkirche on 3 April, following Mozart's* Requiem, and on 26 April, after Cherubini's* Requiem. (*See also* Grillparzer.*)

In 1832 Seyfried published *Ludwig van Beethoven's Studien im Generalbasse, Contrapuncte und in der Compositions-Lehre.* The value of the main body of the book has been largely discredited by Gustav Nottebohm, who was able to demonstrate that most of the items presented by Seyfried were not, as alleged, studies executed by Beethoven for Haydn* or Albrechtsberger; they been culled by

Beethoven later from various theoretical works for use in his lessons with Archduke Rudolph.* However, the supplement, which offers, among other items, the author's personal recollections of Beethoven, is not without interest; it contains also the earliest printed reproduction of the Heiligenstadt Testament.

(Branscombe⁵, Nottebohm¹, Seyfried)

Seyfried, Joseph von (b. Vienna, 24 March 1780; d. Vienna, 28 June 1849). Librettist, editor, and writer; brother of Ignaz von Seyfried.* He adapted numerous Italian, French, and English opera librettos. Among the Viennese journals which he edited were the *Allgemeine musikalische Zeitung* (1819–20), *Der Sammler*, and *Der Wanderer*. He is the author of the text set by Beethoven for three male voices in 'Abschiedgesang' (WoO 102), composed at Mathias von Tuscher's* request on the occasion of Leopold Weiss's departure for Steyr. (*See also* Gesellschaft der Musikfreunde.*)

Shakespeare, William (bapt. Stratford-upon-Avon, 26 April 1564; d. Stratford-upon-Avon, 23 April 1616). Playwright and poet. The great interest which Beethoven took in Shakespeare and his close knowledge of a number of the plays has been amply demonstrated. A useful summary in English of the main evidence will be found in Donald W. MacArdle's article 'Shakespeare and Beethoven', but his suggestion that Beethoven took the name 'Fidelio' directly from *Cymbeline* is not necessarily correct, for the name was already used by Jean-Nicolas Bouilly* in his libretto *Léonore* which served as Joseph Sonnleithner's* and Beethoven's model (in Bouilly's text, the heroine is identified as 'épouse de Florestan, et porte-clef sous le nom de Fidélio'). Of course, Bouilly himself may well have adapted the name from the character Fidele in Shakespeare's play.

No composition of Beethoven's has been convincingly identified as having been directly inspired by a Shakespearian text; Arnold Schering's assertion (in his *Beethoven und die Dichtung*, Berlin, 1936) that several of the string quartets and piano sonatas are based on plays by Shakespeare has not been generally accepted. Beethoven might have composed an opera on the subject of *Macbeth*, if Heinrich von Collin* (for whose play *Coriolan* he had written an overture in 1807) had persisted in his intention of preparing a libretto based on the play; as it was, it remained incomplete at Collin's death in 1811. (The choice of subject was probably prompted by a successful production of Schiller's* version of *Macbeth* at the Kärntnertor-Theater; the première on 13 February 1808 was followed by ten more performances that same year.) Beethoven made some sketches for the witches' chorus, with which Collin's libretto opened. When Heinrich Anschütz* spoke to him about *Macbeth* in 1822 as a possible subject for a musical composition, it was clear from Beethoven's reaction that the story still fascinated him.

(Anschütz, MacArdle¹², Pečman)

Simrock, Nikolaus (b. Mainz, 23 August 1751; d. Bonn, 12 June 1832). Horn player and music publisher. After he joined the elector's orchestra at Bonn in 1775 he became friendly with the Beethovens. In 1793 he founded his own music publishing business. For his third publication that year he chose Beethoven's variations on the arietta 'Es war einmal ein alter Mann' from Dittersdorf's opera *Das rote Käppchen* (WoO 66). He was an enterprising and energetic businessman —the firm was to publish some 3,000 items under his direction—and his interests were broad. Thus he published not only contemporary composers, such as Haydn,* Carl Maria von Weber,* Johann Friedrich Reichardt,* Andreas Jakob Romberg,* and Zumsteeg, but also Bach (including *Das wohltemperierte Klavier*, Masses, cantatas, and several sonatas for solo violin). Of Beethoven's compositions he was to issue, in addition to reprints, a number of first editions, notably of the *Variations on a Theme by Count Waldstein*,* WoO 67 (in 1794), the 'Kreutzer' Violin Sonata (in 1805, *see also* Kaspar Karl Beethoven*), the Sextet Op. 81b (in 1810), and the two Cello Sonatas Op. 102 (in 1817—*see* Peter Joseph Simrock*). In 1820 he published the first continental edition of the *Variations* Op. 107. (*See also* Nägeli, regarding the Sonatas Op. 31.) Furthermore, the possibility of a collective edition was discussed more than once, but nothing came of the idea.

It was in his letter of 10 February 1820 that Beethoven first offered to Simrock his new mass (*Missa solemnis*), which, he stated rather optimistically, would be performed shortly (it was still far from completed—*see* Rudolph*). Although terms were agreed, and Beethoven promised imminent delivery on more than one occasion and even received an advance payment of part of the fee through Franz Brentano,* he continued to hold out for better terms and to negotiate with other publishers. Eventually he wrote to Simrock on 10 March 1823: 'You will most certainly receive a Mass from me, but I have also composed another Mass and am undecided which one to give you . . . Just be patient until after Easter and I shall then inform you when I shall be sending off one of these Masses.' These statements were less than honest, for Beethoven had no other Mass ready for dispatch. If Simrock replied to this letter, his answer has been lost. He appears, in any case, to have abandoned all hope at this stage of ever obtaining the music. (The advance payment was later returned by Beethoven. The Mass was finally accepted by Schott's Söhne* on 19 July 1824 (*see Corr.* B1852) and was published by them in 1827.)

The absence of any further correspondence—at any rate, none has survived— may well reflect a strain in their relations. Another pointer to Simrock's likely irritation over the matter of the Mass may be the fate of his projected edition of the full scores of Beethoven's first six symphonies (none of which, unlike the separate orchestral parts, had previously been published on the Continent). On 13 May 1822 he had written to Beethoven: 'I have resolved to issue your six *symphonies* in score. I had intended to do so on more than one occasion, and have even announced it publicly, but it has not happened until now, since it is not a profitable venture. I know that only too well, but I wanted to set my worthy old friend a worthy monument, and I hope that you will be pleased with the edition, for I have done my best!' (*Corr.* B1464). The scores of the First and Second Symphonies appeared that spring, that of the 'Eroica' a few months later, and that of the Fourth Symphony in 1823, the critical year in their negotiations concerning the *Missa solemnis*. It may be more than a coincidence that Simrock never published the scores of the Fifth and Sixth Symphonies. (They were first issued by Breitkopf & Härtel* in 1826.)

Nikolaus's brother Heinrich (1754–1839) had settled in Paris by 1792/3 at the latest. He played in the orchestras of several theatres as well as in that of the *Garde nationale*, and also taught singing and the horn at the Conservatoire. In 1802 he set up a branch of the Bonn firm in Paris. He has been credited (notably by J. G. Prod'homme) with significantly promoting interest in Beethoven's compositions in France by making Nikolaus's editions available to the music-loving public there.

(Orel[1], Ottendorff-Simrock[1,2], Prod'homme[2])

Simrock, Peter Joseph [Seppel] (b. Bonn, 18 August 1792; d. Cologne, 13 December 1868). Music publisher; son of Nikolaus Simrock.* In 1812 he opened a branch of the firm at Cologne. In September 1816 he travelled to Vienna at his father's request, in the hope of concluding fresh contracts with Beethoven. He visited Beethoven both at Baden and in Vienna, and also lunched with him at a restaurant. On 28 September, shortly before his departure, Beethoven signed a contract for the publication of his two Cello Sonatas Op. 102. They were published by the firm at Bonn the following year, as was the song 'Das Geheimnis' (WoO 145). Years later, Simrock communicated some memories of his meetings with Beethoven to Thayer.*

After his father's death in 1832 he took charge of the Bonn firm, running it at first together with his brother Franz Carl Anton [Fritz] (1790–1872), and from 1833 on his own. At his death he was succeeded by his son Friedrich August [Fritz] (1837–1901), who moved the firm to Berlin in 1870.

(Elvers[2], Ottendorff-Simrock[1,2])

Sina, Ludwig (1778–1857). Violinist. According to Thayer,* he studied with Emanuel Aloys Förster.* He was among the young musicians who regularly performed chamber music at Prince Karl Lichnowsky's* house in the later 1790s, and he played second violin in the Razumovsky* Quartet (*see* Schuppanzigh*). He was furthermore a member of the orchestra at the Theater an der Wien. On 8 December 1813 he took part in the first performance of *Wellingtons Sieg*.

He is believed to have settled in Paris around 1820. Schindler* states that he was among the small band of Beethoven enthusiasts who promoted interest in his orchestral works in Paris. In particular, according to Schindler, he was responsible for bringing the Fifth Symphony to the attention of François-Antoine Habeneck, the French conductor who did so much to introduce Beethoven's music to French audiences. Sina died at Boulogne-sur-Mer, in straitened circumstances.

Smart, Sir **George (Thomas)** (b. London, 10 May 1776; d. London, 23 February 1867). Conductor, organist, and composer. He became organist at St James's Chapel, Hampstead Road, in 1791, and also played as a violinist at Johann Peter Salomon's* concerts. Through his manifold activities, he came to occupy an increasingly prominent position in British musical life during the first half of the nineteenth century. Thus he was a founder member of the Philharmonic Society* and conducted many of its concerts, and, from 1813 to 1825, he was also in charge of the oratorio concerts regularly presented in London during Lent. In addition, he directed numerous music festivals throughout Great Britain; and in 1822 he was appointed an organist of the Chapel Royal. He was knighted in 1811.

'I was very happy to find that your partiality to Mr. B's compositions is not diminished,' Beethoven's friend Johann von Häring,* who knew Smart from one or several visits to London, wrote to him in March 1815 (*Corr.* A534/B790). Beethoven, having read in the *Wiener Zeitung* that Smart had conducted highly successful performances of *Wellingtons Sieg* at Drury Lane Theatre on 10 and 13 February, had asked Häring to enlist Smart's help in finding English publishers for some of his compositions. He added a brief note to Häring's letter, in which he thanked him 'for the trouble you have taken several times, as I understand, in taking my works under your protection'. (Both Häring's letter and Beethoven's note are in English.)

Wellingtons Sieg, which was repeatedly performed in London that season, was not the first major work by Beethoven which Smart introduced to English audiences. The previous year he had conducted the oratorio *Christus am Ölberg* no fewer than ten times (with an English text and under the title *The Mount of Olives*). He seems to have been particularly fond of the work, for in addition to conducting it in London and elsewhere, he published his own piano reduction of the orchestral score. He even offered to commission a new oratorio from Beethoven for a fee of 100 guineas, specifying that it should be modelled on *The Mount of Olives* ('but with a Bass Song in it'—*see* Smart's letter to Richard Huddlestone Potter in January 1818, *Corr.* B1236); but Beethoven did not take up the offer. In his Philharmonic Society concerts, Smart conducted various works by Beethoven (e.g. the 'Eroica' on 24 April 1820, and during the 1821 season alone, the Seventh (26 February), First (30 April), and Sixth Symphonies (28 May). But the Beethoven work with which Smart's name is most famously associated is the Ninth Symphony, of which he gave the first English performance on 21 March 1825. While Smart was thus instrumental in making Beethoven's works known in

England (Percy M. Young calls him 'Beethoven's English Advocate'), it is less clear what action, if any, he took in response to the composer's request that he should arrange for their publication there.

It was mainly his interest in the Ninth Symphony which led Smart to travel to the Continent in 1825, for, in his own words, 'my principal reason for this journey was to ascertain from Beethoven personally the exact times of the movements of his characteristic [i.e. Ninth]—and some of his other—Sinfonias'. During his stay in Vienna from 4 to 20 September he met many prominent musicians. On 9 September he was introduced to Beethoven at the hotel Zum wilden Mann [17 Kärntnerstrasse], where he heard a private performance of the String Quartet in A minor (Op. 132) by Schuppanzigh,* Holz,* Weiss,* and Linke,* which had been arranged at the request of the visiting music publisher Maurice Schlesinger.* (Schlesinger bought the quartet the next day, but it was not published until September 1827.) Smart returned to the hotel on 11 September, when, again in Beethoven's presence, the same quartet and also two of his piano trios were performed. Finally, on 16 September, he called on Beethoven at his lodgings at Baden, on which occasion Beethoven presented him with a canon on the words 'Ars longa, vita brevis' (WoO 192). Smart wrote detailed accounts of these different events, as well as of his other activities in Vienna, in his diary. (Excerpts from his private papers were published in 1907 in a somewhat bowdlerized form by H. Bertram Cox and C. L. E. Cox under the title *Leaves from the Journals of Sir George Smart*; they include a chapter on his stay in Vienna.) Smart planned to give a further performance of the Ninth Symphony in 1828, based on what he had learned from Beethoven regarding its interpretation, but he had to abandon the idea because of the costs involved. He did, however, conduct the symphony again at a benefit concert for Charles Neate* on 26 April 1830.

Smart was one of the musicians living in London to whom Beethoven appealed for help in obtaining financial assistance from the Philharmonic Society in 1827 (*Corr.* A1555/B2259, A1559/B2271). On 12 August 1845, Smart attended the unveiling of the Beethoven statue in Bonn as a guest of the organizing committee.

(Husk/Temperley, Smart, Young)

Smetana, Carl von (1774–1827). Physician. On 18 September 1816 he successfully operated on Beethoven's nephew Karl* for hernia at Giannattasio's* school. Beethoven remained in contact with him during the rest of his life, and at different times consulted him about various ailments, including his hearing problems.

Sonnenfels, Joseph von (b. ?Nikolsburg [Mikulov, Czech Republic], ?1733; d. Vienna, 25 April 1817). Lawyer, teacher, and writer. Of Jewish origin, he was baptized at the Schottenkirche in Vienna on 18 September 1735, at the same time as his father and two brothers, In 1746 the father, who had changed his name 'Lipmann Perlin [or Berlin]' to 'Aloys Wienner', was ennobled and granted the title 'von Sonnenfels', under which name the family was henceforth known. After attending schools at Nikolsburg and in Vienna, Joseph von Sonnenfels served in the army (1749–54) and then studied law in Vienna (1755–7). Subsequently he held a junior post in the Lower Austrian administration, but in 1761 he re-enlisted in the army, from which he was finally released in 1763. In that year he was appointed to the newly created chair in political science at the University of Vienna. Also in 1763, he married Maria Theresia von Hay (1748–1820), whose sister Carolina Josepha would in 1778 become the wife of Johann Melchior von Birkenstock.*

Through his teaching and his writings—his collected works, published between 1783 and 1787, ran to ten volumes—and also as a member of a number of important committees, Sonnenfels was to be instrumental in bringing about certain reforms in the spirit of the Enlightenment. Characteristically, he named a periodical he founded in 1765 *Der Mann ohne Vorurteil* [The Man without Prejudice]. He was, moreover, a prominent freemason. While his liberal views naturally made him some enemies, they also brought him respect and recognition. In 1780 he was awarded the title 'Hofrat'; in 1794 he was appointed rector of the university; in 1797 he was created a baron; and in 1806 he was granted honorary citizenship of the city of Vienna. In 1811 he was became president of the Akademie der bildenden Künste.

That Beethoven should have dedicated his Piano Sonata in D major, Op. 28, to Sonnenfels in August 1802 has rather puzzled scholars, since there is no known evidence of any contact between them. Thayer* surmises that it must have been simply an expression of the composer's profound regard for a man of high principles, with whose general philosophy he found himself in sympathy. Frimmel, for his part, assumes that the directors of the Kunst- und Industrie-Comptoir,* which published the work, had acted as intermediaries. While either, or both, of these explanations may be correct, there could yet be another one: if Beethoven knew Sonnenfels's brother-in-law Johann Melchior von Birkenstock, a possibility that cannot be ruled out entirely (*see* Birkenstock*), he might have made Sonnenfels's acquaintance through him.

(Lindner)

Sonnleithner (family). Viennese family of lawyers, closely connected with the world of music and the theatre. Three of its members are of particular interest to Beethoven's biographers.

Ignaz von Sonnleithner (b. Vienna, 30 July 1770; d. Vienna, 27 November 1831), the son of Christoph Sonnleithner (1734–86), a lawyer and composer (of church music, symphonies, quartets), himself practised successfully as a lawyer and notary, and he furthermore lectured on law at the University of Vienna and also at the Polytechnisches Institut. At the latter establishment Karl von Beethoven* was among his students in 1825—'Dr Sonnleithner pays great attention to me, because he knows you very well,' Karl told his uncle (*BKh*7/283). Sonnleithner was also active in humanitarian causes. He was ennobled in 1828.

A great music lover and popular amateur singer, he gave regular musical soirées between 1815 and 1824 in his apartment at the Gundelhof [4 Bauernmarkt/5 Brandstätte], which brought together professional as well as leading amateur performers. These concerts, the programmes of which were chosen by his son Leopold (see below), constituted a focal point of Viennese musical life and were of particular importance for Franz Schubert's* career. Among the compositions performed were several works by Beethoven.

It is not clear whether it was Ignaz or his brother Joseph (see below) whom Beethoven consulted in connection with his dispute with Artaria & Co.* about the String Quintet Op. 29. On 13 November 1802 he informed Breitkopf & Härtel:* 'Sonnleitner [*sic*] and I intend to take whatever other steps we consider advisable.'

Ignaz's elder brother **Joseph Sonnleithner** (b. Vienna, 3 March 1766; d. Vienna, 26 December 1835) was also a qualified lawyer. He was employed at court from 1787, at first in Emperor Joseph II's* private office, later in the chancellery. At the same time, he gave early evidence of his interest in the theatre by publishing the *Wiener Theater-Almanach* (1794–6). In 1802 he became a partner in the Kunst- und Industrie-Comptoir.* For a brief period (February–August 1804) he was artistic director of the Theater an der Wien under Baron Braun;* from September 1804 until 1814 he served as secretary of the court theatres. During his tenure of the latter post, he prepared German versions of a number of French plays by such authors as Charles Guillaume Étienne and Pigault-Lebrun, as well as opera librettos, again mostly from French models (e.g. for Cherubini's* *Faniska*, after R. C. G. de Pixérécourt's *Les Mines de Pologne*). The libretto for which he is best remembered is the one he wrote for Beethoven's *Fidelio*, based on Jean-Nicolas Bouilly's* *Léonore, ou L'Amour conjugal*. It was also Sonnleithner who successfully petitioned the police authorities in October 1805 to withdraw their ban on the performance of Beethoven's opera.

Beethoven is known to have attended some of Sonnleithner's musical soirées. It was at one of these, in about 1805, that the young Grillparzer,* who was a nephew of Sonnleithner, saw Beethoven for the first time; also present on that occasion were Cherubini and the Abbé Vogler.* Sonnleithner was a founder member of the Gesellschaft der Musikfreunde,* and its secretary from its establishment in 1814 until his death.

Ignaz's son **Leopold von Sonnleithner** (b. Vienna, 15 November 1797; d. Vienna, 4 March 1873) was, like his father, a successful lawyer. He was also an accomplished musician; his role in planning the concerts given by his father has been mentioned above. He was moreover a prominent member of the Gesellschaft der Musikfreunde. Between 1820 and 1822 he conducted four of the society's regular concerts, at each of which he directed a performance of a work by

Beethoven: on 19 November 1820, the Eighth Symphony; on 18 November 1821, the Seventh Symphony; on 3 March 1822, the Overture to *Egmont*; and on 15 December 1822, the First Symphony.

Leopold von Sonnleithner, who later wrote extensively on musical matters, is a valuable source of information on his period. In a letter dated 24 March 1864 to the editor of the Leipzig *Allgemeine musikalische Zeitung*, concerning the Ninth Symphony, he quoted Carl Czerny* as telling him on several occasions that, some time after the first performance of that symphony, Beethoven had admitted to certain friends, Czerny among them, that he now considered the final movement a mistake and intended to replace it by a purely orchestral one. The letter was printed in the journal on 6 April under the title '*Ad vocem*: Contrabass-Recitative der 9. Symphonie von Beethoven'. (Czerny told a similar story to Gustav Nottebohm.) Beethoven had evidently overcome his doubts about the appropriateness of the original music by the time he sent the score to the publisher.

(Seemann, Sonnleithner. For further information about the activities of these three members of the Sonnleithner family, *see* Clive², 216–21.)

Sontag [Sonntag], **Henriette (Gertrud Walpurgis)** (b. Koblenz, 3 January 1806; d. Mexico City, 17 June 1854). Soprano. Daughter of the actor Franz Sontag (1783–1819) and the actress and singer Franziska Sontag, née Mar(c)kloff (1789–1865). From 1816 to 1823 she lived with her mother in Prague. In 1817 she enrolled at the Conservatoire where she studied singing with Anna Czegka-Aurhammer, theory with Joseph Triebensee, and the piano with Friedrich Wilhelm Pixis. She made her debut as a mature performer in Prague in 1819 as the Princess of Navarre in Boieldieu's opera *Jean de Paris*. (She had already appeared on the stage as a young child in Germany, and later in Prague.) Between 22 July and 17 August 1822 she made a series of highly acclaimed guest appearances at the Theater and der Wien and the Kärntnertor-Theater in Vienna; in addition to the Princess of Navarre, her roles included Agathe in *Der Freischütz* and Rosina in *Il barbiere di Siviglia*. As a result she was offered a contract in Vienna, jointly with her mother, starting in the spring of 1823. When Weber* heard her as Elena in Rossini's *La donna del lago*, he was so impressed that he offered her the title role in his new opera *Euryanthe*, which had its première in Vienna on 25 October 1823. (The first time he had heard her, in Prague in February 1822, he had liked her singing, but had considered her 'still a novice'.)

On 8 September 1822 Beethoven wrote to his brother Nikolaus Johann:* 'Two women singers have visited me to-day, and since they fervently wished to kiss my hands and were quite pretty, I suggested that they kiss my mouth instead.' As the conversation books for this period have not survived, their identities cannot be established from the entries they will almost certainly have made. However, it is generally believed that the two attractive young singers were Sontag and Karoline

Unger.* Emily Anderson, in her edition of Beethoven's correspondence, qualifies this assumption with an 'almost certainly' (*Corr.* A1097 n. 4), while it is stated as a fact in the new German edition (*Corr.* B1493 n. 8). As far as Unger is concerned, the identification may be correct, but it is wrong in Sontag's case. This is evident from two entries in the conversation books. In December 1823, in the course of a discussion about suitable singers for the opera *Melusina* which Beethoven was proposing to compose to Grillparzer's* libretto, Schindler* wrote about Sontag in terms which make it clear that she had not yet visited Beethoven at that time: 'The girl shows exceptional application and is unusually well educated. She has long wished to take the liberty of visiting you, but cannot quite summon up the courage to do so. Sontag is excellent, a model of rare morality' (*BKh*5/34). And when Sontag finally accompanied Unger to Beethoven's lodgings in mid-March 1824 (in late January she had been prevented from calling by bad weather, which, however, had not deterred Unger), she herself told Beethoven that she had come 'to make your acquaintance, an honour to which I have long looked forward' (*BKh*5/219).

By then Beethoven was, of course, well aware of her growing reputation and, more particularly, of her recent successful appearance in *Euryanthe*. Moreover, he had been told by Count Moritz Lichnowsky* in November 1823 that she was to sing in a new production of *Fidelio*, and had received the same information from Schindler in December; but no performance of the opera is known to have taken place in Vienna during the period in question. In due course she was chosen (in preference to Therese Grünbaum) to sing the solo soprano parts in the Ninth Symphony and in sections of the *Missa solemnis* at the concert on 7 May 1824. When rehearsals began, she, like Unger—who took the solo alto parts— found some of the music extremely difficult, but Beethoven refused their repeated requests for changes (*see also* Unger*). In the end, though, she felt confident enough: 'I stake my life on it that I shall not miss a single note this evening,' she declared (*see BKh* 6/195). And indeed, she acquitted herself well and was rewarded with a letter of appreciation from Beethoven who addressed her as 'My dear, lovely Sonntag' and signed himself 'Your friend and admirer' (*Corr.* A1289/B1832). She sang again at the second concert at the Grosser Redoutensaal on 23 May, at which the symphony and the Kyrie from the Mass were repeated.

Sontag left Vienna on 23 April 1825, having given a farewell concert six days earlier. After some guest appearances at Leipzig she took up an engagement at the Königstädtisches Theater, Berlin, where she made a splendid debut on 3 August as Isabella in Rossini's *L'italiana in Algeri*. The following year she had an even greater triumph in Paris. But in 1830, when the marriage into which she had secretly entered with the Sardinian diplomat Count Carlo Rossi (?1797–1864) some three years earlier became common knowledge, she was obliged to retire from the stage in order to protect his career. Her last appearance was as Semiramide in Rossini's opera of that name in Berlin on 22 May 1830. However, after her husband left the diplomatic service in 1849 she was able to resume her own career, her first engagement being at Her Majesty's Theatre in London on 7 July 1849 in the title role of Donizetti's *Linda di Chamounix*. For five more years she enjoyed great acclaim and adulation until her life was suddenly cut short by cholera while she was fulfilling an engagement in Mexico City. She had become one of the most celebrated singers of her age. Her voice, her artistry, and her personal beauty made her a legendary figure; Hector Berlioz declared that she possessed 'all the gifts of art and nature'.

(Kühner[4], Pirchan, Stümcke, Warrack[2])

Sophie, Archduchess (b. Munich, 27 January 1805; d. Vienna, 28 May 1872). Daughter of King Maximilian I Joseph of Bavaria* and his second wife, Karoline Friederike, née princess of Baden. On 4 November 1824 she married Archduke Franz Karl of Austria (1802–78). Their first child was the future Emperor Franz Joseph (1830–1916).

Beethoven's Waltz in D major for piano (WoO 85) was dedicated to her in 1825 by its publisher, Carl Friedrich Müller.

Spiker, Samuel Heinrich (b. Berlin, 24 December 1786; d. Berlin, 24 May 1858). Librarian at the Königlich-Preussische Bibliothek in Berlin; translator, journalist, and editor. His interest in British affairs—he travelled through England and Scotland in 1816, and translated Shakespeare* and Walter Scott—earned him the nickname 'Lord Spiker'. The sobriquet probably also owed something to his flamboyant lifestyle; Ignaz Franz Castelli* described him as being almost as great a bon vivant as the Viennese, paid tribute to the excellent table he kept, and admired his wit which was without a hurtful barb. Spiker edited the *Journal für Land- und Seereisen* from 1819 to 1827, and in the latter year acquired the prominent Berlin newspaper *Berlinische Nachrichten von Staats- und gelehrten Sachen*, which he published until his death.

Spiker was commissioned by the Berlin publisher Adolph Martin Schlesinger* to prepare the German translations for the bilingual edition of Scottish songs (*Fünfundzwanzig schottische Lieder*, Op. 108) which was published in July 1822. However, his name was not mentioned until the second edition, which, according to Kinsky-Halm, appeared between 1845 and 1850. Spiker visited Vienna from 2 September to 9 October 1826, and during his stay he called on Beethoven together with Tobias Haslinger,* probably on 23 September (*see Corr.* A1527/B2207). When he left Vienna, he took with him a splendidly bound manuscript copy of the Ninth Symphony, corrected in Beethoven's own hand, for the king of Prussia to whom the work was dedicated (*see* Friedrich Wilhelm III* and *Corr.* A App.D, 6/B2214). Spiker gave an account of his visit to Beethoven in the *Berlinische Nachrichten* on 25 April 1827.

(Castelli, Pröhle)

Spohr, Louis [Ludewig, Ludwig] (b. Brunswick, 5 April 1784; d. Kassel, 22 October 1859). Composer, violinist, and conductor. He arrived in Vienna in late 1812 to give concerts and direct performances of his oratorio *Das jüngste Gericht*. While he was in Vienna, he was engaged by Count Pálffy* as leader of the orchestra at the Theater an der Wien, a post he held until 1815. He became friendly with Beethoven and was among the well-known musicians who took part in the first performance of *Wellingtons Sieg* on 8 December 1813. In his *Selbstbiographie* (Kassel, 1860–1) he described his contacts with Beethoven and gave an interesting account of the effect which Beethoven's increasing deafness had on the way he played the piano and conducted. Before his departure, Beethoven composed for him the canon 'Kurz ist der Schmerz, ewig ist die Freude' (WoO 166); the text is taken from the final line of Schiller's* drama *Die Jungfrau von Orleans*.

From 1817 to 1819 Spohr was director of the Frankfurt opera, and in 1822 he accepted an appointment as Kapellmeister at Kassel. In 1823 Beethoven asked him to persuade the Elector Wilhelm II of Hesse to subscribe to the *Missa solemnis* (*Corr.* A1213/B1716), but without success.

(Spohr)

Sporschil [Sporschill], **Johann Chrysostomus** (b. Brünn [Brno], 23 January 1800; d. Vienna, 16 December 1863). Historian, translator, and journalist. In January 1823 Nikolaus Johann van Beethoven* wrote in his brother's conversation book: 'Spohrschild [*sic*] came to see me today and asked me to give you his respects, and if you should wish it, he will write an opera [libretto] for you' (*BKh*2/348). The suggestion was favourably received and Sporschil produced in due course a libretto entitled *Die Apotheose im Tempel des Jupiter Ammon*, which dealt with certain historical and imaginary episodes in the life of Alexander the Great. Beethoven made some preparatory notes and a few sketches, and gave consideration to using music originally written for *Die Ruinen von Athen* and a chorus from *Die Weihe des Hauses*, but he soon abandoned the project. He seems to have shown even less interest in a proposal by Sporschil for a three-act opera on the life of St Vladimir.

There are a few other references to Sporschil in the conversation books, but he never appears as a participant in the conversations, and it is not known what contacts he had with Beethoven. On 5 November 1823 the *Stuttgarter Morgenblatt für gebildete Stände* published an article by him (signed only 'S.....l') about Beethoven, which showed a certain familiarity with the composer's circumstances and way of life; it was reprinted in the *Wiener Theaterzeitung* on 15 November. Four years later, an obituary of Beethoven written by Sporschil appeared in the Dresden *Abendzeitung* (11–12 July 1827).

Sporschil lived in Germany for many years: from 1827 at Leipzig, in 1832–3 at Brunswick, and from 1833 until 1858 again at Leipzig. He was a prolific writer and translator (from both English and French); in addition to his numerous contributions to various newspapers and journals, he published books on historical and other subjects.

(Pečman, Wurzbach[1])

Stadler, Maximilian [Abbé] [baptismal names: Johann Karl Dominik] (b. Melk, Lower Austria, 4 August 1748; d. Vienna, 8 November 1833). Composer, music historian, and keyboard performer. After teaching at Melk Monastery (1775–82) and serving as its prior (1784–5), he held various ecclesiastic appointments in Lower and Upper Austria until 1796 when he went to live in Vienna in a private capacity. There he devoted much of his time to music, for, in addition to being a composer, he was an accomplished violinist, pianist, and organist. From 1803 until 1815 he was in charge of parishes at Alt-Lerchenfeld, a suburb of Vienna, and Böhmisch Krut [Grosskrut] in Lower Austria. In 1815 he retired on a pension and moved to Vienna, where he prepared a history of Austrian music up to the death of Joseph II.* He himself composed much church music, as well as instrumental works, songs, and music for plays.

He was a highly respected figure in musical circles and his opinions carried much weight, especially among the older music lovers. Perhaps it was for this reason that early in 1803 Beethoven was planning to dedicate one of his compositions, the *Fifteen Variations* (Op. 35), to him (*see Corr.* B127). However, on 8 April he asked the publishers, Breitkopf & Härtel,* to dedicate them to Count Moritz Lichnowsky* instead, because the count 'has quite recently done me an unexpected favour'. Curiously enough, Beethoven never thought of dedicating any of his later works to the Abbé.

Stadler, who venerated Mozart,* found Beethoven's music little to his taste. Ignaz Franz Castelli* quotes him as describing it as 'barer Unsinn' [utter nonsense] and adds that Stadler regularly fled from the concert hall when one of Beethoven's compositions was about to be performed. Nevertheless Stadler was among the signatories to the letter sent to Beethoven by Viennese music lovers in February 1824, in which he was urged, in the most flattering terms, to present his new Mass and symphony at a concert in Vienna and to compose a new German opera.

Stadler's personal relations with Beethoven were very cordial. Castelli relates an amusing anecdote, according to which Beethoven knelt down before Stadler in Steiner's* music shop one day and asked for his blessing, whereupon Stadler made the sign of the cross over him, while murmuring 'If it does you no good, it won't do you any harm.' This anecdote is probably the reason why the canon 'Signor Abate, io sono ammalato. Santo Padre! Vieni e datemi la benedizione!' (WoO 178) is believed to be addressed to Stadler. There are numerous references to Stadler in the conversations books, and even some entries in his own hand, made on the occasion of a visit he paid to Beethoven in March 1826. Shortly before, he had sent

Beethoven a copy of his monograph *Vertheidigung der Echtheit des Mozartischen Requiem*, in which he affirmed the authenticity of Mozart's Requiem, on which Gottfried Weber had cast doubt in an article in the periodical *Cäcilia*. Beethoven had warmly congratulated Stadler on the tract in a letter on 6 February.

(Castelli)

Stainhauser von Treuberg, Gandolph Ernst (b. Salzburg, 21 December 1766; d. Vienna, 30 September 1805). Portrait painter; son of the jurist Johann Philipp Stainhauser von Treuberg (1719–99). Among his portraits was one of Beethoven. It is lost, but an engraving made from it by Johann Joseph Neidl* in 1801 has survived.

(*ALBK*)

Starke, Friedrich (b. Elsterwerda, Saxony, 1774; d. Döbling, near Vienna, 18 December 1835). Horn player and composer. He began his career as a professional musician in his native Saxony, later played in the Salzburg court Kapelle, was subsequently employed as a piano teacher at Wels in Upper Austria, and then became Kapellmeister in an Austrian regiment. During those years he acquired a thorough knowledge of various string and wind instruments. Eventually he settled in Vienna, where he studied theory with Albrechtsberger.* He is believed to have met Beethoven around 1812, and he soon established a friendly relationship with him. He gave Beethoven's nephew Karl* piano lessons (*c*.1815), and Beethoven helped him to get a position as horn player in the court opera orchestra. There are several references to him in the conversation books, and even an entry in his hand in February 1823. But most of the available information concerning his personal contacts with Beethoven derives from anecdotes later communicated by Starke to Ferdinand Simon Gassner, director of music at Karlsruhe, who was planning to write a biography of Beethoven (*see* Holz*). Ludwig Nohl was granted access to these anecdotes and published them in his *Beethoven nach den Schilderungen seiner Zeitgenossen*; they were reprinted by Friedrich Kerst in *Die Erinnerungen an Beethoven*. Of particular interest is the description of Beethoven's improvisations; Starke also heard him play the organ. On one occasion they decided to play Beethoven's Horn Sonata Op. 17 together, but discovered that the piano sounded a half-tone too low. Thereupon Beethoven transposed the piano part from F major to F sharp major: 'We began and Beethoven played wonderfully well; the passages rolled forth so clearly and beautifully that one would never have thought that he was transposing.'

Starke composed a considerable number of works, including church and chamber music. He had a special talent for writing and arranging music for military bands; among the compositions he adapted was Beethoven's *Egmont* Overture. He furthermore published a piano tutor, *Wiener Pianoforte-Schule* (3 parts, 1819–21), for which he solicited contributions from Vienna's leading composers. Beethoven wrote for him the five Bagatelles Op. 119, Nos. 7–11, which appeared in the third part of the book. In addition, Starke included the Andante and Rondo from the Piano Sonata in D major, Op. 28, and some passages from the Piano Sonata in D minor, Op. 31, No. 2, as well as a free arrangement, made by Beethoven himself, of the Coda from the last movement of the Third Piano Concerto. He also printed twenty-five of the forty variations written by Archduke Rudolph* on a theme proposed by Beethoven (WoO 200). In the tutor Starke paid homage to Beethoven, calling him 'a star of the first magnitude in the musical firmament'.

(Jancik[6], Kerst, Nohl[4])

Staudenheim, Jakob von (b. Mainz, 1764; d. Vienna, 17 May 1830). Physician. He studied in Paris, Augsburg, and under Maximilian Stoll in Vienna, where he eventually set up in practice. He became both the teacher and medical adviser of Count Karl Borromäus Harrach, later a well-known humanist, philanthropist, and doctor. When the count fell gravely ill, Staudenheim succeeded in curing him, which not only earned him a very generous fee, but also made his reputation, and he soon became one of the most fashionable doctors in Vienna. In 1826 he successfully treated Emperor Franz I during a serious illness and was rewarded with a valuable present and public honours. He was furthermore named personal physician to the duke of Reichstadt.

Beethoven consulted Staudenheim when he felt unwell while at Teplitz [Teplice] in July 1812; according to Frimmel, Staudenheim had accompanied the imperial family to the Bohemian spa. This is usually regarded as their first meeting. The doctor advised Beethoven to move to Karlsbad [Karlovy Vary], later from there to Franzensbad [Františkovy Lázně], and finally from there back to Teplitz. As Beethoven wrote to Breitkopf & Härtel* from Teplitz on 17 September: 'My Aesculapius has pretty well led me round in a circle, for the best treatment is after all available here. These fellows do not really know how to produce an effect; I believe that we are far more proficient in that respect in our art.'

It is not known whether Staudenheim was in professional contact with Beethoven during the next few years. In any case, it was not until after Beethoven had fallen out with Malfatti* that Staudenheim became his regular doctor, probably in April 1817 (see Corr. A783/B1132); he was still attending Beethoven in 1824. In 1825, however, he was replaced by Dr Braunhofer, in circumstances which remain unclear. Schindler* states that Beethoven made the change because he was displeased with the brusque manner in which Staudenheim, who insisted on strict observance of his instructions, had reprimanded his 'disobedient patient'. Yet, while Beethoven may have felt some irritation with Staudenheim, he nevertheless tried to contact him when he was afflicted with severe stomach pains on 18 April 1825. Only when Staudenheim proved to be unavailable did Beethoven turn to Braunhofer. The truth might well be that it was Staudenheim who, offended by an outburst of ill temper on Beethoven's part, had severed the link.

By December 1826, Beethoven had apparently quarrelled with Braunhofer as well. Reportedly neither Braunhofer nor Staudenheim, whom he also summoned, responded to his call for medical assistance when he arrived in Vienna from Gneixendorf at the beginning of that month, and he was obliged to enlist the services of Dr Wawruch.* But Staudenheim did hold a consultation with Wawruch shortly afterwards, during which he confirmed Wawruch's opinion as to the urgent need to draw off fluid from Beethoven's abdomen. This operation (the first of several) was carried out by Dr Johann Seibert* on 20 December. Staudenheim may also have joined in a consultation with Wawruch and Malfatti on 11 January 1827.

(Schindler[1], Wurzbach[1])

Steibelt, Daniel (b. Berlin, 22 October 1765; d. St Petersburg, 20 September 1823). Composer and pianist. While popular with the general public, he was regarded as something of a charlatan by many professional musicians. During a visit to Vienna in 1800, he was decisively defeated by Beethoven in an informal contest at Count Fries's* house. When his turn came, Beethoven improvised so brilliantly on a theme taken from one of Steibelt's piano quintets that Steibelt left the room before he had finished. Steibelt thereafter avoided any further contact with Beethoven during the remainder of his stay in Vienna. According to Ferdinand Ries,* he even made his acceptance of any invitation conditional on Beethoven not being among the guests.

It is worth pointing out that Ries, whose account (in *Biographische Notizen*) constitutes the only written source for our knowledge of this incident, was not himself a witness to it, since he most probably did not arrive in Vienna until late 1801. However, brief confirmation of the overall veracity of the anecdote is supplied by an entry made by Beethoven's nephew Karl* in a conversation book in September 1825 (*BKh*8/126): 'Schuppanzigh* is describing how you triumphed over Steipelt [*sic*].' The entry was made on the occasion of a private performance of Beethoven's Quartet in A minor, Op. 132, at the hotel Zum wilden Mann. Schuppanzigh may have been telling the story to Sir George Smart* who was among the guests.

(Dawes, Müller[1], Wegeler/Ries)

Stein (family). Musicians and instrument makers. The most celebrated member of the family was the Augsburg organist and piano and organ maker **Johann (Georg) Andreas Stein** (b. Heidelsheim, 6 May 1728; d. Augsburg, 29 February 1792). It is very likely that Beethoven made his acquaintance at Augsburg in 1787, either on the outward or the return journey of his trip to Vienna. This supposition is based mainly on an entry by Karl von Beethoven* in a conversation book in 1824 (*BKh6/321*); but it also draws support from the very reasonable assumption that he would have been eager to meet Stein and examine his pianos. He may have been introduced to Stein by Joseph Wilhelm von Schaden* or his wife Nanette. The latter, an excellent pianist, was friendly with Stein's daughter Maria Anna and presumably knew her father well.

Stein's daughter **Maria Anna** [Nannette] (b. Augsburg, 2 January 1769; d. Vienna, 16 January 1833) took over the business after her father's death. In 1794 she moved with her husband Johann Andreas Streicher* to Vienna, where she founded a new piano-making firm together with her brother **Matthäus Andreas** (b. Augsburg, 12 December 1776, d. Vienna, 6 May 1842). The partnership split up in 1802, and Matthäus Stein then set up his own business. (On the Streichers' relations with Beethoven, *see* the separate article devoted to them.)

Beethoven is known to have been in contact with Matthäus Stein at various times, especially during the last ten years of his life, when his deafness was seriously affecting his work as a musician and the standard pianos no longer satisfied his requirements. In December 1817 he told Nannette Streicher that Matthäus had done him 'a very great favour'—almost certainly a reference to some improvements made by Matthäus to his piano. In 1820, Matthäus devised a sound amplifier for him, and in 1824, with some assistance from Johann Andreas Stumpff,* he completely overhauled Beethoven's Broadwood* piano. In 1826 the piano was repaired once more, this time by Matthäus's son **Karl Andreas** (1797–1863), who worked in his father's firm. (It was on this occasion that Conrad Graf* lent Beethoven one of his own instruments.)

Nannette's brother **(Andreas) Friedrich** (b. Augsburg, 26 May 1784; d. Vienna, 5 May 1809) arrived in Vienna in 1804. A pianist by training, he studied composition with Albrechtsberger,* and performed concertos by Beethoven and Mozart* at public concerts. In 1809 the Kunst- und Industrie-Comptoir* published his arrangement for two pianos of Beethoven's Fourth Symphony. Beethoven informed Breitkopf & Härtel* on 4 March of the same year that Stein was offering to make similar arrangements of the Fifth and Sixth Symphonies (both of which the firm was about to publish). It is not known whether Breitkopf & Härtel accepted the offer; in any case, Stein died soon afterwards. According to Kinsky/Halm, Johann Baptist Traeg* published Stein's arrangement of the *Coriolan* Overture for piano duet in 1811.

(Bolte, Göthel[1])

Stein, Anton Joseph (b. Bladen, Upper Silesia, 24 April 1759; d. Vienna, 4 October 1844). Philologist and poet. In 1806, after teaching in Viennese schools for some twenty years, he was appointed professor of Latin literature and Greek philology at the University of Vienna; he remained on its faculty until 1825. In 1843 he published his collected poems, in German, Latin, and Greek.

He wrote the text for 'Hochzeitslied' (WoO 105), the wedding hymn composed by Beethoven on the occasion of the marriage of Anna Giannattasio del Rio* to Leopold von Schmerling on 6 February 1819. Anna's daughter Anna Pessiak-Schmerling later told Thayer* that Stein had been a friend of her grandfather, Cajetan Giannattasio del Rio.* He was cited by Beethoven, in his letter to the Vienna Magistracy on 1 February 1819 (*Corr.* A App.C, 9/B1286), as one of the learned persons who considered boarding schools to be unsuitable institutions for his nephew Karl,* because they did not provide adequate supervision.

(Wurzbach[1])

Steiner, Sigmund Anton; S. A. Steiner & Co. Sigmund Anton Steiner (b. Weitersfeld, Lower Austria, 26 April 1773; d. Vienna, 28 March 1838) moved to Vienna in 1789, and later worked as secretary for Joseph Hartl von Luchsenstein. In 1803 he was appointed manager of the newly founded Chemische Druckerei, a printing-house started by Alois Senefelder with financial assistance from Hartl. Steiner took over the firm in 1805 (together with Rochus Krasniczky), and the following year he bought Franz Anton Hoffmeister's* complete stock of music, together with the plates and publication rights. In 1807 he registered a new music publishing firm under the name 'S. A. Steiner', which he ran together with Krasnitzky until 1812, when he became its sole proprietor; by then the firm had published some 2,000 musical works. In 1813 Tobias Haslinger* was engaged as manager; two years later he became Steiner's partner, whereupon the firm was renamed 'S. A. Steiner & Co.'. In addition to its music publishing activities, the firm launched the periodical *Allgemeine musikalische Zeitung* in 1817; it appeared until 1824. The music store in Paternostergassel, near the Graben, became a favourite meeting place for Viennese and visiting musicians, and Beethoven was to be regularly found there for many years. In his dealings with the firm he made amusing use of a scale of military ranks: he styled himself 'Generalissimus', whilst Steiner was called 'Generalleutnant', Haslinger 'Adjutant', and Anton Diabelli,* who was for a time employed there as proof-reader, 'Grossprofos' ['provost marshal']; in this connection *see also* Esterházy von Galántha, Almerie*.

Beethoven's business contacts with Steiner were, at the outset, closely linked with the loan of 1,500 florins which the composer had granted his brother Kaspar Karl* in April 1813 and which had been guaranteed by the latter's wife Johanna.* It is therefore desirable to trace the history of that loan in as much detail as the somewhat confusing available evidence allows. (Part of that history concerns Kaspar Karl and Johanna as directly as it does Beethoven himself, and due reference is made to it in the articles relating to them.) When the original loan remained unpaid in the autumn of 1813, Beethoven took legal steps to recover his money. A settlement was reached on 22 October which provided for the repayment of 1,000 florins within six months (i.e. by April 1814) and of the remaining

500 florins three months later (July 1814). But in December 1813 Beethoven, presumably in urgent need of cash, ceded his claim to Steiner, who thereupon paid out the full amount to him. An agreement dated 10 December stipulated, however, that if Steiner had not received repayment from Kaspar Karl and Johanna within nine months (i.e. by September 1814), the onus for discharging the debt would fall on Beethoven, to whom Steiner would then be prepared to grant a three-month grace period. In return for this concession Beethoven was to make available to Steiner, for the latter's free use and without charge, 'his entirely new and still unpublished piano sonata with or without accompaniment by another instrument' for a period of three months, and, in addition, offer Steiner first option on certain future compositions.

Evidently Kaspar Karl and Johanna did not meet their obligation, for in September 1814 Steiner took steps to have a lien placed on the guarantor's (i.e. Johanna's) half of a house which she owned jointly with her husband in the Alser suburb; this was duly done on 21 October. Beethoven appears to have been thereby relieved of any responsibility for the discharge of the still outstanding debt, and it accordingly becomes inappropriate to speculate, as some of his recent biographers have done, whether he ever actually paid the 1,500 florins to Steiner. On the other hand, it is very likely that Johanna eventually did so (perhaps with the help of Johann Kaspar Hofbauer), for it transpires from a letter she addressed to Steiner on 28 March 1818 (*Corr.* B1250) that she had repaid a loan of that amount eleven days earlier, as well as another one of 700 florins in 1817. In the same letter she promised to pay Steiner by 1 August 1818 the interest of 280 florins which was still due in respect of those loans. However, she did not keep this promise, and later Beethoven voluntarily assumed responsibility for that sum (*see Corr.* B1422 n. 5, and A1087/B1486).

If, as has been argued above, the agreement of 10 December 1813 did not, in the end, involve Beethoven in the actual discharge of Johanna's debt, it may very well at least partly account for the fact that Steiner's firm displaced Breitkopf & Härtel* as his principal publisher. In that case, the 'new piano sonata' mentioned in that agreement turned out to be the Sonata Op. 90 which Steiner published in June 1815. (It was, incidentally, the only one of Beethoven's works to bear the imprint 'S. A. Steiner', as against 'S. A. Steiner & Co.') Furthermore, Steiner bought a number of works from Beethoven for 250 ducats on 20 May 1815. The most important of these—with the exception of *Fidelio* (the score of which was eventually issued by A. Farrenc in Paris in 1826) and the oratorio *Der glorreiche Augenblick* (issued by Haslinger in 1837)—were published by S. A. Steiner & Co. in 1816–17. Among them were the Seventh and Eighth Symphonies, *Wellingtons Sieg*, the String Quartet Op. 95, the Violin Sonata Op. 96, and the Piano Trio Op. 97. (The first work by Beethoven to be issued by the new firm S. A. Steiner & Co. was, however, not one of those included in the May 1815 package, but the piano arrangement of 'Es ist vollbracht' (WoO 97), the final number of Georg

Friedrich Treitschke's* *Die Ehrenpforten*, which, according to Kinsky/Halm, appeared in July 1815.)

In 1816 S. A. Steiner & Co. also published the song cycle *An die ferne Geliebte*, composed that same year, as well as two other songs (Opp. 94, 98, 100); in 1817 the firm brought out the first edition of the Piano Sonata Op. 101. This almost marked the end of the firm's association with Beethoven, except for a number of relatively minor works during the 1820s: settings of Goethe's poems 'Meeresstille' and 'Glückliche Fahrt' (Op. 112) in 1822; the Overture to *Die Ruinen von Athen* (Op. 113) in 1823; the variations on 'Ich bin der Schneider Kakadu' (Op. 121a) in 1824; the Overture *Zur Namensfeier* (Op. 115) in 1825; and the March with chorus from *Die Ruinen von Athen* (Op. 114), the Overture to *König Stephan* (Op. 117), and the trio 'Tremate, empi, tremate' (Op. 116) in 1826. (This last composition, like the three overtures, had been among the music purchased in May 1815.)

As already indicated, Beethoven's connection with Steiner went beyond that of composer and publisher, for, in addition to taking over the aforementioned loan in 1813, Steiner rendered him some other financial services. In 1816 Beethoven invested 4,000 florins with Steiner, who paid him 8 per cent interest; Beethoven withdrew the money in 1819 in order to buy eight bank shares (*see* Eskeles*). During the same period Beethoven obtained several loans from the firm, and although he made occasional repayments, his debt eventually reached 3,000 florins. But when Steiner requested settlement of the debt in 1820, Beethoven reacted angrily. Steiner justified his demand in his letter of 29 December 1820 (*Corr.* B1422) which was both dignified and cordial in tone: 'I assisted you as a friend in need, I trusted and believed in your word of honour, I did not press for repayment nor have I ever harassed you in any other manner. I must therefore protest solemnly against the reproaches you have addressed to me . . . When you consider that a part of the loan I have made you goes back five years, you will recognize that I have been anything but an importunate creditor. I would go easy on you even now and wait patiently, if, on my honour, I was not myself in urgent need of cash for my business.' Steiner pointed out, moreover, that he had allowed Beethoven, at his request, to withdraw his entire capital of 4,000 florins in 1819, without deducting the money Beethoven owed him at the time. In 1823, Beethoven had to sell one of his bank shares (*see* Eskeles*) to meet some of his obligations; even so, it was not until April 1824 that his debt to Steiner was completely repaid. The matter appears to have engendered lasting resentment in Beethoven, for in a letter to Schott's Söhne* on 5 February 1825 he described Steiner as 'an extremely avaricious scoundrel'. Steiner, on the other hand, retained his high regard for Beethoven. Writing to Haslinger from Leipzig on 24 May 1824, he thus commented on the difficulties which Beethoven had encountered in connection with his recent concerts: 'I also feel sorry for our one and only Beethoven. No one here will believe that so great and rare a man is being treated so callously' (*see Corr.* B1840 n. 5).

On 11 March 1826 Steiner's partnership with Haslinger was dissolved. Two days later he registered a new firm in his own name, but shortly afterwards he decided to turn in his licence. Like Haslinger, he was a torchbearer at Beethoven's funeral. (For first editions of works by Beethoven published by Haslinger's firm, *see* the separate article devoted to him.)

(Slezak[4], Wurzbach[2])

Sterkel, Johann Franz Xaver [Abbé] (b. Würzburg, 3 December 1750; d. Würzburg, 12 October 1817). Composer, pianist, and organist. Between the years 1778 and 1797 he lived mainly at Mainz; but it was at Aschaffenburg (where the summer palace of the elector of Mainz was located) that Beethoven was introduced to him in the autumn of 1791, while travelling to Mergentheim with the rest of the Bonn court Kapelle. The occasion, which greatly impressed those who witnessed it, was later described by Franz Gerhard Wegeler* in *Biographische Notizen*, and also by Nikolaus Simrock* in a letter to Schindler.* After Sterkel had played one of his own violin sonatas with Andreas Romberg,* Beethoven, at Sterkel's request, performed some of his own recently published variations on Vincenzo Righini's arietta 'Venni Amore' (WoO 65)—'entirely in [Sterkel's] manner, with the utmost delicacy and a brilliant, light touch, to the amazement of the visitors from Bonn who had never heard him play in that style before' (Wegeler).

(Schiedermair[1], Wegeler/Ries)

Stich, Johann Wenzel: *see* Punto.*

Stieler, (Kaspar) Joseph (b. Mainz, 1 November 1781; d. Munich, 9 April 1858). Portrait painter. He studied with Christoph Fesel at Würzburg (1798–1800) and Friedrich Heinrich Füger in Vienna, where he lived from 1800 to 1805. His early travels also took him to Poland (1805–7) and Italy (1809–12). Between 1812 and 1816 he executed several portraits of the Bavarian royal family, and although he continued to travel extensively, mainly in Germany, throughout the rest of his life, Munich remained his principal place of residence. In 1816 King Maximilian I Joseph* sent him to Vienna to paint the portraits of Emperor Franz I and Empress Karoline Auguste, who was Maximilian's daughter. Stieler resided in Vienna until 1820. In addition to painting the imperial couple, he fulfilled numerous commissions from the local aristocracy. This was, in fact, the third time he had stayed in Vienna, for apart from his student years he had spent several weeks there in 1807, on his return from Poland. In the diary he had kept on that occasion he had described in some detail the city's musical life, in which he had participated as a singer and guitarist. Among the musicians he had met had been Muzio Clementi* who was on a visit to Vienna at the time; but there is no evidence of his having been introduced to Beethoven then.

In February–March 1820, a few months before his return to Munich, he painted Beethoven at the request of Franz Brentano* (whose portrait, as well as that of his wife Antonie, he had done some years previously). Beethoven granted him several sittings, at least one of which appears to have taken place in Stieler's rooms on the Mölkerbastei. The portrait shows Beethoven in the process of composing the *Missa solemnis*. Opinions among Beethoven's acquaintances were divided as to whether Stieler had achieved a true likeness of his subject. Oliva* thought quite highly of the painting, but Schindler* declared that he preferred Schimon's* portrait. It is, above all, an idealized depiction of an inspired genius, and as such it was to become a powerful element in the development of the Romantic Beethoven myth.

Stieler stated that, after publicly exhibiting the portrait, he would send it to Franz Brentano. But after it was shown at an exhibition of the Akademie der bildenden Künste in Vienna in April 1820, Stieler decided to keep it— perhaps, as Frimmel suggests, because he did not regard it as completed. Instead, he painted a (now lost) miniature portrait on ivory for the Brentanos. A lithograph of the Viennese portrait, made by Stieler's nephew Friedrich Dürck and printed by Joseph Anton Selb in Munich, was offered for sale by Mathias Artaria* in 1826. The original painting, as well as a preparatory sketch in oils, is now at the Beethoven-Haus at Bonn. Reinhold Schmitt-Thomas's suggestion that another Beethoven portrait, which in 1970 was in the possession of a private collector at Schweinfurt, may likewise be the work of Stieler has been rejected on stylistic grounds by Stieler's biographer Ulrike von Hase-Schmundt.

(*Beethoven-Haus*[3], Frimmel[1,3], Hase[2], Kalischer, Schmitt-Thomas)

Stoll, Joseph Ludwig (b. Vienna, 1778; d. Vienna, 22 June 1815). Poet and dramatist; son of the well-known physician Maximilian Stoll (1742–88). In 1801, after extensive travels in Europe, he settled at Weimar, where he wrote comedies for the court theatre (*Das Bild Amors, Scherz und Ernst, Streit und Liebe*). In 1807 he was engaged as resident dramatist at the Burgtheater in Vienna. There, the following year, he founded the literary periodical *Prometheus* with Baron Leo Seckendorf. In 1811 the first part of his *Poetische Schriften* was published at Heidelberg (the second part never appeared.) During his final years Stoll lived in increasing poverty, having lost his post at the theatre and squandered a not inconsiderable inheritance.

Stoll was in contact with Beethoven by 1808 at the latest; in May of that year the latter's song 'Sehnsucht' (WoO 134, first version) was published as a supplement to the third number of *Prometheus*. But for the premature demise of that periodical, the song 'Andenken' (WoO 136) would likewise have appeared there. In December 1811 Beethoven set a poem by Stoll in 'An die Geliebte' (WoO 140; Schubert set the same poem in 1815).

In his recollections of Beethoven, Grillparzer* recalls having seen Beethoven and Stoll together at coffee houses, and he also mentions rumours that they were planning to write an opera together. Nothing came of the project, if indeed it was ever seriously considered. Beethoven is known to have tried to help Stoll, for whom he evidently felt some sympathy. On one occasion, probably in the summer of 1809, he asked Hammer-Purgstall* to secure free or cheap transport for Stoll to Paris, where Stoll hoped to make arrangements for a teaching post in Westphalia (*Corr.* A227/B391); but there is no evidence that Stoll actually travelled to Paris at this time. Two years later Beethoven offered to guarantee a loan which Stoll wished to obtain from the firm Gebrüder Offenheimer (*Corr.* A293/B522). (*See also* Oliva.*)

(Fischer³, Orel², Sauer)

Streckfuss, (Adolf Friedrich) Karl (b. Gera, 20 September 1779; d. Berlin, 26 July 1844). Civil servant in Saxony, and later in Prussia; poet. He arrived in Vienna in 1803 from Trieste, where he had been employed as a private tutor. He soon became a popular figure in Karoline Pichler's circle, admired for his poems and greatly liked for his personal qualities. He remained in Vienna until 1806. As a poet, he became particularly well known for his translations from the Italian, especially of Dante.

In 1804 he published in Vienna a collection of verse (*Gedichte*) which included German versions of some of Petrarch's* sonnets. The book was found among Beethoven's possessions after his death. Beethoven made sketches for settings of two of the sonnets (*see* Petrarch*). It is not known whether he ever met Streckfuss.

(Schürmann, Virneisel)

Streicher (family). Musical instrument makers. **Maria Anna** [Nannette] **Streicher** (b. Augsburg, 2 January 1769; d. Vienna, 16 January 1833) was a daughter of the famous Augsburg organ and piano manufacturer Johann Andreas Stein.* She learned to play the piano at an early age and was hailed as an infant prodigy, but Mozart,* while recognizing her great talent, severely criticized her technique when he heard her in 1777. After her father's death she took over the business, with the assistance of her younger brother Matthäus Andreas (*see* Stein (family)*). On 7 January 1794 she married the pianist and teacher **Johann Andreas Streicher** (b. Augsburg, 2 January 1769; d. Vienna, 16 January 1833) who had in his youth been a close friend of Friedrich Schiller* and had helped him escape from Stuttgart to Mannheim in 1782.

In July 1794 the Streichers and Matthäus Stein moved to Vienna, where Nannette and her brother founded the piano manufacturing firm 'Frère et sœur Stein', while Johann Andreas devoted himself mainly to teaching (among his pupils was Mozart's son Franz Xaver Wolfgang). Nannette was the guiding spirit of the firm, which quickly made its mark. In 1796 J. F. von Schönfeld, in his

Jahrbuch der Tonkunst von Wien und Prag, described the Streichers and Anton
Walter as the only truly inventive instrument makers then active in Vienna. The
firm was renamed 'Nannette Streicher, née Stein' when the two partners separated
in 1802; Matthäus subsequently set up his own business. Henceforth Johann
Andreas Streicher was to play an increasingly important part in the firm, which
continued to flourish. Its growing eminence in the field is reflected in a contract
it signed on 1 October 1802 with Breitkopf & Härtel,* under which it undertook
not to sell its instruments to anyone in Saxony except the Leipzig publishers,
who were that year commencing what was to become an extremely successful
trade in pianos.

The Streichers must have established contact with Beethoven soon after their
arrival in Vienna—or, more probably, re-established it, for it is very likely that he
had made Nannette's (and her father's) acquaintance at Augsburg in 1787, while
certain remarks in Johann Andreas's letters indicate that he had known Beethoven
since about 1788; where he had met Beethoven—whether at Augsburg in 1787,
or elsewhere the following year—is a matter for conjecture. Both Streichers felt a
profound admiration for Beethoven's music and deeply respected him as a man.
Johann Andreas went out of his way to assure Breitkopf & Härtel that Beethoven
was incapable of an ignoble action (letter of 18 December 1802, cited by
W. Lütge).

Beethoven's relationship with the Streichers appears to have been uniformly
serene, but it was inevitably closer at certain periods than at others. His numerous
letters and notes to Nannette, which date almost entirely from the years 1817–18,
when he was, for the most part, living in the Landstrasse suburb not far from the
Streichers, concern predominantly his personal affairs and relate above all to his
health and still more to his household. It was during this period that he first set
about engaging a housekeeper and a kitchenmaid, a matter in which he greatly
depended on Nannette's advice and assistance, both of which she provided most
generously. His correspondence with Johann Andreas, on the other hand, dealt
mainly with aspects of his professional life as a pianist and composer. Thus
Streicher did his best to further Beethoven's early contacts with Breitkopf
& Härtel, and later he tried to interest Carl Friedrich Peters* in the idea of publishing an edition of Beethoven's collected works (*Corr.* B1883). Naturally, his
discussions with Beethoven also bore on the subject of pianos. In this connection
it is worth noting that Beethoven had initially some reservations about the
Streicher piano. Writing to Streicher from Pressburg [Bratislava] on 19 November
1796, he praised the piano which the firm had sent him there as 'truly excellent',
but added that it was 'too good' for him, 'because it takes away my freedom to
create the tone for myself'. Subsequently Streicher modified his pianos (according to Johann Friedrich Reichardt,* on Beethoven's advice) so as to give a virtuoso
pianist greater control over its tonal quality, and years later, in a letter on 7 July
1817, Beethoven assured Nannette that their pianos had been his preferred instru-

ments since 1809. In the same letter he asked them to rent him one of their pianos, after adapting it to the special needs occasioned by his faulty hearing.

The Streichers regularly held concerts in their music room, which were attended by the cream of Viennese music lovers; the guests included Archduke Rudolph.* Both husband and wife frequently performed on those occasions. The room was adorned with busts of composers which the Streichers had commissioned; among them was Franz Klein's* bust of Beethoven (later probably replaced by Anton Dietrich's*). Dr Karl von Bursy,* who was present at a concert given by the Streichers in 1816, noticed that during the performance of Carl Czerny's* two-piano arrangement of the 'Pastoral' Symphony the listeners would, at certain particularly delightful passages, look up lovingly at Beethoven's bust. In 1827 Streicher was among Beethoven's last visitors, for he accompanied Hummel* to the Schwarzspanierhaus on 8 March. On seeing his old friend so ill, he burst into tears, as did Hummel (according to Schindler's* letter to Moscheles* of 14 March, *Corr.* B2282).

From 1823 on Nannette played a less active role in the business and her son **Johann Baptist** (b. 3 January 1796; d. Vienna, 28 March 1871), who had worked in the firm for many years, was made a full partner; the firm's name was thereupon changed to 'Nannette Streicher & Sohn'. It was Johann Baptist who delivered to Beethoven the Handel* edition which Johann Andreas Stumpff* had sent from England. After the deaths of his parents in 1833, he became the firm's sole owner. He devised several important improvements in piano-making; in 1839 he was appointed court piano manufacturer. He married twice: in 1822 Auguste André (1802–47), a daughter of the Augsburg music publisher Johann Anton André, and in 1849 the pianist Friederike Müller (1816–95), a pupil of Chopin.

Johann Baptist's sister **Sophie** (1797–1840), who was also a competent amateur musician and performed at her parents' concerts, married Ernst Pauer, a Lutheran minister. She was the mother of the pianist and teacher Ernst Pauer (1826–90) who became a professor at the Royal Academy of Music and later at the Royal College of Music in London, and the grandmother of the pianist and teacher Max von Pauer (1866–1945).

(Bolte, Clemen, Göthel[3], Hirt, Lütge[1])

Stumpff, Johann Andreas (b. Ruhla, Thuringia, 27 January 1769; d. London, 2 November 1846). Harp maker; poet. He settled in London in 1790, but subsequently travelled to the Continent more than once. Over the years he came to know several of the leading musicians, both in England and in Germany; he was also a friend of Goethe.*

In 1824 he visited Vienna, and shortly after his arrival on 25 September, accompanied by Tobias Haslinger* and armed with a letter of introduction from Johann Andreas Streicher* whom he had previously met in London, he called on Beethoven at Baden. According to Ludwig Storch, Stumpff was a man of imposing appearance and of a noble and sweet character. 'Never have I encountered a more friendly, more loving eye in any man . . . ,' Storch wrote in the Leipzig periodical *Die Gartenlaube* in 1857, 'and even before he spoke one was subjugated by the beam of love emanating from this splendid mirror of his soul. And when he then spoke in his soft, sonorous, warm voice, no one could resist him; he conquered every heart in an instant.' No wonder, then, that he was cordially received by Beethoven and quickly established a friendly relationship with him. Although he stayed in Vienna for less than a month (he probably left on 19 October), he was able to see Beethoven several times. He wrote down a very detailed account of their meetings and conversations, which Thayer* was able to consult and which he printed in his Beethoven biography. Stumpff was particularly impressed by the very profound admiration which Beethoven expressed for Handel's* music, and decided there and then that he would try to procure for him a collection of Handel's works, since Beethoven lacked the means to purchase them himself. This he managed to do two years later, to Beethoven's great delight (*see* the article on Handel). More immediately, Stumpff endeared himself to Beethoven by arranging and supervising the complete overhaul of his Broadwood* piano by Matthäus Andreas Stein.* On his departure, Beethoven presented him with a print of a portrait of himself.

In 1827 Stumpff was among the English acquaintances to whom Beethoven appealed in his distress over his financial problems (*see also* Moscheles* and Smart*). On 1 March, Stumpff was able to inform him of the Philharmonic Society's* decision to send him £100 (*Corr.* B2267). Beethoven was highly appreciative of the part Stumpff had apparently played in the discussions which had led to this gift. Two weeks after Beethoven's death, Schindler* wrote to Moscheles: 'My very best regards to Herr Stumpf [*sic*], and tell him that it was Beethoven's intention to dedicate one his most recent compositions to him. This shall be done if we can find one that is complete.' Nothing came of this idea. It is, however, interesting to note that among Stumpff's belongings auctioned after his death was 'a chased silver snuff-box with a lock of Beethoven's hair set in a locket outside and original verses by J. A. Stumpff engraved within'; it fetched 7 guineas. The lock of hair may well have been sent to him by Schindler.

Another composer whom Stumpff revered was Mozart,* and he reportedly derived considerable pleasure from having been born on the same day of the year. On his journey to Vienna he had stopped at Salzburg, where he had made the acquaintance of Mozart's widow Constanze, now married to Georg Nikolaus Nissen, and had been shown the room in which Mozart was born. He remained in contact by letter with Constanze, and on being informed by her in 1829 that Mozart's sister was living in straitened circumstances he organized a collection among London musicians and sent her a gift of £63 through Vincent Novello, who was visiting Salzburg that year. He had also acquired a number of Mozart autographs in 1811, which he claimed to have bought from Constanze herself but had more probably purchased from Johann Anton André of Offenbach, to whom Constanze had sold most of her husband's autographs. Subsequently Stumpff tried unsuccessfully on two occasions to sell these autographs, which included ten quartets. They were eventually sold at auction after his death; the autographs of the quartets were bequeathed to the British Museum by a later owner in 1907.

(King, Moscheles, Storch, Willetts)

Stutterheim, Joseph, Baron (b. Mährisch-Neustadt [Uničov, Czech Republic], 18 June 1764; d. Lemberg [Lwiw, Ukraine], 21 July 1831. Army officer. He reached the rank of lieutenant-field marshal in 1815, having distinguished himself in the wars against Napoleon; in 1819 he was awarded a barony.

In 1815 he became co-owner of the 8th Infantry Regiment, whose principal owner was Archduke Ludwig. When Stephan von Breuning,* who was a colleague of his in the war department, approached him on Beethoven's behalf after Karl's* attempted suicide, Stutterheim agreed to take Karl into his regiment. He interviewed Karl in Vienna in December 1826, and on 2 January 1827 Karl left for Iglau [Jihlava, Czech Republic] where the regiment was stationed. The grateful Beethoven dedicated to Stutterheim his String Quartet in C sharp minor, Op. 131, which he had originally intended to dedicate to Johann Nepomuk Wolfmayer:* 'It must be dedicated to Lieutenant Field-Marshal Baron Stutterheim to whom I am indebted for great kindnesses,' he informed Schott's Söhne* on 10 March. The quartet appeared posthumously, in June 1827.

Swieten, Gottfried (Bernhard), Baron van (b. Leyden, 29 October 1733; d. Vienna, 29 March 1803). Diplomat and civil servant; composer and patron of music; son of the distinguished physician Dr Gerhard van Swieten (1700–72). He held diplomatic posts in Brussels (1755–7), Paris (1760–3), Warsaw (November 1763–middle of 1764), and in Berlin (1770–7), where he served as ambassador extraordinary to the Prussian court. During this last posting he fell under the spell of the music of Handel* and J. S. Bach which was particularly cherished in the circle of Frederick the Great's sister, Princess Anna Amalia of Prussia. After his return to Vienna, where he was appointed director of the court library (and in 1782 president of the Education and Censureship Commission), he endeavoured to make the works of those two composers better known by having them performed at concerts at his town residence [3 Renngasse] and also elsewhere, for he was the leader of a group of aristocrats (Gesellschaft der Associierten Kavaliere) who sponsored regular private concerts which were mainly held at the Schwarzenberg and the Lobkowitz palaces. It was, furthermore, at his suggestion that Mozart* re-orchestrated four works by Handel (*Acis and Galatea*, *Messiah*, *Ode for St Cecilia's Day*, and *Alexander's Feast*). Another contemporary musician who greatly benefited from his patronage was Haydn,* for whose oratorios *Die Schöpfung* and *Die Jahreszeiten* he himself wrote the texts.

In Beethoven's case, Swieten did not live long enough to witness his growth into a major composer. The admiration Swieten felt for him was thus inspired primarily by his performances and improvisations on the piano, but Swieten did also encourage him to acquire a thorough command of counterpoint. Their acquaintance commenced soon after Beethoven's arrival in Vienna in late 1792, and Beethoven became a welcome visitor to Swieten's home. According to Schindler,* Swieten was 'musically insatiable' and would not let Beethoven leave after a concert until he had played several Bach fugues. In a brief note on 15 December 1794 Swieten wrote: 'If you have no other engagement next Wednesday, I should be glad to see you here at half past eight with your nightcap in your bag' (*Corr.* B18). No doubt Beethoven's contact with Swieten provided him with valuable opportunities to enrich his knowledge of Handel's music, for which he was to feel an abiding love for the rest of his life. He expressed his gratitude to Swieten by dedicating his First Symphony to him (following the death in July 1801 of the Elector Maximilian Franz,* to whom he had originally intended to dedicate the work).

Swieten, who reportedly studied composition during his Berlin years with Johann Philipp Kirnberger,* wrote a number of undistinguished symphonies and two *opéras comiques*.

(Bernhardt, Olleson[1], Schindler[1], Schmid[2])

Tejček, Martin [Taiček, Teiczek] (b. Prague, 1780; d. Prague, 1847). Lithographer and painter, mostly of landscapes. In 1821 he was deputy director of the Lithographisches Institut in Vienna. The following year he founded a similar business in Prague, together with Anton Machek. In 1841 he produced a lithographed portrait of Beethoven, based on a drawing he had made in *c*.1826 (according to S. Bettermann). It shows Beethoven wearing a smart overcoat and a top hat. There is no evidence that Tejček ever met Beethoven, but he presumably had opportunities to observe him while out walking.

(*ALBK*, Bettermann)

Teltscher, Joseph Eduard (b. Prague, 15 January 1801; d. by drowning, near Athens, 7 July 1837). Portraitist, lithographer, and painter on ivory. In *c*.1820 he moved to Vienna where his uncle Franz Teltscher kept a shop; in 1823 he enrolled as a student at the Akademie der bildenden Künste. He belonged to the circle around Franz Schubert.*

Teltscher made at least two drawings of Beethoven on his deathbed: one is a 'close-up' of the face and upper body, the other, drawn from a certain distance, shows him lying in the bed. While the drawings themselves do not permit one to conclude with certainty that Beethoven was still alive when they were made, the generally held view is that he was (H. C. Robbins Landon, for instance, labels the drawings 'Beethoven in a coma'). In the account of Beethoven's final hours which

Anselm Hüttenbrenner* gave Thayer* in a letter on 20 August 1860 (later printed in the Graz *Tagespost* on 23 October 1868), he states that Teltscher was present in Beethoven's bedroom when he himself arrived there at about 3 o'clock on 26 March 1827, but that Teltscher left before death occurred some two and a half hours later; during all of which time, except at the very end, Beethoven had been unconscious and 'emitting the death-rattle'. Only he himself and one other person were in the room when Beethoven died (*see* Johanna van Beethoven* and Therese van Beethoven*). From the absence of any reference to the drawings, one might deduce that if they were made on that day, they had been completed before Hüttenbrenner's arrival.

A different story was, however, told by Johann Baptist Jenger* to Marie Pachler*—in a letter written, not thirty-three years after the event, like Anselm Hüttenbrenner's (when the memory of the events described may well have been less than sharp), but at 10 o'clock on the morning of 27 March 1827, the day following Beethoven's death. In it Jenger states that Teltscher stood with Hüttenbrenner at Beethoven's bedside when he died and that Teltscher drew him shortly afterwards ('Teltscher zeichnete den Verblichenen unmittelbar nach dem Hinscheiden'). Since it is clear from Jenger's letter that he had not himself been present at the time, he had presumably been given this information either by Teltscher himself, or by Anselm Hüttenbrenner who returned to Graz on 26 March, a few hours after Beethoven's death, but may well have spoken to Jenger before his departure. Or Jenger may possibly have received the information from Tobias Haslinger,* to whom Hüttenbrenner had, by his own account, given the news of Beethoven's death before leaving Vienna.

The matter is still further confused by a letter written by Anselm Hüttenbrenner's brother Joseph to an unknown correspondent in 1868. (It is printed in *Schubert: Die Erinnerungen seiner Freunde*, ed. O. E. Deutsch, Leipzig, 1957 (reissued Wiesbaden, 1983); an English version, *Schubert: Memoirs by his Friends*, appeared in London in 1958.) In this letter Joseph states that Schindler* took him, Anselm, Schubert,* and Teltscher to visit Beethoven a few days before he died: 'When I approached his bed with Anselm and Schubert, he smiled . . . Teltscher drew him, my brother has the drawings . . . A few days later Anselm closed his eyes!'

It therefore appears possible that Teltscher made drawings of Beethoven on two separate occasions: the first time a few days before his death, and the second time on the very day he died, either not long before or shortly after his death. In that case, not all his drawings have survived. The two extant ones described above were first published by Frimmel in his *Blätter für Gemäldekunde* (5/3) in 1909, at which time they were in the possession of the well-known collector August Heymann; later they were acquired by Stefan Zweig. They are now at the British Library in London.

(Deutsch[1], Kerst, Landon[3])

Thayer, Alexander Wheelock (b. South Natick, Mass., 22 October 1817; d. Trieste, 15 July 1897). Writer, biographer of Beethoven. He graduated from Harvard College in 1843, and in 1848 completed his studies at the Harvard University Law School; during his last years there he was employed as an assistant librarian. His interest in Beethoven originally led him to plan a revised edition of Moscheles's* English edition of Schindler's* biography, but, struck by the discrepancies between Schindler's book and the *Biographische Notizen* published by Franz Gerhard Wegeler* and Ferdinand Ries,* he soon concluded that much research still needed to be done first. He spent 1849–51 collecting material, first at Bonn and then mainly in Berlin. By the time he returned for a further two-year spell of research in the summer of 1854, he had decided to write a detailed biography of Beethoven for American readers. This time he worked mainly on the conversation books and other biographical material preserved at the Königlich-Preussische Bibliothek (*see* Schindler*). In the spring of 1856 he headed back to America, in ill health and short of funds (he had kept himself going by writing for the *New York Tribune* and other papers). Finally, in August 1858, thanks to the generosity of two persons, Mehetabel Adams of Cambridge, Massachusetts, and Lowell Mason of South Orange, New Jersey, he was able to settle permanently in Europe, where, in Berlin, Bonn, Vienna, and elsewhere, he pursued his investigations and contacted numerous persons who had associated with Beethoven. Eventually he obtained employment at the American embassy in Vienna, and from 1865 until 1882 he served as American consul at Trieste. Throughout his very extensive research he was motivated by only one desire, that of establishing as precisely and as accurately as possible the true facts of Beethoven's life. 'I fight for no theories and cherish no prejudices; my sole point of view is the truth,' he wrote to Hermann Deiters in 1865. Thayer did not concern himself with the analytical discussion or aesthetic interpretation of the music, but devoted all his time and effort to discovering 'Beethoven the man'.

While it was still Thayer's intention to bring out his biography in English, he now decided to publish it in the first place in German. For this purpose he handed over the text in 1865 to Hermann Deiters, a young teacher and already a promising writer on music (that very same year he published articles in the *Allgemeine musikalische Zeitung* on Beethoven's dramatic compositions and on Schumann as a writer). The first volume of Thayer's *Ludwig van Beethovens Leben*, covering the period up to 1795, appeared in Berlin in 1866 (Deiters was himself to publish a revised edition of it in 1901); the second (1796–1806) and third (1807–16) volumes were likewise published in Berlin, in 1872 and 1879 respectively. Increasingly suffering from ill health, Thayer was unable to complete the remainder of his biography, and it was on the basis of the material he had gathered that Deiters applied himself to that task after Thayer's death. Not long before the fourth volume (1817–23) was ready for publication Deiters himself died, and that volume and the final one appeared at Leipzig in 1907 and 1908 in editions prepared by the well-known musicologist Hugo Riemann, who subsequently also brought out revised editions of the first three volumes (vol. i in 1917, vol. ii in 1910, and vol. iii in 1911). Contrary to Thayer's own stated principle of confining himself strictly to biographical aspects, Deiters and Riemann added numerous and frequently lengthy discussions of the music. These were omitted in the English version published in New York in 1821 by Henry Edward Krehbiel, whose aim was to return to Thayer's original text, at any rate as far as the period covered by the first three volumes was concerned. On the other hand, he felt free to present the material relating to the final ten years of Beethoven's life (corresponding to vols. iv and v of the German edition) in the manner he judged best. Lastly, a reworked and updated edition of the English version was published by Elliot Forbes in 1964 (Princeton University Press; 2nd, rev., edn., 1967). In Forbes's own words, it aims 'to present Thayer's *Life of Beethoven* to an English-reading public as I believe he would have wanted it, using all the new research on Beethoven that Thayer would have used himself had it been available'.

(Forbes[3])

Thomson, George (b. Limekilns, Fife, 4 March 1757; d. Leith, 18 February 1851). Editor and publisher. From 1780 until he retired in 1839 he was employed by the Board of Trustees for the Encouragement of Art and Manufactures in Scotland at Edinburgh, at first as a junior clerk, eventually as principal clerk. His great passion was music, and he was himself a competent amateur violinist. He was deeply moved when he heard two Italian singers, Domenica Corri and the celebrated male soprano Giusto Ferdinando Tenducci, perform Scottish songs at the St Cecilia Society concerts. He was particularly enchanted by the beauty of Tenducci's renditions: 'He it was who inoculated me for Scottish song,' he recalled in a letter to Robert Chambers in 1838. 'Oh that Mrs. Chambers had heard him! He would have beguiled her of her tears as he oft drew mine. I have heard all the great singers of the last fifty years, and not one of them surpassed him for singing to the heart.' As a result of this experience, Thomson conceived the idea of collecting and publishing folk songs. Originally concerned only with traditional Scottish songs, he later extended the project to cover also Welsh and Irish airs. In order to make the songs attractive and suitable for the drawing room, he commissioned several well-known composers (notably Haydn,* Kozeluch,* Pleyel,* and Beethoven) to set them for a small group of instruments, including the piano, and to provide each, in addition, with an introduction and a coda; and at the same time he arranged for the often rather crude texts to be replaced by new and more refined ones (among the poets he approached were Robert Burns, Byron, and Sir Walter Scott). Thomson's initial edition of the Scottish songs appeared in four sets between 1793 and 1799; it was subsequently greatly expanded. The collection of Welsh songs comprised three volumes (1809, 1811, 1817), that of Irish songs two (1814, 1816).

In his first letter to Beethoven, on 20 July 1803, Thomson enquired about his fee for composing six sonatas based on Scottish national airs (*Corr.* B149). In his reply (5 October) Beethoven demanded 300 ducats, a price which Thomson considered unacceptably high. Further correspondence the following year led nowhere, nor did a proposal made by Thomson in July 1806 that Beethoven should compose six trios and six quintets (*Corr.* B253). But Thomson's suggestion that he should harmonize a number of British folk songs eventually bore fruit when Beethoven sent him fifty-three arrangements of such melodies on 17 July 1810 (in this connection, *see Corr.* B253, A136/B259, B401, A229/B409, B426, and A266/B457). Altogether, Thomson was to publish Beethoven's arrangements for one or several voices, with newly composed accompaniments for piano trio, of 125 folk songs: 40 Scottish, 59 Irish, and 26 Welsh (Op. 108, WoO 152–7).

It was Thomson's habit to provide his composers only with the melodies, and in some cases he did not even commission the new texts until he had received their settings of the old tunes. Beethoven complained more than once about this practice, explaining that it was essential for him to know the words if he was to evoke the required emotion in the music, and he even threatened to refuse future commissions unless he was provided with the texts (letter of 29 February 1812); there are indeed indications that he had access to the texts for some of the later settings. Thomson congratulated Beethoven repeatedly on the excellence of his arrangements; and the sincerity of his praise is proved by the following note which he wrote on the flyleaf of one volume: 'Original and beautiful are these arrangements by that inimitable genius Beethoven.' But he did not hesitate to ask for any to be revised if he thought them inappropriate or, as was more likely, too difficult for the limited pianistic skills of the young Scottish ladies for whom the editions were principally intended. 'You are forever writing "easy, very easy",' Beethoven once protested with some exasperation (letter of 25 May 1819, *Corr.* A945/B1303). He must nevertheless have enjoyed making these settings, for he also made arrangements of certain continental folk songs which he had selected himself (WoO 158). Thomson bought these also, but he never published them. He did, on the other hand, bring out the first editions of the variations Op. 105 and of Nos. 2, 6, and 7 of Op. 107.

In September 1813 Thomson informed Beethoven that he and some friends had recently spent a few days in the country, during which they had, among other compositions, played his Quintet (Op. 29) and the first 'Razumovsky' Quartet. 'Each day we played them with increased pleasure,' he wrote, 'and each day we enthusiastically drank the composer's health.' As for the Adagio of the quartet, its theme 'would bring balm to my soul if I heard it even as I lay dying' (*Corr.* B671). And about the oratorio *Christus am Ölberg* which Sir George Smart* conducted at Edinburgh in 1819: 'It is a sublime work which alone would suffice to ensure your immortality' (*Corr.* B1357). The correspondence between Thomson and Beethoven was conducted almost entirely in French.

(Cooper³, Hadden, Hopkinson/Oldham, MacArdle¹)

Thun-Hohenstein, (Maria) Wilhelmine, Countess (b. Vienna, 12 June 1744; d. Vienna, 18 May 1800). Daughter of Imperial Count of the Realm Anton Corfiz Ulfeld (1699–1770), who held several high political and court appointments, and his second wife, Maria Elisabeth, née Princess Lobkowitz (1726–86). On 30 July 1761 Wilhelmine married Count Franz Joseph Anton Thun-Hohenstein (1734–1801), who later became an imperial chamberlain. Her house near the Minoritenkirche was a focal point of the social and musical life of Vienna's aristocracy. Charles Burney described her as 'a most agreeable and accomplished lady of very high rank, who, among many other talents, possesses as great a skill in music as any person of distinction I ever knew'. She was one of Mozart's* principal patrons. On 24 March 1781, shortly after arriving in Vienna from Munich, he wrote to his father: 'I have already lunched twice at Countess Thun's and go there almost every day. She is the most charming and delightful lady I have met in my whole life, and she also thinks highly of me.' In 1798 Beethoven dedicated his Piano Trio Op. 11 to her.

One of the countess's daughters, Maria Elisabeth (1764–1806), married Count [later Prince] Andrei Kyrillovich Razumovsky,* and another one, Maria Christiane (1765–1841), married Prince Karl Lichnowsky.* (*See also* Maria Christiane Lichnowsky*.)

(Burney)

Tieck, (Johann) Ludwig (b. Berlin, 31 May 1773; d. Berlin, 28 April 1853). Poet, novelist, and critic. He visited Vienna, where his sister Sophie was then living, in 1808 (1 August to mid-October), and during his stay there he met several prominent members of the city's literary circle, among them Heinrich von Collin* and his brother Matthäus, Friedrich von Schlegel, Karoline Pichler, and the historian Baron Joseph Hormayr. Another of his acquaintances was Beethoven's friend Johannes Büel.* Tieck was repeatedly received by Beethoven himself, who would readily improvise for his visitor. However, according to his biographer Rudolf Köpke, Tieck felt only qualified admiration for Beethoven's music, recognizing the original and powerful quality of his instrumental works, but caring little for the songs and for his opera. Above all, he found Beethoven's tempestuous character disturbing and greatly displeasing. Indeed, Beethoven's unpredictable behaviour made a lasting impression on him. After spending an evening with Tieck on 25 November 1847, Eduard von Bülow (the father of the pianist and conductor Hans von Bülow) recorded in his notes on their conversation that Tieck had 'once again vehemently expressed his hatred of Beethoven . . . His aversion for Beethoven has also a personal element.' One image which had remained in Tieck's memory for some forty years was that of Beethoven picking up and smashing, in a fit of sudden fury, 'a small marble bust of a count . . . which stood on his writing-desk and in whose palace he had lived'. The nobleman in question was presumably Prince Lichnowsky.* (On the background of the incident, *see* Karl Lichnowsky.*)

(Kopitz, Köpke, Schweikert)

Tiedge, Christoph August (b. Gardelegen, 14 December 1752; d. Dresden, 8 March 1841). Poet, best known for *Urania: Über Gott, Unsterblichkeit und Freiheit* (Halle, 1801), a philosophical poem which, in its rationalism, showed the influence of Kant and Schiller.*

He met Beethoven in 1811 while staying at Teplitz [Teplice] with Elisabeth von der Recke,* whose life he had shared for the past eight years. Beethoven was greatly attracted to him, as is evidenced by a letter he sent to Tiedge after the latter's departure, in which he writes: 'Every day I scold myself for not having made your acquaintance at Teplitz sooner. It is dreadful to come to know goodness so briefly and then to lose it once more . . . Let us embrace like men who have cause to love and honour one another' (*Corr.* A324/B521). In his (lost) reply, Tiedge apparently addressed Beethoven with the familiar 'Du', a mark of intimacy willingly accepted by Beethoven, who assured Tiedge on 11 October that 'brief though our contacts were, we quickly recognized one another as kindred spirits' (*Corr.* A327+335/B525). In spite of their warm relationship, no further correspondence between them is known, nor is there any record of their having met at Teplitz in 1812, although both visited the spa again that year. Perhaps Tiedge had left by the time Beethoven arrived in early July.

Beethoven twice set stanzas from *Urania*, each time under the title 'An die Hoffnung'. The first setting (Op. 32), was written for Josephine von Brunsvik* in 1805 and published later that year by the Kunst- und Industrie-Comptoir,* though without a dedication; the second, on a slightly longer text (Op. 94), was composed in 1815 and published the following year by S. A. Steiner & Co.,* with a dedication to Princess Karolina Kinsky.* According to the tenor Franz Wild,* the latter version was written for him, and he and Beethoven performed it 'at a matinée before a select audience' (in May 1816). For the Ukrainian song WoO 158, No. 16, Beethoven used a German text by Tiedge (*see* Schürmann).

(Schürmann, Wild[1])

Tomášek, Václav Jan Křitel [Tomaschek, Wenzel Johann] (b. Skutsch [Skuteč, Czech Republic], 17 April 1774; d. Prague, 3 April 1850). Composer and teacher. His considerable output includes operas, choral music, a large number of songs, and numerous compositions for the piano. The most interesting of these works, certainly the ones which most influenced other composers, notably

Schubert, were the short lyrical piano pieces. By 1827, the year in which Schubert wrote his Impromptus (D899, D935), Tomášek had published some ten sets of Eclogues, Rhapsodies, and Dithyrambs; his pupil Jan Václav Voříšek,* who had settled in Vienna in 1813, himself published a set of Impromptus there in 1822.

Tomášek was immensely impressed and moved when he first heard Beethoven play at a public concert in Prague in (probably October) 1798: 'Beethoven's magnificent playing, and especially the daring development of his improvisation, stirred me strangely to the depth of my soul. Indeed I was so profoundly shaken in my innermost being that I could not touch my piano for several days.' At this concert Beethoven had performed his First Piano Concerto and two movements from the Piano Sonata Op. 2, No. 1, and had improvised on the theme of the Annio–Servilia duet 'Ah perdona al primo affetto' from Act I of Mozart's* *La clemenza di Tito*. But after Tomášek had heard Beethoven play on two further occasions in Prague (at another public concert, at which Beethoven performed his Second Piano Concerto, and then at a private house), his admiration was tempered with certain reservations. Commenting on Beethoven's improvisation on 'Ah vous dirai-je, Maman', he wrote later: 'While I admired his powerful and brilliant playing, I could not help noting his frequent daring leaps from one theme to another, thereby disrupting the organic connection, the gradual development of ideas. His most splendid compositions are often weakened by such defects . . . What seemed to count most for him in composing was to be unconventional and original.' Tomášek, whose musical idol was Mozart, never lost his profound regard for Beethoven's music, but he found it difficult to come to terms with some of his compositions. Eduard Hanslick, who studied with him, recalled that the twin poles of his lessons were Bach's *Das wohltemperierte Klavier* and Beethoven's piano sonatas, with the exception of the last ones.

Tomášek made Beethoven's acquaintance during his visit to Vienna in the autumn of 1814. He called on him on 10 October and 24 November, and later described their conversations in great detail in the memoirs which he published in the Prague periodical *Libussa* between 1845 and 1850. (These memoirs, written in German, span the period from his youth to the year 1823 and are based on diaries he had kept at the time, so his account of what Beethoven said is likely to be largely accurate.) While in Vienna, he attended a performance of *Fidelio* and a rehearsal for Beethoven's forthcoming concert of 29 November; at the rehearsal he heard the Seventh Symphony, the cantata *Der glorreiche Augenblick*, and *Wellingtons Sieg*. He did not warm either to the opera or to the other three works.

(Bužga[2], Nettl[2], Simpson[1,4])

Traeg, Johann (bapt. Gochsheim, Franconia, 20 January 1747; d. Vienna, 5 September 1805). Music publisher. He moved to Vienna in *c*.1779 and set up as an art and music dealer, trading both in printed editions and in manuscript copies prepared in his own workshop. In a letter on 2 August 1794 Beethoven recommended him as a potential Viennese agent to Nikolaus Simrock,* describing him as 'an excellent and capable fellow'; in 1798 he became an agent for Breitkopf & Härtel.* According to A. Weinmann, Traeg's own publishing career was launched in April 1794 with three string quartets by Joseph Leopold Eybler; but F. Slezak states that he was not granted an official licence until October 1795. Shortly afterwards (December 1795), he published Beethoven's variations for piano on the theme 'Quant' è più bello l'amor contadino' from Paisiello's opera *La molinara* (WoO 69). This was the first of several sets of variations for the piano by Beethoven which were first issued by Traeg. It was followed by variations on the duet 'Nel cor più non mi sento' from the same opera, WoO 70 (March 1796), on 'Ein Mädchen oder Weibchen' from Mozart's* *Die Zauberflöte*, Op. 66 (September 1798), on 'Mich brennt ein heisses Fieber' from Grétry's *Richard Löwenherz* [*Richard Cœur-de-lion*], WoO 72 (November 1798), and on Vincenzo Righini's arietta 'Venni Amore', WoO 65 (2nd version, 1802). Traeg also published first editions of the String Trios Op. 9 in July 1798, and of the songs 'Zärtliche Liebe', WoO 123 (*see* Herrosee*), and 'La partenza', WoO 124, in June 1803.

In September 1803 Traeg made his son **Johann Baptist Adalbert** (bapt. Vienna, 15 September 1781; d. Vienna, 10 November 1839) a partner in the firm. Its name was thereupon changed to 'Johann Traeg und Sohn', but sometime after the father's death it reverted to 'Johann Traeg' (April 1808), a fact which was to cause some confusion to later students of its history. In 1807 Traeg Jr. announced the publication of *Twelve Écossaises* for orchestra, as well as in an arrangement for piano (WoO 16), but no copies have been found. It has, however, been suggested that the *Six Écossaises* for piano, WoO 83, which were published in the collected edition issued by Breitkopf & Härtel, may have been a part of the piano arrangements in question.

Beethoven appears to have been less impressed by the son than he had been by the father: 'bey hrn Traeg ist alles träg', he complained in a letter to Breitkopf & Härtel on 28 January 1812; and the pun ('träg' means 'slack') was evidently more than empty wordplay, for he added: 'In particular, I find none of [Gottfried Christoph] Härtel's hard work there.' In 1817 Traeg declared bankruptcy, and he gave up his licence in 1820. The dissolution of the firm led to legal proceedings regarding the publication rights of Beethoven's three String Trios Op. 9, for whereas the plates were bought in 1818 by Artaria & Co.* (who, as a result, considered themselves entitled to sell the music and did so), Beethoven's original contract with Traeg's firm, and with it the copyright, was acquired in 1823 by S. A. Steiner & Co.,* with the composer's blessing. In 1829 Tobias Haslinger,* who had been running the latter firm under his own name since 1826, took legal steps to establish his sole right to publish the trios, and the courts ruled in his favour and against Artaria & Co.

(Slezak[4], Weinmann[8])

Treitschke, Georg Friedrich (b. Leipzig, 29 August 1776; d. Vienna, 4 June 1842). Playwright, theatre manager, and librettist. He was trained to take over his father's business affairs, but soon abandoned commerce for the theatre. His first play, *Das Bauerngut*, was produced with some success in Leipzig and elsewhere. In 1802 he was engaged as producer and dramatist at the court opera in Vienna; in 1809 he was appointed deputy director of the Theater an der Wien, but he returned to the Kärntnertor-Theater as producer and dramatist in 1814. In 1822 he was made responsible for the financial management of the court theatres. Treitschke wrote several plays and numerous opera librettos, mainly based on French models; he was also a noted lepidopterist. In 1805 he married the Italian-born dancer Magdalena Decaro [de Caro] (1788–1816) who was a member of the court theatre ballet from 1803 until 1814.

Beethoven must have known Treitschke long before his earliest known efforts to collaborate with him, for, according to Joseph August Röckel,* Treitschke was among the persons attending the celebrated meeting at Prince Karl Lichnowsky's* in December 1805, at which the first revision of the libretto of *Fidelio* was discussed. (*See also* Kuffner.*) In 1811 Beethoven asked him to prepare a libretto from R. C. G. de Pixérécourt's drama *Les Ruines de Babylone* which had been produced with great success in Paris the previous year, but nothing came of that project. However, when it was proposed in 1814 to revive *Fidelio*, Beethoven turned to Treitschke for assistance with the changes he deemed necessary. Treitschke later described his contribution to the revised libretto in his article 'Die Zauberflöte. Der Dorfbarbier. Fidelio' which appeared in the Viennese periodical *Orpheus* in 1841. (The new version was presented at the Kärntnertor-Theater on 23 May 1814.) Beethoven seems to have been well pleased with Treitschke's efforts.

While engaged on the revision of *Fidelio*, he also wrote the music for the concluding number 'Germania! Germania! Wie stehst Du jetzt im Glanze da!' (WoO 94) of Treitschke's Singspiel *Die gute Nachricht*. This patriotic work, which celebrated the entry of the Allies into Paris on 31 March 1814, used music by several composers; it was first performed at the Kärntnertor-Theater on 11 April. The bass solo in WoO 94 was sung by Karl Weinmüller,* the Rocco in the forthcoming production of *Fidelio*. Beethoven also furnished the music (WoO 97) for the final number, 'Es ist vollbracht', of *Die Ehrenpforten*, another Singspiel by Treitschke inspired by a victory over Napoleon—this time the Battle of Waterloo, which was followed by the second entry of the allied armies into Paris on 7 July 1815. This Singspiel was produced at the Kärntnertor-Theater on 15 July 1815. The soloist in 'Es ist vollbracht' (WoO 97) was once more Weinmüller. Another collaboration envisaged at this time did not come to fruition. Although Beethoven's correspondence reveals his interest in a libretto by Treitschke, to be based on one of the latter's plays, *Romulus und Remus*, and even though *Der Sammler* announced on 16 December 1815 Beethoven's intention of setting the text, he eventually abandoned the project. One final instance of his artistic association with Treitschke appeared in the latter's volume of poetry, *Gedichte*, published in 1817: a setting (WoO 147) of Treitschke's poem 'Ruf vom Berge'. (*See also* WoO 205f and *Corr.* A1068/B1216.)

(Griep, Hess[5])

Trémont, Louis-Philippe-Joseph Girod de Vienney, Baron (b. Besançon, 2 October 1779; d. Saint-Germain-en-Laye, 1 July 1852). French army officer; public official. Having been appointed a junior member of the Conseil d'État in 1808, he was the following year instructed to deliver the council's dispatches to Napoleon* in Vienna. He arrived there soon after 22 May and remained until an armistice had been arranged at Znaim [Znojmo] on 12 July, after which he was appointed an intendant in Moravia. Following the conclusion of the Treaty of Vienna (14 October) he returned to that city, but shortly afterwards he took over an intendancy in Croatia. Subsequently he served as prefect of Aveyron and of the Ardennes, and later, in 1831–2, of Dijon, after which time he held no further public office. He had been created a baron of the Empire in 1810. In his will, he bequeathed six volumes of manuscript notes and recollections to the Bibliothèque Nationale. Extracts, including the account of his meetings with Beethoven, were later published (notably by Jean Chantavoine in *Le Mercure musical* in 1906 and J.-G. Prod'homme in the *Musical Quarterly* in 1920). Trémont was himself a competent amateur musician and regularly held concerts at his Paris residence.

He called on Beethoven in Vienna in 1809 and, to his great delight, was very cordially received and invited back more than once; Beethoven even played for him. Trémont claims that Beethoven agreed to travel to Paris with him, where he was to stay at his house; he explains that the plan was abandoned when he was posted to Moravia and later to Croatia. Trémont also suggests that Beethoven, notwithstanding his hostility towards Napoleon, admired him for having risen so high from such humble beginnings, and would not have been averse to receiving some mark of distinction from him. Trémont comments: 'Thus does human pride bow down before what flatters it.'

(Chantavoine, Kinsky, Prod'homme[1])

Troxler, Ignaz Paul Vital (b. Beromünster, 17 August 1780; d. Aarau, 6 March 1866). Swiss philosopher, physician, politician, and teacher. He studied medicine and philosophy at Jena (1800–3). After qualifying as a doctor, he spent some time (1804–5) in Vienna, where, according to his biographer Emil Spiess, he wished to complete his studies in ophthalmology with Dr Johann Malfatti* (in a letter to Friedrich Wilhelm Joseph von Schelling he indicated that he was staying with Malfatti). He was again in Vienna from the summer of 1807 until shortly after his wedding to Wilhelmine Polborn on 16 October 1809, and, finally, during the Congress, from late October 1814 to late February 1815. In Switzerland he practised as a doctor, and he also taught philosophy at Aarau and at the universities of Basle (1830–1) and Berne (1834–53).

Spiess states that Troxler met Beethoven through the Malfattis during his first stay in Vienna in 1804–5. However, Beethoven probably did not make the acquaintance of Dr Malfatti's cousin Jakob Friedrich* and his family until 1810, and there is no firm evidence that he knew Dr Malfatti himself before 1809. It may well be that Troxler did not meet Beethoven until his second visit to Vienna in 1807–9. The only known written communication between them is a letter sent by Beethoven to Troxler from Baden in August/September 1809 (*Corr.* A225/B399). Its purpose was to request Troxler to accompany Beethoven as interpreter to a meeting with Muzio Clementi.* The tone of the letter—the rather informal address 'Lieber Doctor' (as opposed to 'Lieber Herr Doktor') and the concluding phrase 'Halten Sie lieb Ihren Freund' [Think fondly of your friend]—suggests a certain intimacy.

(Geiser, Spiess)

Tuscher, Mathias von (*c.*1775–1860). Magistratsrat [magisterial councillor] in Vienna at the time of Beethoven's dispute with Johanna van Beethoven.* His friendship with the composer went back at least as far as May 1814, when, at his request, Beethoven had composed 'Abschiedsgesang' (WoO 102—*see* Joseph von Seyfried*).

In 1819 Tuscher obliged Beethoven by offering to assume the co-guardianship of his nephew Karl.* The appointment was approved by the Magistracy on 26 March and took effect the next day. Tuscher supported Beethoven in his efforts to obtain permission to have Karl educated by Johann Michael Sailer* at Landshut, but this new attempt to reduce Johanna's contacts with her son failed (*see* Piuk*). On 5 July Tuscher applied to be relieved of the guardianship, on the grounds that 'the multiplicity of his official duties, as well as various other considerations' made it impossible for him to continue in that function, which he described as 'irksome and onerous in every respect' (*Corr.* B1311 n. 4). His request was granted on 17 September 1819 when the Magistracy named Johanna and Leopold Nussböck co-guardians. Beethoven felt annoyed with Tuscher for not curbing Johanna's influence more effectively, but later he recognised that Tuscher could not really be held responsible for this; moreover, as he wrote to Johann Baptist Bach* in February 1820, 'an old friendship cannot be denied' (*Corr.* A1006/B1366).

It is not clear why, when the Philharmonic Society of Laibach [Ljubljana] awarded its honorary membership to Beethoven, the diploma (dated 15 March 1819) should have been sent to him through Tuscher. In acknowledging receipt of the diploma on 4 May 1819, Beethoven promised to send the society in due course—likewise through Tuscher—the manuscript of an as yet unpublished composition. (He never did so, but may instead have presented to the society the manuscript of the 'Pastoral' Symphony which is today in the library of Ljubljana

University.) Perhaps Tuscher's role in this matter was connected with his membership of the Gesellschaft der Musikfreunde* in Vienna, of which he was one of the original fifty *Repräsentanten* [representatives]. He also sang in some of its concerts.

(Pohl³)

Ueltzen, Hermann Wilhelm Franz (b. Celle, 29 September 1759; d. Langlingen, near Celle, 5 April 1808). Tutor, preacher, and poet. Beethoven set one of his poems in 'Das Liedchen von der Ruhe' (Op. 52, No. 3) and used its opening words 'Im Arm der Liebe ruht's sich wohl' in a canon (WoO 159).

(Timmermann)

Umlauf [Umlauff], **Ignaz** (b. Vienna, 1746; d. Meidling, near Vienna, 8 June 1796). Composer, conductor, and viola player. His most successful stage works were *Die Bergknappen* (1778), *Die schöne Schusterin, oder Die pücefarbenen Schuhe* (1779), and *Das Irrlicht* (1782). In 1796 Beethoven composed two arias (WoO 91), one for tenor, the other for soprano, for performances of *Die schöne Schusterin*. This Singspiel was based on *Les Souliers mordorés, ou La Cordonnière allemande*, an *opéra comique* by Alessandro Mario Antonio Fridzeri and A. de Ferrières (Paris, 1776). It had first been produced at the Burgtheater, with a German text by Johann Gottlieb Stephanie, on 22 June 1779; it was altogether performed twenty-five times between 1779 and 1782. Subsequently it was produced also at other Viennese theatres, including the Freihaus-Theater auf der Wieden (27 April 1795) and the Kärntnertor-Theater (30 May 1795). At the latter theatre, according to Franz Hadamowsky, *Die schöne Schusterin* was performed eight times in 1795 and seven times in 1796 (in which year it was also given once at the Burgtheater). But Beethoven may well have first seen the Singspiel at Bonn, where it was presented during the 1789–90 and 1790–1 seasons. The text of the soprano aria was already in Stephanie's libretto; for the tenor aria Beethoven revised his earlier song 'Maigesang' (Op. 52, No. 4), based on a poem by Goethe.*

(Branscombe⁶, Hadamowsky, Hess³)

Umlauf [Umlauff], **Michael** (b. Vienna, 9 August 1781; d. Baden, near Vienna, 20 June 1842). Composer, conductor, and violinist; son of Ignaz Umlauf.* He started his career as a violinist in the court orchestra and later became one of its conductors. From 1819 to 1834 he also directed the concerts of the Wiener Tonkünstler-Societät. In 1840 he became, for a short time, music director of both court theatres. He wrote music for a number of ballets and some Singspiels, as well as a Mass and various other works, but as a composer he never attained the prominence which his father had enjoyed.

Umlauf is of interest to Beethoven scholars for his association with several important performances. Some well-known anecdotes describe occasions during rehearsals or performances when he saved the orchestra (and singers) from being hopelessly confused by Beethoven's conducting, which was determined by the progress of the composition as he imagined it in his mind rather than by the performance he was directing—which, of course, he was unable to hear. The tenor Franz Wild* tells of one such crisis occurring at a performance of *Wellingtons Sieg* (either on 8 December 1813 or 2 January 1814), when Umlauf took charge at the decisive moment, without Beethoven even being aware of it. And Treitschke* relates that when Beethoven failed to keep correct time at the première of the final version of *Fidelio* on 23 May 1814, 'Kapellmeister Umlauf, standing behind him, guided everything to success with his eyes and hands'. Umlauf also conducted the new production of the opera on 3 November 1822. Finally, he played a major role in the rehearsals and at the first two performances of the Ninth Symphony on 7 and 23 May 1824. His name frequently appears in the conversation books in this connection, and there are even some entries in his own hand. The announcements of the two concerts clearly show that the responsibility for directing them was largely his: 'Herr Schuppanzigh* will lead the orchestra, and Herr Kapellmeister Umlauf will conduct the whole performance. Herr L. v. Beethoven will take part in the direction of the whole performance.' Beethoven's nephew Karl* fully recognized how essential Umlauf's contribution had been for the success of that first performance of the symphony ('Ohne Umlauf wär es gewiss nicht gegangen', *BKh*6/176). He added that Umlauf had been so concerned that the orchestra might not be up to the task that as he stepped on the stage he made the sign of the cross over the players.

(Branscombe[7])

Unger [Ungher, Ungher-Sabatier], **Karoline** [Caroline, Carolina, Carlotta] (b. Stuhlweissenburg [Székesfehérvár, Hungary], 28 October 1803 (place of birth according to Kutsch/Riemens and *New Opera Grove; MGG* and *New Grove* give Vienna); d. Florence, 23 March 1877). Contralto; daughter of the teacher, writer, and amateur singer Johann Karl Unger (1771–*c*.1836). Among her singing teachers were Joseph Mozatti, Mozart's* sister-in-law Aloisia Lange, and Johann Michael Vogl;* she also studied the piano with Mozart's son Franz Xaver Wolfgang. In 1821 she was engaged at the Kärntnertor-Theater, having already made a certain name for herself in concerts. She appeared in the title role of Rossini's* *Tancredi* in January 1821, and the following month in *Mädchentreue* [*Così fan tutte*] in the part of Isabella [Dorabella], in which Schubert* had coached her. Under Domenico Barbaia's management she frequently appeared with the Italian opera company. She even tried to persuade Beethoven to compose an Italian opera, but although he promised to, he never did.

Her first documented visit to Beethoven took place around 20 January 1824, but she may already have called on him on 8 September 1822 (*see* Sontag*). In any case, as she told Ludwig Nohl in 1872, she had repeatedly met him while he was walking in the country near Vienna, and he had on those occasions encouraged her to pursue her musical studies; she attributed his kindness towards her to his friendship with her father. In the years 1823–4 her name is frequently mentioned in the conversation books. She obviously felt the greatest admiration for Beethoven, but was not overawed by him; Schindler* once described her as a 'splendid girl, full of fire and natural high spirits'. She encouraged Beethoven to give another concert in Vienna. 'If you give a concert, I guarantee there will be a full house,' she wrote in January 1824. 'You have too little self-confidence. Has not the homage of the whole world given you a little more pride . . . Won't you believe and accept that everyone is longing to worship you again in new works? Oh, such obstinacy!' (*BKh*5/105–6). When eventually a concert was arranged for 7 May 1824, the programme of which included three sections from the *Missa solemnis* and the first performance of the Ninth Symphony, she was chosen to take the solo contralto parts. Like Henriette Sontag (who sang the solo soprano parts), she found the music difficult and pleaded, though without success, for certain changes. Finally, in exasperation, she accused Beethoven of being 'a tormentor of all vocal organs'—but the resigned exclamation 'Well then, in God's name, let's go on torturing ourselves' which has been attributed to Unger (*see* Thayer/Forbes, 1967, i. 907) was in fact, according to Schindler, uttered by Sontag. At the concert, Unger was involved in an incident which has become famous. Schindler relates that at the end of the symphony Beethoven was unaware of the audience's enthusiastic response until Unger plucked him by the sleeve and drew his attention to it. (In 1860 Sigismond Thalberg, who had been 12 at the time of the concert, told Thayer* that the incident had taken place after the Scherzo.) Unger also sang at the concert at the Grosser Redoutensaal on 23 May, at which the symphony and the Kyrie from the Mass were again performed.

In March 1825 she left for Italy, where she performed for several years, in Naples, Milan, and various other cities. In 1833–4 she sang in Paris, in 1837–40 in Vienna, and in 1840–2 at Dresden. She was as much admired for the beauty of her voice as for the subtlety of her interpretations. In 1843, two years after her marriage to the French writer François Sabatier (1818–91), she retired from the stage and thereafter resided at Florence.

(Schindler[1], Thayer/Forbes)

Usteri, Johann Martin (b. Zurich, 12 April 1763; d. Rapperswil, 29 July 1827). Poet and graphic artist. Beethoven's canon 'Freu' dich des Lebens' (WoO 195), which he wrote out for Theodor Molt* on 16 December 1825, was based on the text of a very popular song, 'Gesellschaftslied'. This text (the opening line of which actually reads 'Freut euch des Lebens . . .') had been written by Usteri; the melody has been ascribed to Nägeli,* though this attribution has been questioned.

(Friedländer, Hahn[1], Unger[1])

Varena, Joseph von (b. Marburg, Styria [Maribor, Slovenia], 15 October 1769; d. Graz, 4 November 1843). He attended school at Marburg and the university at Pest [Budapest], qualifying as a lawyer in 1790. He then settled at Graz, where he practised law and became a notary public. From 1804 he held senior positions (Gubernialrat, Kammerprokurator) in the regional treasury office. Later he was appointed head of the department of law and politics at the local Lyceum. A great music lover, he was a member of the Steiermärkischer Musikverein.

Beethoven made his acquaintance at Teplitz [Teplice] in the summer of 1811. Towards the end of 1811 they began a correspondence which was to continue for at least three and a half years. (The last of Beethoven's known eighteen letters to Varena is dated 23 July 1815; Varena's letters are lost.) Varena asked Beethoven to send him some recent compositions for the charity concerts he was organizing in Graz, and Beethoven provided printed editions or manuscript copies of a number of his works, without charging any fees. As a result, Graz audiences came to know various Beethoven works which they might not otherwise have had an opportunity to hear at this time. Thus the Choral Fantasia (which had been published in July 1811) was performed at a concert on 22 December of that year, with the young Marie Leopoldine Koschak (*see* Pachler*) as soloist; and another concert on 29 March 1812, in aid of a girls' school run by the Ursuline nuns, included the Overture to *König Stephan* and a march with chorus from *Die Ruinen von Athen*, both of them recent and still unpublished compositions (also on the programme were the *Egmont* Overture and the Septet Op. 20). Beethoven probably met Varena again at Baden in the summer of 1814. His last three letters to Varena, all written in 1815, do not concern music for charity concerts, but deal with more personal matters, principally the selection of a piano for Varena's daughter. Beethoven arranged for the delivery of an instrument made by Johann Schanz.

(Deutsch[2], Suppan)

Varnhagen von Ense, Karl August (b. Düsseldorf, 21 February 1785; d. Berlin, 10 October 1858). Diplomat and man of letters; on 27 September 1814 he married Rahel Levin [Rahel Robert] (b. Berlin, 19 May 1771; d. Berlin, 17 March 1833) who had been a prominent literary hostess at the beginning of the century. Varnhagen joined the Austrian army in 1809 and was wounded at the Battle of Wagram (5–6 July). Captured by the French, he was held 'at liberty' in Vienna in August–September before being set free in a prisoners-of-war exchange. He again spent some time in Vienna in 1810. During the next four years, he at first continued to serve in the Austrian army, was later commissioned in the Russian forces, and finally joined the Prussian state service. He returned to Vienna for the Congress as a member of the Prussian delegation which was headed by Prince Karl August Hardenberg and Baron Wilhelm Humboldt. In 1816 he was appointed Prussian chargé d'affaires (from 1817, resident minister) at the ducal court of Baden at Karlsruhe (but he certainly never served as 'prime minister in Karlsruhe', as stated in P. Nettl's *Beethoven Encyclopedia*). Suspected of holding liberal political views, he was recalled to Berlin in 1819. Though remaining in government service there until 1834, he devoted his time increasingly to writing, particularly biographies and memoirs. Among the most notable of his works are the *Biographische Denkmale* (5 vols., 1824–30), and *Denkwürdigkeiten und vermischte Schriften* (7 vols., 1837–46, followed by two posthumous vols. in 1859). His diaries and much of his correspondence have also been published.

In *Denkwürdigkeiten* he describes his first contacts with Beethoven in the late summer of 1811 at Teplitz [Teplice]. He had been staying there with Rahel since 17 June, while Beethoven did not arrive until early August. Their first meeting, arranged by Franz Oliva,* took place at the end of that month or the beginning of September. On 4 September Varnhagen wrote to his friend and military superior Count (later Prince) Friedrich Wilhelm Belgicus zu Bentheim-Steinfurth: 'I have made Beethoven's acquaintance. The wild man behaved very cordially and pleasantly towards me.' Beethoven even agreed to play for Rahel, on condition that she told no one. (According to Varnhagen, Beethoven had been eager to make their acquaintance because Rahel, of whom he had caught sight during a walk in a local park, had reminded him of a person who was dear to him.) After that, they saw each other daily. In *Denkwürdigkeiten* Varnhagen recalled that he had been even more impressed by Beethoven the man than by the artist. But the association was short-lived, for Rahel left for Dresden on 14 September, and Varnhagen returned to Prague, where his regiment was stationed, on 16 September. Beethoven, who left Teplitz two days later, stopped briefly at Prague and may well have met Varnhagen there. Varnhagen expected to hear further from Beethoven during the autumn, especially as they had discussed the possibility of collaborating on an opera (to Rahel, Varnhagen wrote on 18 September: 'Perhaps I shall adapt a French play as an opera libretto for Beethoven . . . It is called *Giafar*'). But he received no communication either from Beethoven or from Oliva, with whom he and Rahel had become very friendly at Teplitz. 'From Beethoven or Oliva I hear and see nothing,' he informed Rahel on 24 October; and on 8 December: 'I have not heard a single word from Beethoven or Oliva.'

However, even if the opera project was silently buried, contact with Vienna was re-established in March 1812 through a letter from Oliva. On 3 June Oliva sent Varnhagen, who was still at Prague, a letter addressed to Prince Kinsky,* in which Beethoven requested his patron to pay his annuity henceforth in redemption bonds at the original figure; Varnhagen was asked to deliver the letter in person and to persuade the prince to take a prompt decision in the matter (*see Corr.* B578). Varnhagen successfully fulfilled the commission on 8 June, and reported back to Oliva the following day (*Corr.* B579). He met Beethoven himself when the latter passed through Prague on his way to Teplitz at the beginning of July. Beethoven wrote to him from Teplitz on 14 July, but nothing is known about a meeting between the two men at Teplitz that year, although Beethoven returned there from Karlsbad [Karlovy Vary, Czech Republic] in the middle of September, while Varnhagen is mentioned in a list of visitors to Teplitz on 19 September.

Varnhagen did meet Beethoven once more, when he called on him together with Prince Radziwill* during the Congress of Vienna. His account of the visit in *Denkwürdigkeiten* is remarkable chiefly for its cool tone, greatly at variance with the warm feelings he had earlier expressed for Beethoven. Now Varnhagen portrays him as a surly and unsociable individual, fiercely hostile towards the aristocracy; and he adds that, in view of Beethoven's uncouth behaviour, he refrained from taking him to meet Rahel, who was also in Vienna. It is tempting to speculate that Varnhagen's changed attitude may have had other causes.

(Feilchenfeldt, Jacobs[1], Pickett, Varnhagen[1,2])

Vering, Gerhard von (b. Oesede, near Osnabrück, 28 January 1755; d. Vienna, 8 November 1823). Physician. He studied medicine first at Münster, and later in Vienna where he moved not later than 1775. He enjoyed a long and distinguished career as a senior medical officer in the Austrian army, retiring in 1822. In a letter to Franz Gerhard Wegeler* on 29 June 1801 Beethoven mentions that he has been consulting Vering during the past month about his persistent attacks of colic and his hearing problems, and that Vering's treatment has been particularly beneficial for the stomach complaint. At the same time, Beethoven's statement 'I had always had confidence in him' indicates that he had known Vering for some time and had most probably consulted him before. However, his confidence was not to last much longer, for less than five months later he complained to Wegeler that Vering did not take sufficient interest in his ailment: 'If I did not go to his house once in a while, which entails great inconvenience for me, I should never see him.' Moreover, he considered Vering to be too much of a 'practical' doctor 'to derive many new ideas from reading' (*Corr.* A54/B70). Shortly afterwards Beethoven sought the advice of Dr Johann Adam Schmidt,* a good friend of Wegeler's.

(Wurzbach[1])

Vigà, Salvatore (b. Naples, 25 March 1769; d. Milan, 10 August 1821). Choreographer, dancer, and composer; son of the dancer, choreographer, and impresario Onorato Vigà (1739–1811) and his wife Maria Ester, also a dancer and a sister of Luigi Boccherini. Vigà was dancing in public by 1783, and he also studied music with Boccherini. In 1789, while performing at the coronation festivities of King Charles IV at Madrid, he met the dancer Maria Medina (?1765–?1833) who became his wife and regular partner. In Madrid he also became acquainted with the French dancer and choreographer Dauberval [real name: Jean Bercher], a pupil of Noverre, and he subsequently studied with Dauberval at Bordeaux. Back in Italy, he choreographed his first ballet, *Raoul signore di Créchi*, at Venice in 1791.

In 1793 Viganò and his wife accepted a joint engagement in Vienna, where they made their debut on 13 May in Antonio Muzzarelli's ballet *Diana und Endymion, oder Der Triumph der Liebe*. They were, on the whole, highly successful, although Salvatore's reform of the traditional ballet and Maria's style of dancing gave rise to some controversy, mainly fanned by the supporters of Salvatore's rival Muzzarelli. As Heinrich von Collin,* a great admirer of Salvatore, wrote: 'Of course there was something disconcerting in suddenly seeing dramatic action, depth of feeling, and pure plastic beauty of movement in a particular form of spectacle in which one was hitherto accustomed to seeing nothing but leaps and contorsions, constrained positions, and contrived and complicated dances, all of which gave one no sense of any unity.' Stendhal, who later attended several performances of Viganò's ballets in Milan, declared that he, together with Canova and Rossini,* constituted the glory of contemporary Italy.

Between 1795 and 1798 the Viganòs performed together in Prague and various German cities, and in 1798–9 at Venice, but there they separated. From 1799 to 1803 Salvatore was ballet-master at the Vienna court theatre. After returning to Italy he worked in many cities before being engaged in 1811 at La Scala in Milan. There he spent the final ten years of his life, which were to prove the most successful and satisfying of his career.

Beethoven's and Viganò's artistic paths first converged in 1795/6, in connection with the romance 'Une fièvre brûlante' from Grétry's opera *Richard Cœur-de-lion* (originally produced at the Comédie-Italienne, Paris, on 21 October 1784). The opera was presented at the Kärntnertor-Theater on 7 January 1788 under the title *Richard Löwenherz*, with a German text by Johann Gottlieb Stephanie. It was to receive eight more performances, the last on 3 February 1788, after which it was not heard again in Vienna until it was performed at the Freihaus-Theater on 14 June 1800. However, Viganò had, in the meanwhile, produced a ballet with the same title, to music by Joseph Weigl,* into which the romance from Grétry's opera was inserted. This ballet had its première on 2 February 1795, the title role being taken by Salvatore's brother Giulio Viganò (whose engagement in Vienna ran from 1793 to 1815). The ballet was given eleven more times in February and nine times in March, and altogether thirty-two times, the final performance being on 30 August. It was presumably this highly successful ballet which inspired Beethoven to write a set of variations on the romance (WoO 72). He began to work on them in 1796 (or perhaps already in 1795); they were published by Johann Traeg* in 1798.

A closer association between Beethoven and Viganò arose in the case of the 'allegorical' ballet *Die Geschöpfe des Prometheus* which had its première (a benefit performance for its leading female dancer, Maria Casentini*) at the Burgtheater on 28 March 1801. For this Viganò devised and choreographed the story, while Beethoven was invited to provide the music; Viganò also danced in the ballet. The music was received with respect rather than with enthusiasm, being considered somewhat too 'learned' for a ballet. For his part, Beethoven was not entirely satisfied with Viganò's contribution. 'I have composed a ballet,' he informed Franz Anton Hoffmeister* on 22 April 1801, 'but the ballet-master did not do his work quite as well as he might have done.' Notwithstanding these reservations, the spectacle proved sufficiently popular to be repeated fourteen times in 1801 and thirteen times the following year.

(Derra de Moroda, Hadamowsky, Levinson, Raab, Sartori)

Vogl, Johann Michael (b. Ennsdorf, near Steyr, Upper Austria, 10 August 1768; d. Vienna, 20 November 1840). Baritone. Shortly after completing his law studies at Vienna University, he took up an engagement at the court opera on 1 May 1794 and soon became one of its leading singers, excelling in both German and Italian opera. His most successful roles included Mikély in Cherubini's* *Les Deux Journées* [*Der Wasserträger*], Oreste in Gluck's *Iphigénie en Tauride*, Dr Berg in Gyrowetz's *Der Augenarzt*, Jacob in Méhul's *Joseph*, Almaviva in Mozart's* *Le nozze di Figaro*, Télasco in Spontini's *Fernand Cortez*, Sternberg in Joseph Weigl's* *Das Waisenhaus*, and Jakob Friburg in the same composer's *Die Schweizerfamilie*. In February or March 1817 he made the acquaintance of Franz Schubert,* with whom he formed a close musical as well as personal association. He retired from the Kärntnertor-Theater at the end of 1822.

Vogl sang Pizarro at the première of the third version of *Fidelio* on 23 May 1814 (*see also* Weinmüller*), and also in several further performances. However, his voice was not quite deep and strong enough for the part and Beethoven was glad to have an opportunity, when Vogl fell ill, to entrust the role to Anton Forti,* who took it over on 18 July.

(Clive[2])

Vogler, Georg Joseph [Abbé] (b. Pleichach, near Würzburg, 15 June 1749; d. Darmstadt, 6 May 1814). Composer, organist, pianist, theorist, and teacher. A controversial figure, both as composer and performer, he was admired by some—including his pupils Meyerbeer* and Weber*—but regarded as a charlatan by others, Mozart* among them. From late 1802 until 1805 he lived in Vienna, where he was given a contract by Schikaneder* to write three operas for the Theater an der Wien; but he only completed one, *Samori*, which was produced there on 17 May 1804.

Sometime in 1804, Joseph Sonnleithner* gave a musical soirée to which he invited both Vogler and Beethoven, and at which each improvised on a theme proposed by the other. The young Johann Baptist Gänsbacher (later a well-known composer and conductor, and incidentally one of the eight Kapellmeisters who acted as pallbearers at Beethoven's funeral) recorded the occasion in his diary. Although he was greatly impressed by Beethoven's improvisation, it had not, he wrote, aroused in him 'the enthusiasm inspired by Vogler's learned playing, incomparable in its treatment of harmony and counterpoint'. Gänsbacher was very probably influenced by the fact that he was then studying with Vogler; for a different assessment of the respective merits of the two pianists, *see* Junker.*

(Clive¹, Grave)

Vořišek, Jan Václav [Worzischek, Johann Hugo] (b. Wamberg [Vamberk, Czech Republic], 11 May 1791; d. Vienna, 19 November 1825). Composer and pianist. He toured Bohemia as a child virtuoso, and later studied law at the University of Prague (1810–13), while continuing to give concerts and studying composition with Václav Jan Křitel Tomášek.* Adrienne Simpson states (in *New Grove*) that he was particularly enthusiastic about Beethoven's music, and 'it was with the hope of closer contact with Beethoven' that he moved to Vienna in 1813. There he became acquainted with two compatriots who were also passionate music lovers, Johann Nepomuk Zizius* and Raphael Georg Kiesewetter.* Perhaps it was Zizius who introduced him to Beethoven. In any case, he was soon received by Beethoven, who told Tomášek in October 1814 that Vořišek had visited him several times and had recently shown him some of his compositions, which were very well worked out.

Vořišek enjoyed a successful musical career in Vienna (he also briefly worked as a clerk at the war department). When Hummel,* who had given him some tuition, left Vienna in 1816, he handed his pupils over to Vořišek. The latter repeatedly performed in public, as well as at private concerts such as those given by Kiesewetter, and in 1819 he conducted two concerts of the Gesellschaft der Musikfreunde;* the programme of the second, on 18 April, included Beethoven's Second Symphony. In 1822 he was appointed assistant court organist, and the following year he succeeded Wenzel Růžička as court organist. He wrote sixteen songs (which were indebted to Schubert*), some chamber music, and a number of works for the solo piano (which influenced Schubert). One of his models was Beethoven, with whose works his compositions present thematic and rhythmic affinities.

In the summer of 1825, Karl Holz* told Beethoven that Vořišek was dying (*BKh*8/30). According to A. Simpson, Beethoven sent his own doctor to attend him. Vořišek died of tuberculosis, from which he had suffered for many years.

(Simpson⁵, Štědroň²,Tomášek)

Voss, Johann Heinrich (b. Sommersdorf, Mecklenburg, 20 February 1751; d. Heidelberg, 29 March 1826). Poet and translator. Beethoven composed a melody for his song 'Minnelied', but never wrote an accompaniment to it.

(Schürmann)

Wagner, Johann (b. Braunau [Brumov, Czech Republic], 1800; d. Vienna, 1832). Physician. It fell to Wagner, then an assistant at the Pathologisch-anatomisches

Museum, Vienna, to carry out the autopsy of Beethoven's body on 27 March 1827, the day following his death. The original of Wagner's report in Latin, dictated and signed by him, was long believed to have been lost, but was found in 1970. It has been published by Hans Bankl and Hans Jesserer in their book *Die Krankheiten Ludwig van Beethovens . . .*

A man of great professional conscientiousness and considerable talent, Wagner was highly regarded by his colleagues, and when Dr Lorenz Biermayer was dismissed from his post of professor of pathological anatomy in 1829, Wagner was chosen to succeed him. He died only two years later, of tuberculosis.

(Bankl/Jesserer, Neumayr)

Wähner, Friedrich (b. Raguhn, near Dessau, 1786; d. Vienna, 6 September 1839). Journalist. Little is known about his life. According to Franz Gräffer, he was active as a preacher at Dessau before moving to Vienna. There, in 1818, he founded a short-lived literary magazine, *Janus* (3 October 1818 to 30 June 1819). He was obliged by the police to leave in 1825, but returned to Vienna ten years later. Among the journals which carried his articles were *Der Telegraph, Hermes,* and the *Wiener Zeitschrift für Kunst, Literatur, Theater und Mode*; he also contributed to Ignaz Jeitteles's* *Ästhetisches Lexikon.* He was a man of some accomplishments; in particular, he was reputed to be an excellent Hellenist. But his acerbic wit— according to Franz Gräffer, 'his ink was nitric acid'—made him more enemies than admirers. He became increasingly addicted to alcohol and died in poverty.

The article 'Ludwig van Beethoven' which appeared in the first two issues of *Janus* (3 and 7 October 1818) was probably written by Wähner himself. It contained some biographical notes (including the statement 'He was born at Bonn in 1772'), as well as favourable comments on Beethoven's music. There is a reference by Karl van Beethoven* to this article in the conversation books in 1823 (*BKh* 5/24). Following Beethoven's death, Wähner wrote down his recollections of the composer, which were first published in the *Wiener Zeitschrift für Kunst . . .* in 1837. They were subsequently reprinted, entirely or in part, in various periodicals and newspapers in Vienna and Germany. Important extracts were later reproduced in F. Kerst's *Die Erinnerungen an Beethoven* and T. Frimmel's *Beethoven-Handbuch.* Wähner paints a highly sympathetic portrait of Beethoven, which was evidently based in part at least on direct observation and personal contact, as is evident from such phrases as 'Once I asked him . . .' and 'Another time I found him in a state of excitement . . .', as well as from a passage on Beethoven's great love for his nephew.

(Gräffer, Wurzbach[1])

Waldmüller, Ferdinand Georg (b. Vienna, 15 January 1793; d. Hinterbrühl, near Mödling, Lower Austria, 23 August 1865). Painter. His enormous output consists primarily of landscapes, genre paintings, and portraits. In 1823 he was commissioned by Breitkopf & Härtel* to paint Beethoven's portrait; the firm's letter, apparently sent in January, did not reach him until mid-April. He accepted the commission in a letter written on 18 April, in which he also stated that on the previous day Beethoven had promised to sit for him briefly. In a further letter on 3 May he mentioned that the picture was already half finished.

Schindler,* in the *Allgemeine musikalische Zeitung* in 1835 and later in his Beethoven biography, gave detailed accounts of what he described as the one and only session granted to Waldmüller. Beethoven, he writes, had at that time little inclination or patience to sit for a painter, being under great pressure of work and furthermore suffering from eye trouble, with the result that he was constantly in a bad temper. He was therefore predisposed to being irritated by Waldmüller, whom he called the worst painter he had ever met, and he refused any further sittings. In consequence, Waldmüller was obliged to finish the portrait from memory, a fact which, Schindler asserts, explains its 'worthlessness'. Whether Schindler's statement that there was only one sitting is correct it is impossible to say. Certainly there is no mention of this fact in Waldmüller's second letter to Breitkopf & Härtel, but since, according to Schindler, he was anxious to get his fee, he might have deliberately kept the information from the publishers.

Waldmüller's portrait is known to have existed in at least two versions, one of which was destroyed during the Second World War, while the other was, at any rate in the early 1990s, in a private collection in Brussels. However, in an article published in *Studien zur Musikwissenschaft* in 1979, Ellmar Worgull argued that there must have been altogether three versions, of which the first, painted during the sitting in Beethoven's rooms, could have been no more than a quick study or sketch in oils. It was on the basis of this sketch that Waldmüller subsequently painted the full portrait in his studio, which he then sent to Breitkopf & Härtel, in whose possession it remained until it was fatally damaged during an air raid on Leipzig in 1943. (Fortunately a full-size colour copy had earlier been made by a Munich printer (Piperdruck No. 118).) As for the third (and only surviving) version, which very closely resembles the Breitkopf and Härtel portrait, Worgull concluded that it was either copied from it or was painted, like it, directly from the original sketch.

The portrait regarded by Worgull as the third version was shown publicly in Vienna in 1990, and it was subsequently included in an exhibition of items from the Brussels collection which was held at the Beethoven-Haus in Bonn from 15 December 1991 until 12 March 1992. On the latter occasion R. Feuchtmüller published a short article in which he challenged Worgull's conclusions and asserted that there had never been more than two versions: the painting in the Brussels collection, which was in fact the one done during the sitting and which was accordingly the earlier of the two; and the portrait sent to Breitkopf & Härtel.

By an interesting coincidence, both these paintings could for many years be admired in Leipzig. For the 'Brussels' portrait was acquired, at an unknown date, by Carl Friedrich Kistner, who had bought Heinrich Albert Probst's* publishing firm in 1831. Kistner's firm continued in business after his death in 1844, until it was finally sold in 1919 to Carl and Richard Linnemann by Magdalene Gurckhaus, the widow of the firm's last owner Ludwig Gurckhaus who had died the previous year. She reportedly sold the portrait at a public auction. In 1968 it was offered for sale by the music dealer and publisher Hans Schneider (Tutzing, near Munich), and it was later acquired by the Brussels collector. Lastly, it should be mentioned that the Beethoven-Haus in Bonn possesses a copy of Waldmüller's portrait, which was painted in oils by a local artist, Willy (or Wilhelm) Fassbender, at the beginning of the twentieth century and has been in its collection ever since. Its model appears to have been the version then owned by Breitkopf & Härtel.

The quality of Waldmüller's portrait and its resemblance to Beethoven's appearance has been the subject of some controversy. Gottfried Wilhelm Fink, writing in the *Allgemeine musikalische Zeitung* in 1835, praised it as a most excellent likeness of the composer; Schindler, replying in the same journal, dismissed it as the worst of all Beethoven portraits. As for Richard Wagner, he admired it so much—even though, never having seen Beethoven, he obviously had no way of assessing its likeness—that he commissioned the Leipzig painter Isidor Robert Krausse to make a copy for him in 1869. In Worgull's judgement, Waldmüller painted a true picture of Beethoven, which does not idealize him as other painters tended to do, but shows him as he really looked during the sitting(s): sullen and resentful at being kept from his work.

(Feuchtmüller, Lütge[3], Schindler[1], Worgull)

Waldstein, Ferdinand Ernst Joseph Gabriel, Count (b. Vienna, 24 March 1762; d. Vienna, 26 May 1823). A son of Count Emanuel Philibert Waldstein and his wife Maria Anna Theresia, née princess of Liechtenstein, he came from an old Bohemian family which had connections with many of the leading aristocrats of the day. He joined the Teutonic Order and, after spending his year's novitiate partly at Ellingen, in Württemberg, and from 1 February 1788 at Bonn (where he had been summoned by the Elector Maximilian Franz,* the grand master of the Order), he was made a knight on 17 June 1788. Thereafter he was entrusted with a number of duties and diplomatic missions by the elector, with whom he was on excellent terms until opposing political views placed a strain on their relations. Waldstein took an active part in the cultural life of the town and became a member of the *Lesegesellschaft* [Reading Society], and in 1794 its president; he was very musical, being both a pianist and a composer.

From 1795 until 1805 he served in the British army, and subsequently undertook certain military and diplomatic tasks. He did not return to Austria until May 1809. On 9 May 1812, having left the Teutonic Order, he married Countess Isabella Rzewuska (1785–1818), a daughter of Count Seweryn Rzewuski, in Vienna (on her family, *see* Rzewuski*). The couple had a daughter, Ludmila (1816–47). They divided their time between Vienna (Waldstein owned a house at nearby Baden) and the family's estates in Bohemia; after his wife's death, the count lived mostly in Vienna. Crippled by debts, he died penniless.

In the *Biographische Notizen*, Franz Gerhard Wegeler* calls Waldstein 'Beethoven's first, and in every respect most important, Maecenas' and describes him as the first person to recognize Beethoven's great talent. Wegeler furthermore credits Waldstein with discreetly supporting the young musician financially, and, even more importantly, with being responsible for his appointment as organist and for his being sent to Vienna by the elector. It is, however, highly unlikely that Waldstein, who, as far as is known, did not visit Bonn before 1788, had anything to do with Beethoven's appointment as organist in 1784. As for his alleged involvement in Beethoven's journey to Vienna, Wegeler's remark could conceivably have some validity—at least, from a chronological point of view—if applied to the 1792 journey, but not to that of 1787. The most plausible conclusion which can be drawn from the available evidence is that Waldstein had not met Beethoven prior to his arrival in Bonn in early 1788, although the possibility of Beethoven having been introduced to him during his short stay in Vienna in April 1787 cannot be entirely discarded. (Waldstein's biographer Josef Heer speculates that Beethoven may have gone to Prague in early 1787 to meet Mozart* prior to travelling to Vienna, and could have made Waldstein's acquaintance on that occasion. There appear to be no grounds to support such a suggestion.)

In Bonn, Waldstein became very friendly with Beethoven. He visited him at the flat occupied by the Beethovens in Wenzelgasse, no doubt met him frequently at the Breunings'* with whom he was for a time on excellent terms, and also saw him elsewhere. At his request, Beethoven composed music for a *Ritterballet* which was devised by the count and performed by the local nobility on Carnival Sunday, 6 March 1791. The music (WoO 1) was subsequently described in H. Reichard's *Theater-Kalender auf das Jahr 1792* (published at Gotha) as the work of Waldstein himself—perhaps, as Ludwig Schiedermair suggests, because the count had contributed some of the melodies. Furthermore, Beethoven, while still at Bonn, composed a set of variations for piano duet on a theme by Waldstein (WoO 67), which was published by Nikolaus Simrock* in 1794. When Beethoven left in 1792 to study with Haydn,* Waldstein wrote in his album: 'You are now going to Vienna in fulfilment of your long-held wish . . . By dint of unremitting effort you shall receive *Mozart's spirit from Haydn's hands*.' A letter written by Beethoven to Simrock about the above-mentioned variations on 18 June 1794 indicates that he was at that time still in touch with the count, who had, in fact, just spent several months in Vienna.

According to Heer, Waldstein returned to England from an expedition to the West Indies at the beginning of 1798 and, except for a journey to Paris in 1802, is unlikely to have left England again before 1807 at the earliest. During all those years there is no record of any contact between him and Beethoven. It is accordingly rather curious that Beethoven should have decided in 1805 to dedicate his Piano Sonata Op. 53, composed in 1803–4, to the count—whom, for all he knew, he might never see again; perhaps there was some communication between them after all. There is no evidence that their friendship was renewed following Waldstein's return to Vienna.

(Heer, Schaal[3], Schiedermair[1], Wegeler/Ries)

Wallishausser [Wallishauser], **Johann Baptist** (b. Vienna, 13 January 1790; d. Vienna, 11 October 1831). Printer, publisher, and bookseller. In 1819 he took over the firm which had been founded by his identically named father (1758–1810). His publications included numerous plays by contemporary Austrian dramatists, notably Castelli* and Grillparzer.*

Beethoven's song 'Ruf vom Berge' (WoO 147), a setting of a poem by Georg Friedrich Treitschke,* was first published as a musical supplement to an edition of Treitschke's *Gedichte* which Wallishausser brought out in 1817. Beethoven's extant correspondence contains one letter to Wallishausser. Probably written in 1822, it opens with an example of his well-known love for wordplay: 'I present my greetings to Herr Vallis and Herr Hauser, as also to Herr Hauser and Herr Vallis, and especially to Herr VallisHauser' (*Corr.* A1046/B1521). The letter concerned a book which Beethoven wished to order. The following year he was in contact with Wallishausser in connection with the planned composition of an opera to Grillparzer's libretto *Melusina*, Grillparzer having ceded the rights to the work to Wallishausser; but nothing came of the project.

(Czeike)

Wawruch, Andreas Johann Ignaz (b. Niemtschitz, near Olmütz [Němčice, near Olomouc, Czech Republic], 22 November 1773; d. Vienna, 21 March 1842). Physician. He first studied philosophy and theology at the University of Olmütz, but soon switched to medical studies at Prague University. After qualifying, he became an assistant at the Medical Clinic of the University of Vienna; from 1811 he also lectured on the history of medicine. In 1812 he returned to Prague, where, during the next seven years, he occupied a chair in pathology and pharmacology. In 1819 he was appointed director of the Medical Clinic in Vienna and, at the same time, professor of the pathology and therapy of internal diseases; he exercised these functions until his death. In his leisure hours, he indulged his love of music. He was reportedly a very good cellist, and Aloys Fuchs* recalled singing in many vocal quartets at his house. He owned furthermore a number of scores and theoretical works on music.

Wawruch attended Beethoven during his final illness. After two of the composer's previous physicians, Dr Braunhofer* and Dr Staudenheim,* failed to call when summoned, Wawruch was approached by Karl Holz,* who assured

Beethoven that he was regarded as one of the ablest physicians in Vienna. Wawruch visited Beethoven on 5 December 1826; in his first entry in the conversation book he described himself as a fervent admirer of Beethoven's music and assured his patient that he would do everything possible to give him speedy relief. Thereafter he visited Beethoven regularly until the end. As a New Year's present, Beethoven gave him the score of Handel's* *Messiah* (*see Corr.* B2243). Inevitably though, when his condition failed to improve, Beethoven lost confidence in his new doctor. Wawruch, perhaps at Beethoven's urging, consulted other physicians, notably Dr Johann Malfatti;* but although he followed certain suggestions made by Malfatti, he always remained in overall charge of the case, and he did not hesitate to discontinue Malfatti's remedies when he thought it advisable. After Beethoven's death, Wawruch wrote a medical report on the final period of his life (*Ärztlicher Rückblick auf Ludwig van Beethovens letzte Lebensepoche*), which offers a detailed account of his medical condition and of the various treatments prescribed for him. This document, which is dated 20 May 1827, did not appear in print in Wawruch's lifetime; it was first published by Aloys Fuchs in the *Wiener Zeitschrift für Kunst, Literatur, Theater und Mode* on 30 April 1842.

In his Beethoven biography, Schindler* accuses Wawruch of incompetence in his diagnosis and treatment of Beethoven's illness, and so does Gerhard von Breuning* in *Aus dem Schwarzspanierhause*. (Breuning, who was only 13 years old at the time, also criticizes Wawruch's 'indifference and mercenary attitude'.) However, a well-known modern physician, Dr Anton Neumayr, has firmly rejected these allegations of Wawruch's professional ineptitude, asserting that he showed himself fully acquainted with the medical knowledge available in his day.

(Bankl/Jesserer, Breuning, Franken, Neumayr, Schindler[1], Staehelin[1])

Weber, Carl Maria (Friedrich Ernst) von (b. Eutin, ?18 November 1786; d. London, 5 June 1826). Composer, conductor, and pianist. He visited Vienna on at least four occasions while Beethoven resided there: from October 1803 to October 1804, during which time he studied with the Abbé Vogler;* in March 1813, to recruit artists for the Estates Theatre in Prague, of which he had recently been appointed conductor; in February–March 1822, having received a proposal from Domenico Barbaia, the manager of the Kärntnertor-Theater, to write an opera for that theatre (during his stay he conducted a performance of *Der Freischütz*); and in the autumn of 1823, to prepare and direct the première of the new opera, *Euryanthe*, on 25 October. It was apparently only during this last visit that he came into close contact with Beethoven. At the latter's invitation, Weber called on him at his lodgings at Baden on 5 October, together with Julius Benedict, Tobias Haslinger,* and Ferdinand Piringer.* Both Weber and Benedict subsequently described the meeting, the former in a letter to his wife the next day, the latter in one addressed to Thayer* many years later; a somewhat less reliable account is given by Max Maria von Weber in his biography of his father. All three agree on the essential point: Beethoven received Weber most cordially. This is not surprising, for in April of that year Weber had presented a highly successful production of *Fidelio* at Dresden. Furthermore, the production had led to a friendly correspondence between them which had extended from January until the summer. Beethoven had thus much cause to entertain warm feelings for Weber, who, moreover, had already years earlier shown his admiration for *Fidelio* by introducing it to Prague audiences (27 November 1814). This had been the first performance of the opera outside Vienna.

Weber had not always been so enthusiastic about Beethoven's music. In a frequently quoted letter to the Swiss composer and publisher Hans Georg Nägeli* on 21 May 1810 he wrote: 'The fiery, indeed almost unbelievable, gift for invention which inspires [Beethoven] is coupled with such confusion in the ordering of his ideas that only his earlier compositions appeal to me; the more recent ones strike me merely as a bewildering chaos, an incomprehensible struggle for novelty, from which some odd strokes of genius shine forth, which show how great he could be if he were only willing to rein in his exuberant imagination.' His appreciation of Beethoven's compositions increased as he became more familiar with certain of them during the years he spent in Prague (1813–16), and his deeper understanding of them may well have owed something to the influence of Franz Clement,* whom he brought from Vienna to lead his orchestra and who was well acquainted with Beethoven and his music. In later life, Weber spoke admiringly of Beethoven's genius, but even so he felt out of sympathy with the works written during the composer's final period. As for Beethoven, he was reportedly impressed by *Der Freischütz*: 'I would never have thought that mild little man was capable of this,' he is said to have remarked after looking through the score. Grillparzer* may have been right in suggesting that it was probably the success of Weber's operas which gave Beethoven the idea of composing another opera himself.

(Kroll, Lühning)

Wegeler, Franz Gerhard (b. Bonn, 22 August 1765; d. Koblenz, 7 May 1848). Physician. He studied medicine under Franz Wilhelm Kauhlen at Bonn and from 1787 in Vienna, where he attended the lectures given by the well-known surgeon Johann Nepomuk Hunczovsky.* Shortly after qualifying as a doctor on 1 September 1789 he was appointed a professor of medicine at the University of Bonn. A sound rather than a brilliant or particularly innovative scholar, he nevertheless enjoyed the high respect of his peers, and he was elected rector for the year 1793–4. At the approach of the French army he fled to Vienna in October 1794, having been politically compromised by signing a resolution passed by the university senate which had forbidden the students to have any personal contact with the French prisoners passing through Bonn en route to Austria, for fear that they might contract typhus. He remained in Vienna until June 1796, when he left to resume his lectures in Bonn at the invitation of his colleagues. After the university was abolished in 1797, he struggled to make ends meet in private practice; from 1800 he taught at a school in the town. On 28 March 1802 Wegeler married Eleonore von Breuning* (1771–1841), who was to bear him two children, Helene (1803–32) and Julius Stephan (1807–83). In 1807 the family moved to Koblenz, where Wegeler gave courses for midwives at a teaching department of the local hospital. He had a distinguished career at Koblenz which was crowned by the bestowal of the titles of Royal Prussian Geheimrat and Regierungs-Medizinalrat, and by the award of the Order of the Red Eagle. He was, however, disappointed in his hopes of being invited to join the new university which was established at Bonn in 1818.

Wegeler is of great importance to Beethoven studies as a valuable source of information on the composer's youth. His recollections appeared, together with those of Ferdinand Ries,* at Koblenz in 1838 under the title *Biographische Notizen über Ludwig van Beethoven*; the volume also contains a number of letters written by Beethoven to Wegeler and Ries. In 1845, on the occasion of the unveiling of the Beethoven statue at Bonn, Wegeler published a supplement, again at Koblenz (*Nachtrag zu den biographischen Notizen über Ludwig van Beethoven*). Precisely when he met Beethoven is uncertain. Most of the composer's biographers have been reluctant to accept Wegeler's own statement that he 'became acquainted with the 12-year-old boy, who was already an author [i.e. composer], in 1782'. It has been suggested that he may, in fact, not have met Beethoven until a year or two later.

Until Beethoven left Bonn permanently in 1792 he enjoyed a close friendship with Wegeler. It was, moreover, Wegeler who introduced him to the Breuning family. After Wegeler arrived in Vienna in 1794, there was, according to his own account, 'hardly a day when we did not see one another'. If this close relationship did not later produce a frequent exchange of letters, the fault lay with Beethoven, who was, by his own admission, an extremely poor correspondent. However, they probably received occasional news of each other's activities through such mutual friends as Ries, Stephan von Breuning, and Nikolaus Simrock.* When they did write, the tone was warm and affectionate. It was to Wegeler that Beethoven revealed the anguish which his failing hearing was causing him (letter of 29 June 1801), and it was to Wegeler that he turned (*Corr.* A256/B439) when he required a copy of his birth certificate in 1810 (but he did not mention that he needed it in connection with a hoped-for marriage—see Malfatti (family)*). In 1815 he sent Wegeler Höfel's* lithograph based on Letronne's* portrait (*Corr.* A661/B979), and in 1826 a lithograph of Joseph Stieler's* portrait, inscribed 'To his greatly admired and beloved friend of many years' (*Corr.* A1542/B2236). On 1 February 1827 Wegeler, informed of Beethoven's illness, proposed that they should meet at Karlsbad [Karlovy Vary, Czech Republic] once he had recovered, and that Beethoven should afterwards visit the family at Koblenz. Too ill to write himself, Beethoven dictated a brief reply to Schindler* (*Corr.* A1551/B2257).

Beethoven never dedicated any of his compositions to Wegeler, although he promised to do so in his letter of 2 May 1810. (Wegeler later commented: 'My fate was the same as that of his pupil Ries: the dedication remained in the letters. But are these not of higher value?') However, Wegeler bequeathed to his son a manuscript in Beethoven's hand containing two movements of a sonatina (WoO 50), which, according to a note by Wegeler, had been 'written' for him by Beethoven. (The note has been interpreted as signifying that the piece had been composed for him, rather than that Beethoven had simply copied it out for him.) Also of some interest is the fact that Wegeler wrote new words, suitable for performance at masonic lodges, for two of Beethoven's songs, 'Der freie Mann' (WoO 117) and 'Opferlied' (WoO 126). The music of the former, with Wegeler's text, was issued separately by Simrock under the title 'Maurerfragen' in 1806, and thus appeared two years before the publication (likewise by Simrock) of the song, with Pfeffel's* text, in *Drei deutsche Lieder*. Wegeler furthermore provided the text for a song entitled 'Die Klage', which was based on the Adagio of the Piano Sonata Op. 2, No. 1, and published by Simrock in 1807. Wegeler wrote the three poems in 1797.

(Braubach[1], Wegeler/Ries)

Weidner, Joseph (b. Vienna, 5 June 1801; d. Vienna, 13 February 1871). Viennese painter known for his genre pictures and his portraits, including one of his sister, the court opera singer Katharina Weidner, who married Ferdinand Georg Waldmüller.* He made a drawing (which he coloured) showing Beethoven from the back while out walking. According to Frimmel, he also painted a portrait of Beethoven which is lost.

(*ALBK*, Frimmel[3])

Weigl, Joseph (b. Eisenstadt, 28 March 1766; d. Vienna, 3 February 1846). Composer and conductor; son of the cellist Joseph Franz Weigl (1740–1820) and the soprano Anna Maria Josepha Weigl. He composed more than thirty operas and also wrote music for ballets, cantatas, and sacred works. A pupil of Salieri,* he was appointed deputy Kapellmeister at the court theatre in 1790, and Kapellmeister two years later. In 1804 he became director of music for both German and Italian opera.

Beethoven is said to have esteemed Weigl highly, but little is known about their personal relations, which are unlikely to have been intimate. For the last movement of his Piano Trio Op. 11, composed in 1798, Beethoven wrote a set of variations on the trio 'Pria ch'io l'impegno' from Weigl's opera *L'amor marinaro, ossia Il corsaro*, which had had its première on 15 October 1797.

Weigl was a pallbearer at Beethoven's funeral.

(Angermüller[2])

Weinkopf, Johann Michael (1780–1862). Singer (bass). He began his professional career at the Theater an der Wien, and there, at the première of *Fidelio* on 20 November 1805, he created the role of Don Fernando. He appeared in the same role in the revised version on 29 March 1806. From 1814 he sang at the Kärntnertor-Theater; he was also choirmaster at the Michaelerkirche. (In the production of the 1814 version of *Fidelio*, Don Fernando was sung by Ignaz Saal.)

Weinmüller, Karl Friedrich Joseph (bapt. Dillingen, Bavaria, 8 November 1763; d. Ober-Döbling, near Vienna, 16 March 1828). Singer (bass). He studied law in Vienna, but, possessing a pleasing voice and a talent for music, was soon drawn to the theatre. Following an unsuccessful attempt to launch his career at the Kärntnertor-Theater, he joined Zöllner's company at Wiener Neustadt in December 1783 and reportedly made his debut there as Sander in Grétry's *Zémire et Azor*. He remained for five years with the troupe, which gave performances in provincial theatres during the winter and at the residence of Count Philipp Batthyány at Hainburg an der Donau, near Pressburg [Bratislava], in the summer. Subsequently he moved to Budapest, where he was active as a singer and director of operatic performances from 1788 to 1796. Towards the end of this period, he made a highly acclaimed guest appearance at the court opera in Vienna. (According to Eisenberg, he appeared there as the village apothecary Stössel in *Doktor und Apotheker* on 6 November 1795, but according to F. Hadamowsky (*Die Wiener Hoftheater . . .*), the only performance at the Kärntnertor-Theater of Dittersdorf's Singspiel that month took place on the 11th; the theatre was closed on the 6th.) Weinmüller's excellent performance on that occasion led to a full-time engagement as a singer and actor at the Viennese court theatres; at the same time his wife, an actress, was also offered a contract. He made his official debut as Jakob in Joseph Wölfl's* *Das schöne Milchmädchen*, probably at the première on 5 January 1797.

Weinmüller became one of the most admired performers on the Viennese stage, widely praised not only for the beauty and artistry of his singing, but also for the excellence of his acting. Ignaz Franz Castelli* described him as 'the dramatic singer *par excellence*'. He particularly distinguished himself in Mozart* operas: Figaro, Leporello, Alfonso, and Sarastro were among his most famous roles (he sang Sarastro when *Die Zauberflöte* was first performed at the Kärntnertor-Theater, on 24 February 1801). Among his other great successes were the roles of Zamosky in Cherubini's* *Faniska*, Thoas in Gluck's *Iphigénie en Tauride*, Steinau in Gyrowetz's* *Der Augenarzt*, and Kranz in the same composer's *Der Samtrock*, Axur in Salieri's* *Axur, re d'Ormus*, and Richard Boll in Joseph Weigl's* *Die Schweizerfamilie*; but he earned praise also for many other interpretations. He and Johann Michael Vogl,* with whom he seems to have enjoyed very friendly relations and whom he frequently partnered on the stage, were long considered the male stars of the company. Weinmüller was a member of it for over twenty-five years; he made his last appearance, as Leporello, on 21 November 1823. In addition to his operatic performances, he was highly appreciated as a singer of church music and oratorios (e.g. in Joseph Leopold Eybler's *Die vier letzten Dinge* and Haydn's* *Die Jahreszeiten* and *Die Schöpfung*). One year after joining the court theatres he was appointed a court Kapellsänger, and a year later a court Kammersänger; in 1810 he was awarded a diploma of citizenship by the city of Vienna.

For Beethoven scholars, Weinmüller's association with his music centres on the final version of *Fidelio*. Not only did Weinmüller sing Rocco when that version was produced at the Kärntnertor-Theater on 23 May 1814, as a benefit performance for Weinmüller, Vogl (Pizarro), and Ignaz Saal (Don Fernando); it may well be that the three singers had, in fact, been responsible for persuading Beethoven to revise the opera (which had not been heard in Vienna since 10 April 1806) for the occasion. Incidentally, Rocco's aria 'Hat man nicht auch Gold beineben', which had been dropped in 1806, was not restored to the score until the seventh performance of the new version on 18 July 1814. Beethoven inscribed a copy of the piano reduction of *Fidelio*, which he presented to Weinmüller, 'To his dear— dear—beloved friend Weinmüller, supreme bass of the Austrian empire'.

Weinmüller also performed other compositions by Beethoven in 1814. At Beethoven's concert at the Grosser Redoutensaal on 27 February he sang the high priest's aria from the music for *Die Ruinen von Athen* (Op. 113, No. 7) and took part in the first performance of the trio 'Tremate, empi, tremate' (Op. 116). (*See also* Treitschke.*)

(Castelli, Eisenberg, Layer[1,2])

Weiss, Franz (b. Glatz, Silesia [Kładzko, Poland], 18 January 1778; d. Vienna, 25 January 1830). Violist and composer. It is not known exactly when and under what circumstances he settled in Vienna. He eventually came to be regarded as the outstanding violist performing there and gave frequent concerts; but he is best remembered as a member of several celebrated string quartets. From 1794 to 1799 he was regularly engaged by Prince Karl Lichnowsky* to perform, together with Ignaz Schuppanzigh,* Ludwig Sina,* and Nikolaus (or Anton) Kraft,* at the prince's Friday morning concerts; from 1808 to 1816 he played in the quartet formed by Schuppanzigh for Count [later Prince] Razumovsky;* from 1821 he performed in chamber music concerts directed by Joseph Böhm;* and following Schuppanzigh's return from Russia in 1823, he became a member of the new Schuppanzigh Quartet. As a result of his numerous appearances with these different groups, he must have been very familiar with much of Beethoven's chamber music. He also took part in the performance of *Wellingtons Sieg* at Beethoven's concert on 8 December 1813. His own compositions include orchestral and chamber music, works for the piano, and songs.

(Wessely[5])

Weisse, Christian Felix (b. Annaberg, 28 January 1726; d. Leipzig, 16 December 1804). Government official; poet, dramatist, and editor—from 1759 until 1788 he edited the Leipzig periodical *Bibliothek der schönen Wissenschaften und der freyen Künste* (retitled *Neue Bibliothek der Wissenschaften und schönen Künste* in 1765). Several of his plays were produced at the Burgtheater, including *Romeo und Julie* (3 October 1776), an adaptation of Shakespeare's tragedy, and the comedies *Die Freundschaft auf der Probe* (16 August 1777) and *Amalia* (27 September 1783). Beethoven set one of his poems in the arietta 'Der Kuss' (Op. 128).

(Wild[2])

Weissenbach, Aloys (b. Telfs, Tyrol, 1 March 1766; d. Salzburg, 26 October 1821). Physician; poet and dramatist. He was educated at Innsbruck and later studied medicine in Vienna. In 1804, after serving as a doctor in the Austrian army for sixteen years, he settled in Salzburg. There he enjoyed a successful career as a physician and surgeon, as well as a professor of surgery and veterinary science. In addition, he made a name for himself as a playwright and poet. His drama *Die Barmeciden, oder Die Ägypter in Bagdad* was produced at the Burgtheater on 4 October 1799, and the tragedy *Der Brautkranz* at the Kärntnertor-Theater on 14 January 1809; a dramatic poem for several speakers, 'Der zehnte November', was presented at the Burgtheater on 10 November 1816 to mark the arrival in Vienna of Karoline Auguste of Bavaria, who became the fourth wife of Emperor Franz I. Weissenbach's poem 'Der heilige Moment' celebrated the victory of the Allies over Napoleon at the Battle of Leipzig (16–19 October 1813); it was published at Salzburg in 1814. In September of that year Weissenbach went to Vienna, and while there he wrote the text for Beethoven's cantata *Der glorreiche Augenblick*, a work conceived in honour of the Congress of Vienna. According to Schindler,* Beethoven found Weissenbach's text impossible to set and asked Karl Joseph Bernard* to revise it. The cantata was first performed, before an illustrious audience, at Beethoven's concert at the Grosser Redoutensaal on 29 November 1814; it was repeated at the concerts of 2 and 25 December. (It was not published until 1837, when Tobias Haslinger* brought out parallel editions of it, one with the original text, the other with a new text entitled *Preis der Tonkunst* by Friedrich Rochlitz.*)

Weissenbach recounted his experiences in Vienna in *Meine Reise zum Congress: Wahrheit und Dichtung* (Vienna, 1816). It is of particular importance for Beethoven scholars because the author devotes some thirty pages to the composer, for whom he evidently felt great reverence. He met Beethoven repeatedly during his stay, and the physical and moral portrait which he draws is based on his observations and on their various conversations. The latter did not always proceed easily, for Weissenbach, like Beethoven, was hard of hearing; as a fellow-sufferer and a physician, he was particularly interested in the origin of Beethoven's affliction and in the effect it had on his personality. He sent a copy of his book to

Beethoven, among whose belongings it was found after his death. Beethoven even made reference to it in his letter to the Magistracy of the City of Vienna of 1 February 1819, where he declares that 'not only is the probity of my moral character generally and publicly recognised, but also excellent authors such as Weissenbach and others have considered it worth their while to write about it' (*Corr.* A App. C, 9/B1286).

Beethoven met Weissenbach again at Mödling in October 1819. On that occasion, he seriously considered withdrawing his nephew Karl* from Blöchlinger's* boarding school and sending him to Salzburg to be educated under Weissenbach's supervision; he even thought that Weissenbach might take him into his own house. On 15 November, in a letter composed in a flowery language not untypical of his literary style, Weissenbach urged his 'Herzensfreund' ['most beloved friend', lit. 'friend of my heart'] to come to Salzburg with his nephew; once there, he would be so enchanted by the beauty of the scenery that he would not wish to leave again, and as for Karl, a suitable arrangement could no doubt be made for his education (*Corr.* B1353). But in spite of this encouragement and Weissenbach's extravagant protestations of devotion and admiration, Beethoven abandoned the plan.

(Nottebohm[2], Wurzbach[1])

Weissenthurn, Johanna: *see* Franul von Weissenthurn.*

Wennington, William. English man of letters and amateur composer who published a number of songs and pieces for the piano in London, several of them in 1790. During a visit to Vienna in 1798 he met Beethoven, probably at Prince Karl Lichnowsky's.* Beethoven set his poem 'La tiranna' (WoO 125), and Wennington brought the completed song back to London the following year. He arranged to have the composition printed there and registered it at Stationers Hall as his property on 12 December 1799. The imprint states that it was published 'in Vienna, by the Principal Music Shops, and in London, by Messrs. Broderip & Wilkinson,* Hodsoll, & Astor & Co.', but no Viennese edition has been found.

(Blaxland, Tyson[3,10])

Werner, Friedrich Ludwig Zacharias (b. Königsberg, East Prussia [Kaliningrad, Russia], 18 November 1768; d. Vienna, 17 January 1823). Dramatist and poet. Beethoven set Werner's 'Kriegslied für die zum heiligen Krieg verbündeten deutschen Heere' (Hess 123, *see also Corr.* A472/B712). The composition is lost.

Wessenberg, Ignaz Heinrich Carl, Baron (b. Dresden, 4 November 1774; d. Konstanz, 9 August 1860). Cleric; bishop of Konstanz, 1814–27. His poems appeared in two volumes in Zurich in 1800–1. Beethoven set one of them in 'Das

Geheimnis' (WoO 145) in 1815. The song was published by Nikolaus Simrock* in 1817.

Wetzlar von Plankenstern, Raimund, Baron (b. 1752; d. Grünberg, 29 September 1810). Son of the wealthy merchant and banker Karl Abraham Wetzlar von Plankenstern (1715/16–99), a native of Offenbach am Main (Germany) who converted from Judaism to Catholicism in 1777 and was later ennobled.

Baron Raimund Wetzlar was married to Maria Theresia, née Calmer [Balmer] de Piquenay (d. 1793). A patron of musicians and himself a fine guitarist and a competent singer, he was well acquainted with Mozart,* who, in letters to his father, described him as an 'honest' and 'good and true' friend. He was Mozart's landlord in 1782–3 and, at his own request, became in 1783 godfather to Mozart's first child, Raimund Leopold. In *c.*1799 his summer residence, near the Meidling Gate [309 Schönbrunnerstrasse], was the scene of a piano contest between Beethoven and Joseph Wölfl,* whom Wetzlar greatly admired. (The house was known as the Villa Chairé, after the Greek word 'XAIPE' [Welcome] inscribed above a central window.) Ignaz von Seyfried* gives an account of this contest in an appendix to his book *Ludwig van Beethoven's Studien im Generalbasse . . .*

In May 1803 Beethoven provided the violinist George Polgreen Bridgetower* with a letter of introduction (*Corr.* A73/B137) to Baron Raimund's brother Alexander (1769–1810).

(Schönfeld, Seyfried)

Wieck, (Johann Gottlieb) Friedrich (b. Pretzsch, near Torgau, 18 August 1785; d. Loschwitz, near Dresden, 6 October 1873). Music teacher; father of the pianist and composer Clara Schumann (1819–96). In early July 1823 he was introduced by Matthäus Andreas Stein* to Beethoven, who was then staying at Hetzendorf (*see* Prónay*). His account of the visit appeared in 1873 in the *Dresdener Nachrichten* (6 December) and *Signale für die musikalische Welt* (37, p. 897). The conversation bore upon a variety of subjects, including music making at Leipzig (where Wieck was living at the time), Italian opera, politics, and current methods of treating hearing problems (*BKh* 3/365–8). Concerning the latter, Wieck spoke favourably of the homoeopathic methods developed by two doctors practising at Leipzig, Christian Friedrich Samuel Hahnemann and Moritz Wilhelm Müller. Finally, Beethoven improvised for his visitor. (In his account, Wieck mistakenly places the meeting at Hietzing, in 1826.)

Wild, Franz (b. Nieder-Hollabrunn, Lower Austria, 31 December 1792; d. Ober-Döbling, near Vienna, 1 January 1860). Tenor. He received his musical training as a boy chorister at Klosterneuburg Monastery and later (1804–7) as a choirboy in the court Kapelle and a pupil at the Stadtkonvikt in Vienna. After singing in the chorus at the Theater in der Leopoldstadt and the Theater in der Josefstadt and as soloist in Prince Nikolaus Esterházy's* Kapelle at Eisenstadt, he was engaged at the Theater an der Wien, where he made his debut in 9 July 1811 as Ramiro in Isouard's *Cendrillon*. Among his other early successes was Tamino (*Die Zauberflöte*). From 1814 he also sang at the court theatre. He soon became a great favourite, for he possessed a powerful, noble, and highly distinctive voice of exceptional beauty, which was judged to be ideal for dramatic tenor roles and also certain baritone parts. He was, moreover, in the words of a contemporary critic, 'a splendid exception' to the rule that tenors tend to be mediocre actors.

Wild left Vienna in August 1816 and, following successful appearances in various German cities, he became one of the stars of the Darmstadt court theatre (1817–24); subsequently he settled at Kassel (1825–29). As a result of highly acclaimed guest appearances in Vienna in June–July 1829, he was offered an excellent contract at the Kärntnertor-Theater, and there he sang from 1830 until 1845, while accepting, from time to time, brief engagements elsewhere (in Frankfurt, Mainz, London, Berlin, etc.). His very extensive repertoire included, notably, Florestan (*Fidelio*), Max (*Der Freischütz*), Masaniello (*La Muette de Portici*), Georges Brown in Boieldieu's *La Dame blanche*, and the title roles in *Don Giovanni*, Hérold's *Zampa*, and Rossini's* *Otello*. His final role at the Kärntnertor-Theater was Abayaldos in Donizetti's *Dom Sébastien*, which he sang at the Viennese première (conducted by the composer) on 6 February 1845, and at ten further performances, the last on 24 March. (Some reference works mistakenly have him continue his stage career until 1855.) It has been calculated that he sang altogether no fewer than 117 different operatic roles. His final appearance at a concert took place on 8 November 1859, only a few weeks before his death.

Wild came into contact with Beethoven in late 1814, when he was a solist at the first performance of the cantata *Der glorreiche Augenblick* on 29 November. (The concert was repeated on 2 and 25 December.) He became much better acquainted with Beethoven soon afterwards. In autobiographical notes which were published shortly after his death in the periodical *Rezensionen über Theater und Musik*, he recalled that when Beethoven heard of his intention of singing 'Adelaide' at a gala concert before the court and numerous dignitaries attending the Congress, he called on him and offered to accompany him at the concert, which he duly did. The concert took place on 25 January 1815 (not, as Wild states, on 23 December 1814). Wild adds that Beethoven was so pleased with his rendition that he considered orchestrating the song—presumably so that Wild might perform it in that setting—but he did not get around to doing so. However, Wild continues, Beethoven wrote 'An die Hoffnung', to a text by Tiedge, for him. This was evidently the second setting (Op. 94) of that text, which Beethoven made in the spring of 1815. It was published in April 1816, and they performed it together 'at a matinée before a select audience' the following month.

In his memoirs, Wild also left a striking account of how Beethoven's deafness affected his conducting, making him crouch down during loud passages and dramatically 'reappear' during soft ones, to the utter confusion of the orchestra. Wild reports having observed this bizarre behaviour at the first performance of *Wellingtons Sieg* (Op. 91) at the Grosser Redoutensaal, but if the performance was indeed the first one, Wild was mistaken about the venue, for the first two performances of *Wellingtons Sieg* were given on 8 and 12 December 1813 at the university, and only the next two, on 2 January and 27 February, took place at the Grosser Redoutensaal.

(Wild[1])

Willmann, (Johann) Ignaz (bapt. Wolfach, Germany, 2 November 1739; d. Breslau [Wrocław], 28 May 1815). Violinist. In 1767 he joined the court orchestra at Bonn and thus became a colleague of Beethoven's father and grandfather. He remained at Bonn at least until 1774. Information about his activities during the next fourteen years is scanty, but he is known to have served for a time as director of music to Count Johann Pálffy von Erdöd (from ?1784 to April 1786) and to have devoted some time and effort to displaying the musical gifts of his children (see below). From 1788 until 1793 he was again a member of the Bonn orchestra. Later he lived in Vienna; from June 1805 until early 1808 he held the post of Kapellmeister and director of the court theatre at Kassel.

His marriage, in 1765, to Maria Elisabeth Erdmannsdorff(er) was to produce five children, three of whom—Max(imilian Friedrich Ludwig) (1767–1813), (Maximiliana Valentina) Walburga (1769–1835), and (Johanna) Magdalena* (1771–1801)—showed musical talent at an early age. Willmann presented them at a concert at the Kärntnertor-Theater on 16 March 1784, and they appeared together at another concert in Vienna on 7 March 1787. Max was a cellist who later played in the orchestra of Prince Thurn und Taxis at Regensburg until 1798, and subsequently with Schikaneder's* company in Vienna. Walburga was an excellent pianist who is said to have studied with Mozart.* Later she was appointed *virtuosa di camera* at the court theatre at Bonn, but she left the town with her family in July 1793. On 28 September 1797, in Vienna, she married Franz Xaver Huber.* Between 1800 and 1804 she toured as a concert artist. (On Magdalena, *see* the next article.)

Willmann's wife died at Bonn on 27 September 1789, and in May 1793 he married Marianne de Tribolet (1768–1813), a soprano at the Bonn court theatre who later joined Schikaneder's company at the Freihaus-Theater in Vienna. In March 1795 she sang Konstanze in *Die Entführung aus dem Serail*. For the next ten years she appeared at that theatre and at its successor, the Theater an der Wien; from 1805 until 1812 she sang at Kassel. The couple had only one child, Maria Anna Antonetta, known as Caroline (1796–*c*.1860), who became a well-known soprano. She performed at Pest, Vienna, and several cities in Germany.

There is no doubt that the Willmann and Beethoven families knew each other well at Bonn, professionally and personally. (Five months after Willmann started his engagement at Bonn, Beethoven's grandfather, by virtue of his position as Kapellmeister, represented the elector—who had agreed to be godfather to Willmann's newly born son Maximilian—at the baptismal ceremony.) After he moved to Vienna, Beethoven continued his contacts with the Willmanns (*see also* Magdalena Willmann*). In this connection, certain observations made by K. M. Pisarowitz in his articles on the Willmanns in *Musik in Geschichte und Gegenwart* and *New Grove* merit closer consideration. In both articles he suggests that Willmann, while in Vienna in 1786–7, probably initiated Beethoven's trip to study with Mozart. It is certainly true that Willmann was in Vienna during the period preceding Beethoven's arrival, as is proved by his children's participation in the above-mentioned concert of 7 March. It is, moreover, very likely that the Willmanns were in contact with Mozart at that time, for quite apart from the fact that Walburga may have been receiving tuition from him, she performed one of his concertos (perhaps K503) at that concert. Thus, while there is no documentary evidence to support it, Pisarowitz's suggestion is not an impossible one.

On the other hand, his grounds for stating (in *New Grove*) that Willmann was also the 'initiator' of the proposed appointment of Beethoven as court composer to the king of Westphalia, Jérôme Bonaparte,* are less clear. His assertion is made more puzzling by the confused chronology of his *New Grove* article: 'After another stay in Vienna during which he tried unsuccessfully to arrange Beethoven's appointment as court conductor to King Jérôme Buonaparte, Willmann was conductor and director of the court theatre in Kassell (1 June 1805 to Easter 1808).' In the first place, Willmann could not have tried to obtain the post in question for Beethoven prior to June 1805, for it was not until August 1807 that Jérôme Bonaparte became ruler of the kingdom of Westphalia, which had itself only been created the previous month. Secondly, it is rather difficult to imagine why Willmann should have had anything to do with the offer that was made to Beethoven in the autumn of 1808, for he had been replaced as Kapellmeister and director of the court theatre at Kassel by Johann Friedrich Reichardt* several months earlier (probably already at the beginning of the year 1808, rather than at Easter, as Pisarowitz states). Regrettably, Pisarowitz offers no explanation for his statement.

(Fischer-Dieskau, Pisarowitz[1,3,4])

Willmann, (Johanna) Magdalena (b. Bonn, 13 September 1771; d. Vienna, 23 December 1801). Soprano. Daughter of the violinist (Johann) Ignaz Willmann.* She studied with Vincenzo Righini in Vienna, and made her concert debut there, together with her brother Max and sister Walburga, on 16 March 1784 (*see* under Ignaz Willmann*); they all appeared there again on 7 March 1787. Magdalena sang also in other cities, and in 1789 she became a member of the court Kapelle at Bonn. After hearing her as Lisetta in Paisiello's *Il rè Teodoro in Venezia* at Mergentheim on 11 October 1791, Carl Ludwig Junker* warmly praised her elegant and expressive singing, and her lively and delightful acting (in a report published in *Musikalische Korrespondenz der teutschen filharmonischen Gesellschaft*, Speyer). On 13 July 1793, the Willmanns left Bonn and during the following winter Magdalena sang at Venice, apparently in new operas composed by Peter Winter for the Teatro San Benedetto (*I fratelli rivali* had its première there in November 1793, and *Belisa, ossia La fedeltà riconosciuta* on 5 February 1794). On 30 July 1794, on her way to Vienna, she gave a concert at Graz, and during the next season she performed, but without much success, in Berlin. From 1 April 1795 she was engaged at the Vienna court theatre. On 13 July 1796, in Vienna, she married Anton(io) Galvani, a merchant born in Trieste. During the last two years of her life she sang at concerts at Leipzig, Dresden, and Hamburg.

Beethoven must have been quite well acquainted with Magdalena and all her family while he was at Bonn. (Like Magdalena and her father, he was among the court musicians who performed at Mergentheim in September–October 1791.) He was also in contact with the Willmanns in Vienna, both before and after Magdalena's marriage. On at least one occasion (30 January 1801) he played at a concert in which she also participated (on this concert, *see* Gerhardi*). He performed his Horn Sonata Op. 17 with Giovanni Punto,* while she sang in extracts from Sebastiano Nasolini's *Merope* and Cimarosa's *Gli Orazi ed i Curiazi*. (*See also* Jahn.*)

Beethoven's feelings for Magdalena are said to have at one time transcended those of mere friendship and to have even led him to propose marriage, only to be rebuffed. There are no contemporary sources for this incident which, if true, is most likely to have occurred in 1795 or early 1796. The story was related by Thayer,* who had heard it in 1860 from Max Willmann's daughter Maria Magdalena. When Thayer asked why her aunt had refused Beethoven's proposal, 'Frau S.' (she had married Karl Viktor Sales, the son of the Italian composer Pietro Pompeo Sales) said, with a laugh, 'because he was so ugly and half-crazy'.

(Pisarowitz[1,3,4], Schiedermair[1])

Wölfl [Wölffl, Woelfl], **Joseph** (b. Salzburg, 24 December 1773; d. London, 21 May 1812). Pianist and composer. As a chorister at Salzburg Cathedral (1783–6) he was taught by Leopold Mozart and Michael Haydn. In 1790 he went to Vienna, where he may have studied with Mozart.* During his subsequent stay in Warsaw (1792–5) he became a prominent piano teacher, much sought after by the local aristocracy. After his return to Vienna in 1795 he achieved increasing renown as a virtuoso pianist and also as a composer. His heroic-comic opera *Der Höllenberg*, to a text by Emanuel Schikaneder,* was produced at the Freihaus-Theater on 21 November 1795. As a pianist, he was considered to have no equal except Beethoven, and a friendly rivalry developed between the two men which was encouraged by the Viennese music lovers and led to 'a highly interesting contest between the two athletes' (Ignaz von Seyfried*) in *c*.1799 at the house of Baron

Raimund Wetzlar von Plankenstern* who was Wölfl's champion (Beethoven's greatest admirer was Prince Karl Lichnowsky*). A perceptive comparison of the two pianists appeared in the *Allgemeine musikalische Zeitung* on 22 April 1799, whilst a dramatic account of their contest at Wetzlar's was published by Seyfried as an appendix to his *Ludwig van Beethoven's Studien im Generalbasse . . .*

In addition to several works for the stage, Wölfl wrote much instrumental and keyboard music. In 1798 he dedicated a set of three piano sonatas to Beethoven.

(Baurn, Hamann², Seyfried)

Wolfmayer, Johann Nepomuk (1768–1841). Wealthy Viennese cloth merchant, senior partner in the firm Johann Wolfmayer & Co. A great music lover, he was among Beethoven's earliest and staunchest admirers: 'Wolfmayer is happy that he championed your compositions as long as twenty-five years ago; now the public is beginning to appreciate them too,' Karl Holz* wrote in Beethoven's conversation books in 1826 (*BKh*10/123). The previous year he had reported (*BKh*8/109) that Wolfmayer had 'wept like a child' while listening to the slow movement of the String Quartet in A minor (Op. 132). According to Schindler,* he was also 'one of Beethoven's most discreet and supportive benefactors'. Aloys Fuchs* told Otto Jahn that Wolfmayer would occasionally have a new coat made for Beethoven which he discreetly substituted for an old one during a visit to his lodgings. He also commissioned Beethoven in April 1818 to compose a requiem for 100 gulden. (His letter is addressed to 'Ludwig v. Beethoven, most celebrated composer and musical genius' (*Corr.* B1252).) But although Beethoven agreed to write a suitable composition, he did not do so. No doubt Wolfmayer must have supported Beethoven also in other ways, to merit Schindler's tribute. He last saw Beethoven when he called on him in February 1827. As he left the the sick man's apartment, he exclaimed, with tears in his eyes; 'The great man! Alas, alas.' He was a torchbearer at the funeral.

Beethoven intended to dedicate the String Quartet in C sharp minor, Op. 131, to Wolfmayer, but at the last minute decided to dedicate it to Baron Joseph Stutterheim* instead. Eventually, the String Quartet in F major (Op. 135) appeared posthumously with the dedication 'à son ami Jean Wolfmeier'. Schindler states that a week before his death Beethoven asked him to take care of the matter of the dedication of the quartet and to choose for this purpose one of the composer's 'worthiest friends'; accordingly, shortly after Beethoven's death, he instructed the publisher Adolph Martin Schlesinger* to dedicate the work to Wolfmayer. There is, however, some evidence that the suggestion had in the first place been made by Holz.

(Schindler¹)

Wolf-Metternich [Wolff-Metternich], **Antonie**, Countess (1744–1827). Daughter of Baron Hermann Werner Asseburg; wife of Count Johann Ignaz Wolf-

Metternich zur Gracht (1740–90), head of the Bonn court treasury (1772), later minister (1784) and president of the High Court of Appeal (1786). Their house was one of the main centres of musical life at Bonn. One of their daughters, Felice [Felicitas] (*c.*1767–97) was included by Christian Gottlob Neefe,* in an article on musical life at Bonn (C. F. Cramer's *Magazin der Kunst*, 8 April 1787), in his list of highly competent local amateur pianists; two years later he dedicated his song 'Klementine' to her.

It was to Countess Antonie, whom Max Braubach describes as the 'soul' of the Metternich family, that Beethoven dedicated one of his earliest compositions, the *Variations on a March by Dressler** (WoO 63). In Kinsky/Halm, the dedicatee's name is mistakenly given as 'Felice'.

(Braubach³, Leux²)

Wranitzky [Vranický], **Anton** [Antonín] (b. Neureisch [Nová Říše, Czech Republic] 13 June 1761; d. Vienna, 6 August 1820) and **Paul** [Pavel] (b. Neureisch, 30 December 1756; d. Vienna, 26 September 1808). Brothers; composers and violinists of Moravian origin. Anton, who counted Mozart,* Haydn,* and Albrechtsberger* among his teachers, was appointed choirmaster at the chapel of the Theresianisch-Savoyische Akademie in Vienna not later than December 1783. By 1790 he had joined the household of Prince Joseph Franz Maximilian Lobkowitz* as composer, music teacher, and Konzertmeister, and later became Kapellmeister of the prince's private orchestra. After Lobkowitz assumed responsibility for operatic performances in 1807, Anton Wranitzky was appointed director of the court theatre orchestra; from 1814 he also held a similar post at the Theater an der Wien. Furthermore, from 1812 to 1816, he assisted Lobkowitz in the management of the Hoftheater-Musik-Verlag.* His brother Paul arrived in Vienna in *c.*1776 to pursue theological and musical studies. In *c.*1785 he became music director to Count Johann Nepomuk Esterházy, and some five years later he was appointed orchestra director of the court theatres. Later he became secretary of the Tonkünstler-Societät.

Beethoven was in contact with both brothers. Carl Czerny* recalled in his memoirs that the first time he visited Beethoven's rooms (i.e. in 1800/1), they were both present. In 1796 Beethoven had composed a set of twelve variations (WoO 71) on a Russian dance which Maria Casentini* had executed in *Das Waldmädchen*, a ballet by Giuseppe Traf(f)ieri to music by Paul Wranitzky, which had been first produced at the Kärntnertor-Theater on 23 September of that year. After Beethoven's concert of 2 April 1800, at which the First Symphony and the Septet Op. 20 were first performed in public, the Leipzig *Allgemeine musikalische Zeitung* reported that there had been a quarrel about who should conduct it: Beethoven had favoured Paul Wranitzky, but the orchestra of the Italian opera, which played at the concert, had refused to perform under him and had preferred Giacomo Conti (who had been leading the orchestra since 1793). The article was highly critical of the quality of the orchestra's playing.

(Poštolka[4,5])

Würfel, Václav Vilém [Wenzel Wilhelm] (b. Plaňan [Plaňany, Czech Republic], 6 May 1790; d. Vienna, 23 March 1832). Composer and pianist. From 1815 he was active as a music teacher in Warsaw, where he was also a professor of organ and theory at the Conservatoire. In 1824, following a brief stay in Prague, he settled in Vienna; in 1826 he was appointed Kapellmeister at the Kärntnertor-Theater. He wrote two operas, *Rübezahl* and *Der Rotmantel*, as well as a number of Singspiels. (*Rübezahl* was produced in Prague on 7 October 1824 and at the Theater an der Wien in Vienna on 10 March 1825.)

Würfel made Beethoven's acquaintance on 2 September 1825, when he accompanied Tobias Haslinger* and others (*see* Kuhlau*) on an excursion to Baden. He had been eager to meet Beethoven, since he had a profound admiration for his music. He told Beethoven that he had conducted the Seventh Symphony at St Petersburg, and that he had given public performances of all the sonatas and of the First Piano Concerto 'before 4,000 persons'. He promised to play Beethoven's works at his concerts in Vienna 'as they had been written' and indicated that he would be glad to receive appropriate instructions from Beethoven (*see* BKh8/79–83). On 13 April 1825 Würfel took part in a performance of the Piano Trio Op. 70, No. 1, at one of Schuppanzigh's* subscription concerts.

(Bauer[1], Freemanová)

Zelter, Carl Friedrich (b. Berlin, 11 December 1758; d. Berlin, 15 May 1832). Composer, conductor, and teacher. Beethoven most probably made Zelter's acquaintance during his visit to Berlin in 1796. At that time Zelter was assistant conductor of the Berlin Singakademie; in 1800 he succeeded the founder, Carl Friedrich Fasch, as its principal conductor. In 1809 he also founded the Liedertafel, a men's choral society.

Zelter's letters to Goethe* offer a fascinating insight into his evolving attitude to Beethoven's music. Originally uncomprehending and highly critical, though not totally unaware of Beethoven's genius, he eventually came to feel a profound admiration for him. While staying in Vienna in 1819, he was anxious to meet him again ('Beethoven, whom I should have liked to see once more in my life, is staying in the country,' he informed Goethe). They met, if only very briefly, on 12 September, when their coaches crossed on the road between Vienna and Mödling, Zelter being on his way with Sigmund Anton Steiner* to visit Beethoven at Mödling, while Beethoven was heading for Vienna. 'We got down and embraced most warmly,' Zelter reported to Goethe. They arranged to meet later that day at Steiner's music shop, but both Beethoven and Zelter were, for different reasons, unable to keep the appointment. When Beethoven sent a note expressing his regret (*Corr.* A972/B1332), Zelter replied: 'To see once more in my life the face of the man who brings joy and edification to so many worthy persons, among whom I, of course, am glad to count myself, such was my intention in wishing to visit you, dear friend, at Mödling' (*Corr.* B1333; this letter is known only from the draft, or copy, which Zelter wrote down on Beethoven's note).

In 1823 Zelter, in response to an invitation from Beethoven to subscribe to the *Missa solemnis* (*Corr.* A1135/B1563), declared his readiness to purchase the Mass for the Singakademie, provided that Beethoven was willing to prepare an *a capella* arrangement (*Corr.* B1577). Beethoven was evidently not disposed to do so, for on 25 March he wrote that, if the Mass were ever published, he would send Zelter a free printed copy, from which Zelter could then make the required arrangement himself. That appears to have been the end of the matter. The final contact between them occurred in 1825, on the occasion of Ludwig Rellstab's* visit to Vienna. Zelter provided him with a letter of introduction 'to the noble and peerless Beethoven' (*Corr.* B1946). In his conversation with Rellstab, Beethoven spoke warmly of Zelter as 'a worthy champion of true art'.

(Blumner, Kalischer, Rellstab, Taubert)

Zizius, Johann Nepomuk (b. Heřmanměstetz [Heřmanův Městec, Czech Republic], 7 January 1772; d. Vienna, 5 April 1824). Lawyer and teacher. He was educated at Chrudim, Brünn [Brno], and Olmütz [Olomouc], and completed his law studies in Vienna. He taught political science at a school for the imperial guards and at the Theresianische Akademie from 1803, and later also held a professorship at the university. A wealthy bachelor, he was able to gratify his love for music by giving parties, at which leading Viennese artists as well as visiting musicians performed before 'a very select audience drawn from the aristocratic and plutocratic classes' (Leopold von Sonnleithner*). Zizius' sister Antonia acted as hostess, and the entertainment would frequently be followed by a supper and a small ball. Zizius's position as a prominent patron of music led to his being elected to the executive committee of the new Gesellschaft der Musikfreunde.* He himself played the violin.

Beethoven knew Zizius and regularly attended his parties. Zizius furthermore acted as Beethoven's legal adviser on at least one occasion, namely in his dispute with Artaria & Co.* over the String Quintet Op. 29.

(Schindler[1b] (Moscheles's preface), Sonnleithner, Ullrich[5], Wurzbach[1])

Zmeskall von Domanovecz, Nikolaus (b. Lestin, Hungary [Leštiny, Slovak Republic], 20 November 1759; d. Vienna, 23 June 1833). Civil servant. After legal studies he settled in Vienna, where, from 1784 until his retirement in 1825, he was employed at the Hungarian court chancellery. Afflicted by gout, he became increasingly incapacitated in the early 1820s. When he attended Beethoven's concert on 7 May 1824, he had to be carried to his seat in a sedan chair.

Zmeskall was a prominent figure in Viennese musical circles. He was himself an excellent cellist and took part in the chamber music concerts arranged by Prince Karl Lichnowsky.* For many years he regularly held string quartet sessions in his flat at the Bürgerspital, a vast housing complex in central Vienna; sometimes he gave concerts which were open to a select audience. Many well-known musicians performed on those occasions. It may be assumed that Beethoven's works were frequently on the programme, as were Haydn's,* for Zmeskall was a great admirer of both. (Haydn dedicated a new edition of his 'Sun' Quartets Op. 20 to him in 1800.) At a concert at Zmeskall's which he attended during his visit to Vienna in 1808–9, Johann Friedrich Reichardt* heard a 'difficult quintet' by Beethoven (Op. 16 or 29), as well as a 'great Beethoven fantasia' (probably the Sonata Op. 27, No. 2), brilliantly executed by Dorothea Ertmann.* He was able to admire her playing again on another occasion at Zmeskall's, when he also heard 'some of my favourites among the older Haydn quartets'. Zmeskall was, moreover, himself a composer, specializing in string quartets. He never published any of his compositions, however, and at his death bequeathed them to the Gesellschaft der Musikfreunde,* in whose archives they remain to this day. He had been a founder member of the society, and had served on the first executive committee.

Beethoven made Zmeskall's acquaintance soon after arriving in Vienna, perhaps at Prince Lichnowsky's. His published correspondence includes a very large number of letters and notes to Zmeskall, most of them very short and of no particular interest to the biographer other than as evidence of a long relationship which was close and remained untroubled. They reveal that the two friends frequently took their midday meal together at the Zum weissen Schwan restaurant [24 Kärntnerstrasse/6 Neuer Markt]. Beethoven consulted Zmeskall on a variety of matters, especially concerning the engagement and behaviour of his servants, and he also occasionally requested small favours, such as the loan of a small sum of money, or the purchase of a mirror, or a supply of quills. But while the style of Beethoven's communications is generally humorous and he employs some amusing forms of address, his tone does not shed a certain formality and he never uses the intimate 'Du'. The earliest of his known letters to Zmeskall was written on 18 June 1793, the last on 18 February 1827; but there are some gaps in the published correspondence, notably between January 1819 and February 1827, except for a note from Zmeskall in May 1822 (*Corr.* B1463).

Beethoven originally planned to dedicate the Mass Op. 86 to Zmeskall (*see* his letter to Breitkopf & Härtel* of 15 October 1810), but he eventually dedicated it to Prince Ferdinand Kinsky* instead. To Zmeskall he later dedicated the String Quartet in F minor, Op. 95; he probably also wrote for him the Duet in E flat for viola and cello, WoO 32. Two letters (*Corr.* A29/B39, A65/B115) contain brief musical jokes (WoO 101, WoO 205a).

(Pisarowitz[2], Sandberger, Sonnleithner, Ullrich[2], Vörös)

Zulehner, Georg Carl (b. Mainz, 20 July 1770; d. Mainz, 27 December 1841). Composer and music publisher. He studied with Johann Franz Xaver Sterkel* at Mainz and Johann Gottfried Eckard in Paris. He was particularly well known for his very numerous piano arrangements, including one of *Don Giovanni* (he had probably met Mozart* during the latter's visit to Mainz in 1790).

Between 1802 and 1811 he was active as a music publisher. His announcement, in 1803, of a projected collected edition of Beethoven's works for pianoforte and string instruments led Beethoven to issue a furious 'Warning', which appeared in the *Wiener Zeitung* on 22 October and in the Leipzig *Allgemeine musikalische Zeitung* the following month. In it he informed 'all music lovers' that he did not have the slightest part in the proposed edition, which, he asserted, was premature and, moreover, certain to be faulty and incomplete. He intended to announce himself in due course a collection of his works, which would be prepared under his own supervision and be based on a careful examination of previously published editions.

The warning evidently did not lessen Zulehner's interest in Beethoven's music or his belief in its commercial potential, for he went on to publish what W. Matthäus has described as 'the most complete series of [Beethoven] reprints after Simrock's'. In addition, Zulehner later arranged certain of Beethoven's works (e.g. the first two symphonies and the *Coriolan* Overture) for piano duet, piano and violin, and string quartet; these arrangements were published by Simrock* and Schott's Söhne.*

(Matthäus[2], Thayer[1])

Zumbusch, Caspar von (b. Herzebrock, Westphalia, 23 November 1830; d. Rimsting, near Prien am Chiemsee, 27 September 1915). Sculptor. When he was 18, he became a pupil of Johann Halbig at the Polytechnisches Institut in Munich and worked in his studio. He soon made a name for himself. His earliest patrons included Count Karl August Reisach, archbishop of Munich and Freising, for whom he made an ivory crosier and whose bust he modelled. Among the numerous works created by him during his Munich years were the following: a marble bust of King Ludwig II (1864); a bust of Richard Wagner, and statuettes of several characters from his operas; various funerary monuments (including one for the celebrated actress Sophie Schröder); and statues of the medieval historian Otto of Freising (erected at Freising), of the famous physician Johann Lukas Schönlein (for Bamberg), and of King Maximilian II of Bavaria (for Munich). From 1873 until 1901 he taught at the Akademie der bildenden Künste in Vienna. During this period he also received a number of important commissions. Among his most prestigious works were the monumental statues of Beethoven (see below), of the Empress Maria Theresa (on Maria-Theresien-Platz, unveiled 13 May 1888), of Field Marshal Count Johann Joseph Radetzky (unveiled in Am Hof Square on 24 April 1892 and moved to its present location on the Stubenring in 1912), and of Archduke Albrecht (before the Albrechtsrampe, unveiled on 21 May 1899). Zumbusch finally left Vienna in 1908. He had been ennobled in 1888; in 1911 he was awarded an honorary doctorate by the University of Vienna.

On 7 February 1871, more than twenty-five years after Ernst Julius Hähnel's* Beethoven monument had been unveiled in Bonn, the Gesellschaft der Musik-freunde* established a Beethoven Monument Committee, which, on 14 June, elected Nikolaus Dumba as its chairman. In May 1873 the committee invited designs from Johannes Benk (a sculptor who had studied with Hähnel in Dresden), Karl Kundmann (whose Schubert statue had been unveiled in the Stadtpark the preceding year), Anton Paul Wagner, and Zumbusch. Kundmann declined to take part in the competition because of other commitments. On 18 February 1874 a jury unanimously decided in Zumbusch's favour, and, after he had made certain modifications, his design received formal approval on 4 March 1875. A significant part of the costs, which amounted to some 84,000 florins, was borne by private individuals and cultural institutions and associations. (*See also* Liszt.*)

At the unveiling ceremony on 1 May 1880, which was presided over by Dumba, the emperor (who was indisposed by a cold) was represented by the Archdukes Karl Ludwig and Rainer. Among the guests of honour was Karoline van Beethoven, the widow of Beethoven's nephew Karl,* and one of their daughters. Dumba's speech was followed by an address given by the mayor of Vienna, Julius von Newald, who announced that the city council was bestowing honorary citizenship on Dumba and Zumbusch.

The square in which the statue stands has, since 1904, been known as 'Beethovenplatz'. Originally the statue faced the Palais Gutmann, the residence of the industrialist Max von Gutmann [3 Beethovenplatz/12 Fichtegasse]. However, after the river Wien had been covered over in 1899, the statue was turned to face towards it in 1901. Incidentally, Zumbusch's statue was not the first Beethoven monument in the Vienna area. That honour probably belongs to the metal bust modelled by Anton Dominik von Fernkorn which was unveiled at Heiligenstadt in June 1863.

(*Beethoven Statue*[1], Mittig, Schmoll)

Bibliography and Abbreviations

CONVERSATION BOOKS

BKh   *Ludwig van Beethovens Konversationshefte*, herausgegeben von K.-H. Köhler, G. Herre, D. Beck, et al. (11 vols., Leipzig, 1972–).

CORRESPONDENCE

Corr. A   *The Letters of Beethoven*, collected, trans. and ed. with an introduction, appendices, notes, and indexes by E. Anderson (3 vols., London, 1961).

Corr. B   *Briefwechsel Ludwig van Beethoven: Gesamtausgabe*, herausgegeben von S. Brandenburg (8 vols., Munich, 1996–).

ADB   *Allgemeine deutsche Biographie* (56 vols., Munich, 1875–1912; repr. Berlin, 1967–71).

ALBK   *Allgemeines Lexikon der bildenden Künstler von der Antike bis zur Gegenwart*, begründet von U. Thieme und F. Becker (37 vols., Leipzig, 1907–50; repr. Leipzig, 1970–1).

Albrecht[1]   Albrecht, S., 'Leben und Werk von Johann Malfatti, Edler von Montereggio', diss. (University of Heidelberg, 1974).

Albrecht[2]   *Letters to Beethoven and Other Correspondence*, trans. and ed. T. Albrecht (3 vols., Lincoln, Nebr., 1996).

Allan   Allan, J. M., 'Thomson, George', in *MGG*.

Allroggen[1]   Allroggen, G., 'Dressler', in *New Grove*.

Allroggen[2]   —— 'Himmel', in *New Grove*.

Alth/Obzyna   Alth, M. von, and Obzyna, G., *Burgtheater 1776–1976: Aufführungen und Besetzungen von zweihundert Jahren* (2 vols., Vienna, n.d.).

Altman   Altman, G., *Beethoven: A Man of his Word. Undisclosed Evidence for his Immortal Beloved* (Tallahassee, Fla., 1996).

Anderson[1]   Anderson, E., 'The Text of Beethoven's Letters', *Music & Letters*, 34 (1953), 212–23; *see also* p. 363.

Anderson[2]   —— *The Letters of Beethoven*, collected, transl., and ed. with an introduction, appendices, notes, and indexes by E. Anderson (3 vols., London, 1961).

Anderson[3]   —— 'Charles Neate: A Beethoven Friendship', in *Festschrift Deutsch*, 196–202.

Angermüller[1]   Angermüller, R., *Antonio Salieri: Sein Leben und seine weltlichen Werke . . .* (3 vols., Munich, 1971–4).

Angermüller[2]   —— 'Weigl, Joseph', in *New Grove*.
Anschütz   Anschütz, H., *Erinnerungen aus dessen Leben und Wirken* (Vienna, 1866).
Antonicek[1]   Antonicek, T., 'Cartellieri', in *MGG*.
Antonicek[2]   —— 'Dietrichstein-Proskau-Leslie', in *MGG*.
Antonicek[3]   —— 'Ignaz von Mosel (1772–1844): Biographie und Beziehungen zu den Zeitgenossen', doctoral diss. (University of Vienna, 1962).
Antonicek[4]   —— *Musik im Festsaal der Österreichischen Akademie der Wissenschaften* (Vienna, 1972).
Antonicek[5]   —— 'Musiker aus den böhmischen Ländern in Wien zu Beethovens Zeit', in *Beethoven und Böhmen*, 43–61.
Antonicek[6]   —— 'Empfindungen und geregelte Töne: Ignaz von Mosel im ästhetischen Spannungsfeld der bürgerlichen Musikkultur', *ÖMZ*, 49 (1994), 539–44.
Arendt   Arendt, H., *Rahel Varnhagen: Lebensgeschichte einer deutschen Jüdin aus der Romantik. Mit einer Auswahl von Rahel-Briefen . . .* (Munich, 1962).
Arneth   Arneth, A. Ritter von, *Aus meinem Leben* (2 vols., Vienna, 1891–2).
Arnim[1]   *Bettinas Briefwechsel mit Goethe . . .* , herausgegeben von R. Steig (Leipzig, 1922).
Arnim[2]   Arnim, H. von, *Louis Ferdinand, Prinz von Preussen* (Berlin, 1966).
Asow   *Ludwig van Beethoven: Heiligenstädter Testament*, Faksimile, herausgegeben von H. M. von Asow (Vienna, 1957).
Asshoff   Asshoff, C., 'Huber', in *LL*.
Atterbom   *Aufzeichnungen des schwedischen Dichters P. D. A. Atterbom über berühmte Männer und Frauen nebst Reiseerinnerungen aus Deutschland und Italien aus den Jahren 1817–1819*, aus dem Schwedischen übersetzt von F. Maurer (Berlin, 1867).
Auer   *Wien und seine Gärten*, herausgegeben von A. Auer (Vienna, 1974).
Bab   Bab, J., *Die Devrients: Geschichte einer deutschen Theaterfamilie* (Berlin, [1932]).
Bachmann   Bachmann, L. G., *Beethoven contra Beethoven: Geschichte eines berühmten Rechtsfalles* (Munich, 1963).
Badstüber   Badstüber, H., *Christoph Kuffner, ein vergessener Poet des Vormärz: Ein Beitrag zur österreichischen Literaturgeschichte* (Leipzig, 1907).
Badura-Skoda[1]   Badura-Skoda, E., 'Schimon', in *MGG*.
Badura-Skoda[2]   —— 'Umlauff [Umlauf]', in *MGG*.
Badura-Skoda[3]   —— 'Probleme einer Dokumentar-Biographie Beethovens', in *Beethoven Congress[2]*, 331–3.
Badura-Skoda[4]   —— 'Zum Charakterbild Anton Schindlers', *ÖMZ*, 32 (1977), 241–6.
Badura-Skoda[5]   —— 'Der Bildhauer Anton Dietrich: Ein Beitrag zur Ikonographie Beethovens und Schuberts', in *Festschrift Henle*, 30–52.
Badura-Skoda[6]   —— 'Reminiszenzen an Beethoven, Schubert und einige Maler der Wiener Biedermeierzeit: Aus den *Gedenkblättern* von Franz Stohl', in *Festschrift Wessely*, 53–65.
Bankl/Jesserer   Bankl, H., and Jesserer, H., *Die Krankheiten Ludwig van Beethovens: Pathographie seines Lebens und Pathologie seiner Leiden* (Vienna, 1987).
Barbarisi   Barbarisi, G., 'Bondi', in *DBI*.
Barton   Barton, D. P., *Bernadotte: The First Phase, 1763–1799* (New York, 1914).

Bate   Bate, P., 'Oboe', in *New Grove*.

Bauer[1]   Bauer, A., *150 Jahre Theater an der Wien* (Zurich, 1952).

Bauer[2]   —— *Opern und Operetten in Wien: Verzeichnis ihrer Erstaufführungen in der Zeit von 1629 bis zur Gegenwart* (Graz, 1955).

Bauer[3]   Bauer, E. E., *Wie Beethoven auf den Sockel kam: Die Entstehung eines musikalischen Mythos* (Stuttgart, 1992).

Bauernfeld   Bauernfeld, E., *Erinnerungen aus Alt-Wien*, herausgegeben von J. Bindtner (Vienna, 1923).

Baum   Baum, R., *Joseph Wölfl (1773–1812): Leben, Klavierwerke, Klavierkammermusik und Klavierkonzerte* (Kassel, 1928).

Beahrs[1]   Beahrs, V. O., 'The Immortal Beloved Reconsidered', *Musical Times*, 129 (1988), 64–70.

Beahrs[2]   —— 'The Beethoven-Malfatti Connection Revisited', *Beethoven Journal*, 13 (1998), 12–16.

Becker   Becker, H., 'Henning, Carl Wilhelm', in *MGG*.

Beck/Herre[1] Beck, D., and Herre, G., 'Anton Schindlers fingierte Eintragungen in den Konversationsheften', in *Zu Beethoven*, 11–89.

Beck/Herre[2] —— 'Anton Schindlers "Nutzanwendung" der Cramer-Etüden: Zu den sogenannten Beethovenschen Spielanweisungen', in *Zu Beethoven 3*, 177–208.

Beethoven and Quebec   *Beethoven and Quebec* (Montreal, 1966).

Beethoven Congress[1]   *Beethoven-Symposion Wien 1970: Bericht* (Vienna, 1971).

Beethoven Congress[2]   *Bericht über den internationalen musikwissenschaftlichen Kongress Bonn 1970*, herausgegeben von C. Dahlhaus *et al.* (Kassel, [1971]).

Beethoven Congress[3]   *Beiträge '76–78: Beethoven-Kolloquium [Wien] 1977. Dokumentation und Aufführungspraxis*, Redaktion: R. Klein (Kassel, 1978).

Beethoven Congress[4]   *Bericht über den internationalen Beethoven-Kongress 20. bis 23 März 1977 in Berlin*, herausgegeben von H. Goldschmidt *et al.* (Leipzig, 1978).

Beethoven Congress[5]   *Beethoven, Performers, and Critics: The International Beethoven Congress, Detroit, 1977*, ed. R. Winter and B. Carr (Detroit, 1980).

Beethoven Exhibition   *'Die Flamme lodert': Beethoven-Ausstellung der Stadt Wien. Rathaus, Volkshalle, 26. Mai bis 30. August 1970*, catalogue (Vienna, 1970).

Beethoven-Haus[1]   *Verein Beethoven-Haus in Bonn. Bericht über die ersten fünfzehn Jahre seines Bestehens* (Bonn, [1804]).

Beethoven-Haus[2]   *Zimelien aus den Sammlungen des Beethoven-Hauses: 21 ausgewählte Neuerwerbungen der letzten drei Jahrzehnte. Dr. h.c. Hermann J. Abs zum 90. Geburtstag* (Bonn, 1991).

Beethoven-Haus[3]   *Beethoven und sein Bonner Freundeskreis: Ausgewählte Dokumente aus der Sammlung Wegeler im Beethoven-Haus*, bearbeitet und herausgegeben von M. Ladenburger (Bonn, 1998).

Beethoven Statue[1]   *Zur Enthüllung des Beethoven-Denkmals in Wien am 1. Mai 1880* (Vienna, 1880).

Beethoven Statue[2]   *Monument für Beethoven: Zur Geschichte des Beethoven-Denkmals (1845) und der frühen Beethoven-Rezeption in Bonn. Katalog zur Ausstellung des Stadtmuseums Bonn und des Beethoven-Hauses*, herausgegeben von I. Bodsch (Bonn, 1995).

Beethoven und Böhmen   *Beethoven und Böhmen: Beiträge zu Biographie und Wirkungsgeschichte Beethovens*, herausgegeben von S. Brandenburg und M. Gutiérrez-Denhoff (Bonn, 1988).

Beichler   Beichler, C., *Therese von Brunswick und ihr Lebensauftrag zwischen Beethoven und Pestalozzi* [Rendsburg, 1993].

Benyovszky   Benyovszky, K., *J. N. Hummel: Der Mensch und Künstler* (Bratislava, 1934).

Berger[1]   Berger, A., *Felix, Fürst zu Schwarzenberg: Ein biographisches Denkmal* (Leipzig, 1853).

Berger[2]   Berger, K., *Theodor Körner* (Bielefeld, 1912).

Berlioz   Berlioz, H., 'Antoine Reicha', *Journal des débats* (3 July 1836).

Bernhardt   Bernhardt, R., 'Aus der Umwelt der Wiener Klassiker: Freiherr Gottfried van Swieten (1734–1803)', *Der Bär* (1929–30), 74–164.

Bettermann   *Erinnerungen an Beethoven: Skizzen, Zeichnungen, Karikaturen*, ausgewählt und erläutert von S. Bettermann (Bonn, 1987).

Biach   Biach, R., *Johann Peter Frank, der Wiener Volkshygieniker* (Vienna, 1962).

Bianchi   Bianchi, J., 'Vier unveröffentliche Briefe von Leopold von Sonnleithner', *Studien zur Musikwissenschaft*, 31 (1980), 49–66.

Biba[1]   Biba, O., 'Beethoven als "Klaviermeister" einer Wiener Bürgerfamilie', *ÖMZ*, 32 (1977), 136–8.

Biba[2]   —— 'Beethoven und die "Liebhaber Concerte" in Wien im Winter 1807/8', in *Beethoven Congress*[3], 82–93.

Biba[3]   —— 'Concert Life in Beethoven's Vienna', in *Beethoven Congress*[5], 77–93.

Biba[4]   —— 'Beethovens Schüler Erzherzog Rudolph', *Musikblätter der Wiener Philharmoniker*, 35 (1981), 209–11.

Biba[5]   —— 'Unbekannte oder wenig beachtete Schriftstücke Beethovens', *Beethoven-Jahrbuch*, 2nd ser. 10 (1983), 21–85.

Biba[6]   —— 'Neue Beethoveniana in den Sammlungen der Gesellschaft der Musikfreunde in Wien', *ÖMZ*, 41 (1986), 635–9.

Biberhofer   Biberhofer, R., '*Vestas Feuer*: Beethovens erster Opernplan', *Die Musik*, 22 (1929–30), 409–14.

Biesterfeld   Biesterfeld, W., 'Tiedge', in *LL*.

Birke   Birke, V., 'Danhauser', in *DicArt*.

Bisanz   Bisanz-Prakken, M., *Gustav Klimt. Der Beethovenfries: Geschichte, Funktion und Bedeutung* (Salzburg, 1977).

Bischoff[1]   Bischoff, F., *Chronik des Steiermärkischen Musikvereines* (Graz, 1890).

Bischoff[2]   —— 'Beethoven und die Grazer musikalischen Kreise', *Beethoven-Jahrbuch*, 1 (1908), 6–27.

Bischoff[3]   —— 'Zu Beethovens Briefwechsel mit Varena 1811–1815', *Beethoven-Jahrbuch*, 2 (1909), 155–60.

Bissing   Bissing, W. M. von, *Friedrich Wilhelm II, König von Preussen: Ein Lebensbild* (Berlin, 1967).

Blaxland   Blaxland, J. H., 'Eine unbekannte Canzonetta Beethovens', *Zeitschrift für Musikwissenschaft*, 14 (Oct. 1931), 29–34.

Blittersdorff   Blittersdorff, J., 'Versuch einer Genealogie der Familien v. Birkenstock und v. Hay', *Adler*, 9/49–50 (Feb. 1925), 227–30, 250.

Blumner   Blumner, M., *Geschichte der Sing-Akademie zu Berlin* (Berlin, 1891).

Bolte   Bolte, T., *Die Musikerfamilien Stein und Streicher* (Vienna, 1917).

Bory   Bory, R., *La Vie et l'œuvre de Ludwig van Beethoven par l'image* (Zurich, 1960).

Brandenburg[1]   Brandenburg, S., 'Bemerkungen zu Beethovens Op. 96', *Beethoven-Jahrbuch*, 2nd ser. 9 (1977), 11–25.

Brandenburg[2]   —— *Der Freundeskreis der Familie Malfatti in Wien, gezeichnet von Ludwig Ferdinand Schnorr von Carolsfeld* (Bonn, 1985).

Brandenburg[3]   —— *Beethoven: Der Brief an die unsterbliche Geliebte* (Bonn, 1986).

Brandenburg[4]   —— 'Beethovens Oratorium *Christus am Ölberg*: Ein unbequemes Werk', in *Festschrift Massenkeil*, 203–30.

Brandenburg[5]   —— 'Die Beethovenhandschriften in der Musikaliensammlung des Erzherzogs Rudolph', in *Zu Beethoven 3*, 141–76.

Brandenburg[6]   *Briefwechsel Ludwig van Beethoven: Gesamtausgabe*, gerausgegeben von S. Brandenburg (8 vols., Munich, 1996–).

Brandenburg[7]   —— 'Johanna van Beethoven's Embezzlement', in *Festschrift Tyson*, 237–51.

Brandenburg/Staehelin   —— and Staehelin, M., 'Die "erste Fassung" von Beethovens Righini Variationen', in *Festschrift Rosenthal*, 43–66.

Branscombe[1]   Branscombe, P., 'Gallenberg', in *New Grove*.

Branscombe[2]   —— 'Gläser', in *New Grove*.

Branscombe[3]   —— 'Kanne', in *New Grove*.

Branscombe[4]   —— 'Schenk', in *New Grove*.

Branscombe[5]   —— 'Seyfried', in *New Grove*.

Branscombe[6]   —— 'Umlauf, Ignaz', in *New Grove*.

Branscombe[7]   —— 'Umlauf, Michael', in *New Grove*.

Braubach[1]   Braubach, M., *Die erste Bonner Universität und ihre Professoren: Ein Beitrag zur rheinischen Geistesgeschichte im Zeitalter der Aufklärung* (Bonn, 1947).

Braubach[2]   —— *Eine Jugendfreundin Beethovens: Babette Koch-Belderbusch und ihr Kreis* (Bonn, 1948).

Braubach[3]   —— *Kurköln: Gestalten und Ereignisse aus zwei Jahrhunderten rheinischer Geschichte* (Münster, 1949).

Braubach[4]   —— *Maria Theresias jüngster Sohn, Max Franz, letzter Kurfürst von Köln und Fürstbischof von Münster* (Vienna, 1961).

Braubach[5]   —— 'Die Mitglieder der Hofmusik unter den vier letzten Kurfürsten von Köln', in *Festschrift Schmidt-Görg*[2], 26–63.

Braubach[6]   —— 'Beethovens Abschied von Bonn: Das rheinische Erbe', in *Beethoven Congress*[1], 25–41.

Braubach[7]   —— *Die Stammbücher Beethovens und der Babette Koch*, in Faksimile mit Einleitung und Erläuterungen herausgegeben von M. Braubach (Bonn, 1970).

Braubach[8]   —— 'Vom Schicksal der Bonner Freunden des jungen Beethovens', *Bonner Geschichtsblätter*, 28 (1976), 95–138.

Braunbehrens   Braunbehrens, V., *Salieri: Ein Musiker im Schatten Mozarts* (Munich, 1989).

Brauneis   Brauneis, W., ' ". . . COMPOSTA PER FESTEGGIARE IL SOVVENIRE DI UN GRAND UOMO": Beethovens "Eroica" als Hommage des Fürsten Franz Joseph

	Maximilian von Lobkowitz für Louis Ferdinand von Preussen', *ÖMZ*, 53/12 (1998), 4–24.
Breidenstein[1]	Breidenstein, H. K., *Festgabe zu der am 12ten August 1845 stattfindenden Inauguration des Beethoven Monuments* (Bonn, 1845). *See also* next item.
Breidenstein[2]	—— *Zur Jahresfeier der Inauguration des Beethoven-Monuments: Eine actenmässige Darstellung dieses Ereignisses, der Wahrheit zur Ehre und den Festgenossen zur Erinnerung* (Bonn, 1846); repr., together with the preceding item, under the title *Inauguration des Beethoven-Monuments zu Bonn* (Bonn, 1983).
Brennecke	Brennecke, W., 'Grosheim', in *MGG*.
Brenneis[1]	Brenneis, C., 'Das Fischhof-Manuskript: Zur Frühgeschichte der Beethoven-Biographie', in *Zu Beethoven*, 90–116.
Brenneis[2]	—— 'Das Fischhof-Manuskript in der Deutschen Staatsbibliothek: Text und Kommentar', in *Zu Beethoven 2*, 27–87.
Brentano	Brentano, J. Freiherr von, *Die Brentano: Aufsätze zur Familiengeschichte* (Munich, 1990).
Bresch	Bresch, S., 'Beethovens Reisen zu den böhmischen Bädern in den Jahren 1811 und 1812', in *Beethoven und Böhmen*, 311–48.
Breuning	Breuning, G. von, *Aus dem Schwarzspanierhause: Erinnerungen an L. van Beethoven aus meiner Jugendzeit* (Vienna, 1874); English trans.: *Memories of Beethoven: From the House of the Black-Robed Spaniards*, ed. M. Solomon; trans. from the German by H. Mins and M. Solomon (Cambridge, 1992).
Breyer	Breyer, H., *Johann Peter Frank, Fürst unter den Ärzten Europas* (Leipzig, 1983).
Brosche[1]	Brosche, G., 'Aus Beethovens Alltag: Neue Forschungsergebnisse über einige Wiener Bekannte des Meisters in den Jahren 1819/20', *ÖMZ*, 26 (1971), 381–6.
Brosche[2]	—— 'Zur Datierung der Beethoven-Konversationshefte', *ÖMZ*, 32 (1977), 119–24.
Brown	Brown, M. J. E., 'Sechter', in *New Grove*.
Bunge	Bunge, R., '*Fidelio*: Nach persönlichen Mitteilungen des Herrn Professor Joseph Röckel', *Die Gartenlaube* (Leipzig) (1868), 38: 601–6.
Burney	Burney, C., *The Present State of Music in Germany, the Netherlands and United Provinces. A Facsimile of the* [2nd, corrected] *1775 London Edition* (London, 1969).
Burnham	Burnham, S., 'Criticism, Faith, and the *Idee*: A. B. Marx's Early Reception of Beethoven', *19th Century Music*, 13 (1989–90), 183–92.
Buschmann	Buschmann, B., 'Fannys Tagebuch: Neue Überlegungen zu einer vielzitierten Quelle', in *Zu Beethoven 3*, 31–42.
Bužga[1]	Bužga, J., 'Reicha', in *MGG*.
Bužga[2]	—— 'Tomášek', in *MGG*.
Carse	Carse, A., 'The Choral Symphony in London', *Music & Letters*, 32 (1951), 47–58.
Castelli	Castelli, I. F., *Memoiren meines Lebens: Gefundenes und Empfundenes, Erlebtes und Erstrebstes*, herausgegeben von J. Bindtner (2 vols., Munich, 1913).

Celeda	'Beethoven's "Immortal Beloved": Oldrich Pulkert's Presentation and Edition of Jaroslav Celeda's Manuscript "Immortal Beloved" ', further rev. by Hans-Werner Küthen and trans. by William Meredith', *Beethoven Journal*, 15 (2000), 2–18. (*See also* Meredith, W., 'Moral Musings: Testing the Candidacy of Almerie Esterházy against the Antonie Brentano Theory', ibid., 42–7.)
Černy	Černy, M. K., 'Kaňka', in *New Grove*.
Chantavoine	Chantavoine, J., 'Une visite à Beethoven', *Mercure musical*, 9 (1906), 393–8.
Charlton	Charlton, D., 'Kreutzer, Rodolphe', in *New Grove*.
Chitz	Chitz, A., 'Une œuvre inconnue de Beethoven pour mandoline et piano', *Revue musicale* (15 Dec. 1912), 24–31.
Chorley[1]	Chorley, H. F., *Modern German Music* (London, 1854; repr. New York, 1973).
Chorley[2]	—— *Thirty Years' Musical Recollections* (London, 1862); slightly abridged edn. by E. Newman (London, 1926, repr. New York, 1972).
Chrysander	Chrysander, F., 'Beethovens Verbindung mit Birchall und Stumpff in London', *Jahrbücher für musikalische Wissenschaft*, 1 (1863), 429–52.
Churgin	'Beethoven and Mozart's Requiem: A New Connection', *Journal of Musicology*, 5 (1987), 457–77.
Clemen	Clemen, O., 'Andreas Streicher in Wien', *Neues Beethoven-Jahrbuch*, 4 (1930), 107–17.
Clive[1]	Clive, P., *Mozart and his Circle: A Biographical Dictionary* (London, 1993).
Clive[2]	—— *Schubert and his World: A Biographical Dictionary* (Oxford, 1997).
Cloeter[1]	Cloeter, H., *Zwischen gestern und heute: Wanderungen durch Wien und den Wienerwald* (Vienna, n.d.).
Cloeter[2]	—— *Geist und Geister aus dem alten Wien: Bilder und Gestalten* (Vienna, 1922).
Collin	*Heinrich Joseph von Collin und sein Kreis: Briefe und Aktenstücke*, herausgegeben von M. Lederer (Vienna, 1921).
Cone	Cone, E. T., 'Schubert's Beethoven', *Musical Quarterly*, 56 (1970), 779–93.
Converse	Converse, J. K., 'Burlington Female Seminary', *Vermont Historical Gazetteer*, 1 (1867), 531–5.
Cooper[1]	Cooper, B., 'Beethoven's Revisions to "Für Elise" ', *Musical Times*, 125 (1984), 561–3.
Cooper[2]	—— *The Beethoven Compendium: A Guide to Beethoven's Life and Music*, ed. B. Cooper (London, 1991).
Cooper[3]	—— *Beethoven's Folksong Settings: Chronology, Sources, Style* (Oxford, 1994).
Cooper[4]	—— 'Beethoven's Oratorio and the Heiligenstadt Testament', *Beethoven Journal*, 10 (1995), 19–24.
Cooper[5]	—— 'The Newly Discovered Quartet Movement by Beethoven', *Beethoven Journal*, 15 (2000), 19–24.
Cooper[6]	Cooper, M., *Beethoven: The Last Decade* (London, 1970).
Craig	Craig, K. M., Jr., 'The Beethoven Symphonies in London: Initial Decades', *College Music Symposium*, 25 (1985), 73–91.
Criste	Criste, O., *Feldmarschall Johannes Fürst von Liechtenstein: Eine Biographie* (Vienna, 1905).

Czeike   Czeike, F., *Historisches Lexikon Wien* (5 vols., Vienna, 1992–7).

Czeke   Czeke, M. de, 'Séjours de Beethoven en Hongrie', *Neues Beethoven-Jahrbuch*, 6 (1935), 52–8.

Czeke/Révész   —— and Révész, M., *Gróf Brunsvik Teréz: Élet-és jellemrajza* (Budapest, 1926).

Dadelsen   Dadelsen, G. von, 'Kirnberger', in *MGG*.

Dale   Dale, K., 'The Three C's: Pioneers of Piano Playing', *Music Review*, 6 (1945), 138–48.

Dalton   Dalton, D., 'Goethe and the Composers of his Time', *Music Review*, 34 (1973), 157–74.

Danhauser   *Danhauser, Josef (1805–1845): Gemälde und Zeichnungen*, [Katalog] bearbeitet von V. Birke (Vienna, 1983).

Davenport   Davenport, A. D., 'Beethoven: A Study in Hypothesis of the Events Leading up to, and Surrounding, the Summer of 1802', *Music Review*, 31 (1970), 21–31.

Davey   D[avey], H., 'Salomon', in *DNB*.

David/Charlton   David, P., and Charlton, D., 'Clement', in *New Grove*.

Dawes   Dawes, F., 'Steibelt', in *New Grove*.

DBI   *Dizionario biografico degli Italiani* (Rome, 1960–   ).

DBL   *Deutsch-baltisches biographisches Lexikon 1710–1960*, herausgegeben von W. Lenz (Cologne, 1970).

Deissinger   Deissinger, H., *Ferdinand Sauter: Sein Leben und Dichten. Auf Grund einer Dissertation von H. D.*, herausgegeben, ergänzt . . . von O. Pfeiffer (Vienna, 1926).

DeNora[1]   DeNora, T., *Beethoven and the Construction of Genius: Musical Politics in Vienna, 1792–1803* (Berkeley, Calif., 1995).

DeNora[2]   —— 'Musical Patronage and Social Change in Beethoven's Vienna', *American Journal of Sociology*, 97 (1991), 310–46.

Derra de Moroda   Derra de Moroda, F., 'Viganò, Salvatore', in *New Grove*.

Deutsch[1]   Deutsch, O. E., 'Aus Beethovens letzten Tagen: Briefe Johann Baptist Jengers an Marie Leopoldine Pachler-Koschak', *Österreichische Rundschau*, 10 (1907), 189–205.

Deutsch[2]   —— *Beethovens Beziehungen zu Graz: Neue Beiträge zur Biographie des Meisters und zur Konzertgeschichte der Stadt* (Graz, 1907).

Deutsch[3]   —— 'Beethovens gesammelte Werke: Des Meisters Plan und Haslingers Ausgabe', *Zeitschrift für Musikwissenschaft*, 13 (1930–1), 60–5.

Deutsch[4]   —— 'Der Liederdichter Reissig: Bestimmung einer merkwürdigen Persönlichkeit', *Neues Beethoven-Jahrbuch*, 6 (1935), 59–65.

Deutsch[5]   —— 'Beethovens Textdichter Reissig', *Anbruch* (1936/4), 69–71.

Deutsch[6]   —— 'Kozeluch ritrovato', *Music & Letters*, 26 (1945), 47–50. *See also* ibid. 121–2, and 27 (1946), 24–5; and correspondence in 33 (1952).

Deutsch[7]   —— 'Count Deym and his Mechanical Organs', *Music & Letters*, 29 (1948), 140–5.

Deutsch[8]   —— 'Ein wiedergefundenes Beethovenhaus', *ÖMZ*, 18 (1963), 433–6.

Deutsch[9]   —— 'Festkonzerte im alten Universitätssaal: Haydn, Beethoven, Schubert', *ÖMZ*, 18 (1963), 428–33.

Deutsch[10] —— 'Musik im Burgtheater', *ÖMZ*, 18 (1963), 439–42.

Deutsch[11] —— 'Musik in der "Josefstadt" ', *ÖMZ*, 18 (1963), 549–52.

Deutsch[12] —— 'Schikaneders Testament', *ÖMZ*, 18 (1963), 421–5.

Deutsch[13] —— 'Zu Beethovens Grossen Akademien von 1824', *ÖMZ*, 19 (1964), 426–9.

DicArt *The Dictionary of Art*, ed. J. Turner (34 vols., London, 1996).

DNB *Dictionary of National Biography* (63 vols., London, 1885–1900; 3 supplements, 1901).

Dömling Dömling, W., 'Die Kunstausstellung als Weihfestspiel: Max Klinger und sein "Beethoven" in Wien', *ÖMZ*, 48 (1993), 87–91.

Dorfmüller *Beiträge zur Beethoven-Bibliographie; Studien und Materialen zum Werkverzeichnis von Kinsky-Halm*, herausgegeben von K. Dorfmüller (Munich, 1978).

Dressler 'Lebensumstände des im Jahr 1779 verstorbenen Hessen-Casselchen Cammermusikus Dressler', *Magazin der Musik*, 2/1 (1785), 482–9.

Dürr[1] Dürr, W., 'Wer vermag nach Beethoven noch etwas zu machen? Gedanken über die Beziehungen Schuberts zu Beethoven', *Beethoven-Jahrbuch*, NS 9 (1977), 46–67.

Dürr[2] —— ' "Die Grenzen der Kunst möglichst zu erweitern": Beethoven und Schubert', *Programme: Schubertiade Hohenems 1988*, 10–30.

Ealy Ealy, G. T., 'Of Ear Trumpets and a Resonance Plate: Early Hearing Aids and Beethoven's Hearing Perception', *19th Century Music*, 17 (1993–4), 226–73.

Edwards E[dwards], F. G., 'George P. Bridgetower and the Kreutzer Sonata', *Musical Times*, 49 (1908), 302–8.

Ehinger[1] Ehinger, H., *Friedrich Rochlitz als Musikschriftsteller* (Leipzig, 1929).

Ehinger[2] —— 'Hoffmann, E. T. A.', in *MGG*.

Ehinger[3] —— 'Rochlitz', in *MGG*.

Ehinger[4] —— *E. T. A. Hoffmann als Musiker und Musikschriftsteller* (Olten, 1954).

Eichner Eichner, S., 'Beethoven in Budapest', *Deutsche Musiker-Zeitung* (17 Sept. 1927).

Eisenberg Eisenberg, L., *Grosses biographisches Lexikon der deutschen Bühne im XIX. Jahrhundert* (Leipzig, 1903).

Elkin Elkin, R., *Royal Philharmonic: The Annals of the Royal Philharmonic Society* (London, n.d.).

Elliott Elliott, P., 'Thayer's Beethoven', *Beethoven Newsletter*, 2/1 (Spring 1987), 13–14.

Elvers[1] Elvers, R., 'Schlesinger', in *MGG*.

Elvers[2] —— 'Simrock', in *New Grove*.

Engel Engel, H., 'Clementi', in *MGG*.

Engelbrecht Engelbrecht, C., *et al.*, *Theater in Kassel: Aus der Geschichte des Staatstheaters Kassel von den Anfängen bis zur Gegenwart* (Kassel, 1959).

Engländer[1] Engländer, R., 'Ferdinando Paer als sächsischer Hofkapellmeister', *Neues Archiv für sächsische Geschichte und Alterthumskunde*, 1 (1929), 204–24.

Engländer[2] 'Paers *Leonora* und Beethovens *Fidelio*', *Neues Beethoven-Jahrbuch*, 4 (1930), 118–32.

Eschenhagen   Eschenhagen, B., 'Recke', in *LL*.

Esterházy[1]   *Mémoires du Cte Valentin Esterhazy*, avec une introduction et des notes par E. Daudet (2nd ed., Paris, 1905).

Esterházy[2]   *Lettres du Cte Valentin Esterhazy à sa femme, 1784–1792*, avec une introduction et des notes par E. Daudet (Paris, 1907).

Esterházy[3]   *Nouvelles Lettres du Cte Valentin Esterhazy à sa femme, 1792–1795*, publiées par E. Daudet (Paris, 1909).

Federhofer[1]   Federhofer, H., 'Halm', in *MGG*.

Federhofer[2]   —— 'Hüttenbrenner', in *MGG*.

Federhofer[3]   —— 'Schenk', in *MGG*.

Federhofer[4]   —— 'Ein thematischer Katalog der Dorothea Graumann (Freiin von Ertmann)', in *Festschrift Schmidt-Görg*[1], 100–10.

Federhofer-Königs[1]   Federhofer-Königs, R., 'Rasumowsky', in *MGG*.

Federhofer-Königs[2]   —— 'Rudolph Johann Joseph Rainer, Erzherzog von Österreich', in *MGG*.

Feilchenfeldt   Feilchenfeldt, K., 'Varnhagen von Ense', in *LL*.

Fellinger[1]   Fellinger, I., 'Kanne', in *MGG*.

Fellinger[2]   —— 'Friedrich August Kanne als Kritiker Beethovens', in *Beethoven Congress*[2], 383–6.

Festschrift Abs   *Divertimento für J. Abs: Beethoven-Studien dargebracht zu seinem 80. Geburtstag . . .*, herausgegeben von M. Staehelin (Bonn, 1981). *See also Beethoven-Haus*[2].

Festschrift Deutsch   *Festschrift Otto Erich Deutsch zum 80. Geburtstag am 5. September 1963*, herausgegeben von W. Gerstenberg *et al.* (Vienna, 1963).

Festschrift Fellerer   *Festschrift Karl Gustav Fellerer zum sechzigsten Geburtstag am 7. Juli 1962*, herausgegeben von H. Hüschen (Regensburg, 1962).

Festschrift Forbes   *Beethoven Essays: Studies in Honor of Elliot Forbes*, ed. L. Lockwood and P. Benjamin (Cambridge, Mass., 1984).

Festschrift Hantsch   *Österreich und Europa: Festgabe für Hugo Hantsch zum 70. Geburtstag* (Graz, 1965).

Festschrift Henle   *Musik, Edition, Interpretation: Gedenkschrift Günter Henle*, herausgegeben von M. Bente (Munich, 1980).

Festschrift Kaufmann   *Music East and West: Essays in Honor of W. Kaufmann*, ed. T. Noblitt (New York, 1981).

Festschrift La Laurencie   *Mélanges offerts à M. Lionel de La Laurencie* (Paris, 1933).

Festschrift Massenkeil   *Beiträge zur Geschichte des Oratoriums seit Händel: Festschrift Günther Massenkeil zum 60. Geburtstag*, herausgegeben von R. Cadenbach und H. Loos (Bonn, 1986).

Festschrift Müller-Blattau   *Zum 70. Geburtstag von Joseph Müller-Blattau*, herausgegeben von C.-H. Mähling (Kassel, 1966).

Festschrift Richel   *Frankfurter Beiträge A. Richel gewidmet* (Frankfurt am Main, 1933).

Festschrift Rosenthal   *Festschrift Albi Rosenthal*, herausgegeben von R. Elvers (Tutzing, 1984).

Festschrift Schmidt-Görg[1]   *Festschrift Joseph Schmidt-Görg zum 60. Geburtstag*, herausgegeben von D. Weise (Bonn, 1957).

Festschrift Schmidt-Görg[2]   *Colloquium amicorum: Joseph Schmidt-Görg zum 70. Geburtstag*, herausgegeben von S. Kross und H. Schmidt (Bonn, 1967).

Festschrift Strecker   *Festschrift für einen Verleger: Ludwig Strecker zum 90. Geburtstag*, herausgegeben von C. Dahlhaus (Mainz, 1973).

Festschrift Stummvoll   *Festschrift Josef Stummvoll . . .* , herausgegeben von J. Mayerhofer und W. Ritzer (2 vols., Vienna, 1970).

Festschrift Tyson   *Haydn, Mozart, & Beethoven: Studies in the Music of the Classical Period. Essays in Honour of Alan Tyson* (Oxford, 1998).

Festschrift Wessely   *Festschrift Othmar Wessely zum 60. Geburtstag*, herausgegeben von M. Angerer *et al.* (Tutzing, 1982).

Fétis   Fétis, F. J., *Biographie universelle des musiciens et bibliographie générale de la musique* (2nd edn., 8 vols., Paris, 1868–70). *Supplément et complément* (2 vols., Paris, 1878–81).

Feuchtmüller   Feuchtmüller, R., 'Das Beethoven-Portrait von Ferdinand Georg Waldmüller (1823)', in *Eine Brüsseler Beethoven-Sammlung: Ausstellung im Beethoven-Haus Bonn, 15. Dezember 1991–12 März 1992* (Bonn, 1991), 5–7.

Fischer[1]   Fischer, C., 'Castelli', in *LL*.

Fischer[2]   —— 'Kuffner', in *LL*.

Fischer[3]   —— 'Stoll, Joseph Ludwig', in *LL*.

Fischer[4]   *Des Bonner Bäckermeisters Gottfried Fischer Aufzeichnungen über Beethovens Jugend*, herausgegeben von J. Schmidt-Görg (Munich, 1971).

Fischer-Dieskau   Fischer-Dieskau, D., *'Weil nicht alle Blümenträume reiften': Johann Friedrich Reichardt, Hofkapellmeister dreier Preussenkönige. Portrait und Selbstportrait* (Stuttgart, 1992).

Fischman[1]   Fischman, N., 'Autographen Beethovens in der UdSSR', *Beiträge zur Musikwissenschaft*, 3 (1961), 22–9.

Fischman[2]   —— 'Die Uraufführung der *Missa solemnis*', *Beiträge zur Musikwissenschaft*, 12 (1970), 275–81.

Fischman[3]   —— 'Verzeichnis aller in der UdSSR ermittelten und registrierten Beethoven-Autographe: Stand am 1. Januar 1980', in *Zu Beethoven 3*, 113–40.

Fojtíková/Volek   Fojtíková, J., and Volek, T., 'Die Beethoveniana der Lobkowitz-Musiksammlung und ihre Kopisten', in *Beethoven und Böhmen*, 219–58.

Forbes[1]   Forbes, E., 'Forti', in *New Grove*.

Forbes[2]   —— 'Schuppanzigh', in *New Grove*.

Forbes[3]   —— 'Thayer', in *New Grove*.

Franke   Franke, W., *Der Theaterkritiker Ludwig Rellstab* (Berlin, 1964).

Franken   Franken, F. H., *Die Krankheiten grosser Komponisten* (2 vols., Wilhelmshaven, 1986). On Beethoven, *see* i. 61–110.

Freeman   Freeman, R. N., 'Albrechtsberger', in *New Grove*.

Freemanová   Freemanová, M., 'Würfel', in *New Opera Grove*.

Frey   'Das Wiener Tagebuch des Mannheimer Hofkapellmeisters Michael Frey, [herausgegeben] von J. Schmidt-Görg', *Beethoven-Jahrbuch*, 2nd ser. 6 (1965–8) [1969], 129–204.

Friedländer   Friedländer, M., *Das deutsche Lied im 18. Jahrhundert: Quellen und Studien* (2 vols., Stuttgart, 1902; repr. Hildesheim, 1970).

Friedrich   Friedrich, A., 'Klinger', in *DicArt*.

Fries   Fries, A. Graf von, *Die Grafen von Fries: Eine genealogische Studie* (Dresden, 1903).

Frimmel[1]   Frimmel, Theodor, *Beethoven-Studien* (2 vols., Munich, 1905–6). Vol. i: *Beethovens äussere Erscheinung*; vol. ii: *Bausteine zu einer Lebensgeschichte des Meisters* (contains, among other studies, the following: 'Beethovens Kopisten', 'Beethovens letzter Landaufenthalt', 'Beethoven und der französische Geiger Alex. Boucher', 'Beethoven und sein Neffe in Blöchlingers Erziehungsanstalt', 'Besuche in Pressburg', 'Beziehungen zu Baron Johann Baptist Pasqualati', 'Carl Friedrich Hirsch', 'Der kleine Franz Liszt').

Frimmel[2]   —— 'Der Geiger Josef Mayseder und Beethoven', *Beethoven-Forschung*, 2 (July 1911), 49–58.

Frimmel[3]   —— *Beethoven im zeitgenössischen Bildnis* (Vienna, 1923).

Frimmel[4]   —— 'Beethoven als Gasthausbesucher in Wien', *Neues Beethoven-Jahrbuch*, 1 (1924), 124–41.

Frimmel[5]   —— *Beethoven-Handbuch* (2 vols., Leipzig, 1926).

Fürst   Fürst, R., *August Gottlieb Meissner: Eine Darstellung seines Lebens und seiner Schriften mit Quellenuntersuchungen* (Stuttgart, 1894).

Gábry   Gábry, G., 'Das Klavier Beethovens und Liszts', *Studia musicologica Academiae Scientiarum Hungaricae*, 8 (1966), 379–90.

Geck   Geck, M., 'Zelter', in *MGG*.

Geiser   Geiser, S., *Beethoven und die Schweiz* (Zurich, 1976).

Gelderblom   Gelderblom, G., 'Antonie Brentano, Edle von Birkenstock', in *Festschrift Stummvoll*, 774–80.

Ginsburg[1]   Ginsburg, L., *Istorija violonchelnovo iskusstva* (3 vols., Moscow, 1950–65). On Golitsïn, *see* vol. ii (1957), 223–77.

Ginsburg[2]   —— 'Ludwig van Beethoven und Nikolai Galitzin', *Beethoven-Jahrbuch*, 2nd ser. 4 (1959–60) [1962], 59–71.

Ginsburg[3]   —— 'Ludwig van Beethoven und Nikolai Fürst Golitzin', *ÖMZ*, 19 (1964), 523–9.

Ginsburg[4]   —— 'Zur Geschichte der Aufführung der Streichquartette Beethovens in Russland', in *Beethoven Congress*[2], 135–9.

Gläser   'Franz Gläser: Autobiographie. Erinnerungen an Beethoven. [Veröffentlicht] von F. Lorenz', *Die Musikforschung*, 31 (1978), 43–6.

Glück[1]   Glück, F., 'Das Mählersche Beethoven-Bildnis von 1804/05 im Historischen Museum der Stadt Wien', *ÖMZ*, 16 (1961), 111–14.

Glück[2]   —— 'W. J. Mählers Beethovenbildnisse und seine Porträte anderer Persönlichkeiten', *Alte und moderne Kunst* (Apr. 1961), 11–16.

Glück[3]   —— 'Prolegomena zu einer neuen Beethoven-Ikonographie', in *Festschrift Deutsch*, 203–12.

Goedeke   Goedeke, K., *Grundriss zur Geschichte der deutschen Dichtung* (2nd, rev., edn., Dresden, 1884–   ).

Goethe[1]   *Goethes Briefwechsel mit Friedrich Rochlitz* (Leipzig, 1887).

Goethe[2]   *Goethes Briefwechsel mit Antonie Brentano 1814–1821*, herausgegeben von R. Jung (Weimar, 1896; repr. Berne, 1970).

Goethe[3]   *Goethes Briefwechsel mit Marianne von Willemer*, neu herausgegeben von M. Hecker (Leipzig, n.d.).

Goldschmidt[1]   Goldschmidt, H., *Die Erscheinung Beethoven* (Leipzig, 1974).

Goldschmidt[2]   —— 'Beethoven in neuen Brunksvik-Briefen', *Beethoven-Jahrbuch*, 2nd ser. 9 (1973–7) [1977], 97–146.

Goldschmidt[3]   —— *Um die 'Unsterbliche Geliebte': Eine Bestandsaufnahme* (Leipzig, 1977).

Goldschmidt[4]   —— 'Aspekte gegenwärtiger Beethoven-Forschung', in *Zu Beethoven*, 167–242.

Goldschmidt[5]   —— ' "Und wenn Beethoven selber käme . . .": Weitere Aspekte zum Mälzelkanon', in *Zu Beethoven 2*, 185–204.

Goldschmidt[6]   —— ' "Auf diese Art mit A geht alles zu Grunde": Eine umstrittene Tagebuchstelle in neuem Licht', in *Zu Beethoven 3*, 8–30.

Göllerich   Göllerich, A., *Franz Liszt* (Berlin, 1908).

Goos   Goos, H., 'Albrechtsberger', in *MGG*.

Göthel[1]   Göthel, F., 'Stein, Familie', in *MGG*.

Göthel[2]   —— 'Radicati', in *MGG*.

Göthel[3]   —— 'Streicher', in *MGG*.

Gottschalk   Gottschalk, R., 'Die drei Beethovenbriefe Bettinas', *Neue Zeitschrift für Musik*, 94/1 (1927), 154–9.

Grab   Grab, W., 'Schneider, Eulogius', in *LL*.

Gräffer   Gräffer, F., *Kleine Wiener Memoiren . . .* (3 vols., Vienna, 1845).

Grasberger[1]   Grasberger, F., 'Weigl', in *MGG*.

Grasberger[2]   —— 'Beethovens "Zärtliche Liebe" ', *ÖMZ*, 14 (1959), 508–10.

Grasberger[3]   —— 'Gustav Nottebohm: Verdienste und Schicksal eines Musikgelehrten', *ÖMZ*, 22 (1967), 739–41.

Grasberger[4]   —— 'Beethoven-Handschriften in Wien', *ÖMZ*, 26 (1971), 41–5.

Grasberger[5]   —— 'Ludwig van Beethoven: "Zärtliche Liebe" ', in his *Kostbarkeiten der Musik*, i: *Das Lied* (Tutzing, 1968), 33–72.

Graue   Graue, J. C., 'Cramer', in *New Grove*.

Grave   Grave, M. H., 'Vogler', in *New Grove*.

Griep   Griep, W., 'Treitschke', in *LL*.

Griesinger   *'Eben komme ich von Haydn . . .': Georg August Griesingers Korrespondenz mit Joseph Haydns Verleger Breitkopf & Härtel, 1799–1819*, herausgegeben und kommentiert von O. Biba (Zurich, 1987).

Gugitz   Gugitz, G., 'Ein Stück Altwiener Lebenskunst: Gastwirt Jahn und seine Unternehmungen', *Unsere Heimat: Monatsblatt des Vereines für Landeskunde und Heimatschutz von Niederösterreich und Wien*, NS 3 (1930), 309–25, 340–58.

Guhde   Guhde, E., *Gottlieb Konrad Pfeffel: Ein Beitrag zur Kulturgeschichte des Elsass* (Winterthur, 1964).

Günzel   Günzel, K., *Die Brentanos: Eine deutsche Familiengeschichte* (Zurich, 1993).

Gutiérrez   Gutiérrez-Denhoff, M., ' "O unseeliges Dekret": Beethovens Rente von Fürst Lobkowitz, Fürst Kinsky und Erzherzog Rudolph', in *Beethoven und Böhmen*, 91–145.

Haas[1]   Haas, R., 'Zur Wiener Ballettpantomine um den Prometheus', *Neues Beethoven-Jahrbuch*, 2 (1925), 84–103.

Haas[2]   —— 'The Viennese Violinist Franz Clement', *Musical Quarterly*, 34 (1948), 15–27.

Haas³   ——— 'Franz Martin Pechatschek—endlich richtig bestimmt', *Mozart-Jahrbuch* (1954), 73–7.

Hadamowsky   Hadamowsky, F., *Die Wiener Hoftheater (Staatstheater)* . . . (2 pts., Vienna, 1966–75).

Hadden   Hadden, C., *George Thomson, the Friend of Burns: His Life and Correspondence* (London, 1898).

Hadley   Hadley, D. W., 'Beethoven and the Philharmonic Society of London: A Reappraisal', *Musical Quarterly*, 59 (1973), 449–61.

Hager   Hager, N., 'The First Movement of Mozart's Sonata, K.457 and Beethoven's Opus 10, No. 1: A C-Minor Connection?', *Music Review*, 47 (1986–7), 89–100.

Hahn¹   Hahn, A., 'Usteri', in *LL*.

Hahn²   Hahn, K., 'Marx, Adolf Bernhard', in *MGG*.

Halem   *G. A. v. Halem's Selbstbiographie nebst einer Sammlung von Briefen an ihn* . . . , bearbeitet von seinem Bruder L. W. C. v. Halem und herausgegeben von C. F. Strackerjan (Oldenburg, 1840; repr. Berne, 1970).

Hamann¹   *Die Habsburger: Ein biographisches Lexikon*, herausgegeben von B. Hamann (Vienna, 1988).

Hamann²   Hamann, H. W., 'Wölfl', in *MGG*.

Hammer-Purgstall   Hammer-Purgstall, J. von, *Erinnerungen aus meinem Leben 1774–1852*, bearbeitet von R. Bachofen von Echt (Vienna, 1940).

Hansell   Hansell, S., 'Lucchesi', in *New Grove*.

Hanslick   Hanslick, E., *Geschichte des Concertwesens in Wien* (2 pts., Vienna, 1869–70).

Hanson¹   Hanson, A. M., 'Income and Outgoings in the Vienna of Beethoven and Schubert', *Music & Letters*, 64 (1983), 173–82.

Hanson²   ——— *Musical Life in Biedermeier Vienna* (Cambridge, 1985).

Häntzschel   Häntzschel, G., 'Bürger', in *LL*.

Harich   Harich, J., 'Beethoven in Eisenstadt: Die Beziehungen des Meisters zum Fürsten Nikolaus Esterházy', *Burgenländische Heimatblätter*, 21 (1959), 168–88.

Harten   Harten, U., 'Preindl', in *New Grove*.

Hase¹   Hase, Oskar von, *Breitkopf & Härtel: Gedenkschrift und Arbeitsbericht* (4th edn., 2 vols., Leipzig, 1917–19).

Hase²   Hase [Hase-Schmundt], U. von, *Joseph Stieler, 1781–1858: Sein Leben und sein Werk. Kritisches Verzeichnis der Werke* (Munich, 1971).

Hase³   ——— 'Das Beethoven-Bildnis des Isidor Neugass: Entstehung und kunstgeschichtliche Stellung', in *Verein Beethoven-Haus Bonn, Jahresgabe 1983* . . . , herausgegeben von M. Staehelin (Bonn, 1983), 9–34.

Haubold   Haubold, H., *Johann Peter Frank, der Gesundheits- und Rassenpolitiker des 18. Jahrhunderts* (Munich, 1939).

Haupt¹   Haupt, G., 'Gräfin Erdödy und J. X. Brauchle', *Der Bär* (1927), 70–99.

Haupt²   ——— 'J. N. Mälzels Briefe an Breitkopf & Härtel', *Der Bär* (1927), 122–45.

Haupt³   Haupt, H., 'Wiener Instrumentenbauer von 1791 bis 1815', *Studien zur Musikwissenschaft*, 24 (1960), 120–84.

Heckel   *150 Jahre Kunst und Musik. K. Ferd. Heckel* (Mannheim, 1971). Contains an important survey of the firm's history by R. Würtz.

Heer	Heer, J., *Der Graf von Waldstein und sein Verhältnis zu Beethoven* (Siegburg, n.d.).
Heers	Heers, A., *Das Leben Friedrich von Matthissons* (Leipzig, 1913).
Hellmann-Stojan[1]	Hellmann-Stojan, H., 'Unger [Ungher]', in *MGG*.
Hellmann-Stojan[2]	—— 'Vogl', in *MGG*.
Hellsberg	Hellsberg, C., 'Ignaz Schuppanzigh (Wien 1776–1830): Leben und Wirken', doctoral diss. (University of Vienna, 1979).
Helm	Helm, E., 'Reichardt', in *New Grove*.
Henseler	Henseler, T. A., *Das musikalische Bonn im 19. Jahrhundert* (Bonn, 1959).
Herrmann	Herrmann, J., 'Emanuel Alois Förster, Joseph Linke: Zwei schlesische Musiker im Lebenskreis Beethovens', *Schlesien*, 11 (1966), 30–4.
Hess[1]	Hess, W., '24 unbekannte italienische A-capella-Gesänge Beethovens', *Die Musik*, 33 (1941), 240–4.
Hess[2]	—— '*Vestas Feuer* von Emanuel Schikaneder: Zum Erstdruck des Textbuches', *Beethoven-Jahrbuch*, 2nd ser. 3 (1957–8) [1959], 63–106.
Hess[3]	—— 'Das Singspiel *Die schöne Schusterin*', *Beethoven-Jahrbuch*, 2nd ser. 4 (1959–60) [1962], 142–86.
Hess[4]	—— '*Tarpeja*', *Beethoven-Jahrbuch*, 2nd ser. 5 (1961–4) [1966], 92–147.
Hess[5]	—— 'Zwei patriotische Singspiele von Friedrich Treitschke', *Beethoven-Jahrbuch*, 2nd ser. 6 (1965–8) [1969], 269–319.
Hess[6]	—— *Beethoven-Studien* (Bonn, 1972).
Hess[7]	—— *Beethoven: Studien zu seinem Werk* (Winterthur, 1981).
Hess[8]	—— *Das Fidelio Buch: Beethovens Oper 'Fidelio', ihre Geschichte und ihre drei Fassungen* (Winterthur, 1986).
Hesselmann	Hesselmann, P., 'Halem', in *LL*.
Heussner	Heussner, H., 'Rellstab', in *MGG*.
Hevesy	Hevesy, A. de, *Petites Amies de Beethoven* (Paris, 1910).
Hill	Hill, C., 'Ries', in *New Grove*.
Hiller[1]	Hiller, F., *Aus dem Tonleben unserer Zeit: Gelegentliches* (3 vols., Leipzig, 1868–71).
Hiller[2]	—— 'In Wien vor 52 Jahren', *Nord und Süd* (Feb. 1880), 180–95.
Hilmar	Hilmar, R., *Der Musikverlag Artaria & Comp.: Geschichte und Probleme der Druckproduktion* (Tutzing, 1977).
Hirsch/Oldman	Hirsch, P., and Oldman, C. B., 'Contemporary English Editions of Beethoven', *Music Review*, 14 (1953), 1–35.
Hirt	Hirt, F. J., *Meisterwerke des Klavierbaus: Geschichte der Saitenklaviere von 1440 bis 1880* (Olten, 1955).
Hirth	Hirth, F., *Johann Peter Lyser: Der Dichter, Maler, Musiker* (Munich, 1911).
Hitzig[1]	Hitzig, W., 'Das Hochzeitslied für Giannatasio del Rio von Beethoven', *Zeitschrift für Musikwissenschaft*, 7 (1924–5), 164–5.
Hitzig[2]	—— 'Aus den Briefen Griesingers an Breitkopf & Härtel entnommene Notizen über Beethoven', *Der Bär* (1927), 23–34.
Hitzig[3]	—— 'Beethoven und das Haus Breitkopf & Härtel', *Der Bär* (1927), 1–22.
Hitzig[4]	—— 'Zu der Erstveröffentlichung des Beethovenschen Hochzeitslieds für Giannatasio del Rio', *Der Bär* (1927), 157–9.

Hoffmann-Erbrecht   Hoffmann-Erbrecht, L., 'Neefe', in *New Grove*.

Holst   Holst, N. von, 'Ein unbekanntes Beethoven-Portrait in den USA', *ÖMZ*, 39 (1984), 94–5.

Hopkinson/Oldham   Hopkinson, V., and Oldham, C. B., 'Haydn and Beethoven in Thomson's Collections', *Transactions of the Edinburgh Bibliographical Society*, 2 (1940), 1–64.

Hornstein   'Memoiren von R. von Hornstein', *Süddeutsche Monatshefte*, 4/2 (July–Dec. 1907), 30–60, 145–69, 289–316, 453–82, 551–77.

Horovitz-Barnay   Horovitz-Barnay, I., 'Im Hause Franz Liszts: Erlebnisse und Gespräche mit dem Meister', *Deutsche Revue* (July–Sept. 1898), 76–84.

Howell   Howell, S., 'Beethoven's Maelzel Canon: Another Schindler Forgery?', *Musical Times*, 120 (1979), 987–90. German version: 'Der Mälzelkanon— eine weitere Fälschung Schindlers?', in *Zu Beethoven 2*, 163–71.

Hüffer   Hüffer, E., *Anton Felix Schindler, der Biograph Beethovens* (Münster, 1909).

Humboldt   *W. von Humboldt: Briefe an Christian Gottfried Körner*, herausgegeben von A. Leitzmann (Berlin, 1940).

Humphries   Humphries, C., 'Smart, Familie', in *MGG*.

Humphries/Smith   —— and Smith, W. C., *Music Publishing in the British Isles, from the Beginning until the Middle of the Nineteenth Century* (2nd edn., Oxford, 1970).

Hunziker   Hunziker, R., *Hans Georg Nägeli* (Zurich, 1938).

Husk/Carr   Husk, W. H., and Carr, B., 'Neate', in *New Grove*.

Husk/Jones   —— and Jones, P. W., 'Chappell', in *New Grove*.

Husk/Temperley   —— and Temperley, N., 'Smart', in *New Grove*.

Igálffy-Igály   Igálffy-Igály, L., 'Stammtafel der Ritter, Freiherrn, Grafen und Fürsten Lichnowsky v. Woszczyk vom 14. Jahrhundert bis zur Gegenwart', *Adler*, 3[17]/9–10 (May–Aug. 1954), 117–43.

Jacobs[1]   Jacobs, E., 'Beethoven, Goethe und Varnhagen von Ense. Mit ungedruckten Briefen von Beethoven, Oliva, Varnhagen u.a.', *Die Musik*, 4 (1904–5), 387–402.

Jacobs[2]   Jacobs, H. C., *Literatur, Musik und Gesellschaft in Italien und Österreich in der Epoche Napoleons und der Restauration: Studien zu Giuseppe Carpani (1751–1825)* (2 pts., Frankfurt am Main, 1988).

Jancik[1]   Jancik, H., 'Blahetka', in *MGG*.

Jancik[2]   —— 'Mosel', in *MGG*.

Jancik[3]   —— 'Schuppanzigh', in *MGG*.

Jancik[4]   —— 'Seyfried', in *MGG*.

Jancik[5]   —— 'Sonnleitner', in *MGG*.

Jancik[6]   —— 'Starke', in *MGG*.

Jander   Jander, O., 'Adolph Bernhard Marx, Victim of the Post-Schering Syndrome', *Beethoven Journal*, 10 (1995), 6–18.

Johnson[1]   Johnson, D., 'Fischhof', in *New Grove*.

Johnson[2]   —— 'Music for Prague and Berlin: Beethoven's Concert Tour of 1796', in *Beethoven Congress*[5], 24–40.

Johnson/Tyson/Winter   —— Tyson, A., and Winter, R., *The Beethoven Sketchbooks: History, Reconstruction, Inventory* (Berkeley, Calif., 1985).

Joost   Joost, U., 'Matthisson', in *LL*.

Just-Kaiser   Just-Kaiser, U., 'Moritz Schwinds Gemälde "Eine Symphonie": Neuartige Aspekte zur Beethoven-Rezeption, insbesondere der Chorfantasie Op. 80', *Zeitschrift für Musikpädagogik*, 12 (1987), 33–8.

Kaden   Kaden, W., 'Beethovens Lehrer Christian Gottlob Neefe', in *Beethoven Congress*[4], 395–400.

Kagan   Kagan, S., *Archduke Rudolph, Beethoven's Patron, Pupil, and Friend: His Life and Music* (Stuyvesant, 1988).

Kahl[1]   Kahl, W., 'Cramer', in *MGG*.

Kahl[2]   —— 'Czerny, Karl', in *MGG*.

Kahl[3]   —— 'Diabelli', in *MGG*.

Kahl[4]   —— 'Duschek [Dušek]', in *MGG*.

Kahl[5]   —— 'Neefe', in *MGG*.

Kahl[6]   —— 'Zur Geschichte des Bonner Beethovendenkmals. Mit einem Brief Anton Schindlers', *Beethoven-Jahrbuch*, 2nd ser. 1 (1953–4) [1954], 63–79.

Kaiser   Kaiser, H., *Das grossherzogliche Hoftheater zu Darmstadt, 1810–1910* (Darmstadt, 1964).

Kalischer   Kalischer, A. C., *Beethoven und seine Zeitgenossen* (4 vols., Berlin, 1908–10).

Kalkschmidt   Kalkschmidt, E., *Moritz von Schwind: Der Mann und das Werk* (Munich, 1943).

Kallmann   Kallmann, H., 'Molt', in *New Grove*.

Kantner   Kantner, L., 'Anton Diabelli: Ein Salzburger Komponist der Biedermeier Zeit', *Mitteilungen der Gesellschaft für Salzburger Landeskunde*, 98 (1958), 51–88.

Karstädt   Karstädt, G., 'Reichardt', in *MGG*.

Keiler   Keiler, A., 'Liszt and Beethoven: The Creation of a Personal Myth', *19th Century Music*, 12 (1988–9), 116–31.

Kerman   Kerman, J., 'An die ferne Geliebte', in *Beethoven Studies*, ed. A. Tyson (New York, 1973), 123–57.

Kerst   *Die Erinnerungen an Beethoven*, gesammelt und herausgegeben von F. Kerst (2 vols., Stuttgart, 1913).

Kidson   Kidson, F., *British Music Publishers, Printers and Engravers: London, Provincial, Scottish, and Irish. From Queen Elizabeth's Reign to George the Fourth's* (London, 1900; repr. New York, 1967).

Kidson/Smith/Jones   —— Smith, W., and Jones, P. W., 'Goulding & Co.', in *New Grove*.

Kier   Kier, H., *Raphael Georg Kiesewetter (1773–1850): Wegbereiter des musikalischen Historismus* (Regensburg, 1968).

Kinderman   Kinderman, W., *Beethoven* (Oxford, 1995).

Kindermann   Kindermann, H., *Theatergeschichte Europas* (10 vols., Salzburg, 1957–74).

King   King, A. H., *Mozart in Retrospect* (London, 1955).

Kinsky   Kinsky, G., 'Beethoven's Brief an Baron de Trémont', in *Festschrift La Laurencie*, 269–73.

Kinsky/Halm   —— *Das Werk Beethovens: Thematisch-bibliographisches Verzeichnis seiner sämtlichen vollendenten Kompositionen*, nach dem Tode des Verfassers abgeschlossen und herausgegeben von H. Halm (Munich, 1955).

Kircheisen   Kircheisen, F., *König Lustig, Napoleons jüngster Bruder* (Berlin, 1928).

Klein[1]	Klein, R., *Beethovenstätten in Österreich* (Vienna, 1970).
Klein[2]	—— 'Der Saal des Ignaz Jahn', *Acta Mozartiana*, 3 (Nov. 1970), 51–7.
Klein[3]	—— 'Beethoven im "Klepperstall": Ein unbekannter Brief von Zmeskall v. Domanovecz', *ÖMZ*, 26 (1971), 3–9. *See also* p. 380.
Klein[4]	—— 'Forschungsbericht zur Beethoven-Topographie', in *Beethoven Congress*[2], 455–7.
Klein[5]	—— 'Das Beethovenhaus am Heiligstädter Pfarrplatz', *ÖMZ*, 28 (1973), 35–7.
Klein[6]	—— 'Ein Alt-Wiener Konzertsaal: Das Etablissement Jahn in der Himmelpfortgasse', *ÖMZ*, 28 (1973), 12–18.
Klein[7]	—— 'Musik im Augarten', *ÖMZ*, 28 (1973), 239–48.
Klein[8]	—— 'Gerhard von Breuning über Beethovens Beziehungen zu seinen Verwandten', *ÖMZ*, 29 (1974), 67–75.
Klein[9]	—— 'Sensationelle Enthüllung beim Ost-Berliner Beethoven-Kongress', *ÖMZ*, 32 (1977), 202–3.
Klein[10]	—— 'Neue Hypothesen um Beethovens "Unsterbliche Geliebte" ', *ÖMZ*, 35 (1980), 28–31.
Klessmann	Klessmann, E., *Prinz Louis Ferdinand von Preussen, 1772–1806: Gestalt einer Zeitenwende* (Munich, 1972).
Klöber	Klöber, A. von, in 'Miscellen', *Allgemeine musikalische Zeitung*, NS 2 (1864), 325–6.
Köhler[1]	Köhler, K.-H., 'Beethovens Gespräche: Biographische Aspekte zu einem modernen Beethovenbild. Bemerkungen zur Edition der noch unveröffentlichen Konversationshefte', in *Beethoven Congress*[1], 159–74.
Köhler[2]	—— 'The Conversation Books: Aspects of a New Picture of Beethoven', in *Beethoven Congress*[5], 147–61.
Köhler[3]	Köhler, V., 'Marschner', in *New Grove*.
Kolisko	Kolisko, M., *Caspar von Zumbusch* (Zurich, 1931).
Komma	Komma, K. M., 'Hauschka', in *MGG*.
Komma/Vernillat	—— and Vernillat, F., 'Gelinek', in *MGG*.
Komorzynski	Komorzynski, E., 'Das Urbild des Verschwenders', *Raimund-Almanach* (1959), 18–24.
Kopitz	Kopitz, K. M., 'Das Beethoven-Erlebnis Ludwig Tiecks und Beethovens Zerwürfnis mit Fürst Lichnowsky', *ÖMZ*, 53 (1998), 16–23.
Köpke	Köpke, R., *Ludwig Tieck: Erinnerungen aus dem Leben des Dichters nach dessen mündlichen und schriflichen Mitteilungen* (2 pts., Darmstadt, 1970).
Körner[1]	*Theodor Körners Werke*, herausgegeben von A. Stern (3 vols., Stuttgart, 1890–1).
Körner[2]	*Theodor Körners Briefwechsel mit den Seinen*, herausgegeben von A. Weldler-Steinberg (Leipzig, 1910).
Kramer[1]	Kramer, L., 'The Strange Case of Beethoven's *Coriolan*: Romantic Aesthetics, Modern Subjectivity, and the Cult of Shakespeare', *Musical Quarterly*, 79 (1995), 256–80.
Kramer[2]	Kramer, R., 'Notes on Beethoven's Education', *Journal of the American Musicological Society*, 28 (1975), 72–101.

Kramer[3]   —— '*Gradus ad Parnassum*: Beethoven, Schubert, and the Romance of Counterpoint', *19th Century Music*, 11 (1987–8), 107–20.

Krasa   Krasa, S., *Josef Kriehuber, 1800–1876: Der Portraitist einer Epoche* (Vienna, 1987).

Krasa-Florian Krasa-Florian, S., 'Franz Klein: Ein Wiener Bildhauer des Klassizismus', *Mitteilungen der Österreichischen Galerie*, 14 (1970), 58: 99–149.

Kratochvil   Kratochvil, V., 'Beethoven und Fürst Kinsky', *Beethoven-Jahrbuch*, 2 (1909), 3–47.

Krauthausen   Krauthausen, U., 'Die rheinische Fischerfamilie Wistorff und ihre Nachkommen, zugleich ein Beitrag zur Verwandschaft Ludwig van Beethovens', *Mitteilungen der westdeutschen Gesellschaft für Familienkunde*, 22/3 (Apr. 1966), 253–66.

Kriegleder   Kriegleder, W., 'Gleim, Johann Wilhelm Ludwig', in *LL*.

Kroll   Kroll, E., 'C. M. von Weber und Beethoven', *Neues Beethoven-Jahrbuch*, 6 (1935), 124–40.

Krones[1]   Krones, H., ' "... der schönste und wichtigste Zweck von allen ...": Das Conservatorium der Gesellschaft der Musikfreunde des österreichischen Kaiserstaates', *ÖMZ*, 43 (1988), 66–83.

Krones[2]   —— ' "... er habe ihm seine Liebesgeschichte in Musik setzen wollen": Ludwig van Beethovens E-moll-Sonate, Op. 90', *ÖMZ*, 43 (1988) 592–601.

Kübeck   *Tagebücher des Carl Friedrich Freiherrn Kübeck von Kübau*, herausgegeben und eingeleitet von seinem Sohne Max Freiherr von Kübeck (Vienna, 1909).

Kühner[1]   Kühner, H., 'Lablache', in *MGG*.

Kühner[2]   —— 'Milder-Hauptmann', in *MGG*.

Kühner[3]   —— 'Schröder-Devrient', in *MGG*.

Kühner[4]   —— 'Sontag', in *MGG*.

Kümmerling   Kümmerling, H., 'Beethovens Akademien am 8. und 12. Dezember 1813 und ihre Vorgeschichte', in *Beethoven Congress*[2], 486–7.

Kunze   *Ludwig van Beethoven. Die Werke im Spiegel seiner Zeit: Gesammelte Konzertberichte und Rezensionen bis 1830*, herausgegeben und eingeleitet von S. Kunze (Laaber, 1987).

Küthen[1]   Küthen, H.-W., 'Neue Aspekte zur Entstehung von *Wellingtons Sieg*', *Beethoven-Jahrbuch*, 2nd ser. 8 (1971–2) [1975], 73–92.

Küthen[2]   —— 'Die erste Pariser Originalausgabe: Ermittlungen zu den Violinsonaten Op. 23 und 24', *Beethoven-Jahrbuch*, 2nd ser. 10 (1978–81) [1983], 121–40.

Küthen[3]   —— '*Quaerendo invenietis*: Die Exegese eines Beethoven-Briefes an Haslinger vom 5. September 1823', in *Festschrift Henle*, 282–313.

Kutsch/Riemens Kutsch, K. J., and Riemens, L., *Grosses Sängerlexikon* (4 vols., Berne, 1987–94).

Laaff   Laaff, E., 'B. Schott's Söhne', in *MGG*.

Laban   Laban, F., *Heinrich Joseph Collin: Ein Beitrag zur Geschichte der neueren deutschen Literatur in Oesterreich* (Vienna, 1879).

La Garde   La Garde, Graf A. de, *Gemälde des Wiener Kongresses 1814–1815: Erinnerungen, Feste, Sittenschilderungen, Anekdoten*, eingeleitet und erläutert von G. Gugitz (2 vols., Munich, 1914).

La Mara¹   La Mara [pseud. of Marie Lipsius], *Beethovens Unsterbliche Geliebte: Das Geheimnis der Gräfin Brunsvik und ihre Memoiren* (Leipzig, 1909).

La Mara²   —— *Beethoven und die Brunsviks: Nach Familienpapieren aus Therese Brunsviks Nachlass* (Leipzig, 1920).

Landon¹   Landon, H. C. R., 'Gallenberg', in *MGG*.

Landon²   —— *Haydn* (5 vols., London, 1976–80).

Landon³   *Beethoven: A Documentary Study*, compiled and ed. H. C. R. Landon (London, 1970).

Laube   Laube, H., *Reisenovellen* (6 vols., Leipzig, Mannheim, 1834–7).

Layer¹   Layer, A., 'Weinmüller', in *MGG*.

Layer²   —— 'Karl Friedrich Weinmüller (1763–1828): Ein Wiener Sänger der Beethovenzeit. (Zur 200. Wiederkehr seines Geburtsjahres.)', *Jahrbuch des Historischen Vereins Dillingen an der Donau*, 64–5 (1962–3), 94–111.

Lebe   Lebe, R., *Ein deutsches Hoftheater in Romantik und Biedermeier: Die Kasseler Bühne zur Zeit Feiges und Spohrs* (Kassel, 1964).

Ledebur   Ledebur, C. Freiherr von, *Tonkünstler-Lexicon Berlins von den ältesten Zeiten bis auf die Gegenwart* (Berlin, 1861; repr. Tutzing, 1965).

Leeder   Leeder, C., 'Beethovens Widmungen', *Die Musik*, 3 (1904), 367–80.

Legge   L[egge], R. H., 'Smart, Sir George Thomas', in *DNB*.

Lesure   Lesure, F., 'Les Premières Éditions françaises de Beethoven', in *Henle Festschrift*, 326–31.

Leuchtmann   Leuchtmann, H., 'Lachner', in *New Grove*.

Leux¹   Leux, I., 'Neue Neefiana', *Neues Beethoven-Jahrbuch*, 1 (1924), 86–114.

Leux²   —— *Christian Gottlob Neefe (1748–1798)* (Leipzig, 1925).

Levien   Levien, J. M., *Beethoven and the Royal Philharmonic Society* (London, 1927).

Levin   Levin, T. Y., 'Integral Interpretation: Introductory Notes to Beethoven, Kolisch and the Question of the Metronome', *Musical Quarterly*, 77 (1993), 81–9.

Levinson   Levinson, A., *Meister des Balletts*, aus dem Russischen übertragen von R. von Walter (Potsdam, 1923).

Lewald   Lewald, F., *Zwölf Bilder nach dem Leben: Erinnerungen* (Berlin, 1888).

Ley¹   *Beethoven als Freund der Familie Wegeler-v. Breuning*, nach den Familien-Sammlungen und Erinnerungen herausgegeben von S. Ley (Bonn, 1927).

Ley²   Ley, S., 'Grundsätzliches zur Beethoven-Ikonographie', *Neues Beethoven-Jahrbuch*, 8 (1938), 84–103.

Ley³   —— 'Urkundliches über Beethovens Beerdigung und erste Grabstätte', *Neues Beethoven-Jahrbuch*, 10 (1942), 25–35.

Ley⁴   —— *Wahrheit, Zweifel und Irrtum in der Kunde von Beethovens Leben* (Wiesbaden, 1955).

Liess   Liess, A., *Johann Michael Vogl, Hofoperist und Schubertsänger* (Graz, 1954).

Lindner   Lindner, D., *Der Mann ohne Vorurteil: Joseph von Sonnenfels, 1733–1817* (Vienna, 1983).

Linnemann   Linnemann, R., *Fr. Kistner 1823/1923* (Leipzig, 1923).

Lippmann   Lippmann, F., 'Pacini', in *MGG*.

Litschauer   *'In questa tomba oscura': Giuseppe Carpanis Dichtung in 68 Vertonungen (1808–1814)*, veröffentlicht von W. Litschauer (Graz, 1986).

Little	Little, W. A., *Gottfried August Bürger* (New York, 1974).
LL	*Literatur Lexikon: Autoren und Werke deutscher Sprache*, herausgegeben von W. Killy (15 vols., Gütersloh, 1988–93).
Lockwood[1]	Lockwood, L., 'Beethoven's Early Works for Violoncello and Contemporary Violoncello Technique', in *Beethoven Congress*[3], 174–82.
Lockwood[2]	—— 'Beethoven's Early Works for Violoncello and Pianoforte: Innovation in Context', *Beethoven Newsletter*, 1/2 (Summer 1986), 17–21.
Lohberger	Lohberger, H., 'Marie Pachler', *Blätter für Heimatkunde. Herausgegeben vom Historischen Verein für Steiermark*, 36 (1962), 81–4.
Longyear	Longyear, R. M., 'Förster', in *New Grove*.
Loos	Loos, H., 'Beethoven in Prag 1796 und 1798', in *Beethoven und Böhmen*, 63–90.
Lorenz	Lorenz, S., 'Kotzebue', in *LL*.
Lorenzen[1]	Lorenzen, K., 'Brentano', in *MGG*.
Lorenzen[2]	—— 'Claudius', in *MGG*.
Lorenzen[3]	—— 'Fouqué', in *MGG*.
Lorenzen[4]	—— 'Gleim', in *MGG*.
Lück	Lück, R., 'Peters', in *MGG*.
Lühning	Lühning, H., '*Fidelio* in Prag', in *Beethoven und Böhmen*, 349–91.
Luise	Luise von Preussen, Fürstin Anton Radziwill, *Fünfundvierzig Jahre aus meinem Leben (1770–1815)*, herausgegeben . . . von Fürstin Radziwill, geb. von Castellane, aus dem Französischen übertragen von E. von Kraatz (Brunsvik, 1912).
Lund	Lund, S., *Raptus: A Novel about Beethoven Based on the Source Material* (Royston, 1995).
Lütge[1]	Lütge, W., 'Andreas und Nanette Streicher', *Der Bär* (1927), 53–69.
Lütge[2]	—— 'Anton Reicha', *Der Bär* (1927), 100–9.
Lütge[3]	—— 'Waldmüllers Bild', *Der Bär* (1927), 35–41.
MacArdle[1]	MacArdle, D. W., 'The Family Van Beethoven', *Musical Quarterly*, 35 (1949), 528–50.
MacArdle[2]	—— 'Four Unfamiliar Beethoven Documents', *Music & Letters*, 36 (1955), 331–40.
MacArdle[3]	—— 'Beethoven and George Thomson', *Music & Letters*, 37 (1956), 27–49.
MacArdle[4]	—— 'The Brentano Family in its Relations with Beethoven', *Music Review*, 19 (1958), 6–19.
MacArdle[5]	—— 'Beethoven and Grillparzer', *Music & Letters*, 40 (1959), 44–55.
MacArdle[6]	—— 'Beethoven and Handel', *Music & Letters*, 41 (1960), 33–7.
MacArdle[7]	—— 'Beethoven and the Philharmonic Society of London', *Music Review*, 21 (1960), 1–7.
MacArdle[8]	—— 'Beethoven, Matthisson, Kotzebue, and Gaveaux', *Music Review*, 22 (1961), 288–93.
MacArdle[9]	—— *An Index to Beethoven's Conversation Books* (Detroit, 1962).
MacArdle[10]	—— 'Beethoven and the Archduke Rudolph', *Beethoven-Jahrbuch*, 2nd ser. 2 (1959–60) [1962], 36–58.
MacArdle[11]	—— 'Anton Felix Schindler, Friend of Beethoven', *Music Review*, 24 (1963), 50–74.

MacArdle[12]   —— 'Shakespeare and Beethoven', *Musical Times*, 105 (1964), 260–1.
MacArdle[13]   —— 'Beethoven and Ferdinand Ries', *Music & Letters*, 46 (1965), 23–34.
MacArdle[14]   —— 'Beethoven and Schuppanzigh', *Music Review*, 26 (1965), 3–14.
MacArdle/Misch   *New Beethoven Letters*, trans. and annotated by D. W. MacArdle and
                 L. Misch (Norman, Okla., 1957).
Macek[1]   Macek, J., 'Beethovens Freund Karl Peters und seine Frau', in *Beethoven und
                 Böhmen*, 393–407.
Macek[2]   —— 'Franz Joseph Maximilian Lobkowitz, Musikfreund und Kunstmäzen',
                 in *Beethoven und Böhmen*, 147–201.
Macnutt[1]   Macnutt, R., 'Pacini, Antonio', in *New Grove*.
Macnutt[2]   —— 'Schlesinger', in *New Grove*.
Madjera   Madjera, W., 'Beethovens Wohnung im Pasqualatihaus zu Wien', *Der
                 Merker*, 12 (1921), 33–6.
Mair   Mair, C., *The Chappell Story, 1811–1961* (London, 1961).
Major   Major, E., 'Beethoven in Ofen im Jahre 1800', *Zeitschrift für Musikwis-
                 senschaft*, 8 (1925–6), 482–4.
Mann[1]   Mann, A., 'Beethoven's Contrapuntal Studies with Haydn', *Musical
                 Quarterly*, 56 (1970), 711–26.
Mann[2]   —— 'Haydns Kontrapunktlehre und Beethovens Studien', in *Beethoven
                 Congress*[2], 70–4.
Marchi   Marchi, G. P., 'Carpani', in *DBI*.
Marks   Marks, A., 'Die alten Linzer Apotheken', *Oberösterreich* 9/1–2 (Summer
                 1959), 59–63.
Marretta-Schär   Marretta-Schär, L., 'Schnyder von Wartensee', in *New Grove*.
Marston   Marston, N., 'Schumann's Monument to Beethoven', *19th Century Music*, 14
                 (1990–1), 247–64.
Martinet   Martinet, A., *Jérôme Napoléon, roi de Westphalie* (Paris, 1902).
Marx   Marx, A. B., *Ludwig van Beethoven: Leben und Schaffen* (Berlin, 1859).
Massin   Massin, B., 'L' "Unique Bien-aimée" de Beethoven: Joséphine de Brunsvik',
                 in J. Massin and B. Massin, *Recherche de Beethoven* (Paris, 1970).
Massin/Massin   Massin, J., and Massin, B., *Ludwig van Beethoven* (Paris, 1967).
Matthäus[1]   Matthäus, W., 'Bossler', in *MGG*.
Matthäus[2]   —— 'Zulehner', in *MGG*.
Matthews   Matthews, B., 'George Polgreen Bridgtower', *Music Review*, 29 (1968), 22–6.
May   May, J., 'Beethoven and Prince Karl Lichnowsky', *Beethoven Forum*, 3 (1994),
                 29–38.
Meissner   Meissner, A., *Rococobilder. Nach Aufzeichnungen meines Grossvaters*
                 (Gumbinnen, 1891).
Mell   Mell, A., 'Radicati', in *New Grove*.
Mendheim   Mendheim, M., 'Treitschke', in *ADB*.
Merk   Merk, M., 'Franz Clement (1780–1842)', doctoral diss. (University of
                 Vienna, 1969).
MGG   *Die Musik in Geschichte und Gegenwart: Allgemeine Enzyklopädie der Musik*,
                 herausgegeben von F. Blume (14 vols., Kassel, 1949–68). Supplement (2 vols.,
                 Kassel, 1973–9). *Register* (Kassel, 1986).

Michel   Michel, A., 'Rellstab', in *LL*.

Michotte   Michotte, E., *Souvenirs personnels. La Visite de R. Wagner à Rossini (Paris 1860)* (Paris, 1906).

Mies[1]   Mies, P., '"Sehnsucht" von Goethe und Beethoven', *Beethoven-Jahrbuch*, 2nd ser. 2 (1955–6) [1956], 112–19.

Mies[2]   —— 'Beethovens letzter Flügel: Geschichte und Probleme', in *Verein Beethoven-Haus, Bonn, 1889–1964* (Bonn, 1964), 19–48.

Mikoletzky[1]   Mikoletzky, H. L., 'Schweizer Händler und Bankiers in Österreich (vom 17. bis zur Mitte des 19. Jahrhunderts)', in *Festschrift Hantsch*, 149–81.

Mikoletzky[2]   —— *Österreich: Das entscheidende 19. Jahrhundert. Geschichte, Kultur und Wissenschaft* (Vienna, 1972).

Misch   Misch, L., *Neue Beethoven-Studien und andere Themen* (Bonn, 1967).

Mitchell   Mitchell, A. L., 'Czerny, Carl', in *New Grove*.

Mittig   Mittig, H.-E., 'Das Wiener Beethoven-Denkmal von Zumbusch und die Wende der Beethoven-Darstellung', *Alte und moderne Kunst* (May–June 1969), 25–33.

Mix   Mix, Y.-G., 'Goeckingk', in *LL*.

Mondolfi   Mondolfi, A., 'Paer', in *MGG*.

Monson   Monson, D. E., 'The Classic–Romantic Dichotomy: Franz Grillparzer and Beethoven', *International Review of the Aesthetics and Sociology of Music*, 13 (1982), 161–75.

Morley/Fitzpatrick Morley-Pegge, R., and Fitzpatrick, H., 'Punto', in *New Grove*.

Morrow   Morrow, M. S., *Concert Life in Haydn's Vienna: Aspects of a Developing Musical and Social Institution* (Stuyvesant, 1989). Important review by D. Edge in *Haydn Yearbook*, 17 (1992), 108–66.

Moscheles   *Aus Moscheles' Leben: Nach Briefen und Tagebüchern*, herausgegeben von seiner Frau [C. Moscheles] (2 vols., Leipzig, 1872–3).

Moser[1]   Moser, A., *Geschichte des Violinspiels* (2nd, corrected and augmented, edn. by H.-J. Nösselt, 2 vols., Tutzing, 1966–7).

Moser[2]   Moser, H. J., 'Wer war Herrosee?', *Neues Beethoven-Jahrbuch*, 2 (1925), 43–51.

Moser[3]   —— *Goethe und die Musik* (Leipzig, 1949).

Moyer   Moyer, B., 'Marx', in *New Grove*.

Müller[1]   Müller, G., *Daniel Steibelt: Sein Leben und seine Klavierwerke* (Leipzig, 1933; repr. Baden-Baden, 1973).

Müller[2]   Müller, W. C., *Briefe an deutsche Freunde von einer Reise durch Italien über Sachsen, Böhmen und Oestreich* [*sic*] *1820 und 1821 . . .* (2 vols., Altona, 1824).

Müller[3]   —— 'Etwas über Ludwig van Beethoven', *Allgemeine musikalische Zeitung*, 29 (1827), 345–54.

Müller/Daunton Müller, H.-C., and Daunton, F., 'Schott', in *New Grove*.

Münch   *Julius Schneller's Lebensumriss und vertraute Briefe an seine Gattin und seine Freunde*, herausgegeben von E. Münch (Leipzig, 1834). The letters are preceded by Münch's detailed biography of Schneller.

NDB   *Neue deutsche Biographie* (Berlin, 1952–   ).

Neighbour   Neighbour, O., 'The Stefan Zweig Collection', *Musical Times*, 127 (1986), 331–2.

Nettheim   Nettheim, N., 'How the Young Schubert Borrowed from Beethoven', *Musical Times*, 132 (1991), 330–1.

Nettl[1]   Nettl, P., 'Kanka', in *MGG*.

Nettl[2]   —— *Forgotten Musicians* (New York, 1951).

Nettl[3]   —— *The Beethoven Encyclopedia* (New York, 1956; repr. New York, 1994).

Nettl[4]   —— 'Beethoven's Grand-Nephew in America', *Music & Letters*, 38 (1957), 260–4.

Nettl[5]   —— 'Jewish Connections of Some Classical Composers', *Music & Letters*, 45 (1964), 337–44.

Neumann[1]   Neumann, Werner, 'Kistner & Siegel', in *MGG*.

Neumann[2]   Neumann, Wilhelm, *Baltische Maler und Bildhauer des XIX Jahrhunderts. Biographische Skizzen mit den Bildnissen der Künstler und Reproductionen nach ihren Werken* (Riga, 1902).

Neumayr   Neumayr, A., *Musik und Medizin* (3 vols., Vienna, 1987–91).

New Grove   *The New Grove Dictionary of Music and Musicians*, ed. S. Sadie (20 vols., London, 1980).

Newman[1]   Newman, W. S., 'On the Rhythmic Significance of Beethoven's Annotations in Cramer's Studies', in *Beethoven Congress*[2], 43–7.

Newman[2]   —— 'Yet Another Major Beethoven Forgery by Schindler?', *Journal of Musicology*, 3 (1984), 397–422.

New Opera Grove   *The New Grove Dictionary of Opera*, ed. S. Sadie (4 vols., London, 1992).

Noack   Noack, E., 'Schlösser', in *MGG*.

Nohl[1]   *Neue Briefe Beethovens. Nebst einigen ungedruckten Gelegenheitskompositionen und Auszügen aus seinem Tagebuch und seiner Lektüre*, herausgegeben von L. Nohl (Stuttgart, 1867).

Nohl[2]   Nohl, L., *Beethoven, Liszt, Wagner: Ein Bild der Kunstbewegung unseres Jahrhunderts* (Vienna, 1874).

Nohl[3]   —— *Eine stille Liebe zu Beethoven. Nach dem Tagebuch einer jungen Dame* (Leipzig, 1875).

Nohl[4]   —— *Beethoven nach den Schilderungen seiner Zeitgenossen* (Stuttgart, 1877).

Noll   Noll, H., *Hofrat Johannes Büel von Stein am Rhein, 1761–1830: Ein Freund grosser Zeitgenossen* (Frauenfeld, 1930).

Nottebohm[1] Nottebohm, G., *Beethoven's Studien*, i: *Beethoven's Unterricht bei J. Haydn, Albrechtsberger und Salieri* (Leipzig, 1873; repr. Niederwalluf, 1971).

Nottebohm[2] —— *Beethoveniana: Aufsätze und Mittheilungen* (Leipzig, 1872). Includes 'Beethoven und Weissenbach'.

Nottebohm[3] —— *Thematisches Verzeichniss der im Druck erschienenen Werke Ludwig van Beethovens* (2nd edn., Leipzig, 1868).

Nováček   Nováček, Z., 'Beethovens Schülerin Babette Keglevich aus der Slowakei und ihre Familie', in *Beethoven Congress*[2], 526–8.

Nowak   Nowak, L., 'Esterházy', in *MGG*.

Nowak-Romanowicz   Nowak-Romanowicz, A., 'Radziwill, Prince Antoni Henryk', in *New Grove*.

ÖBL   *Österreichisches biographisches Lexikon 1815–1950* (Vienna, 1957–   ).

Oldman   Oldman, C. B., 'A Beethoven Friendship: Lost Documents Recovered', *Music & Letters*, 17 (1936), 328–36.

Olleson[1]	Olleson, E., 'Gottfried van Swieten, Patron of Haydn and Mozart', *Proceedings of the Royal Musical Association*, 89 (1962), 63–74.
Olleson[2]	—— 'Georg August Griesinger's Correspondence with Breitkopf & Härtel', *Haydn Yearbook*, 3 (1965), 5–53.
ÖMZ	*Österreichische Musikzeitschrift* (Vienna).
Oppersdorff	Oppersdorff, W. H., Graf von, 'Beethoven und der Graf von Oppersdorff: Zur vierten und fünften Symphonie', *Schlesien*, 26/2 (1981), 65–76.
Orel[1]	*Ein Wiener Beethoven Buch*, herausgegeben von A. Orel (Vienna, 1921). Includes: A. Orel, 'Beethoven und seine Verleger', and A. Trost, 'Moritz von Schwinds Bild *Die Symphonie*'.
Orel[2]	Orel, A., *Grillparzer und Beethoven* (Vienna, 1941).
Orel[3]	—— 'Förster, Emanuel Alois', in *MGG*.
Orel[4]	—— 'Mälzel', in *MGG*.
Orel[5]	—— 'Gräfin Wilhelmine Thun (Mäzenatentum in Wiens klassischer Zeit)', *Mozart-Jahrbuch* (1954), 89–101.
Ottendorff-Simrock[1]	Ottendorff-Simrock, W., 'Simrock', in *MGG*.
Ottendorff-Simrock[2]	—— *Das Haus Simrock: Ein Beitrag zur Geschichte der kulturtragenden Familien des Rheinlandes* (Ratingen, 1954).
Pachler	Pachler, F., *Beethoven und Marie Pachler-Koschak: Beiträge und Berichtigungen* (Berlin, 1866).
Pagler	Pagler, J. L., *Biographisches Lexikon hervorragender Ärzte des neunzehnten Jahrhunderts* (Berlin, 1901; repr. Leipzig. 1989).
Palmer[1]	Palmer, A., *Bernadotte: Napoleon's Marshal, Sweden's King* (London, 1990).
Palmer[2]	Palmer, F. M., *Domenico Dragonetti in England (1794–1846): The Career of a Double Bass Virtuoso* (Oxford, 1997).
Panzerbieter[1]	Panzerbieter, E., 'Beethovens erste Reise nach Wien im Jahre 1789', *Zeitschrift für Musikwissenschaft*, 10 (1927–8), 153–61.
Panzerbieter[2]	—— 'Beethoven in Regensburg 1795', *Neues Beethoven-Jahrbuch*, 6 (1935), 48–51.
Parsons	Parsons, J., 'Footnotes, Fantasies, and *Freude*: Once More on Schiller and Beethoven's "An die Freude"', *Beethoven Journal*, 9 (1994–5), 114–18.
Parthey[1]	*Jugenderinnerungen von G. Parthey* . . . (2 pts., Berlin, 1907).
Parthey[2]	Parthey, L., *Tagebücher aus der Berliner Biedermeierzeit*, herausgegeben von B. Lepsius (Berlin, 1928).
Paulig	Paulig, F. R., *Friedrich Wilhelm III, König von Preussen (1770 bis 1840): Sein Privatleben und seine Regierung im Lichte neuerer Forschungen* (2nd edn., Frankfurt an der Oder, 1905).
Payne	[Payne, S. B.], 'A Visit to Beethoven. (Extract from a Letter Written by an English Lady; Dated Vienna, October 1825)', *Harmonicon* (1825), 222–3.
Peake	Peake, L. E., 'The Antecedents of Beethoven's Liederkreis', *Music & Letters*, 63 (1982), 242–60.
Pečman	Pečman, R., *Beethovens Opernpläne* (Brno, 1981).
Pederson	Pederson, S., 'A. B. Marx, Berlin Concert Life, and German National Identity', *19th Century Music*, 18 (1994–5), 87–107.
Pendle	Pendle, K., 'Bouilly', in *New Opera Grove*.

Perger/Hirschfeld   Perger, R., and Hirschfeld, R., *Geschichte der k.k. Gesellschaft der Musikfreunde in Wien* (Vienna, 1912).

Perreau   Perreau, R., 'Une grande pianiste colmarienne: Marie Kiené, épouse Bigot de Morogues', *Annuaire de la Société historique et littéraire de Colmar*, 12 (1962), 59–67.

Pete   Pete, C., 'Geschichte der Wiener Tonkünstler-Societät', doctoral diss. (University of Vienna, 1996).

Pfannhauser   Pfannhauser, K., 'Mayseder', in *MGG*.

Pfohl   Pfohl, E., *Ortslexikon Sudetenland* (Nuremberg, 1987).

Pfrimmer   Pfrimmer, A., 'Beethoven und Frankreich', *Beethoven-Jahrbuch*, 2nd ser. 3 (1957–8) [1959], 7–31.

Pichler[1]   Pichler, K., *Leonore: Ein Gemälde aus der gewöhnlichen Welt* (2 vols., Vienna, 1804).

Pichler[2]   —— *Denkwürdigkeiten aus meinem Leben . . .* , herausgegeben von E. K. Blümml (2 vols., Munich, 1914).

Pickett   Pickett, T. H., *The Unseasonable Democrat: Karl August Varnhagen von Ense (1785–1858)* (Bonn, 1985).

Pidoll   Pidoll, C., *Verklungenes Spiel: Erinnerungen des Herrn Nikolaus Zmeskall von Domanovetz* (Innsbruck, 1950).

Pierre   Pierre, C., *Histoire du Concert spirituel 1725–1790* (Paris, 1975).

Pirchan   Pirchan, E., *Henriette Sontag, die Sängerin des Biedermeier* (Vienna, 1946).

Piroth   Piroth, M., 'Beethovens letzte Krankheit auf Grund der zeitgenössischen medizinischen Quellen', *Beethoven-Jahrbuch*, 2nd ser. 4 (1959–60) [1962], 7–35.

Pisarowitz[1]   Pisarowitz, K. M., 'Willmann, (Johann) Ignaz', in *MGG*.

Pisarowitz[2]   —— 'Zmeskáll von Domanovecz', in *MGG*.

Pisarowitz[3]   —— 'Die Willmanns: Der restituierte Roman einer potenzierten Musikerfamilie', *Mitteilungen der Internationalen Stiftung Mozarteum* (Salzburg), 15 (1967), 7–12.

Pisarowitz[4]   —— 'Willmann', in *New Grove*.

Platinga   Platinga, L., *Clementi: His Life and Music* (London, 1977).

Plesske   Plesske, H.-M., 'Bossler', in *New Grove*.

Plevka   Plevka, B., 'Ludwig van Beethoven und Joseph Franz Maximilian Lobkowicz', *Beethoven-Jahrbuch*, 2nd ser. 10 (1978–81) [1983], 307–12.

Pohl[1]   Pohl, C. F., 'Beethovens Maske betreffend', *Signale für die musikalische Welt*, 29 (1871), 100.

Pohl[2]   —— *Denkschrift zum Anlass des hundertjährigen Bestehens der Tonkünstler-Societät* (Vienna, 1871).

Pohl[3]   —— *Die Gesellschaft der Musikfreunde des österreichischen Kaiserstaates und ihr Conservatorium* (Vienna, 1871).

Pohl/Warrack   —— and Warrack, J., 'Gebauer', in *New Grove*.

Pohl/Zingel   —— and Zingel, H. J., 'Krumpholtz, Wenzel', in *New Grove*.

Polski słownik   *Polski słownik biograficzny* (Wrocław, 1935–   ).

Poštolka[1]   Poštolka, M., 'Dušek', in *New Grove*.

Poštolka[2]   —— 'Gelinek', in *New Grove*.

Poštolka[3]   —— 'Kozeluch', in *New Grove*.

Poštolka[4]   —— 'Wranitzky, Anton', in *New Grove*.

Poštolka[5]   —— 'Wranitzky, Paul', in *New Grove*.
Potter   Potter, C., 'Recollections of Beethoven, with Remarks on his Style', *Musical World*, 1/7 (29 Apr. 1836), 101–3; repr. *Musical Times*, 10 (1861–2), 150–3.
Pougin   Pougin, A., *Notice sur Rode, violiniste français* (Paris, 1874).
Prod'homme[1]   Prod'homme, J.-G., 'The Baron de Trémont: Souvenirs of Beethoven and Other Contemporaries', *Musical Quarterly*, 6 (1920), 366–91.
Prod'homme[2]   —— 'Die Entdecker Beethovens in Frankreich', *Die Musik*, 19 (1927), 400–11.
Prod'homme[3]   —— 'From the Unpublished Autobiography of Antoine Reicha', *Musical Quarterly*, 22 (1936), 339–53.
Pröhle   Pröhle, H., 'Spiker', in *ADB*.
Puschmann   Puschmann, T., *Die Medicin in Wien während der letzten 100 Jahre* (Vienna, 1884).
Raab   Raab, R., *Biographischer Index des Wiener Opernballetts von 1631 bis zur Gegenwart* (Vienna, 1994).
Racek[1]   Racek, J., 'Beethoven auf Schloss Grätz (Hradec) bei Troppau in den Jahren 1806 und 1811: Ein Beitrag zur Frage Beethoven und die böhmischen Länder', in *Beethoven Congress*[1], 215–35.
Racek[2]   —— 'Beethovens Beziehungen zur mährischen Musikkultur im 18. und 19. Jahrhundert', *Beethoven-Jahrbuch*, 2nd ser. 9 (1973–7) [1977], 377–94.
Reckziegel   Reckziegel, W., 'Vogler, Georg Joseph', in *MGG*.
Rector   Rector, M., 'Pfeffel', in *LL*.
Redlich   Redlich, H. F., 'Dragonetti', in *MGG*.
Redlich/Harman   —— and Harman, R. A., 'Chappell & Co. Ltd.', in *MGG*.
Rehm[1]   Rehm, J., *Zur Musikrezeption im vormärzlichen Berlin: Die Präsentation bürgerlichen Selbstverständnisses und biedermeierlicher Kunstanschauung in den Musikkritiken Ludwig Rellstabs* (Hildesheim, 1983).
Rehm[2]   Rehm, W., 'Kreutzer, Konrad', in *MGG*.
Reichardt   Reichardt, J. F., *Vertraute Briefe geschrieben auf einer Reise nach Wien und den österreichischen Staaten zu Ende des Jahres 1808 und zu Anfang 1809*, eingeleitet und erläutert von G. Gugitz (2 vols., Munich, 1915).
Reimann   Reimann, H., 'Beethoven und Graf Oppersdorf: Ein Beitrag zur Geschichte der C-moll Symphonie . . .', in his *Musikalische Rückblicke* (2 vols., Berlin, 1900), i. 111–15.
Reinitz[1]   Reinitz, M., 'Beethovens Prozesse', *Deutsche Rundschau*, 162 (1915), 248–82.
Reinitz[2]   —— *Beethoven im Streit mit dem Schicksal* (Vienna, 1924).
Reinöhl   Reinöhl, F. von, 'Neues zu Beethovens Lehrjahr bei Haydn', *Neues Beethoven-Jahrbuch*, 6 (1935), 36–47.
Rellstab   Rellstab, H. F. L., *Aus meinem Leben* (Berlin, 1861).
Rheinwald   Rheinwald, E., 'Die Brüder Ludwig Friedrich Griesinger, Jurist und Politiker, 1767–1845, und August von Griesinger, Sächsischer Legationsrat in Wien, Musikfreund, 1769–1845', *Schwäbische Lebensbilder*, 5 (1950), 115–38.
Rice   Rice, J. A., 'De Gamerra', in *New Opera Grove*.
Richter   Richter, M., 'Schmidt, Klamer Eberhard Karl', in *LL*.
Ries   *Ferdinand Ries: Briefe und Dokumente*, bearbeitet von C. Hill (Bonn, 1982).

Rietsch[1]   Rietsch, H., 'Aus Briefen Johanns van Beethoven', *Neues Beethoven-Jahrbuch*, 1 (1924), 115–27.

Rietsch[2]   Rietsch, H., 'Nochmals Johann van Beethoven und anderes', *Neues Beethoven-Jahrbuch*, 3 (1927), 42–8.

Ringer   Ringer, A. L., 'Clementi and the *Eroica*', *Musical Quarterly*, 47 (1961), 454–68.

Roche   Roche, J., 'Moscheles', in *New Grove*.

Rochlitz[1]   Rochlitz, F., 'Zusatz aus einem spätern Briefe [Baden, den 9ten Julius (1822)]', *Allgemeine musikalische Zeitung* (Jan. 1828), 6–16.

Rochlitz[2]   —— *Für ruhige Stunden* (2 vols., Leipzig, 1828).

Rochlitz[3]   —— *Für Freunde der Tonkunst* (2nd edn., 4 vols., Leipzig, 1830–2).

Rochlitz[4]   'Der Besuch des Hofrats Friedrich Rochlitz bei Ludwig van Beethoven in Wien', *Der Bär* (1927), 166–73.

Rosenbaum   'The Diaries of Joseph Carl Rosenbaum 1770–1829', ed. E. Radant, *Haydn Yearbook*, 5 (1968).

Rowland   Rowland, H., *Matthias Claudius* (Boston, 1983).

Rumph   Rumph, S., 'A Kingdom Not of This World: The Political Context of E. T. A. Hoffmann's Beethoven Criticism', *19th Century Music*, 19 (1995–6), 50–67.

Russell   Russell, J., *A Tour of Germany and Some of the Southern Provinces of the Austrian Empire in 1820, 1821, 1822* (2 vols., Edinburgh, 1828).

Rzewuska   Rzewuska, R., *Mémoires de la comtesse Rosalie Rzewuska (1788–1865)*, publiées par son arrière-petite fille G. Caetani Grenier (3 vols., Rome, 1939–50).

Sachs   Sachs, J., 'Hummel', in *New Grove*.

Sakka   Sakka, K., 'Beethovens Klaviere: Der Klavierbau und Beethovens künstlerische Reaktion', in *Festschrift Schmidt-Görg*[2], 327–37.

Sams   Sams, E., 'E. T. Hoffmann, 1776–1822', *Musical Times*, 117 (1976), 29–32.

Sandberger   Sandberger, A., *Ausgewählte Aufsätze zur Musikgeschichte* (2 vols., Munich, 1921–4). Vol. ii (*Forschungen, Studien und Kritiken zu Beethoven und zur Beethovenliteratur*) contains, among others, the following articles: 'Antonie Brentano an Johann Michael Sailer wegen Beethovens Neffen', 'Beethovens Freund Zmeskall als Komponist', 'Beethovens Stellung zu den führenden Geistern seiner Zeit in Philosophie und Dichtung', 'Franz Xaver Kleinheinz', '*Léonore* von Bouilly und ihre Bearbeitung durch Joseph Sonnleithner', 'Zur Geschichte der Beethovenforschung und des Beethovenverständnisses', 'Zur Reise nach Mergentheim und Aschaffenburg'.

Sartori   Sartori, C., 'Viganò', in *MGG*.

Sauer   Sauer, E., 'Joseph Ludwig Stoll', *Germanisch-Romanische Monatsschrift*, 11 (1921) 313–19.

Schaal[1]   Schaal, R., 'Lichnowsky', in *MGG*.

Schaal[2]   —— 'Lobkowitz', in *MGG*.

Schaal[3]   —— 'Waldstein, Ferdinand Ernst Joseph Gabriel, Graf von', in *MGG*.

Schaal[4]   —— 'Die Autographen der Wiener Musiksammlung von Aloys Fuchs. Unter Benutzung der Originalkataloge bearbeitet von R. Schaal', *Haydn Jahrbuch*, 6 (1969), 5–191.

Schaal[5]   Schaal, S., 'Das Beethoven-Denkmal von Ernst Julius Hähnel in Bonn', in *Beethoven Statue*[2], 39–133.

Schafer   Schafer, R. M., *E. T. A. Hoffmann and Music* (Toronto, 1975).

Schanzlin/Walter   Schanzlin, H. P., and Walter, G., 'Nägeli', in *MGG*.

Schattner   Schattner, H. J., *Volksbildung durch Musikerziehung: Leben und Wirken Hans Georg Nägelis* (Otterbach, 1960).

Schenk[1]   Schenk, E., 'Beethovens Reisebekanntschaft von 1787: Nanette von Schaden', in *Festschrift Fellerer*, 461–73.

Schenk[2]   Schenk, J. B., 'Autobiographische Skizze', *Studien zur Musikwissenschaft*, 11 (1924), 75–85; English version in Nettl[2], 265–79, 330–1.

Scherf   Scherf, H., 'Beethovens Krankheit und Tod', *ÖMZ*, 32 (1977), 125–34.

Schering   Schering, A., 'Zum Bildnis der Amalie Sebald', *Neues Beethoven-Jahrbuch*, 5 (1933), 5–6.

Schiedermair[1]   Schiedermair, L., *Der junge Beethoven* (Leipzig, 1925).

Schiedermair[2]   —— 'Zur Biographie Johann van Beethovens (Vater)', *Neues Beethoven-Jahrbuch*, 3 (1927), 32–41.

Schiedermair[3]   —— 'Neue Schriftstücke zu Beethovens Vormundschaft über seinen Neffen', *Neues Beethoven-Jahrbuch*, 8 (1938), 59–64.

Schiel[1]   Schiel, H., 'Frankfurter Erinnerungen Antonie Brentanos', in *Festschrift Richel*, 68–72.

Schiel[2]   —— *Johann Michael Sailer: Leben und Briefe* (2 vols., Regensburg, 1948–52).

Schindler[1]   (*a*) Schindler, A., *Biographie von Ludwig van Beethoven* (Münster, 1840); 2nd edn., with two supplements (Münster, 1845); 3rd, rev., edn. (Münster, 1860).
                 (*b*) English trans. of 1st edn.: *The Life of Beethoven, Including his Correspondence with his Friends, Numerous Characteristic Traits, and Remarks on his Musical Works*, ed. Ignace Moscheles (2 vols., London, 1841).
                 (*c*) English trans. of 3rd edn.: *Beethoven as I Knew Him. A Biography by Anton Felix Schindler*, ed. D. W. MacArdle and trans. C. S. Jolly (Chapel Hill, NC, 1966).

Schindler[2]   —— *Beethoven in Paris. Nebst anderen den unsterblichen Tondichter betreffenden Mittheilungen und einem Facsimile von Beethoven's Handschrift. Ein Nachtrag zur Biographie Beethoven's* (Münster, 1842).

Schindler[3]   *Anton Schindler, der Freund Beethovens: Sein Tagebuch aus den Jahren 1841–43*, herausgegeben von M. Becker (Frankfurt, [1939]).

Schletterer   Schletterer, [H. M.], 'Schechner', in *ADB*.

Schmid[1]   Schmid, E. F., 'Artaria', in *MGG*.

Schmid[2]   —— 'Gottfried van Swieten als Komponist', *Mozart-Jahrbuch* (1953), 15–31.

Schmidt[1]   Schmidt, H., 'Verzeichnis der Skizzen Beethovens', *Beethoven-Jahrbuch*, 6 (1965–8), 7–128.

Schmidt[2]   —— 'Das Bonner Beethoven-Archiv', *ÖMZ*, 25 (1970), 769–74.

Schmidt[3]   —— 'Die Beethovenhandschriften des Beethovenhauses in Bonn', *Beethoven-Jahrbuch*, 2nd ser. 7 (1969–70) [1971], pp. vii–443; 'Addenda und Corrigenda . . .', 8 (1971–2) [1975], 207–20.

Schmidt[4]   —— 'Aus der Werkstatt eines Handschriftenfälschers: Ein Liebesbrief Beethovens', *ÖMZ*, 29 (1974), 57–66.

Schmidt[5]   Schmidt, H., 'Das Bonner Beethoven-Archiv: Zum fünfzigsten Bestehen', *Beethoven-Jahrbuch*, 2nd ser. 9 (1973–7) [1977], 405–25.

Schmidt[6]   —— 'Eeden, van den', in *New Grove*.

Schmidt-Görg[1]   Schmidt-Görg, J., 'Schindler', in *MGG*.

Schmidt-Görg[2]   —— 'Wegeler', in *MGG*.

Schmidt-Görg[3]   —— 'Neue Briefe und Schriftstücke aus der Familie Brunsvik', *Beethoven-Jahrbuch*, 2nd ser. 2 (1955–6) [1956], 11–23.

Schmidt-Görg[4]   *Beethoven: Die Geschichte seiner Familie* (Bonn, 1964).

Schmidt-Görg[5]   —— 'Wasserzeichen in Beethoven-Briefen', *Beethoven-Jahrbuch*, 2nd ser. 5 (1961–4) [1966], 7–74.

Schmidt-Görg[6]   —— 'Wer war "die M." in einer wichtigen Aufzeichnung Beethovens?', *Beethoven-Jahrbuch*, 2nd ser. 5 (1961–4) [1966], 75–9.

Schmidt-Görg[7]   —— 'Zur Entstehungszeit von Beethovens Gellert-Lieder', *Beethoven-Jahrbuch*, 2nd ser. 5 (1961–4) [1966], 87–91.

Schmidt-Görg[8]   —— 'Neue Schriftstücke zu Beethoven und Josephine Gräfin Deym', *Beethoven-Jahrbuch*, 2nd ser. 6 (1965–8) [1969], 205–8.

Schmidt-Görg[9]   —— 'Verleger Verlegenheiten: Ein besonderes Kapitel bei Beethoven', in *Festschrift Strecker*, 135–48.

Schmidt-Görg[10] —— 'Ein Schiller-Zitat Beethovens in neuer Sicht', in *Festschrift Henle*, 423–6.

Schmidt-Görg[11] *Dreizehn unbekannte Briefe zu Josefine Gräfin Deym, geb. v. Brunsvik. Faksimile*, Einführung und Übertragung von J. Schmidt-Görg (Bonn, 1986).

Schmitt-Thomas   Schmitt-Thomas, R., 'Über ein wenig bekanntes Beethoven-Bildnis. (Der Beethoven II von Josef Karl Stieler.)', in *Beethoven Congress*[2], 557–8.

Schmitz   Schmitz, A., *Das romantische Beethovenbild: Darstellung und Kritik* (Berlin, 1927; repr. Darmstadt, 1978).

Schmoll   Schmoll, J. A. [Eisenwerth], 'Zur Geschichte des Beethoven-Denkmals: Das Künstlerdenkmal', in *Festschrift Müller-Blattau*, 242–77.

Schmutzenhofer   Schmutzenhofer, W., 'Leidesdorf', in *MGG*.

Schnaus   Schnaus, P., *E. T. A. Hoffmann als Beethoven-Rezensent der Allgemeinen musikalischen Zeitung* (Munich, 1977).

Schneider   Schneider, H., *Der Musikverleger Johann Michael Götz (1740–1810) und seine kurfürstlich privilegirte Notenfabrique* (2 vols., Tutzing, 1989).

Schnyder   Schnyder von Wartensee, X., *Lebenserinnerungen* (Zurich, 1887).

Schofield   Schofield, B., 'Letter of Anton Schindler', *British Museum Quarterly*, 21/2 (1957), 30–1.

Scholes   Scholes, P. A., *The Great Dr. Burney: His Life, his Travels, his Works, his Family and Friends* (2 vols., London, 1948).

Schonberg   Schonberg, H. C., *The Great Pianists* (New York, 1963).

Schöne   *Briefe an Marie Gräfin Erdödy, geb. Gräfin Niszky, und Mag. Brauchle*, herausgegeben von A. Schöne (Leipzig, 1867).

Schönfeld   Schönfeld, J. F. von, *Jahrbuch der Tonkunst von Wien und Prag* (Vienna, 1796; repr. Munich, 1976).

Schrötter-Firnhaber   Schrötter-Firnhaber, H. von, 'Antonia Brentano', *Alt-Frankfurt*, 3 (1930), 105–8.

Schultz   [Schultz, J. R.], 'A Day with Beethoven', *Harmonicon* (Jan. 1824), 10–11.

Schulz	Schulz, G., 'Fouqué, Friedrich, Baron de La Motte', in *LL*.
Schünemann	Schünemann, G., 'Czernys Erinnerungen an Beethoven', *Neues Beethoven-Jahrbuch*, 9 (1939), 47–74.
Schürmann	*Ludwig van Beethoven: Alle vertonten und musikalisch bearbeiteten Texte*, zusammengestellt und herausgegeben von K. E. Schürmann (Münster, 1980).
Schwaiger	Schwaiger, G., *Johann Michael Sailer, der bayerische Kirchenvater* (Munich, 1982).
Schwarz[1]	Schwarz, B., 'Rode, Pierre', in *MGG*.
Schwarz[2]	—— 'Beethoveniana in Soviet Russia', *Musical Quarterly*, 47 (1961), 4–21; 'Addenda', 48 (1962), 148.
Schwarz[3]	—— 'More Beethoveniana in Soviet Russia', 49 (1963), 143–9.
Schwarz[4]	—— 'Zur Uraufführung von Beethovens *Missa solemnis* in St. Petersburg', in *Beethoven Congress*[2], 559–61.
Schwarz[5]	—— 'Polledro', in *New Grove*.
Schwarz[6]	—— *Great Masters of the Violin, from Corelli and Vivaldi to Stern, Zukerman and Perlman* (New York, 1983).
Schwarz[7]	Schwarz, V., 'Musikalische Kindererziehung im Hause des Fürsten Joseph Franz Maximilian Lobkowitz', *ÖMZ*, 32 (1977), 253–5.
Schweikert	Schweikert, U., 'Eduard von Bülow: Aufzeichnungen über Ludwig Tieck', *Jahrbuch des freien deutschen Hochstifts* (1972), 318–68.
Seemann	Seemann, O., 'Bibliographia Sonnleithneriana', *Wiener Geschichtsblätter* (1998), Beiheft 4.
Serwer	Serwer, H., 'Kirnberger', in *New Grove*.
Seyfried	Seyfried, I. von, *Ludwig van Beethovens Studien im Generalbass, Contrapunkt und in der Compositionslehre, aus dessen handschriftlichen Nachlass gesammelt und herausgegeben.* (2nd, rev., edn. by H. H. Pierson, Leipzig, 1853; repr. Hildesheim, 1967).
Shamgar	Shamgar, B., 'Three Missing Months in Schubert's Biography: A Further Consideration of Beethoven's Influence on Schubert', *Musical Quarterly*, 73 (1989), 417–34.
Sharp	S[harp], R. F., 'Neate, Charles', in *DNB*.
Siegert	Siegert, R., 'Sauter, Samuel Friedrich', in *LL*.
Sietz[1]	Sietz, R., 'Hiller', in *MGG*.
Sietz[2]	—— 'Kuhlau', in *MGG*.
Sietz[3]	—— 'Radziwill', in *MGG*.
Sietz[4]	—— 'Ries', in *MGG*.
Sietz[5]	—— 'Röckel', in *MGG*.
Simpson[1]	Simpson, A., 'Beethoven through Czech Eyes', *Musical Times*, 111 (1970), 1203–5.
Simpson[2]	—— 'Bohemian Piano Music of Beethoven's Time', *Musical Times*, 113 (1972), 666–7.
Simpson[3]	—— 'Doležálek', in *New Grove*.
Simpson[4]	—— 'Tomášek', in *New Grove*.
Simpson[5]	—— 'Voříšek', in *New Grove*.
Skrine	Skrine, P., 'Collin, Heinrich Joseph von', in *LL*.

Slatford[1]   Slatford, R., 'Domenico Dragonetti', *Proceedings of the Royal Musical Association*, 97 (1970–1), 21–8.

Slatford[2]   —— 'Dragonetti', in *New Grove*.

Slezak[1]   Slezak, F., 'Josef Riedl Leuenstern (1786–1856): Ein altwiener Verleger, Staatsbeamter und Gelehrter', *Tradition: Zeitschrift für Firmengeschichte und Unternehmerbiographie*, 15 (1970), 84–96.

Slezak[2]   —— 'Zur Widmung des Klavierkonzerts Op. 19', *Beethoven-Jahrbuch*, 2nd ser. 8 (1971–2) [1975], 93–6.

Slezak[3]   —— 'Zur Firmengeschichte von Artaria & Compagnie', *Beethoven-Jahrbuch*, 2nd ser. 9 (1973–7) [1977], 453–68.

Slezak[4]   —— *Beethovens Wiener Originalverleger* (Vienna, 1987).

Sloane   Sloane, D. F., 'Beethoven and Mälzel: A Re-evaluation of Mälzel's Character and the History of *Wellington's Victory*', *Beethoven-Jahrbuch*, 12 (1997), 54–64.

Smart   *Leaves from the Journals of Sir George Smart*, ed. H. B. Cox and C. L. E. Cox (London, 1907).

Smidak   Smidak, E. F., *Isaak-Ignaz Moscheles: Das Leben des Komponisten und seine Begegnungen mit Beethoven, Liszt, Chopin, Mendelssohn* (n.p., 1988).

Smith/Jones   Smith, W. C., and Jones, P. W., 'Dale, Joseph', in *New Grove*.

SML   *Schweizer Musiker-Lexikon/Dictionnaire des musiciens suisses*, bearbeitet von/rédigé par Willi Schuh *et al.* (Zurich, 1964).

Smolle   Smolle, K., *Wohnstätten Ludwig van Beethovens von 1792 bis zu seinem Tod* (Munich, 1970).

Solomon[1]   'Beethoven's Tagebuch of 1812–18' (bilingual edn. with commentary by M. Solomon), in *Beethoven Studies 3*, ed. A. Tyson (Cambridge, 1982), 193–287 (rev. edn., in English only, in Solomon[5], 233–95); rev. edn. in German: *Maynard Solomon: Beethovens Tagebuch*, herausgegeben von S. Brandenburg (Mainz, 1990).

Solomon[2]   Solomon, M., *Beethoven* (New York, 1977; 2nd, rev., edn., New York, 1998).

Solomon[3]   —— 'Schubert and Beethoven', *19th Century Music*, 3 (1979–80), 114–25.

Solomon[4]   —— 'A Beethoven Acquaintance: Josef von Hammer-Purgstall', *Musical Times*, 124 (1983), 12–15.

Solomon[5]   —— *Beethoven Essays* (Cambridge, Mass., 1988). Contains the following: 'Antonie Brentano and Beethoven', 'Beethoven and his Nephew: A Reappraisal', 'Beethoven and Schiller', 'Beethoven's Birth Year', 'Beethoven's Creative Process: A Two-Part Invention', 'Beethoven's *Magazin der Kunst*', 'Beethoven's *Tagebuch*', 'On Beethoven's Deafness', 'Recherche de Josephine Deym', 'The Creative Period of Beethoven', 'The Dreams of Beethoven', 'The Ninth Symphony: A Search for Order', 'The Nobility Pretense', 'The Posthumous Life of Ludwig Maria van Beethoven', 'The Quest for Faith', 'Thoughts on Biography'.

Solomon[6]   —— 'Some Romantic Images in Beethoven', in *Festschrift Tyson*, 253–81.

Sonnleithner   'Leopold von Sonnleithner's Erinnerungen an die Musiksalons des vormärzlichen Wiens. Eingeleitet von O. E. Deutsch', *ÖMZ*, 16 (1961), 49–62, 97–110, 145–57.

Spehr   Spehr, F., 'Birkenstock', in *ADB*.

Spiel	*Der Wiener Kongress in Augenzeugenberichten*, herausgegeben und eingeleitet von H. Spiel (2nd edn., Düsseldorf, 1965).
Spiess	Spiess, E., *Ignaz Paul Vital Troxler: Der Philosoph und Vorkämpfer des schweizerischen Bundesstaates. Dargestellt nach seinen Schriften und den Zeugnissen der Zeitgenossen* (Berne, 1967).
Spohr	Spohr, L., *Selbstbiographie* (2 vols., Kassel, 1860–1). English trans.: *Louis Spohr's Autobiography* (London, 1865; repr. New York, 1969).
Springer	Springer, P., 'Hähnel', in *DicArt.*
Squire[1]	Squire, W. B., 'Broadwood, John', in *DNB.*
Squire[2]	—— 'Dragonetti', in *DNB.*
Squire[3]	—— 'Röckel', in *New Grove.*
Stadlen[1]	Stadlen, P., 'Beethoven and the Metronome', *Music & Letters*, 48 (1967), 330–49.
Stadlen[2]	—— 'Schindler's Beethoven Forgeries', *Musical Times*, 118 (1977), 549–52.
Stadlen[3]	—— 'Zu Schindlers Fälschungen in Beethovens Konversationsheften', *ÖMZ*, 32 (1977), 246–52.
Stadlen[4]	—— 'Beethoven und das Metronom', in *Beethoven Congress*[3], 57–75.
Stadlen[5]	—— 'Schindler und die Konversationshefte', *ÖMZ*, 34 (1979), 2–18.
Staehelin[1]	Staehelin, M., 'Aus der Welt der frühen Beethoven-"Forschung": Aloys Fuchs in Briefen an Anton Schindler', in *Festschrift Henle*, 427–46.
Staehelin[2]	—— *Beethovens Brief an den Freiherrn von Schaden von 1787* (Bonn, 1982).
Staehelin[3]	—— *Hans Georg Nägeli und Ludwig van Beethoven: Der Zürcher Musiker, Musikverleger und Musikschriftsteller in seinen Beziehungen zu dem grossen Komponisten* (Zurich, 1982).
Staehelin[4]	—— 'Die Beethoven-Materialen im Nachlass von Ludwig Nohl', *Beethoven-Jahrbuch*, 2nd ser. 10 (1978–81) [1983], 201–19.
Staehelin[5]	—— 'Übersicht über die neuerworbenen Beethoven-Autographen des Beethoven-Hauses 1975–1980', *Beethoven-Jahrbuch*, 2nd ser. 10 (1978–81) [1983], 327–30.
Staehelin[6]	—— 'A Veiled Judgment of Beethoven by Albrechtsberger?', in *Festschrift Forbes*, 46–52.
Stainhauser	'Stainhauser', in *ALBK.*
Steblin[1]	Steblin, R., 'The Newly Discovered Hochenecker Portrait of Beethoven (1819): "Das ähnlichste Bildnis Beethovens"', *Journal of the American Musicological Society*, 45 (1992), 468–97.
Steblin[2]	—— 'Beethoven's Life Mask of 1812 Reconsidered', *Beethoven Newsletter*, 8/3 and 9/1 (Winter 1993–Spring 1994), 66–70.
Štědroň[1]	Štědroň, B., 'Doležálek', in *MGG.*
Štědroň[2]	—— 'Voříšek', in *MGG.*
Stekl	Stekl, H., *Österreichs Aristokratie im Vormärz: Herrschaftsstil und Lebensformen der Fürstenhäuser Liechtenstein und Schwarzenberg* (Munich, 1973).
Stenzl	Stenzl, J., 'Gyrowetz', in *New Grove.*
Stephenson[1]	Stephenson, K., 'Duport', in *MGG.*
Stephenson[2]	—— 'Romberg, Familie', in *MGG.*
Stephenson[3]	—— 'Romberg (family)', in *New Grove.*

Sterba/Sterba   Sterba, E., and Sterba, R., *Beethoven and his Nephew: A Psychoanalytic Study of their Relationship*, trans. W. R. Trask (New York, 1954); German version: *Ludwig van Beethoven und sein Neffe: Tragödie eines Genies. Eine psychoanalytische Studie* (Munich, 1964).

Sternfeld   Sternfeld, F. W., 'Goethe and Beethoven', *Beethoven Congress*[2], 587–90.

Stieler   'Stieler', in *ALBK*.

Stock   Stock, W. H., 'Schlösser', in *MGG*.

Stockhammer   Stockhammer, R., 'Dr. Malfattis Beziehungen zu Beethoven', *ÖMZ*, 14 (1959), 412–16.

Stone   Stone, P. E., 'Reicha, Antoine', in *New Grove*.

Storch   Storch, L., 'Ein hochherziger Mann aus dem Volke [J. A. Stumpff]', *Die Gartenlaube* (Leipzig) (1857), 437–40, 455–7, 468–70.

Stümcke   Stümcke, H., *Henriette Sontag* (Berlin, 1913).

Suppan   Suppan, W., *Steirisches Musiklexikon* (Graz, 1962–6).

Swinburne   Swinburne, H., *The Courts of Europe at the Close of the Last Century* (2 vols., London, 1841).

Taddey   *Lexikon der deutschen Geschichte: Personen, Ereignisse, Institutionen, von der Zeitwende bis zum Ausgang des 2. Weltkrieges*, herausgegeben von G. Taddey (2nd, rev., edn., Stuttgart, 1983).

Taubert   Taubert, K. H., *Carl Friedrich Zelter (1758–1832): Ein Leben durch das Handwerk für die Musik* (Berlin, n.d.).

Tellenbach[1]   Tellenbach, M.-E., *Beethoven und seine 'Unsterbliche Geliebte' Josephine Brunswick: Ihr Schicksal und der Einfluss auf Beethovens Werk* (Zurich, 1983).

Tellenbach[2]   —— 'Beethoven e Josephine, contessa Brunswick, 1799–1821', *Nuova rivista musicale italiana*, 25 (1991), 355–74.

Tellenbach[3]   —— 'Psychoanalyse und historisch-philologische Methode: Zu Maynard Solomons Beethoven und Schubert-Deutungen', *Analecta musicologica*, 30 (1997), 661–719.

Teltscher   'Teltscher', in *ALBK*.

Temperley   Temperley, N., 'Beethoven in London Concert Life, 1800–1850', *Music Review*, 21 (1960), 207–14.

Thayer[1]   Thayer, A. W., *Ludwig van Beethovens Leben*, ed. and trans. H. Deiters, vol. i (Berlin, 1866; rev. 1901; rev. H. Riemann, 1917); vol. ii (Berlin, 1872; rev. H. Riemann, 1910); vol. iii (Berlin, 1879; rev. H. Riemann, 1911); vol. iv, ed. H. Riemann (Leipzig, 1907); vol. v, ed. H. Riemann (Leipzig, 1908). English versions by H. Krehbiel (New York, 1921) and E. Forbes (see Thayer/Forbes below).

Thayer[2]   —— 'The Lobkowitz Family: An Original Investigation', *Musical World* (1879), 307, 325–6, 335.

Thayer[3]   —— 'Maelzel', in *New Grove*.

Thayer/Forbes   *Thayer's Life of Beethoven*, rev. and ed. E. Forbes (2 vols., Princeton, 1964; 2nd, rev., edn. 1967).

Thomas-San-Galli[1]   Thomas-San-Galli, W., *Die 'unsterbliche Geliebte' Beethovens: Amalie Sebald. Lösung eines vielumstrittenen Problems* (Halle an der Saale, n.d.).

Thomas-San-Galli[2]   —— *Beethoven und die unsterbliche Geliebte: Amalie Sebald, Goethe, Therese Brunswik und anderes* (Munich, n.d.).

Thürheim   Thürheim, Gräfin L., *Mein Leben: Erinnerungen aus Österreichs grosser Welt*, in deutscher Übersetzung . . . herausgegeben von R. van Rhyn (4 vols., Munich, 1914–23).

Timmermann   Timmermann, H., 'Ueltzen', in *LL*.

Tomášek   Tomášek, V. J. K., 'Excerpts from the Memoirs of J. W. Tomaschek. Transl. by A. Loft', *Musical Quarterly*, 32 (1946), 244–64.

Trier   Trier, E., 'Der Beethoven-Schrein in der Julius-Wegeler-Familienstiftung', in *Festschrift Abs*, 229–70.

Trost   Trost, A., 'Moritz von Schwinds Bild *Die Symphonie*', in Orel[1], 239–44.

Tyson[1]   Tyson, A., 'Maurice Schlesinger as a Publisher of Beethoven, 1822–1827', *Acta musicologica*, 36 (1962), 182–91.

Tyson[2]   —— 'Beethoven in Steiner's Shop', *Music Review*, 23 (1962), 119–27.

Tyson[3]   —— *The Authentic English Editions of Beethoven* (London, 1963).

Tyson[4]   —— 'The First Edition of Beethoven's Op. 119 Bagatelles', *Musical Quarterly*, 49 (1963), 331–7.

Tyson[5]   —— 'Beethoven's Oratorio', *Musical Times*, 111 (1970), 372–5.

Tyson[6]   —— 'Conversations with Beethoven', *Musical Times*, 111 (1970), 25–8.

Tyson[7]   —— 'Notes on Five of Beethoven's Copyists', *Journal of the American Musicological Society*, 23 (1970), 439–71.

Tyson[8]   —— 'An Angry Letter from Beethoven', *Musical Times*, 112 (1971), 842–5.

Tyson[9]   —— 'Beethoven's English Canzonetta', *Musical Times*, 112 (1971), 122–5.

Tyson[10]   —— 'J. R. Schultz and his Visit to Beethoven', *Musical Times*, 113 (1972), 450–1.

Tyson[11]   —— 'The "Razumovsky" Quartets: Some Aspects of the Sources', in *Beethoven Studies 3*, ed. A. Tyson (Cambridge, 1982), 107–35.

Tyson[12]   —— 'Ferdinand Ries (1784–1838): The History of his Contribution to Beethoven Biography', *19th Century Music*, 7 (1983–4), 209–21.

Ueberfeldt   Ueberfeldt, L., *Ferdinand Ries' Jugendentwicklung* (Bonn, 1915).

Ullrich[1]   Ullrich, H., 'Beethovens Freund Friedrich August Kanne', *ÖMZ*, 29 (1974), 75–80.

Ullrich[2]   —— 'Beethovens Freund Nikolaus Zmeskall von Domanovecz als Musiker', *ÖMZ*, 32 (1977), 79–85.

Ullrich[3]   —— 'Franz Oliva: Ein vergessener Freund Beethovens', *Jahrbuch des Vereins für Geschichte der Stadt Wien*, 36 (1980), 7–29.

Ullrich[4]   —— 'Karl Holz, Beethovens letzter Freund', *Studien zur Musikwissenschaft*, 31 (1980), 67–189.

Ullrich[5]   —— 'Beethovens Wiener Rechtsanwälte: Eine Studie', *Studien zur Musikgeschichte*, 32 (1981), 147–203.

Ulrich[6]   Ulrich, P. S., *Theater, Tanz und Musik im 'Deutschen Bühnenjahrbuch': Ein Fundstellennachweis von biographischen Eintragungen, Abbildungen und Aufsätzen* . . . (2 vols., Berlin, 1985).

Unger[1]   Unger, M., 'Der Kanon für Theodor Molt', *Neue Zeitschrift für Musik*, 81/40–1 (1914), 504A.

Unger[2]   Unger, M., *Muzio Clementis Leben* (Langensalza, 1914).

Unger[3]   —— *Ludwig van Beethoven und seine Verleger S. A. Steiner und Tobias Haslinger in Wien, Ad. Mart. Schlesinger in Berlin: Ihr Verkehr und Briefwechsel* (Berlin, 1921).

Unger[4]   —— 'Beethoven und das Wiener Hoftheater im Jahre 1807', *Neues Beethoven-Jahrbuch*, 2 (1925), 76–83.

Unger[5]   —— 'Beethoven und Therese von Malfatti', *Musical Quarterly*, 11 (1925), 63–72.

Unger[6]   —— 'Zu Beethovens Briefwechsel mit B. Schott's Söhnen in Mainz', *Neues Beethoven-Jahrbuch*, 3 (1927), 51–61.

Unger[7]   —— 'Die Beethovenbilder von Neugass', *Zeitschrift für Musik*, 102/11 (1935), 1211–26.

Unger[8]   —— 'Kleine Beethoven-Studien', *Neues Beethoven-Jahrbuch*, 8 (1938), 65–83.

Unger[9]   —— 'Beethovens letzte Briefe und Unterschriften', *Die Musik*, 34 (1942), 153–8.

Unger[10]   —— 'Beethovens vaterländische Musik', *Musik im Kriege*, 1 (1943), 170–5.

Unger[11]   —— 'Vom geselligen Beethoven', *ÖMZ*, 12 (1957), 91–101.

Unverricht[1] Unverricht, H., articles on Anna Jacobina, Anna Maria, Johann Peter, and Philipp Salomon in *Rheinische Musiker 4*, herausgegeben von K. G. Fellerer (Cologne, 1966), 129–35.

Unverricht[2] —— 'Salomon', in *New Grove*.

Vallat   Vallat, G., *Études d'histoire, de mœurs et d'art musical sur la fin du XVIIIe siècle et la première moitié du XIXe siècle* (Paris, 1890).

Van der Zanden   Van der Zanden, J., 'A Dutch Visitor to Beethoven', *Beethoven Journal*, 14/2 (Winter 1999), 50–5.

Van Hasselt   Van Hasselt, L., 'Beethoven in Holland', *Die Musikforschung*, 18 (1965), 181–4.

Varnhagen[1]   Varnhagen von Ense, K. A., *Denkwürdigkeiten des eignen Lebens*, pt. 2: *1810–15*, herausgegeben und eingeleitet von J. Kühn (Berlin, 1925).

Varnhagen[2]   Varnhagen von Ense, R., *Briefwechsel mit August Varnhagen von Ense*, herausgegeben von F. Kemp (Munich, 1967).

Vetterl   Vetterl, K., 'Der musikalische Nachlass des Erzherzogs Rudolf im erzbischöflichen Archiv zu Kremsier', *Zeitschrift für Musikwissenschaft*, 9 (1926–7), 168–79.

Virneisel   Virneisel, W., 'Kleine Beethoveniana', in *Festschrift Schmidt-Görg*[1], 361–76.

Volek/Macek[1]   Volek, T., and Macek, J., 'Beethoven's Rehearsals at the Lobkowitz's', *Musical Times*, 127 (1986), 75–80.

Volek/Macek[2]   —— 'Beethoven und Fürst Lobkowitz', in *Beethoven und Böhmen*, 203–17.

Volkmann   Volkmann, H., *Beethoven in seinen Beziehungen zu Dresden: Unbekannte Strecken seines Lebens* (Dresden, 1942).

Vörös   Vörös, K., 'Beiträge zur Lebensgeschichte von Nikolaus Zmeskáll', *Studia musicologica Academiae Scientiarum Hungaricae*, 4 (1963), 381–409.

Voss   Voss, E., 'Das Beethoven-Bild der Beethoven-Belletristik: Zu einigen Beethoven-Erzählungen des 19. Jahrhunderts', in *Beethoven und die*

	Nachwelt: Materialen zur Wirkungsgeschichte Beethovens, herausgegeben von H. Loos (Bonn, 1986), 81–94.
Wacha[1]	Wacha, G., 'Johann van Beethoven: Neue Quellen zur beruflichen Tätigkeit des Linzer und Urfahrer Apotheker', *Historisches Jahrbuch der Stadt Linz* (1972), 105–53.
Wacha[2]	—— 'Dreihundert Jahre Wasserapotheke', *Historisches Jahrbuch der Stadt Linz* (1973), 177–232.
Wackernagel	Wackernagel, R. H., 'Zur Restaurierung des Beethoven-Bildnisses des Isidor Neugass', in *Verein Beethoven-Haus Bonn, Jahresgabe 1983* . . . , herausgegeben von M. Staehelin (Bonn, 1983), 35–40.
Wainwright	Wainwright, D., *Broadwood by Appointment: A History* (London, 1982).
Waldmüller	'Waldmüller', in *ALBK*.
Walker	Walker, A., *Franz Liszt* (3 vols., Ithaca, NY, 1987–96).
Wallace	Wallace, R., *Beethoven's Critics: Aesthetic Dilemmas and Resolutions during the Composer's Lifetime* (Cambridge, 1986).
Walter[1]	Walter, F., 'Der Musikverlag des Michael Götz in Mannheim', *Mannheimer Geschichtsblätter*, 16/3–4 (1915), 36–42.
Walter[2]	Walter, H., 'Die biographischen Beziehungen zwischen Haydn und Beethoven', in *Beethoven Congress*[2], 79–83.
Walter[3]	—— 'Haydns Schüler', in *Joseph Haydn in seiner Zeit. Eisenstadt, 20. Mai–26. Oktober 1892* [exhibition catalogue, Eisenstadt, 1982].
Walther	Walther, P. F., 'Memorandum [dated 26 March 1860]' in English trans., *Annals* of the Royal Philharmonic Society, London (1871), 9–10.
Warrack[1]	Warrack, K., 'Boucher', in *New Grove*.
Warrack[2]	—— 'Sontag', in *New Grove*.
Wates[1]	Wates, R. E., 'Karl Ludwig Junker (1748–1797): Sentimental Music Critic', Ph.D. diss. (Yale University, 1965).
Wates[2]	—— 'Junker', in *New Grove*.
Watson	Watson, J., 'Beethoven's Debt to Mozart', *Music & Letters*, 18 (1937), 248–58.
Weber[1]	Weber, G., 'Einiges aus dem Leben von Xaver Schnyder von Wartensee', *Schweizerische Musikzeitung und Sängerblatt*, 29 (1884), 19–20, etc.
Weber[2]	Weber, W., 'Meissner', in *LL*.
Webster[1]	Webster, J., 'The Falling-Out between Haydn and Beethoven: The Evidence of the Sources', in *Festschrift Forbes*, 3–45.
Webster[2]	—— 'Music, Pathology, Sexuality, Beethoven, Schubert', *19th Century Music*, 17 (1993–4), 89–93.
Wegeler	Wegeler, F. G., *Nachtrag zu den biographischen Notizen über Ludwig van Beethoven* (Koblenz, 1845). Supplement to Wegeler/Ries (*see* next item).
Wegeler/Ries	—— and Ries, F., *Biographische Notizen über Ludwig van Beethoven* (Koblenz, 1838; repr., together with the preceding item, Hildesheim, 1972).
Wegerer	Wegerer, K., 'Beethovens Hammerflügel und ihre Pedale', *ÖMZ*, 20 (1965), 201–11.
Wegmann	Wegmann, L., *Ferdinand Sauter: Ein Lebensbild des wienerischen Dichters, nach Mitteilungen seiner Zeitgenossen* (Vienna, 1904).

Wehmeyer   Wehmeyer, G., 'Carl Czerny und die Einzelhaft am Klavier', *ÖMZ*, 36 (1981), 622–30.

Weidmann   Weidmann, F. C., *Moriz Graf von Dietrichstein: Sein Leben und Wirken aus seinen hinterlassenen Papieren dargestellt* (Vienna, 1867).

Weidner   'Weidner', in *ALBK*.

Weigmann   Weigmann, O., *Schwind: Des Meisters Werke in 1265 Abbildungen* (Stuttgart, n.d.).

Weinmann[1]   Weinmann, A., 'Haslinger', in *MGG*.

Weinmann[2]   —— 'Hoffmeister, Franz Anton', in *MGG*.

Weinmann[3]   —— 'Löschenkohl', in *MGG*.

Weinmann[4]   —— 'Mollo', in *MGG*.

Weinmann[5]   —— 'Pennauer', in *MGG*.

Weinmann[6]   —— 'Sauer, Ignaz', in *MGG*.

Weinmann[7]   —— 'Steiner', in *MGG*.

Weinmann[8]   —— 'Traeg', in *MGG*.

Weinmann[9]   —— *Vollständiges Verlagsverzeichnis Artaria & Comp.* (Vienna, 1952).

Weinmann[10]   —— *Wiener Musikverleger und Musikalienhändler von Mozarts Zeit bis gegen 1860: Ein firmengeschichtlicher und topographischer Behelf* (Vienna, 1956).

Weinmann[11]   —— *Die Wiener Verlagswerke von Franz Anton Hoffmeister* (Vienna, 1964).

Weinmann[12]   —— *Verlags-Verzeichnis Pietro Mecchetti quondam Carlo* (Vienna, 1966).

Weinmann[13]   —— *Verzeichnis der Musikalien der Verlage Maisch-Sprenger-Mathias Artaria* (Vienna, 1970).

Weinmann[14]   —— 'Hoffmeister', in *New Grove*.

Weinmann[15]   —— 'Löschenkohl', in *New Grove*.

Weinmann[16]   —— 'Mollo', in *New Grove*.

Weinmann[17]   —— 'Traeg', in *New Grove*.

Weise   *Beethoven: Entwurf einer Denkschrift an das Appellationsgericht in Wien vom 18. Februar 1820. Erste vollständige Faksimile Ausgabe . . .* , Einführung, Übertragung und Anmerkungen von D. Weise (Bonn, 1953).

Weiss   Weiss, K., 'Collin, Heinrich Joseph von', in *ADB*.

Werba   Werba, E., 'Beethoven und seine Gönner', *ÖMZ*, 15 (1960), 240–7.

Wessely[1]   Wessely, O., 'Glöggl', in *MGG*.

Wessely[2]   —— 'Kiesewetter, Raphael Georg', in *MGG*.

Wessely[3]   —— 'Koželuch', in *MGG*.

Wessely[4]   —— 'Kraft', in *MGG*.

Wessely[5]   —— 'Weiss, Franz', in *MGG*.

Wessely[6]   —— 'Linz und die Musik: Von den Anfängen bis zum Beginn des 19. Jahrhunderts', *Jahrbuch der Stadt Linz* (1950), 96–197.

Wessely[7]   —— 'Das Linzer Musikleben in der ersten Hälfte des 19. Jahrhunderts', *Jahrbuch der Stadt Linz* (1953), 283–442.

Wessely[8]   —— 'Fuchs, Aloys', in *New Grove*.

Wessely[9]   —— 'Kiesewetter, Raphael Georg', in *New Grove*.

Weston[1]   Weston, P., 'Beethoven's Clarinettists', *Musical Times*, 111 (1970), 1212–13.

Weston[2]   —— *Clarinet Virtuosi of the Past* (London, 1971).

Weston[3]   —— *More Clarinet Virtuosi of the Past* (London, 1977).

Wild[1]   Wild, F., 'Autobiographie', *Rezensionen über Theater und Musik* (Vienna), 4 (1860), 19–20, 53–6, 68–71, 83–6, 100–6, 123–4, 174.

Wild[2]   Wild, R., 'Weisse', in *LL*.

Willetts   Willetts, P. J., 'Johann Andreas Stumpff, 1769–1846', *Musical Times*, 118 (1977), 29–32.

Williams[1]   Williams, A., *Portrait of Liszt by Himself and his Contemporaries* (Oxford, 1990).

Williams[2]   Williams, M. D., 'Rodolphe Kreutzer vs. Beethoven and Berlioz', in *Festschrift Kaufmann*, 273–82.

Wirsta   Wirsta, A., 'Kreutzer, Rodolphe', in *MGG*.

Witzmann   Witzmann, R., *Hieronymus Löschenkohl: Bildreporter zwischen Barock und Biedermeier* (Vienna, 1978).

Wodtke[1]   Wodtke, F. G., 'Kotzebue', in *MGG*.

Wodtke[2]   —— 'Klopstock', in *MGG*.

Wodtke[3]   —— 'Matthisson', in *MGG*.

Wolf   Wolf, S., *Beethovens Neffenkonflikt: Eine psychologisch-biographische Studie* (Munich, 1995).

Wolff   Wolff, H. C., 'Dressler', in *MGG*.

Worgull   Worgull, E., 'Ferdinand Georg Waldmüller malt Ludwig van Beethoven: Beethovenikonographie und Kunstgeschichte', *Studien zur Musikwissenschaft*, 30 (1979), 107–53.

Wright   Wright, J. R. B., 'George Polgreen Bridgetower: An African Prodigy in England, 1789–99', *Musical Quarterly*, 66 (1980), 65–82.

Würtz   Würtz, R., 'Götz', in *New Grove*.

Würz   Würz, A., 'Lachner', in *MGG*.

Wurzbach[1]   Wurzbach, C. von, *Biographisches Lexikon des Kaiserthums Oesterreich, enthaltend die Lebensskizzen der denkwürdigen Personen, welche 1750 bis 1850 im Kaiserstaate und in seinen Kronländern gelebt haben* (60 vols., Vienna, 1856–91).

Wurzbach[2]   Wurzbach, W. von, *Josef Kriehuber und die Wiener Gesellschaft seiner Zeit* (2 vols., Vienna, 1955–7).

Wythe   Wythe, D., 'The Pianos of Conrad Graf', *Early Music*, 12 (1984), 446–60.

Young   Young, P. M., *Beethoven: A Victorian Tribute. Based on the Papers of Sir George Smart* (London, 1976).

Zanetti   Zanetti, E., 'Carpani', in *MGG*.

Zekert   Zekert, O., 'Apotheker Johann van Beethoven', *Pharmazeutische Monatshefte* (1928), 29–35, 62–8, 90–3, 107–10, 130–4, 151–5.

Zeman   Zeman, H., ' "Sendung von Schubert aus Wien, von meinen Liedern Compositionen": Gedichte Goethes im Liedschaffen Beethovens und Schuberts', *ÖMZ*, 54/3 (1999), 4–15.

Zenger   Zenger, M., *Geschichte der Münchener Oper*, nachgelassenes Werk herausgegeben von T. Kroyer (Munich, 1923).

Ziegler   *Leonhard Ziegler und Xaver Schnyder von Wartensee im Briefwechsel*, herausgegeben von P. O. Schneider (Zurich, 1941).

Zimmer   Zimmer, H., *Theodor Körners Braut: Ein Lebens- und Charakterbild Antonie Adambergers* (2nd edn., Stuttgart, 1918).

Zingel   Zingel, H. J., 'Krumpholtz', in *MGG*.

Zu Beethoven   *Zu Beethoven: Aufsätze und Annotationen*, herausgegeben von H. Gold-
                  schmidt (Berlin, 1979).

Zu Beethoven 2 *Zu Beethoven 2: Aufsätze und Dokumente*, herausgegeben von H. Gold-
                  schmidt (Berlin, 1984).

Zu Beethoven 3 *Zu Beethoven 3: Aufsätze und Dokumente*, herausgegeben von H. Gold-
                  schmidt (Berlin, 1988).

Index of Beethoven's Works

❧

Index of Names

❦